MW00512141

THE GROWTH AND COLLAPSE OF ONE AMERICAN NATION:
The Early Republic 1790-1961

"His behind-the-scenes portraits of such players as Jefferson, Hamilton, Jackson, and Lincoln will make the book more than just history for readers who appreciate facts delivered in a personal and, at times, cinematic manner. Given the situations, and the protagonists, the tale Fraser is telling is riveting throughout. He is adept at combining factual information and enough creative liberty to make these well-known moments come alive, while still retaining historical accuracy. Fraser's many footnotes leave no doubt as to his diligent research, overlaid with the zeal for his subject matter."

—Self-Publishing Review ★★★★★

"This is an exhaustive history, but its delivery is clear. Topics from law to philosophy to war are covered to support a complex argument that the United States is a creedal nation defined by a shared set of values, including individual liberty, equality, freedom of religion, and the rule of law. *The Growth and Collapse of One American Nation* adds to the ongoing conversation about American identity and the nation's future."

—Foreword Reviews ★★★★

"This book subscribes to the storytelling tradition of historical analysis and continues chronologically from the author's first book... The narrative's clarity, precision, and detail make this book highly readable... This work's strength lies in exploring broader political themes that we continue to face, such as what defines an American (or makes one un-American)."

—Blueink Review

"Fraser's massive work proves Santayana's theory that those who do not learn history are doomed to repeat it. The author deftly shows that, even from this nation's earliest days, there were those who were concerned only with the prosperity of themselves and their families and others who thought it was morally proper to help those who were less fortunate. So what's happening in the U.S. today isn't something that's new and different...He succeeds in putting human faces on what could be dry, drab history."

—**Kirkus Reviews**

"*The Growth and Collapse of One American Nation* is an erudite history of the country's early development as a republic. Author Donald J. Fraser traces the leaders, movements and events involved in building the American form of government and politics, and shaping its identity. Fraser's readable style and scholarship, as exhibited by the copious primary and secondary sources cited, give the volume its vigor...Fraser reminds us that American unity is not certain, but depends on shared ideals that are always contested."

—**Indie Reader 4.5 stars**

The GROWTH *and* COLLAPSE *of* ONE AMERICAN NATION

ALSO BY DONALD J. FRASER

THE EMERGENCE OF ONE AMERICAN NATION:
The Revolution, the Founders, and the Constitution

The GROWTH *and* COLLAPSE *of* ONE AMERICAN NATION

The Early Republic 1790-1861

DONALD J. FRASER

FRASER & ASSOCIATES
ROSEVILLE, CA

For information contact:
Fraser & Associates
Roseville, California
www.perspectiveshistory.com

978-0-9970805-2-0 (paperback)
978-0-9970805-3-7 (ebook)

Library of Congress Control Number: 2020900955

Book Design by Dotti Albertine

Printed in the United States of America

For Chris, Christine and Alby—

I write about the past and you are the future.

The Timeline of the Early Republic

Growth: The Founding Era (1790-1819)	Decay: The Age of Jackson (1820-1846)	Collapse: The Rise of Lincoln (1847-1861)
❖ What type of nation? ❖ Building blocks of nationhood established ❖ Westward Expansion ❖ Unsolved: Federalism and slavery (and who can be an American)	❖ Westward Expansion / Missouri Compromise ❖ Market economy ❖ Continuing battles over what type of nation ❖ Abolitionist movement begins	❖ Mexican-American War and new territories ❖ North and South begin to split ❖ Free Soil Movement ❖ Compromise of 1850 ❖ Rise of the Republican Party

CONTENTS

CONTENTS

ACKNOWLEDGMENTS

*R*esearching and writing history has become my passion in life. Since I published my first book, I have also started teaching history courses to adults through the Osher Lifelong Learning Center at U.C. Davis and Sierra College. This has further enriched my life and reminded me of the thirst that people have for how the past relates to events in our current world. My books are written for a general audience, to meet people's need for better historical knowledge so they can be better citizens. In a book review written by Steven E. Woodworth of Texas Christian University, he wrote that "increasing the public's knowledge and understanding of—and whetting its appetite for—accurate history is a worthwhile goal." I hope that this volume helps to meet that goal.[1]

An author has many people to thank in writing a book. First to my wife Patty, for her continued support of what I am doing. To my close family, who attend my classes, read my books, and provide great feedback. For those who attend my classes, who learn history from me, but also teach me. Finally, to my team of top-flight professionals. Vicki Gibbs, my copy editor, has been of immeasurable help in the production of both of my books. Without her, the final product would not be the work before you. Brittany Dowdle, whose attention to detail is unsurpassed, did the final proof reading of the book and corrected all of those nagging errors that get missed in earlier drafts. Any remaining errors in this book are mine alone. I would also like to thank AElfwine Mischler for her expertise in preparing the index and to Dotti Albertine for her work in compiling my books and creating the cover artwork, which has made this a professional looking endeavor.

If by your legislation you seek to drive us from the territories of California and New Mexico, purchased by the common blood and treasure of the whole people, I am for disunion.
　—ROBERT TOOMBS OF GEORGIA[2]

The first shot was fired in the early morning hours just before dawn. Major Robert Anderson of the United States Army, a West Point graduate, had been warned to surrender the fort or suffer the consequences. The mortar shell, fired over Fort Sumter in Charleston Harbor on April 12, 1861, was not fired by a foreign nation, but by Americans shooting at Americans. The Civil War had begun.

The great experiment in nationhood, under which a republic would be established over a large land mass with a heterogenous population, had collapsed. The founding generation had launched this experiment in self-government first by declaring independence in 1776 and then by framing a new and unifying Constitution in 1787. The proximate cause of the sectional split of the country into North and South was the election of Abraham Lincoln in November of 1860, but the deeper reasons went back to the founding generation, who had been unable to resolve the twin problems that split the nation: slavery and the ultimate locus of political power in a federal system, whether at the state or federal level. In some ways the issue went even deeper, to a debate over what made America a nation and just who could be a member of that nation.

While these problems had vexed the United States since its founding, the split became unmanageable in the 1850s. In the aftermath of the Mexican-American War in 1848, the United States had added a large swath of new territory that included the future states of California, Arizona, Utah, Nevada, and New Mexico. Many in the North wanted to see these territories remain open for free labor. The Compromise of 1850 seemed to settle the matter by allowing the California legislature to select whether to allow slavery within its borders but placed no restrictions on slavery in the balance of the territory. Since California's political leaders were known to oppose slavery, the settlement benefited the North by adding that state, but gave the South the possibility of adding future slave states in the remaining territory.[3]

But the issue erupted again over whether Kansas and Nebraska should be admitted as free or slave states. Lincoln made his national reputation in the 1850s debating his old rival, Stephen A. Douglas, over the issue of expansion of slavery. Douglas's position, which was incorporated into the Kansas-Nebraska Act that he sponsored, allowed those territories to decide the issue based on popular sovereignty, by the people of the territories voting whether they wanted to allow slavery or not. The Kansas-Nebraska Act undid the Missouri Compromise of 1820, which had barred slavery in the area that runs "east along the [original] Mason-Dixon line and headed westward to the Ohio River and along the Ohio to its mouth at the Mississippi River and then west along 36 degrees 30 minutes North."[4]

Lincoln, who in the 1850s was a little-known yet ambitious Illinois politician, thought that Douglas's position on popular sovereignty was absurd. Lincoln grounded his argument against the expansion of slavery in the nation's founding documents, the Constitution and the Declaration of Independence. The Founding Fathers had "eschewed and rejected" slavery, Lincoln maintained. The Constitution they framed "forbore to so much as mention the word 'slave' or 'slavery' in the whole instrument." To Lincoln, the idea that self-government could be used to justify the expansion of slavery was a perversion of republican government and of the Declaration of Independence. "Near eighty years ago we began by declaring that all men are created equal; but now from that beginning we have run down to the other declaration, that for some men to enslave OTHERS is a 'sacred right of self-government.'" While in his speeches he indicated sympathy for Southerners, that "they are just what we would be in their situation," the core of Lincoln's view was that slavery was immoral. "Because the Negro was a man, there could be no moral right to slavery," historian David Donald has written of Lincoln's position. "No man is good enough to govern another man, without that other's consent. I say this is the leading principle—the sheet anchor of American republicanism," according to Lincoln.[5]

Lincoln parlayed his position on slavery, which reflected a middle ground between the abolitionists on one side and defenders of slavery on the other, into a prominent role in the newly emerging Republican Party. The party combined the disaffected elements of the old Whig Party with antislavery Democrats. Lincoln further enhanced his reputation during 1858, running for the Senate seat occupied by Stephen Douglas. The two men engaged in a series of debates that focused on the issue of slavery in the new territories. Although Lincoln lost that election, he emerged as the dark horse candidate for the presidency as the Republican nominee in 1860. In the aftermath of Lincoln's election, one in which he received no votes from the Southern states,

South Carolina seceded from the Union. It was quickly followed by six other states of the South and led to the confrontation at Fort Sumter.

⚘ ⚘ ⚘

John C. Calhoun, the senator from South Carolina, was a champion of states' rights and had in the past attempted to nullify federal laws that his home state disagreed with. In 1850, he issued a warning about the perils that the Union would soon face. "It is a great mistake to suppose that disunion can be affected by a single blow. The cords which bind these States together in one common Union are far too numerous and powerful for that. Disunion must be the work of time." Calhoun warned that "agitation of the slavery question has snapped" some of the most important cords, and that eventually "nothing will be left to hold the States together except force."[6]

What were these common cords that bound the nation together? How had they developed between 1789 and 1850? Why did the twin issues of slavery and federalism finally tear these cords apart? These are the questions that volume two of the American Nation series considers. But before that, we should first consider the nature of the American nation.

Two Views of Nation

The concept of a nation is at the center of this second volume. In *The Emergence of One American Nation*, the term *nation* was defined as "a collective identity of a people as a result of common history, expectations of a shared future, and, usually, a common language."[7]

To that, I would add that individuals must be aware of or conscious of their own unity and have a common vision of the future. There are numerous elements that help create a common identity, including ethnicity, race, a common culture and language, and control over land. At the time of the American Revolution, these elements were present, yet the most important, self-identification of America as a nation, was missing. Winning independence and forming the first government for the United States under the Articles of Confederation were important underpinnings for nationhood, but they were insufficient to hold together in one nation thirteen separate states, which considered themselves individually sovereign. The framing and ratification of the Constitution was the seminal act in nation building, providing a roof over the new nation, and allowing the time needed to build the wall of shared experience central to nationhood. Yet the founders left behind the twin problems of slavery and federalism, which were often two sides of the same coin, and they continue to bedevil their progeny.[8]

There have always been two views of what makes America a nation. One is tied to a traditional racial or ethnic view, ethnonationalism for short, the other that America is an idea. Gunnar Myrdal of Sweden dubbed the second one the American Creed, that Americans were bound together by "the ideals of the essential dignity and equality of all human beings, of inalienable rights to freedom, justice and opportunity."[9] Myrdal was referring to Jefferson's natural-rights section of the Declaration of Independence, in which Jefferson wrote:

We hold these truths to be self-evident; that all men are created equal; that they are endowed by their Creator with certain inalienable rights; that among these are life, liberty, and the pursuit of happiness; that to secure these rights, governments are instituted among men, deriving their just powers from the consent of the governed.

Today, the United States is religiously, culturally, and ethnically diverse. Yet we see ourselves as Americans in large part due to this creedal notion of America. In 2018, two scholars at Grinnell College "polled Americans on what they most associate with being a real American." They found that a "vast majority of respondents identified a set of values as more essential than any particular identity." As historian Mark Byrnes has written, "The United States is fundamentally an idea, one whose basic tenets were argued in the Declaration of Independence and given practical application in the Constitution." These ideas revolve around liberty, equality, self-government, and equal justice for all, and have universal appeal. "Since America was an idea, one could become an American by learning and devoting oneself to" those universal ideas, Byrnes observes. This is, in fact, what our citizenship tests do. People have come from all over the world, from diverse backgrounds, religions, and races, and have become Americans. And we pride ourselves on hyphenated identifiers: Italian-American; Irish--American; Chinese-American, African-American. Nowhere else in the world can this occur except in a place that is dedicated to a set of broad ideas. It also allowed people whose rights were initially denied to them, including women and African-Americans, to stake their claim based on our founding creed. "This creedal understanding of American identity emerged as the result of a long struggle stretching over nearly two centuries," political scientist Francis Fukuyama writes. The universal ideals expressed in the Declaration of Independence and memorialized in the law through the Constitution and the Bill of Rights have not always been achieved, certainly not at the time they were written, and not today as we continue with the struggle to meet them. Nor are they self-actualizing. One way to view American history is as a struggle by individuals and groups to claim their share of these rights, from the abolishment of slavery, to the women's movement to gain the vote and a share of equal rights, to today's clash over gay and transgender rights. To fully share in the American dream, numerous immigrant groups have also had to overcome resistance from those who have a restricted view of what makes America one nation. Over the course of American history, the American Creed would animate many who felt their rights were denied and wanted the nation to live up to its highest ideals.[10]

Despite the strong appeal of the American Creed, 25 percent of those polled by Grinnell College held nativist views similar to those espoused by Donald Trump during his 2016 election campaign for president, which in part helped elect him to the highest office in the United States. The view that ethnicity and race made the United States one people predominated in the early American republic, as we will explore in this book. John Jay, in *Federalist* No. 2, made the argument that the United States was one nation at the time of the debate over ratification of the Constitution by appealing to ethnonationalism. He wrote that we are "one united people—a people descended from the same ancestors, speaking the same language, professing the same religion, attached to the same principles of government, very similar in their manners and customs and who, by their joint counsels, arms, and efforts ... established their general liberty and independence."[11]

Jay's thesis largely reflected the traditional view of nationhood. "It is based on shared religion (Protestantism), ethnicity (descent from the English), [and] common language (English)," Fukuyama notes. It was certainly true that speaking a common language helped to establish a sense of nationhood, especially among a group of states that had been founded over a long period of time during the colonial era and which were at great distances from one another. As Noah Webster would later write, a "national language [is] ... a band of national union." At the time of ratification of the Constitution, a majority of people were of English descent, and most of the rest were European in origin. They viewed America as a nation for white people, with Caucasians as the superior race and Anglo-Saxons superior among whites. The late Samuel P. Huntington, who was a Harvard political scientist, argued that there were also important cultural elements that came from our Anglo-Saxon heritage and that pervaded American society. He, too, includes among these Christianity, the rule of law, individualism, and a work ethic, all of which were rooted in the Protestant religion or were inherited from the English. These cultural elements had an effect on the American Creed. "Out of this culture the settlers developed in the eighteenth and nineteenth centuries the American Creed with its principles of liberty, equality, individualism, representative government and private property."[12]

But John Jay also overstated the extent of national unity that existed in 1788. The *Federalist Papers* were written to convince the state of New York to join the stronger federal union laid out by the recently framed American Constitution, and as such they present an argument in favor of nationhood. However, this was but one side of a debate on how strong the central government should be, a debate that did not end with ratification of the Constitution. As *The Emergence of One American Nation* shows, the United States did not begin as one nation, far from it. The time that elapsed between the establishment of the colonies and the geographical distance between them made the European people that populated the Eastern Seaboard largely strangers to each other. Prior to the revolution, the colonists identified themselves as loyal British subjects and members of the colony they lived in. The occupants of those colonies "discovered that they really did not like each other very much, but that they needed common trust to survive" a war with Great Britain, as historian John Murrin has written. In 1775, John Adams noted that the differences between New England and the other colonies made them seem like "several distinct nations." After taking over the Continental Army, Washington found he did not much like the New England troops he commanded, calling them "an exceedingly dirty and nasty people." In a 1785 letter, Jefferson described Northerners as "cool" and "laborious" while Southerners were "fiery" and "indolent."[13]

The ethnonationalist perspective cannot describe the United States today—it was inaccurate even in 1790, when we were already a diverse people. While white Anglo-Saxon Protestant men came to dominate the United States, they were not the only ethnic or racial group present in 1790. Black people, most of them enslaved, were almost 20 percent of the total population of the South in 1790. The middle colonies were quite diverse. In Pennsylvania, 33 percent of the people were of German ancestry in 1790. Both New York and New Jersey had large numbers of German and Dutch peoples. There were also conflicts between the English and these other groups, including the Irish, the Scottish, and the Welsh, who were themselves from the British Isles. Even the term *British* had only come into existence in 1707, and the "English, Welsh, Scottish and Irish settlers were all quite different from each other in folkways, language and religion," Ed Simon writes.[14]

The Founding Fathers differentiated between the people who inhabited the original thirteen colonies, who were largely drawn from Northern Europeans, even if today we see few differences between people of European descent. Benjamin Franklin complained about the "Palatine Boors" who swarmed "into our Settlements ... herding together" and creating a "Colony of Aliens." "Thomas Jefferson doubted that he shared the same blood as the 'Scotch' and worried about immigrants from the wrong parts of Europe coming to the United States," Fukuyama writes. These conflicts had deep roots, as historian Roger Daniels notes. "In the nearly two centuries before the Revolution, the attitudes of the predominant English American blew hot and cold about 'foreign immigrants,' prefiguring an ambivalence that has continued to prevail in American society." Still, the founders knew that in order to conquer the entire continent, they would need to allow immigrants to come to America. In the Constitution, the only office that a naturalized citizen could not hold was the presidency. "In addition, the natural-rights philosophy that inspired so many of the leaders of the revolution tended them toward tolerance and non-sectarianism," Daniels writes. These tensions were on display in 1790, when an immigration act was passed that allowed an immigrant to become a citizen after two years, which was then increased to five years with the Naturalization Act of 1795. New citizens were required to swear allegiance to the Constitution, yet the act was only applicable to "free-born white persons." Still, it advanced "belief rather than birth as the principal criteria for citizenship," Daniel A. Gerber writes.[15]

While ethnonationalism has deep roots in the United States, so does the American Creed. Jay noted how the United States was "attached to the same principles of government." To Thomas Paine, the country was drawn from "people from different nations, speaking different languages" who were melded together "by the simple operation of constructing governments on the principles of society and the Rights of Man" in which "every difficulty retires and all the parts are brought into cordial union." Unlike Europe, the United States was a place without a hereditary hierarchy, and outside of the South, originally a nation made up primarily of small land-owning farmers. As such, equality was an essential value in the founding of the nation, placed on the same footing as freedom and the pursuit of happiness in the Declaration of Independence. America was also an experiment in self-government, a republic unlike any in history, which would ultimately expand over an entire continent. Given the country's size and diversity, its historical development during colonial times, and its revolt against a centralized system of British power, there was always a tension between nationalism, with its tendency toward centralization, and the need for autonomy at the state level.[16]

Washington saw America as a place that was "open to receive not only the Opulent and respectable Stranger, but the oppressed and persecuted of all Nations and Religions." As with many of the founders, Washington had a nonsectarian conception of the role of religion in American life, arguing that each person should "be protected in worshipping the Deity according to the dictates of his own conscience." Both Jefferson and Madison worked to disestablish Anglicanism as the recognized religion for Virginia, and they played key roles in establishing freedom of religion in the new nation. While Huntington has argued that Protestant Christianity was of importance in establishing an underlying American culture, part of what helped religion grow in the country was the freedom each person had to worship God as they wished, or to not worship at all.[17]

Hector St. John de Crevecoeur was another adherent of the concept of America as an idea. Originally from France, he immigrated to New York during the colonial period. Crevecoeur talked about the amazing "mixture of English, Scotch, Irish, French, Dutch, Germans, and Swedes" who were "a strange mixture of blood." He referred to people who came to the United States as Americans, saying it was a place where "individuals of all nations are melted into a new race of men." But, of course, people do not actually melt. As we have already seen, there were significant tensions between the early settlers who mostly came from England and later immigrants. The early republic would experience some tension over immigration, as witnessed by the Alien and Sedition Acts that were targeted against France.

But the tensions were not as significant as they would later become, partly because so little immigration took place between the end of the Revolutionary War and 1812. By 1820, and the rise of Andrew Jackson, this would begin to change as more immigrants came to the United States from Ireland and Germany (many of whom would be Catholics) an influx that would lead to "a full-blown movement that exalted bigotry to a matter of principle," Daniels observes.[18]

For people of color, America has rarely been a welcoming place, as we shall see in the pages of this book. Blacks were brought here as slaves, and native peoples were overrun as the insatiable desire for land led to ever-greater westward expansion. Any history of the early republic must take into account "the shameful fact: historically the United States has been a racist nation," as the historian Arthur Schlesinger framed it. "The curse of racism has been the great failure of the American experiment, the glaring contradiction of American ideals." Nonwhites were excluded from who could be considered a part of the people. Fukuyama goes so far as to say that the "American Civil War was, at its root, a fight over American national identity. The Southern states explicitly linked identity to race by excluding nonwhites from citizenship." We will also see that the North was racist, although the rise of the abolitionists in the 1830s would eventually lead to the rise of the Republican Party in the 1850s, a group committed to stopping the spread of slavery. Abraham Lincoln would become one of the party's leaders, a man committed to a creedal view of America who would extend the rights enshrined in the Declaration of Independence to all people, black and white, native born and immigrant.[19]

The United States emerged as a unique nation after the ratification of the Constitution, but it was far from a settled question whether any nation of this type could long endure, in Lincoln's famous words at Gettysburg. One of the elements not yet deeply engrained was a set of shared experiences, a shared history that creates unity. This volume explores some of those key experiences during the period from 1789 to 1860 that formed the common bonds that Calhoun spoke of. It also analyzes in greater depth the issues of slavery and federalism that finally tore the nation apart, and how these were connected. The issue of slavery is paramount in this telling, of whether we would live up to our founding creed that all people are created equal and have a right to freedom or continue to deny this and treat black people as property.

There are many ways to tell the story of the development of American nationhood. This volume focuses on the major events that occurred in the early republic in a chronological manner, not only to manifest the development of one American nation and the events that tore it apart, but also as a way to discuss a broad outline of American history during this period.

Endnotes

1 (from Acknowledgments) Steven E. Woodworth, review of *A Fierce Glory: Antietam—The Desperate Battle That Saved Lincoln and Doomed Slavery*, by Justin Martin, The Journal Of American History, September 2019, p. 474

2 Quoted in Doris Kearns Goodwin, *Team of Rivals: The Political Genius of Abraham Lincoln* (New York, 2005), p. 141.

3 Goodwin, p. 143.

4 Goodwin, p. 160; Matt Rosenberg, "The Mason-Dixon Line Divided the North and South," retrieved June 21, 2014, from http://geography.about.com/od/politicalgeography/a/masondixon.htm.

5 Abraham Lincoln, *Selected Speeches and Writings* (New York, 1992), p. 93–99. The quotes are from Lincoln's speech on the Kansas-Nebraska Act at Peoria, Illinois, on October 16, 1854; David Herbert Donald, *Lincoln* (New York, 1995), p. 176, which also contains the Lincoln quote at the end of the paragraph.

6 Goodwin, p. 142.

7 Donald J. Fraser, *The Emergence of One American Nation*, (Roseville, 2015), p. 3, as taken from Gordon Bowen. *Foundations of Political Science: Defining Concepts.* The URL that this was taken from no longer exists.

8 The metaphor of the roof comes from John M. Murrin, "A Roof without Walls: The Dilemma of American National Identity," in Richard Beeman, Stephen Botein, and Edward C. Carter III, *Beyond Confederation: Origins of the Constitution and American National Identity* (Chapel Hill, 1987).

9 Arthur M. Schlesinger, *The Disuniting of America: Reflections on a Multicultural Society* (New York, 1998), p. 33, for the quote from Myrdal. See also Samuel P. Huntington, *Who Are We: The Challenges to American's National Identity* (New York, 2004), p. 66–68 for an analysis of Myrdal's American Creed and others who have expressed similar sentiments.

10 Caleb Elfenbein and Peter Hanson, "What does it mean to be a real American?" retrieved January 4, 2019, from https://www.washingtonpost.com/outlook/2019/01/03/what-does-it-mean-be-real-american/; Mark Byrnes, "What Was 2016 About? Who We Are and What Values We Cherish," retrieved December 16, 2016, from the History News Network at http://historynewsnetwork.org/blog/153856; Francis Fukuyama, *Identity: The Demand for Dignity and the Politics of Resentment* (New York, 2018), p. 158.

11 Alexander Hamilton, James Madison, and John Jay, *The Federalist Papers* (New York, 1961), p. 38.

12 Fukuyama, p. 155; Huntington, p. 40–41.

13 Murrin, p. 343; the quote from Washington was taken from Joseph J. Ellis, *His Excellency: George Washington*, (New York, 2004), p. 78.

14 Roger Daniels, *Coming To America: A History of Immigration and Ethnicity in American Life*, (New York, 2002), p. 31, p. 66–67; Ed Simon, "What the People Who "Want their Country Back" Forget," retrieved August 20, 2018 from the History News Network at http://historynewsnetwork.org/blog/169710;

15 Daniels, p.101–118; David A. Gerber, *American Immigration: A Very Short Introduction* (Oxford, 2001), p. 19; see also Gordon S. Wood, *Empire of Liberty: A History of the Early Republic, 1789-1815* (Oxford, 2009), p. 147-149.

16 Fukuyama, p. 156.

17 Jon Meacham, *American Gospel: God, the Founding Fathers, and the Making of a Nation* (New York, 2006), p. 77–78 for the Washington quote. The universal nature of the founder's religion runs throughout this volume.

18 Schlesinger, p. 15–16; Daniels, p. 117.

19 Schlesinger, p. 18; Fukuyama, p. 156.

CHAPTER 1

The Development of the First American Party System

If I could not go to heaven but with a party, I would not go there at all.
—THOMAS JEFFERSON, 1789

*I*t would seem an unusual place to begin a book about the evolution of American nationhood with a discussion of political parties. By their nature parties divide, while nations unify. But in fact, people within every society have differences of opinion and pursue interests that can clash. Recent scholarship in the field of political science indicates that the liberal/conservative divide may be innate to human beings, that individuals are predisposed to certain political orientations and beliefs.[1] In authoritarian societies, governments use brute force to stamp out political differences. This approach is inappropriate in democratic societies, and so governments must find some means to organize these differences and give voice to them, and then allow governing institutions to craft the compromises needed to solve societal problems and avoid a reversion to violence. Well-formed democratic political institutions play this role, including elected legislative and executive bodies, courts, and political parties.

The new American republic faced the same challenge. Despite the anti-party bias of the founders, they soon found it necessary to coalesce into two antagonistic political parties that differed over both domestic and foreign policy issues. Beyond even these policy disputes, they differed over a vision for the future of the newly emerging nation. Because they had little experience working in a partisan environment, each party began to see the other as illegitimate. This tendency was especially strong in the Federalist Party, which held power during the Washington and Adams administrations. As historian Richard Hofstadter writes: "One of the great dangers in newly organized states is that the party in power ... claims for itself the exclusive custodianship of the essence of nationality and the exclusive right to interpret the meaning of national welfare."[2]

The Federalist view of their opponents, the Republican Party of Jefferson and Madison, was that their criticism on issues was "criticism of all government," that would ultimately lead to "anarchy, subversion, and disloyalty." For their part, the Republicans charged the Federalists with undermining popular consent and wanting to create a monarchy in America that would lead to rule by the aristocratic few and overturn the republic.[3] The 1790s were a period when the founding generation needed to manage these extensive differences of opinion without allowing the political system to fall either into chaos or dictatorship. The outcome of these disputes was by no means assured as the decade unfolded, and the nation's experiment with a republic almost failed before the founding generation discovered a path for organizing political differences through competition, debate, and elections, rather than violence. The two-party system would ultimately become one of the hallmarks of American nationhood.

The Nature of Political Differences

Before launching into the history of the 1790s, it may be instructive to take a step back and analyze the nature of political differences that have existed since the beginning of human history. Aristotle wrote that "Man is by nature a political animal." The Greek philosopher, who lived around 300 BC, was probably onto something. Political scientists John R. Hibbing, Kevin B. Smith, and John R. Alford, in their book, *Predisposed: Liberals, Conservatives and the Biology of Political Differences*, argue that political differences may in fact be rooted, at least in part, in distinct biological differences between individuals.

It turns out that liberals and conservatives have different tastes not just in politics, but in art, humor, food, life accoutrements, and leisure pursuits; they differ in how they collect information, how they think, and how they view other people and events; they have different neural architecture and display distinct brain waves in certain circumstances; they have different personalities and psychological tendencies; they differ in what their autonomic nervous systems are attuned to; they are aroused by and pay attention to different stimuli; and they might even be different genetically. At least at the far ends of the ideological spectrum, liberals and conservatives are emotionally, preferentially, psychologically, and biologically distinct.[4]

Political differences fall along a continuum from liberal at one end to conservative at the other end. Most people have views that are a mix of liberal and conservative perspectives and fall somewhere along the continuum. It should also be kept in mind that some people have little to no interest in politics. "Certain people are in possession of powerful political predispositions ... other people have much weaker political predispositions," the authors argue.[5]

While specific issues vary over time and between different societies, the authors posit that certain "bedrock social dilemmas" have always divided people and they lie at the heart of our political differences. They divide these bedrock differences into four distinct areas. One involves the importance of tradition versus the need for change. Some people are committed to the tried and true way of doing things, and to traditional values. They feel suspicious when it comes to making changes in society, and they want change to occur slowly, if at all. Others are more open to new experiences and approaches to solving problems in society and are willing to change the moral code as society evolves. A second set of differences deals with the importance of the welfare of the group versus that of the individual. Numerous political disagreements are rooted in divergent views of the extent to which individuals should assume personal responsibility for themselves versus the responsibility we share as a group toward one another. Liberals and conservatives also differ on how to deal with those who exist outside of one's own kin group, tribe, ethnic group, or nation. Some view outsiders as a threat to their own group, while others see them as nonthreatening and similar to themselves. The final area of difference involves the best way to make decisions in society. Some people prefer top-down leadership, while others believe leaders should act based on input from the group. This area also includes whether leaders should cooperate with each other and find ways to compromise, or whether they should stick with their principles.

Hibbing and his co-authors have measured responses to these issues based on a series of questions they have developed, which they call the "Society Works Best" Index. Not surprisingly, conservatives, more so than liberals, tend to score higher on issues involving "traditional values, unbending leaders, punishment for rule breakers ... and rewards assigned on the basis of merit rather than need." And an individual's score on bedrock social dilemmas also tends to mirror that person's position on current political issues.[6]

Not only do people have varying tastes and preferences based on deeply imbedded biological predispositions, but these differences seem to extend to placing greater or lesser emphasis on different moral values. Liberals tend to be more concerned with how individuals are treated, whether fairly or unfairly, and are more interested in the "new and novel, a commitment to individual expression, and a tolerance of differences." Conservatives have a "greater desire for order and security, a commitment to tradition, and group loyalty."[7] The evolutionary biologist Avi Tuschman contends that ethnocentrism, the belief in the superiority of one's own ethnic group, is a hallmark of a conservative point of view. "Conservatives have more positive feelings towards members of their in-group and higher levels of patriotism,"Tuschman writes. "That is why the political right extols the altruistic sacrifice of individual interest for the benefit of the tribe."[8] This may explain why conservatives tend to support the use of public resources to pay for national defense and public safety programs, but are opposed to funding programs that involve group sacrifice for individuals, such as welfare or health care programs.

During the course of evolution, both liberal and conservative political orientations have played a role in the survival of our species. As Hibbing and his co-authors point out, early hunter-gatherer societies were likely suspicious of other tribes, since they posed a potential danger. Life during pre-agricultural days was much more dangerous, with deaths in battle as high as 500 out of 100,000 people, compared to the modern world where only .3 out of 100,000 people will die in war. In such an environment, suspicion of out-groups was a smart survival strategy. But as human society began to move to an agricultural base, dangers began to fade. "In such an altered environment, selection pressures for heightened negativity bias, for the tried and true way of doing things, and for deep suspicion of out-groups likely would start to fade," the authors write. Openness toward new ideas and a willingness to trust outside groups brought certain advantages as well, including the ability to trade with other groups and to learn innovative ways to solve societal problems. Jared Diamond has argued that one of the great advantages that allowed the fertile crescent to become the dominant region was the lack of geographic barriers (rivers, mountains, etc.), allowing for the free flow of new ideas and innovation in that area.[9]

Given the biological foundation for political differences and its deep roots in humankind's evolution, the founders would have found it impossible to not fall into political disagreement with each other. Tuschman, in his book, *Our Political Nature: The Evolutionary Origins of What Divides Us*, organizes his concepts differently but comes to remarkably similar conclusions on the importance of biological evolution in influencing political views. One of his core arguments is that a person's view of inequality is heavily influenced by their political orientation. Liberals tend to "believe in the innate, inner equality of all people, [and] attribute the world's inequalities to outer, structural injustices." Liberals want to break down differences that occur due to power relationships, believing this will lead to a more just world. Thomas Jefferson, perhaps more than any other member of the founding generation, represents this point of view. Conservatives believe that "hierarchies reflect inner, individual capabilities," and that inequalities "reveal the worth of the powerful and the weak," which makes them more tolerant of inequalities. Alexander Hamilton, more than any other founder, believed in this point of view. Finally, George Washington and James Madison fall somewhere between the two extremes. [10]

Let's see how the core societal problems identified by Hibbing and his co-authors, and the importance of inequality that Tuschman discusses, relate to Jefferson, Madison, Washington, and Hamilton. Historian Stuart Leibiger places these men on the political continuum from Jefferson at the furthest left, to Madison just left of center,

Washington just right of center, and Hamilton furthest to the right.[11] This analysis not only reveals the applicability of these problems in American history, but also helps to explain why these men fell into disagreement so quickly. John Ferling has written of Jefferson and Hamilton that "their opposing views are like the twin strands of DNA in the American body politic."[12] First, we will explore the broadest area of disagreements over human nature, which affects each man's views on authority and leadership (whether it flows up or down) in society. Then we will review the specific domestic policy issues that divided these men, which illustrate differing views on inequality, tolerance for change, whether authority should flow up or down, and individual versus group interests. In chapter 2, we will explore how each individual's view of outsiders divided the founding generation in terms of the foreign policy they advocated.

Human Nature and the Founders

Is human nature good or evil? Is mankind cooperative or competitive? Those who view human nature as generally good believe that people are naturally cooperative and altruistic, that man is other centered and concerned with the public good. Evil, in this worldview, "comes primarily from undeserved inequalities in strength or power," according to Tuschman, which requires certain actions that can ameliorate these unequal situations. Such instances could involve the relationship between aristocrats and common people; the power which a business owner holds over his workers; "soldiers and police who abuse civilians"; "men who mistreat women"; or the power that slave owners held over African Americans in the world of the founders. Those who view man as sinful believe that people act only out of their own self-interest and lack empathy for the plight of others. Many religious people, particularly Christians, tend to view man as generally sinful due to the fall of Adam, and believe that "people are prone to pride, arrogance, and oppressive use of power for selfish ends." But they also believe that man can be redeemed through a loving God. Political philosophers from Aristotle to Locke to Rousseau have subscribed to a generally favorable view of human nature. On the other side stood Plato and Thomas Hobbes, who both tended to see that man was by nature evil.[13] One's views on human nature will drive the types of political systems that are favored and whether authority should flow from the top down or from the bottom up.

Among all our founders, Thomas Jefferson had the most favorable view of human nature. He believed that man was essentially cooperative, a social creature that tended to act altruistically, and that man had an innate moral sense. Jefferson falls furthest to the left on the political spectrum. Gordon Wood describes him as "high minded, optimistic, visionary, and often quick to grab hold of new and sometimes outlandish ideas ... he was also a radical utopian ... [who] often dreamed of the future and was inspired by how things might be." In an 1814 letter to Thomas Law, Jefferson wrote that "the Creator" had made the "moral principle so much a part of our constitution." He went on to say that he viewed "our relations with others as constituting the boundaries of morality ... Self-love, therefore, is no part of morality. Indeed, it is exactly its counterpart. It is the sole antagonist of virtue, leading us constantly by our propensities to self-gratification in violation of our moral duties to others." While he admitted that this moral sense of duty to others was "not planted in every man, because there is no rule without exceptions; but it is false reasoning which converts exceptions into the general rule." Political scientist Garrett Ward has summarized Jefferson's philosophy as being threefold: 1) the capacity for humans to choose good over evil; 2) "an innate identification with others" and a feeling of sympathy toward others; and 3) a natural sense of justice that makes social life possible. As Jefferson once wrote to John Adams, "the essence of virtue is in doing good to others." The political scientist Richard K. Matthews adds an important component to this view: that Jefferson believed man's nature evolves over time and that this "evolution can lead to human progress and perfectibility."[14]

Jefferson subscribed to the view that evil in the world was a product of outside structural injustices that were put in place by an elitist few. This belief caused friction with Hamilton, who he thought was placing just such societal barriers in place that would lead to rule by a new monarchy in America. Jefferson believed that injustice in the world was a product of governing institutions that were inflicted on the common person by elites. That point of view comes across most clearly in his *Summary Views of the Rights of British Citizens*, which he wrote in 1774 during the ferment that led to American independence. In it, Jefferson argued that there was a time in England, before the Norman conquest, when the people lived in perfect harmony without the rule of kings and princes. That this was fictitious did not matter, since for Jefferson it "told a story that fitted perfectly with the way his mind worked ... [The] romantic endorsement of a pristine past, a long-lost time and place where men had lived together in perfect harmony without coercive laws or predatory rules, gave narrative shape to his fondest imaginings and to utopian expectations with deep roots in his personality," writes Joseph Ellis.[15]

Utopian expectations may also have formed his view on the need for limited government. Jefferson looked at the Indian population of North America as living in a state of nature, without the need for extensive government. Since man is by nature a moral creature who has a "sense of justice," little by way of government is needed among the Indian tribes to maintain peace. Jefferson writes of the Indians:

This practice [of breaking up into many small societies] results from the circumstances of their having never submitted themselves to any laws, any coercive power, any shadow of government. Their only controls are their manners, and that moral sense of right and wrong, which like the sense of tasting and feeling in every man, makes a part of his nature ... It will be said, the great societies cannot exist without government. The savages therefore break them into small ones.[16]

In a letter to Madison, Jefferson indicated that he saw three types of societies: "1. [Those] without government, as among our Indians. 2. Under governments wherein the will of every one has a just influence ... 3. Under governments of force." He indicates that "it is a problem, not clear in my mind, that the 1st condition is not the best," but he was resigned to the fact that some government is needed due to the "great degree of population" in the United States. Jefferson believed that a better world could be created if the privileges bestowed on the few by government were removed. To the extent that overarching authority could be removed, men would once again live in harmony. That is, in part, why he wanted government power to largely reside at the local level where the people could rule themselves, what Sheldon refers to as ward democracy under which each local county would be further subdivided down to the ward level.[17]

Jefferson's faith was in the people, and not in rulers. In his book, *Notes on the State of Virginia*, he wrote that "every government degenerates when trusted to the rulers of the people alone. The people themselves therefore are its only safe depositories." He was a strong proponent of public education as a way to enlighten the masses and to "render even them safe, their minds must be improved to a certain degree." An educated populace would be able to participate in government at the local ward level. He also believed that elites were needed as elected representatives at higher levels of government, a group he referred to as the "natural aristocracy," who would be distinguished by their "genius and virtue." "The natural aristocracy I consider as the most precious gift of nature for the instruction, the trusts, and the government of society," Jefferson wrote. Jefferson also differentiated between the natural aristocracy, made up of those with "virtue and talent" and an artificial aristocracy "founded on wealth and birth." Ultimately, authority would flow up from the bottom, from the mass of people to their elected representatives, in Jefferson's worldview.[18]

☙ ☙ ☙

James Madison had a more balanced view of human nature, one that was closer to Alexander Hamilton's than Jefferson's. Perhaps that was, in part, why he and Hamilton were able to work so closely together in establishing the American Constitution. Madison thought that man was both capable of goodness and virtue, but also could act in a self-interested and at times depraved way. Madison's view of human nature led him to draft a Constitution which relied on a balance among branches of government, between the states and the federal government, and between officeholders themselves and the public they served. His views can place him either just to the left or right of center, but because he ultimately became closer to Jefferson's views on political issues and collaborated with him on the establishment of the Republican Party, I believe he belongs just to the left of center.

His writings in the *Federalist Papers*, and especially *Federalist* No. 10 and No. 51, expose the pessimistic side of Madison. In *Federalist* No. 10, Madison attempts to balance the need for majority rule (what he and the other founders referred to as majority factions) in a republic with protection for individual rights to life, liberty, and property. Factions arise due to "the diversity in the faculties of men," which give them differing opinions "concerning religion, concerning government, and many other points." To Madison, "the latent causes of faction are thus sown in the nature of man," with the most "common and durable source of factions" being the "unequal distribution of property." Men break into factions because they have differing interests that are caused by their differing abilities and resulting accumulation of wealth. For Madison, the best method to control majority factions and protect the rights of individuals is through an extended republic that incorporates a multiplicity of interests and factions so as to "make it less probable that a majority of the whole will have a common motive to invade the rights of other citizens."[19]

Federalist No. 51 reflects Madison's concern that human nature is sinful, that people are focused on their own selfish desires, and specifically, that some people, especially those that are attracted to political power, have a need to dominate others. *Federalist* No. 51 focuses on the need to control officeholders, and Madison's solution is to ensure that politicians check each other's ambitions for power. "Ambition must be made to counteract ambition. The interest of the man must be connected with the constitutional rights of the place."[20]

While each of these writings from the *Federalist* can be read as exhibiting a solely negative view of human nature, a better view is that these were attempts by Madison to achieve a balance in the political sphere. The need to control factions had arisen because of Madison's experience at the state level in the 1780s, where he saw that an overreliance on the legislative branch and its direct dependence on the public had led to a series of bad laws. "Madison's suspicion ... [of government power] was based on his fear that the elected officials were only too representative, only too expressive of the passions of the people who had elected them," according to Gordon Wood. He saw the Virginia legislators as "parochial, illiberal, [and] small minded," as a group that only served a "particular interest."[21] He was especially concerned in the 1780s with state laws that favored debtors over creditors through the issuance of paper money, which he feared would lead to inflation, as it had during the Revolutionary War. His solution was to shift more power to the central government to balance the state governments.

While Madison saw the less honorable side of human nature, he also saw the good. He balanced the negative with a belief that man also had a "capacity for reason and justice," as historian Clinton Rossiter has framed it.[22] Without the ability to see both sides of human nature, he would likely have become a supporter of the views of Thomas Hobbes, who thought that only an overarching authority figure, a leviathan, could control man. Madison would not have been the strong supporter of a republican government that he was if he did not believe that the people also had the capacity for self-government.

At the Federal Convention, Madison was one of the strongest supporters for the direct election of the House of Representatives. He "considered the popular election of one branch of the National Legislature as essential to every plan of Free Government." The House should be the "grand depository of the democratic principle," and the government "would be more stable and durable, if it should rest on the solid foundation of the people themselves." He also opposed attempts to limit voting for federal officers to property holders, because this would violate "the fundamental principle that men cannot be justly bound by laws" that they have no part in making. At one point during the Constitutional Convention, Madison also supported the direct election of the president, although this may have been a ploy to eliminate the possibility of appointment by the legislature, a move he feared would reduce the independence of the executive.[23]

Madison's views on the direct role of the public in the government had its limits. He was not a supporter of direct democracy, since it offered "no cure for the mischiefs of faction." He believed that a republic, one in which "the scheme of representation takes place," offered the means to control faction. To Madison, the capacity to act with reason, wisdom, and judgment was thought to reside largely in those men "who possess the most attractive merit and the most diffusive and established characters," as he wrote in *Federalist* No. 10.[24] In other words, Madison and the other Framers wanted to rely on the elite of society, on the natural aristocracy that rose to prominence due to merit and achievement.

On the political spectrum, George Washington was just to the right of center. He was the ultimate realist. In a 1786 letter to John Jay on the problems of governing under the Articles of Confederation, Washington wrote: "We have errors to correct; we have probably had too good an opinion of human nature in forming our confederation. Experience has taught us, that men will not adopt and carry into execution measures the best calculated for their own good, without the intervention of a coercive power." In other words, some type of top-down leadership was required in order to promote the public good. Ultimately, "we must take human nature as we find it; perfection falls not to the share of mortals," Washington wrote to Jay.[25]

Washington was not a political theorist, but rather a man of action. He did not leave extensive writings on his views of human nature, politics, or society, as did others in the founding generation. Rather, we must look at his life to discern what influenced his views on the nature of man.

On the one hand, Washington believed, based on his own experience, that people often acted based on their own self-interest, and that passion and emotion often ruled human behavior. He had spent a good deal of his early life learning to control his own emotions, especially his explosive temper. His need to master self-control may have been what made him so hard to know, both to his contemporaries and to us today. Washington was "the original marble man ... an intensely passionate man, whose powers of self-control eventually became massive because of the interior urges they were required to master," according to Joseph Ellis. Yet for all his self-control in the public arena, he never totally mastered his emotions in private. Alexander Hamilton, who knew him as well as anyone, could attest to this. While serving as his aide-de-camp during the Revolutionary War, Hamilton took the brunt of much of Washington's ill temper. "A stoic figure who strove to be perfectly composed in public, Washington needed to blow off steam in private, and the proud, sensitive young Hamilton grew weary of dealing with his boss's varying moods," according to biographer Ron Chernow. Ultimately, Washington's temper and Hamilton's thin skin would cause a falling out between the two in early 1781 over a minor incident in which Hamilton kept Washington waiting. The two would later reunite, most famously when Washington selected Hamilton to be his treasury secretary in 1789 under the new Constitution.[26]

Washington also knew from firsthand experience that people sometimes made bad judgments based on their own self-interest. During the French and Indian War, Washington had gotten into a heated dispute with General Forbes over the best route for the army to take to attack Fort Duquesne (present-day Pittsburgh). Washington wanted to follow the established route that went through Northern Virginia, since it would solidify his own colony's claim to the Ohio country. When Forbes selected a more direct route that went through Pennsylvania, Washington complained bitterly and attempted to go over Forbes's head to have the decision overturned. "At this stage of his life, Washington sometimes found it difficult to distinguish his own from the general interest," explains Chernow.[27]

Washington's judgment improved over time, to the point where he could successfully lead the United States to victory in the Revolutionary War. While Washington understood the need for a top-down command structure in military matters, he also elicited opinions from his top generals, and sometimes changed his mind when their advice seemed superior to his own judgment. Early in the war, he decided to have the Continental Army evacuate New York based on the advice of others, even though his own preference was to stand and fight. That decision, in all likelihood, kept the army from being annihilated by the British in 1776, an outcome that would have ended the American quest for independence.[28] As president, Washington served as "the hub of the wheel," according to Jefferson, with the various cabinet officers as the spokes, providing him advice and recommendations.

Washington has variously been called a "cautious optimist" and a "guarded optimist." He needed that spirit of optimism to sustain him during some of the darkest days of the Revolutionary War, and to maintain a sense of hope during the trying times of the 1780s. But he was also the ultimate realist, and while his public writings were often profoundly optimistic, his private ones were much more pessimistic. Perhaps this attitude is what placed him squarely in the ideological center of the American political scene.[29]

❧ ❧ ❧

Alexander Hamilton, who was the furthest right on the political spectrum, saw human nature as competitive, as driven largely by self-interest. He no doubt agreed with Madison's statement that interest was the "immediate augmentation of property and wealth." Political scientist Michael P. Federici has described Hamilton's view of human nature as moral realism, a view he shared with Madison. At the Constitutional Convention, Hamilton said that "we must take man as we find him," which meant as acting from self-interest and not necessarily toward outcomes that would serve the public good. "As found, humans are too selfish for the interests of the public good to rely solely on their patriotism and virtue," wrote Federici.[30]

Hamilton believed that the elite in society could break through their own self-interest and act from "more worthy motives." In this regard, Washington was his model. He was distrustful of democracy and of the common man and thought that "the interests of the political and social elites were more likely to coincide with the commonweal than would those of the general population." Hamilton believed that only the elite could act in a disinterested and objective manner. In this regard, he thought authority in society needed to flow down from the elites, and not up from the masses, as Jefferson believed. But he shared with Jefferson a belief in an aristocracy of talent, of which he was one. He did not support the establishment of a monarchy in America, nor the creation of a hereditary aristocracy, a charge that Jefferson and the Republicans would repeatedly level against him. In 1792 he wrote, "I am *affectionately* attached to the republican theory. I desire *above all things* to see the *equality* of political rights, exclusive of all *hereditary* distinction, firmly established by a practical demonstration of it being consistent with the order and happiness of society."[31]

Government needed sufficient power to control man's baser instincts in Hamilton's worldview. He especially supported a strong and "energetic" executive, which opened him to charges of being a closet monarchist. Hamilton had an abiding fear of disorder due to the evil he felt existed in human nature. Government was needed "because the passions of men will not conform to the dictates of reason and justice without constraint." He also saw that men were capable of good, but that the capacity to act with virtue was largely found in society's elite, which made him distrust democracy. "Hamilton's offending view may be that he did not think virtue equally present in all individuals," according to Federici.[32]

Given his view of human nature, Hamilton had little concern for inequality, an issue that would create a major fissure between him and Jefferson's emerging Republicans. The Revolutionary War had unleashed changes in the hierarchal society that had existed during the colonial period, ones that Hamilton and other Federalists were determined to hold back. "Hamilton accepted that there would always be inequalities in society, and that they would increase over time," John Ferling writes. His views were "an expression of the elite's overarching desire to preserve their exalted status."[33]

Hamilton's economic policies, which will be explored next, would open him up to charges that his goal was to enrich himself and his supporters. But Hamilton was in fact opposed to policies that benefited individuals at the expense of society, and subscribed to the eighteenth-century theory of disinterestedness, a condition in which one is "not influenced by private profit."[34] Hamilton's real goal was to see the United States develop into a great economic and political power in the world, one intended "for the accomplishment of great purposes" and that would have the means to defend itself from the other great powers.[35] In order to accomplish this, the economic system of the nation would need to be diversified to include a better balance between agriculture and industry. But before this could occur, the credit worthiness of the new government would first need to be established.

Federalist Economic Policies

Between January of 1790 and the end of 1791, Alexander Hamilton put forward a three-pronged approach to the economic problems of the United States. The first was to restore the credit of the new nation through a plan both to repay the domestic debt and to assume all of the debts of the states. Second, to establish a first Bank of the United States that would manage the repayment of the debt and establish a stable currency. And finally, Hamilton proposed a series of policies to promote industry. Each of these initiatives would prove to be controversial, lead to charges that Hamilton and the Federalists wanted to establish a monarchy in America, and eventually lead Jefferson and Madison toward the creation of their own political party.

Hamilton had done as much as anyone to bring about the stronger central government contained in the Constitution. Since his days in the Continental Army, he had seen the deleterious impact that a weak government produced on the war effort and the troops, who were badly provisioned and rarely paid. As early as 1781, he had proposed a system for propping up the credit of the country and establishing a national bank. He had also been a strong proponent throughout the 1780s of calling for a convention to rewrite the Articles of Confederation. Although his role at the Constitutional Convention had been limited, largely because his views were too far outside of the mainstream, his role in the ratification fight had been crucial in bringing New York into the new union.

Washington initially asked Robert Morris to serve as the first treasury secretary, but Morris, who had performed a similar role for the Confederation Congress, declined to accept and instead recommended Hamilton.[36] Treasury was a unique department compared to the State and War departments, whose incumbents reported to the president, since the treasury secretary was to report directly to Congress. As such, Hamilton had far greater autonomy than the other two major cabinet officers. Besides, Washington was comfortable managing foreign and military affairs, but not economic policy. This caused Jefferson to later conclude that Washington's support of Hamilton's economic policies was grounded in "confidence in the man [Hamilton]" rather than in the policies themselves. In fact, the two men shared a similar worldview in terms of the need for a strong central government led by an energetic executive and of the need for a stable system of public credit for the new nation.[37]

Hamilton's first great task was to unravel the debt left over from the Revolutionary War, which at the time ran to somewhere around 40 percent of the gross domestic product of the country.[38] That debt included money owed to foreign countries, the domestic debt of the federal government, and the accumulated state debts. The United States had been unable to manage the debt under the old Articles of Confederation because the central government lacked the power to tax. Instead, the Confederation Congress had to rely on requests to the states for money. The United States had missed making interest payments on the debt for many years under the articles, and it was one of the problems that led to the creation of a stronger central government under the Constitution.

In January of 1790, Hamilton released his *First Report on the Public Credit*, a forty-thousand-word tour de force on the makeup of the debt and a comprehensive plan to manage it. The debt of the United States was a "bewildering array of bills, notes, and certificates issued by the various agencies of both the Confederation and the state governments," according to Gordon Wood.[39] Hamilton indicated in the report that the debt was the "price of liberty," a remnant from the pursuit of independence. But for the country to succeed, the government would need the ability during times of emergency "to borrow upon good terms," and the essential ingredient for this is "that the credit of a nation should be well established," which required that the country, no less than individuals, repay its debts.

In total, the debt from all sources exceeded $79 million. Of this, about $12 million was money owed to foreign governments, primarily France and Holland. Repaying this part of the debt was not controversial. State debts amounted to about $25 million. Approximately $42 million of the debt was made up of money owed by the federal government to its citizens. This included members of the Continental Army and farmers, who had been paid with certificates for their wartime service and goods. "In many cases, these upright patriots, either needing cash or convinced they would never be repaid, had sold their securities to speculators for as little as fifteen cents on dollar," Chernow writes. Additional speculation had been fueled in the aftermath of the ratification of the Constitution and as Hamilton prepared his report on the public credit, with speculators seeking out and buying up the debt. Since Hamilton's plan was to issue new securities to replace these old certificates, the question was whether the current owners of the debt should receive the full par (face) value of the bonds, or whether the windfall they would receive should be shared with the original owners, a concept called discrimination. Hamilton came down firmly opposed to discrimination for two primary reasons. First, he believed that the "security of transfer" was of paramount importance in the issuance of public debt. An investor would be unwilling to purchase government securities in the open market if they were not assured that the government would repay them at full face value. Government securities under such an approach would become illiquid and would not be available to serve as a source of productive capital or be used as part of the money supply of the country. [40]

The second reason Hamilton opposed discrimination had both political and economic elements to it and lay at the core of what would become Federalist philosophy. Hamilton wanted the new federal debt to be concentrated in the hands of an investor class who would use it to make productive investments in the economy. By concentrating wealth, they would form a capitalist class that would invest in and grow the economy and be loyal to the federal government. He was probably the first to make use of the "trickle down" theory of economic activity. The Scottish philosopher, David Hume, who Hamilton had clearly studied, had written that capital would not help an economy "if it is dispersed into numberless hands, which either squander it in idle show and magnificence, or employ it in the purchase of the common necessaries of life."[41]

Hamilton also proposed that the federal government assume all the state debts. This was another idea that would prove controversial, since some states had almost fully repaid their debts, while other states had large remaining obligations. Here, once again, Hamilton had political considerations in mind. He did not want the states competing with the federal government for the loyalty of the wealthy. "He knew that nothing would strengthen the government more than the loyalty of wealthy and propertied creditors," John Ferling has written.[42]

Under Hamilton's proposed plan, new government securities would be issued to replace the old array of notes, bonds, and certificates. But Hamilton faced a dilemma, which was that the old debt was to be repaid with 6 percent interest, which would overwhelm the government's ability to repay. He decided to issue the new debt with interest paid at 4 percent, which reflected a partial write-off of the old debt. He assumed that investors would be satisfied with such a trade, knowing they would actually be repaid, since the new debt would have a specific pledge of federal revenues. In addition to using import duties, Hamilton proposed a series of excise taxes to repay the debt and established a sinking fund to be financed with postal revenues as a means to retire the principal over time. Many of his opponents, and even some modern historians, have charged Hamilton with wanting a permanent debt. But in fact, as he wrote in the report, he "ardently [wished] to see it incorporated as a fundamental maxim in the system of public credit of the United States that the creation of debt should always be accompanied with the means of extinguishment."[43]

Congress had also charged the treasury secretary to make other recommendations to support the public credit. In December of 1790, Hamilton submitted his second report on the public credit, which proposed the creation of the first Bank of the United States, generally modeled after the Bank of England. The bank represented one of the first public-private partnerships in America, chartered by the federal government with total capital of $10 million. Of this, $2 million would come from the federal government, and the balance from private investors who could use their holding of the newly issued debt to make their investment. While the bank would be independently run by a board of directors, the government would be a minority stockholder and have the ability to monitor the bank's activities, including auditing its books. Hamilton too had concerns about concentrating too much power in either public or private hands.

The treasury secretary's goals in establishing the bank were multi-faceted. First, it would serve as the paying agent for federal debt. Second, it would serve as a source of a stable money supply in an "economy traditionally short of specie." It would also be a source of lending to larger commercial enterprises. The bank would issue notes redeemable in gold or silver, which would expand the money supply; but the creation of paper money would be restricted because those holding the notes could always redeem them for specie. In this way, Hamilton intended to place a check on the issuance of an oversupply of paper money by the government and avoid the rapid inflation that had occurred during the war.[44]

The bank would only make short-term loans of less than ninety days to large merchants and business enterprises, making it of little or no value to small farmers, plantation owners, and middle-class merchants. These groups would form the core of the opposition to the bank and make up the Republican constituency that was beginning to form. Eventually, the states would charter banks to fill the role of lending to these groups. But as with each of Hamilton's economic programs, the focus was on the wealthy few at the top of society who could invest in the growth and expansion of the economy.[45]

❧ ❧ ❧

One year later, Hamilton submitted his final major report to Congress, which had requested a study on how to promote manufacturing in the new nation. At the time of its issuance in late 1791, the United States was an overwhelmingly rural and agricultural country. Of the 3.9 million that lived in the country in 1790, only 202,000 were considered urban dwellers. There were no cities with a population of over 50,000, and only two that had a population of between 25,000 and 50,000.[46] These were New York, at approximately 33,000, and Philadelphia, at 29,000. The *Report on Manufactures* envisioned what the United States would later become.

With the public credit stabilized and a national bank in place, Hamilton saw the opportunity to diversify the American economy. Part of his objective was to ensure that the country could produce its own goods during wartime. "As the War of Independence had revealed, the United States was largely dependent upon foreign supplies in time of war and these supplies could easily be cut off by an enemy possessed of superior sea power," one of Hamilton's biographers, John C. Miller, points out. Much of the public debt had been concentrated into the hands of wealthy foreign and domestic investors, and Hamilton wanted to guide that wealth into productive investments in manufacturing. His plan to do this would involve the government providing subsidies, what he called "bounties," for new business enterprises. "To maintain between the recent establishments of one country and the long matured establishments of another country, a competition upon equal terms ... is in most cases impracticable," Hamilton wrote in the report, rejecting Adam Smith's invisible hand of the marketplace, at least for new industries that were trying to compete with established firms in other countries. As part of the report, the treasury secretary also proposed the "judicious regulation" of manufactured products by the government in order to "prevent fraud upon consumers at home, and exporters to foreign countries." Finally, he saw the need for investment in infrastructure, "good roads, canals, and navigable waterways," as a further means to promote economic development. The *Report on Manufactures* was well ahead of its time, and most of its recommendations were never acted on by Congress.[47]

🐦 🐦 🐦

Hamilton's economic policies, particularly the management of the public debt and the creation of a stable money supply, were widely successful. Between 1790 and 1794, the number of American ships doubled, the price of wheat rose, and the value of land increased. The United States saw "a five-fold increase in the value of exports," from 1793 to 1801. The assumption of state debts allowed states to reduce taxes "between 50 and 90 percent." The value of imported goods rose from $23.5 million in 1790 to $63 million in 1795. "Daily wages for both ship carpenters and laborers in Philadelphia doubled between 1790 and 1796," Gordon Wood writes.[48] While one might expect that this level of prosperity would lead to domestic tranquility, much of this growth was centered in the eastern cities and aided those who were already wealthy. Still, prosperity kept the Federalists' program quite popular through the middle part of the 1790s. But Hamilton's economic plans had also unleashed powerful forces of opposition that led to the creation of the first political party in America, the Republicans. The Republicans of the 1790s should not be confused with the modern Republican Party, which arose right before the Civil War. The Republicans of this era, led by Jefferson and Madison, would later evolve to be the Democratic-Republicans, and later be known as the Democrats.

The Republican Response

In May of 1791, Jefferson and Madison set off on a month-long tour of New York and New England. The two were old friends, having first worked together when Jefferson was governor of Virginia and Madison was a member of the Council of State. They were also neighbors, and today the road from Monticello to Montpelier, less than sixty miles, is known as the Constitution Highway.

They opened the trip by cruising up the Hudson River, then switched to travel by land. Surprisingly, they were the guests of

Hamilton's father-in-law, Philip Schuyler, when they arrived in Albany. The trip was ostensibly a scientific venture to explore "the botanical objects which continually presented themselves," according to Jefferson. Madison described his objective for the trip as "health, recreation & curiosity." But, in fact, their travels also had a political goal, with the two exploring Northern unhappiness with the Federalists in meetings with Hamilton's enemies, including Aaron Burr and Philip Freneau. Freneau was an old classmate of Madison's and was recruited to start a newspaper, the *National Gazette*, which would serve as the public relations arm of the newly emerging Republican Party and a counterweight to the pro-Federalist newspaper the *Gazette of the United States*. So began the era of a partisan press in the United States. Freneau would also be placed on the payroll of the State Department by Jefferson and would be paid by the very government he would extensively criticize.[49]

The two men were in an awkward position to launch an opposing party. For one thing, they lived in an age when party was equated with narrowly based factional politics. More importantly, Jefferson was secretary of state in Washington's cabinet, so his opposition would need to occur behind the scenes. His actions would often appear self-deceptive at best and duplicitous at worst, as Joseph Ellis has written. Madison had led the movement, along with Washington and Hamilton, for the creation of a stronger central government embodied in the Constitution. During the ratification debates, he and Hamilton had collaborated in writing perhaps the most brilliant political tract defending the Constitution in the form of the *Federalist Papers*. In the aftermath of the establishment of the new government, Madison was elected to the House of Representatives, where he helped craft Washington's inaugural address, and the House's response to it. During the early part of Washington's administration, Madison was "not only Washington's closest advisor but a virtual prime minister, linking the executive and legislature together" according to Stuart Leibiger.[50]

Madison had opposed the most controversial parts of Hamilton's plan to restore public credit. He thought that the proposal to repay the debt at par would only benefit speculators, the people he and Jefferson both referred to as the "stockjobbers." His alternative proposal for discrimination would pay off the securities at face value but redistribute the proceeds between the original and current holders of the debt. He offered a compromise in which the current holders would receive "the highest price which has prevailed in the market" with "the residue [going] to the original sufferers." Madison's discrimination plan was impractical and would have imperiled the transferability of securities and was easily defeated in the House. But he had much greater success in his opposition to the assumption of states' debts and was able to bottle up that part of Hamilton's proposal in the House. Madison's opposition to assumption was less a matter of principle than a reflection of the interests of his home state of Virginia, which had largely paid off its debts. Surprisingly, it was Jefferson, recently returned from France to serve as secretary of state, who brokered a compromise over the issue. He hosted a dinner that Madison and Hamilton both attended at which Madison agreed to remove his opposition to assumption, without actually voting for the bill, and Hamilton agreed to use his influence in support of placing the permanent national capital in Virginia, along the Potomac. It was a political bargain that Jefferson would later regret.[51]

❧ ❧ ❧

Opposition to the bank bill was fought largely over constitutional principles, which made it more dangerous in dividing the two sides.

Madison took the position that Congress had no power to charter a bank since no such power was enumerated in the document. He believed it would "strike at the very essence of the Govt. as composed of limited & enumerated powers." While his constitutional arguments may well have been sincere, they also met the ends he wanted. "Many Southerners in particular saw no need for banks," wrote Gordon Wood. "In their agricultural world banks seemed to create an unreal kind of money that benefited only Northern speculators." One must wonder if he would have taken a similar stand had the circumstances been different, since his prior writings had suggested a more expansive view of congressional power. After all, it was Madison who had written in *Federalist* No. 44 that "no axiom is more clearly established in law, or in reason, than that wherever the end is required, the means are authorized; wherever a general power to do a thing is given, every particular power necessary for doing it is included."[52]

Washington was confronted with a major dilemma, with two of his primary advisors now at odds. The president's mind-set was that such divisions were dangerous in a republic. Hoping to find an answer, he asked Jefferson and Edmund Randolph, the attorney general, to provide their opinions on the constitutionality of the bank. Both sided with Madison, in what has become known as the strict constructionist view. Washington then provided Jefferson's opinion to Hamilton, who put forward what one of his biographers has called "the most brilliant argument for a broad interpretation of the Constitution in American political literature." Hamilton posited that the necessary-and-proper clause gave Congress the means to carry out all of its ends, even if the specific power was not listed in the document. The government had the "right to employ all the means requisite, and fairly applicable to the ends of such power; and which are not precluded by restrictions & exceptions specified in the constitution." He must have taken great pleasure in throwing Madison's own words from the *Federalist* back at him. Washington signed the bank bill on February 25, 1791, in large measure because he was as much a supporter of a strong central government as Hamilton. Both Madison and Jefferson, who had the utmost respect for Washington, began to believe that the treasury secretary had duped the unwitting president, who by his own admission was not well versed in economic matters. They found it easier to believe that Washington had been misled than to believe that he actually agreed with Hamilton. Shortly thereafter, the two men set off on their journey North to gauge the level of discontent with the policies of Hamilton.[53]

The emerging Republican opposition was motivated by a mix of interests and ideology, which the bank bill unleashed. In terms of interests, the Southerners feared that placing the bank in Philadelphia would threaten moving the permanent national capital to a site along the Potomac. It was a fear shared by Washington and may have been one of the reasons he hesitated before signing the bank bill. More importantly, the Southerners may well have been concerned that an all-powerful federal government of the kind that Hamilton was putting in place could also threaten the existence of slavery in the South.[54]

But the ideological components were even more important, and had economic, social, and political elements to them. They also connect to some of the core societal dilemmas that divide liberals and conservatives, including equality, how authority should flow in a society, and tradition versus change.

In the latter part of the eighteenth century, a debate was unfolding on whether the process of industrialization and urbanization reflected progress or decay. David Hume, who so influenced Hamilton, stood on one side and believed industrialization "promoted all kinds of beneficial intercourse, resulting in a more civilized, refined and learned culture," as historian Drew McCoy wrote. Rousseau and a number of other traditionalists stood on the other side, believing that industrial societies created major inequality and placed workers under the power of the owners of capital. The Virginians, including Jefferson and Madison, stood on this side of the question. Their vision was to maintain the United States as a largely agricultural society and avoid the development of large cities teaming with people who owned no property. George Mason, also a Virginian who had attended the Constitutional Convention, framed it this way: "will the manners of populous commercial cities be favorable to the principles of free government? Or will not the vice, the depravity of morals, the luxury, venality, and corruption, which invariably prevail in great commercial cities, be utterly subversive of them?"[55]

There was a body of belief that the only way a republic could survive was in a system without major inequalities of wealth. Jefferson was also committed to the expansion of political participation for ordinary men, at least ordinary white men. For such a political system to work, the Jeffersonian Republicans believed that the economy of the United States would need to be decentralized and grounded in a community of independent yeoman farmers endowed with a high degree of equality. Jefferson's views on the virtues of an agrarian lifestyle are well known, as when he wrote that "those who labor in the earth are the chosen people of God, if ever he had a chosen people, whose breasts He has made His peculiar deposit for substantial and genuine virtue." For Jefferson, "economic freedom [is] the basis for a democratic society," as Matthews writes. Jefferson proposed governmental policies to deal with the problem of wealth concentration, in part by the elimination of primogeniture, which focused on reducing inequality caused by passing wealth from one generation to another. By eliminating primogeniture, Jefferson was attempting to eliminate an aristocracy of inherited wealth. Jefferson, when he wrote Virginia's constitution, also proposed that: "every person of full age" should be "entitled to an appropriation of [50] acres" of land, an idea that was rejected by his fellow Virginians.[56]

Jefferson was aghast at the inequality he found in Europe, and he equated this to their overdependence on an industrial economic system. Jefferson wrote to Madison about the extremes of wealth he saw in prerevolutionary France. He told about a conversation he'd had with a peasant woman who had difficulty finding work and often had no bread for her children. Jefferson lamented a situation in which "property is absolutely concentrated in a very few hands." He went on to say, "I am conscious that an equal division of property is impracticable. But the consequences of this enormous inequality producing so much misery to the bulk of mankind, legislators cannot invent too many devices for subdividing property ... Another means of lessening the inequality of property is to exempt all from taxation below a certain point, and to tax the higher portions of property in geometrical progression as they rise."[57] While generally opposed to high taxation, Jefferson was willing to use that power to ameliorate gross inequality, a tactic he believed would not be needed if the United States remained a largely agrarian society.

Both Jefferson and Madison opposed Hamilton because they believed that his economic policies would lead to the expansion of an industrial society with power in the hands of a few wealthy oligarchs and the creation of cities that would be made up of people trapped in "ignorance, poverty and vice," which would make them incapable of sustaining a republic. After spending time in Europe, Jefferson found "the general fate of humanity here most deplorable." He thought that the "great mass of the people are ... suffering under physical and moral oppression," in large part because they were trapped in a system where they were wage earners for other people, which stripped them of their economic independence. Matthews writes of Jefferson that "while the accumulation of property is not the essence of humanity, a sufficient amount of property is necessary in order to guarantee individual freedom," with an ultimate goal of guaranteeing "freedom from an exploitative economic system."[58]

Jefferson and Madison did not oppose all industry or commerce in America. Rather, they felt that the country should have the right types of manufacturing. "For the well-being of the nation's agriculture, a commerce functioning primarily as a carrier of surplus produce to worldwide markets was indispensable," explained historians Stanley Elkins and Eric McKitrick.[59] Industry should support a primarily agricultural economy, and provide basic goods that could be supplied through home industries and artisan production, without the need for large-scale industrial production. As Joyce Appleby has written, Jefferson had a vision of America "that was both democratic and capitalistic, agrarian and commercial." Later in life, particularly after the War of 1812, Jefferson began to accept that some level of manufacturing was going to be needed to ensure the economic independence of the United States. But even here, Jefferson thought that the need for manufacturing was caused by England and France, which had required that America move "from a peaceable and agricultural nation" to a "military and manufacturing one." And Jefferson never made his peace with modern banking and the need for credit markets, which he thought were a particularly corrupt method of making a living. In 1792, he wrote that "agriculture, commerce, & every thing useful must be neglected, when the useless employment of money is so much lucrative."[60]

The Republican view was that the consolidation of economic power in the hands of the few would also lead to the introduction of an aristocratic government in the United States, which is why the Republicans sometimes referred to the Federalists as the monocrats. They justified this view, in part, by claiming that the Federalist program was attempting to replicate the British system of a funded debt, the creation of a national bank, and the movement toward an industrial society. The Republicans charged that Hamilton's program had led to a government that favored a small group of monied men, the so-called stockjobbers, some of whom were members of Congress. This gave the treasury secretary too much control over the legislature, which would no longer be able to act independently in the public interest.[61] The Republicans saw the Federalists as wanting to maintain a traditional and hierarchical political system in which power flowed down from the elites on top to the common people below.

John Taylor of Virginia typified this point of view. In one of his pamphlets, he pointed out that "a faction of monarchic speculators had seized upon" the legislative functions in combination with Hamilton. This faction had created "a dangerous inequality of rank" and laid "the foundation for the subversion of the government itself by undermining its true principles ... The corruption of principles included having legislators that acted in the interest of the rich instead of "the duty they owe their constituents" and in converting the "government from a limited to an unlimited one." Taylor thought the "chief design [of the national bank] was to make the rich, richer and the poor, poorer," and that it was clearly intended as a "design for ... erecting aristocracy and monarchy."[62] The late historian Lance Banning summarizes the core of the Republican ideology as follows:

*Republicans were levelers, at least to a degree ... America had come
to be defined, in part, in terms of its relatively equal agrarian
balance of property. Republicans held it as a first principle that
private morality and public virtue depended on the maintenance
of this distribution of wealth, a distribution profoundly threatened
in their minds by the rise of the monied favorites of a Federalist
administration.*[63]

It is easier to understand Jefferson's opposition to Hamilton and
the Federalists than Madison's. As he wrote to Madison in 1797
regarding the Constitution, "I am not a friend to a very energetic
government. It is always oppressive."[64] But it is impossible to overlook
Madison's movement from a strong advocate for a powerful federal
government in the 1780s to a champion of state's rights and minimal
government in the 1790s. Part of his shifting position was clearly
tied to his home state of Virginia, which did not see any benefit from
Hamilton's financial plans. Like any practical politician, Madison had
to conform his views to those of his constituents. He may also have
been influenced by Jefferson, who had always been the senior partner
in their relationship. But Madison had his own principled reasons
for his evolving views, which were tied to maintaining balance in the
system of federalism.

In the 1780s, Madison had thought that the states had become too
powerful and that policy makers were too dependent on the whims
and momentary passions of the voters. In this environment, he supported a "middle ground, which may at once support a due supremacy
of the national authority, and not exclude the local authority whenever
they can be subordinately useful," as he wrote to Washington in 1787.
By the 1790s, Madison believed that Hamilton's policies were tilting
the system out of balance, favoring Northern commercial interests

over the broader public good. He had always favored a system of checks and balances, which was rooted in his realistic assessment that human nature had both good and bad elements to it, and that government needed to be structured to take both into account. The Constitution was designed to balance the national and state governments, the different branches of government, the few and the many, and even individual politicians. But the policies of Hamilton had thrown the system out of balance by favoring monied interests. "As he saw repeatedly how concentration of power inclined toward tyranny or the triumph of selfish interests, his devotion to checks and balances and separation of powers increased," argued his biographer Ralph Ketcham.[65] While he did not believe that the majority should trample the rights of the minority, he also opposed government by a minority, which would destroy the most important element of a republic, which was government grounded in the consent of the governed. For Madison, the Federalists appeared to be a minority that had captured the government.

Madison also saw a connection between equality and the survival of the republic. He wrote a series of essays for Freneau's *National Gazette*, including one that defended the creation of political parties as "unavoidable," given the different interests in society. The key was to make "one party to serve as a check on the other." He also urged that the pernicious effects of party could be controlled by promoting greater equality. Madison wanted to withhold "unnecessary opportunities from a few, to increase the inequality of property" and "reduce extreme wealth toward a state of mediocrity."[66]

❦ ❦ ❦

In addition to differences over the economy, which were rooted in differing views of equality, the two sides clashed over the role of the common person in politics, and specifically whether power should flow from the top down or the bottom up. To a certain extent, these differences were a matter of degree. The Federalists believed in the core element of republicanism, which was that government needed to be grounded in the consent of the governed. Even Hamilton, no friend to democracy, supported the election of the lower house of the legislature by the people. But once elections were over, the common people should allow the natural aristocracy to then run the government. Jefferson and Madison also both believed that the natural aristocracy should rule. Both sides were attempting to preserve a traditional view of republican government in which a disinterested group of "autonomous individuals, free of interested ties and paid by no masters," would rule. Only the wealthy, and particularly those who were part of the "learned professions ... truly form no interest in society," according to Hamilton, and could act as an "impartial arbiter" between differing interests in society.[67]

But in politics, matters of degree can make a huge difference, and the Federalists would cling to the notion of a society where authority flowed downward, from the elite to the masses. The Republicans, on the other hand, were open to a more expansive, if still limited, role for the people. The Federalist tendency revealed itself early on over the discussion of what to call Washington as the newly elected president. Some Federalists, like John Adams, favored formal titles, which led to a Senate committee that recommended the title "His Highness the President of the United States of America and Protector of the Liberties." Fortunately, the House rejected the use of titles. The Washington administration also carried a certain high tone about it, even though the president himself had concerns about appearing to be monarchical. Many of his advisors had no such qualms, which led to charges from the Republicans that they intended to establish a monarchy in America.[68]

Much of the rhetoric used by the Republicans, which they carried out through pamphlets and Freneau's *National Gazette*, was overstated, specifically the charges regarding monarchy. "By any neutral standard, the picture that Jefferson and Madison saw in their heads was a preposterous distortion," Ellis writes. It would have meant that Washington, who had already rejected "the crown at the end of the war," was part of a conspiracy to implement a monarchy. Yet, Jefferson believed that this was indeed Hamilton's intent. As the battle between the two men worsened (Jefferson referred to them as being "daily pitted in the cabinet like two cocks"), each man attempted to get the other fired. In a letter to Washington, Jefferson charged that Hamilton was preparing "the way for a change, from the present republican form of government, to that of monarchy, of which the English constitution is the model." When Washington met with Jefferson to respond to this letter, and to determine if he should seek a second term, he tried to reassure his secretary of state that introduction of monarchy in American was highly unlikely, since "the main body of the people in the eastern states were steadily for republicanism as in the Southern." He further explained to Jefferson that "he did not believe there were ten men in the United States whose opinions were worth attention who entertained such a thought," and that Hamilton was not one of them. Washington, who had wanted to stay above the fray, could not. He had sided with Hamilton on both the debt plan and also the national bank. Given Jefferson's great love of Washington, he could only attribute the decisions the president had made to being "duped by the Secretary of the treasury, and made a tool for forwarding his schemes," a charge that Washington resented deeply.[69]

In a letter to Hamilton a few weeks after meeting with Jefferson, Washington listed numerous complaints he had heard about his policies, including that Hamilton wanted to "prepare the way for a change from the present republican form of government to that of monarchy, of which the British Constitution is to be the model." He asked both men to end their infighting and to achieve "mutual forebearances and temporizing yieldings *on all sides*," since without such a change in direction the union would be endangered. About the only thing the two sides could agree on was that Washington should stay on for a second term, since, as Madison framed it, only Washington could "reconcile the warring parties."[70]

But Washington may have also inadvertently contributed to the disagreements between the two sides. He could never see that political differences were the norm in society, nor the value of parties in organizing those differences into a competition for political power without reverting to violence. Washington also exhibited a certain degree of hostility toward the emergence of democratic forces in the nation. A group known as the Democratic-Republican Societies had sprung up after Washington's 1792 reelection. "The membership was galvanized by alarm at the growing reach and power of the national government, and particularly by signs of presidential omnipotence and the monarchical overtones of Washington's presidency," according to Ferling. They had formed in the aftermath of the French Revolution and the war that began between the British and the French in 1793. The Washington administration maintained a policy of neutrality between the two sides, which Jefferson initially opposed and only begrudgingly supported. Many in the Republican camp thought that the United States should side with their fellow revolutionaries in France, including the members of the Democratic Societies. "These political clubs were outspokenly pro-French and pro-Republican," according to Richard Hofstadter, and "asserted themselves as lively pressure groups functioning on" the left wing of the Republican Party. Both Jefferson and Madison also kept their distance from them, largely because there was still a large question over the legitimacy of such groups to lobby the government since they were not elected by the people. Madison, and to a lesser extent Jefferson, also held to a traditional, top-down approach to politics in 1793. But the two men also never denounced the groups, unlike Washington. And as the 1790s progressed, the two men began to see the need to harness public opinion in order to achieve their goal of having the government under the control of those with republican views.[71]

Washington blamed the societies for igniting the Whiskey Rebellion, in which distillers in western Pennsylvania used violence and intimidation to keep from paying the excise tax on spirits which Congress had approved as part of Hamilton's revenue-raising measures. In response, Washington was forced to call out the militia to restore order. But Washington ignited a firestorm when he implied that the type of opposition the societies represented were seditious and had no right to exist. Jefferson felt that Washington's position was an "attack on freedom of discussion," and even Adams thought that "political clubs must and ought to be lawful in every free country." Madison went even further, fearing that Washington's attack was an attempt "to connect the democratic societies with the odium of insurrection, to connect the Republicans in Congress with these societies," thereby making all opposition to the government equal to sedition. While Washington's approach to the societies worked in the short term, since they disappeared from the scene within a few years after 1793, it placed him and the Federalists on the wrong side of an emerging democratic society.[72]

John Adams also contributed to the Federalist view of the proper role for the many and the few in society. Adams was a revolutionary, a man who contributed as much as anyone to independence for the United States. But he was also a conservative revolutionary, and his political views had become more pessimistic over time. When he wrote *Thoughts on Government* in the 1770s, which was used as the basis for many of the state constitutions in the aftermath of declaring independence, he still believed that the people could act in a virtuous manner and place the public good above individual interests. But by the 1790s, he had abandoned this view and came to believe that the many and the few needed to be balanced against one another in different houses of the legislature. The only way to keep the two in balance was to have a strong executive "who would share in the law-making and mediate the basic social struggle between the few and the many," wrote Gordon Wood.[73]

Adams's evolving views contributed to the perception that he was a supporter of monarchy and aristocracy, a charge he always denied. He fostered this view through his support for titles for the president and other government officials. He also had a great fear of mob rule and preferred to maintain the existing social order, maintaining that "the time would come when the American people, weary of corrupt presidential elections, would demand a hereditary Executive," according to Elkins and McKitrick.[74]

How did the divergent parties stack up on the issue of tradition versus change? They were a mix of each. On the economic side, Hamilton and the Federalists fell clearly on the side of change, attempting to move the United States from a primarily agricultural society to one that would have a combination of both agriculture and industry. Hamilton also moved the country toward a modern nation-state with a banking system and administrative mechanisms to manage the debt.

Historians have long maintained that Hamilton was trying to

mimic the British economic system.[75] The colonies had been a backwater for the emerging British industrial system, a farming area that supported British industry. The Federalists also supported maintaining a much more hierarchal society, as had existed during the period prior to the revolution. Hamilton and the Federalists did not intend to introduce a monarchy into America, but they believed in a more top-down system than did the Republicans. "In the eyes of their Jeffersonian Republican opponents the Federalists seemed to be taking America back to the monarchy that had been repudiated in 1776," wrote Gordon Wood.[76]

Jefferson and the Republicans were much more open to political change in America. They also loathed all things British. As we have seen, their views were a product of numerous political predispositions and environmental factors. They feared governments that were too strong because aristocratic governments used strong government actions to promote one group over another and to create significant levels of inequality. Jefferson saw this firsthand in France.

Both Jefferson and Madison, men from rural areas, needed to protect those interests, and also slavery. This made them more apt to protect the status quo in America, which would normally be a very conservative position. Still, Jefferson's view of agriculture was quite progressive and not mired in a world of subsistence farming. He was always looking for changes "in cultivation, processing, and marketing that would enhance its profitability," Appleby writes.[77] Both Jefferson and Madison were also trying to stop what they perceived as Hamilton's attempt to graft the British system onto America, which they saw as creating a much more unequal society. Politically, they were both more committed to an emerging democratic and egalitarian America, one that opened up participation more widely than Hamilton and the Federalists were comfortable with.

❧ ❧ ❧

Washington's second term was largely dominated by the war in Europe, as Great Britain and revolutionary France fought for dominance of the continent. The Republicans identified with the French and the Federalists with England, making the party disputes ever more intense and treacherous. This was the environment as Adams was elected president in 1796, with Jefferson as his vice president. Unlike Washington, Adams did not have the respect of both sides (perhaps neither side), and partisanship began to spin out of control. The open question became whether power could be peacefully transferred as Adams and Jefferson faced each other in the election of 1800.

Endnotes

1 John R. Hibbing, Kevin B. Smith, and John R. Alford, *Predisposed: Liberals, Conservatives and the Biology of Political Differences* (New York, 2014).

2 Richard Hofstadter, *The Idea of a Party System: The Rise of Legitimate Opposition in the United States, 1780-1840* (Berkeley, 1969), p. 86.

3 Hofstadter, p. 87.

4 Hibbing (et al.), p. 6.

5 Hibbing (et al.), p. 24.

6 Hibbing (et al.), p. 53–55.

7 Hibbing (et al.), p. 107 and p. 110.

8 Avi Tuschman, *Our Political Nature: The Evolutionary Origins of What Divides Us* (Amherst, 2013), p. 67 and p. 339.

9 Hibbing (et al.), p. 221–223; Jared Diamond, *Guns, Germs, and Steel: The Fate of Human Societies* (New York, 1997), chapter 10.

10 Tuschman, p. 250-251.

11 Stuart Leibiger, *Founding Friendship: George Washington, James Madison, and the Creation of the American Republic* (Charlottesville, 1999), p. 2. Leibiger measures the four men based on "a scale running from liberty, localism, and states' rights on the left to order, cosmopolitanism, and consolidation on the right."

12 For the disagreements between the historians on Madison's conversion from a strong

nationalist, some believe that Madison had changed his mind while others maintain that his thinking was consistent throughout and that he never intended to support the type of program that Hamilton put forward. For those who think he changed his mind, see Jack N. Rakove, *James Madison and the Creation of the American Republic* (New York, 2007), p. 110–111, and Ralph Ketcham, *James Madison: A Biography*, (Charlottesville, 1971), p. 314–315. For the opposing view, see Lance Banning, *The Sacred Fire of Liberty: James Madison & the Founding of the Federal Republic* (Ithaca, 1995), whose book is dedicated almost entirely to this issue, especially chapter 10. Wood also deals with this issue in *Revolutionary Characters* in chapter 5; John Ferling, *Jefferson and Hamilton: The Rivalry That Forged a Nation* (New York, 2013), p. X.

13 The quotation on the sinful nature of man to Christians comes from Garrett Ward Sheldon, *The Political Philosophy of James Madison* (Baltimore, 2001), p. xv, who argues that Madison's views on human nature were heavily influenced by a Christian realist view. Tuschman has a good overview of the views of different philosophers on human nature on p. 299–306.

14 Gordon Wood, *Revolutionary Characters: What Made the Founders Different* (New York, 2006), p. 145. The quotes from the letter to Thomas Law dated June 13, 1814, are from Adrienne Koch and William Peden, *The Life and Selected Writings of Thomas Jefferson* (New York, 1972), p. 636–638; Garrett Ward Sheldon, *The Political Philosophy of Thomas Jefferson* (Baltimore, 1991), p. 55–56; the quote from the letter to Adams is from Sheldon, p. 58. Richard K. Matthews, *The Radical Politics of Thomas Jefferson: A Revisionist View* (Lawrence, 1984), p. 53.

15 See Sheldon, *Jefferson*, p. 25–29, and Joseph J. Ellis, *American Sphinx: The Character of Thomas Jefferson* (New York, 1998), p. 36–37, for a general discussion of Jefferson's view of a mythical English past.

16 Koch and Peden, p. 221.

17 For a more detailed analysis of Jefferson's views on native Americans, see Matthews, p. 57–65, which I find compelling and have summarized in this paragraph. Sheldon makes the case for Jefferson's views on government being best at the local level on pages 60–72.

18 Koch and Peden, p. 265; Sheldon, *Jefferson*, p. 79.

19 The quotes are from the edition of the *Federalist Papers* with an introduction by Clinton Rossiter, (New York, 1961). All quotes footnoted based on the primary author and page number. The quote from Madison is from p. 78–79 and p. 83.

20 Madison, p. 322.

21 Wood, p. 145 and 148.

22 From Rossiter's introduction to the Federalist Papers, in which he is making a broad generalization about how the essays reflect "both the light and dark sides of human nature," on p. xiv.

23 The quotes are from two sources. The first is Winton Solberg, ed., *The Federal*

Convention and the Formation of the Union of the American States (Indianapolis, 1976), p. 85 and 86. The second is Ketcham, p. 197 and 220. The insight on Madison's view of the direct election of the president is from Ketcham, p. 219.

24 The quote from Rossiter is taken from his introduction to the *Federalist Papers*, p. xiv; Madison, p. 83.

25 George Washington to John Jay, August 1, 1786. Retrieved 11/19/2014 from http://press-pubs.uchicago.edu/founders/documents/v1ch5s11.html.

26 Joseph J. Ellis, *His Excellency: George Washington* (New York, 2004), p. 37–38; Ron Chernow, *Washington: A Life* (New York, 2010), p. 392.

27 Chernow, *Washington*, p. 89.

28 Joseph J. Ellis, *Revolutionary Summer: The Birth of American Independence* (New York, 2013), p. 165–170.

29 For a good discussion of both Washington's optimistic and pessimistic sides, see Richard J. Behn, "History – Essays," retrieved November 19, 2014 from http://www.lehrmaninstitute.org/history/founders-optimism.html.

30 Michael P. Federici, *The Political Philosophy of Alexander Hamilton* (Baltimore, 2012), p. 7 and p. 51.

31 Federici, p. 51 and p. 53; Chernow, *Hamilton*, p. 398–401.

32 Federici, p. 62 and p. 64.

33 Ferling, p. 187.

34 Gordon S. Wood, *The Idea of America: Reflections on the Birth of the United States* (New York, 2011), p. 142.

35 Quoted from Gordon S. Wood, *Empire of Liberty: A History of the Early American Republic 1789-1815* (Oxford, 2009), p. 91.

36 Ron Chernow, *Alexander Hamilton* (New York, 2004), p. 286. Not all historians accept that Washington first asked Morris to take the position. See Ferling, p. 203.

37 See Wood, *Empire*, p. 91 on Hamilton's free reign at Treasury, and Chernow, *Washington*, p. 620 on Jefferson's view and the sympathy that Washington had for Hamilton's economic proposals.

38 Simon Johnson and James Kwak, *White House Burning: The Founding Fathers, our National Debt, and Why it Matters to You* (New York, 2012), p. 21.

39 Wood, *Empire*, p. 95.

40 Chernow, *Hamilton*, p. 297–298.

41 Leibiger, p. 126; Chernow, *Hamilton*, p. 298; Wood, *Empire*, p. 95–96; Stanley Elkin and Eric McKitrick, *The Age of Federalism: The Early American Republic 1788-1800* (New York, 1993), p. 117; John C. Miller, *Alexander Hamilton: Portrait in Paradox* (New York, 1959), p. 23.

42 Ferling, p. 205.

43 For example, see Ferling, p. 205, who states that the new bonds would never mature but does not mention the sinking fund proposal. The quote is from Chernow, *Hamilton*, p. 300.

44 Elkins and McKitrick, p. 226; Chernow, *Hamilton*, p. 348; Miller, p. 259.

45 Wood, *Empire*, p. 99.

46 Douglass C. North, *The Economic Growth of the United States 1790-1860* (New York, 1966), p. 17.

47 Miller, p. 285.

48 North, p. 46; Miller, p. 279; Wood, *Empire*, p. 201–202.

49 Ketchum, p. 232–326.

50 Ellis, *American Creation*, p. 168; Leibiger, p. 109.

51 Elkins and McKitrick, p. 143-151. Joseph J. Ellis, *Founding Brothers: The Revolutionary Generation*, (New York, 2001), p. 48–50.

52 Leibiger, p. 134; Wood, *Empire*, p. 144; *The Federalist Papers*, p. 285.

53 The biographer mentioned is Jacob E. Cooke, and the quote is found in Chernow, *Hamilton*, p. 352. See also Ferling, *Jefferson and Hamilton*, p. 220–221, for the quote from Hamilton's opinion. Ferling also makes the point that Washington and Hamilton shared a similar perspective on the need for a strong national government.

54 Ellis raises the point on slavery in *American Creation*, p. 174–175.

55 Drew R. McCoy, *The Elusive Republic: Political Economy of Jeffersonian America* (Williamsburg, 1980). McCoy's work is one of the best at describing this debate, especially the introduction and chapter 1, from which the quotes are drawn.

56 Koch and Peden, p. 280; Matthews, p. 34; Sheldon, *Jefferson*, p. 74.

57 Thomas Jefferson letter to James Madison, October 28, 1785, retrieved from http://press-pubs.uchicago.edu/founders/print_documents/v1ch15s32.html.

58 Matthews, p. 41–42 and p. 50.

59 Elkins and McKitrick, p. 20.

60 Joyce Appleby, *Liberalism and Republicanism in the Historical Imagination* (Cambridge, 1992), p. 269; Matthews, p. 49; and Sheldon, *Jefferson*, p. 77.

61 See Lance Banning, *The Jeffersonian Persuasion: Evolution of a Party Ideology* (Ithaca, 1978), which goes into detail on this issue, especially chapters 5–7.

62 The quotes are from Banning, *The Jeffersonian Persuasion*, p. 194–195 and 197.

63 Banning, p. 204.

64 Thomas Jefferson letter to James Madison, December 20, 1787, from Koch and Peden, p. 440.

65 Ketcham, p. 301.

66 James Madison, *Parties*, retrieved September 3, 2015 from http://press-pubs.uchicago. edu/founders/documents/v1ch15s50.html.

67 Sheldon, p. 79. The quote is from Gordon Wood, *The Idea of America: Reflections on the Birth of the United States* (New York, 2011), p. 143, as is the quote attributed to Hamilton, p. 147.

68 Elkin and McKitrick, p. 48; see also Wood, *Empire*, p. 76, for the high tone that the Washington administration set.

69 Ellis, *American Creation*, p. 171; Ferling, *Jefferson and Hamilton*, p. 230–232; Chernow, *Washington*, p. 679.

70 The quotes are primarily from Chernow, *Washington*, 677–681; also see Ellis, *His Majesty*, p. 218.

71 Hofstadter, p. 92; see also Stanley Elkin and Eric McKitrick, *The Age of Federalism: The Early American Republic 1788-1800* (New York, 1993), p. 455–461; Ferling, *Jefferson and Hamilton*, p. 249; Sean Wilentz, *The Rise of American Democracy: Jefferson to Lincoln* (New York, 2005), p. 49–62, has a good discussion of the relationship between the Republican elite like Jefferson and Madison and the members of the Democratic Republican societies, which consisted primarily of "ordinary artisans" along with "minor public officials" and a smattering of "self-made men of wealth."

72 Hofstadter, p. 94–95, and Elkin and McKitrick, p. 461.

73 Wood, *Empire*, p. 214; see also Wood, *Revolutionary Characters*, chapter 6, in which he makes the full argument on Adams's evolving views, which have influenced my view on the subject.

74 Elkins and McKitrick, p. 536.

75 See the introduction from Elkins and McKitrick for a useful summary on this issue.

76 Gordon Wood, *The Radicalism of the American Revolution* (New York, 1991), p. 263.

77 Appleby, p. 269.

CHAPTER 2

The Peaceful Transfer of Power

*The changes of administration, which in every government
and in every age have most generally been epochs of confusion,
villainy and bloodshed, in this our country take place without
any species of distraction, or disorder.*[1]
—MARGARET BAYARD SMITH, 1801

*The American tradition of transferring or reaffirming immense
power ... we do this in a peaceful and orderly way.*[2]
—SENATOR LAMAR ALEXANDER, 2013

While the author was touring Independence Hall in May of 2015, the docent mentioned that the election of John Adams in 1796 to replace George Washington was the first peaceful transfer of power in the world. In 1796, the peaceful transition did not transfer power to a rival political party, since both men were Federalists. It was the election of 1800 that really represented the first peaceful transfer of power, one that was in doubt until the moment Thomas Jefferson took the oath of office on March 4, 1801. Politics in the late 1790s had turned ugly, making it much less likely that a peaceful transfer of power would occur. But it did, and it became another of those elements that knitted the newly emerging American nation together and allowed democracy to eventually flourish.

The Adams Presidency

Adams and Jefferson first faced off against each other in the election of 1796, during a time in our history when candidates did not actually campaign for president, since to do so would indicate that they were unworthy to hold the office. Instead, their friends and supporters advanced their cause. For those who believe that the politics of an earlier age was more elevated, elections from the founding era will disabuse them of that notion. This was an ugly campaign, as many presidential elections are, with two rival parties seeking power. "Jefferson was decried as a Jacobin, an atheist, and charged with cowardice for having fled Monticello from the British cavalry in 1781," David McCullough writes. Adams was depicted as a monarchist and ridiculed as "his rotundity."[3]

Alexander Hamilton went after Jefferson with gusto. In a series of newspaper essays, "he maligned Jefferson from pillar to post," according to John Ferling. The most damning claim Hamilton made was an oblique reference that Jefferson was having an affair with Sally Hemings, writing that Jefferson "must have seen all around him sufficient marks of this *staining of blood*," a reference to race mixing on Southern plantations. Although Hamilton was not running for any office at the time, he had to defend himself shortly thereafter from a pamphlet that was published about an affair that Hamilton had with Maria Reynolds in 1791. As part of the affair, Reynolds's husband James had attempted to extort money from Hamilton. The whole sordid affair had been privately investigated in 1791 by a committee of three congressmen, including James Monroe, who were looking into whether Hamilton had been guilty of corruption in his role as treasury secretary, a charge he was exonerated from. Politics in the early republic could be quite brutal.[4]

Each party attempted to bring regional balance to their ticket, with Thomas Pinckney of South Carolina running with Adams for vice president on the Federalists' side, and Aaron Burr of New York as Jefferson's running mate. Due to the provision of the Constitution that allowed electors to vote for two people, it was possible for a vice-presidential candidate to be elected president, or for men from different parties to hold the two highest offices in the land. Hamilton, who had left the Treasury Department in January of 1795 to alleviate his financial problems, worked to get Pinckney elected. While he feared the election of Jefferson, Hamilton also knew he could not control the always independent Adams.

Adams ultimately prevailed in the electoral college, receiving seventy-one votes to Jefferson's sixty-eight, Pinckney's fifty-nine, and Burr's thirty. The election produced more of a regional than a party split, with Adams winning the Northern states and Jefferson the South and Pennsylvania.[1] Due to the anomaly of the Constitution, which the ratification of the Twelfth Amendment in 1804 would ultimately fix, Jefferson became Adams's vice president.

The two men were old friends, having served together in the Continental Congress in the months prior to independence. Adams led the committee that was designated to draft the Declaration of Independence, with Jefferson its primary author. Adams had been sent to France in 1779 to work alongside Franklin in negotiating a peace treaty with Great Britain. They did not get along well, with Adams believing that Franklin had only a "passion and reputation for fame."[2] Because of this, Adams spent much more of his time in Holland, and was able to secure a $2 million loan from Dutch bankers in 1782, in the aftermath of the American victory at Yorktown. Ultimately, Franklin and Adams, along with John Jay, managed to negotiate the peace treaty with the British that achieved all that the United States had hoped for.

Adams remained in France during most of the tumultuous 1780s, and in 1784, Abigail and his family joined him. The Confederation Congress also assigned Jefferson to join Adams as foreign minister in that same year. Their friendship had continued through a series of letters they exchanged prior to Jefferson's posting, and the two men were glad to be in one another's company once again. Jefferson immediately fell in love with France, which he considered a "great and good country." But he also understood that his primary job was to represent American interests in Paris, where he attempted, through the power of France, to counterbalance continuing threats from Great Britain. The bonds of friendship grew during the time Adams and Jefferson spent together in France, with the two families (Jefferson's daughter Patsy had joined him) dining together often. Abigail also became close to Jefferson, commenting that "Mr. Adams colleague Mr. Jefferson is an excellent man." Jefferson became so close to John Quincy that Adams would later write, "He appeared to me as much your boy as mine."[3]

In 1784, Adams and his family set off for England to serve as America's envoy. He continued his relationship with Jefferson through numerous letters, discussing the issues of the day. When the Constitution was completed, Adams and Jefferson traded observations about it. Adams viewed it with "great satisfaction" and wrote to Jefferson that it "seems to be admirably calculated to preserve the Union ..." Jefferson was not so enthusiastic, likening the president to a "bad edition of a Polish King," who could be "reelected from 4 years to 4 years for life." Always wary of too much power in one man's hands, Jefferson preferred that the president be ineligible for reelection. Their views of the Constitution reflected the differing views they held toward human nature and politics. Adams succinctly summarized their differences when he wrote "You are afraid of the one, I, the few."[4]

Given their mutual regard for each other, it should surprise no one that the two men initially attempted to achieve a bipartisan administration. But their failure to achieve this outcome should give pause to those today who continue to hope for such an outcome in modern politics. It is difficult to achieve bipartisan cooperation when individuals have deep-seated differences of political philosophy and prefer different policy outcomes.

Jefferson made a first attempt when he wrote a supportive letter to Adams on December 28, 1796. In it, he indicated his continuing affection for the newly elected president, "and that your administration may be filled with glory and happiness." He told Adams that he retained "for you the solid esteem of moments when we were working together for our independence, and sentiments of respect and affectionate attachment." Jefferson then sent the letter to Madison, asking that he deliver it to Adams. In his letter to Madison, he wrote "I can particularly have no feelings that would revolt at a secondary position to Mr. Adams. I am his junior in life, was his junior in Congress, his junior in the diplomatic line, his junior lately in civil government." Madison thought that the letter was a major mistake and provided six reasons why the letter should not be delivered. Most importantly, the letter could end up embarrassing Jefferson at some point in the future, since there was a strong "probability that Mr. A's course of administration may force an opposition to it from the Republican quarter ..." The letter was never delivered.[5]

Adams, for his part, also made an attempt at bipartisanship. He initially discussed the possibility that Jefferson might undertake a mission to France as the head of a three-man commission, but realized it was not "justifiable for him to send away the person destined to take his place in case of an accident to himself." Adams then told Jefferson that he was considering asking Madison, who had retired from Congress, to fill the position, and would Jefferson ask him. Adams quickly rescinded the offer when Washington and other Federalists objected. Madison also had no intention of accepting the job. Both sides had walked to the edge of working together and then pulled back. Adams later recalled that they "consulted very little afterward"; Jefferson that Adams never "consulted me as to any measure of the government."[6]

Foreign Policy Differences

One might expect that the Federalists, as the more conservative group, would be hostile to outsiders and that Republicans would be more open. But both parties distrusted outsiders, just different ones. The Federalists came to distrust France as its revolution began to spin out of control. The Republicans were Anglophobic. The positions the two sides took had more to do with tradition versus change, but not in the way one would expect. As we saw in chapter 1, the Hamilton-led Federalists wanted to change the American economy so that it would be more balanced between industry and agriculture. To do this, they needed to create a financial system that included a central bank and a funded debt. Their model was England. Politically, they did not want change but wished to maintain the remnants of a top-down, deferential society in which elites were the sole rulers.[7] The Republicans wanted to retain the traditional agricultural base of the economy, and distrusted banks, industry, and urbanization. Politically, they were more open to the participation of the average person and would begin to pave the way toward a more democratic society. Much of the vitriol that would come from foreign policy disputes was rooted in resolving different approaches to change. Foreign policy differences would also harden opposition between the two political parties.

❦ ❦ ❦

The war between Great Britain and France that began in 1793 had a profound impact on American politics. The war was an outgrowth of the French Revolution, which began in 1789 with the first meeting of the Estates General since 1614; the formation of the first National Assembly to represent common people; and the storming of the Bastille. Initially, Americans were universally supportive of the French Revolution, seeing it as an expansion of the twin goals of liberty and equality, and they wanted to repay the French for their support of the American movement for independence. By 1792, the European continent was engulfed in war, and the Reign of Terror ensued in France when King Louis XVI was beheaded, and a French republic declared. At that point, the Federalists turned against the French Revolution, rightfully seeing that it had descended into "popular anarchy," in the words of Gordon Wood. The Republicans continued to support the French, despite the excesses of the revolution, while the Federalists were generally pro-British. "Indeed, the bitterness of the division of the next few years has been exceeded only once in American history, and that resulted in a civil war," explained Lance Banning. Jefferson too saw things this way, writing to James Monroe in 1793, the "war has kindled ... the two parties with an ardour which our own [domestic] interests ... could never excite."[8]

The Washington administration, as we have seen, attempted to steer a neutral course between the French and the British, an unpopular position with many Republicans, who saw it as in fact favoring the British. Madison, for one, had long favored a discriminatory trade policy toward England. The policy was in response to Great Britain's navigation acts in the aftermath of the Treaty of Paris in which American shipping was excluded from the lucrative trade with the West Indies. "In 1789, Madison had sought unsuccessfully to levy discriminatory tariffs on British imports in order to force Britain to open its ports in the West Indies and Canada to American shipping," Wood writes.[9] He resurrected this policy once again in 1794. Madison was operating under the false assumption that Great Britain needed the United States more than the Americans needed the British. He thought that the British had become dependent on "fashion and superfluities," on luxury items, whereas the Americans operated in an "independent situation," since they produced essential products "on their own soil."[10]

Part of the ideology of the American Revolution was that the elimination of monarchies and the opening of free trade between peoples of the world would break down barriers and ultimately end wars. While even Washington and the Federalists subscribed to this theory, it was the Republicans who clung to it the longest and made it the centerpiece of their foreign policy. Great Britain was the one country that stood in the way of their vision. The Republicans wanted "to destroy Britain's commercial hegemony in the world and end America's commercial, and hence political, dependence on the former mother country," according to Wood. It was a policy the Federalists opposed, since commercial trade with the British provided the prosperity and import taxes needed to fund the federal government and repay the debt. British trade was predominant in the United States, making up 87 percent of manufacturing imports during the period from 1787 to 1790.[11]

Not only would commercial discrimination harm the ability of the United States to pay its debt, it would destroy the prosperity upon which much of the country depended. Despite the war between Britain and France, American trade expanded rapidly between 1790 and 1796, with the nation's ships almost doubling the tonnage of foreign goods they carried into the country. American trade continued to expand during the 1790s despite the overt attempt by the British to exclude the Americans from the West Indies. "The shadow trade—not simply smuggling, but the repeated opening of the ports to American ships by dispensation of the island governors ... was flourishing," explained Elkins and McKitrick. By the mid-1790s, the carrying trade in the United States was booming.[12]

The attempts by Madison and Jefferson, who had retired to Monticello at the end of 1793, to impose commercial discrimination failed in the Congress. But the problems with Great Britain continued to fester. In addition to enacting a formal blockade of American shipping to France and the French West Indies, the British had also seized numerous ships and their cargo and had taken American sailors captive or forced them to serve in Great Britain's navy. There were also problems that remained from the 1783 peace treaty. The British still retained their outposts in the Northwest Territories, where they encouraged attacks by local Indian tribes on American settlers, and Southerners had never received compensation for their loss of slaves at the end of the Revolutionary War.

In the aftermath of the capture of American vessels, war fever swept the country. The Federalist response was to propose a major expansion of the army, a move that both Madison and Jefferson opposed, given their fear of standing armies. They also both saw it as a further attempt to expand the power of the central government. As Jefferson wrote to Madison, "the monocrats and papermen ... [do not want war]; but they want armies and debt." Indeed, the Federalists did not want war with Great Britain, and knew that the embryonic nation was in no position to do battle once again with the greatest military power on the face of the earth. Washington, therefore, appointed John Jay, the chief justice of the Supreme Court, as a special envoy to negotiate a settlement with the British.[13]

The Jay Treaty

John Jay was perhaps America's most experienced diplomat. Born to an affluent New York family in December of 1745, he was the sixth child of Peter Jay and Mary van Cortlandt. At the age of fourteen, he entered Kings College (present-day Columbia University in Manhattan) and graduated four years later. He became enmeshed in revolutionary politics in the 1770s as a part of the moderates from the mid-Atlantic states that attempted to steer a middle course between the movement toward independence and negotiations with the British.[14]

In 1778, Jay was appointed president of the Continental Congress. He soon saw that the structure of the government was too weak, and joined the ranks of the nationalists, those who pursued a stronger central government. A year later he was asked to serve as an envoy to Spain, and then was part of the three-man mission (along with Franklin and Adams) that negotiated the end of hostilities with Great Britain with the Treaty of Paris in 1783. It was Jay who decided to ignore the orders of Congress to follow the lead of the French in the negotiations, understanding that their interests diverged from those of the United States. He also recognized the importance of the Mississippi River as the westward boundary of the country, since the future success of the United States was inextricably linked to continental expansion.[15]

Jay may have had an inkling of the difficulties he would have in negotiating a treaty with the British in the 1790s, in particular the political ramifications of such an agreement. In 1784, the Spanish had closed the Mississippi to the United States. Jay, as foreign minister under the Confederation Congress, was unable to get the Spanish to reopen the river. Instead, they insisted on a twenty-five-year ban on the use of the river and in return offered a commercial treaty that gave the United States "most favored nation" status, which would provide trade advantages such as lower tariffs. The proposed terms of the treaty split the North from the South, was never approved by the Congress, and became part of the impetus for the call for a Constitutional Convention, since the United States was unable to speak with one voice on foreign policy.[16]

Numerous events in the late 1780s led to the call for the convention, and Jay was one of the most committed of the nationalists. He was blocked from attending the convention by the then governor of New York and those who opposed a stronger central government. Still, he played an important role in the process by assisting in writing the *Federalist Papers* and serving as a delegate to the New York ratifying convention, where he and Hamilton were able to convince that state to ratify the Constitution.

Jay arrived in Great Britain in June of 1794 with instructions that had largely been crafted by Hamilton. The key American objectives were to end the deprivation of American shipping in the West Indies, receive compensation for spoliation of goods received and slaves captured during the war, and end the occupation of the Northwest forts. Depending on the outcome of the negotiations, the Americans hoped that success on these issues might also lead to the formal reopening of trade with the British West Indies and most-favored-nation status for each side.[17]

Viewed from the perspective of the instructions that Jay carried with him, he accomplished much of what he set out to do. The British had already revoked the previous order seizing all American ships carrying goods to the French West Indies, the prime event that had triggered the crisis. The treaty included provisions that the British would finally abandon all of its posts in the Northwest Territory; a commission would be established made up of British and American representatives that would decide on compensation for ships that had been seized; and the British West Indies would be open to American ships of less than seventy tons. This last provision was not of great benefit to the United States, since it would open trade only to small American ships, something Jay knew since he had originally proposed a limit of ships up to one hundred tons. But Jay was unable to obtain any compensation for slaveholders, although he probably did not make a great effort in this area, given his opposition to slavery.[18]

The real problem with the Jay Treaty was one of perspective. Neither Hamilton nor Washington was overjoyed with the terms of the treaty, but it reflected the relative power of the two sides to the negotiations. "Washington wanted peace, fearing disaster for the weak, strife-torn United States in another round of warfare," wrote John Ferling. The treaty implicitly abandoned the "principle of freedom of the seas and neutral rights" that had been at the core of American revolutionary ideology and which was the centerpiece of the Republican view of foreign relations. It also appeared to place the United States on the side of the British, abandoning neutral rights and banning discrimination against British trade for ten years. "There is virtual unanimity among historians that the drawn-out battle over

Jay's treaty represented the maturation of America's First Party System," according to historian Jacob E. Cooke.[19]

❧❧❧

Washington had his own reservations about the Jay Treaty, specifically the provision that gave most-favored-nation status to the British but denied it to the United States, and Article XII, which only allowed small vessels into the British West Indies and restricted American ships from carrying "Melasses, Sugar, Coffee, Cocoa or Cotton." He also suspected the treaty would trigger a major controversy, so he submitted it in secret to the Senate for its advice and consent. The Senate ultimately ratified the treaty in June of 1795 on a 20–10 vote, the bare two-thirds minimum required. Every Federalist voted for it, and every Republican voted against it.[20]

Before Washington could release the terms of the Jay Treaty, it was leaked by a Republican congressmen, and set off the firestorm of protest he had feared. Jay was hung in effigy in so many towns and cities "that he declared he could have traversed the entire country by the glare of his flailing figure," Ron Chernow writes. When Hamilton, who had retired as treasury secretary during the time when Jay was in England, attempted to defend the treaty in New York, he was hit in the head by a stone. Countless meetings were held up and down the new nation between early July and the end of August, protesting the treaty and urging Washington to reject it.[21]

Washington withdrew to Mount Vernon to contemplate whether to sign the treaty or not. To further exacerbate the problem, the British had issued new Orders in Council directing that American ships bound for France with grain be seized. Washington considered making the signing of the Jay Treaty contingent on the British reversal of the order, but new Secretary of State Edmund Randolph badly bungled the negotiations with the British envoy. Randolph was also under a cloud, having been suspected of engaging in treason with the French, a charge that, while not true, did reveal that Randolph had "strong pro-Republican sentiments." Washington turned to his most trusted advisor, Hamilton, who provided him with a detailed analysis that justified his signature. Hamilton also took up his pen in support of the treaty, writing a series of brilliant essays that caused Jefferson to admit, in grudging admiration, that "Hamilton is really a colossus to the antirepublican party. Without numbers, he is like a host within himself."[22]

In August 1795, Washington signed the Jay Treaty. He did so largely to avoid war, having commented that the immature American nation would not be ready to fight the British "for about twenty years." His decision was also grounded in his concerns about the opposition that had arisen, to the tactics that were used, and to the personal invective that was hurled his way. Some of the resolutions he had received in opposition were so indecent that Washington refused to answer them: "No answer given. The address too rude to merit one," he wrote in response to one from New Jersey. He also found himself now caught in the middle of a partisan divide, one that he could no longer transcend, and had grave concerns over the "future of an ordered society in the United States," as Wood writes. There was also dissonance in his own cabinet, where Randolph's conversations with the French "conveyed the impression that Washington was a dazed, over-the-hill patriarch, the dupe of scheming Northern bankers and closet monarchs," language that reflected much of what Jefferson and the Republican opposition were saying and writing about him.[23]

But the story did not end with the signing of the Jay Treaty. Both Jefferson and Madison decided to make their final stand in the House of Representatives. It was a bizarre place to fight the battle, since the Constitution so clearly gave treaty-making power to the president, with the advice and consent of the Senate. Madison had defended the Senate's role in foreign affairs in *Federalist* No. 62, when he wrote that there is a "necessity of some stable institution in the government," since without this the United States would forfeit "the respect and confidence of other nations ..." At the time, Jefferson agreed, writing to Madison after the signing of the Constitution that he considered the House "illy qualified for [affairs of] the union, for foreign nations, etc." Still, Madison attempted to take up the issue in the House, initially using that body's power over money matters to defund the treaty. But he went even further, supporting other Republicans in the House in their demand that the Washington administration turn over its records on how the treaty was negotiated. "He was claiming a power in the House to nullify treaties after their ratification by the Senate," according to Madison biographer Garry Wills. "This was more than 'loose construction' of the Constitution. It amounted to reversal of its plain sense." Washington not only refused to comply, claiming for the first time executive privilege, he submitted the records he was in possession of that showed the Framers at the convention had rejected any role for the House in making treaties, and that Madison had voted with Washington and the majority on this measure. Madison's attempts to defund the treaty in the House ultimately failed. But the loss for Madison went beyond this, as his long friendship with Washington ended. "Never again did he ask Madison's advice or invite him to family dinners," Stuart Leibiger has written. Washington's relationship with Jefferson also ended over the feud that had erupted over the Jay Treaty. Although Jefferson had been conspiring behind Washington's back since his days as secretary of state, Washington refused to believe it. By July of 1796, Washington could no longer ignore the role Jefferson had played in opposing him and the vilification that had taken place in the Republican press. The Jay Treaty marked the end of any sense of bipartisan cooperation between the two sides.[24]

❧ ❧ ❧

This was the environment Adams confronted when he became president. Even Washington, the major symbol of the American nation, had been unable to hold the two sides together. Adams would fare no better and was also distrusted by many of the members of his own party, especially Hamilton and his followers, sometimes referred to as the high Federalists. While the furor over the Jay Treaty subsided, and the avoidance of war led to a period of economic growth, a new problem arose in America's relationship with France that was directly related to the Jay Treaty. It would further divide the two sides and harden party loyalties.

Other than the support of his wife, Abigail, Adams was alone. They had been married since 1764, and she was very much his equal, a remarkable person, incredibly intelligent, a person who could quote large passages of poetry from memory. Adams always leaned on his wife, and as his problems as president continued to mount, she became his only ally. At one point, he wrote to her, saying: "The times are critical and dangerous, and I must have you here to assist me. I must now repeat with zeal and earnestness. I can do nothing without you."[25]

While Washington had a firm group of loyalists and was held in high esteem by almost everyone, Adams had no close friends. He initially had the good will of the Republicans, who rightly saw him as independent from the high Federalists. One Republican had written of Adams's "incorruptible integrity." But this type of praise from the other side did not last long. Adams also made a major strategic error when he kept Washington's cabinet. "They belonged to the ardently anti-French, pro-British wing of the party who considered Alexander Hamilton their leader ... and they were inclined to look down on John Adams," McCullough writes.[26]

Trouble with the French began before Washington left the presidency, and Adams inherited the problem. The French read the Jay Treaty as favoring the British, and in the spring of 1797, just as Adams assumed office, began to seize American ships and sailors. In fact, this was not something new, since the French had, at irregular intervals, violated America's neutral shipping rights. Their policy was not much different from the British, and the new nation found itself caught between the two great European powers.[27]

Adams, taking a page from Washington, adopted a two-prong policy to deal with France's belligerence. In a speech to Congress in May of 1797, he described how the French Directory had refused to receive Charles Cotesworth Pinckney, whom Washington had appointed to replace James Monroe. Adams announced that he would "institute a fresh attempt at negotiations," and that a three-man commission would be sent to France to work toward a peace agreement "compatible with the rights, duties, interests, and honor of the nation." He also requested that Congress authorize "effectual measures of defense," primarily the building of a navy that could protect the commerce of the United States.[28]

It was the three-man commission which Adams had originally considered Jefferson for, and then Madison. Adams wanted Madison, the "embodied authority of the pro-French party in America, and thus as strong an inducement as the United States government could give them to take its representatives seriously," say Elkins and McKitrick. Hamilton, who did not agree with Adams on much, did agree on this and worked to convince the high Federalists to support Madison's selection. But Adams's cabinet was totally opposed to sending any Republican to negotiate with the French, and Pickering went so far as to propose declaring war on France. Madison also chose not to be a member of the commission, believing that it would require him to accept the Jay Treaty as the representative of a Federalist administration. In addition, Madison had a grave fear of sailing across the ocean, writing to Jefferson in 1785 "that crossing the sea would be unfriendly to a singular disease of my constitution." Instead, Adams selected future Supreme Court justice John Marshall, Elbridge Gerry, and Charles Cotesworth Pinckney as members of the commission.[29]

✿ ✿ ✿

Jefferson almost immediately went into opposition mode, considering Adams's announcement the first step toward war with France. It is somewhat difficult to understand his position, given that Adams's policy seems so reasonable today: attempt to negotiate peace but be prepared for war. With Madison recently retired from Congress, Jefferson assumed the mantle of party leadership, albeit behind the scenes since he was the vice president. In terms of his role in the administration, he decided to confine himself "to legislative functions" and "not take part whatever in executive consultations," as he wrote to Elbridge Gerry in May of 1797. Jefferson's party activities were clearly revealed when he, Aaron Burr, and Albert Gallatin (who replaced Madison as the Republican's party leader in the House) met James Monroe's ship as he returned from France in June of 1797. The men spent "two hours in a consultation that had all of the appearances of a conclave of party leaders," according to one of Jefferson's biographers. A few days later, Jefferson attended a dinner thrown by the Republicans for Monroe.[30]

Why did Jefferson, who held Adams in high esteem, so quickly turn against his friend and lead the Republican opposition from behind the scenes? Historian John Ferling ascribes this largely to Jefferson's fear that Adams would lose control of his foreign policy to Hamilton's manipulations of the cabinet. Jefferson also believed that Adams was being alienated from him by "the Hamiltonians by whom he is surrounded, and who are only a little less hostile to him than me." Perhaps this is the whole story, but Jefferson is a very complicated individual, a man who is difficult to fully understand. Given this, it might be helpful to view two distinct sides of his personality. One is how he dealt with interpersonal relations and the other is his strongly held political views.[31]

On the personal side, Jefferson abhorred conflict. In a letter to his grandchildren in 1802, he wrote: "It is a charming thing to be loved by everybody; and the way to obtain it is never to quarrel or be angry with anybody ... do all the kind things you can to your companions." He later wrote to another grandchild: "Whenever you feel warmth of temper rising, check it at once, and suppress it, recollecting it will make you unhappy within yourself, and disliked by others." One of Jefferson's biographers, Jon Meacham, argues that his need to be personally liked by all was often mistaken for duplicity. This may be a somewhat overly kind observation, given that Jefferson could indeed be duplicitous, as we saw in his relations with Washington while serving as secretary of state. One need look no further than his hiring of Philip Freneau as a translator in the State Department, when his real job was to run opposition newspaper articles opposed to the very administration that Jefferson served in.[32]

Jefferson willingly did things behind the scenes that he was unwilling to do in an aboveboard manner because he thought that the republic was, in fact, in danger. He believed that Adams was "for war" and that "war was the object" for which the Congress was called into special session. The ultimate goal of that war was to break relations with France, set up an alliance with England, and graft an English-style monarchy onto the United States. That this was not true is beside the point, since he believed it was. Jefferson's state of mind during this period can be seen most clearly in a May 1797 letter he wrote to Gerry. In it, he paints a picture of the new nation as being completely dominated by Great Britain, which has "in fact obtained" a "monopoly of commerce and influence within the United States." This had been brought about by a small cadre of Federalists, who wished to see the country enter into a war with France on the side of the British. In fact, the British were not dominating the United States during this period and very few Federalists wished for war. "Jefferson's fear of war was nothing if not genuine," Elkins and McKitrick write, making him unable to see "the prudential side of Adams's policy" of negotiation and defense preparations.[33] Ultimately, however, the Federalists would adopt a series of policies that would confirm Jefferson's worst fears.

Jefferson's words could sometimes get him into deep trouble. During the crisis over the Jay Treaty, Jefferson had written a private letter in which he criticized "an Anglican monarchical aristocratical party ... whose avowed object is to draw over us the substance, as they have already done the forms, of the British government." He complained of "the apostates who have gone over to these heresies, men who were Samsons in the field and Solomons in the council, but who have had their heads shorn by the harlot England." When the letter became public during the controversy over relations with France during the Adams administration, "nearly everyone who read the letter reached the same conclusion," according to Ferling. Jefferson was referring to Washington. It was another episode that ratcheted up the partisan feuding during this period, and the Federalist press charged Jefferson with being both "treasonable" and "traitorous." The letter cost Jefferson his friendship with Washington, who never spoke to him again.[34]

❧ ❧ ❧

Charles Cotesworth Pinckney had been appointed by Washington as foreign minister to replace James Monroe, but the French had refused to see him, which had helped trigger the crisis. Pinckney had attended the Constitutional Convention as a delegate from South Carolina and was one of the most ardent defenders of slavery, ensuring that the document would protect the peculiar institution. Marshall was a strong Federalist from Virginia who had served in the army during the revolution. As a veteran, he was a strong nationalist who was "confirmed in the habit of considering America as my country, and Congress as my government." He would go on to become perhaps the most important chief justice of the Supreme Court by establishing the court's role as the arbiter of the Constitution based on the principle of judicial review. The final member of the commission was Gerry of Massachusetts. Gerry had been involved in revolutionary politics and had also attended the Constitutional Convention, although he refused to sign the document. He was a rather odd person, difficult to get along with, a man who often disagreed with those he met. But Adams knew him well and felt "he needed someone on the commission whose friendship and loyalty were beyond doubt," according to McCullough.[35]

At the time of the commission's arrival, the French government was in the hands of the Directory, but the real power was beginning to emerge in the person of Napoleon Bonaparte, whose army was amassing victories across Austria and Italy, stretching as far as Egypt.

The commissioners were to meet with France's wily foreign minister Charles Maurice de Talleyrand-Perigord. A former bishop in the Catholic Church, he was a chameleon who knew how to survive. He had gravitated quickly from a supporter of the king to a part of the revolutionary movement, but then fled France before it could turn on him. Returning in 1796, he plotted his way to become foreign minister, where he intended to "make an immense fortune," as the Americans would soon find out.[36]

The Americans arrived in France in the first week of October 1797 and held a brief fifteen-minute meeting with Talleyrand in which they presented their credentials. A few days later, his agents began a shakedown of the American envoys. Before negotiations could even begin, the commissioners would need to denounce the president's speech to Congress as belligerent, the United States would have to agree to loan France $10 million, and a "sweetener" of $250,000 would need to be paid to Talleyrand. Despite threats from the agents, the Americans refused to negotiate under such conditions. A series of dispatches were prepared and sent to the president late in November, but due to bad weather they would not arrive until the following spring. Marshall was the primary author of the dispatches, which referred to the agents as X, Y, and Z. In March of 1798, the dispatches were decoded and read by Adams, who privately fumed over the way in which the envoys had been treated, and rashly considered asking Congress to declare war on France immediately. He calmed down and publicly did not overreact, instead informing Congress that the peace mission had failed, but he didn't mention a declaration of war against France.[37]

The Republicans, unaware of the content of the XYZ dispatches, now made a massive mistake. They attacked Adams, with Jefferson calling the president's policy "almost insane." "The Republicans called for the release of the commission's dispatches, unaware of how damaging they were to their cause," Wood writes. Adams was only too happy to comply. When the country discovered what had occurred, there was a wave of patriotic support for the president, whose "popularity soared." War fever spread throughout the nation. The Republicans had overplayed their hand and given the Federalists a gift, which they used to their advantage. "Over the remainder of 1798 and into 1799 the Federalists won election after election," Wood writes. The Republicans lost the ability to block Adams's policy toward the French as the Federalists took charge of Congress, approving further preparations for war. Going beyond the president's recommendation, they also proposed the formation of a standing army of 12,500 men. The Quasi-War with France, as it became known, was now fully underway.[38]

The Alien and Sedition Acts

As with so many wars in American history, the party in power also overplayed their hand. Adams, whose finest moments as president could be found in his resistance to declaring war on France during this period, also succumbed to some ill-considered legislation passed by Congress known as the Alien and Sedition Acts. Less than ten years after the ratification of the Bill of Rights, it became illegal to criticize the government.[39] Jefferson would acquit himself no better in response to the acts.

Congress adopted the legislation during a period marred by a poisonous atmosphere. The fear of a French invasion was real. Adams received a dispatch from his son John Quincy that France intended to "attack the trans-Appalachian west (near today's Alabama and Mississippi) and sever the entire territory from the eastern half of the United States," the historian Jay Winik writes. French warships were patrolling off the country's coast, and American vessels were captured in New York harbor. It was in this context that Congress approved the formation of a large army, although due to longstanding fears of a standing army they called it the "Provisional Army." In July of 1798, the intense atmosphere of fear led the Federalists to approve an army of twelve new regiments. Adams chose Washington to lead the lead the new forces, who demanded that Hamilton be his second in command. Washington was sixty-six and in failing health. He had no intention of commanding the army in the field, which meant that in reality Hamilton would be in charge. Adams attempted, through various means, to resist the appointment of his foe Hamilton, who was already manipulating the cabinet against him, but to no avail. It was the price he needed to pay to secure the support of Washington for his policies.[40]

War fever further divided the two sides, as passions ran high. In Congress, two members got into a physical fight, one using a cane and the other fire tongs. Republicans were called Jacobins (after the most radical of the French revolutionaries that participated in the Reign of Terror) while Federalists were "Anglomen." Any sense of proportionality was lost. Jefferson commented that "men who had been intimate all their lives cross the street to avoid meeting, and turn their heads another way, lest they should be obliged to touch their hat." Each side saw the other in the worst terms. "Republicans feared that the unacknowledged agenda behind this burgeoning military establishment was not to defend America from France so much as to save America for the Federalists and stifle domestic dissent," Chernow writes. Hamilton, in a seven-part newspaper article known as "The Stand," castigated Jefferson over his claim that Talleyrand and not the Directory was to blame for the XYZ affair. "The recourse to so pitiful an evasion betrays in its author a systematic design to excuse France at all events, to soften submission to every violence she may commit, and to prepare for subjection to her," Hamilton wrote.[41]

In the overheated summer of 1798, the Federalists passed a series of measures that became known as the Alien and Sedition Acts. The Alien bills were designed to rid the country of French émigrés and "the hordes of wild Irishmen," who were considered pro-French and primarily Republicans. As we saw in chapter 1, those with a more conservative bent tend to distrust outsiders, and the Alien bills were the epitome of such thinking. The Federalists may also have been motivated by a genuine fear that some foreigners were "enemy agents" plotting against the United States. The final bill allowed the president to deport any immigrant who had not become a naturalized citizen if the person was thought to be "dangerous to the United States." But this part of the law was "a dead letter" since Adams never deported a single immigrant under the act until it expired in 1800.[42]

The most clearly partisan of the measures was the Sedition Act passed in July of 1798. The act made it a crime to speak or publish "any false, scandalous, and malicious writings against the United States, or either House of the Congress of the United States, with intent to defame ... or to bring them ... into contempt or disrepute ..." The Sedition Act, in what Madison viewed as a violation of the First Amendment, was clearly directed at the Republicans, making it essentially illegal to criticize the government. Political scientist James MacGregor Burns wrote that "the act was a clear declaration by the Federalists that opposition to a particular group of leaders in power was in fact opposition to the whole government and an effort to subvert the Constitution."[43]

While Adams had not proposed the bills, he later conceded "that there was need enough of both," and he signed all of the acts. Hamilton supported the Alien bills and wanted "the mass of aliens to leave the country." One of his biographers called it "a disappointing stance from America's most famous foreign-born citizen and once an influential voice for immigration." And while Hamilton opposed the original and more draconian version of the Sedition Act, urging his fellow Federalists to "not establish a tyranny," he did support the final bill that emerged from Congress. The Sedition bill was used to prosecute Republican newspaper editors, with fifteen of sixteen cases that were heard in the North by overzealous Federalist judges resulting in guilty verdicts. War, or the fear of war, has a way of creating bad policy decisions when it comes to civil liberties, and the Alien and Sedition bills were the first example of this under the Constitution. Madison summarized this best in May 1798 when he wrote to Jefferson: "Perhaps it is a universal truth that the loss of liberty at home is to be charged to provisions against danger real or pretended from abroad."[44]

❦ ❦ ❦

Jefferson initially thought that patience was needed in response to the Federalists' program, but this was before the Sedition bill passed in July. "A little patience and we shall see the reign of witches pass over, their spells dissolved, and the people recover their sight," he wrote in June. But as the Sedition Act went into effect, he decided something more needed to be done. Eventually, five of the six Republican newspapers were prosecuted under what Ron Chernow describes as "trumped up charges." Even a Republican Congressman, Matthew Lyons, was jailed for criticizing the president.[45]

Jefferson's response was to secretly prepare a resolution for the newly added state of Kentucky to adopt that maintained that a state could nullify federal laws that it found unconstitutional. It was a dangerous precedent on his part, one that would have more far-reaching implications over the next sixty years than the Sedition Act. Madison saw the danger in his friend's approach and left any mention of nullification out of the resolution he prepared for Virginia, also in secret. Both men correctly feared prosecution for sedition had they acted openly. Fortunately, the Kentucky legislature stripped the nullification language from the resolution it adopted.

Why did Jefferson overreact? He certainly thought that the Federalists were now in their final act that would culminate in war with France, the overthrow of the republic, and the installation of a monarchy in the United States, so the stakes were extremely high in his mind. He also felt he had little choice. The principle of judicial review had not yet been firmly established by the Supreme Court, and "the Republicans already had good reason to expect the [Supreme Court] to be highly partisan," according to one of Jefferson's biographers.[46]

Still, Jefferson was an ardent nationalist, a man who loved the union, even if he wanted to devolve power downward. He was looking for a better balance, what he called "that beautiful equilibrium on which our constitution is founded," between the states and the federal government. Jefferson's nationalism was tied to a decentralized vision of the future where power would flow up from the people through wards at the local level, to the states and ultimately the federal government. "Americans could only sustain a decentralized union ... if they were truly a united people," according to the historian Peter Onuf. Jefferson feared the amount of power that the Federalists had placed in the federal government. To his mind, the government had grown dependent on a permanent debt and high taxes to sustain a standing army that could be used to crush dissent and overthrow the republic with a monarchy. The Sedition Act was the latest and most egregious example of this, since no opposition party could survive and convince the public of the government's errors if dissent and freedom of the press were forbidden. Yet Jefferson also knew that the federal government could not survive if every disagreement led to the end of the union. "But if on a temporary superiority of the one party, the other is to resort to a scission of the Union, no federal government can exist," Jefferson wrote in 1798.[47]

Despite Jefferson's position on nullification, he took a stand against the use of force to overcome the opposition of the Federalists. In a letter to a fellow Virginian, Jefferson wrote: "Anything like force would check the progress of the public opinion and rally them around the government. This is not the kind of opposition the American people will permit." Rather, the Republicans needed to use "the constitutional means of election and petition." The rejection of violence is another of the important way stations on the route to a peaceful transfer of power and the ability for two opposing parties to compete with each other for power within a democratic framework.[48]

One way to view the Kentucky and Virginia resolutions is as the first great clash between pulling the nation together and pushing it apart. Leaders needed to find a balance to avoid separation of the union. The Federalists had pushed too far with their attempts to eliminate those who opposed them. Jefferson came right to the brink of calling for a dissolution of the union, but was pulled back by Madison and other Republicans, including the Kentuckians, who saw the danger. Perhaps another of his biographers, Jon Meacham, came closest to capturing Jefferson's mood when he wrote the following:

Viewed in terms of philosophy, the contradictions between Jefferson the nationalist and Jefferson the nullifier seem irreconcilable.

Viewed in terms of personality and of politics, though, Jefferson was acting in character. He was always in favor of whatever means would improve the chances of his cause of the hour.[49]

Jefferson's response to the crisis and his position on nullification of federal laws would repeat itself multiple times over the next half century leading up to the Civil War. In part, this was caused by the Framers at the Constitutional Convention, who had been unable to resolve the issue of where sovereignty resided, whether in the states or in the federal government. They developed a novel approach that sovereignty resided in the people, who doled out power to the different levels of government. But while that may work in theory, in practice it does not, since sovereignty must reside somewhere. As James Garfield, the twentieth president of the United States wrote at the end of the Civil War, the Kentucky resolution "contained the germ of nullification and secession, and we are today reaping the fruits." The fact that the Kentucky legislature ultimately removed the nullification language did not lesson its full impact in the future, since it later became common knowledge that Jefferson had originally included this language.[50]

❦ ❦ ❦

Perhaps Jefferson should have taken his own advice on patience, because the Federalists would soon split apart over the best course of action to take with regard to France. Adams had received word, from numerous sources, that Talleyrand was ready to open peace negotiations once again. Discussions with Gerry, who had finally returned from France in October of 1798, gave Adams reassurance that the French were serious. On February 18, 1799, Adams, acting very much alone, sent word to the Senate that he would dispatch William Vans Murray (who was the minister to The Hague) "to discuss and conclude all controversies between the two Republics by a new treaty." Ultimately, Murray was joined by two other commissioners, who set sail for France in October of 1799.[51]

While Adams had become convinced that the French were now serious about peace, there was a further reason he decided to send the new peace mission. He, too, feared the army that had been put into place with Hamilton at its head. The previous November, he had attempted to shrink the size of the army, but both his cabinet and the high Federalists opposed this action. A shift in public opinion was underway as the threat of a French invasion faded and "both Adams and Jefferson believed that the Alien and Sedition Acts, and the new taxes levied to pay for the army, had tempered the firm and belligerent mood" of the nation, according to Ferling. Adams also became aware of private letters that Hamilton had written in which he argued that the army should be used to suppress "internal disorders," a clear reference to the Republican Party. Rumors swirled that Hamilton planned to use the army to invade Virginia, causing Adams to write that "this man is stark mad." Adams "thought Hamilton and a Party were endeavoring to get an army on foot to give Hamilton the command of it & then proclaim a Regal Government, place Hamilton at the Head of it & prepare the way for a Province of Great Britain." It is surprising how much Adams and Jefferson agreed about where the plans of Hamilton and the high Federalists would lead. The Federalists were now completely split, and Adams would not have the full support of his own party as he headed into the election of 1800. As one historian has written, had Adams been a different man and seized on "anti-French feeling to precipitate a war," the Union itself may have been destroyed instead of the Federalist Party.[52]

While the Federalists were splintering, the Republicans were uniting. The threat that the Federalists posed to their very existence made them rally around the protection of civil liberties that were now threatened by the Sedition Act. Their electoral prospects brightened considerably when they captured the New York state legislature in April of 1799, led by the efforts of Aaron Burr.

Burr was born in 1756 to one of the most influential families in the North. Both his father and grandfather had been presidents of Princeton, but he never knew either of them, since both died, leaving him orphaned at a young age. He and his sister lived a nomadic existence, moving between different family members. At the age of sixteen he graduated with distinction from Princeton, and then became involved in revolutionary politics. He served in the war as an aide-de-camp and endured the harsh winter at Valley Forge. In the aftermath of independence, he became a successful lawyer in New York, ran for office, and ultimately unseated Hamilton's father-in-law as a senator. He was known to be a womanizer and "loved luxury, abhorred boredom, and was never good at managing money," according to Gordon Wood.[53]

Burr's two cardinal sins were that he was overly ambitious in an age when such behavior was unacceptable, and he lacked any known political principles or philosophy. He pursued politics for "fun and honor & profit," he admitted later in life. Wood has written that "one searches in vain for a single thoughtful letter about political philosophy" in Burr's papers. At the time, his opponents wrote that "he had no theory" and that he was "a mere matter of fact man." His overriding ambition ultimately made enemies of both Hamilton and Jefferson.[54]

In one way, Burr was ahead of his time. While today we take for granted that politicians actively seek office, this was frowned upon during the late eighteenth century. In the spring of 1799, Burr actively campaigned to elect Republicans to the New York state assembly. He and other members of the party "addressed meetings, distributed literature, and stationed themselves in force at the polls in all three days of the election," according to Elkins and McKitrick. Both the Alien and Sedition Acts and the increase in tax burdens triggered by the military buildup were major campaign issues, and the Republicans used that to elect a majority in the New York Assembly. It was that body that would choose the state's twelve delegates to the electoral college and would prove crucial in their support for Jefferson. In 1796, Adams had won those delegates. In return for his work in New York, Burr was rewarded with the vice president's slot in the election of 1800 once again. It was a fateful decision.

The Election of 1800

The election of 1800 ended in a tie in the electoral college between Jefferson and Burr. "Each elector cast two votes, and the man who received the most votes became president, the runner up vice president, regardless of their political affiliations; any candidate could win either office," Joanne B. Freeman succinctly writes. It was a byproduct of the founders' anti-party bias, since those who attended the Constitutional Convention could not envision two candidates running together with a party. The Twelfth Amendment, approved in 1804, would require that separate ballots be cast for president and vice president. But in 1800, the tie threw the decision to the House of Representatives, with each state receiving one vote. The House did not meet again until February of 1801, even though the tie was confirmed at the end of December.[55]

In the intervening period, rumors began to swirl that the Federalists were considering extraconstitutional measures to deprive Jefferson of the presidency. One involved waiting until Adams left office in March and then installing the president pro tempore of the Senate or the Speaker of the House as president under a 1792 statute. As events unfolded, it was becoming apparent that a peaceful transfer of power was at stake. "Talk was rife about militias arming, a possible civil war, and the breakup of the union," James Roger Sharp writes. "There were even reports that Jefferson would be assassinated." While many of these rumors were overblown, the participants at the time believed them. After the election was decided, Jefferson said that "in the event of a usurpation, I was decidedly with those who were determined not to permit it." Jefferson also told Adams that any attempt at usurpation "would probably produce resistance by force and incalculable consequences."[56] The Federalists ultimately decided to pursue a different method of denying Jefferson the presidency by supporting Burr.

The Federalists met in mid-January to hatch their scheme to support Burr. "After a decade of intense rivalry and hyperbolic rhetoric, many Federalists so hated Jefferson that they were feverishly anxious to keep him out of the presidency," Ferling writes. Theodore Sedgwick, the Federalist senator from Massachusetts, framed their view best when he wrote to Hamilton that while Burr's "ambition was of the worst kind," he was a man that lacked any political philosophy or "pernicious theories." Sedgwick thought that Burr could be controlled since he "must depend on good men for his support & that support he cannot receive but by a conformity to their views." Hamilton disagreed vehemently, and in the irony of all ironies, decided to support Jefferson as the lesser of two evils. To Hamilton, Burr had no character, "a man who has no principle public or private." "There is no doubt but upon every virtuous and prudent calculation Jefferson is to be preferred," Hamilton wrote in December of 1800. "He is by far not so dangerous a man and he has pretensions to character."[57]

In a December 23, 1800, letter, Hamilton made it clear that Burr could not be trusted to stick with any deal he made since he was only interested in his own ambition. "How then should we be able to rely upon any agreement with him," Hamilton wrote. On the other hand, Jefferson was not "zealot enough to do anything in pursuance of his principles," and he was as likely to "temporize" and preserve many of those systems he opposed. Hamilton proposed that the Federalists attempt to strike a deal with Jefferson to preserve the "Fiscal System," maintain neutrality with Britain and France, maintain the naval buildup, and keep Federalists in office, other than for the "great departments," the major cabinet positions. But alas, Hamilton's influence in the Federalist Party had waned. With the death of Washington, his great patron, in December 1799 and some missteps of his own, Hamilton no longer held an esteemed place in the party. Those missteps included the fifty-four-page pamphlet he had written in October of 1800 that attacked Adams and all but destroyed his own party's nominee for president. "Nothing that Hamilton ever wrote about Jefferson was half so contemptuous," McCullough writes.[58]

Burr was the great anomaly of the election of 1800–1801. It was clear that Jefferson was at the top of the ticket, and that Burr should have stepped aside for him, but instead he left the door open for Federalist members of Congress to back him. While the Republicans had swept to victory in the legislative elections, it was the lame-duck House, still under Federalist control, that would meet in February to cast ballots to break the tie. Initially, Burr indicated he would "utterly disclaim all ambition" for the presidency, but this was in mid-December before it became clear that there was a tie. While Burr "did nothing to actively draw the presidency away from Jefferson," according to Freeman, "he never promised to decline the office if it were offered." Ultimately, Burr would find himself frozen in place, and alienate both sides before Jefferson was finally elected.[59]

The balloting began on February 11, 1801. While the Federalists had a majority of members in the House, voting was by state, and they only controlled six state delegations. Eight states were controlled by the Republicans, and two were split (Vermont and Maryland). Nine states were needed to win the election, since there were now sixteen states in the Union. It would take thirty-six ballots over the next six days to decide the election.[60]

Finally, on February 14, James Bayard of Delaware informed his Federalist colleagues that he planned to change his vote. As the sole representative from his state, he did not need to consult with anyone to swing the election to Jefferson. Once his fellow party members realized they could not change his mind, they had little choice but to go along with him. While Bayard voted a blank ballot on February 17, the Federalist members from Vermont and Maryland withdrew from the chambers, and Jefferson was elected president with the vote of ten states. The crisis of 1800–1801 was over.[61]

Why did Bayard change his vote? First, he had been attempting to get certain assurances from Burr, which were not forthcoming. As we have seen, Burr was immobilized, unable to move in either direction. If "Burr had intrigued with the Federalists and failed ... [his] political future would have been wrecked then and there," Elkins and McKitrick point out. Second, Bayard seemed to have been genuinely concerned that the election of anyone but Jefferson could lead to a civil war. Bayard later said he "was chiefly influenced by the current of public sentiment, which I thought it neither safe nor politic to counteract." Finally, and perhaps most importantly, he thought that he had reached an agreement with Jefferson. Bayard went to one of Jefferson's friends to seek a deal. If Jefferson would agree to the terms that Hamilton had outlined, Bayard would throw his support to him. According to Bayard's account, he received Jefferson's endorsement and the deal was struck.[62]

When this became public knowledge many years later, Jefferson denied it. Some of Jefferson's most prominent biographers have denied there was any deal. Jefferson was certainly aware of the framework of a deal, and President Adams had requested he "calm the worst of opposition's fears," Jon Meacham writes. Jefferson also told one Federalist that "he should never go into the office of president by capitulation, not with my hands tied by any conditions which should hinder me from pursuing the measures which I should deem for the public good."[63]

Was there a deal? It's an unsolvable question given the historical record and the contradictory accounts of the two men involved. Still, Jefferson was a very savvy and astute politician, a man who knew how to phrase vague answers that could be interpreted in a myriad of ways. It is possible that whatever he relayed to Bayard fit such parameters. "It seems likely that Bayard *believed* he had sufficient assurance that Jefferson was not going to tear down the whole works of the previous dozen years," Jon Meacham writes. Jefferson also knew that he had to pull the nation back from the brink of dissolution. And so perhaps he gave some indefinite assurances that in reality were short of a deal. It would soon become clear from his inaugural address that Jefferson intended to reach out to moderate Federalists and convert them to Republicans.[64]

❦ ❦ ❦

In 1819, Jefferson referred to the events that occurred in 1800 and 1801 as the "revolution of 1800," which was as real as the first revolution of 1776, only this one was brought about by the "suffrage of the people." His victory over the Federalists, and then his attempts to merge them into his own party, would be more successful than he probably ever imagined.[65]

While the Federalists would continue as a party for many years, they would never again win the presidency. This was, in part, due to the advantages that the Constitution bestowed upon the South from the provision that allowed three-fifths of slaves to be counted for the purpose of representation. The number of Federalists in Congress would also shrink over time, from a high of twenty-two senators and sixty representatives in the 1799–1801 period to only five senators and twenty-four representatives in 1823–1825, when the party finally disappeared. Gradually, Federalists became isolated to the New England states.[66] This occurred despite the successes of federalism, including: 1) bringing about the Constitution (in the period before Madison shifted alliances to the Republicans); 2) stabilizing the finances of the United States; and 3) steering the country away from war. Eventually, a new conservative party would arise, one more capable of competing in this newly emerging democratic age.

The political scientist James MacGregor Burns has explained the demise of the Federalists as follows:

A major reason for Federalist Party decline lay in their hallowed but increasingly anachronistic beliefs in the stewardship of gentlemen of learning and virtue, in the need to protect the rights of property, in order as a prerequisite to liberty, in the natural hierarchical order among citizens, in the need for balance and harmony among classes and interests ... Their ideas were not necessarily wrong, but rather mean and elitist and outdated at the time of rising democratic sentiment.[67]

Endnotes

1 Wood, *Empire*, p. 212.

2 Quoted from Jack Rakove, *Revolutionaries: A New History of the Invention of America* (New York, 2010), p. 263.

3 See Jon Meacham, *Thomas Jefferson: The Art of Power* (New York, 2012), p. 182, p.179–180, and McCullough, p. 311.

4 This paragraph is largely drawn from Meacham, p. 212–213, and McCullough, p. 379–380.

5 The quote from the letter to Adams is from McCullough, p. 465; Thomas Jefferson's letter to James Madison, January 1, 1797, from Koch and Peden, p. 539; James Madison, *Writings* (New York, 1999), letter to Jefferson dated January 15, 1797, p. 583.

6 McCullough, p. 474–475.

7 Wood, *Radicalism*, is the best work on the deferential structure of colonial society and how the Federalists attempted to maintain that system.

8 Wood, *Empire*, p. 174–177; Banning, *The Jeffersonian Persuasion*, p. 209; Ferling, *Jefferson and Hamilton*, p. 246 for the Jefferson quote.

9 Wood, *Empire*, p. 193.

10 Elkins and McKitrick, p. 130–131; James Madison, *Writings* (New York, 1999), p. 514.

11 Wood, *Empire*, p. 192–193.

12 For American trade statistics, see Elkins and McKitrick, p. 71 and p. 381–382.

13 Ferling, p. 263.

14 Joseph J. Ellis, *The Quartet: Orchestrating the Second American Revolution 1783–1789* (New York, 2015), p. 69–70; Rakove deals with the moderates in chapter 2 of *Revolutionaries*.

15 Ellis, *The Quartet*, p. 67–69.

16 Donald J. Fraser, *The Emergence of One American Nation: The Founders, the Revolution and the Constitution* (Roseville, 2015), p. 178–179; Ellis, *The Quartet*, p. 87–89.

17 Elkins and McKitrick, p. 397.

18 Elkins and McKitrick have the most in-depth analysis of the treaty negotiations on pages 396–410, which is where this account is largely drawn from. For the lack of benefit for ships under seventy tons, see Ferling, p. 272.

19 Wood, *Empire*, p. 197; Jacob E. Cooke, "Organizing the New National Government." In Leonard W. Levy and Daniel J. Mahoney, *The Framing and Ratification of the Constitution* (New York, 1987), p. 329.

20 Chernow, *Washington*, p. 729–730; the language on the products banned from shipping is taken from the terms of the Jay Treaty, retrieved October 22, 2015, from http://avalon.law.yale.edu/18th_century/jay.asp; the outcome of the Senate vote is from Ferling, p. 272.

21 Chernow, *Washington*, p. 731; Elkins and McKitrick, p. 420.

22 For a detailed discussion of the British order and Washington's response, see Elkins and McKitrick, p. 421–423; the Jefferson quote is from Ferling, p. 275.

23 Ellis, *His Excellency*, p. 227–228, which is where the quote about being over the hill is from; Wood, *Empire*, p. 198.

24 Rossiter, p. 380; Garry Wills, *James Madison* (New York, 2002), p. 41–43; Leibiger, p. 209; Ellis, *His Excellency*, p. 231–232, has a concise description of the split between Washington and Jefferson.

25 McCullough, p. 54–57, for the portrait of Abigail Adams and p. 479 for the quote.

26 McCullough, p. 469–472.

27 Elkins and McKitrick, p. 538; Wood, p. 238.

28 Wood, *Empire*, p. 239; "John Adams Special Message to the Senate and the House, May 16, 1796," retrieved February 10, 2016, from http://avalon.law.yale.edu/18th century/ja97-03.asp.

29 I have followed Elkins and McKitrick's description of these events on p. 543–548; I became aware of Madison's fear of sailing in Ferling, p. 286, who refers to Madison's letter to Jefferson of April 27, 1785, from which I have drawn the quote that was retrieved February 27, 2016, from http://founders.archives.gov/documents/ Jefferson/01-08-02-0070.

30 Koch and Peden, p. 541; Noble E. Cunningham Jr., *In Pursuit of Reason: The Life of Thomas Jefferson* (New York, 1987), p. 210.

31 Ferling, p. 288; for a useful short summary of Jefferson and his biographers, see Fawn M. Brodie, *Thomas Jefferson: An Intimate History* (New York, 1974), p. 4–7.

32 The quotes are from Meacham, p. xxiv, and M. Andrew Holowchak, *Thomas Jefferson: Uncovering His Unique Philosophy and Vision* (New York, 2014), p. 154.

33 For Jefferson's state of mind, see James Roger Sharp, *American Politics in the Early Republic: The New Nation in Crisis* (New Haven, 1993), p. 168; Jefferson's letter of June 17, 1797, to Aaron Burr, retrieved March 5, 2016, from http://founders.archives. gov/documents/Jefferson/01-29-02-0345; Koch and Peden, p. 540–542; Elkins and McKitrick, p. 554–555, have a complete analysis of the actual American position vis-à-vis the British during the period, which is where the quotes come from.

34 Koch and Peden, p. 537; Ferling, p. 290–291.

35 Elkins and McKitrick, p. 556–561, give a good overview of the members; McCullough, p. 486.

36 Elkins and McKitrick, p. 561–562.

37 Wood, *Empire*, p. 242–243; McCullough, p. 495; Elkins and McKitrick, p. 571.

38 Wood, *Empire*, p. 243; Elkins and McKitrick, p. 588.

39 David A. Strauss, *The Living Constitution* (Oxford, 2010), p. 61, argues that many of the founders, including Adams and Hamilton, did not think that the Sedition

Act violated the First Amendment. "So there are serious doubts about whether the founding generation understood the First Amendment to stand even for what is, for us today, the central principle of a system of free expression."

40 Jay Winik, *The Great Upheaval: America and the Birth of the Modern World 1788-1800* (New York, 2007), has an excellent discussion of the atmosphere in the country during this period on p. 541–543; see Chernow, p. 554–560, for a detailed discussion of the wrangling that took place over Hamilton's appointment as second in command of the Army.

41 Ferling, p. 289; Chernow, p. 551–553.

42 Winik, p. 542, discussed the fear of foreign agents; Elkin and McKitrick, p. 591–592, use the term *dead letter* in regard to the Alien bill.

43 Elkins and McKitrick, p. 592; James MacGregor Burns, *The Vineyard of Liberty* (New York, 1982), p. 127.

44 Elkins and McKitrick, p. 592; Chernow, p. 572; Burns, p. 128; the Madison quote is from Meacham, p. 314.

45 Meacham, p. 319; Chernow, p. 575.

46 Dumas Malone, *Jefferson and the Ordeal of Liberty* (Boston, 1962), p. 375.

47 My thinking in this paragraph has been influenced by Hofstadter, p. 109–120, which is where I became aware of Jefferson's letter to John Taylor of June 4, 1798. See also Peter S. Onuf, *Jefferson's Empire of Liberty: The Language of American Nationhood* (Charlottesville, 2000), which is an excellent analysis of Jefferson's nationalism. See especially the introduction and chapter 3. The quote from him is from page 12. The quote on equilibrium is mentioned in Onuf on p. 95 and is from Jefferson's letter to Peregrine Fitzhugh dated February 23, 1798, and was retrieved on April 7, 2016, from http://founders.archives.gov/documents/Jefferson/01-30-02-0089. The Jefferson quote from 1798 was from the letter to John Taylor mentioned above and was retrieved April 7, 2016, from http://teachingamericanhistory.org/library/document/letter-to-john-taylor-2/.

48 Hofstadter, p. 119–120.

49 Meacham, p. 318.

50 Chernow, p. 574, contains the quote from Garfield; Meacham, p. 319.

51 McCullough, p. 511–523; Winik, p. 552, which is where the Adams quote is taken from.

52 John Ferling, *A Leap in the Dark: The Struggle to Create the American Republic* (Oxford, 2003), p. 442–444; Elkins and McKitrick, p. 615–616; Chernow, p. 595; Hofstadter, p. 110.

53 Gordon S. Wood, *Revolutionary Characters: What Made the Founders Different* (New York, 2006), p. 231–232; Ferling, p. 279; Elkins and McKitrick, p. 744.

54 Wood, *Revolutionary Characters*, p. 234, 229, and 231.

55 Joanne B. Freeman, *Affairs of Honor: National Politics in the New Republic* (New

Haven, 2001), p. 199; on the founders' view on parties, see Fraser, p. 287–289.

56 Sharp, p. 250–252; Meacham, p. 334; Ferling, *A Leap in the Dark*, p. 475; Malone, *The President*, p. 8.

57 Ferling, *A Leap in the Dark*, p. 468; Elkins and McKitrick, p. 748–749.

58 See Hamilton's letter to Harrison Gray Otis of December 23, 1800, and his letter to Oliver Wolcott Jr., from December 1800 that were retrieved April 10, 2016, from http://founders.archives.gov/documents/Hamilton/01-25-02-0140; excerpts from Hamilton's letter to James Bayard were drawn from Elkins and McKitrick, p. 748–749; McCullough, p. 549.

59 Freeman, p. 248; Elkins and McKitrick, p. 748–749, make the point that Burr was, in their words, "immobilized."

60 Sharp, p. 265; Ferling, *A Leap in the Dark*, p. 472.

61 Sharp, p. 271–272.

62 Elkins and McKitrick, p. 748 and footnote 166 on p. 907; Sharp, p. 272; Ferling, *A Leap in the Dark*, p. 473; and Meacham, p. 338.

63 The biographers mentioned are from Malone, *The President*, p. 491, and Cunningham, p. 236; the quote from Jefferson can be found in Meacham, p. 339.

64 Meacham, p. 338.

65 Jefferson letter of September 6, 1819, to Spencer Roane retrieved April 19, 2016, from http://press-pubs.uchicago.edu/founders/documents/a1_8_18s16.html.

66 These numbers were retrieved on April 19, 2016, from https://en.wikipedia.org/wiki/Party_divisions_of_United_States_Congresses.

67 Burns, p. 228.

CHAPTER 3

The West and Jefferson's Empire of Liberty

*The old charters of Massachusetts, Virginia, and the Carolinas
had given title to strips of territory extending from the Atlantic
westward to the Pacific.*
—ALBERT BUSHNELL HART

Go West, young man, Go West and grow up with the country.
—HORACE GREELEY

Westward expansion has always been an important element in
understanding the United States. We were populated by people
looking for virgin land and new opportunities. But westward expansion would prove to be a double-edged sword. On the one hand, it
opened new opportunities for many people in the vastness of the West
and it ultimately allowed the United States to become a continental
power, implementing Jefferson's vision of an empire of liberty. But it
came at a high price, pushing Indians ever further from their ancestral
lands, and leading to the expansion of slavery, which would almost
destroy the union.

The West Prior to 1800

Albert Bushnell Hart, an American historian from the late 1800s, points to an important truth about westward expansion. Even before independence, the various colonies had their sights set on expansion to the west, to the area beyond their settled boundaries. Both Virginia and Massachusetts came out of the same original colonial charter. In 1609, a second charter was granted by King James I that extended the boundaries of Virginia to the Pacific Ocean. Similarly, the Charter of Carolina in 1663 stretched across the continent.[1]

In the aftermath of the French and Indian War, Great Britain issued the Proclamation of 1763, which closed the area west of the Appalachians to further settlement. George Washington, who had been pursuing claims to western lands that had been promised to veterans of the war, considered the proclamation a "preposterous joke," according to Joseph Ellis. Washington saw the future of Virginia, and his own financial well-being, as tied to development in the Ohio River valley. It was one more grievance that the colonists held against the British in the run-up to the Revolutionary War.[2]

Disputes over claims to lands in the West slowed the approval of the Articles of Confederation by the Continental Congress during the Revolutionary War. The articles, which were drafted in 1776 in the aftermath of declaring independence, originally envisioned that the central government would have the power over western lands. Virginia refused to approve the Confederation unless its right to western lands was recognized. Maryland, for its part, refused to ratify until Virginia removed its claims. The issue wasn't resolved until 1780, when the British implemented their Southern strategy, attacking the Carolinas. In order to secure continued French support for the war effort, then Governor Thomas Jefferson agreed to relinquish Virginia's claims to western lands. The Articles of Confederation finally went into effect on March 1, 1781.[3]

Washington had always been enamored with the idea that there was a way to use the Potomac River as the main mode of transportation to the west, even though it would prove to be a wholly unrealistic idea. By the 1780s, he owned vast tracts of western land spread over the Shenandoah Valley, western Pennsylvania, and areas on the Ohio and Great Kanawha Rivers. He was a main proponent of internal improvements to the Potomac, including locks and canals, which would allow it to flow to the Ohio River. The improvements would serve the dual purpose of allowing Washington to prosper by selling western lands and tying the settlers in the area to the United States. In 1785, Washington hosted a conference on navigation of the Potomac River at Mount Vernon with representatives of both Virginia and Maryland. At the conclusion of the conference, Virginia proposed that a larger conference be held of all the states to discuss possible reforms to the central government that existed under the Articles of Confederation. It was the beginning of efforts to organize the Constitutional Convention.[4]

Jefferson was also a major proponent of westward expansion. Monticello faced west, which was the future direction of the United States in Jefferson's mind. Although he never traveled past the Natural Bridge on the western edge of the Blue Ridge Mountains, he had a "peculiar confidence in the men from the western side of the mountains."[5] For Jefferson, westward expansion and the new nation went hand in hand. Peter S. Onuf writes that:

Jefferson envisioned 'an empire of liberty,' an expanding union of republics held together by ties of interest and affection. For this bold experiment in republicanism to succeed, Americans would have to be a united people, conscious of themselves as a nation with a crucial role to play in world history.[6]

The Northwest Territory

The Northwest Territory included the land west of Pennsylvania and Northwest of the Ohio River. The future states of Ohio, Indiana, Illinois, Michigan, and Wisconsin would ultimately be formed from this area. The Ohio frontier was the first to be occupied by white settlers, along with the future state of Kentucky, as people moved through the Cumberland Gap in the middle of the 1700s. Those who came to the Ohio valley were confronted by the Shawnees, the Wyandots, and the Delawares, who had settled in the area in the 1730s. These tribes had been forced west by white settlement further east and lived both as hunters and as farmers. They quickly became dependent on both the French and British for weapons, which they acquired with beaver and fur skins. During the French and Indian War, the tribes kept shifting alliances between the British and the French.[7]

As we have seen, the British attempted to close the Ohio and Kentucky frontiers in the aftermath of the French and Indian War in order to reach a peaceful settlement with the Indians and secure the western border from French and Spanish influence. But they had little success, and by the eve of the Revolutionary War, over five thousand settlers lived in the Ohio valley. The goal of the settlers was the removal of the Indian tribes from the area. "Hatred and violence characterized the actions of both Indians and whites on the Ohio frontier," writes historian R. Douglas Hurt. By the mid-1770s, Indian tribes had largely agreed to cede their land in Kentucky, with a promise from the Pennsylvanians and Virginians that the lands in the Ohio River valley would remain for the Indians. It was one of many promises that would not be kept.[8]

The Treaty of Paris ceded all the land east of the Mississippi to the United States. It made no mention that much of this land was already occupied by Indians. The policy of the United States during the Confederation period was that westward expansion would occur by right of conquest. Treaties were imposed on the tribes in the Ohio River valley, even though the government had no means to enforce its will. "The Indians, still resentful of the manner in which they had been forced to sign treaties after 1783, were engaged in open hostilities," according to historian Reginald Horsman. The Indians were aided by the British, who refused to abandon their Northwest posts. During this period, North Carolina and Georgia maintained control over their western land claims, which meant Congress did not have total control over Indian policy.[9]

Expansion into the Northwest Territory was hindered by continued fighting between the white settlers and the Indian tribes. In the aftermath of the Revolutionary War, the Confederation Congress grappled with how to incorporate the area into the United States. A committee headed by Thomas Jefferson put forward the Land Ordinance of 1784. It proposed that the new territories could form their own governments based on the Constitution and laws of the existing states, and that once they reached a population at least equal to "any one of the thirteen original states," they could be admitted to the union on an equal basis "with the said original states."[10]

The Ordinance of 1784 also included a clause that banned slavery in the territories after 1800. Not surprisingly, it proved to be controversial and split the Confederation Congress along geographic lines. Only one other Southern representative voted with Jefferson. The inclusion of the slavery ban lost by one vote when the representative from New Jersey was sick and did not attend the session when the matter came up for a vote. "The voice of a single individual would have prevented this abominable crime from spreading itself over the new country ... Heaven was silent in that awful moment," Jefferson wrote in 1786. Had it passed, the future of slavery in the United States may have been limited to the original Southern states and not been allowed to expand into the future new territories.[11]

Two problems continued to plague westward expansion. One was the problem of squatters. The Land Ordinance of 1785 subdivided the land into one-square-mile lots of 640 acres. The government attempted to sell the lots for $1,240, or $2.00 per acre. The Confederation Congress hoped that the sale of western land would help to pay off the debt that had been accumulated from the drive for independence, but the price proved too high and instead encouraged people to squat on the land. "Then they built a log cabin, planted corn, and dared anyone, red or white, to move them off," according to Hurt. To bring some order to the process, the Confederation Congress approved the Northwest Ordinance of 1787. It called for a more gradual movement toward statehood, with the original territories "to be governed dictatorially by a federally appointed governor" until such time as the population reached at least five thousand people, at which point a representative assembly could be formed. In order to be eligible to enter the union as a state, the population would be required to grow to sixty thousand people. In 1787, the Congress also began to sell land to eastern speculators who promised to bring order to the sale of land. But this too proved illusory, at least initially. The settlers "shunned the speculators lands and refused to buy land at the expensive prices at which it was offered," according to Wood, since they could have it for free. Eventually, the land was offered at a discount and in smaller lots by the private companies, who in the 1790s began to sell fifty- to one-hundred-acre plots at one dollar per acre. "Most settlement occurred on privately held lands, because settlers could afford it" as Hurt writes, and the problem of squatting gradually began to wane, even if it did not disappear totally.[12]

The other problem the United States needed to confront was the continuing war with native tribes, a problem that would vex Americans for the next century and lead to one of the greatest failures of the new nation, causing the near eradication of the native tribes. As the new Constitution was implemented in 1789, the Washington administration, under the leadership of Secretary of War Henry Knox, implemented a more liberal and moral policy toward the Indians. Knox had occupied the same position during the latter years of the Confederation and believed that the Indians "possess the right of the soil. It cannot be taken from them unless by their free consent, or by the right of conquest in case of a just war." He pointed out that both the British and the colonial governments had always purchased land from the Indians, and the new American government should return to this policy. Knox wanted the federal government to take over control of Indian policy from the Southern states and proposed that the native people be treated as sovereign nations subject to American foreign policy. But the new policy was grounded in two illusions: first, that the Indians were prepared to sell their land; and second, that as white settlers advanced, the Indians would be absorbed into western society as farmers. Knox also left a rather large opening for the use of force against the Indians with his position on "just war." "All wars are just in the eyes of the nation that fights them, and as the Indians would undoubtedly resist the cession of large areas of land, this provision could come in for considerable use," wrote Horsman.[13]

The new reality set in as the Washington administration found that it needed to defend from Indian attacks the settlers that had been pouring into Kentucky and the Northwest Territory. "Though the talk was of conciliation, concession, and the bringing of civilization, the

United States could not give back the lands forced from the Indians in the 1780s," states Horsman.[14] Development in the Ohio valley really began to take off in the mid-1790s. Washington appointed Anthony Wayne to lead an army of some two thousand regulars and fifteen hundred Kentucky militia against the continued British presence in the Northwest Territories. The British had been arming the Indians in the area, who continued to resist white encroachment on their land. In June of 1794, General Wayne's troops defeated the Indians at Fallen Timbers. This victory, along with the Jay Treaty, removed Great Britain from the Northwest, and led to the Treaty of Greenville, where the Indians ceded the Ohio River valley to the United States.[15]

The war with the native peoples was over, at least temporarily, and the white population began to expand rapidly, growing from forty-five thousand in 1800 to over two hundred and thirty thousand in 1810. The people who settled in the Ohio frontier primarily came from western Pennsylvania and Virginia, although some came from as far away as New England, Maryland, and New Jersey. Land ownership was highly concentrated in the hands of the speculators that the federal government sold it to, with one-third of the land owned by 10 percent of the population. But of the land that was ultimately sold, most of it was held by small farmers. By 1810, "90 percent of the population who owned land held fewer than 480 acres, with the median holding being 15 acres," Hurt writes. Most started as subsistence farmers, but very quickly commercial farming developed, with surplus crops and livestock being sold into the market economy. Roswell Caulkin was typical. He lived "comfortably" with "good beef, pork, turnips and potatoes, wheat, rye and indian corn, [and] tallow for candles." Ohio farmers planted wheat for sale to the markets, which created the need for flour mills. Both the Ohio and Mississippi Rivers made for a convenient mode of transporting the wheat crop for export, and many goods were shipped through New Orleans. The farmers also kept farm animals, including pigs, cattle, and sheep. What wasn't used for personal consumption was sold to the markets, which led to the development of a meatpacking industry in towns throughout the Ohio valley.[16]

The Ohio valley was an area where the American dream could be realized. Young men without wealth could come to the area, and if they were willing to work hard as an agricultural laborer, they could earn enough to purchase land within a few years. It was a very different pattern of settlement than that which would occur in the Southern part of the United States, including major portions of the Louisiana Territory that Jefferson would acquire in 1803.

Pinned down fighting the Indians in the Northwest Territory, the Washington administration could not afford any further warfare in the South. Knox negotiated treaties with the Creeks in Georgia and the Cherokees in the western part of North Carolina and Tennessee. Neither the tribes nor the states were happy with the results. As Horsman observes, "the Southern frontier was the scene of continued frontier advance, sporadic warfare, and bloodshed." The settlers in the South continued to infringe on Indian lands, and the lack of a federal troop presence in the area to keep them safe soured them on the new government. Andrew Jackson warned that if the federal government did not provide protection from the Indians, the settlers would need to find it "from some other Source."[17]

The Louisiana Purchase

When King Ferdinand and Queen Isabella bankrolled the voyages of Columbus, Spain became the first of the European imperial powers to occupy this continent, launching the era of expansion in the New

World. Spain controlled much of South and Central America, Mexico, and parts of western North America to the Canadian border. They also controlled Florida and the territory known as Louisiana. By the start of the nineteenth century, Spain was an empire in decline, its treasury empty, a process that had begun when Great Britain defeated the Spanish Armada in 1588. The Spanish were spread too thin and had too many enemies, including the newly rising powers of France and Great Britain.[18]

In 1795, the United States negotiated the treaty of San Lorenzo, which opened trade through New Orleans. In the autumn of 1802, the Spanish intendent closed the port to the Americans, in violation of the treaty. Jefferson had been hearing rumors since early in his first year as president that the Spanish intended to cede Louisiana to Napoleon, and the closure created a public controversy. Jefferson's response was to move slowly and with patience, and through a combination of skill, luck, and pragmatism, he would achieve an unexpected triumph.[19]

The president's first move was to send his friend and fellow Virginian James Monroe to France to assist the American minister, Robert Livingston, in negotiations with Napoleon. It was one thing for the "feeble" Spanish to hold New Orleans, but "France and the U.S. [cannot continue] long friends" under such circumstances. "From that moment we must marry ourselves to the British fleet and nation," Jefferson wrote to Livingston.[20] It was quite an admission from the Anglophobe president who had been attempting to break ties with the former motherland since his days as a young revolutionary. But it also showed his grave concern about an expansionist France under Napoleon controlling land in the West. In a letter to Livingston, Jefferson explained that if France would sell "the island of New Orleans and the Floridas" to the United States, then the two sides might reconcile their interests. The president knew that New Orleans was the key, since "the produce of three eights of our territory must pass to market" through its ports.

The Federalists condemned Jefferson's policy toward the French. "The obvious line for critics to take was that the policies of the administration in the face of the crisis were feeble," Dumas Malone writes. Hamilton proposed that the United States attempt to purchase Louisiana through negotiation, and if that failed, then "go to war [and] seize at once on the Floridas and New Orleans, and then negotiate." In the Senate, a resolution was introduced by the Federalists that would authorize Jefferson to seize New Orleans and call out up to fifty thousand men. The resolution was defeated by the Republicans.[21]

It was at this point that luck intervened to assist Jefferson. The French had been attempting to put down a slave revolt led by Toussaint L'Ouverture on the island of Santo Domingo (present-day Haiti) that had begun in 1791, in part spurred by the French Declaration of Rights. France was dependent on sugar from Santo Domingo, which made up 20 percent of its exports. Bonaparte also looked upon Louisiana as "dumping ground for French malcontents and a source for provisioning the lucrative French sugar islands," Wood writes. In 1801, Napoleon sent his brother-in-law and forty thousand men to put down the slave revolt. Although they were successful in capturing L'Ouverture through subterfuge, claiming they were there to support him, the overall mission ultimately failed. By 1802, the French troops succumbed to a combination of attacks by the Haitians and yellow fever, and only two thousand men remained alive. The loss of Santo Domingo caused Napoleon to change his mind and "renounce Louisiana," which he now planned to sell to the United States.[22]

As Bonaparte soaked in his cologne-scented bath, his brothers attempted to change his mind, arguing that he needed the permission of the French legislature. Napoleon dismissed their concerns, stating that he alone would make the decision. When apprised of the situation, Livingston decided to exceed his instructions, noting that the moment "must not be missed," as he wrote to Madison. He and Monroe ultimately negotiated a price of $15 million for a land mass that doubled the size of the United States. On July 3, 1803, word finally reached Jefferson, who was ecstatic. "This removes the greatest source of danger to our peace," Jefferson wrote. The Louisiana Purchase "freed America from Europe's colonial entanglements and prepared the way for the eventual dominance of the United States in the Western Hemisphere," Wood notes.[23]

The final element needed to bring the purchase to a successful conclusion was pragmatism. Jefferson's personality was an interesting mix: part dreamer, part radical, but overwhelmingly practical, especially when it suited his purposes. As we have seen, he was a strict constructionist when it came to the Constitution. If the document did not provide explicit authority to do something, then it could not be done. That was why, in part, he opposed Hamilton's bank proposal in the 1790s. Whereas Hamilton relied on implied powers when he interpreted the Constitution, Jefferson believed that the document needed to be amended to undertake powers not explicitly granted.

Jefferson faced a dilemma with the Louisiana Purchase. He and his fellow Republicans were ideologically committed to a very narrow view of the role of the federal government and of executive power. Jefferson already thought just negotiating the treaty exceeded his authority. But as Joseph Ellis points out, Jefferson now needed to face the fact that "republican government at the national level simply could not function if Republican political values were strictly enforced." His personal view was that he and the Congress lacked the power to ratify the treaty, so he originally favored a constitutional amendment. "I think it will be safer not to permit the enlargement of the Union but by an amendment of the Constitution," Jefferson wrote to his treasury secretary, Albert Gallatin. In part he seemed to fear that some future president, lacking his own scruples, would expand executive power even further. Both Gallatin and Madison tried to steer Jefferson away from this course, maintaining that the treaty-making power contained in the Constitution was sufficient to add the Louisiana Territory without the need for an amendment.[24]

What finally changed his mind was the potential loss of the treaty. On August 18, Livingston sent a dispatch saying that Napoleon was having second thoughts and would be only too happy if the Americans failed to ratify by October 30. There simply was not enough time to pursue a constitutional amendment, and so Jefferson submitted the treaty to the Senate for its ratification. As Jon Meacham writes, Jefferson's actions expanded the power of the presidency beyond what he was truly comfortable with. "The philosophical Jefferson had believed an amendment necessary. The political Jefferson, however, was not going to allow theory to get in the way of reality," observes Meacham. Jefferson would later write that "to lose our country by a scrupulous adherence to written law" would result in "absurdly sacrificing the end to the means." In a contest between his theoretical and practical side, the practical generally won.[25]

The Senate quickly ratified the treaty by a vote of 21–7 on October 20, 1803. But in the House, which needed to act to provide the funding to take possession of the Louisiana Territory, the constitutional questions were publicly raised. In a bizarre twist such as our history is replete with, the Republicans were forced to defend the treaty by referring to the implied powers granted by the necessary-and-proper clause. The Northern Federalists, who were rightly worried over the expansion of the slaveholding South, took on the mantle of the strict constructionist. "In effect, both sides switched, suggesting how one interpreted the Constitution was less a matter of principle than a function of one's location in or out of power," Ellis has observed. The Republicans ultimately prevailed in the House, although many of their members defected, making the vote extremely close.[26]

The Louisiana Purchase was momentous for the United States, opening a vast new area for the expansion of Jefferson's empire of liberty. The president had, even before the purchase, seen the future through the lens of the West. In 1802, Jefferson had authorized the Lewis and Clark expedition, an overt scientific venture with "a covert military and commercial" purpose underlying it, to explore the lands from west of the Mississippi River to the Pacific Ocean. But it would also hasten the twin problems that would bedevil the young nation. One was America's troubled relations with its native population. The other, the expansion of slavery into the West, which would almost destroy the country.[27]

Jefferson and the Indians

Despite the major differences between the Republicans and the Federalists on public policies, there was almost no difference on matters of relations with the Indians. "If the Indian were transformed, if he adopted civilization and lived like a white man, his savage ways would disappear, and he would endure to become a useful member of the white man's world," historian Bernard W. Sheehan has written. Or so the theory went. The reality was far different.[28]

Jefferson had always had an interest in the native population. This was, in part, spurred by his need to refute the theories of the French naturalist George Comte de Buffon. Buffon had written that the American environment was deficient, and he called into question whether progress could actually occur on the North American continent in comparison to the far better environment of Europe. One of Buffon's associates "insisted that the hardiest European would 'degenerate' in the new world," according to historian Nicholas Guyatt. The deficiency of the environment extended to the native peoples of North America, who Buffon viewed as "no more than the first among animals," as a group of savages stuck in an early stage of development. Jefferson, in his *Notes on the State of Virginia*, refuted the claims of Buffon that the North American environment was detrimental to plant, animal, and human life. As Gordon Wood has written, Buffon's claims called into question "the success of the new American republican experiment" and Jefferson felt compelled to respond.[29]

On the Indians, Jefferson wrote "that his vivacity and activity of mind is equal to ours in the same situation." It wasn't the environment of America that caused the Indians to fall behind, but simply "that letters have not yet been introduced among them," or, in other words, that the Indian had not yet been exposed to education and a more advanced way of life. As he wrote in 1785, "the proofs of genius given by the Indians of N. America place them on a level with Whites in the same uncultivated state." But Jefferson definitely believed that the Indians were in an earlier stage of development, that they needed to move "from a savage to a civilized state," says Jefferson scholar Peter Onuf. The key to this was to "teach them agriculture and the domestic arts," as Jefferson explained in his second inaugural. To the Delaware Indians, Jefferson said, "You will unite yourselves with us, and we shall all be Americans. You will mix with us by marriage." Jefferson's policy of integration would fail and ultimately provide "the moral and intellectual rationale for the removal of Indians across the Mississippi under President Andrew Jackson," Onuf notes.[30]

The Jefferson administration's initial dealings with the Indians were generally fair and rather benign. In 1786, he wrote "that not a foot of land will ever be taken from the Indians without their own consent," and his administration attempted, at least at first, to follow this dictate. But Jefferson also envisioned an ever-expanding empire of liberty, and to achieve this goal, he needed the land that the Indians occupied. This became ever more acute when the Spanish ceded the Louisiana Territory to France. In order to avert the influence of the French on the Indian tribes, the new country needed to acquire more western land near the Mississippi. Increasingly, the administration became more and more aggressive in its attempts to pressure the Indians to sell land. Jefferson also had to deal with the white settlers in the West who saw the Indians as a threat and often violated the terms of treaties that were established with the tribes.[31]

Jefferson's policy also had a fatal flaw within it: his belief that the Indians would be willing participants in selling their land and joining Western society. There was no sense of the value of Indian culture, or that change of the type and magnitude that was contemplated could not be accomplished immediately. Most of the Indians were being asked to change from a hunter-gatherer society, one in which all land was held by the tribe, to an agricultural society based on private owner-ship of land. Even for those tribes that had been practicing agriculture since before Columbus, like the Five Civilized Tribes, land was held in common, and the tribes had no intent of selling land to the United States. American policy was not grounded in an evolutionary process that would unfold over many generations but rather was one that was being imposed on the current generation of Indians. While the policy had some success in the South with the Cherokees, who were part of the Five Civilized Tribes, it was an overall failure. As we will see in greater detail later, by the time of the presidency of Andrew Jackson, Indian removal would become the official policy of the United States.

The 1791 Treaty of Holston, in which the American government had agreed to assist the Cherokees "to become herdsmen and cultivators" would be abrogated and the Indians in Georgia, Alabama, and Mississippi would be forcibly removed.[32]

It was no wonder the policy met resistance from the tribes, or that in 1805 the Shawnee chief Tecumseh and his half brother, who was known as the Prophet, began a resistance movement in the Northwest Territories. The basis of their movement was that the Indians should no longer sell land to the United States, and that they should resist attempts to be incorporated into American society. When Jefferson became aware that the Shawnees might try to play the British off against the United States, he wrote to his secretary of war that the Indians should be aware that if the United States lifted "the hatchet against any tribe, we will never lay it down till the tribe is exterminated, or driven beyond the Mississippi."[33]

Joseph Ellis makes the case that the Louisiana Purchase hastened the process of Indian removal, since it opened a vast new domain to the west of the Mississippi that the Indians could be relocated to. Jefferson, always the optimist, wrote in August 1803 that the United States would endeavor "to exchange some of the country there unoccupied by Indians for the lands held by the Indians on this side of the Mississippi, who will be glad to cede us their country." And the land acquired from the Indians would then be sold to new settlers, who would "pay the whole debt contracted before it becomes due." Out of this came the policy in which removal went hand in hand with attempts to civilize the tribes and have them adopt Western ways. Some Indians also began to voluntarily leave the areas east of the Mississippi as hunting became more difficult in the face of ever-expanding settlers. Ultimately, removal would prevail, as it "became widely accepted that the Indian could not, or would not, be civilized and that, even if he did accept the outward forms of civilization, he would not be admitted into the white man's world," Sheehan writes.[34]

The Expansion of Slavery

Jefferson's views on slavery and black people often mirrored those of his fellow countrymen, yet sometimes his views were out of step with them. It is illuminating to compare Jefferson's beliefs to the prevailing national mood to see how each went through a period of wanting to end the peculiar institution, only to accept its ultimate growth and see the nation begin to split over its expansion in the West.

"Slavery bounded his life from cradle to grave," Annette Gordon-Reed and Peter S. Onuf write. Jefferson's first memory was of being handed to a slave on a pillow for a long journey when he was two or three. On his deathbed, he was attended to by his grandson and his manservant, Burwell Colbert, a nephew of Sally Hemings. It was Colbert who understood, as the old man mumbled, that Jefferson wanted his head elevated. He died shortly thereafter.[35]

Jefferson believed that slavery was evil, even though he owned a large plantation and enslaved African Americans. He thought that slavery degraded not only those who were forced into it, but also had a deleterious effect on those who owned other human beings. "The whole commerce between master and slave is a perpetual exercise of the most boisterous passions, the most unremitting despotism on the one part, and degrading submissions on the other," Jefferson wrote in *Notes on the State of Virginia*. In 1768, the twenty-five-year-old Jefferson wanted the House of Burgesses to allow owners the choice of emancipation of their slaves, which was promptly rejected by his fellow Virginians. He had asked an older member of the House to introduce the measure, who "was denounced as an enemy to his country, & was treated with the grossest indecorum." Perhaps it was the exuberance of youth that made him think emancipation could be accomplished so easily, but the response made Jefferson think that his generation was not yet ready to eliminate slavery. This experience may also have affected Jefferson's future unwillingness to lead on the issue of slavery, since he absolutely hated conflict and went to great lengths to disguise his role in events that caused major disputes. And his own ambivalence about slavery was on display when, a year after he proposed the emancipation of slaves, he took out a newspaper ad and offered a reward for one of his runaway slaves.[36]

It was Jefferson's immortal words in the Declaration of Independence, that all men have certain natural rights, that called into question whether slavery could exist in a society dedicated to such ideals. The gradual elimination of slavery was particularly strong in the North and the upper South during the revolutionary period. By 1774, Rhode Island and Connecticut prohibited new slaves from being brought into their colonies. Vermont abolished slavery in 1777. Pennsylvania began the process of gradual abolition in 1780, and in 1783 the Massachusetts Supreme Court found that slavery was unconstitutional. Other New England states soon followed suit with their own plans for gradual elimination. New York and New Jersey took much longer, in large part because they had a larger number of slaves. But by the early 1800s, they too adopted plans for the gradual elimination of slavery.[37]

In the upper South, including Virginia and Maryland, those that owned slaves questioned slavery's compatibility with their own ideology. Not only Jefferson, but Washington, Madison, Mason, and other leaders of the revolution found it difficult to square their support of liberty and equality with owning human beings. In 1786, Washington stated, "I never mean to possess another slave by purchase; it being among my first wishes to see some plan adopted by the Legislature, by which slavery in this Country may be abolished by slow, sure, and imperceptible degrees." Madison wrote that he wished "to depend as little as possible on the labor of slaves." At the Constitutional Convention, George Mason said that "every master of slaves is born a petty tyrant." Perhaps that is why Virginia, Delaware, and Maryland all allowed for the private manumission of slaves by the early 1780s. But while many of those in the upper South saw the pernicious impact of slavery, they also could never find a way to be free of the system without bringing financial ruin on themselves and the economy of their states.[38]

Jefferson saw clearly that the North and the upper South were moving toward some form of emancipation. As he wrote in a 1785 letter, in the North "there being but few slaves, they can easily disencumber themselves of them." As for Maryland and Virginia, "the bulk of the people will approve it in theory," although it would need to wait for the next generation to put this into practice. As he wrote a year later, "those who desire it, form as yet a minority of the state." But in the Deep South, he saw little hope of abolition.[39]

The leadership of South Carolina and Georgia were the great defenders of slavery. Their ancestors had come from Barbados, where slaves were treated particularly brutally. At the Constitutional Convention, the delegates from those two states were the ones that pushed for the protection of slavery as the price for their agreement to join the new and stronger union. They were able to not only have slaves counted as three-fifths of people for purposes of representation in the House (and indirectly for the presidency through the electoral college), but they also protected the importation of slaves until 1808. Many of the Northern delegates would have preferred that the Constitution place slavery "on the road to ultimate extinction," as Ellis writes. Still, the document never mentions the word slavery, and as Ellis also points out, "any clear resolution of the slavery question one way or the other rendered ratification of the Constitution virtually impossible."[40]

In the aftermath of ratification of the Constitution, it was clear that the elimination of slavery was becoming more and more difficult in the South. The two regions had begun to grow apart in how they viewed slavery, in part predicated on how many slaves there were in each part of the country, as shown in the chart below.

The 1790 Census and Slavery			
	Total	Slaves	Percent
Northern States			
• Vermont	85,539	16	0.02%
• New Hampshire	141,885	158	0.11%
• Maine	96,540	0	0.00%
• Massachusetts	378,787	0	0.00%
• Rhode Island	68,825	948	1.38%
• Connecticut	237,946	2,764	1.16%
• New York	340,120	21,324	6.27%
• New Jersey	184,139	11,423	6.20%
• Pennsylvania	434,373	3,737	0.86%
Total	1,968,154	40,370	2.05%
Southern States			
• Delaware	59,094	8,887	15.04%
• Maryland	319,728	103,036	32.23%
• Virginia	747,610	292,627	39.14%
• Kentucky	73,677	12,430	16.87%
• North Carolina	393,751	100,572	25.54%
• South Carolina	249,073	107,094	43.00%
• Georgia	82,548	29,264	35.45%
Total	1,925,481	653,910	33.96%

Source: Census data as shown in Ellis, Founding Brothers, p. 102

While total population was evenly split between North and South, slaves made up only 2 percent of the population in the North but almost 34 percent in the South. In South Carolina, slaves made up 43 percent of the population. It was no wonder that emancipation was easier in the North than in the South. As Gordon Wood writes, Northerners "had little or no appreciation that slavery in the South was a healthy, vigorous, and expansive institution." Population trends were adding to the problem of emancipation. The black population was nearly doubling every twenty to twenty-five years. The importation of slaves was adding to the problem. Property rights were of central importance to the revolutionary generation, one of John Locke's core rights of "life, liberty and estate." Any scheme for the emancipation of slaves would be dependent on compensating slave owners for their property and would also require some plan for relocating those that were freed. "The larger the enslaved population grew, the more financially and politically impractical any emancipation scheme became," Ellis writes.[41]

The Quakers of Pennsylvania found this out when they submitted two petitions to Congress in 1790, one that would end the slave trade and another that would end slavery altogether. Congress could hardly ignore them, since they were signed by Benjamin Franklin, who feared that the impetus from the revolution for the elimination of slavery would soon dissipate. The conversations and arguments that had ensued in private at the convention now became public. Two members from South Carolina led the opposition to the petitions, foreshadowing many of the positions that would be put forward in defense of slavery in the future. Their arguments were twofold. First was that their states had only joined the union because they were assured that the Northern states would not meddle with slavery. As one of them stated it, "the Southern states must be left to themselves on this subject." The second was a racial argument, that emancipation of the slaves would result in the extinction of the white race as inter-marriage began to occur. The racial arguments were meant to scare whites in both the North and South, holding out the specter that "the American people would all be of the mulatto breed."[42]

Jefferson's personal view on the equality of black slaves was stated in *Notes on the State of Virginia.* "I advance it, therefore, as a suspicion only, that the blacks, whether originally a distinct race, or made distinct by time and circumstances, are inferior to the whites in the endow-ments both of mind and body," Jefferson wrote. While he proffered this as a suspicion only, his view clearly diverged from his view of Indi-ans, whom he saw as equal to whites. The man who wrote that "all men are created equal" did not completely believe this statement when it came to blacks of African descent. This view diverged from Jefferson's general viewpoint that all of life was a product of its environment. His response to Buffon's theory that the environment of North America was debilitating had caused him to defend the native population, as we have seen. Jefferson's view that blacks were inferior to whites was criticized by more liberal members of white society. Dr. Benjamin Rush of Philadelphia wrote that "the unhappy sons of Africa, in spite of the degrading influence of slavery, are in no wise inferior to the more fortunate inhabitants of Europe and America." Yet Jefferson's position on racial inequality probably reflected the view of many whites and would later be echoed by none other than Lincoln. Since colonial times, slave masters had created an environment in which poor whites were made to feel superior to blacks as a means to elicit their support in controlling the slave population. Perhaps Jefferson's need to rationalize his role as a slave owner, part of an institution he clearly believed was evil, caused him to view blacks as lacking in the same innate abilities as whites. He also made allowances for the theory that the condition of slavery had in fact led "to the degraded condition of their existence," as he later wrote in 1791.[43]

Jefferson, like many of his contemporaries, thought that a mixing of the races would result in the "staining of the blood of the master." But just as with many of his contemporaries, Jefferson engaged in a long-term relationship with one of his slaves, Sally Hemings, who was his wife's half sister. Martha Jefferson's father had six children with one of his slaves, making Sally her half sister. "According to Hemings family lore, Jefferson promised his wife on her deathbed [in 1782] that he would not remarry," Gordon-Reed and Onuf write. He indeed did not remarry, but instead entered into a long-term relationship with the sixteen-year-old Sally while he served as foreign minister in France between 1784 and 1789. When he was recalled to the United States, Sally Hemings initially refused to leave with him, since she was essentially a free person under French law. Jefferson "suggested that her return to Virginia would not, in fact, be a return to slavery, as she knew it. He promised that she would lead a life of extraordinary privilege on the mountain and that their children would be free once they became adults," according to Gordon-Reed and Onuf.[44]

While in France, Jefferson seems to have become reconciled to his role as a slave owner and of slavery's continued existence in American society. As a young man he thought that the emancipation of slaves could begin right away, at least on a gradual basis, but as he grew older, he began to believe that this might be the work of the next generation, since "they have sucked in the principles of liberty as it were with their mother's milk, and it is to them I look with anxiety to turn the fate of this question" he wrote in 1785. As for his own generation, "those who desire it, form as yet the minority of the whole," he wrote in 1786 about Virginia, yet "I flatter myself it will take place there at some period of time not very distant." Jefferson was always ambivalent, not about the need for emancipation, but about his playing a leadership role in bringing it about. He was concerned that his proposal to emancipate slaves after a certain date, which was contained in *Notes*, would become public and wrote that these were "the parts which I do not wish to have made public, at least till I know whether their publication would do most harm than good." When approached to become a member of an abolition society while in France, he responded that such an association "would be too public a demonstration of my wishes to see it abolished" and "might render me less able to serve it [the pursuit of abolition] beyond the water," or, in other words, at home. Jefferson's biggest evolution was not his lack of support for emancipation, but his thoughts on how long it would take. By 1814, he had even despaired that the younger generation would pursue a plan of gradual emancipation.[45]

Jefferson thought emancipation would need to be accompanied by some form of colonization. He never believed that whites and blacks could live in the same society. As he wrote in *Notes*:

> *Deep-rooted prejudices entertained by whites; ten thousand recollections by the blacks, of the injuries they have sustained; new provocations; the real distinctions which nature has made; and many other circumstances, will divide us into parties, and produce convulsions, which will probably never end but in the extermination of one or the other race.*[46]

The fear of a racial war runs through Jefferson's correspondence about slavery. Three related events would cause Jefferson and the minority of his fellow Southerners to change their mind on gradual emancipation and colonization of slaves, lead to the expansion of slavery, and eventually drive an irreconcilable wedge between the North and the South. The events were the slave uprising in Santo Domingo, the rise of the cotton economy, and Jefferson's own dream of westward expansion.

☞☞☞

We have already seen that the slave uprising on Santo Domingo had contributed to Napoleon abandoning the North American continent and selling Louisiana to the Americans. But it also put the fear of God into the slaveholders of the South, nowhere more so than in a Virginia which was attempting to liberalize its practice of slavery. The slave revolt began in 1790, motivated in part by the principles of freedom promised by the French Revolution, would last for over a decade, and result in the death of many black slaves and white plantation owners. Widespread newspaper stories were published in America, and so both slaves and slave owners were aware of what was happening on the island. Many of the Southern states barred those slaves fleeing from Santo Domingo from entering their states, but not Virginia, "which stimulated wild fears of slave insurrections in the state," Wood writes. The events that occurred in the West Indies caused Jefferson to pursue his goal of colonizing emancipated slaves. As he wrote in a 1797 letter, Americans needed to "furnish an answer" to the question "Whither shall the colored emigrants go?" By 1801, he thought that the answer might be the West Indies, since he could not envision free blacks living as peaceful neighbors in the still Spanish-held Louisiana. Fear of slave uprisings pretty much put the death knell to any liberalization of slave policy. In 1800, a slave named

Gabriel attempted to lead a slave rebellion in Richmond. The rebellion was doomed to failure when two slaves told their masters about the plan, and a major rainstorm "flooded roads and bridges, making it impossible for the rebels to meet and coordinate their plans," Wood has written. Gabriel and twenty-seven other blacks were tried and hung for insurrection. "The emancipation fume has long evaporated and not a word is now said about it," one Virginian said.[47]

The growing of cotton in the South gave the expansion of slavery a new lease on life as well, one that would lead to its diffusion west to present-day Alabama, Mississippi, and Louisiana. Demand for cotton had been rising as improvements in technology allowed British man-ufacturers to make ever-greater products. "Rapidly falling yarn prices created ever larger groups of consumers, especially in Europe, where cotton, once a luxury product only accessible to the rich, could now be consumed by the many," according to historian Sven Beckert. The problem was how to secure the supply of cotton. Originally, the British and French looked to the Caribbean, especially Santo Domingo. Just before the slave revolt, the island was exporting 6.8 million pounds of cotton to France. But the slave uprising led to a significant drop in cotton production. In Great Britain, cotton from Santo Domingo went from 24 percent of total imports in 1791 to under 5 percent by 1795. A new source of supply was needed, and the American South was the ideal candidate.[48]

Cotton had been grown in the South since the Jamestown set-tlement, but it was primarily used for domestic consumption and not as a commercial crop for export. But it was indigenous to the South, and weather and growing conditions were ideal. Still, the growth of cotton was limited in the South because long-staple cotton would only grow in the lowland areas. As prices began to rise for cotton in Great Britain, Southern planters turned to the crop for exportation, and growers from Santo Domingo immigrated to the United States and established new cotton plantations. In 1793, Eli Whitney invented the cotton gin, which now made it practical to easily remove the seed from short-staple cotton, which could be grown in many more areas. Ironically, it was Jefferson while secretary of state who had approved Whitney's patent for the cotton gin. Cotton production then began to rise rapidly in the up-country of South Carolina and Georgia. An area that had been made up primarily of small yeoman farmers with only a few slaves was transformed into the site of large plantations of cotton growers. The need for slaves grew rapidly, nearly doubling in Georgia during the 1790s and increasing from twenty-one thousand in the up-country of South Carolina in that same year to over seventy thousand by 1810. Some of these new slaves were brought in from Africa as part of the slave trade, but most of them were transported from Maryland and Virginia.[49]

Like tobacco, cotton was particularly hard on the soil. "Yet even soil exhaustion did not slow the cotton barons; they simply moved farther west and farther South," Beckert writes. In 1798, Congress prohibited the importation of slaves from Africa into the Mississippi Territory but allowed slaves already in the country to be transported there. A similar law was passed for the Louisiana Territory in 1804. But demand was so great that the laws were soon overturned. Over time, the new territories of the Southwest would become dominated by large slave-owning plantations. The population of slaves increased rapidly in the Mississippi Territory, growing from thirty-five hundred in 1800 to over seventeen thousand by 1810. States west of South Carolina and Georgia produced approximately one-third of all cotton grown in the United States by 1820. "Since everyone presumed that only slaves could work the cotton fields, any effort to limit slavery in the Southwest was met with fierce opposition," Wood argues.[50]

The question arises, why did Jefferson not ban slavery from the territories that had been acquired with the Louisiana Purchase? After all, Congress had essentially given President Jefferson the sole "responsibility for federal policy in the Louisiana Territory," Ellis writes. In 1782, Jefferson had proposed a gradual scheme of emancipation in Virginia, and he had also pursued the elimination of slavery from the Northwest Territory.[51]

The answer seems twofold: First was Jefferson's great fear of race mixing. In a letter to James Monroe in 1801 where he talked about the "empire of liberty" that he envisioned for the West, he cautioned that the empire must avoid any "blot or mixture," a reference to blacks. It was another example of Jefferson's hypocrisy on the issue of race, given he was by then in a long-term relationship with Sally Hemings, who would bear his mixed-race children. Still, Jefferson could have banned slavery from the Louisiana Territory without resettling freed blacks in the area, so this is not the most compelling reason for his hesitancy. The second reason for his reticence would not become apparent until the issue of the expansion of slavery arose in the 1820s, culminating in the Missouri Compromise. At that point, Jefferson's thinking on the matter became clear. Jefferson never raised the issue of banning slavery in the Louisiana Territory because he feared it would lead "to a destructive debate that might lead to civil war," according to Ellis. Jefferson could not bear any form of overt conflict, although he was not shy about acting behind the scenes so long as his fingerprints could not be detected. It was Thomas Jefferson's great failure that he would not expend his political capital nor provide leadership to eliminate the great moral stain on the revolution that he had helped to lead.[52]

The expansion of slavery into the new western territories was, in part, justified by a philosophy of diffusion. One member of Congress from Virginia thought that allowing the expansion of slavery would "spread the blacks over a large space, so that in time it might be safe" to emancipate "this class of men." Jefferson shared this view as early as 1785, when he observed that it was easier for the Northern people to free their slaves since they had "but few." Later in life, he was even more explicit in his support for the diffusion of slaves. In an 1820 letter over the issue of whether slaves should be allowed into Missouri, Jefferson wrote "so their diffusion over a greater surface would make them individually happier, and proportionally facilitate the accomplishment of their emancipation, by dividing the burthen on a greater number of coadjustors."[53]

The slaves who were sent to the Southwest came primarily from Virginia and Maryland. A surplus of slaves existed in these states, caused by the gradual exhaustion of the soil from growing tobacco. The owners in the upper South had operated with a sense of propriety toward their slaves, knowing that the practice was wrong and could not be justified under their founding creed. Diffusion was thought of as a way to ultimately free slaves, since whites would never support emancipation where too many slaves lived. But it was a myth that allowed slavery to expand and grow, creating a whole new generation of slave owners whose livelihood depended on owning other people.

Diffusion was a brutal process, almost as brutal as the journey from Africa in the hold of slave ships. The movement of slaves west led to the breakup of families, with husbands separated from their wives and children separated from their parents. Historian Edward E. Baptist describes the experience of one slave as he began his journey. "As those who were about to be led away formed before dawn, he saw men and women fall on the damp ground behind the old I-style house on their knees[,] begging to be purchased to go with their wives or husbands.'" Large groups of men were fit together with iron collars, manacles, and chains. Women were roped together. This was called a "coffle, an African term derived from the Arabic word *cafila*: a chained slave caravan," Baptist writes. Once chained, any hope of escape vanished, although men would often search for any weaknesses in their manacles. They marched in the heat, in rain, in snow, often at a pace that ran from ten to twenty miles a day. It was not unusual for fights to break out between slaves that were chained together, and the strong would prey on the weak. Sleep was difficult, and the slavers would often wake them in the night. Women suffered the crime of rape. Some traveled as far as seven hundred miles under such ghastly conditions. By 1859, just before the outbreak of the Civil War, over eight hundred thousand slaves were transported into the Southwest.[54]

While compromises over slavery at the Constitutional Convention had contributed to the formation of one American nation, the accommodation would ultimately not hold. The North and the South were growing apart on the issue of slavery by the time of Jefferson's presidency. While the North was gradually eliminating slavery, the South was expanding its use, fueled by the cotton economy. The expansion of slavery into the new territories would make its eradication all but impossible and ultimately lead to the Civil War. While the masters from the upper South knew that slavery was wrong, those who settled into the newly expanding areas felt no such qualms. Many shared Jefferson's view that African slaves were inherently inferior, which gave them a basis upon which to justify slavery. Gordon Wood writes that "if the Africans were not and could never be equal to whites, then their subjugation made sense; slavery became a means of civilizing them."[55]

John Adams, for one, saw the concept of diffusion of slavery as a means to eliminate it, as lunacy. In letters to his son and daughter-in-law in 1819 and 1820, he declared that "the Virginia dynasty [Jefferson, Madison, and Monroe] had lost its collective mind," Ellis writes. By 1824, just a scant few years after he had so forcefully advocated for diffusion, Jefferson confronted the difficulty of emancipating black people now that slavery had expanded so rapidly. He estimated that it would cost $900 million to deport all 1.5 million slaves over a twenty-five-year period, which caused him to conclude "it is still impossible to look at the enterprise a second time." While he ruminated over other means to accomplish the emancipation of slaves and their colonization, he recognized that many "will say, we will not go." Ellis succinctly writes that "by 1820 it had become abundantly clear that procrastination and avoidance, which were Jefferson's cardinal convictions on the subject, had rendered any Southern-sponsored solution extremely unlikely." In fact, any solution short of war would prove impossible.[56]

The Jefferson Quandary

All historians of the founding era, this one included, must ultimately come to grips with the quandary of Thomas Jefferson. He was a life-long opponent of slavery, seeing it as distinctly evil, yet he was also a lifelong slave owner who was dependent on it for his economic survival. He viewed blacks as inferior to whites yet had a long-term relationship with his wife's half sister, Sally Hemings, who bore him six children. Jefferson never believed that white and black people could live together in a racially mixed society, and so he proposed numerous schemes for the colonization of black people somewhere else upon their emancipation.

Jefferson's view on the elimination of slavery underwent a major evolution over the course of his life in terms of when it would occur.

When he was young, he thought it could be accomplished by his generation. Later in life, he thought the next generation could accomplish it. The date when it could occur was continually pushed out, until the growth of the peculiar institution began to make its elimination all but impossible. It seems that Jefferson's real failure was twofold. One issue was his personal unwillingness to free his own slaves, even when he died. He may have released at most ten of the over two hundred slaves he owned at one time or another. The second was his unwillingness to lead on an issue that was clearly not popular in parts of Virginia and the Deep South. This runs through his writings in the 1780s, when he feared the release of *Notes on the State of Virginia* due to the stir it would raise over his view on gradual emancipation. Perhaps part of his hesitation was caused by his belief in majority rule. As he wrote to James Madison in 1787 about the new Constitution, "it is my principle that the will of the majority should prevail." If the majority did not support the elimination of slavery, then neither would Jefferson. His aversion to conflict may also have played a role in his unwillingness to be in the forefront on this issue, although he did lead on other contentious issues of the day and started the first political party in the United States, albeit from behind the scenes.[57]

Some historians have treated Jefferson quite harshly, parts of which are deserved. Paul Finkelman has called Jefferson a "creepy, brutal hypocrite" who held pro-slavery views. Conor Cruise O'Brien, the Irish politician and historian, wrote a book on Jefferson claiming that his support of the French Revolution waned when he thought its egalitarian ideas endangered slavery. The writer Henry Wiencek has argued that Jefferson abandoned his antislavery views by the 1790s due to economic considerations. "It was all about the money. By the 1790s, he saw them as capital assets and was literally counting his babies," Wiencek is quoted as saying.[58]

But most Jeffersonian scholars take a more balanced approach to the man. They reveal his inconsistencies and shortcomings, but also his strengths and contributions to the founding of our nation. One can simply list those and see how they begin to add up. He was the author of both the Declaration of Independence and the Virginia Statute for Religious Freedom. He was a primary supporter of "individual sovereignty as a starting point for thinking about democratic government," Sean Wilentz writes. He was the major proponent for the role of the common man in politics, which led to the growth of democracy in America. Perhaps most importantly, he stood for equality (at least for white men) and feared that the concentration of wealth would destroy self-government. One must also remember all of the various roles and offices he held and the contributions he made in those offices: representative in the House of Burgesses; member of the Second Continental Congress; governor of Virginia; diplomat; secretary of state; vice president; and president of the United States for two full terms.[59]

Jefferson certainly gets his share of the blame for allowing slavery to continue unabated and to expand into the new territories. But it is simply too great a historical burden to place so much blame on one man for America's original sin. There is plenty of blame to go around that must be shared by the founding generation. This is especially true for the man who gave us the American Creed as expressed in the Declaration of Independence. Those immortal words may not have applied to blacks, women, and Indians at the time that they were written. But once written, they can and have been claimed by many who say, yes, I too can be equal and free. Much of American history has been the story of the excluded claiming their rights, a struggle that continues to this day. Yet we must also face the Jefferson quandary, that the person who wrote "all men are created equal" also believed that blacks were inferior to whites. Jefferson's ambivalence has also been our nation's quandary over the issue of race and has plagued America ever since, making the Declaration's call for human equality an ongoing struggle.

Endnotes

1 This information was retrieved from two sites on May 24, 2016: http://www.virginiaplaces.org/boundaries/charters.html and http://www.learnnc.org/lp/multimedia/6182.

2 Ellis, *His Excellency*, p. 55; see also Chernow, *Washington*, p. 147–151, for his pursuit of land in the west.

3 Fraser, p. 128 and 146–147; Ferling, *A Leap in the Dark*, p. 230–232.

4 Fraser, p. 182–186.

5 Ellis, *American Creation*, p. 211; the quote is from Malone, *The President*, p. 240.

6 Peter S. Onuf, *Jefferson's Empire of Liberty: The Language of American Nationhood* (Charlottesville, 2001), p. 2.

7 R. Douglas Hurt, *The Ohio Frontier: Crucible of the Old Northwest, 1720-1830* (Bloomington, 1996), p. 1–55.

8 Hurt, p. 59–60.

9 Reginald D. Horsman, *Expansion and American Indian Policy: 1783-1812* (Norman, 1992), p. 20–24.

10 Willard Sterne Randall, *Thomas Jefferson: A Life* (New York, 1993), p. 362; the text of the 1784 Ordinance was retrieved on May 29, 2016, from http://www.Northwestordinance.org/p/ordinance-of-1784.html.

11 Randall, p. 363.

12 Hurt, p. 145 and p. 168–169; Wood, *Empire*, p. 119–122.

13 See Horsman, chapter 4, for a complete discussion. The quote is from p. 55.

14 Wood, *Empire*, p. 130–133.

15 Wood, *Empire*, p. 130–131.

16 The statistics on population growth were retrieved on May 31, 2016, from http://www.encyclopedia.com/topic/Ohio.aspx; Hurt, p. 175 and p. 233. Chapter 8 has an extensive discussion of the development of commercial farming in Ohio.

17 Horsman, chapter 5; Wood, *Empire*, p. 133.

18 Ellis, *American Creation*, p. 212.

19 Malone, *The President*, p. 240; Meacham, p. 383.

20 Meacham, p. 384; Wood, p. 368; Jefferson letter of April 18, 1802, to Robert

Livingston was retrieved June 20, 2016, from http://www.let.rug.nl/usa/presidents/thomas-jefferson/letters-of-thomas-jefferson/jefl146.php.

21 Malone, *The President*, p. 276–280.

22 Wood, *Empire*, p. 367–368; Ellis, *American Creation*, p. 219–220.

23 Ellis, *American Creation*, p. 221–222; Meacham, p. 382; Wood, *Empire*, p. 369.

24 Ellis, *American Creation*, p. 224–225; Meacham, p. 389.

25 Meacham, p. 391; the Jefferson quote is taken from Malone, *The President*, p. 320, and is from a letter to John B. Colvin on September 20, 1810.

26 Ellis, *American Creation*, p. 227; Wood, *Empire*, p. 370–372.

27 Wood, *Empire*, p. 377, makes the observation that the Lewis and Clark expedition had a covert meaning.

28 Bernard W. Sheehan, *Seeds of Extinction: Jeffersonian Philanthropy and the American Indian* (Chapel Hill, 1973), p. 4.

29 Sheehan, p. 66–68; Wood, *Empire*, p. 388.

30 Koch and Peden, p. 211; Horsman, p. 105; Onuf, p. 19–20; Nicholas Guyatt, *Bind Us Apart: How Enlightened Americans Invented Racial Segregation* (New York, 2016), p. 24.

31 Horsman, p. 104–157, has a detailed description of Indian policy and treaties during the Jefferson administration. The tribes were under ever more pressure to sell land, often at bargain prices for the United States. Bribery was often used to buy off tribal leaders.

32 Howe, p. 342–345.

33 Appleby, p. 108.

34 Ellis, *American Creation*, p. 232–234; Sheehan, p. 246–250.

35 Annette Gordon-Reed and Peter S. Onuf, *Most Blessed of the Patriarchs: Thomas Jefferson and the Empire of Imagination* (New York, 2016), p. 70.

36 Gordon-Reed and Onuf, p. 59; Randall, p. 142–143.

37 Wood, *Empire*, p. 517–520; Joseph J. Ellis, *Founding Brothers: The Revolutionary Generation* (New York, 2000), p. 88–90.

38 Fraser, p. 58, p. 187, and p. 304 for the quotes; Wood, *Empire*, p. 522.

39 Jefferson's letter to Richard Price from August 7, 1785, and to J. N. Demeunier from June 26, 1786, retrieved July 21, 2016, from https://www.monticello.org/site/jefferson/quotations-slavery-and-emancipation-0.

40 Ellis, *Founding Brothers*, p. 92–93.

41 Wood, p. 523–524; Ellis, *Founding Brothers*, p. 104 .

42 Ellis, *Founding Brothers*, p. 100–101.

43 Koch and Peden, p. 262; Guyatt makes the case that more enlightened and liberal people were critical of Jefferson's views on blacks in chapter 1. The quote from Rush is found in Joseph J. Ellis, *American Dialogue: The Founders and Us* (New York, 2018), p.

26, who also quotes a number of other individuals who were critical of Jefferson. See also Sheldon, p. 133. On the use of racism to control the slave population, see Alan Taylor, *American Colonies: The Settling of North America* (New York, 2001), p. 156–157.

44 Gordon-Reed and Onuf, p. 121–132.

45 One way to see Jefferson's evolution is to read his various statements on the subject of slavery over a period of years. The website for Monticello has a compendium of his quotes on slavery and emancipation, retrieved July 21, 2016, and can be found at https://www.monticello.org/site/jefferson/quotations-slavery-and-emancipation-0, where the quotes used in this paragraph are found.

46 Koch and Peden, p. 256.

47 Wood, *Empire*, p. 533–537; Jefferson's views and quotes are from his August 28, 1797, letter to George Tucker and his November 24, 1801, letter to James Monroe, taken from the website shown in endnote 45.

48 Sven Beckert, *Empire of Cotton: A Global History* (New York, 2014), p. 88–97.

49 Beckert, p. 102–103; Wood, *Empire*, p. 528.

50 Beckert, p. 103–104; Wood, *Empire*, p. 522 and p. 528.

51 Ellis deals with this issue in much greater detail in both *American Creation*, chapter 6, and *American Dialogue*, chapter 1, which I have summarized in this section.

52 Ellis, *American Creation*, p. 237.

53 Wood, *Empire*, p. 522; Joseph J. Ellis, *American Sphinx: The Character of Thomas Jefferson* (New York, 1996), p. 321.

54 This paragraph is based on Edward E. Baptist, *The Half Has Never Been Told: Slavery and the Making of American Capitalism* (New York, 2014), p. 1–37.

55 Wood, *Empire*, p. 540–541.

56 Ellis, *American Sphinx*, p. 320–322; Jefferson letter to Jared Sparks, February 4, 1824, retrieved July 28, 2016, from http://www.let.rug.nl/usa/presidents/thomas-jefferson/letters-of-thomas-jefferson/jefl276.php.

57 Koch and Peden, p. 440; for the number of slaves that Jefferson freed, see Sean Wilentz, *The Politicians & The Egalitarians: The Hidden History of American Politics* (New York, 2016), p. 87.

58 The Finkelman quote was retrieved July 28, 2016, from http://www.nytimes.com/2012/12/01/opinion/the-real-thomas-jefferson.html?_r=2; for information about O'Brien, see Wilentz, p. 84–97; the Wiencek quote was retrieved July 28, 2016, from http://www.nytimes.com/2012/11/27/books/henry-wienceks-master-of-the-mountain-irks-historians.html.

59 Most of the scholars I am referring to have been used in this book. The quote from Wilentz is from p. 119. His chapter on Jefferson is an example of what I consider a balanced approach.

CHAPTER 4

The War of 1812 and the Rise of New Leadership

The War of 1812 is the strangest war in American History.
—GORDON WOOD

They are more Americans; they feel and act more as a nation ...
—ALBERT GALLATIN, MAY 7, 1816, ON THE IMPACT OF THE WAR[1]

*W*ars often spur nationalism and can sometimes lead to xeno-phobia. For the United States, the War of 1812 was a seminal act in nation building. In some ways it represented the final battle in the war for independence. But the war was not without controversy. While it solidified support for the Union in the South and West, it was largely a partisan war that was opposed by the Federalists in New England. The war also led to the rise of new leadership, men who would help guide, and in some cases challenge, the existence of the new nation in the future.

Buildup to the War

Relations between the United States and Great Britain had been rocky since the Revolutionary War ended. Despite the controversy it generated, the Jay Treaty had stabilized the relationship and allowed American shipping to flourish. While the British continued to block larger American vessels from directly participating in the lucrative West Indies trade, the Americans took advantage of a loophole known as the "broken voyage." As a neutral during the war between France and England in the 1790s, American shippers would pick up exports from the West Indies, stop in an American port and pay duties, and then re-export the goods to Europe, giving rise to the concept of the "broken voyage." "The expansion of the carrying and re-export trades was a result of the disappearance from international trade of the ships of every belligerent [including Holland, France, and Spain] save England," economic historian Douglass C. North wrote. Those countries simply found it too risky to do their own shipping from the Caribbean islands with the war in Europe going on, so American shippers came to dominate the trade. Between 1795 and 1801, the combined value of exports and re-exports went from $56.3 million to over $140 million. American prosperity became tied to trade. While this initially aided New England and the other major seaports of New York and Philadelphia, where shipbuilding and the carrying trade was centered, it soon also helped the Southern planters, whose exports of cotton began to skyrocket in the early 1800s.[2]

In 1802, the Treaty of Amiens went into effect, temporarily ending the European war. While this reduced tensions with both the French and British, American trade plummeted as the great European powers returned to the carrying trade. The value of exports and re-exports fell in 1803 to $69 million. The peace lasted little over a year, and by May 1803 the European continent was once again engulfed in war. In 1805 Great Britain won a great naval victory at Trafalgar and controlled the seas. Later that year, Napoleon's army defeated Austria and Russia at Austerlitz and controlled the continent. The United States was now caught between the two belligerent nations that were fighting for their existence.[3]

Great Britain has never been a land power, and their best hope in the war was to blockade the French from receiving supplies. Given this, by 1805 the British had "decided to drive American ships from the West Indies and from the European carrying trade," historian Ralph Ketcham writes, in order to deny Napoleon any means of support outside of the continent. They relied on the Rule of 1756, which stated that trade that was prohibited in peace time was also forbidden in a time of war. As we have seen, the United States had evaded the Rule of 1756, and the British had not enforced it, through the concept of the "broken voyage."[4]

"In the *Essex* decision (1805), the High Court of Admiralty ruled that landing goods and paying duties in the United States was no longer proof" of a broken voyage, writes historian Donald Hickey. James Madison, who was serving as Jefferson's secretary of state, wrote an extensive pamphlet that refuted the British position. But for Great Britain, this was not a matter of law or legalism, but of survival. Not only did the British maintain their right to stop American ships from carrying goods to France, they also asserted their right to board American ships to find British sailors that had fled service and impress them back into the navy. The American merchant fleet paid better and offered better working conditions, so there was no shortage of British sailors willing to abandon their own navy. By some estimates, over 25 percent of American sailors were British citizens. The French contributed to the war at sea when they issued the Berlin Decree in 1806 that banned British trade to the continent. Napoleon saw this as a way to subvert the British economy. The British responded with their own Orders in Council, with the two sides essentially making all neutral commerce illegal and subject to confiscation.[5]

The Jefferson administration attempted to settle the issues with the British through diplomacy in 1806 when James Monroe was sent to negotiate with the British foreign secretary. Jefferson was not particularly supportive of any agreement that would eliminate the ability of the Americans to implement commercial retaliation against the British, but his hand was forced by Congress, which wanted the negotiators to settle a whole range of issues, not just impressment and restoring the re-export trade. The British immediately refused to abandon impressment, since their navy was dependent on it to keep more sailors from deserting. "But they did offer to observe 'the greatest caution' in impressing British seamen and afford 'immediate and prompt redress' to any Americans mistakenly forced into service," Hickey writes. Ultimately, Jefferson rejected the treaty and refused to send it to the Senate. "Jefferson considered the British concessions trifling and was unwilling to give up the weapon of commercial sanctions without a British promise to end impressment," according to Hickey. In fact, the treaty had terms that were more favorable to the United States than the Jay Treaty, and an opportunity to avoid war with the British was lost. Jefferson's rejection of the treaty also poisoned, at least in the short term, his and Madison's relationship with James Monroe. Since Monroe looked upon Jefferson as his mentor, he blamed Madison for the rejection of the treaty.[6]

Matters worsened in June of 1807 when the USS *Chesapeake* was attacked off American waters near Hampton Roads, Virginia, by the HMS *Leopard*. The captain of the *Leopard* had sent a boarding party to search the American ship for deserters. When the *Chesapeake* refused, they were fired on, killing three American sailors and injuring eighteen others. The British removed four sailors from the *Chesapeake*, although only one of them turned out to be a deserter.[7]

Both Jefferson and the country were outraged. Jefferson began preparations for war, telling Congress after the fact that "the moment our peace was threatened, I deemed it indispensable to secure a greater provision of those articles of military stores" that would be needed. But the president also knew that the country was not ready for war. This was, in large part, due to his policies and those of his fellow Republicans. The ideology of the Republican Party was that wars were fought by monarchies for their own aggrandizement and that these led to large standing armies and navies, high taxes, and debt designed to sustain the war machine. Both Jefferson and Madison believed that the ability to withhold American trade could change international behavior without the need for war, a proposition that would soon be tested and found wanting.[8]

Jefferson and the Republicans had adopted policies that paid down the debt and reduced taxes and cut governmental expenditures for defense purposes. Treasury Secretary Gallatin, when he came into office, had recommended to Jefferson that the federal debt of $83 million could be eliminated over the next sixteen years by annually appropriating $7.3 million a year. Much of the debt reduction was paid for from duties generated by the shipping industry, and by decreasing military expenditures. The army was reduced from 5,400 to 3,300 men in 1802, and the navy was ordered to decommission six of the thirteen frigates that had been built during the era of Federalist rule, and six ships of the line that were under construction were canceled. In the future, the Republicans under Jefferson would rely on the militia and on coastal gun boats to provide for the defense of the nation. While the gun boats were effective in shallow water, they were "prone to capsize when they reached the choppy Atlantic" and the cost to finance "177 such boats ... could have paid for eight new frigates," historian Michael Beschloss writes.[9]

As Jon Meacham explained, Jefferson was no pacifist. During his first term in office he had gone to war with the Barbary States

(Morocco, Algiers, Tunis, and Tripoli), having long opposed paying tribute to them for the right to ship through the Mediterranean Sea. "Jefferson expected a quick, easy and cheap victory in the Barbary War," Alan Taylor writes. Instead, he got four years of frustrating wars in the first American conflict in the Islamic world. The American navy did finally win a number of victories, and in June 1805 a peace treaty was signed ending the war on favorable terms for the United States. Still, it was one thing to fight the Barbary States, a totally different matter to declare war on Great Britain. The question for Jefferson, as he phrased it, was "whether War, Embargo or Nothing shall be the course." He settled on the embargo.[10]

The Embargo

Both Jefferson and Madison had an overly optimistic view of the effects that an embargo could have on the British. Jefferson's view on the efficacy of economic coercion may well have been rooted in the lessons he learned prior to the Revolutionary War. The British Stamp Act had been reversed, in part, by the economic embargo the colonies had implemented. In 1769, Virginia and the other colonies had boycotted British goods in response to the Townshend Act, and once again in response to the Intolerable Acts. "On Jefferson, the impression of this experience of successful commercial pressure would be lifelong," Elkins and McKitrick write.[11]

Madison was also a supporter of the use of commercial coercion to sway British foreign policy. One of his first acts as a member of the new House of Representatives in 1789 was to propose a tariff act that would discriminate against Great Britain to force them to open up trade in the parts of the West Indies they controlled. Madison's views were based on a major misconception: that American prosperity was grounded in "the independent situation and manly sentiments of American citizens, who live on their own soil, or whose labour is necessary to its cultivation." Whereas the British were dependent on "fashion and superfluity," Madison wrote in 1793, and so the Americans would prevail in any contest. As he also wrote in 1793, "what a noble stroke would be an embargo ... It would probably do as much good as harm at home, and would force peace on the rest of the world, and perhaps liberty along with it." By 1807, Madison was again pushing the idea of economic coercion on his friend Jefferson, writing that "the efficacy of an embargo also cannot be doubted [by forcing] all the nations having colonies in this quarter of the globe to respect our rights." As Elkin and McKitrick write, "there was no evidence ... for such an assumption" on Madison's part, but he was able to convince a willing Jefferson that an embargo would work.[12]

In December of 1807, Jefferson proposed, and Congress approved, an embargo that prohibited trade with all nations. The president initially saw it as a purely defensive measure that would keep "at home our vessels, cargoes & seamen, [and save] us the necessity of making their capture the cause of immediate war ... "[13] But the embargo hurt American trade much more than it did that of the British, who were its main target. Between 1807 and 1808, the value of American exports and imports, including those from the cotton trade, dropped precipitously. The chart below shows the impact of the embargo on exports and imports.

Impact of 1808 Embargo			
	1807	1808	%
Exports / Re-exports	$167,989,000	$35,428,000	-78.91%
Imports	144,470,000	58,101,000	-59.78%
Cotton Exports	66,213,000	12,064,000	-81.78%
Source: North, p. 221, p. 228, and p. 231			

While exports dropped by close to 80 percent, the Non-Importation Act continued to allow some imports from Britain, including rum, coarse woolens, and salt. The impacts were felt most acutely in New England and the other seaport cities, where most of American shipping was centered. "Ships rotted at the wharves; forests of bare masts were silhouetted in the harbors; grass grew on hitherto humming wharves; bankruptcies, suicides, and crime increased; soup kitchens were established," one historian writes. Political leaders in New England supported active resistance to the Embargo Act, and goods were smuggled through Canada. Talk of secession was heard from the North, and Jefferson was burned in effigy in a village in New York. But Jefferson refused to yield and engaged in his own self-delusion that the embargo was working. Madison was no better, stating that "the public mind everywhere is rallying to the policy." Jefferson, who was an opponent of centralized power, was forced to take on ever more executive power to implement the embargo, calling on the military to enforce it and stop the smuggling going on. As Joyce Appleby writes, "Jefferson allowed [the embargo] to threaten every political principle he held dear."[14]

The embargo contributed to Jefferson's withdrawal from the presidency, as he longed to return to Monticello and began to send "his furniture, wine, and books" home, Appleby writes.[15] He left the decision of what to do about the embargo to his hand-picked successor, James Madison. By the time Madison took office, Congress had repealed the embargo.

The United States was a new and still tenuous nation. New England was not the only area where secession was a potential possibility. American leaders had always worried about the allegiance of the newly emerging areas of the West. During the 1780s, Washington was concerned that without a stronger central government the settlers "would in a few short years be as unconnected to us, indeed more so, than we are with South America." Joyce Appleby argues that while our political map looks inevitable to those of us living in the twenty-first century, it was a true struggle "to gain the nation its ocean-to-ocean borders." So, it should come as no surprise that the Jefferson administration would face a potential attempt to establish a new nation in the American West, although the surprise was the person who would attempt to lead it: the former vice president.[16]

Due to his disloyalty during the election of 1800–1801, Jefferson had kept Burr off the ticket in 1804. Burr decided to run for governor of New York, a race he ultimately lost. But Hamilton's opposition to his bid to be governor, and numerous remarks that Burr found disparaging, ultimately led to their duel in Weehawken, New Jersey. While Hamilton may well have shot into the air, Burr fatally wounded Hamilton, who died on July 11, 1804, at the age of forty-seven.[17]

In 1805, Aaron Burr headed west and began a plot to start his own country in the West. Even before he left office as vice president, he had told the British ambassador of his plans "to affect a separation of the United States from that which lies between the Atlantic and the mountains." He allied himself with, of all people, the commander of the American army, James Wilkerson. Wilkerson had long been a spy for the Spanish, and he had become convinced "that most residents of the West could be lured into a new political unit by an intrepid leader," according to Appleby. But Wilkerson got cold feet and told Jefferson about Burr's plot, and Burr was arrested in March of 1807. In a bizarre treason trial, Jefferson's nemesis and cousin, Chief Justice John Marshall, so narrowed the definition of treason that Burr got off. Soon thereafter Burr left for Europe, his political career in tatters.[18]

☞ ☞ ☞

Certainly, Jefferson's attempt to avoid war was laudable. War should always be the last resort for any president. But the embargo leaves us with one final question: Is economic coercion as an alternative to war always a failure? A quick search through Google indicates a range of scholarly opinion on the issue, from outright opposition to the use of economic sanctions to general support within certain limits. One interesting article, published by the Institute for International Economics, makes two points that are relevant to the lack of efficacy of Jefferson's embargo:

1. that the goal must be relatively modest, such as winning the release of political prisoners; and

2. that the target country is much smaller, economically weak, and more politically unstable than the country imposing the sanctions.[19]

Obviously, neither of these conditions applied to the Unites States vis-à-vis Great Britain or France in 1808. The goal of the United States was not a limited one, but rather an attempt to change both of the superpowers' overarching policies during a time of all-out war so that they would respect the rights of the United States. A policy of respecting neutral rights was clearly not in the interest of either Great Britain or France, who were each attempting to destroy the other's economy and ability to wage war. Jefferson was also attempting to impose an embargo on two countries with superior power to the United States. Madison, for his part, was operating under a false assumption, which was that Great Britain needed the United States more than we needed them. It was based on a perception that trade with the British only brought in luxury items that the Americans could easily do without. This ignored that New England and the port cities of the middle states were dependent on the carrying trade, as were the plantations of the South, especially with the growth of the cotton economy. Garry Wills writes that Madison engaged in "two equal-but-opposite errors, two misreadings of the British Empire—as frighteningly powerful inside the boundaries of the United States and as surprisingly weak outside those borders," that contributed to both the embargo and that later made him "welcome the prospect of war with England," after he became president.[20]

The Madison Administration and the March to War

James Madison was Jefferson's choice to succeed him—not a surprising decision. The two men had been close friends since Jefferson's stint as Virginia's governor in 1779. As Madison biographer Ralph Ketcham writes, "both had a fondness for words and ideas and books that over and over gave them reason to seek each other out for the sheer joy of learning." They had been political comrades in arms since the 1790s in their battles with Hamilton and the Federalists, and Madison had served as Jefferson's secretary of state. In some ways, Madison's selection was a way for Jefferson to vindicate his two terms as president, a way to prove that he deserved a third term.[21]

But Madison faced a Republican Party that had begun to split apart as the fortunes of the Federalists waned. Perhaps this was inevitable since, as we saw in chapter 1, political differences are natural.

First, there were the Old Republicans, or "quids" as they were some-times called, who were more Jeffersonian than Jefferson and opposed the extension of federal power and any military buildup. Second was another group of Republicans that wanted to break the domination of the Virginians in controlling the presidency. And third, there was a group called the Invisibles that formed a separate faction in the Senate. Finally, there were the regular Republicans, of which Madison was the new leader.[22]

The quids were able to quietly get James Monroe to run against Madison. Monroe was still miffed about the rejection of the treaty he had negotiated with England and largely blamed Madison for Jefferson's refusal to send it to the Senate. In a very strange move, George Clinton of New York both ran for the presidency and also for the vice presidency (the office he already held under Jefferson) on the Republican ticket. The Federalists nominated Charles C. Pinckney. "Had the embargo become law a year earlier, the backlash against it might have hurt Madison's chances with the party or against his Federalists opponent," Jack Rakove argues. As it was, Madison prevailed rather easily, winning the electoral college by a vote of 122–47 over Pinckney. Clinton received six electoral votes, all from New York, and Monroe none.[23]

For those who have read my previous book, *The Emergence of One American Nation*, it should be clear that I am a great admirer of James Madison. More than any person, he helped to bring about the Constitutional Convention and was the intellectual father of the new government that replaced the failed Articles of Confederation, earning him the well-deserved title of the Father of the Constitution. Madison was also a talented legislator, crafting the Bill of Rights and then getting it passed through the first Congress. He excelled at committee work and behind-the-scenes activities, including his co-authorship of the *Federalist Papers*. But he generally played a subordinate role, first to Washington at the convention and during the early years of the republic and later to Jefferson. He had no executive experience and "seemed awed by the prospect of becoming president," according to Gordon Wood. He could sometimes be indecisive until he had studied an issue intensively, an important skill for a legislator but a deadly trait for an executive when rapid action based on insufficient information can be crucial. And in two instances leading up to the War of 1812, Madison would make quick decisions that backfired. One of his biographers believes that his problems stemmed from a combination of his own "provincialism with regard to the rest of the world and a certain naiveté with regard to the rest of his fellow human beings." His name never leads the list of best presidents as rated by various historians or publications, although he occasionally is included in the top 10, and always appears in the top quartile, above such modern presidents as Reagan and Clinton.[24]

Madison had two interrelated problems as president. First, he lacked the commanding presence of Washington and Jefferson. Given his diminutive size and his weak voice, he could not put the fear of God into other men, a characteristic that Washington possessed as a war hero and the dominant figure from the American Revolution. Nor did he elicit the type of personal support that Jefferson did from his backers. Second, "he fully accepted the Republican principle of executive deference to the people's representatives in Congress but made none of the necessary efforts to manage the legislature as Jefferson had," Wood writes. This was true even in the field of foreign policy, which most presidents assume is theirs to fully command.[25]

The problem of Madison's weak leadership was apparent immediately when he could not even select his own cabinet members. He had wanted to move Albert Gallatin, the treasury secretary under

Jefferson, over to the State Department as the secretary. Gallatin, who had been born in Geneva, Switzerland, had immigrated to the United States in 1780 at age nineteen. Elected to the House of Representatives in 1795, he headed the House Committee on Finance. During his short time in the Senate, he had become a thorn in the side of Alexander Hamilton, leading the effort to investigate the treasury secretary. When Jefferson was elected president in 1801, he used a recess appointment to install Gallatin as secretary of the treasury, since he knew how controversial the selection was. Gallatin's opponents in the Federalist Party taunted him as a man that "could not speak the English language intelligibly, and that he was French in spirit as well as accent," according to Jefferson biographer Dumas Malone. But Gallatin proved to be a very able treasury secretary, helping Jefferson not only to pay down the debt of the United States but also to finance the purchase of Louisiana.[26]

Gallatin proved no less controversial when Madison attempted to appoint him as secretary of state. In order to keep his fragile coalition together in the Senate, Madison decided to keep Gallatin at Treasury, since he was told that the Senate would never consent to him being secretary of state. Instead, Madison appointed Robert Smith to the post, the brother of the leader of the Senate Invisibles, Samuel Smith. The new secretary of state would prove not only incompetent, forcing Madison to serve as both president and secretary of state, but he was disloyal, "conspiring with his [brother's] faction to undermine Gallatin in the cabinet," Wills observes. Smith also fancied himself a future president and made a practice of telling foreign leaders that there were "powerful forces in the country [that] disagreed with the President."[27]

It took two years, but Madison finally fired Smith. Gallatin gave an assist to the whole process when he tendered his resignation, unless Smith was removed. Jefferson had been working behind the scenes to repair the relationship between Monroe and Madison, who had been friends for over thirty years. On March 20, 1811, Monroe accepted the position of secretary of state.[28]

There were numerous missteps and incidents that occurred on the road to war with Great Britain. French deprivations of American shipping and their continued violation of neutral rights almost led to war with both of the major powers. Madison and the Republicans had always been more suspicious of the British, and ultimately the War of 1812 was viewed by many at the time as the final battle in the American quest for independence from the former mother country.

One of these missteps occurred just as Madison assumed office in March of 1809. Congress had adopted a new Non-Intercourse Act to replace the embargo, which prohibited trade with both Britain and France. Trade would be reopened with the first of the belligerents that removed their trade restrictions. The British minister to the United States, David Erskine, told the secretary of state that the Orders in Council were going to be revoked. Acting on this information before fully confirming it, Madison reached an agreement with Erskine that called for both sides to remove their trade restrictions. It looked like a great victory for the United States, but Erskine had, in fact, "exceeded his instructions, omitting three conditions for England's repeal of the Orders, including the continued right of the British to intercept and board American vessels" and a provision that trade with France would continue to be prohibited. Great Britain's repudiation of the Erskine agreement further soured relations between the two nations and "convinced [Madison of] England's implacable, unreasonable hostility," Ketcham writes.[29]

"The weakness of Madison's leadership became evident after the Eleventh Congress reassembled in November 1809," Rakove writes. The Non-Intercourse Act was set to expire, and Congress passed a new law referred to as Macon's Bill Number 2 (so named for its author, whose first bill, which Gallatin had crafted, failed to pass). The bill removed all trade restrictions with both France and Great Britain but included "the remarkable proviso that if either nation ceased violating America's neutral rights, the President could prohibit trade with the other." Madison called it a "botch of a bill," but he made no attempt to lobby Congress against it. The bill actually favored Great Britain, which would now gain the benefit of trade with America while its navy kept the French bottled up in Europe. Madison's one hope was that the bill might entice France to remove their trade restrictions, which Napoleon did, or at least so it appeared. Napoleon had his foreign minister inform the Americans that the Milan and Berlin Decrees, which had established the French blockade of Great Britain, would be revoked so long as the United States "shall cause their rights to be respected by the English." In fact, this was a bit of trickery that Napoleon was using under which he could interpret whether the United States had met such a test. In addition, there were other decrees that remained in effect. Madison knew there were ambiguities in the French actions, but rather than wait for more definitive information from his minister in France, he gambled that Napoleon would fulfill his commitments. In November 1810, he imposed new trade restrictions on Britain that would begin in February 1811 unless the British withdrew their Orders in Council. "By the time that Madison discovered that Napoleon was not observing the terms of Macon Number 2, the bill had done its work," Wills argues. "A momentum toward war with England had been accelerated."[30]

As we have seen, some historians have portrayed Madison's actions as those of a purely naive and provincial actor on the world stage. Others have brought a more nuanced approach, while recognizing his errors. In Madison's defense, he faced a no-win situation, with the infant United States caught between two hostile great powers engaged in a war for survival. In September, Madison wrote that the possible revocation of the French decrees provided the United States with an alternative to "a mortifying peace, or a war with both great belligerents." Ralph Ketcham argues that Madison may have also been concerned that Napoleon would "issue more severely hostile edicts than ever" if the United States did not accept his offer. Still, Madison's real error was in not waiting for additional information from the American envoy in Paris that showed Bonaparte's duplicity, which arrived a week after Madison's proclamation of November 2.[31]

The president was also unable to get his congressional allies to support measures to prepare for war. The charter for the Bank of the United States ended in March of 1811, and Madison, the one-time opponent of the bank, had changed his mind over its constitutionality. He now believed that its long-term existence "amounted to the requisite evidence of the national judgement and intention," and supported its renewal. Gallatin had long favored continuation of the bank and knew that the lack of trade caused by the embargo and the various other measures adopted by Congress had stripped the American treasury of its chief means of support. Given this, he also proposed increases in duties. Due to Madison's prior opposition to the bank, he decided to stay clear of the congressional debate, an error in judgment that may have resulted in the failure of Congress to approve the renewal of the bank or any corresponding tax increases that were needed to support military readiness. In fact, military spending was reduced in order to balance the budget.[32]

One of the opponents of the bank bill was a young and brash Kentuckian named Henry Clay, who had been selected to fill an unexpired Senate seat. Clay was destined to be one of the major political leaders in the coming years. In 1811, he represented a Western-oriented political philosophy of nationalism, a prime supporter of the future expansion of the United States as an empire of liberty. He was shortly to become the Speaker of the House in the new Congress that would meet in November 1811 and the leader of a group known as the War Hawks, which also included Southern leaders like John C. Calhoun. They would help push Madison, who already saw England as the main threat to the United States, toward war with their former colonial master.

Clay and Calhoun

Henry Clay was born on April 12, 1777, in Virginia. His father was a Baptist minister whose family had deep roots in the New World dating back to the Jamestown settlement. His mother's family was quite affluent. "Years later, Clay was inclined to boast of his humble origins, but his parents were actually slaveholding farmers who lived in comfortable circumstances," historian Harry L. Watson writes. When Henry was only four, his father died. It was just after his death that the British invasion of Virginia occurred, led by Lieutenant Colonel Tarleton. Clay would later remember "a visit made by Tarleton's troops to the house of my mother, and of their running their swords into newly made graves of my father and grandfather." It was an early start toward the animus he would later carry toward Great Britain.[33]

His mother remarried within a year of his father's death, and his stepfather later moved the family to Kentucky in 1791, but then fourteen-year-old Henry remained in Richmond to continue his education. Clay always carried a sense of insecurity about his lack of a classical education that men like Jefferson and Madison had received. While in Richmond he came to the attention of the great lawyer George Wythe, who had trained Jefferson, John Marshall, and James Monroe, among others. Wythe helped to mold young Clay "into an educated, cultivated, urbane, and articulate gentleman," according to his biographer Robert V. Remini, and became the father he never had. Clay also joined a debating society during these years and began to hone his oratorical skills as a public speaker. By 1797, he passed the bar and made his way to Kentucky to start his career.[34]

Settling in Lexington, Clay became a successful lawyer. He was a man who could "drink, carouse, swear, and gamble with the best of them," which made him popular with his peers. His great strength was his public speaking ability, which would help advance his political career, a skill he further honed in presentations to juries. "His versatility, his extraordinary verbal range, his powers of argumentation were the reasons for Clay's meteoric rise to prominence in Kentucky," Remini writes. He ultimately joined the elite of society through his marriage to Lucretia Hart, whose father was wealthy.[35]

Clay's initial political instincts leaned toward the liberal side, and he was a strong supporter of Jefferson and the Republicans. When Kentucky was drafting its state constitution, he supported a ban on slavery. Like Jefferson, his antislavery views would abate as he got older. His leanings gradually shifted as his legal career led him to become a champion for Kentucky's business interests, which included manufacturing, interstate commerce, and plantations. While a member of the state legislature, he championed the interests of the Kentucky Insurance Company, which served as both an insurer of cargo on the Mississippi and as a state bank. By 1808, he was elected speaker of the Kentucky lower house.[36]

His rise politically at the state level led him to be appointed twice to fill two unexpired terms in the United States Senate. It was during his second stint as a senator that he made his mark as the leader of the War Hawks. Westerners like Clay believed that Great Britain, from its base in Canada, had been the source of trouble on the frontier by "arming and encouraging Indian attacks," Watson argues. In a speech delivered on February 22, 1810, Clay made the case that economic sanctions had failed, and so he was for "resistance by the sword." While he wanted peace, he preferred "the troubled ocean of war, demanded by the honor and independence of the country ... to the tranquil, putrescent pool of ignominious peace." Clay and others from the West thought that the Indian uprisings could be quelled by invading Canada. In a rather rash statement, Clay argued that the Kentucky militia alone could conquer Canada, which would later become the focus of the land war. While pushing for war, Clay also made a major error when he opposed rechartering the Bank of the United States in early 1811. In this, he was doing the work of his own home state bank, which found the federal bank too conservative and "stifling" of their activities. He would later become a staunch supporter of the Second Bank of the United States. During his short time in the Senate, Clay also began to develop what would later be called the American System, an active federal government engaged in investing in internal improvements and fostering a manufacturing base.[37]

Henry Clay also realized that he preferred the people's House, "losing patience with senatorial deliberativeness and irresolution," Remini writes. While he could have lobbied for and won a full term in the Senate, he instead chose to run for the House, winning a seat in August 1810. He would very quickly be elected as the Speaker of the House as a freshman, supported by the large number of newly elected House members, who were attracted to his strength and charisma.

Clay began to develop the role of Speaker of the House as a powerful office that was the "political leader of the House," an alternative and rival center of political power to the president. He did this, in part, by controlling committee assignments and referring all bills to one of the standing committees. One of the new members he assigned to one of the standing committees was another War Hawk, the young John C. Calhoun.[38]

☞☞☞

Calhoun would become one of the great defenders of states' rights as a means to protect Southern interests, especially slavery. He would later justify the nullification of federal laws that individual states found unconstitutional, an approach he borrowed from Jefferson and the Kentucky resolution against the Alien and Sedition Acts. But early in his career, he was a strong nationalist.

John C. Calhoun was born March 18, 1782, in the backcountry of South Carolina. As a boy, his father, Patrick, had emigrated from Ireland in 1727 with his family and settled in Virginia. In 1756, the senior Calhoun set out on his own to the backcountry of South Carolina, where "land was fertile, abundant, and cheap." The backcountry was lawless, populated with people "addicted to idleness, fornication, bastardy, robbery, drunkenness and brawling," according to Calhoun biographer Irving H. Bartlett. This was the Carolina backcountry before cotton plantations took over. Patrick helped to civilize the area, and his reputation as a surveyor, farmer, and Indian fighter soon led him to be elected to the state legislature. John saw that his father "was deferred to not only for his illustrious public achievements but also because he owned a substantial number of black slaves," according to Bartlett. When John was only thirteen, his father died, and he assumed responsibility for the plantation along with his mother and younger brother. Five years later, his older brother returned from being trained as a merchant and took over operation of the plantation, freeing John to pursue an education.[39]

His formal education began in a small two-room academy in 1801. By 1802 he had been accepted to Yale as a junior, and quickly distinguished himself as one of the intellectual leaders of his class. It was already clear that he was planning a career in politics, and after graduating, he went on to study law. His biographer describes him as a conservative Jeffersonian who stood over six feet tall, and his portraits from the period reveal a very handsome young man. His Republican leanings were likely handed down by his father, who feared too much centralized power and had opposed the ratification of the Constitution.[40]

In 1804, he attended the Litchfield Law School in Hartford. New England was federalist country, and so the young Calhoun had to keep his head down and limit socializing in town. In 1806, he returned to South Carolina to finish his studies in a law office located in Charleston, a city where slaves outnumbered whites by a substantial number and white men "raced, drank, fought, and went to parties." It was a city where the strongly self-disciplined youth did not fit in well, and so he spent most of his time studying the law. Calhoun quickly learned that one of a lawyer's most important duties in South Carolina was to defend slavery. "He could not question the morality of slavery because he had grown up with it in the new nation and watched its expansion bring honor to his father and prosperity and republican civility to the upper country and unity to the entire state," Bartlett has written.[41]

He passed the bar in December of 1807, but very quickly realized he had "a strong aversion to the law." When the British opened fire on the *Chesapeake*, an opportunity opened for Calhoun to launch a political career. He became a member of the committee that wrote resolutions protesting the British attack, accusing them of a "murderous attack." His participation "laid the foundation for his enduring political popularity in the district," his biographer writes. In 1808, he was elected to the lower house of the South Carolina legislature, followed in 1810 by election to the US House of Representatives. During this period, he also fell in love with the daughter of his cousin, Floride Colhoun, who was like a second mother to him. Colhoun's daughter was also named Floride, and in January of 1811 they were married, just before John set off for Washington, DC. They built a plantation known as Bath, and their first child was born nine months later.[42]

Upon Calhoun's arrival in the House, Henry Clay appointed him the number two person on the Committee on Foreign Relations. Southerners had been harmed by British actions in controlling American shipping, since they were unable to export their cotton and other raw materials to England. Calhoun believed that war with Great Britain was necessary to defend the national interest and the honor of the country. Honor was of great importance to Southerners and those, like Clay, from the West. Clay and Calhoun formed part of the leadership of the War Hawks, young men who did not "remember the horrors of the last British war and thus willing to run the risks of another to vindicate the nation's rights," according to Hickey.[43]

The War Begins

Some historians have argued that Madison was dragged by the War Hawks into the War of 1812. Sean Wilentz, Garry Wills, and Michael Beschloss put forth a more plausible explanation. Wilentz, for example, argues that "Madison needed no prodding to change course and begin preparing resolutely for war." Despite the presence of the War Hawks like Clay and Calhoun, Congress was still deeply divided between Federalists and the old-line Republicans like Randolph, who wanted to avoid war with either side. Wills points out that "Congress was hesitant and doubtful, unwilling to vote for the taxes that would make war preparation a reality." Beschloss makes the case that Madison had "made it very clear that he wanted a war against England, which helped to persuade an ambivalent House and Senate."[44]

James Monroe aided Madison in "choreograph[ing] Congressional actions," as did Henry Clay. In Madison's November 1811 annual address to Congress, the president called for preparation for war. He requested that Congress raise ten thousand regular troops, expand the navy, and increase taxes to pay for these defense measures. The proposal immediately ran into trouble in the Senate, which proposed that the number of troops be increased to twenty-five thousand, which was more than could be raised in a short period of time. In Madison's view, the growth of trade between Great Britain and Canada had made economic coercion from the United States less tenable. "Not only could Canada attract a substantial illegal trade from the United States ... its production of timber for the Royal Navy and foodstuffs for the West Indies also threatened to reduce British dependence on American supplies," Jack Rakove writes. Both Jefferson and Clay thought Canada could be easily taken, thereby subduing the British. This would soon prove a myth, as the Canadians were stronger than the Americans thought, and congressional actions weakened the administration's hand when they also failed to expand the navy and would only support increasing taxes once an actual war was declared. As Rakove points out, the office of the presidency was in large measure designed to avoid the problems experienced during the Revolutionary War, when the central government under the Articles of Confederation lacked an executive. But Madison clung to the Republican ideal that the president should defer to Congress. "The idea that a president should seek to direct the debates of Congress was something that Madison had never come to accept," Rakove writes, and it would harm him and the country in terms of war preparations.[45]

In March, the administration proposed a new embargo, which was "in Madison's mind, a way of preparing for war," according to Wills. It would allow time for American ships to return to port. But even as the administration prepared for war, Madison was still unsure which country, or both, the United States would declare war on. As late as May 1812, he wrote to Jefferson that a war with England would not be supported by the Federalists or the old-line Republicans. But "to go to war against both presents a thousand difficulties." Ultimately, he decided that Great Britain presented the greatest threat, while France was an old ally, even if they also continued to prey on American shipping. As Wills points out, "Americans had never been the subjects of France. There was special humiliation in any submission by a former master." On June 1, Madison submitted a request to declare war on Great Britain. Clay quickly moved the declaration through the House, but the Senate took two weeks before it acted. As Madison feared, the vote was highly partisan, with no Federalists supporting the measure and one-quarter of Republicans also breaking away from the president. The vote was also sectional, with Southerners and westerners strongly in support, while New England was opposed.[46] While some wars in American history were solidly supported by almost the entire population (World War II comes to mind), the War of 1812 fit a more normal pattern of splitting the population (like Vietnam or the second Iraq War).

In fact, the war could have been completely avoided in a world with modern communications. Madison's commercial coercion had, in fact, begun to take its toll on the British. On June 20, two days after Madison signed the declaration of war, Great Britain announced that the Orders in Council would be suspended for one year. But the British action came too late.[47]

☞ ☞ ☞

"Right from the start the war was a disaster," historian Robert V. Remini writes. The Republican Party, led by Jefferson and Gallatin's flinty approach to public finance, had spent the past decade reducing military spending, taxes, and the public debt. While laudable goals, they left the country unable to defend itself. The military leadership had aged and was generally incompetent to lead in a new war. About the only saving grace was the war at sea, which should have overwhelmingly favored the British.[48]

The land war followed a three-prong strategy that was initially focused on invading Canada. The campaign near Detroit was led by fifty-nine-year-old William Hull, who had been a lieutenant colonel during the American Revolution. Hull was past his prime "and a stroke and other personal tragedies had further eroded his strength," according to Hickey. Under siege by a British force of sixteen hundred men (including regulars and Indians), Hull surrendered Fort Detroit and his entire two-thousand-man force without firing a shot. He was later court-martialed and sentenced to death, which was suspended due to his age. Combined with other losses in Chicago and Mackinac, the British controlled much of the Northwest.[49]

The campaign in Niagara, New York, went no better. Although the Americans outnumbered the British troops and their Indian allies, they were unable to coordinate their attacks between the regular army and the militia. Men from the state militias of both Pennsylvania and New York refused to enter Canada, forcing the troops under the capable command of Lieutenant Colonel Winfield Scott to surrender. The planned invasion of Montreal also failed, in part because militia troops once again refused to leave the country. The lack of military preparedness and Republican reliance on state militias had proven to be a major disaster.[50]

Surprisingly, the war at sea went much better for the Americans. Washington's administration had built, over opposition from Madison, a total of seven frigates, which were still in service. They were faster and "capable of outfighting and outsailing ships in their class and of outrunning anything larger," according to Hickey. Unlike their army counterparts, the American navy was blessed with young and capable ship captains and excellent sailors. Between August and the end of December 1812, the navy would capture or defeat seven British vessels, including three frigates, and only lose three smaller vessels. While the British had overwhelming numbers on their side (over one thousand ships available), they were spread thin with most of their navy in Europe. Still, the naval victories "gave a tremendous boost to American morale," Hickey writes.[51]

As the war went on, Madison faced reelection in November. During the spring, he had received the support of caucuses held in eight states, followed by the formal endorsement of the congressional caucus, with two-thirds of the Republicans voting for him. Still, there was a split among the Republicans in the Northeast. New York nominated DeWitt Clinton, the nephew of the recently deceased vice president, to run against Madison. The Federalists decided to support Clinton rather than nominating their own candidate. Wills points out that Clinton ran a very dishonest race, "opposing the war in the North but calling for better management of it in the Middle States." Henry Adams would later write that "Clinton strove to make up a majority which had no element of union but himself and money."[52]

Still, the election was very close. Clinton's strategy was to retain the entire North plus Pennsylvania. New York went for Clinton, in large measure due to the work of a young Martin van Buren. Of Dutch descent, Van Buren was the son of a tavern keeper from Kinderhook. He became a lawyer in 1803, and was a strong Jeffersonian, believing in states' rights and small government. With Clinton's support, he won a seat in the state senate. Despite his strong support for the Republicans, he helped secure all of New York's electoral votes for Clinton. Clinton made a strong bid for Pennsylvania, but his attempt to woo Federalist votes caused fence-sitting Republicans to support Madison, who won in the electoral college by a vote of 128–89. Had Pennsylvania gone the other way, Clinton would have been president. Clinton won all of New England except Vermont, plus New York, New Jersey and Delaware, with Madison taking everything else. The Republicans also lost seats in Congress to the Federalists, although they still retained control over the federal government. Despite their gains, the Federalists were increasingly a regional party, and young conservatives would soon need to look elsewhere for a home.[53]

By early 1813, the British navy had established a blockade that stretched from New York to New Orleans. The American navy, so successful in 1812, was now bottled up in port. The only exception was New England, where the British allowed trade to continue, both to reward them for opposition to the war and to continue needed trade with Canada. The lack of trade put continued pressure on the ability of the Americans to finance the war, since so much of the budget was funded from import duties. When combined with the loss of the Bank of the United States, the treasury became depleted. "In March 1813 Gallatin informed the president that the government had scarcely enough funds to carry on for a month," according to Wood. Gallatin was finally able to secure additional loans when the czar of Russia offered to mediate the conflict in the spring of 1813, and Congress finally approved new internal taxes to go into effect in 1814.[54]

The focus of the war in 1813 continued to be the Canadian front around the Great Lakes. Neither side could create a decisive victory. The American war effort improved with new leadership in the war and navy departments, and with the rise of better military leadership. In September of 1813, the American fleet defeated the British on Lake Erie, which opened the way for Harrison's army to secure the Northwest Territory. As part of this battle, Tecumseh was killed, and the Indian threat crushed. "American settlers could now safely move into all of Indiana and Michigan Territories and further west," Wilentz observes.[55]

The British were more successful defending Lake Ontario. The American army had an early victory in 1813 when they took the Canadian capital of York and burned it to the ground. The British would remember this a year later when they returned the favor, razing Washington, DC. But by the end of the year, the British controlled both Fort George and Fort Niagara, which were the entryways to Lake Ontario.[56]

Peace Overtures and Battles in 1814
As 1814 opened, the British finally agreed to direct negotiations with the Americans to end the war. They had previously rejected the

Russian czar's offer to mediate in early 1813, since they were winning the land war. But American victories in the latter part of 1813 made the British foreign secretary reconsider his position. Madison appointed John Quincy Adams, his minister to Russia, to lead the American team, along with Gallatin and Clay, to meet with the British in Ghent, Belgium. "British officials dragged their feet, hoping that victories in America would enhance their bargaining position," Hickey writes.[57]

The British negotiating strategy was dictated by Napoleon's defeat in the spring of 1814. Great Britain could now turn its full attention to the American war, which had been a sideshow to the main event in Europe. By September, the British had added thirty thousand troops in Canada. But the American army had also improved, becoming more professional as the war moved into 1814. New leadership was emerging from military leaders who drilled their troops for many hours preparing them for the battles to come. The Americans were victorious at Chippewa and Lund Lane as part of the Niagara campaign in the summer, "showing that American troops could hold their own against British regulars in close combat." They followed this up with another victory at Plattsburgh near Lake Champlain in September. The British continued to control parts of the Great Lakes, and "the war on the Canadian-American frontier was still a stalemate," according to Hickey.[58]

Financial problems continued to vex the American war effort, despite the stronger government under the Constitution. The loss of the Bank of the United States did not help matters, and the country verged on the brink of bankruptcy by the summer. In November of 1814, the government defaulted on the national debt and public credit was no longer available. Despite this, the middle and western states prospered during the war, while the South and New England, who were tied to trade, suffered. When Congress reconvened in the fall of 1814, the new treasury secretary recommended that taxes be raised and a new national bank established to close a financing gap for 1815 that was estimated at over $40 million. To put matters into perspective, the entire federal revenue stream was estimated at $15 million. Raising that kind of money would likely have been impossible; fortunately for the Americans, the war would end before the new year had barely begun.[59]

Peace negotiations finally opened in August of 1814. The British team, still hoping for a knock-out blow to the Americans, originally offered very draconian terms to end the war. To protect Canada and their Indian allies, the British wanted a large reservation of land to be granted to the Indians in the Northwest that would serve as a buffer zone. America would also be required to give up a portion of its territory in Northern Maine and Minnesota, and New England would lose their rights to Canadian fisheries. "There was no concession to any of the American grievances" that had started the war, according to Wills, including impressment of American sailors and neutral trading rights. The Americans rejected the initial British position.[60]

In the summer of 1814, the British focused their war effort in the Chesapeake by assaulting Washington and Baltimore. "American officials were slow to perceive the danger, believing that since Washington had no strategic significance the British were not likely to attack it," Gordon Wood writes. The result was that the British invaded Washington and burned it to the ground, including the Capitol and the White House. Madison had taken to the field himself on horseback, armed with two pistols, but watched as the ineffective militia broke and ran. His wife, Dolley, was able to save many of the White House papers, and Gilbert Stuart's portrait of Washington. After the British moved on to attack Baltimore, Madison returned to Washington to reestablish the government, and the British invasion had little long-term affect. The British attack on Baltimore was repulsed as Francis Scott Key penned the words to the "Star Spangled Banner." The Chesapeake campaign also resulted in a stalemate.[61]

Meanwhile, negotiations continued in Ghent. The British negotiators had, in fact, overstated their demands. The establishment of a large Indian nation on the Canadian border was not the sine qua non of British policy. "Our Commissioners had certainly taken a very erroneous view of our policy," Britain's Prime Minister Liverpool exclaimed. The British hopes that victories in the war would strengthen their position were gradually dissipating. "If we had either burnt Baltimore or held Plattsburgh I believe we should have had peace on [our] terms," one of the British negotiators commented. Opposition to the war was also beginning to rise in Great Britain. When Lord Wellington was asked to take over the war effort, he replied that "you have no right ... to demand any concession of territory from America."[62]

The Americans had their own problems with a deeply unpopular war. Donald Hickey has called the war even less popular than Vietnam, although that may stretch the truth just a bit. But it was clearly a partisan war, with the Federalists in New England particularly opposed. The Federalists had always been more supportive of the English, while the Republicans tended to side with the French, at least until Napoleon seized power. The governors of Massachusetts, Connecticut, and Rhode Island had refused to let their state militias participate in the war. By late in 1814, there was even talk in those states of making a separate peace with England and seceding from the union. A regional convention was called to meet in Hartford, but New Hampshire and Vermont refused to participate. This caused the remaining delegates to act in a cautious manner, rejecting more extreme measures. They instead put forward "a series of amendments to the Constitution that summed up [their] grievances over the previous decade and a half," Wood writes. One of these amendments was directed at breaking up the power of the South by eliminating the three-fifths representation clause for slaves. Another amendment would limit a president to one term in office and forbid the election of a president from the same state twice in a row. The amendments were clearly directed at eliminating the Virginia dynasty that had dominated the presidency since Washington.[63]

By the time the report from the Hartford Convention reached Washington, the Treaty of Ghent had been signed by the two negotiating teams on December 24, 1814. The treaty restored the status quo ante as it existed prior to the war. However, the British insisted that the war would not end until both sides had ratified the treaty. Given this, the war continued into early 1815. The final major battle of the war was led by General Andrew Jackson in New Orleans, a smashing victory for the Americans that would eventually lead Jackson to the presidency.[64]

Andrew Jackson

Andrew Jackson would transform American politics. The colonial period had been one in which common people had been required to show deference to their social superiors. The revolution had begun to break down those relationships, but the founders were still skeptical of democracy and established a republic designed to give elected officials some distance from the public in running the government. The politics of the 1790s had been partly fought over the role that average people should play, but even Jefferson and the Republicans thought that once elections were over, elites should govern. The early 1800s would see the beginnings of a market revolution and the emergence of the common man in politics. Jackson, a self-made man, would continue this process by opening up politics even further to ordinary white men and expanding America into an ever more democratic and populist era. One of his biographers, Jon Meacham, argues that Jackson reflected the "American character in formation and in action," by encapsulating both a "love of democracy" and a society "prone to racism and intolerance."[65]

His father and mother immigrated to America from Ireland in 1765. His ancestors were part of the wave of Scottish settlers that had inhabited Northern Ireland under King James as a way "to subdue the unruly Irish," according to historian H. W. Brands. The Scotch Irish would go on to settle much of the Midwest and South. They were very much a warlike people, unafraid to confront the Indians in pursuit of land and opportunity. They would eventually form a "folk community bound together by deep cultural and ethnic ties," as the political scientist Walter Russell Mead writes, and form an alternative narrative of what makes America a nation. Rather than a nation bound together by the ideas expressed in the Declaration of Independence, the Jacksonians would come to define America in more racial terms, as a white Anglo-Saxon country. Andrew Jackson, born on March 15, 1767, in the backcountry of the Carolinas, would become their first national leader.[66]

Andrew Jackson exemplified the values of social equality, hard work, self-reliance, and the honor code that he followed during his life. His father died before he was born, and his mother was forced to move in with her sister's family to survive. Andrew was a "wild child, with an almost unmanageable will and a defiant temper," Brands writes. He came of age during the Revolutionary War, and by the time he was thirteen, he was a member of the militia during the British assault on the South in 1780. While trying to defend his aunt's home, he was wounded by a British soldier when he refused to clean the man's boots. "The sword point reached my head and left a mark there ... on the skull, as well as on the fingers," Jackson later reported. Both of his brothers and his mother died during the war, leaving him alone.[67]

He tried his hand as a saddle maker and then as a teacher, but he was not well suited to either of these. Just shy of turning eighteen, Jackson became apprenticed to study law in the town of Salisbury, North Carolina. By the middle of 1787, he was admitted to practice law, but he had not lost any of his wildness. "He was the most roaring, rollicking, game-cocking, card-playing, mischievous fellow that ever lived in Salisbury," according to one of Jackson's friends. He stood about six feet tall "and very slender" according to one young woman who knew him—not particularly good looking, "but his eyes were handsome," and he had a very real "presence."[68]

In late 1788, Jackson made his way west and settled in Nashville, Tennessee. It was little more than an outpost at that point in time, and he soon fell in love with a beautiful married woman, Rachel Donelson Robards, whose husband was unfaithful. They lived together before finally marrying in January of 1794. She became Andrew's life, and he was totally committed to her. He worked as the district attorney for the Southwest territories and began to acquire land, and slaves to work it, on a site he called the Hermitage. At one point, he lost everything when he backed a friend who went bankrupt. "Jackson recouped his losses ... ," Wilentz writes, but he always distrusted "debt, banks, and the entire paper-money credit system" thereafter. In January of 1796, Jackson was invited to attend the convention that wrote the Tennessee constitution, and he was rewarded by being elected to Congress to represent the new state. Three months later, when he turned thirty, Jackson was appointed to the US Senate. But legislative politics were not to his liking, a place where disputes were settled with "sticks and spittle" instead of pistols. Jackson was born to command, a man destined to be a general and then an executive, a person who gave orders. He left the Senate and returned to Tennessee, where he was appointed to the superior court, and then in 1802, he was elected the commander of the state militia. It was his true calling.[69]

Andrew Jackson was a violent man, prone to dueling when he felt his honor or that of his wife was sullied. He carried a bullet in his chest from one duel that he fought. His personality was suited for war, so when hostilities began in 1812, he led his militia troops into battle. "He delights in peace; but does not fear war," the Tennessee governor wrote at the time. Jackson was a popular leader, a man who "cared about his followers [and] thought of them as his family," Meacham writes. They affectionately called him "Old Hickory" in recognition of his toughness. In the autumn of 1813, he led his troops against a faction of Creek Indians known as the Red Sticks, who were affiliated with Tecumseh's forces. At one battle, his men surrounded and slaughtered over two hundred Red Sticks. "We shot them like dogs," the frontiersman Davy Crockett later recalled. At the conclusion of the Creek War, Jackson imposed a treaty that ceded over twenty-three million acres of land to the United States, which encompasses much of present-day Alabama.[70]

In 1814, Jackson, who had been made a major general in the United States Army, moved his troops to defend New Orleans. "Should the Americans lose the city, everyone realized, they would certainly lose the war," Wilentz writes. The loyalty of the residents of New Orleans was still in doubt, so Jackson defied a federal district judge and placed the city under martial law. As the British marched toward New Orleans, Jackson ordered that an extensive system of ramparts be built to protect his badly outnumbered troops. In the decisive battle in January 1815, his men were protected behind the barricades they built and wiped out the British army. Almost eighteen hundred of the five thousand British troops were killed, wounded, or captured. Only thirteen Americans were killed and fifty were lost or wounded. Andrew Jackson became the hero of the battle of New Orleans, and instantly established a national reputation for himself.[71]

Madison biographer Ralph Ketcham argues that victory at the battle of New Orleans "rescued his administration from ... disgrace." Word of the outcome at New Orleans reached the president shortly before the British peace treaty arrived in early February. The Senate quickly ratified the treaty on February 17, and the war was over.[72]

The War and Nation Building

So, we end where we began, with the fact that wars can contribute to nation building. Fighting a war can contribute to that sense of nationhood by creating a sense of a shared history. The War of 1812 had this impact by allowing the United States to stand up to a more powerful adversary in Great Britain. Over the course of the war the United States achieved some significant victories, even though the war ended in a stalemate. During the darkest days of the war, near the end of 1813, Madison attempted to bolster the public's waning confidence. In a speech to Congress, he said that "the war, with its vicissitudes is illustrating the capacity and the destiny of the United States to be a great, a flourishing, and a powerful nation." The "Americans quickly forgot the war's disheartening defeats and chose instead to remember a few proud moments," like the victory at the battle of New Orleans, writer Walter R. Borneman has observed. In Madison's message to Congress on the Treaty of Ghent, he argued that the war was "a necessary resort to assert the rights and independence of nation," and that the military had "contributed to the honor of the American name."[73]

The events leading up to the war, including the embargo, had begun to usher in what historians have referred to as the market revolution, which would accelerate in the coming years. Factories began to emerge in the North to produce goods from cotton that had once been acquired from England. "The rapid development of domestic trade created the heightened demand almost everywhere for internal improvements—new roads, new canals, new ferries, new bridges—anything that would help increase the speed and lower the cost of the movement of goods within the country," according to Wood. This was one of those elements that would help to "bind the republic together," as John Calhoun framed it. A vision of the American character began to emerge in the North, one based on the concept of the self-made man who achieves success through hard work, diligence, and success in business. Joyce Appleby has written that "a new character ideal" was developing, one based on "the man who developed inner resources, acted independently, lived virtuously, and bent his behavior to his personal goals." But this was largely a Northern phenomenon, and "the antebellum South never became a middling commercial-minded society," Wood writes, leading to an ever-greater divergence between the two regions.[74]

The market revolution went hand in hand with the gradual expansion of democracy in America. "Presumptions about the natural superiority of well-born and well-bred gentleman, challenged during the American Revolution, now fell," Sean Wilentz has observed. The remaining property qualifications to vote and hold office were increasingly removed. None of this happened overnight, but by the 1830s a democratic system would set in, one that "came to define the nation as a whole," according to the historian Eric Foner. Federalism became relegated to New England, and the United States experienced a short period of one-party rule under the Republicans. But under the surface, new forms of tension were beginning to emerge, especially over the expansion of slavery.[75]

Endnotes

1   Quoted in Walter R. Borneman, *1812: The War that Forged a Nation* (New York, 2012), p. 304.

2   Wood, *Empire*, p. 622–624; Douglass C. North, *The Economic Growth of the United States 1790-1860* (New York, 1961), p. 36 and p. 221, for the growth in export values. North also delves into the impact of growth on the cities of the Northeast and the South from trade in chapter 5.

3   Ketcham, p. 441; Wilentz, *Rise*, p. 130.

4   Ketcham, p. 442; Donald R. Hickey, *The War of 1812: A Forgotten Conflict* (Urbana, 1989), p. 10.

5   Hickey, p. 10–11; Ketcham, p. 443–444 and p. 450; Wood, *Empire*, p. 624.

6   Hickey, p. 14–16; Wood, *Empire*, p. 645.

7   Wood, *Empire*, p. 647; Ketcham, p. 452; Hickey, p. 16.

8   Meacham, p. 426; Wood, *Empire*, p. 192, discusses the extent to which Republican ideology clung to notions of using trade sanctions to shape international relations.

9   Hickey, p. 5–9; Malone, p. 8–10; Michael Beschloss, *Presidents of War: The Epic Story, from 1807 to Modern Times* (New York, 2018), p. 8–9.

10 Meacham, p. 428–429; on the definition of the Barbary States, see Meacham, p. 182; American success against the Barbary States is succinctly summarized in Appleby, p. 42; for the lack of an easy victory, see Alan Taylor, "The New Nation," retrieved August 25, 2016, from https://www.gilderlehrman.org/history-by-era/essays/new-nation-1783%E2%80%931815.

11 Elkins and McKitrick make this argument about Jefferson on p. 209.

12 Elkins and McKitrick, p. 67 and p. 130; Madison's views on the contrast between American and British citizens is from his article entitled "Fashion" in the *National Gazette* dated March 22, 1792; see also Wills, p. 51–53.

13 Appleby, p. 127.

14 Burns, p. 200; Wood, *Empire*, p. 652; Meacham, p. 433; Wills, p. 54; Appleby, p. 128.

15 Appleby, p. 128.

16 Fraser, p. 183; Appleby, p. 97.

17 Appleby, p. 92–93; Meacham, p. 399–400.

18 Appleby, p. 98–101; Meacham, p. 405 and p. 420–421.

19 Kimberly Ann Elliot and Gary Clyde Hufbaer, "The Concise Encyclopedia of Economics: Sanctions," retrieved August 14, 2016, from http://www.econlib.org/library/Enc/Sanctions.html.

20 Wills, p. 4.

21 Ketcham, p. 84.

22 Wills, p. 69; Appleby, p. 123.

23 Rakove, *Madison*, p. 174; Ketcham, p. 468.

24 Wood, *Empire*, p. 662; Ketcham, p. 473; Wills, p. 5; Wikipedia, which I do not use as a resource for my books, does have a very helpful matrix that allows the user to sort the rankings of presidents by various sources dating back to 1948. See https://en.wikipedia.org/wiki/Historical_rankings_of_Presidents_of_the_United_States.

25 Wood, *Empire*, p. 663; Rakove, *Madison*, p. 180.

26 On Gallatin generally, see Albert Gallatin from Britannica Online Encyclopedia and Gallatin, Albert from Biographical Directory of the United States, retrieved on August 30, 2016, from https://www.britannica.com/biography/Albert-Gallatin and http://bioguide.congress.gov/scripts/biodisplay.pl?index=g000020; Chernow, Hamilton, p. 455; Malone, *The President*, p. 54.

27 Wills, p. 63–64; Ketcham, p. 484–485.

28 Ketcham, p. 486; Rakove, p. 185.

29 Wills, p. 80–81; Ketcham, p. 493–495.

30 This account is drawn from the varying information and interpretations presented by Rakove, p. 180–183; Ketcham, p. 502–505; and Wills, p. 87–88. The quote on Macon's bill number 2 is from Burns, p. 206.

31 Wills is particularly harsh on Madison, while Ketcham takes a more rounded view. The quote from Madison is in Ketchum, p. 504, as is the quote from Ketcham.

32 Wills, p. 75–77; Ketcham, p. 506.

33 Harry L. Watson, *Andrew Jackson and Henry Clay: Democracy and Development in Antebellum America* (Boston, 1998), p. 42. Most of this account of Clay's life is drawn primarily from Robert V. Remini, *Henry Clay: Statesman of the Union* (New York, 1991). See p. 4 for the Clay quote.

34 Remini, p. 6–8; Watson, p. 44.

35 Remini, p. 19–21.

36 Remini, p. 26–29; Watson, p. 46.

37 Hickey, p. 47; excerpts from Clay's speech were taken from Watson, p. 133. On the gradual emergence of the American System, see Remini, p. 61–68.

38 Remini, p. 76–83.

39 Irving H. Bartlett, *John C. Calhoun: A Biography* (New York, 1993), p. 19–36.

40 Bartlett, p. 30 and p. 43–52.

41 Bartlett, p. 43–61.

42 Bartlett, p. 53, p. 64–66.

43 Bartlett, p. 69–73; Hickey, p. 30.

44 See Wilentz, p. 154. In a footnote, Wilentz argues that the argument that Madison was dragged into the war goes all the way back to historian Henry Adams from the

late nineteenth century, who was the great-grandson of John Adams and the grandson of John Quincy; Wills, p.92–93, also points to the work of Robert Allen Rutland, *The Presidency of James Madison* (Lawrence, 1990), who claims that Madison was "little more than a leaf riding the surface of a torrent." Beschloss, p. 92.

45 Rakove, Madison, p. 186–187 and p. 195; Wills, p. 97–99; Wilentz, p. 154.

46 Wills, p. 96–97; Burns, p. 208–209.

47 Wilentz, p. 155.

48 Remini, p. 94.

49 Wood, p. 677; Hickey, p. 80–84.

50 Hickey, p. 85–90.

51 Wills, p. 106–115; Hickey, p. 90–97.

52 Hickey, p. 100–101; Wills, p. 116; Ketcham, p. 545.

53 Hickey, p. 100–105; Wilentz, p. 156–159; Ketcham, p. 545.

54 Hickey, p. 152; Wood, *Empire*, p. 684; Wills, p. 122.

55 Hickey, p. 126–127; Wilentz, p. 160.

56 Wood, *Empire*, p. 684.

57 Wills, p. 121–127; Hickey, p. 285.

58 Wills, p. 128; Hickey, p. 185–194.

59 Hickey, p. 222–247.

60 Wills, p. 142–143; Hickey, p. 289.

61 Wood, *Empire*, p. 690; Rakove, p. 199.

62 Hickey, p. 294–295; Wills, p. 144.

63 Hickey, p. 255–289; Wood, Empire, p. 694.

64 Wills, p. 146; Hickey, p. 296.

65 For the issue of deference during the colonial period, see Gordon Wood, *The Radicalism of the American Revolution* (New York, 1992), especially Part I. See also Wood, *Empire*, p. 710–721, for a discussion of the emerging market revolution and expansion of the democratic spirit in the early 1800s. The quotes are from Jon Meacham, *American Lion: Andrew Jackson in the White House* (New York, 2008), p. xx–xxi.

66 H. W. Brands, *Andrew Jackson: His Life and Times* (New York, 2005), p. 3–16; Walter Russell Mead, *Special Providence: American Foreign Policy and How It Changed the World* (New York, 2001), p. 227.

67 Brands, p. 17–26; Meacham, *American Lion*, p. 10–14.

68 Meacham, p. 20; Brands, p. 41.

69 Brands, p. 62–80 and p. 97–102; Wilentz, p. 170.

70 Meacham, *American Lion*, p. 28; Wilentz, p. 171–172.

71 Meacham, *American Lion*, p. 31–32; Wilentz, p. 173–175.

72 Ketcham, p. 596–597.

73 Borneman, p. 301 and p. 303; the Madison quote is from James Madison, *Writings* (New York, 1999), p. 707.

74 Watson, p. 7; Wood, p. 706 and 732–733; Joyce Appleby, *Inheriting the Revolution: The First Generation of Americans* (Cambridge, 2000), p. 11.

75 Wilentz, p. 177; Eric Foner, *The Story of American Freedom* (New York, 1998), p. 52.

CHAPTER 5

The Era of (Somewhat) Good Feelings

A federalist newsman dubbed the times "an era of good feelings,"
... but bad feelings failed to go away.
—HISTORIAN LEONARD L. RICHARDS[1]

With the end of the war in Europe, the United States was finally free to focus more fully on domestic issues. The Era of Good Feelings, the term applied to the period that coincided with the incoming presidency of James Monroe, would see both numerous contributions to American nationhood and the widening rift between North and South over slavery. The market economy would begin to flourish, and usher in a new sense of the American character, at least in the North. This would be accompanied by the boom and bust cycles that would accompany capitalism. The boundaries of the United States would continue to expand during this period, and for the first time the country would warn the European powers that the Western Hemisphere was off limits to further colonization.

The Monroe Administration

James Monroe was the next and last member of the Virginia dynasty to become president. The Monroes had been in Virginia since the

1600s, although they never rose to be members of the elite planter class. James was born in 1758, and by the time he was fourteen, both of his parents had died. While he was left land, he had no money, a problem that would bedevil him his entire life. His uncle, Judge Joseph Jones, took care of the children, and helped Monroe enroll in the College of William and Mary in the colonial capital of Williamsburg. Wealthy and well-connected, Jones also took young James to the House of Burgesses meetings held in the capital, and in 1774 he met Washington, Jefferson, and Henry, men who had a strong influence on him.[2]

When the Revolutionary War began, Monroe joined the Virginia militia, and was gravely wounded when Washington's army routed the Hessians in Trenton in 1776. Monroe went on to become an aide-de-camp, befriending other young men like Hamilton and Lafayette, and he shared a cabin with his friend and future Supreme Court justice James Marshall at Valley Forge. By 1780, he had left the army and studied law under the guidance of Jefferson, who was the Virginia governor. "During this period Jefferson began his lifelong role as mentor to Monroe," Gary Hart writes in his biography of Monroe. Jefferson helped him to see that his calling was toward public service.[3]

With Judge Jones's support, Monroe was elected to the Virginia legislature, and was then appointed to serve in the Confederation Congress in 1783. During this period his friendship with Jefferson continued to blossom, as the two served together in the Congress. Monroe was essentially broke, having gone directly from the military into politics, and Jefferson invited him to share the house he rented in Annapolis, where Congress was meeting. Monroe's only wealth was in land he had inherited or tracts of western land he had received as compensation for his service in the military. This may account for his early interest in westward expansion, and he became known as a "man of the Western Water." With his military background, he also began to think nationally and believed that the current government under the Articles of Confederation was enfeebled. While in Congress, he opposed Jay's treaty with Spain that would foreclose American navigation of the Mississippi because it would hinder westward expansion. He believed "the whole development of the Union was at stake," and the outcome would determine "whether the United States was to constitute a nation."[4]

Monroe was popular among his peers and enjoyed "card games, dice, billiards ... horse races and cockfights," according to one of his biographers, Harlow Giles Unger. Fortunately, he was a successful gambler, given his lack of money, and once won a substantial sum from Marshall at whist. But with members of the opposite sex he was not so lucky and was considered unattractive by some. That is, until he met and fell in love with seventeen-year-old Elizabeth Kortright, who was "a natural beauty, superbly educated, a gifted artist and musician [who] sang [and] played the piano forte," Unger writes. She was the daughter of the very affluent Lawrence Kortright, who had made his money from trade in the West Indies and owned a townhouse in New York. On February 26, 1786, they were married at New York's Trinity Episcopal Church. Jones once again bailed out the young Monroe, who was still short of money, by helping him establish a law practice in Fredericksburg, Virginia, and letting him live for free in a house he owned.[5]

Given his need to support his wife and recently born baby, Monroe was unable to attend the Constitutional Convention that opened in May 1787 in Philadelphia. As a nationalist, he originally supported the new Constitution, but surprisingly changed his mind as a member of the Virginia ratifying convention. Perhaps it was the influence of Judge Jones, who opposed the ratification of the document, but Monroe joined the antifederalist side. Monroe may also have been swayed by Patrick Henry's argument that "the president's treaty-making powers might allow him to cede Mississippi River navigation rights to Spain," as well as Henry's criticism of the lack of a Bill of Rights. James Madison was able to sway the convention, in part by promising to support a Bill of Rights after ratification. But the vindictive Henry then blocked Madison's election to the Senate and got Monroe to run against his friend for a gerrymandered district in the House. The two actively campaigned against one another, and Madison ultimately won the election, their friendship still intact.[6]

In the early 1790s, Monroe moved his family back to Albemarle County to be near Jefferson in Charlottesville. He was appointed to the US Senate at the age of thirty-two and became a loyal foot soldier in the Republican cause. He voted against the bank bill and was a member of the committee that investigated Hamilton's behavior in the Reynolds affair. "To a degree, Hamilton held Monroe personally responsible for his humiliation, at least as an agent for Jefferson, and a breach was opened between the two that almost resulted in a resort to pistols," Hart writes. In 1794, Washington appointed Monroe as minister to France. He was attempting to balance relations between England and France as war on the continent raged. The pro-British John Jay had been sent to negotiate a treaty in London, and Monroe's sentiments as friend to France were well known. But Monroe was an inexperienced diplomat, and he quickly exceeded the instructions he was given by the secretary of state, "committing the United States unreservedly to the French cause," according to Elkins and McKitrick. He was recalled in 1796 with his career "close to being ruined then and there, and with relations between America and France in a worse state than ever." Gary Hart astutely points out how the incident revealed one of Monroe's character flaws, that he was thin-skinned.

"Monroe felt almost all criticism or disagreement to be a challenge to his intelligence, judgment, or rectitude," Hart writes. Upon his return from France, he wrote a massive book defending his role and criticizing his former commander in chief, which ended their friendship.[7]

In 1799, the Virginia Assembly elected Monroe governor, where he served for three years. Jefferson then called on him again, this time to assist with the negotiations that led to the Louisiana Purchase, and then on to Great Britain to negotiate over the impressment of American sailors and the opening of trade. As we saw in the last chapter, Jefferson's rejection of Monroe's proposed treaty caused a fissure between the two men that was not healed until Monroe agreed to become secretary of state in 1812.[8]

᠁

By the time James Monroe ran for president in 1816, the Republicans had solidified power and the United States had become a one-party state. "Presumptions about the natural superiority of well-born and well-bred gentlemen, challenged during the American Revolution, now fell," according to Sean Wilentz, which played to the Republican advantage. It was increasingly an era of emerging democratic participation that went hand in hand with expanding economic opportunity in a market economy.[9]

As Jefferson had picked Madison to succeed him, so Madison selected Monroe. In March of 1816, the Republican caucus in Congress supported Monroe on a vote of 65–54 over the current treasury secretary, William Crawford. It was a surprisingly close vote and revealed the continuing split among Republicans and a resistance to the Virginia dynasty. The Federalists nominated Rufus King, but he never really stood a chance, and only carried three states. By this point, ten states chose their members to the electoral college based on the winner of the popular vote, with the other nine states appointing them by the state legislature. Monroe easily won in the electoral college by a vote of 183–34. "The antiwar Federalists found themselves stigmatized as disloyal; the Hartford Convention now looked almost treasonable and became a huge political liability," according to the historian Daniel Walker Howe.[10]

Monroe was not a deeply intellectual man in the mold of either Jefferson or Madison, but "was known as a man of common sense, good judgement, and courage," James MacGregor Burns writes. He was also anti-party, and so the new era fit him well. Whereas both of his mentors had made anti-party statements that fit the age they lived in, both also understood that parties were sown into the fabric of human nature. Monroe believed that political parties were caused by "certain defects of those governments rather than in human nature; and that we have happily avoided those defects in our system," as he wrote to Andrew Jackson after his election. He thought that the only form of party division that existed was between those that were "friendly to free government" and those that were committed to "monocracy." With the Federalists now defeated, "discord does not belong to our system."[11]

In part, the Federalists were disappearing because they practiced a top-down brand of politics in which the masses were required to be deferential to elites. Their disappearance was hastened by what appeared to be disloyalty during the Hartford Convention, especially in the aftermath of Jackson's victory in New Orleans. But the Republicans, or at least some of them, were changing, with the rise of new leaders from the West and South that were more nationalistic and wanted to use federal power to bind the nation together. The War of 1812 had caused Madison and other Republicans to rethink their commitment to America as a purely agrarian society of small yeoman farmers that lacked a military, operated under a weak central government, and eschewed banking.

Madison made this clear in his last State of the Union message, which was submitted in writing to Congress in December of 1815. Four things stood out in his address. The first was the importance of military preparedness, given the American experience during the War of 1812. While the state militias were still considered important, the training of professional military officers was also needed "through the enlargement of the Military Academy," and the "completion of the works of defense" including providing for naval ships. The second was a commitment to a new national bank. Although mentioned only in passing, Madison alluded to the need to have a "uniform national currency" and would support a bill that was later worked out between his treasury secretary and John Calhoun, who was then a member of the House of Representatives. A tariff should be continued in order to protect infant industries needed for "public defense or connected with the primary wants of individuals." Finally, "roads and canals" should be built "under the national authority" and a constitutional amendment be pursued to provide Congress with the authority to do this. These proposals became known as the "Madisonian Platform."[12]

Reaction to the Madisonian Platform was not uniformly positive. The old-line Republicans condemned the program and stated that Madison now "out-Hamilton's Alexander Hamilton." However, this was a distinctly minority view, and even Jefferson now supported the new nationalist vision, at least in terms of the need for the United States to be independent "for the comforts of life" by placing "the manufacturer by the side of the agriculturist." Jefferson, however, still retained his skepticism toward banking. Supported by nationalists like Clay, the Congress reacted positively to Madison's plans, and a bank bill, and tariff and military preparations were all approved in early 1816. However, Madison did veto a bill that would have put profits from the Bank of the United States (BUS) toward the cost of internal improvements, arguing that the Constitution would need to be amended to provide for this. It was his last official act before Monroe took over the presidency in the spring of 1817.[13]

Ralph Waldo Emerson once wrote that "a foolish consistency is the hobgoblin of little minds." Perhaps he was thinking of Madison when he wrote these words. In the mid-1780s, Madison had become the great champion for a new and more powerful central government as envisioned in the Constitution that he did so much to bring about. He then went into opposition over Hamilton's program, as we saw in chapter 1. Now he had come full circle, fully supporting a more powerful central government, even if he still believed in a more limited construction of the Constitution. His biographer, Ralph Ketcham, provides one possible explanation, arguing that Madison now believed that republicanism was safe from any attempt to graft an aristocratic edifice on the United States. "By 1816 Madison was far more certain than he could possibly have been twenty years earlier that the nature of American government was firmly free, united, and republican ... and that the benefits of union and national power sought in the seventeen-eighties could safely be pursued by the federal government operating under the Constitution," Ketcham writes. Another biographer, Garry Wills, adds a second reason. "What Madison was forced unconsciously to adopt was not an ideology but a historic phenomenon—modernity." The world was changing, and Madison and the Republicans realized that their proposals needed to also change to keep up with the times, especially the emergence of a market economy.[14]

The Beginning of a Market Economy

As Madison prepared to leave office and Monroe assumed the presidency, America was on the cusp of radical change in its economy, change that would create a new and divergent national character in the North that differed markedly from that in the South. Urban areas would begin to expand, industrialization would be spurred by new inventions, subsistence farming would gradually be replaced by farmers tied to markets, and the cultural gap between the South and the rest of the country would widen.

But this was all in the coming years. "Life in America in 1815 was dirty, smelly, laborious, and uncomfortable," Howe writes. Average life spans were short, about forty-five years for both men and women. Family farms were the norm, in which food was grown for consumption, and surplus produce was just beginning to be sold into the marketplace, at least for those near to modes of transportation. There was little by way of money, and people bartered their goods with their neighbors. Local shopkeepers kept account books to track what was owed to them. Most clothing was made by women working in their home. Land was widely distributed, which "affirmed a resolute egalitarianism among white men," Howe writes. The sense of equality also helped foster a widening democratic society. Neighbors were tied together by small towns that grew up around farms and by the practice of a common religion, which would soon undergo a major revival.[15]

Population was increasing rapidly and had roughly doubled to 8.4 million people since 1790. However, due to inadequate transportation systems, most people still lived along the Eastern Seaboard, this despite the ever-increasing movement westward. "Almost one-half of the population lived in the Northeast, and it was in this region ... that urbanization and the resulting commercial market were most highly developed," economic historian Douglass C. North has written. As we have seen, the Napoleonic Wars had spurred the carrying trade and the rise of port cities by 1815. "The focal points of most urban economics were still the dock, the wharf, the warehouse and the counting house," in places like Boston, New York, Philadelphia, and Baltimore, according to Leonard Richards. The embargo and the War of 1812 had also seen the first industrial development in the United States.[16]

Labor had largely been split between the unskilled, who worked for low wages, and artisans who tended to be independent producers operating from their own shops or homes. Under protection from the embargo and then the war, a gradual transformation occurred where larger factories began to operate in the Northeast, especially in New England. These factories relied on a division of labor to produce clothing, shoes, furniture, and other items that could be produced on a mass scale. Women and children were the primary employees of these early factories. The most successful of these was the textile mill begun by the Boston Manufacturing Company that began production in 1813. In the aftermath of the War of 1812, Great Britain began to dump large quantities of goods into the American market. By 1816, many inefficient manufacturers were put out of business, although the Boston Manufacturing Company was able to compete with the British. They were assisted by the tariff that Congress approved in April of 1816. By 1820, the British had begun to focus more on the Latin American market, easing the pressure on domestic manufacturing, which once again began to expand.[17]

Entrepreneurship and innovation occurred, with new inventions that began to transform society. The first successful steamboat had begun operations in 1807, which opened up farming in more remote areas near inland waterways, especially the Mississippi River, and allowed for "wheat, cotton and other bulky commodities" to be sold to commercial markets. The invention of the cotton gin led to the expansion of both large plantations and slavery in the Southern portions of the Louisiana Territory. High wages, at least in comparison to England, fostered further innovations and the introduction of labor-saving devices in the industrial sector. Improvements in paper manufacturing and the expansion of the postal system led to the wider dissemination of newspapers and books. Libraries began to open, "which helped fuel the expansion of a print culture that itself became an integral part of a national identity rooted in the free and aggressive exchange of opinion," Appleby writes.[18]

The lack of infrastructure, or internal improvements as used in those days, was a major barrier to expansion. While President Monroe was an affirmed nationalist, he agreed with Madison that a constitutional amendment was needed to provide the federal government with the authority to undertake such improvements. Surprisingly, it wasn't as if the federal government had never undertaken any major capital projects. In 1802, Congress had devoted public-land sales in Ohio to build the National Road, which eventually ran from Baltimore to Indiana. Yet when "Congress passed a bill in 1822 to authorize the collection of tolls on the National Road, thereby making it self-funding, Monroe vetoed it," according to Howe. In the aftermath of this action, Monroe requested and received an advisory opinion from the Supreme Court that stated that the federal government had the power to undertake internal improvements. Some in the South agreed with this, including both Clay and Calhoun. Still, there were others that feared that if the federal government could build infrastructure, it could also interfere with slavery. One of the old-line Republicans warned that "if Congress possesses the power to do what is proposed in this bill, they may emancipate the slaves." The bill he was referring to would have undertaken a general survey for what internal improvements were needed.[19]

While the federal government was immobilized in its attempts to upgrade the nation's infrastructure, states began to pick up the slack. As early as 1794, Pennsylvania had built the Lancaster Turnpike, which connected Philadelphia to Lancaster. "By 1816 turnpikes linked the major cities in the Northeast and formed a continuous line from Maine to Georgia," David S. Reynolds writes. The largest project during this period was construction of the Erie Canal. The National Road had given Baltimore an advantage in terms of trade, but a canal that ran from Lake Erie down the Hudson River to New York City would level the playing field. The Erie Canal began in 1817 and was completed eight years later at a cost of just over $7 million. Tolls from its operation repaid New York's investment within nine years. The canal also "facilitated the settlement of Northern Ohio, Indiana, and Illinois by people of Yankee extraction moving west," according to Howe. The Midwest would balance the expansion of slavery in the Southwest.[20]

Cotton, the Economy, and the Divergence between North and South

What really fueled the growth of the American economy in the postwar years was cotton. In 1796, cotton had represented 2.2 percent of US exports. By 1820, this had grown to 32 percent. Great Britain's demand for cotton drove the price upward, from twenty cents a pound in 1815 to a high of thirty-five cents in 1818. The rise in price led to the expansion of lending and credit toward the purchase of ever larger amounts of land in the Southwest to accommodate the growing demand for the product. As a result of the expansion of their populations, Mississippi and Alabama were added as states in 1817 and 1819. By 1820, American cotton production was ten times higher than it had been in 1800.[21] As we saw in chapter 3, the growth of cotton production gave slavery a new lease on life. Slaves were sold from the older Southern states like Maryland and Virginia and transported under terrible conditions. Slaves were typically transported in winter when they weren't needed to work the fields and traveled "up to twenty-five miles a day and [slept] on the ground," according to Howe. Families were often separated during the process. "Conditions of slave labor generally worsened in newly settled areas, where there was much backbreaking work to be done clearing the land and little of the paternalism that could soften the brutality of the 'peculiar institution' among the planter aristocracy of more stable regions," Howe writes.[22]

The historian Edward E. Baptist describes how the growth in cotton production in the American South fueled Western capitalism, both in England and in the North. "The global economy was launching an unexpected and unprecedented process of growth that has continued to the present day." Great Britain was the first major beneficiary of this, converting cotton fabric from a luxury good to a product used by the masses and in the process enriching English factory owners. American investment in factories in the North was also underway, although it lagged behind the British. The Mississippi valley was crucial in this process, providing the land needed to grow cotton and fuel this growth, which was built on the expansion of slavery. Large banks, like England's Baring Brothers, along with state-chartered banks, made available the financing and credit that made this expansion possible. The Second Bank of the United States further contributed to what was increasingly an emerging bubble that was developing, "allowing credit to slosh into every cranny of the expanding nation," Baptist writes.[23]

While there was an integration occurring between the North's business success in creating new factories and the expansion of the shipping industry, which was built on the South's production of cotton, there was an emerging cultural divide between the two regions.[24] In many ways, the South had always been different. Its land and climate were suitable for growing staple crops like tobacco, rice, and indigo, which led to the use of slave labor, large plantations, and an aristocratic lifestyle. Still, Southerners were at the forefront of the break from England, combining with the New Englanders, who they had almost nothing in common with, to launch the American Revolution. Washington led the Continental Army, while Jefferson worked with Adams to compose the Declaration of Independence, which had become the American Creed. James Madison and the Virginians combined their efforts with those of the Pennsylvania delegates to dominate the early days of the Constitutional Convention and create a new and more powerful central government that was one of the keys to creating a new nation out of thirteen disparate states. In the aftermath of the ratification of the Constitution, the North was just beginning to eliminate slavery, and the moral issue had not become paramount, as the debates at the convention revealed. The founding generation left some major unfinished business, particularly over the issue of slavery and where sovereignty would be located between the states and the federal government. The Republican Party was initially born as a Southern movement by Jefferson and Madison to oppose Hamilton's economic policies, which they saw as both inimical to the South and to rural and agrarian interests regardless of location. But by the time Jefferson was elected president in 1800, the Republican Party had adherents throughout the Union, "a fact that may have also retarded the growth of a distinctively Southern political mind-set," argues historian James C. Cobb. But by the 1820s, the South had begun to move away from the national experiment that some of its leaders had done so much to bring about.[25]

Joyce Appleby, one of the foremost experts on development of our national character during the period, attributes the divergence in part to "the passing of the Revolutionary generation of Southerners who had condemned slavery" and who had shared an "understanding of why human chattel contradicted American values" of liberty and equality. She also argues that the different labor systems found in the two regions, one dependent on slavery, the other free labor, contributed to the split between the two regions. The North became a land of "more diverse opportunities in farming, manufacturing and trade," even for those who held little property, where "an unfettered spirit of inquiry [and] personal independence" ruled. "The slave economy maintained an entrenched elite at the top of Southern society," retarding progress toward democracy. While much of the South was made up of small farmers, many of these owned some slaves, and their racist views (which were also prevalent in the North) put them in alignment with the large plantation owners. There also was some opposition to slavery among small farmers of the upper South. Many of these people were Quakers, although there was also a mix of Methodists and Baptists as well who opposed slavery on religious grounds. "By the 1820s, however, this premarket abolitionism was in headlong retreat before a resurgent slavery," one historian writes. Many of these people would eventually leave the upper South to live in free states. This included Thomas Lincoln, Abraham's father, who moved his family from Kentucky to Illinois.[26]

Southerners looked at the system of Northern capitalism that was emerging as crass, while they looked upon their own lifestyle as "genteel, warm, and stable [because] they did not engage in the hard bargaining and unremitting application to business that characterized for them the Yankees' way of life," Appleby writes. They viewed Northerners as "money mad." The differences in viewpoint led one opponent of slavery to observe that there was almost a "national difference of character between the people of the Northern and the people of the Southern States."[27]

While the North began to urbanize and small towns sprang up to serve local farmers, much of the South remained rather desolate. Thomas Jefferson's granddaughter questioned why Virginia had fallen so far behind compared to New England, where she had lived. "The difference, she perceptively saw, was not a matter of profits, but of spirit, of raw energy, and confidence about the future," observes Appleby. Another observer ascribed the differing conditions to the impact of absentee landlords in Alabama, where plantations were run by overseers. "The more fertile the land the more destitute is the country of villages and towns," since the plantation provided all the goods that slaves needed. Slave owners also did not invest in education. By 1850, the South "had less than one-third as many public schools, one-fourth as many pupils, one-twentieth as many public libraries, and one-sixth as many volumes in those libraries," according to North.[28]

One can see during this period a broad divergence in the concept of what makes American a nation. In the North, nationhood was beginning to be defined as an idea tied to those natural rights expressed by Jefferson in the Declaration of Independence. In 1824 one Northern congressman said that America offered a moral example to the world, "a model by which the rights of men may be secured, and the benefit of good government may be obtained ... " However, despite the movement to eradicate slavery in the North, free blacks were increasingly denied the ability to vote, and the expansion of rights was reserved for white men. Racism was a reality in the North. In the South, the concept of nationhood would follow the Jacksonian model that is more closely tied to race and clan. Northerners may also have been complicit in the growing divide between the two regions. James C. Cobb argues that Northern writers showed "the South as an oppositional other situated within the nation's physical boundaries but embodying everything the United States was not about." Ultimately, the regions began to define themselves in opposition to each other. "Simply put, where Southerners have staked their claim to a distinctive regional identity defined in contrast to the North, Northerners have been more likely to characterize their own identity as simply 'American' and define that in contrast with the South," Cobb argues.[29]

The Twin Crisis

Two separate crises would roil the Era of Good Feelings. One would strike at the very core of the nation's politics, the other at its emerging economic system.

"Like a fire-bell in the night, [it] awakened and filled me with terror," Jefferson wrote. He was referring to a February 1819 resolution in the House of Representatives that would ban new slaves from entering Missouri and free all slaves born after its admission to the Union when they reached the age of twenty-five. The resolution caused a rift between the North and the South that would continue, in one form or another, until the Civil War. Up until this point, new states were admitted that were either free or slave in equal number, thereby maintaining a balance of power between the two regions in the Congress. The Missouri resolution may have been partially meant to maintain this balance, since the newly admitted state of Illinois was represented by two pro-slavery senators. "In practical terms, there was an argument to be made that by admitting neighboring Missouri as a slave state, the pro-slavery bloc in the Senate would enjoy not a two-vote majority but a four-vote majority," Wilentz writes.[30]

But the debate that ensued in Congress, which lasted but a few days near the end of the fifteenth session, revealed a widening gap between Northerners and Southerners on the morality of slavery. This differed markedly from the debates that took place during the drafting of the Constitution, which tended to have a transactional focus to them. For example, Northern delegates at the convention were willing to accept a provision continuing the slave trade until 1808 in exchange for a less restrictive provision on navigation acts that controlled tariffs and quotas on the shipping industry. For the Northern representatives, who were a mix of Republicans and the few remaining Federalists, the debate that was unleashed hinged in part on Jefferson's own words from the Declaration of Independence. "If all men were created equal, as Jefferson said, then slaves, as men, were born free and entitled to life, liberty and the pursuit of happiness under any truly republican government," as Wilentz succinctly summarizes the view of the Northern representatives. They argued that the founders had allowed slavery to continue as a local and not a national right in part because they expected it "would fade away, not proliferate." One member of the House from Massachusetts said that Congress had the "right and duty" to end the spread "of the intolerable evil and the crying enormity of slavery."[31]

Southerners saw the issue differently. They reacted to what they viewed as a dangerous argument that was being put forward by the representatives of the North: to restrict and perhaps ultimately eliminate slavery. They grounded their position in that of states' rights. Since "Congress had no power to interfere with slavery in the states where it already existed, so it was powerless to do so in the new states just gaining admission," Wilentz states. Each state should be allowed to enter the Union on an equal basis, with the public able to choose whether slavery existed or not through popular sovereignty. Some even went so far as to state that slavery was a positive good. "The whole commerce between master and slave is patriarchal," according a senator from South Carolina, and could be justified based on the Bible. More moderate Southerners like Jefferson and Madison, who knew that slavery was wrong, made the case that the dispersion of slavery over a larger area would be beneficial. "Diffusion over a greater surface would make them individually happier, and proportionally facilitate the accomplishment of their emancipation, by dividing the burden on a greater number of coadjustors." It was hardly a convincing argument, since the spread of slavery was making it more difficult to end the practice, and transporting blacks was leading to the breakup of families and the very harsh conditions that accompanied their movement. Jefferson also rationalized the entire debate by blaming his old enemies, the Federalists, for pushing forward the restrictions on slavery in the new territories. Referring to them as the "Hartford convention men," he thought that they were using "auspices of morality" to regain power. But, in fact, it was a bipartisan effort to restrict slavery by both Republicans and those few remaining Federalists.[32]

The House approved the Missouri resolutions on a vote of 82–78. Voting was along sectional lines, with the North in support by a vote of 80–14, and the South opposing it 64–2. But the resolutions died in the Senate, when pro-slavery senators from Illinois and Indiana joined with the Southerners to defeat them. The Congress adjourned, unable to resolve the issue of Missouri statehood. Antislavery sentiment spread throughout the North in the aftermath of the vote. "Public meetings, organized by local luminaries, assembled in virtually every major town and city from Maine to New Jersey and as far west as Illinois to cheer pro-restrictionist speakers, pass anti-slavery resolutions, draft circular letters demanding a free Missouri, and instruct their representatives to stand fast," according to Wilentz.[33]

But 1819 was not 1860, and the movement to restrict slavery was but the opening shot in a political war that would go on for the next forty years. Many of the debates that took place in the just-ended congressional session anticipated the great Lincoln-Douglas debate, with one man maintaining that no nation conceived in liberty could allow slavery to expand, and the other man maintaining it was an issue that should be resolved through popular sovereignty. All of this was still to come, and a compromise was still possible, although it was not easy. Maine's request to be admitted to the Union as a free state opened the door to the Missouri Compromise in early 1820. The two admissions were linked together in the Senate, with an additional proviso added that slavery be prohibited in the rest of the Louisiana Territory at the southern boundary of Missouri. While the bill passed the Senate, it ran into a roadblock in the House. Henry Clay feared "that within five years from this time the Union would be divided into three distinct confederacies." He used his very substantial parliamentary skills to move the Senate bill forward in the House. Knowing he could not get a majority vote for the combined bill, he split it into two parts. Eighteen Northern representatives joined with the solid South to pass the admission of Missouri without any restrictions on slavery on a vote of 90–87. A different majority passed the second part of the bill dealing with the restriction of slavery in the balance of the northern portion of the Louisiana Territory on a vote of 134–42, with members from the Deep South and Virginia in opposition. President Monroe, who played no active role in the whole debate over Missouri, signed the bill.[34]

It was also in 1820, at the height of the Missouri crisis, that a new term entered the American political lexicon: doughface. "It referred to Northerners who catered to Southern interests," according to historian Joanne B. Freeman. Southerners used this term to derisively describe those from the North that they cajoled and bullied to go along with legislation that protected or expanded slavery. While those from the South needed the support of a few Northern congressmen and senators to achieve their ends, they viewed those who supported them as supplicants and cowards. "I knew they would give way. They were scared at their own dough faces—yes, they were scared of their own dough faces!" one Southerner said. The bullying of Northern legislators by their Southern counterparts would increasingly occur in the 1830s and 1840s, as disputes over slavery became more tense.[35]

While Jefferson was wrong in his assessment that it was the Federalists who had created the Missouri crisis, he was correct in his fear of the results. "I considered it at once as the knell of the union. It is hushed, indeed, for the moment. But this is a reprieve only, not a final sentence," Jefferson wrote in an 1820 letter. For now, the South was happy that the Missouri Compromise had established the principle that slavery could not be restricted by the federal government in opposition to the popular will of a state. Overt disputes between the North and the South over slavery would be quelled until the 1850s. But the issue would lurk beneath the surface and any "hope for a moderate, peaceful resolution of America's number one social problem dimmed," Howe writes. During this period, there was also some support in both regions for the emancipation of black people, but only if it were accompanied by colonization somewhere else, preferably Africa. The idea that blacks and whites could somehow live together in a biracial society was considered impossible. The slave uprising in Santo Domingo was still fresh in the minds of many Southerners. When Denmark Vesey, a free black man living in Charleston, South Carolina, threatened a slave revolt in 1822, the fear of free blacks living near whites gave credence to Jefferson's warning. The American Colonization Society was founded in 1816, and both James Madison and Henry Clay served as its president. But the concept of colonizing blacks was a fanciful proposal that would later come under attack in the 1830s by the abolitionist William Lloyd Garrison.[36]

The Missouri Compromise, along with the Panic of 1819, would eventually contribute to the breakup of the grand Republican coalition that had ushered in a period of one-party rule. This would take some time, but the fissures were beginning to emerge between those who supported a strong central government and a broad construction of the Constitution, and those who favored states' rights and a strict constructionist approach. The approach of the latter would increasingly be used, not as a protection for liberty, as Jefferson envisioned, but as a defense of slavery. The role of government in American society was the oldest and most long-running debate, one that continues to our day.[37]

*   *   *

The second crisis was the Panic of 1819. It was the first but certainly not the last time that a general depression would affect the lives of people throughout the country. With the coming of a market economy, people were now exposed to the risks of the business cycle. A drop in the price for cotton, caused by its rapidly expanding supply fueled by the extension of credit by state banks for land purchases in the South and West, initially triggered the panic. The price for cotton fell from a high of 32.5 cents in October of 1818 to a low of 14 cents. The price for other agricultural products also fell, causing major hardship in the newly expanding West, where "crops rotted in the fields" and foreclosures and bankruptcies became commonplace. "The Great Migration itself ground to halt, since people could not afford to buy land," according to Howe.[38]

The BUS made matters worse. It was designed initially to rein in the state banks, which had generated too many loans without adequate reserves, thereby creating inflation and a speculative bubble in land and commodity prices. But instead, the BUS also made too many loans under its first director. In 1819, he was replaced by Landon Cheves, who clamped down on loans just as commodities prices collapsed. Cheves turned "what might have been a sharp recession into a prolonged and disastrous depression," Wilentz writes. The bank expanded credit when it should have contracted it, and when the crash ensued, it then contracted credit, making matters worse.[39]

In response to the panic, the federal government was lobbied for help. Manufacturing industries and those dependent on them, "including workers and the neighboring farmers who supplied them supported the manufacturers' demands for sharp tariff protection," writes historian Charles Sellers. While the House passed legislation increasing tariffs, Southerners defeated it in the Senate by one vote. The government also reduced the price for western land from $2 to $1.25 per acre, but no one had money to buy it. In addition, Congress relaxed repayment terms for those who had borrowed to purchase land. The federal budget was reduced as well, including military expenditures.[40]

The Panic of 1819 led to an antibank climate not too dissimilar to those that would occur during future financial collapses. Proposals were made "for the partial or total elimination of [a] paper-money system." Such proposals split the Republicans even further, with those who supported a strong financial system, known as the New Schoolers, pitted against the Old School faction, who were really the original Jeffersonian Republicans. The Old Schoolers came to "regard the banking and paper-money system as a monstrous engine of oppression," Wilentz states. And part of their ire was directed at John

Marshall and the Supreme Court, whose latest decision in *McCulloch v. Maryland* had further raised tensions, especially in light of other court decisions that had done so much to lay the legal precedent for the emerging capitalist economy.[41]

Marshall, the Supreme Court, and Nationalism

No other chief justice has had the influence of John Marshall. When he was appointed by President Adams late in 1800, the Supreme Court was little more than a backwater. Marshall would transform the court into a co-equal branch of government by firmly establishing the principle of judicial review, that the Supreme Court is responsible for interpreting the Constitution.

John Marshall was born in the backcountry of Virginia in September of 1755. His father's family was of Welsh descent, while his mother traced her roots to the famous Randolph clan, which made Thomas Jefferson his cousin. The two men would engage in lifelong rivalry. John was the eldest son in a family of fifteen children raised in humble circumstances. While his father, Thomas, eventually became rich, this did not occur until later in his life, after John left home. Marshall was largely educated at home, although he briefly attended a school with James Monroe, and the two became friends. When the Revolutionary War broke out, Marshall served alongside his father in the Virginia militia. He wintered at Valley Forge, sharing a cabin with Monroe. "There is no question ... that the war, and especially the duty at Valley Forge, helped to form Marshall's character," one of his biographers writes. It was during this period that his commitment to America as a nation was formed. "I was confirmed in the habit of considering America as my country and Congress as my government," Marshall wrote.[42]

In 1779, Marshall took a leave of absence from the army and began to study law under the scholar George Wythe, who had also trained Jefferson. He went on to establish a very successful law practice in Richmond in the 1780s and fell in love with and married Polly Ambler. The Amblers were descendants of the French Huguenots that had fled France during the religious war in the 1500s. Marshall also served for a time in the Virginia legislature, and saw that the states were the reason that the army had been neglected during the war, which strengthened his nationalism.[43]

When Shays' Rebellion broke out in western Massachusetts, it helped convince the Confederation Congress to call for a convention to amend the Articles of Confederation. Instead, the delegates to the Constitutional Convention that met in Philadelphia in the summer of 1787 wrote a whole plan of government. Marshall became a firm supporter, helping to shepherd the creation of a special ratifying convention through the Virginia legislature. When Patrick Henry attempted to provide the ratifying convention with a mandate to pursue amendments to the document, Marshall offered a proposal that allowed for the "full and free investigation" of the new Constitution without committing or precluding amendments. Marshall and the other strong Federalists feared that an endless round of proposed amendments from the states would doom the document. Marshall's support of the Constitution was tied to his fear of "the excessive power of the various state legislatures and their tendency to serve the interests of a growing call of debtors," his biographer Jean Edward Smith writes, and to his belief in the need to establish a strong court system to protect private property and the sanctity of contracts. The ratifying convention was dominated by men like Henry and Madison, but at one point Marshall debated his old friend Monroe, who opposed the Constitution. It was a lawyerly speech that revealed Marshall's view of a broad construction of the Constitution. "What are the objects of the national government? To protect the United States and to promote the general welfare," Marshall argued.[44]

Marshall remained a private citizen for most of the 1790s, until John Adams coaxed him to participate in the negotiation with France in 1797 that culminated in the XYZ affair. Like Adams, Marshall was a moderate federalist. "The key to his politics lay in his nationalism, not his partisanship," Smith states. As a member of Congress, Marshall stood with Adams against both the High Federalists and the Republicans. "Adams, it often seemed, was bereft of a true political friend in all of Philadelphia—except John Marshall," James F. Simon has argued. Adams rewarded him by making him secretary of state in the aftermath of the firing of the members of his cabinet who were more loyal to Hamilton. In the aftermath of Jefferson's 1800 election victory, Adams appointed Marshall as the chief justice of the Supreme Court in the months before Jefferson assumed the office, even though he had no judicial experience.[45]

*** *** ***

"May I have the favor of your attendance to administer the oath?" Jefferson wrote to his cousin in March of 1801. Marshall replied immediately. "I shall with much pleasure attend to administer the oath of office." It was surprising that these two men, such political opposites, would put aside their differences in order to ensure a peaceful transfer of power. There were both personal and political reasons for their hatred of each other. "Jefferson, for his part, thought Marshall was a hypocrite," Smith writes. Jefferson also saw Marshall as part of the Federalist leadership that wanted to institute a monarchical government in the United States. Marshall, for his part, could not forgive Jefferson for his treatment of Washington, acting duplicitous while he occupied a position in the administration. Marshall also feared that Jefferson would weaken the presidency by deferring to the legislative branch. "By weakening the office of President he will increase his personal power," Marshall wrote. With Hamilton out of power, and soon to die at the hands of Aaron Burr in Weehawken, New Jersey, it would be Jefferson and Marshall who would carry on the dispute over the future direction of the nation. "Jefferson opposed an energetic central government as a danger to individual liberty," Smith writes, while "Marshall saw the government in Washington as the keystone of national well-being."[46]

Today, we consider it apparent, almost a truism, that the Supreme Court always decided on the constitutionality of laws passed by Congress and actions of the executive branch. But this was not the case when Marshall became chief justice. The Constitution was viewed as a "political document" and both Congress and the president "maintained primary responsibility for its interpretation," according to Smith. This was Jefferson's view, who feared that giving the court the sole power of judicial review "would make the judiciary a despotic branch." But starting with the famous case of *Marbury v. Madison*, Marshall established this precedent, at least within the sphere of the court's jurisdiction.[47]

The facts of the case were straightforward. In one of his last acts, Adams had appointed several Federalists as justices of the peace, as a way to keep control of the courts from Jefferson and the Republicans. The commissions for these midnight appointments, as they came to be known, were not all delivered by Madison before he left the office of secretary of state. One of them was to go to William Marbury. Jefferson directed that the commission not be delivered, and Marbury sued, requesting that the Supreme Court direct Madison to issue his commission.[48]

The Marbury decision came down during a period of controversy over the court system. The Federalist Congress had passed the Judiciary Act of 1801, which expanded the jurisdiction of federal courts over state courts. Republicans were opposed to the act, in large part because federal courts favored "creditors, absentee landowners, and the commercial establishment" over small farmers and artisans. Marshall had been attempting to tamp down disputes with the new Republican majority, yet he also wanted to establish the court as a co-equal branch of government. He also truly believed that the courts should be nonpartisan. He needed to craft a clever opinion that achieved his objectives, which he did in an opinion that was nothing short of brilliant. He first established that Marbury had a vested legal right to the commission, which made the Federalists happy. Had he stopped there, and directed that the commission be granted, Madison would likely have ignored the order, showing that the court had no power. Instead, Marshall ruled that the Supreme Court had no jurisdiction over the case, since the Constitution only gave the court original jurisdiction (as opposed to appellate jurisdiction) in limited cases "affecting ambassadors, other public ministers and consuls, and those in which a state shall be a party." Even though Congress had granted the Supreme Court jurisdiction to issue writs of *mandamas* (an order from a superior court to an inferior one), it had exceeded its constitutional authority. "It is emphatically the province and duty of the judicial department to say what the law is," Marshall wrote. With these words, Marshall established the principle of judicial review. But as Jean Edward Smith argues, it was not an unlimited power.

Marshall did not say that the Supreme Court was the ultimate arbiter of the Constitution. He did not say that the authority to interpret the Constitution rested exclusively with the Court, and he certainly did not endorse the grandiose schemes that envisaged the Supreme Court as a board of review sitting in judgement on each act of Congress to determine its constitutionality. He simply stated that the Constitution was law, and that as a judicial matter, it could be interpreted by the Court in cases that came before it.[49]

Marshall had avoided a constitutional crisis and removed the court from the partisan wars that were going on. Neither the Federalists nor Jefferson protested the decision at the time. In fact, the Marbury decision probably squared closely with Jefferson's own view that "each branch of government had a right to decide for itself on the constitutionality of matters before it." It was only later that Jefferson denounced the decision.[50]

The Marshall Court went on to establish precedents on the supremacy of federal courts over state authority, and that restrained states from interfering in an individual's acquisition of private property, which lay at the heart of the market revolution that was going on. In the words of one of his biographers, it was "a vital restatement of the Constitution's underlying Lockean premise that government was limited and that property, along with life and liberty, was one of the unalienable rights the law was designed to protect." Each of the major cases was decided without dissent. It was a tribute to Marshall's ability to work closely with his colleagues and to forge consensus. When he first joined the court, Marshall had arranged to have the jurists live together during the term of the session, which built cohesion among the members. In 1819, the court issued perhaps its most important opinion in the case of *McCullough v. Maryland*.[51]

The case arose from the financial Panic of 1819. Outraged over the role the BUS had played in contributing to the depression, Maryland levied a tax on the Baltimore branch. The bank refused to pay, and the case landed at the Supreme Court. The oral argument took nine days, and the parties to the suit were represented by the best legal minds in the country. Daniel Webster was the lead attorney for the bank. Born in New Hampshire, Webster had originally flirted with nullification during the War of 1812, but by the time of the McCullough case he was beginning to develop a reputation as a nationalist and a strong supporter of the federal government. He was known as a great orator, and by 1850 stated, "I was born an American; I will live an American; I shall die an American." In part swayed by Webster, the Marshall Court sided with the bank, finding that the state tax was unconstitutional. In reaching this decision, the court established the following precedents:[52]

> ❯ That the Constitution was a compact among the people of the country, not one between the states. "The government of the Union ... is, emphatically and truly, a government of the people. In form and substance it emanates from them," Marshall wrote.

> ❯ That the Constitution should be interpreted in a broad manner, and that the document bestowed "implied powers." Echoing the words of Hamilton, Marshall wrote: "Let the end be legitimate, let it be within the scope of the Constitution, and all means which are appropriate, which are plainly adapted to that end, which are not prohibited ... are constitutional."

> That the "power to tax is the power to destroy."
> Therefore, the states had no authority "to retard, impede,
> burden, or in any manner control the operations of the
> constitutional laws enacted by Congress to carry into
> execution the powers vested in the general government."

The McCullough case upheld the principle of national supremacy. But the court decision was not without controversy. States'-rights advocates published a series of newspaper articles attacking Marshall's decision. Jefferson sided with the states'-rights advocates, even agreeing that the Supreme Court should have no jurisdiction over the states. This was too much for Madison. Although he thought Marshall had overreached in his decision, he corrected his mentor, indicating that the convention had "intended the Authority vested in the Judicial Department as a final resort in relation to the States" and "that the federal Constitution & laws shall be the supreme law of the land, and that the Judicial Power of the U.S. shall extend to all cases arising under them." But the debate over federal versus state power would go on.[53]

Foreign Policy, John Quincy Adams, and the Monroe Doctrine

President Monroe's foreign policy was an activist one. Part of this was intentional, and part may have been thrust upon him. One of his biographers notes that Monroe was the "first national security president, whose consistent underlying motivation was to expand and establish the borders of the United States and to make it the dominant power in the Western Hemisphere, free of European interference." Peace among the European powers in the aftermath of the Napoleonic Wars certainly helped in this regard, as did the weakness of the Spanish, who were losing their hold on the New World. He was also aided by the ever-able John Quincy Adams, the son of the second president.

John Quincy Adams (JQA)

His portrait as an old man stares out, stern and unsmiling, providing a glimpse of his upbringing and his own sense that he could never meet the expectations thrust upon him. Born the second child of John and Abigail on July 11, 1767, he was called Johnny. While his father was away planning a revolution, young Johnny was raised primarily by his mother until he was ten years old. She was a stern taskmaster who instilled in the young man the need to pursue "moral purity" and "to seek the good and abhor the bad," as one of his biographers, James Traub, frames it. When he was eight years old, he accompanied his mother to see the battle of Bunker Hill, where their close family friend Dr. Joseph Warren was killed. Perhaps it was at this point that Johnny began to see "that a life properly lived required commitment to principle, sacrifice, and suffering," Traub writes.[54]

When Johnny turned ten, his father was assigned to represent the United States in Europe and took his son with him. The senior Adams also had high expectations for his son, but he was also "affable and relaxed" with his children. Father and son developed a strong bond during their time together overseas. For most of the next seven years, JQA traveled to Paris, St. Petersburg, and Amsterdam, where he attended Leyden University. He became fluent in French; learned Greek, Latin, and geometry; and developed skills as a writer. Much of what we know of John Quincy Adams comes from a diary he began as an eleven-year-old and which he maintained for the next seventy years. In the aftermath of the Revolutionary War, Jefferson joined John Adams in Paris, and Quincy "hero worshipped" him. In 1785, JQA was admitted to Harvard and returned to the United States.[55]

Admitted as an upperclassman, JQA quickly sped through college, and would later recall it as one of the happiest times of his life, "when he could grow intellectually," according to Paul C. Nagel's biography. After graduating in 1788, he began to study law. The young JQA fell in a deep depression, perhaps in part caused by the exceedingly high expectations that his parents held for him. His early career as a lawyer was less than successful, and he needed to borrow money from his father to stay afloat financially. He also fell in love, but since he could not yet support a family, the relationship ended.[56]

Involvement in public affairs finally saved him. In 1791, Thomas Paine published *The Rights of Man*, which extolled not just the virtues of the French Revolution, but all revolutions. Like his father, JQA had an abiding fear of mob rule, which revolutions could devolve into. In a series of newspaper articles, Adams challenged Paine and the concept of abolishing "any form of government it finds inconvenient," which "struck him as a form of madness." He argued that a republic did not need to be subject to violent revolutions, since representative government is capable of reforming itself. The articles were so well structured that both Jefferson and Madison assumed that John Adams had written them. JQA also defended President Washington in a series of letters to a Federalist newspaper in Boston in response to the out-of-control French foreign minister, Edmond-Charles Genet, who was recruiting Americans to assist with France's war with England and Spain. Genet condemned Washington for his proclamation of neutrality between the sides. When Washington found out that Quincy Adams was the author of the letters, he appointed him as minister to Holland.[57]

JQA spent the next seven years in Europe and was directly exposed to the ongoing European war. From his perch at The Hague, with the Dutch homeland now occupied by France, he became convinced that states must act solely out of their own interests, and that for the United States to survive, it would need "to have the force required to repel predators." A strong proponent of Washington's policy of neutrality, Adams also supported the controversial Jay Treaty with Great Britain. Biographer Traub argues that JQA's diplomatic dispatches provided "firsthand evidence of the perilous consequences of forsaking neutrality [and] played a crucial role in the forging of the first generation of American foreign policy."[58]

During a trip to London to oversee the ratification of the Jay Treaty, Adams fell in love for a second time. His first experience with love had broken his heart, but this time would be different. He had begun to spend a lot of time with the family of Joshua Johnson, an American who was living in London. Adams courted the youngest daughter, Louisa, and married her on July 26, 1797. Their engagement had been rocky, with JQA attempting numerous times to put off the marriage. Although they would stay married for fifty years, it was indicative of what the future would hold for them. "Adams was stiff; dominant, especially toward females; and rarely could take teasing," Nagel writes. "Louisa was clever, occasionally lighthearted, and impatient with male pretentiousness." Together they departed for Berlin, where President Adams assigned his son as minister to Prussia.[59]

The son watched as his father lost the election of 1800 to Jefferson. Now a father himself, he returned with his family to Boston and resumed his legal career. But his "years in Europe ... had spoiled him for the routine of an ordinary man," Nagel writes, and he began his political career by being elected to the Massachusetts state senate in 1802. He held the view of the founding generation that he could stand above partisanship and act the part of the statesman. He ran for Congress but lost and was appointed by the state legislature to the US Senate in February of 1803. Though a nominal federalist, while in Washington he was often the guest of President Jefferson. But he now had a more realistic view of the man he once revered, sharing in his parents' view of Jefferson's duplicity. He supported the president's acquisition of the Louisiana Purchase, "although it is made in direct violation of the Constitution," and took positions on other issues that were neither purely Federalist nor Republican. "He would not barter votes or join coalitions or make small sacrifices of principle in order to win large victories," Traub notes, which made him a difficult man for other politicians to work with.[60]

Adams was also hard on himself, which led to periods of depression when his life did not seem to meet his own expectations or those of his parents. In 1794, his father had warned him that "if you do not rise to head not only your profession, but of your country, it will be owing to your *Laziness, Slovenliness,* and *Obstinacy.*" In 1805, he was struggling with his finances, but his mood brightened when he was named the Boylston Professor of Rhetoric and Oratory at Harvard, a position that had been endowed by his grandmother. He also retained his Senate seat and split his time between Cambridge and Washington. As the nation became ever more enmeshed in the Napoleonic Wars, Adams sided with the Republicans on Jefferson's embargo. "Simply put, Adams was the boldest and most consequential American nationalist of his time," Wilentz finds, which is why he sided with Jefferson. He even attended the Republican caucus that nominated Madison to replace Jefferson. His actions alienated his constituents back home, even though JQA always maintained that he was "governed solely by public considerations." This even led to a rebuke from his mother, and ultimately cost him his Senate seat. Madison appointed him minister to Russia, where he would spend the next eight years.[61]

In 1814, Adams joined Henry Clay and Albert Gallatin in Ghent for the peace talks with Great Britain. He and Clay bickered constantly over the terms of a peace treaty, with Gallatin playing the peacemaker. When the British finally realized that continuing the war was too costly, the Treaty of Ghent was signed. Adams would spend the next two years as minister to Great Britain, before returning to the United States to serve as Monroe's secretary of state.[62]

The Problem and Opportunity of Florida

Henry Clay was angry. The position of secretary of state was one that Prince Hal coveted, since it was the senior cabinet position and had become the stepping-stone to the presidency. Monroe was striving for regional balance in his cabinet, and his selection of JQA, who was an experienced diplomat, was meant to keep New England in the fold. To placate Clay, the president offered him secretary of war, which Clay turned down. Clay would attempt to "cripple, if not shatter, the administration of James Monroe," and events in Florida would give him a chance to do that. It would also lead to a rift with Andrew Jackson that would dog the two men for the rest of their public lives.[63]

Dating back to the Louisiana Purchase, the US had coveted Florida, and had laid claim to West Florida (a portion of lower Alabama and Mississippi) as part of the treaty with France, which Spain disputed. In 1810, Madison annexed parts of West Florida. When Monroe took office, Spain continued its gradual decline as an imperial power in the New World, with revolutions breaking out in South America. Monroe wished to obtain Florida and knew that this goal would be more difficult if he overtly supported the breakaway republics in South American. General Jackson offered him a way to obtain Florida, although there is great ambiguity over whether Monroe ever authorized the actions Jackson would take.[64]

In 1814, Jackson had defeated a faction of the Creek Indians known as the Red Sticks at Horseshoe Bend in present-day Alabama. He then imposed a "draconian peace ... in which he forced the Creek to surrender twenty-three million acres of land," according to Remini. The remaining Creek warriors fled into Northern Florida, where they combined with escaped slaves and Seminole Indians to attack settlers in the Southern part of Georgia. In December of 1817, Secretary of War Calhoun ordered General Edmund Gaines to subdue the Seminoles (as the combined force was now referred to), but to not attack the Spanish or their forts. In early 1818, Andrew Jackson was assigned to take over command of the Seminole War.[65]

It is here that the exact sequence of events begins to become murky regarding the orders that Jackson operated under. General Jackson clearly knew about the limitations placed on Gaines, since he had sent a letter to Monroe on January 6, before taking command, where he indicated his disagreement with those limitations. Jackson had never considered that the Indians should be treated as sovereign nations, but rather as subjects of the United States, which had the "right to take [Indian land] and dispose of it" whenever Congress so directed. In the letter Jackson told Monroe that "the whole of East Florida [should] be seized" and that he would do that within sixty days should "it be signified to me through any channel." Monroe later maintained that he was sick in bed when he received the letter "and could not read it." Jackson maintained that Monroe had approved his proposal through a third party. On January 30, Monroe sent Calhoun a message that Jackson was "not to attack any post occupied by Spanish troops," but Calhoun never delivered the message. "The question whether Jackson knowingly exceeded his orders remained an open, and controversial, one for decades to come," Gary Hart writes. Either way, Jackson proceeded to occupy Florida, killing two Englishmen in the process, and "evicted the whole Spanish government from Pensacola," according to Howe. This was much further than anyone in the cabinet expected Jackson to go.[66]

Both Calhoun and the treasury secretary denounced Jackson's actions and thought he should be court-martialed. Adams was the lone cabinet member that supported Jackson's actions. His support may have been derived from two related motives, as his biographer James Traub argues. First, he truly seemed mortified by reports of the actions of the Seminole Indians. Second, Adams wanted to expand the American boundaries into Florida and also across the continent and was actively engaged in negotiations with Spain's minister to obtain Florida and draw a line between Spanish holdings and the United States that extended "straight to the Pacific Ocean."[67]

Monroe pursued a middle course. On the one hand, he wanted to use Jackson's actions to the advantage of the United States in obtaining Florida. On the other hand, he knew that Jackson's actions had potentially violated the Constitution, and placed the onus for the decision to attack the Spanish forts back on Jackson, writing that Jackson had transcended "the limit prescribed by those orders" which had been originally given to General Gaines and therefore "you acted on your own responsibility." The order to attack a Spanish post "would authorize war, to which by the principles of our constitution, the Executive is incompetent. Congress alone possess the Power." Yet Monroe did not censure Jackson, perhaps because the general was so popular. Instead, based on pressure from Spain, Monroe ordered the return of the forts to Spain and the evacuation of Pensacola. But he also supported Adams's negotiations to obtain Florida and better define the boundaries of the Louisiana Territory.[68]

Henry Clay took no such middle course over the Florida invasion, seeing the potential to mortally wound the Monroe administration. Instead, he made a lifelong enemy of Andrew Jackson, taking to the floor of the House on January 20, 1819, and speaking for two hours. He attempted to maintain some balance in his remarks, indicating he had the "most profound respect" for Jackson. While the president had the authority to protect the residents of the United States from the Seminoles, neither he nor the general had the "power to authorize any act of hostility against" Spain. Clay made a "blistering assault" on Jackson in his speech, as his biographer Robert Remini indicates, and in the process "crucified poor Jackson." Jackson knew that Clay's real target was Monroe, but he was not a forgiving man. Clay attempted to undo some of the damage a few days later, going to Jackson's boardinghouse to explain that the speech was political, not personal. Jackson was not there at the time, and never responded to his overtures. In February, the full House voted down any attempt to sanction Jackson. Clay had made a powerful enemy of a man who was growing in popularity, one who "would dedicate himself to blocking his political advancement," Remini writes.[69]

Whereas Clay stumbled over the Florida incident, Adams saw opportunity. He used the weakness of Spain to reach agreement over what came to be known as the Transcontinental Treaty. The United States received all of Florida, and the boundary with Spain was "fixed along the Sabine, Red, and Arkansas Rivers and then North to the 42nd parallel of latitude," Howe writes. Adams now had his line to the Pacific, since the forty-second parallel ran to the Pacific Ocean. Adams was making a bet that the United States would one day control the land in the Far West.[70]

The Monroe Doctrine

In the aftermath of the Napoleonic Wars, the victorious powers (Prussia, Russia, Great Britain, and Austria) met at the Congress of Vienna "in September 1814 to plan the postwar world," according to Henry Kissinger. Prior to that, in April, the Bourbons were restored to the throne in France. Prince von Metternich of Austria was one of the main players in designing the new international order, and he considered Prussia, Russia, and Austria forming the Holy Alliance in 1815 as a further means to preserve the status quo in Europe, considering democracies "dangerous and unpredictable." It was a reactionary movement meant to retain the monarchies of Europe as a way to forestall further revolution and war. In the 1820s, the Holy Alliance considered suppressing a revolution that had occurred in Spain, which caused concern in the United States that they would attempt to overthrow the revolutionary regimes that had arisen in Latin America. These events triggered the Monroe Doctrine.[71]

Great Britain also opposed the intrusion of the Holy Alliance into the internal affairs of other nations and in the New World. In August 1823, the British foreign minister approached the Unites States to issue a joint statement opposing any attempt by Spain or the Holy Alliance to interfere in Latin America. President Monroe took the issue seriously and consulted with Jefferson and Madison, who both encouraged him to proceed with the cooperation of Great Britain. When Monroe brought the issue up to the cabinet, Calhoun fully supported the joint statement with Great Britain, but Adams opposed it.[72]

John Quincy Adams's position was a mix of pragmatism and principle. It was pragmatic because Adams was attempting to position himself to run for president and he could not appear as "being pro-British," Howe writes. But it was also a principled position, since Adams had opposed colonialism for many years, and had most forcefully expressed those views in an Independence Day speech he gave in 1821. In that speech, Adams exalted the government established by the founders because it was based on the principle of consent, and not force. Speaking of the Declaration of Independence, he said that "it demolished at a stroke the lawfulness of all governments founded upon conquest." Adams viewed the United States as an exceptional nation that stood behind liberation movements everywhere. "Wherever the standard of freedom and independence has been or shall be unfurled, there will her heart, her benedictions and her prayers be." But he drew the line on attempting to force nations to emulate the United States, or to allow Americans to interfere in the affairs of other nations. "But she goes not abroad in search of monsters to destroy. She is the well-wisher to the freedom and independence of all. She is the champion and vindicator of her own." For to do so would cause the country to violate the very basis on which it was formed, since "the fundamental maxims of her policy would insensibly change from liberty to force."[73]

The Monroe Doctrine reflected the philosophy of Adams in terms of America's relations with the world. But it would be a mistake to think that Monroe was little more than a bit player in the creation of the policy. The president was, as we have seen, an experienced foreign diplomat, and he spent much of his time in office dealing with questions of foreign policy. While he took Adams's advice regarding the proposal from the British, it was the president who ultimately drafted the content of the doctrine that would bear his name, and he also decided to announce the policy in his annual message to Congress.[74] Both men, no doubt, deserve credit for the major principle it espoused, that "the American continents ... are henceforth not to be considered as subjects for future colonization by any European powers." Monroe issued a warning that "it is impossible that the allied powers should extend their political system to any portion of either continent without endangering our peace and happiness," essentially indicating that the Western Hemisphere was an American sphere of influence. It was probably more aspirational than real when Monroe issued his statement, since the United States had a small "navy, no army, a modest population, and a still infant economy," Traub writes.[75]

Endnotes

1 Leonard L. Richards, *The Advent of American Democracy: 1815-1848* (Glenview, 1977), p. 28.

2 Harlow Giles Unger, *The Last Founding Father: James Monroe and a Nation's Call to Greatness* (Philadelphia, 2009), p. 7–17.

3 Unger, p. 17–40; Gary Hart, *James Monroe* (New York, 2005), p. 12.

4 Unger, p. 49–60; Hart, p. 16.

5 Unger, p. 44 and p. 61–63.

6 Unger, p. 79–84.

7 Hart, p. 21 and p. 38; Elkins and McKitrick, p. 499.

8 Hart, p. 39–46.

9 Wilentz, p. 177.

10 Daniel Walker Howe, *What Hath God Wrought: The Transformation of America, 1815–1848* (Oxford, 2007), p. 89–90.

11 Burns, p. 238; Hofstadter, p. 193–197.

12 Madison, p. 714–716; Howe, p. 80–81; Wilentz, p. 204.

13 Ketcham, p. 603; Howe, p. 83–89; Jefferson's evolving views can be found in his letter of January 9, 1816, to Benjamin Austin, retrieved November 29, 2016, from http://www.let.rug.nl/usa/presidents/thomas-jefferson/letters-of-thomas-jefferson/jefl238.php, which I became aware of from Howe, p. 83. For Jefferson's view on banking, see his letter of January 6, 1816, to Charles Yancey in Koch and Peden, p. 657.

14 Ketcham, p. 605; Wills, p. 155.

15 Howe, p. 31–40; Appleby, *Inheriting*, p. 63.

16 North, p. 63; Richards, p. 73.

17 Charles Sellers, *The Market Revolution: Jacksonian American, 1815–1846* (New York, 1991), p. 23–28; Richards, p. 75–80; North, p. 180.

18 Richards, p. 76; Howe, p. 1–2; Appleby, *Inheriting*, p. 241.

19 Howe, p. 211–213 and p. 222.

20 David S. Reynolds, *Waking Giant: American in the Age of Jackson* (New York, 2009), p. 13; Howe, p. 216–218.

21 Beckert, p. 119; Richards, p. 69; North, p. 185; Howe, p. 124.

22 Howe, p. 130.

23 Baptist, p. 75–94.

24 It's a divide I don't completely understand, because I don't understand the South very well. I was born in New York City, the ultimate Yankee. My formative years were spent on the Southern California coast, and my later years in the Sacramento valley.

I have traveled briefly in the South and enjoyed the people and the region and have good friends that are Southerners that I both admire and respect. But I lack an innate understanding of the Southern point of view, and so what I have written has been culled from some of the best sources I could find.

25 See Fraser, especially chapters 1, 3, and 7. Appleby, *Inheriting*, p. 242; James C. Cobb, *Away Down South: A History of Southern Identity* (Oxford, 2005), p. 9–12.

26 Appleby, *Inheriting*, p. 243–249; Sellers, p. 127.

27 Appleby, *Inheriting*, p. 243–249.

28 Appleby, *Inheriting*, p. 246; North, p. 130–131 and p. 133.

29 Cobb, p. 14 and p. 7; Appleby, *Inheriting*, p. 243.

30 Wilentz, p. 223.

31 Fraser, p. 303–304; Wilentz, p. 226.

32 Wilentz, p. 228–230; Howe, p. 149. On diffusion, see Jefferson's letter of April 22, 1820, to John Holmes in Koch and Peden, p. 698. On Jefferson blaming the Federalists, see his letter of August 17, 1821, to Henry Dearborn, retrieved December 26, 2016, from http://founders.archives.gov/documents/Jefferson/98-01-02-2258.

33 Howe, p. 150; Wilentz, p. 224 and p. 231.

34 Wilentz, p. 232–233; Howe, p. 152; Remini, p. 183.

35 Joanne B. Freeman, *The Field of Blood: Violence in Congress and the Road to the Civil War* (New York, 2018), p. 62–65.

36 Howe, p. 154–157; Koch and Peden, p. 256; Richards, p. 155–157.

37 See Howe, p. 158, on the issue of using states' rights and strict construction as a defense of slavery and not liberty.

38 Howe, p. 142–143; Richards, p. 58.

39 Wilentz, p. 205–207.

40 Sellers, p. 148–149.

41 Wilentz, p. 209–213.

42 Jean Edward Smith, *John Marshall: Definer of a Nation* (New York, 1996), p.21–69 and p. 5 for the Marshall quote.

43 Harlow Giles Unger, *John Marshall: The Chief Justice Who Saved the Nation* (Boston, 2014), p. 31–49.

44 Smith, p. 114–132.

45 James F. Simon, *What Kind of Nation: Thomas Jefferson, John Marshall, and the Epic Struggle to Create a United States* (New York, 2002), p. 101; Smith, p. 6 and p. 14–15.

46 Smith, p. 17 and p. 12; Simon, p. 130–131.

47 Smith, p. 283.

48 Simon, p. 173–177.

49 Smith, p. 322–324.

50 Smith, p. 324.

51 Unger, *John Marshall*, has a very useful summary of the major cases decided by the Marshall Court on p. 321–325; Smith, p. 388 and p. 286 for a description of how Marshall built camaraderie on the Supreme Court. For the vote count on major decisions, see information retrieved from Ballotpedia on February 8, 2017, at https://ballotpedia.org/The_Marshall_Court#Major_cases.

52 For a summary of Daniel Webster, see the article in History.com retrieved February 8, 2017, at http://www.history.com/topics/daniel-webster; Smith, p. 440–445, is the source for the quotes from decisions shown in the bullet points below; see also Howe, p. 144–145 for the importance of the decision.

53 Aaron Blake (February 6, 2017). "Constitutional Crisis? What Happens If Trump Ignores Judge's Ruling?" *Sacramento Bee*, p. 3b, is where I first became aware of the dispute between Jefferson and Madison over the role of the Court. Also, see Simon, p. 276–279 and Ketchum, p. 632–63; Madison, letter to Jefferson dated June 27, 1823, p. 801.

54 This section is generally drawn from two excellent biographies. One is James Traub, *John Quincy Adams: Militant Spirit* (New York, 2016), p. 3–17. The second is Paul C. Nagel, *John Quincy Adams, A Public Life, A Private Life*, (Cambridge, 1997), p. 3–8.

55 Traub, p. 18–38; Nagel, p. 8–9.

56 Nagel, p. 45; Traub, p. 48–58.

57 Traub, p. 60–65.

58 Traub, p. 67–78.

59 Nagel, p. 94–106; Traub, p. 81–89.

60 Nagel, p. 131–135; Traub, p. 124–128.

61 Nagel, p. 160–187; Sean Wilentz, *The Politicians & The Egalitarians: The Hidden History of American Politics* (New York, 2016), p. 130–132.

62 Traub, p. 148–211.

63 Remini, p. 150–151.

64 Wood, *Empire*, p. 374–376; Remini, p. 155; Hart, p. 89.

65 Remini, p. 161; Howe, p. 98–99.

66 Brands, p. 319–324; Howe, p. 102–103; Hart, p. 90; Unger, *The Last Founding Father*, p. 288–289.

67 Traub, p. 222–224.

68 Unger, *The Last Founding Father*, p. 292; James Monroe to Andrew Jackson, July 19, 1818, retrieved February 17, 2017, from https://memory.loc.gov/service/mss/maj.old/maj/01049/01049_0271_0274.pdf; Brands, p. 340; Hart, p. 92.

69 Remini, p. 163–168.

70 Howe, p. 108–109; Traub, p. 228.

71 Henry Kissinger, *Diplomacy* (New York, 1994), p. 35 and 83; information on the restoration of the Bourbons was retrieved on February 22, 2017, from https://www.saylor.org/site/wp-content/uploads/2011/05/Bourbon-Restoration.pdf; for the Russian expansion, see Howe, p. 112.

72 Kissinger, p. 35; Burns, p. 249; Jefferson letter to Monroe dated October 24, 1823, is from Koch and Peden, p. 708–709.

73 The Speech on Independence Day by John Quincy Adams was retrieved on February 21, 2017, from http://teachingamericanhistory.org/library/document/speech-on-independence-day/; Traub, p. 259; Burns, p. 254 is the source for the Morgenthau quote.

74 Traub argues that biographers of Adams tend to give him credit, whereas Monroe's biographers give him credit, see p. 285; the case for Monroe can be found in Unger, p. 313–314; Hart presents a balanced view which I find most compelling and have followed on p. 102.

75 Unger, *Monroe*, has a very useful summary of the Monroe Doctrine in the Appendix from which these quotes were derived. Traub, p. 284.

CHAPTER 6

The Changing Society of the Early Republic

The very character of the people seemed changed. Even the
language was strange—"rights of citizens—elections—members
of Congress—liberty"... and other words which were a perfect
babylonish jargon to the bewildered Van Winkle.

—Gordon Wood on Rip van Winkle's America[1]

To be an American means always adapting to change. Certainly,
the late twentieth and early twenty-first centuries have been a
time of great change, where some have flourished, and others have
been left behind. Often, the early eighteenth century is thought to
be a time where little changed, but in fact it was a period of great
political, economic, social, and cultural ferment. Eras of change also
create a backlash, and post-revolutionary America was no different.

Political and Social Change and the American Revolution

Historians have long argued whether the American Revolution was
really a revolution at all. Did it make fundamental changes in society
or simply result in a change in government? Since it did not fit the
mold of the later French, Russian, and Chinese revolutions, in which
societies were completely turned upside down through violence, some

consider the American Revolution to be conservative. Others, most notably Gordon Wood, argue that the American Revolution was quite radical because it transformed the ways in which people related to each other and the larger society.[2] Of the two alternatives, the view that the American Revolution had a transformative impact on American society seems the most persuasive.

These changes would eventually lead to the type of democratic and egalitarian society that began to emerge in the early republic (from about 1789 to 1823) and then through to the Jacksonian era (from 1824 to about 1845). Examples of the changing society included: 1) a breakdown in the social and political hierarchy that marked the colonial era; 2) the expansion of the concept that rights were not bestowed by people but were found in nature and nature's God; 3) the increasing expansion of political participation; 4) the role of women; and, 5) the questioning of slavery.

❧ ❧ ❧

By the time of the early republic, society had been undergoing rapid change from what existed during the colonial era, and at least some of these changes were unleashed by the American Revolution. In the mid-1700s, the colonists lived in a generally hierarchical society that was divided between ordinary people and those elites at the top of society who were considered gentlemen or the gentry. Unlike Europe, "in the colonies there were few peers or titled gentry ... their sense of aristocracy was largely confined to the category of gentry," Wood writes. But as the revolution unfolded, this quasi-feudal system that was rooted in the monarchical system of Great Britain began to unravel. This was part of a larger movement underway in the late seventeenth century, fueled by the Enlightenment thought and philosophy, which began to gradually replace monarchies with republican governments dedicated to liberty, equality, and self-government. America would become the leading edge of this movement, where experience with popular government during the colonial era created a natural fit for the changes that occurred. Wood writes that "the revolutionaries shed monarchy and took up republicanism, as Jefferson put it, 'with as much ease as would have attended their throwing off an old and putting on a new suit of clothes.'"[3]

Part of the reason the colonists were able to make this transition so easily was that America did not have the same level of income inequality as Europe. There were not the great masses of urban poor that were found in cities like Paris and London. In a 1785 letter to Madison, Jefferson bemoaned conditions in France, where "the property of this country is absolutely concentrated in a very few hands." Later in 1814, he wrote of America "... first, we have no paupers who possess nothing ... The great mass of our population is of laborers; our rich, who can live without labor ... being few, and of modest wealth."[4] The United States was largely made up of farmers and planters living in rural areas. Philadelphia was the largest American city, with a population of 42,500 residents in 1774, compared to London's population of 2.5 million people in 1750. "Incomes were more equally distributed in colonial America than in any other place that can be measured," the economists Peter H. Lindert and Jeffrey G. Williamson have written. Land was also more widely distributed than in Europe.[5]

Even though wealth was generally more equally distributed, colonial society was hierarchical. But as the revolution unfolded, the mind-set of the people began to change. Political scientist Scott John Hammond has written that as early as 1761, James Otis of Massachusetts had put forward the idea that "rights are not the product of human will or historic development but are inherent in all human beings by God's design." In 1776, Jefferson would refer to rights which were "endowed by their Creator." This led to the concept that government needed to be grounded in the consent of the governed. People in America were beginning to view themselves less as subjects and increasingly as citizens who hold certain natural rights and possess sovereignty over the government. In 1789, one resident of South Carolina wrote "subjects look up to a master, but citizens are so far equal, that none have hereditary rights superior to others." The vice president of the new Museum of the American Revolution that opened in 2017 in Philadelphia captured this concept when he said: "The idea is that you enter as a subject, but leave as a citizen." Participation in politics began to expand as early as the 1760s as the gentry had to compete for power.[6]

As the states began to write new constitutions in 1776, they created mixed governments that included bicameral legislatures, an executive, and a court system. In the aftermath of the revolution, power began to devolve almost exclusively to the legislative branch, and particularly to the lower house that was elected by the people, as Jefferson observed in 1783. While most states had an executive, typically a governor, the office was particularly weak and often dependent on the legislature. Eight states required the annual election of the governor and limited the number of terms any individual could serve in that role, all in an attempt to limit the power of the office. "An excess of power in the people was leading not simply to licentiousness but to a new kind of tyranny," Wood writes. James Madison, for one, thought that the quality of decision-making at the state level was very poor, and endangered the future of republicanism.[7]

The movement to adopt and ratify a new and more powerful federal government in 1787 had many motives behind it. In my book *The Emergence of One American Nation*, I argue that it was a seminal act creating one nation out of thirteen disparate states. But another motive of the Framers of the new Constitution was to reduce the role of the common people in the affairs of government, to tamp down some of the demands for democracy and political participation that had been unleashed during the revolution. Prior to the convention of 1787, Shays' Rebellion had scared the elite, who feared that a republic could all too easily descend into licentiousness and ultimately anarchy. Many of the comments from the delegates in the early days of the convention bemoaned the fact that democracy was out of control. James Madison most famously expressed some of these concerns in *Federalist* No. 10, written in the heat of the ratification debate in New York in 1788, arguing that a majority faction could act in an overbearing manner and deny the minority its rights. The concern over minority rights was not focused on our modern concerns for the rights of women or ethnic minorities, but rather that a majority would form and expropriate property from the affluent. In Madison's conception of an extended republic, it would be harder for a majority faction to form. Madison also envisioned that representatives to the federal government would come from the elite, from "the purest and noblest which" society contained. Still, Madison also knew that for a republic to survive, it had to be dependent on the will of people. At the convention, he was one of the strongest voices for the participation of the people in the selection of the House of Representatives, and also supported the direct election of the president. And despite the Framers' fear of too much democracy, no property qualifications were required to hold office under the Constitution.[8]

By the 1790s, Madison had begun to believe that the real threat to society was not oppression by an overbearing majority, but rather domination by a minority, in this case Hamilton and his Federalist Party. As we saw in chapter 1, Madison and Jefferson set off to create the Republican Party as a counterweight to the Federalists. The Republicans would champion the role of the common man, at least the common white man. This had the impact of further breaking down the hierarchical barriers that had been established in colonial society. At least part of the battle that would ensue between the Federalists and the Republicans was over the role that average people should play in politics and society. The Federalists were trying to hold back the floodgates and maintain a more traditional society dominated by the elite, which harkened back to the prerevolutionary days.

❧ ❧ ❧

The revolution had also unleashed a sense of equality among women, although there would later be a backlash against this movement. While this sense of equality did not generally extend to the right to vote, women did have an impact in the run-up to and during the revolution. In the 1770s, one of the prime weapons the colonists wielded was the banning of goods from England. "Women made most household purchases," historian Shelia L. Skemp argues, and so colonial leaders needed to persuade women "to refrain from indulging in English luxury items and depend instead on their own spinning and weaving to produce homespun for their families." During the war, many women had to take over the management of the family farm or business while their husbands were fighting. Abigail Adams managed the home front while John was away as a delegate to the Continental Congress and later as a foreign minister. "I find I am obliged to summon all my patriotism to feel willing to part with [John] again. You will believe me when I say that I make no small sacrifice to the publick," Abigail wrote in 1775. "Women needed to subordinate their own private happiness for the sake of the common good," historian Rosemary Zagarri has written. Some, mostly lower-class women, even went to the battlefields with their husbands, where they "washed clothing and bedding, cooked and sewed, tended to the sick and wounded, and occasionally picked up a musket and fired at the enemy," according to Skemp. Martha Washington spent most winters with her husband at his winter encampments, which meant "she spent about half the war with the Continental Army," according to Ron Chernow. Some women raised money for the army, others served as spies, and a few even joined the ranks and fought alongside men.[9]

Legally, married women were still held back by "the common law system of coventure," which made them dependent on their husbands. Still, the revolution opened the question of whether women too should be included as citizens of the new nation, especially one founded on the ideal of liberty and equality. As David McCullough has written, Abigail Adams was every bit the equal of John, and marrying her may have been his single best decision. She was also an advocate for women's rights, reminding him in 1776 to "remember the ladies." Adams, who was always sensitive to the importance of rank in society, attempted to put her off, writing back that men have "only the name of masters," but were never completely in control. But Adams also knew that extending male suffrage could lead to demands from women for the same rights. Some men even admitted that women should be treated as equals. One leader of the revolution told his widowed sister that he "would at any time give my consent to establish their right" to vote. In New Jersey, women who owned at least fifty pounds were allowed to vote in the years between 1776 and 1807, but this was not widely accepted in other states and would eventually be overturned. "Many people at the time believed that female voting degraded the political process, masculinized women, and undermined male authority," Zagarri argues. Still, women like Mary Wollstonecraft, Mercy Otis Warren, and Judith Sargent Murray continued to push for the political rights of women.

Mary Wollstonecraft

Although Wollstonecraft never visited the United States, this Englishwoman was steeped in the same Enlightenment philosophers that animated the American Revolution. John Adams once said that Abigail was a "disciple of Wollstonecraft," and John read her book on the French Revolution twice.[10] She may have been the first feminist, a woman ahead of her time.

Mary Wollstonecraft was born outside of London in 1759, the second child of Edward and Elizabeth. Her grandfather emerged from the middle class to own a silk weaving business, but he always resented how the gentry lorded their status over him. His son also wanted to climb the social ladder, but without much success. "An alcoholic who squandered his family's money, Edward Wollstonecraft brutalized his wife and children," Charlotte Gordon writes. The one thing that Mary shared with both her grandfather and father was a deep sense that she was as good as anyone, regardless of social class or gender. When she was eleven, Mary and her brothers went to school for the first time. But while her brothers learned mathematics and Latin, she was relegated "to needlework and simple addition."[11]

In her teen years, Mary became exposed to the ideas of John Locke and Jean-Jacques Rousseau. It was a time of revolutionary ferment across the ocean, as the American colonies began to pull away from Great Britain. Wollstonecraft identified with Locke's idea that "creatures of the same species and rank ... should ... be equal," and Rousseau's call for independence and freedom for all people. In these philosophers of the Enlightenment she saw the injustice of her own family life, where her father abused his wife and her mother favored her older brother. She longed to escape her family, and at nineteen she moved to Bath to work as a companion to a rich widow. It offered her a degree of independence, although she was alienated by the aristocratic nature of Bath's society. A few years later, she returned home to care for her ailing mother, since her father had run off with another woman and was not there to take care of her. Her mother died in 1783, two years after Mary's return, never having apologized for the mistreatment Mary felt she suffered.[12]

A wealthy widow funded a school that Wollstonecraft opened that same year. Both of her sisters joined her, although they never had Mary's passion for teaching. The school, which primarily accepted girls, focused on considering each student as a unique individual who needed "a different mode of treatment." The school closed after two years, and Wollstonecraft fell into a deep depression after a close friend died in childbirth. It was writing that saved her, as she completed her first book entitled *Thoughts on the Education of Daughters*. It reflected Mary's views on the importance of educating young women in serious subjects such as mathematics, history, and languages so they could earn a living and be independent. Published in 1787 by Joseph Johnson, she was paid ten pounds, a princely sum in those days. Still, she did not make enough from writing to support herself, so she took a job in Ireland as a governess for one of the largest English landowners. Wollstonecraft despised their aristocratic lifestyle, identifying with the poor tenant farmers that surrounded their large estate. She was soon fired, returning to London determined to "earn her living with her pen," according to Gordon.[13]

It was her editor, Joseph Johnson, who helped her, first taking her in and then finding a permanent place for Mary to live. He also hired her to work for a literary magazine, the *Analytical Review*, as a book reviewer. She originally chafed at being relegated to review romance novels, but Johnson soon put her to work on more serious books. As the French Revolution unfolded, Wollstonecraft identified with the radicals who seized power. "For Mary, the revolutionaries in France proclaimed the ideals she held most dear—the renunciation of tyranny and the redemption of the poor and oppressed," Gordon writes. When the conservative politician and theorist Edmund Burke criticized the French Revolution, Mary took up her pen to write a rebuttal. By now, her philosophy was a mix of Enlightenment thought, which relied on the importance of reason, with the emerging Romanticism of the era, which placed equal weight on the importance of passion and emotion. The result was a 150-page book titled *A Vindication of the Rights of Men*, which challenged Burke's views with a "well-reasoned, often witty" rebuttal. Released in 1790, the book sold over three thousand copies and received generally good reviews, although when Johnson revealed Mary as the author during its second publication, some of those that had praised the work when they thought it was written by a man became critical.[14]

In 1792, Wollstonecraft published *A Vindication of the Rights of Women*, her finest work, which echoed Jefferson's Declaration of Independence by stating that rights were given by God alone. She bemoaned that "the rights of humanity have been confined to the male line from Adam downward." Wollstonecraft argued that women were not inherently inferior to men, but they were treated this way by choice. It was a product of "the civilization," which had been "very partial" to men, that had created such a society. Some men preferred to make women "alluring mistresses rather than rational wives." The key was that women should receive an equal education as men, so that they can be truly independent. "Consequently, the most perfect education, in my opinion, is such an exercise of the understanding as is best calculated to strengthen the body and form the heart; or, in other words, to enable the individual to attain such habits of virtue as will render it independent," she wrote in *Vindication*. Although she never traveled to America, her pioneering work seemed to have an impact on the other side of the Atlantic. In 1793 a congressional representative from New Jersey stated: "The Rights of Women are no longer strange sounds to an American ear; they are now heard as familiar terms in every part of the United States."[15]

In 1797, Wollstonecraft married the writer and philosopher William Godwin. His most famous works included *Political Justice* and the novel *Caleb Williams*, and he has been described as "the father of anarchism." When they first met, Mary and Godwin did not much like each other. At a dinner party where the guest of honor was Thomas Paine, Wollstonecraft came to dominate the conversation, while the shy Godwin hung in the background. But by 1796, they had fallen in love, and when Mary became pregnant with his child, they decided to get married. On August 30, 1797, their baby girl, Mary, was born. Ten days later, Wollstonecraft died from an infection. Her daughter would go on to write the famous novel *Frankenstein* under her married name, Mary Shelley.[16]

⚐ ⚐ ⚐

While Wollstonecraft was urging equality for women across the ocean, in America during the 1790s, women began to identify with either the Federalist or Republican parties, and continued their involvement in civic and party affairs, "cooking for events, wearing colors and symbols of the party, and marrying men of the same party," according to Marie Basile McDaniel. Certain women became quite interested in public affairs and became "female politicians" in the words of Zagarri. Women also became caught up in the partisan warfare that was spreading across the nation in the middle to late 1790s. Nellie Parke Custis, the step-granddaughter of Washington, called herself "perfectly federal" and viewed the French as "democratic murderers." Mercy Otis Warren stood on the other side, opposed the ratification of the Constitution, and in 1805 published the *History of the Rise, Progress and Termination of the American Revolution*, in which she attacked the Federalists for "aristocratic elitism" and exalted the election of Jefferson in 1800.[17]

In a bizarre twist, the expansion of voting rights for white men created a backlash against women being involved in politics by 1800. Zagarri argues that the intense partisanship of the era, which threatened to tear the young nation apart, contributed to removal of women from politics. "Men seemed too involved, too distracted, and too passionate to dampen the flames of party conflict and division. Women, on the other hand, might be better positioned than men to" incorporate a more tolerant view of political opposition, which required they withdraw from political life. Republican ideology began to identify itself with manly qualities like "propertied independence, self-reliance, physical strength, and bravery," according to Skemp. Women were viewed as being "weak, emotional, and irrational, and they belonged in the home." This biological basis for excluding women from politics was accompanied by a philosophical point of view that made a distinction in the natural rights possessed by women versus men. Whereas men were viewed as having all the natural rights envisioned by John Locke, including full inclusion in the polity, women's role was considered much more limited. The impact of the Scottish Enlightenment thinkers, who believed that "the social compact consisted not of an agreement among equals but of a hierarchy in which inequality was a given," began to hold sway in terms of women's rights. Zagarri argues that "expressing one's rights meant fulfilling the duties of one's existing social station," especially the role of wife and mother, which were seen as being in conflict with a political role for women. Courts began to issue opinions that women were dependents of their husbands, and the role for women in the political sphere began to recede. Even the Republican Party, which had done so much to expand political participation, began to believe that "universal male suffrage could only be maintained if women remained as a permanent nonvoting class," McDaniel writes.[18]

The parallels to the women's liberation movement of the 1960s and 1970s, and the backlash against it, seem similar to events in the early republic. Coming out of the 1950s, which had been a time of conformity, women began to demand more choice than simply being restricted to the home. New opportunities opened, with women increasingly attending college and pursuing careers, as well as motherhood. Some men began to take greater responsibility for family life and for raising children. In 1972, the Equal Rights Amendment (ERA) passed Congress and was sent to the states for possible ratification. Some form of the ERA had been proposed since women had gained the right to vote with the Nineteenth Amendment in 1920. The ERA, which simply read that "equality of rights under the law shall not be denied or abridged by the United States or by any state on account of sex," quickly gained ratification by twenty-two states in 1972. But then a conservative backlash occurred, with many of the same arguments used in opposition to the ERA that had been used to deny women a political role in the early republic, and later when the Nineteenth Amendment was debated. "Anti-ERA organizers claimed that the ERA would deny woman's right to be supported by her husband, privacy rights would be overturned, [and] women would be sent into combat," according to Roberta W. Francis of the National Council of

Women's Organizations. Martin Luther King Jr. once said that "the arc of the moral universe is long, but it bends toward justice." But it does not do so in a straight line, nor without great effort.[19]

Daily Life in the Early Republic

By the dawn of the nineteenth century, the changes that had swept through America gradually provided white men with the opportunity to vote and hold office regardless of property ownership. The Constitution had not included any provision that required a certain level of wealth to vote or hold office. For voting, the document simply stated that "the Electors in each State shall have the Qualifications requisite for the Electors of the most numerous Branch of the State Legislature." In 1790, this meant that "fewer than half of the original thirteen states provided an approximation to [universal] white manhood suffrage," Wilentz writes. But over time, this began to change. As new western states began to enter the Union, they allowed all white males to vote, which caused a cascading effect in the older states. "By the 1830s, a flourishing democratic system had been consolidated," Eric Foner has written. The Constitution likewise provided no property or wealth requirements to hold office. As Madison wrote in *Federalist* No. 57, "Who are to be the objects of popular choice? Every citizen whose merit may recommend him to the esteem and confidence of his country. No qualifications of wealth, of birth, of religious faith, or of civil permission is permitted to fetter the judgement or disappoint the inclination of the people."[20]

The United States was experiencing rapid population growth, from 3.8 million people in 1790 to almost 13 million by 1830. The chart below shows some of the major population trends from 1800 to 1830 based on census data.

Population Growth in the United States			
	1800	1820	1830
Total Population	5,172,312	9,625,734	12,858,670
Percent Increase		86%	34%
Number of Free White Men over 25 (1)	692,837	1,260,280	2,356,673
Percent of Total Population	13%	13%	18%
Number of Slaves	875,626	1,531,436	2,009,050
Percent of Total Population	17%	16%	16%
Population under 25 (1)	N/A	5,654,620	5,903,622
Percent of total		59%	46%

(1) For 1830 the Census broke it down to those over 20 years old.
Source: US Census data from https://www.census.gov/prod/www/decennial.html

The population was young, with almost 60 percent of the free white population under the age of twenty-five in 1820, and 46 percent under the age of twenty in 1830. The percent of free white men over the age of twenty-five represented only 13 percent of the population in 1800 and 1820, and those over the age of twenty represented 18 percent of the population in 1830. So, while the barriers were coming down, most of the population, "who included women, children, slaves, and free people of color, were in positions of subordination and dependency," according to historian Christopher Clark. Women and children largely lived under the authority of the men in their lives.[21]

American society was largely rural, with most people engaged in farming during the early republic and through the Jacksonian period. Of the 1.9 million people reported to be in the labor force in

1800, almost 75 percent were involved in agriculture. By 1830, the percentage had dropped just slightly, to around 70 percent.[22]

To survive, men and women needed to work together to make the family farm successful. Very few single men could survive as farmers due to the extensive amount of work required, both in the fields and in the home. In fact, the word *husband* originally meant "farmer," but soon came to mean a married man. Both the husband and wife had separate but interrelated roles to play on the farm. Men were responsible for the hard, physical labor of clearing the land; planting and raising the crops; harvesting; and maintaining the property. Women took care of the "garden, house, kitchen and hearth," and raised the children. Families were large, with women having on average seven children in 1800. "American families worked as patriarchal units, governed by their male heads," according to historian Jack Larkin. While the work of men was seasonal and varied based on their location and the length of the growing season, work for women was often much the same on a daily basis, and included "cooking, clearing away, washing, sewing, mending—a daily sequence of time-consuming, physically demanding, constantly repeating tasks," Larkin writes.[23]

Most farmers would start by growing crops for their own consumption, but many found they could not be self-sufficient and needed to trade, both with their fellow farmers and with the people who lived in the local small towns. Money was scarce, and so trading was done on a credit system. Some of this was informal, with people keeping account of balances that were owed orally. "In the rural North, where pupils were most apt to learn arithmetic in school, some farmers and most artisans kept account books that gave each of their transactions a precise monetary value," according to Larkin. Most of the trading farm families did took place in country stores, with shopkeepers maintaining account books to track what they were owed. As banking became more prevalent in the aftermath of the War of 1812, paper money in the form of bank notes began to circulate in rural areas.[24]

Farming was intensely physical labor. Those who lived near a rushing river could set up a waterwheel, which helped with "grinding grain, sawing timber and pulling handwoven woolen cloth," Larkin writes. Animals, like oxen and horses, were used for plowing and hauling loads. But much of the work was simple manual labor. One of the most demanding chores was the harvesting of hay in New York and New England in the summer months. Farmers would go to the local towns to hire store clerks and merchants to assist with the harvest. Young men would take pride in their speed and ability to use the long-handled scythes to cut down the hay. The slower ones risked potential injury from the person that was following them. Picking cotton was also difficult and sometimes dangerous work, with much of this done by slave labor. "All but the most dexterous pickers risked ripped and bleeding hands from the sharp edges of the fibrous calyxes that held the cotton bolls," Larkin explained. Some of the large planters bemoaned the lack of sophistication of the people who farmed the land. James Madison, for example, was part of a movement that "recommended means of conservation such as crop rotation and fertilization," to improve farming methods and outcomes.[25]

The average diet for those who worked on a farm varied by region, but corn and pork were two products that almost all Americans consumed. In the regions where cattle and dairy were available, like New England and the middle states, people consumed butter, cheese, beef, and milk. Bread made from wheat or rye was available in the North and the middle states, while in the South people had corn pone or hoecakes. Apples, found in the North, were made into apple cider and often allowed to ferment. Farmhouses in the North tended to be larger than those in the West, but they still generally consisted of two to three rooms, with single-story homes predominating. In the South were large plantation homes, although the average Southerner had a smaller house than those in the North.[26]

As the nineteenth century unfolded, the life of farmers also began to change, as they became increasingly entwined in the market economy, one in which they raised crops not just for their own subsistence but also to be sold for consumption by others. New consumer products were purchased using the income that was produced from selling farm produce. "The woman of the house led the way in establishing commercial contact with the wider world beyond the local community," Howe writes, "through her desire to introduce amenities into the rustic simplicity of her home." Consumer goods could be purchased that surpassed the quality that could be made at home. Farm life was also affected by "new tools and implements [that] began to alter ancient, laborious patterns," improving the farmers' productivity. For example, the blades for shovels, which had been made of wood, were now made of cast iron. The more successful farmers were able to experiment with new methods of mechanization. "In the wheat-growing regions of the Middle States and Ohio they were trying out horse-powered threshing machines, which replaced the work of men with wooden flails," Larkin writes. Still, the main work of farmers remained largely manual labor. With the emergence of a market economy, farmers needed to find ways to continue to succeed. Dairy farming began to emerge, especially in parts of Pennsylvania, where milk and cheese could be sent to supply a growing urban marketplace. Rice production expanded in South Carolina and Georgia as new methods for water control and planting were developed. And the growth of the cotton economy was spurred by the invention of the cotton gin, causing numerous changes in American society, as we have already seen.[27]

Due to the marginal nature of the soil and the short growing season, New England farmers had always held more than one job. John Adams's father was both a farmer and a shoemaker. Hervey Brooks of Connecticut ran a brick pottery kiln from his farm in the early 1800s, where he made a variety of pots, pitchers, and mixing bowls. Both men were a part of a group known as artisans, who had specialized skills in producing handmade items. While both Adams and Brooks were rural artisans, others lived in cities and small towns. Artisans included coopers, blacksmiths, carpenters, silversmiths, and clockmakers. Some, like Benjamin Franklin, became printers and bookbinders, while others were furniture makers. Numerous surnames came from the work that people did, like Taylor, Mason, or Smith.[28]

Just as the world was changing for farmers, who were increasingly drawn into the market economy, so too artisans were seeing numerous changes in their occupations as the industrial age emerged. Traditionally, their world had been one where people moved from apprentice, to journeymen, to master mechanic. The apprentice was hired as a trainee who would learn the work, sometimes as an indentured servant. In one cabinetmaker's shop, the apprentice was expected to "open the shop in the morning, build and keep fires during the day, wait on Journeymen, and do all chores and go [on] all errands which are necessary for this shop." The journeymen had developed the basic skills of their profession and tended to move between shops. They were biding their time until they could open their own business and become a master mechanic. Owning their own shops, and employing both apprentices and journeymen, gave the master mechanic a sense of independence. But major changes were underway, as industrialization began to replace handmade products with mass production methods. "As widening markets intensified competition, cost cutting masters with access to merchant capital in the major ports intensified the division of labor by subdividing work processes to exploit cheap, unskilled labor under close supervision in workshops," historian Charles Sellers wrote. The work became less interesting and less well paid. One craftsman referred to it as the "bastard artisan system."[29]

Eli Whitney was one of a new entrepreneurial class that helped to foster the manufacturing revolution. Whitney, who was born in 1765 in Westborough, Massachusetts, was raised on a farm. But he had always been interested in mechanical devices. He created the first cotton gin but was unable to corner the market for his invention, and experienced financial difficulties. In 1798, he obtained a contract with the federal government to manufacture ten thousand muskets, which were to be delivered within twenty-eight months. Whitney purchased a "water-power site on the Mill River outside New Haven," according to James MacGregor Burns, and began to experiment with creating weapons with interchangeable parts. Up to this time, arms had been made "lock, stock and barrel" by one worker, who generally learned the craft from his father or a master mechanic. Given the number of weapons to be made in such a short time frame, Whitney had to "to invent an elaborate system of guides, patterns, templates, gauges, and jigs so that his unskilled workers could produce, in large numbers, a musket from a model that skilled craftsmen had previously made," Burns writes. Whitney was not completely successful, since it took ten years to deliver the arms, but he had discovered a method that would change the way many products were made. In addition to weapons, clocks were one of the first items to be made using interchangeable parts built by low-skilled workers.[30]

Much of the new factory work was done by women and children. As we saw in the previous chapter, early manufacturing began in New England. The most successful of these operations were the cotton textile mills started by the Boston Associates, who employed primarily female laborers from the surrounding farm communities. Referred to as the "mill girls," they expected to spend only a short time working in the mills before they married. The days were long, typically lasting fourteen hours, and the girls worked six days a week, with only Sunday as a day of rest. They lived in boardinghouses onsite with little privacy, and "the girls ate in a large communal dining room and slept six to a room, two to a bed," according to Burns. There were also certain benefits that came from working in the cotton mills, including a sense of independence from earning their own money, and the camaraderie that developed among the women who worked there. Still there was a sense of "confinement, noise, and lint filled air" that the women were forced to live with. Sarah Bagley, who went to work in the mills in 1835, believed that they had little choice in what they did. "The ship which brings us to Lowell is NECESSITY," she wrote. "We must have money; a father's debts are to be paid, an aged mother is to be supported." Eventually, the harsh working conditions led Bagley to start a union called the New England Workingmen's Association.[31]

The migration to cities was just beginning as the 1820s unfolded, with just 7 percent of the population living in urban areas. Over the next thirty years, that would grow to over 18 percent. New York was the only city with a population in excess of one hundred thousand people in 1820, but by 1850 there were six cities in that category. Some young men and women were drawn to urban areas in order to "escape the painful thrift and drudgery of a small farm," as Howe frames it. For others, there was less opportunity to make a living through farming as technological improvements meant fewer people were needed to produce an ever-expanding food supply. The expansion of cities was also fueled by a growing number of immigrants to the United States in the 1820s and 1830s, when over 667,000 people entered the country. This would later become a flood of new people entering the United States from Ireland in the aftermath of the potato famine in 1845.[32]

Commerce had always been the economic lifeblood of cities, particularly for those along the Eastern Seaboard. Boston, New York, Philadelphia, Baltimore, and New Orleans were all major seaports, but there were also smaller port towns, like Providence, Salem, and Richmond that were successful. During the Napoleonic Wars, international trade was of prime importance as the Americans faced little overseas competition. In 1820, *seaman* was the second largest occupation in the United States after *farmer*. Although competition rose in the aftermath of the European war, the expansion of the cotton economy helped sustain the growth of cities, and a symbiotic relationship was established between the Southern plantations and the Northern commercial economy. The five largest cities dominated the Atlantic trade, increasing their share from 56 percent of total exports in 1815 to 68 percent in 1840. New cities began to develop inland along waterways, places like Cincinnati, Chicago, and Buffalo. Cities "were *entrepots*, places for the collection and shipment of staple commodities in exchange for provisions, equipment, and services," according to Howe.[33]

As Jefferson feared, cities were much more hierarchal than the countryside, with a much greater gap between rich and poor. James MacGregor Burns describes how the wealthy merchants in Boston set themselves apart from the masses "by their manner of dress ... and by their demand for deference from their inferiors, in the form of a finger to the brow or the tipping of the hat." They tended to live in large and extravagant homes. One wealthy Boston merchant built a four-story home with twenty-three rooms in 1832. Meanwhile, the poor tended to live on the outskirts of the main city, sometimes in areas that were slums. One of the worst was the Five Points area in New York City, where many of the poor lived in overcrowded conditions marked by "filth, disease, gangs, crime, riots, and vice," Howe writes. Municipal services could not keep up with the growing needs for better public safety, including police, fire, sanitation, and water services.[34]

The growth of cities would contribute to the increase in inequality that was being fostered by the shift to a market economy in the early republic. Between 1800 and 1860, inequality expanded rapidly in the United States. Those that were employed in finance, who were mostly in New York City, had gross wealth that was eight times that of all free households. Opportunities in banking were increasing rapidly during this period, with the number of state banks rising by almost 7 percent per year. Meanwhile, the relative earnings for artisans was going down. When compared to the urban unskilled, the earnings for artisans fell by 26 percent in the country as a whole.[35]

Still, many people were drawn to city life to pursue greater opportunity than that which could be found in the existing rural areas. Cities also provided numerous amenities that did not exist in the countryside, from theaters to fine restaurants, to large marketplaces. For the middle class and the rich, city services began to improve over time, and running water became available in New York and Philadelphia in the 1840s. As Howe argues, city life provided a degree of independence that could not be found on farms. "Together, urban places and the western areas opened up to markets by waterways received adventuresome souls fleeing the backbreaking toil, the patriarchal authority, and the stultifying isolation of semi-subsistence farming."[36]

⚘ ⚘ ⚘

Literacy in America was expanding as the nineteenth century unfolded. Reading was seen as a means to create an informed citizenry and also as a way to continue to promote a market economy. "Citizens needed to be informed; commerce conducted over long distances required proficient readers, writers, and calculators," Appleby writes. The expansion of reading led to new career opportunities in publishing, journalism, and writing, even for women. "Reading had become a necessity of life; it had also become a principal activity of nation-building," according to Joyce Appleby. Sarah Buell Hale, who was widowed at the age of thirty-four, had a successful career as writer and went on to edit two successful magazines. *Godley's Ladies Book*, which Hale edited for forty years, had 10,000 subscriptions in 1837, which grew to 160,000 by 1860.[37]

The number of newspapers was also expanding rapidly. By 1810, there were 371 newspapers, compared to 92 in 1790. By 1828 there were 161 newspapers being published in New York City alone, compared to only three during the revolution. The growth of newspapers was occurring on the frontier as well. Ebner Howe, who was born in the state of New York, moved to Cleveland when he was twenty and began his own newspaper, which he delivered on horseback. The expansion of newspapers also played a role in the emerging abolition movement, as Northern reporters began to publish articles critical of slavery in the South.[38]

Commercialization and the need for greater communications throughout the United States also led to a movement for an expanded education system. Up until the 1830s, a private system of education had predominated. One model was the district system found in New York and New England. "Under this system, each community ran its own school, hired its own teachers, chose its own books, determined its own curriculum," Leonard Richards observes. But ultimately, a more uniform system of education would come to predominate. Its hallmarks would be a standardized system of teacher training and an educational system supervised by a professionally trained superintendent who was responsible to a locally elected school board. These "common schools" were pioneered by the secretary for the Massachusetts State Board of Education in 1837. A system of free public education was gradually being implemented in the United States.[39]

As education expanded, new opportunities became available in the teaching profession, which were initially filled by young men. However, teaching was often a stepping-stone for men, who moved on to careers in law, medicine, or business. Despite the backlash against women in politics, many young women were becoming educated as well, and this created a demand for female teachers as well. "To a remarkable degree women were able to capitalize on the general enthusiasm for educating future mothers, now construed patriotically as providing the critical bridge between childhood and republican citizenship," according to Appleby.[40]

❦ ❦ ❦

American society was violent in the early republic, and some of this was fueled by a population that drank heavily. Southern violence seemed to be tied to the honor culture that was prevalent there, with hot-tempered young men engaging in duels. Frontier areas were known for a lack of law enforcement. "The backwoods of Kentucky had a reputation for extreme lawlessness, [where] fisticuffs, eye-gougings, knife and gun play were everyday events," Richards writes. New Orleans was reported to have a much higher murder rate than London, as did the state of Pennsylvania. And New York City had some of the most extreme violence, where young men "proved their manhood by drinking, fighting each other, attacking members of different ethnic groups ... and gang raping women." Public services, especially law enforcement, were limited, allowing a culture of violence to establish itself.[41]

Urban rioting also fed the violence. The breakdown in hierarchy that was occurring came with a price, with "anonymous lowly people, full of class resentment," comprising the main participants. Baltimore was particularly a tinderbox as the War of 1812 began, having experienced significant population growth that included new immigrants and free blacks. The master mechanics were under great pressure from unskilled labor. Mob violence and rioting went on for close to two months, sparked by the beginning of the war and rivalry between Republicans and Federalists in the city. While rioting settled down in the aftermath of the war, it would return in the 1830s, fed once again by political differences and "ethnic, racial, and religious animosities," Howe writes. Between 1834 and 1836, there were eighty-nine reported riots.[42]

There was also the widespread use of alcohol, especially hard liquor, which fueled violence in America. The amount of alcohol consumed rose from two and one-half gallons per person per year to five gallons by 1820, Wood reports. This was triple the consumption in modern American society. By 1825, Americans were drinking seven gallons of alcohol a year. Many workers would drink during their breaks. "All social classes drank heavily [including] college students, journeyman printers, agricultural laborers, and canal diggers," who were especially known for excessive drinking, according to Howe. It was a society ripe for change, and the religious movement known as the Second Great Awakening would help foster the sobering of America.[43]

In many ways, Congress reflected both the violence of American society and the widespread use of alcohol. "Alongside the debating, discussing, conferring, and voting was a healthy (or rather, unhealthy) dose of belligerence, violence, and drunken swaggering with its own logic and tempo," Freeman writes. She has documented that over the three-decade period between 1830 and 1860, there were seventy violent incidents between national political leaders. Initially, these incidents of violence, including fistfights and dueling, centered on party differences. But during the 1840s and 1850s, the disputes were increasingly over slavery. The use of violence tended to be more pronounced from Southerners, who sometimes carried weapons with them. Congressman John B. Dawson of Louisiana, who was elected in 1841, "routinely wore both a bowie knife and a pistol, and wasn't shy about using them," according to Freeman. Some of this violence may well have been fueled by the consumption of alcohol, which was readily available in Washington, DC.[44]

Life for African Americans

Day-to-day life for most African Americans was dismal, since most of them were enslaved. In 1820, there were over 1.2 million African American slaves compared to 233,000 free blacks. While there were free blacks in every state, over one-third were found in New York, New Jersey, Pennsylvania, and Delaware. During the revolution, some states adopted constitutions that allowed free blacks to vote, including Delaware, Maryland, New Hampshire, and New York. Free African Americans during this period had at least nominal rights, although discrimination was rampant. Over time, these rights were lost as free blacks in the North were increasingly facing discriminatory laws, and many of the new states that began to join the Union (Ohio, Indiana, Michigan, etc.) adopted legislation that discriminated against black people. As white male suffrage expanded, free blacks had their right to vote eliminated in many of the states that had originally allowed it.[45]

Slaves had no rights. Nikole Hannah Jones has written that "enslaved people could not legally marry. They were barred from learning to read and restricted from meeting privately in groups." Slaves had "no claim to their children," who could be forcibly separated from their parents and sold on "auction blocks alongside furniture and cattle." Slaves could be raped, tortured, even murdered, without any recourse to the law. As we shall see, by the 1850s the Supreme Court would ultimately find in the *Dred Scott* decision that slaves, even once freed, could not be citizens of the United States.[46]

For black slaves, the conditions they lived under varied depending on whether they worked as field hands, household servants, or lived in urban areas. But all had this in common: they viewed "the South's peculiar institution chiefly as a system of labor extortion," historian Kenneth M. Stampp has written. Those blacks that worked in the fields probably had the most difficult existence. The day would begin before sunrise, either with the ringing of a bell or a horn, and they would then have a morning meal in their slave cabin. Most slave labor was organized either based on the "gang system" or the "task system." Under the gang system, "the field-hands were divided into gangs commanded by drivers who were to work them at a brisk pace," Stampp writes. Under the task system, each individual was given a task to complete, which, according to a Georgian rice planter, allowed the slave driver or overseer to trace imperfect work "to the neglectful worker," who would then be punished. The field hands would receive a break around noon for the midday meal. "Enslaved people in all regions and time periods often did not have enough to eat; some resorted to stealing food from the master," according to the writer Nicholas Boston. He further reports that "enslaved people were clothed, fed, and housed only minimally to ensure their survival and capacity for labor." During most of the year, slaves were expected to work between fifteen and sixteen hours a day in the fields, and then to tend to other chores once the field work was completed.[47] Solomon Northrup, a free black who was captured and enslaved and whose story was made into the movie *Twelve Years a Slave*, described his experience:

The hands are required to be in the cotton field as soon as it is light in the morning, and with the exception of ten or fifteen minutes, which is given at noon to swallow their allowance of cold bacon, they are not permitted to be a moment idle until it is too dark to see, and when the moon is full, they often labor until the middle of the night.[48]

Slaves who lived in urban areas tended to fare better than those that were a part of the plantation system. Frederick Douglass wrote that "a city slave is almost a freeman, compared with a slave on a plantation." Slaves who lived in cities worked in all forms of skilled and unskilled labor, competing with free whites for work in many cases. "Town slaves worked in cotton presses, tanneries, shipyards, bakehouses, and laundries, as dock laborers and stevedores, and as clerks in stores," according to Stampp. They also worked in skilled fields as blacksmiths, cabinet and shoemakers, carpenters, and other work of this nature. Often white mechanics or skilled journeymen used slaves as their assistants.[49]

House slaves tended to have a better life than those that worked in the fields. They did the domestic work of the household, from cooking and cleaning to the maintenance of gardens. Women served as wet nurses and took care of the children of the plantation owner. The men were often personal servants or drivers, who worked in conjunction with the overseers to keep the field hands under control. Typically, the food, clothing, and shelter were better for house slaves, who sometimes occupied a room in the plantation house. As such, "house servants were considered a privileged class among the enslaved population." They were kept separate from field hands in most instances for fear they would serve as spies for those who were planning to escape. Although the house servants lived under marginally better conditions than those that worked in the fields, their world was still "harsh and demeaning. Women house servants in particular were both desired and routinely raped by the plantation owner." One man who was a house servant in the 1840s wrote that "we were constantly exposed to the whims and passions of every member of the family; from the least to the greatest their anger was wreaked upon us."[50]

As we saw in chapter 3, the revolution had spurred a movement to eliminate slavery in the Northern states and the upper South. Many of the founding generation knew that slavery was wrong and hoped to see its gradual elimination. However, this was not the case in the Deep South. By the 1790s, these views began to change in reaction to the slave uprising in Santo Domingo and the expansion of the cotton economy. By the time of the Missouri Compromise in the 1820s, a few slave owners had even begun to define slavery as a positive good that was justified by references to the Bible. Slave owners also rationalized slavery in paternalistic language, "as one of caring for those who could not look after themselves. Negroes as a race, they insisted, were childlike," Howe writes.[51]

Both slave owners and slaves responded in different ways to the system they found themselves in. Some slave owners did attempt to be kind to the people they owned, at least within the bounds of what was permissible in the society of their time. In many cases, there was an ulterior motive, since slaves that were treated better were more productive. "Now I contend that the surest and best method of managing negroes is to love them," one slave owner contended. Some would allow slaves to work plots of land where they could cultivate their own crops and sell these in town. Gifts were sometimes distributed at the end of the year around Christmas time. Other slave owners were crueler, maintaining control over their slaves by having their overseers inflict physical beatings. Numerous fugitive slave advertisements included descriptions of slaves that had "many stripes of lash, large raised scars," or said that the individual was "marked about the shoulders from whipping."[52]

Some slaves attempted to get along with their masters. This was most typical among house slaves, who sometimes identified with their owners. Sojourner Truth, who was freed from slavery in 1827 and went on to become a very powerful preacher and opponent of slavery, remembered her first owner for his "kindness of heart." Thomas Jefferson had close relationships with some of his house slaves, especially those that were related to the Hemings family. Yet even these relationships were a product of the slave system itself. When one of his slaves failed to tell Jefferson he was leaving Monticello to visit his wife in Washington, DC, in 1806, the then president sent a slave catcher after him. Jefferson could not understand why the man had not informed him, since "never in his life [had he] received a blow from anyone."[53]

Resistance was at the heart of the relationship for other slaves. Some would pretend to be ill, while others would do the work slowly and without great care. But all wanted to be free. As a white man said before the Louisiana Supreme Court in 1847, the desire for freedom "exists in the bosom of every slave—whether the recent captive, or him to whom bondage has become a habit." Some slaves attempted to escape, a practice that was aided by the Underground Railroad, "a network of persons who helped escaped slaves on their way to freedom in the northern states or Canada." Although the network was in existence as early as 1786, when Washington complained that one of his slaves had been helped by Quakers, it received its name in early 1831. There are varying estimates of how many slaves were able to escape, although the overall number was small compared to the total number of those held in bondage. For those that were caught, punishment was brutal. The slave would often be stripped naked and whipped, and then salt or another corrosive substance poured into the wounds so that the person would be permanently scared. Severe punishment was inflicted not just on those that had attempted to escape, but on any slave considered uncooperative, insolent, or surly. The most famous of the escaped slaves was Frederick Douglass.[54]

Frederick Douglass

Historians have dated the birth of Frederick Bailey, who later changed his name to Douglass, as 1818. Douglass, in his first autobiographical work, *Narrative Life of Frederick Douglass*, indicates that he never knew his correct age. "I do not remember to have ever met a slave who could tell his birthday," Douglass wrote. It was another indignity inflicted upon African Americans that their births were so unimportant that they should not be memorialized. Frederick Bailey was raised by his grandparents while his mother worked in an adjoining farm. One of Douglass's biographers, William S. McFeely, intimates that his mother, Harriet, may not have had much interest in her son. But Douglass, who only met her four or five times, and always at night, suggests that it was fear that kept her away. "She was a field hand,

and a whipping is the penalty of not being in the field at sunrise," Douglass wrote. His father was a white man, and may well have been their owner, Aaron Anthony.[55]

Anthony worked for a rich plantation owner in Maryland named Edward Lloyd. Lloyd had been the governor of Maryland and a United States senator. He owned Wye House, his headquarters for a vast plantation of ten thousand acres that was worked by over five hundred slaves. Douglass would later refer to it as a "house that groaned under ... blood bought luxuries." When he was six years old, his grandmother Betsey dropped young Frederick off at the great house to live. He felt abandoned, and "he never fully trusted anyone again," according to McFeely.[56]

Two years later, young Frederick was sent to Baltimore to live with Hugh and Sophia Auld. The move would change Frederick Bailey's life forever. He was only too happy to escape the plantation, where he saw instances of great brutality, including the whipping of his aunt. "The louder she screamed, the harder [Anthony] whipped; and where the blood ran fastest, there he whipped longest," Douglass wrote. He was always cold, having only a linen shirt to wear, and hungry, the children being called to eat from mush from a trough "like so many pigs." When he arrived in the Fell Point area of Baltimore, he was greeted by a loving family, especially Sophia. "I saw what I had never seen before; it was a white face beaming with the most kindly emotions," he wrote of Sophia Auld. But when she began to teach him to read, her husband interceded. "He should know nothing but the will of his master, and learn to obey it," Hugh told his wife. "It would forever unfit him to be a slave." In *Narrative*, Frederick writes: "I understood the pathway from slavery to freedom" would be found in reading, and he taught himself. When Douglass was twelve, he obtained a copy of *The Columbian Orator*, and began to learn what it took to become a great speaker. As he entered puberty, he heard about the abolitionist movement, which was just underway, and he dreamed of freedom. He became aware of men like John Quincy Adams, who were working to free the slaves. He also became surly, as most young men in their early teens do, which "put a gulf between him and his family," McFeely writes. This probably led Hugh Auld to send Frederick, now fifteen, to live with Thomas Auld in the port town of St. Michaels.[57]

Thomas Auld was also unable to control Douglass, so he sent him to live with Edward Covey, a known slave breaker. The first six months was a brutal experience for Frederick, long hours of work, insufficient food, and frequent beatings. "I was broken in body, soul, and spirit," Douglass later wrote. Finally, when Covey went to attack him, he decided to fight back. "I seized Covey hard by the throat ... he held on to me and I to him." Douglass reports that the fight went on for almost two hours, and that after this, Covey never attempted to whip him again. "This battle with Mr. Covey was the turning point in my career as a slave ... it was a glorious resurrection, from the tomb of slavery, to the heaven of freedom."[58]

Douglass now committed himself to run away and become a free man. His first attempt failed, and he ended up in jail. Hugh Auld had him released, and took him back to Baltimore, where he became trained as a journeyman caulker. He lived on his own, hired out as a laborer, and was largely independent of Auld. He met and fell in love with Anna Murray, a free black woman who was five years older than he was. In the summer of 1838, Douglass went to a camp social meeting outside the city. Before he left, he failed to pay Auld his wages for the week. Auld ordered Frederick "to give up his independent employment and housing and move back where [he] could keep an eye on him," McFeely writes. At that point, the twenty-year-old

Frederick knew he could no longer live as a slave and he decided to escape once again. Douglass used the Underground Railroad, which the *New York Times* would later describe as "the organized arrangements made in various sections of the country, to aid fugitive slaves." He was able to obtain documents that showed he was a free seaman. On September 3, 1838, Douglass boarded a train headed North. He would eventually arrive in New York after taking multiple trains, a steamboat, and two ferries. Once he arrived there, he was assisted by David Ruggles, who then made arrangements for Anna to join him. They were soon married and departed for New England, where Frederick Douglass would make an indelible mark in the movement to abolish slavery and free his people.[59]

Endnotes

1   From the introduction to Wood, *Empire*, p. 1.

2   For a quick survey of this dispute, the internet has numerous articles on this subject. For example, see the following: https://www.saylor.org/site/wp-content/uploads/2012/11/HIST303-2.6.1-HowRevolutionaryWastheRevolution-FINAL.pdf; http://www.stratford.org/uploaded/faculty/jjordan/Viewpoint_Essays/(Microsoft_Word_-_Did_the_American_Revolution_have_a_revolutionary_impac.pdf; http://www.ettc.net/tah/Summer_Institute_Documents/Summer_Institute_2008/Readings/WEEK%202--Major%20Problems%20in%20American%20History.pdf.

3   See Wood, *Radicalism*, p. 30 and p. 109. For a complete discussion of these changes, readers should review Part I of the book from pages 11 to 109. A condensed summary of the book can be found at http://www.ettc.net/tah/Summer_Institute_Documents/Summer_Institute_2008/Readings/WEEK%202--Major%20Problems%20in%20American%20History.pdf.

4   Koch and William Peden, eds., p. 389 and p. 649.

5   Peter H. Lindert and Jeffrey G. Williamson, *Unequal Gains: American Growth and Inequality Since 1700* (Princeton, 2016), p. 15 and p. 37.

6   The quote from Hammond was retrieved April 17, 2017, from http://www.stratford.org/uploaded/faculty/jjordan/Viewpoint_Essays/(Microsoft_Word_-_Did_the_American_Revolution_have_a_revolutionary_impac.pdf; Jennifer Schuessler, April 13, 2017, "A New Museum of the American Revolution, Warts and All," *The New York Times*, retrieved June 12, 2017, from https://www.nytimes.com/2017/04/13/arts/

design/a-new-museum-of-the-american-revolution-warts-and-all.html?_r=0; Wood, *Radicalism*, p. 169 and p. 173.

7 Gordon Wood, *The Creation of the American Republic: 1776-1787* (Chapel Hill, 1969), p. 403–406; Fraser, p. 236–237.

8 Fraser, p. 197–204, contains a more comprehensive discussion of Madison's views.

9 Shelia M. Skemp, *Women and Politics in the Era of the American Revolution*, p. 1–6, retrieved April 25, 2017, from http://americanhistory.oxfordre.com/view/10.1093/acrefore/9780199329175.001.0001/acrefore-9780199329175-e-216; Rosemary Zagarri, *Revolutionary Backlash: Women and Politics in the Early American Republic* (Philadelphia, 2007), p. 24–25; Chernow, *Washington*, p. 216–217.

10 Charlotte Gordon, *Romantic Outlaws: The Extraordinary Lives of Mary Wollstonecraft & Mary Shelley* New York, 2015), p. 73 and p. 257.

11 Gordon, p. 11–22.

12 Gordon, p. 36–48.

13 Gordon, p. 60–73, p. 92–98, p. 111.

14 Gordon, p. 142–154.

15 Skemp, p. 8–11; David McCullough, *John Adams* (New York, 2001), p. 57; Zagarri, p. 30–42; Mary Wollstonecraft, *A Vindication of the Rights of Woman* (SWB Publishers, 2010), p. 9 and p. 20.

16 Gordon, p. xv and p. 178.

17 Marie Basile McDaniel, Book Review of *Revolutionary Backlash* by Rosemarie Zagarri, p. 2, retrieved April 25, 2017, from http://www.h-net.org/reviews/showrev.php?id=24669; Zagarri, p. 75 and p. 86–87.

18 Zagarri, p. 125 and p. 173–174; Skemp, p. 11–12; McDaniel, p. 3.

19 Roberta W. Francis, "The History Behind the Equal Rights Amendment," retrieved May 15, 2017, from http://www.equalrightsamendment.org/history.htm.

20 Wilentz, *The Rise*, p. 27; Eric Foner, *The Story of American Freedom* (New York, 1998), p. 32; Akhil Reed Amar, *America's Constitution: A Biography* (New York, 2005), p. 69.

21 Christopher Clark, *Social Change in America: From the Revolution through the Civil War* (Chicago, 2006), p.81.

22 The statistics are from Stanley Lebergott, *Labor Force and Employment, 1800-1960*, retrieved May 16, 2017, from http://www.nber.org/chapters/c1567.pdf.

23 Howe, p. 34; Jack Larkin, *The Reshaping of Everyday Life:1790–1840* (New York, 1988), p. 16–17.

24 Larkin, p. 36–39; Howe, p. 35; Clark, p. 118.

25 Larkin, p. 16–20; Howe, p. 37.

26 Larkin, p. 171–172 and p. 112.

27 Larkin, p 47–50; Clark, p. 101–102; Howe, p. 40–41.

28 Larkin, p. 39–42; Howe, p. 536.

29 Larkin, p. 42–48; Sellers, p. 24; Howe, p. 537.

30 Burns, p. 287–290; Howe, p. 532–533.

31 Burns, p. 293–295; Howe, p. 536–547.

32 Howe, p. 526–527.

33 Richards, p. 68–74; Clark, p. 98; Howe, p. 527–528.

34 Burns, p. 221; Larkin, p. 126; Howe, p. 531.

35 Lindert and Williamson, p. 133–135.

36 Howe, p. 532.

37 Appleby, *Inheriting*, p. 92–99.

38 Appleby, *Inheriting*, p. 99–102.

39 Richards, p. 108; Howe, p. 452–453.

40 Appleby, p. 106.

41 Wood, *Empire*, p. 327 and p. 334–335; Richards, p. 5; Howe, p. 528.

42 Wood, *Empire*, p. 336–337; Howe, p. 430–431.

43 Wood, *Empire*, p. 339; Howe, p. 166–167.

44 Freeman, *The Field of Blood*, p. 5, p. 30–31, p. 46 and p. 50–52.

45 The statistics are from https://www.census.gov/prod/www/decennial.html; Kimberly Sambol-Tosco, "Legal Rights and Government," retrieved April 27, 2017 from http://www.pbs.org/wnet/slavery/experience/legal/index.html. This site from the Public Broadcasting System has some very interesting and useful information on the slave experience in America called "Slavery and the Making of America." For a history of free blacks voting "The History of Black Voting Rights" retrieved May 9, 2017, from http://www.freerepublic.com/focus/news/1072053/posts and "Race-based legislation in the North" retrieved May 9, 2017, from http://www.pbs.org/wgbh/aia/part4/4p2957.html.

46 Nikole Hannah-Jones (August 14, 2019), "Our democracy's founding ideals were false when they were written. Black Americas have fought to make them True," *New York Times Magazine*, retrieved August 15, 2019, from https://www.nytimes.com/interactive/2019/08/14/magazine/black-history-american-democracy.html.

47 Kenneth M. Stampp, *The Peculiar Institution: Slavery in the Ante-Bellum South* (New York, 1956), p. 44 and p. 54–55; Nicolas Boston, "Living Conditions," retrieved April 27, 2017, from http://www.pbs.org/wnet/slavery/experience/legal/index.html.

48 Stampp, p. 74.

49 Boston, p. 1, and Stampp, p. 63.

50 *House Slaves: An Overview*, Gale Library of Daily Life: Slavery in America, retrieved April 27, 2017, from Encyclopedia.com http://www.encyclopedia.com/humanities/applied-and-social-sciences-magazines/house-slaves-overview; House Slaves, retrieved

April 27, 2017 from Spartacus Educational http://spartacus-educational.com/USASdomestic.htm.

51 Howe, p. 58.

52 Stampp, p. 162–166 and p. 184–187.

53 Howe, p. 57–59; Reed and Onuf, p. 68–69.

54 Stampp, p. 90–91; information on the Underground Railroad is from "Underground Railroad" retrieved May 10, 2017, from http://www.history.com/topics/black-history/underground-railroad and "The Underground Railroad: 1780–1782," retrieved May 10, 2017, from http://www.pbs.org/wgbh/aia/part4/4p2944.html; information on runaway slave punishments from Jen Shulman, "These 10 Horrific Punishments Were Used To Discipline Slaves Who Misbehaved," retrieved May 10, 2017, from http://www.allday.com/these-10-horrific-punishments-were-used-to-discipline-slaves-who-misbe-2180836601.html.

55 Frederick Douglass, *Narrative of the Life of Frederick Douglass* (Mineola, 1995), p. 1–2; William S. McFeely, *Frederick Douglass* (New York, 1991), p. 3–10.

56 McFeely, p. 10–14.

57 Douglass, p. 4, p. 16, and p. 20; McFeely, p. 23–39; James Oakes, *The Radical and the Republican: Frederick Douglass, Abraham Lincoln, and the Triumph of Antislavery Politics* (New York, 2007), p. 6–7.

58 Douglass, p. 42–43.

59 McFeely, p. 58–73; the quote from the *New York Times* was taken from Eric Foner, *Gateway to Freedom: The Hidden History of the Underground Railroad* (New York, 2015), p. 6.

CHAPTER 7

Religion in the Early Republic

*On my arrival in the United States the religious aspect of the
country was the first thing that struck me.*

*That to enable religions, humanly speaking, to thrive in
democratic periods, not only must they carefully remain within
a circle of religious matters, but also their power depends even
more upon the nature of their beliefs, their external structures,
and the duties they impose.*
  —ALEXIS DE TOCQUEVILLE[1]

As Tocqueville noted upon his arrival, religion played a significant
role in American life and always has. New England was founded
by the Puritans fleeing religious persecution in Great Britain. Other
colonies also had a connection to religion in their establishment,
including the Anglicans in Virginia and the Quakers in Pennsylvania,
although none was quite as strong as that found in Massachusetts and
most of its New England neighbors. By the time of the American
Revolution, ideas from the Enlightenment led many of the founders
to deism and ultimately to the separation of church and state. But in
the aftermath, religion thrived even more.

Religion in the Colonial Era

They left England aboard the Mayflower on August 5, 1620, a small group of Puritans known as the Pilgrims. Unlike their more mainline brethren, the Pilgrims were Separatists who wanted to set up their own church. The journey was full of delays due to leaks that developed in their sister ship the *Speedwell*, which had to turn back. During the second half of the voyage, the seas turned rough as the small ship ran into numerous Atlantic storms. They finally arrived in the New World in November and established the Plymouth colony. They endured a hard winter in which half of the people died. Yet they still believed that God had directed them to come in order to escape the dictates of the Church of England.[2]

The Great Migration followed in 1630, led by John Winthrop, who preached that "We shall be as a city upon a hill." This would become one of the enduring myths that both John F. Kennedy and Ronald Reagan would refer to, that America was destined to be an exceptional nation on the world stage. "It is a vision chiseled into the American ethos, seemingly as indestructible as the presidential faces carved into Mount Rushmore," wrote historian David Lee McMullen. The Puritans would establish a republic on America's shores, and over time New England would become the most egalitarian region in the New World. It was also a society without a division between church and state, a tradition they carried with them from their European roots. "Only through the union of church and state, Puritans believed, could humans produce a Christian society conformed to scriptural teaching," the religious scholar David L. Holmes argues. Everyone was required to attend religious services, and laws were adopted that made immoral acts, including adultery and witchcraft, illegal. Those who disagreed were banished, like Roger Williams, who went on to form a more open and tolerant religious society in Rhode Island. Williams wanted a "hedge or wall of separation between the Garden of the church and the wilderness of the world." As Jon Meacham argues, Williams was concerned not that religion would pervert government, but that the "vices of men could pervert the church, turning faith into a means of temporal power."[3]

The Congregational Church, which the Puritans were a part of, became the established religion throughout most of New England, which was viewed by "visitors as the most conspicuously devout and religiously homogeneous region in British North America," according to Taylor. But full membership in this church was limited to an exclusive few, only those members who took communion. Many of those who attended church may have felt unworthy to participate in the sacrament of communion, which was required for full membership. Due to this, records on actual church membership can be misleading. For example, two historians report that church membership by the end of the eighteenth century was only 10–15 percent of the population. While formal church membership was low, actual church attendance was high.[4]

☙ ☙ ☙

Virginia was originally established by men in search of get-rich-quick schemes, as they pursued the Spanish model of exploiting the local Indian tribes in search of gold and other valuable minerals. This approach was an abject failure, and the Virginians ultimately turned to plantation farming. Religion was used originally as a means of implementing discipline through the "Laws Divine, Moral and Martial" that were introduced in 1609. Twice-daily church services were required, and those who failed to attend would first lose food;

later offenses could result in whipping and even death. Eventually, the Anglican Church became the dominant religion. But its reach was not as strong as the Congregational Church in New England, largely because Anglican ministers were so few. "In 1724, Virginia had 120,000 inhabitants but only twenty-eight Anglican ministers. Further south the situation was even worse," Taylor reports.[5]

In other colonies, the religious experience was present, but never as strong as that of New England. Pennsylvania was established as a colony for Quakers, but also welcomed people from Ireland, Wales, Germany, and the Netherlands, who brought their own religions with them. Anglicanism was also the established church in New York, but it represented only a minority of the population. New Jersey was also open to people of different religious faiths. North Carolina was considered the least religious of the colonies, although in the 1750s the Baptist movement had spread there. In South Carolina, the Anglican Church was predominant, although other churches also flourished. Like North Carolina, "the Anglican establishment in Georgia existed on paper," Holmes writes.[6]

The first great wave of Evangelicalism swept through the colonies in the 1730s and 1740s. The most successful preacher was the Englishman George Whitefield, a disciple of John Wesley and the emerging Methodist religion, who made seven trips to America in the 1740s. The Evangelicals stressed an emotional and personal religious experience, that one must be born again in Jesus Christ and take him as their personal lord and savior. Whitefield was a charismatic and dynamic preacher who attracted large crowds who attended services both in churches and in open fields. He became a friend of Benjamin Franklin, who attended one of his revivals in Philadelphia. Franklin had determined to give no money to Whitefield, but by the end of the service stated that "he finished so admirably, that I emptied my Pocket wholly into the Collector's Dish." The movement would soon burn out, but it left a religious legacy in the form of both the Methodist and Baptist sects that would come to dominate in the West and the South and flourish among African American slaves.[7]

By 1750, about "two-thirds of colonial adults attended or were affiliated with a church." The table below shows the number of churches by denomination.

Sect	Primary Location
Congregationalists	450 churches centered in New England
Anglicans	300 churches, mostly in the South
Quakers	250 meetings in Pennsylvania
Presbyterians	160 churches, mostly in the middle colonies
Baptists	100 churches in the South
Lutherans	95 churches in the South
Dutch Reformed, German Reformed, Catholic, and Jewish	Scattered throughout
Source: Taylor, p. 342	

This was the state of religion as the revolution was about to unfold. Of the thirteen colonies, nine had an established religion. Only Rhode Island, New Jersey, Pennsylvania, and Georgia had none.[8] Since state-established religion was common prior to the Revolutionary War, why did the Founding Fathers decide to separate church and state? It is to that question we now turn.

The Enlightenment and the Founders

The founders were heavily influenced by European Enlightenment thinkers as diverse as Thomas Hobbes, René Descartes, and John

Locke. Each questioned established ways of thinking and considered reason as the means to knowledge. The Enlightenment roughly spanned the eighteenth century. Religion was also affected, as standard Christian orthodoxy came under intense scrutiny. One movement that gained adherents was deism, a belief that God had created all things, but he did not intervene in human affairs. "Its creed is pure and sublimely simple. It believes in God and there it rests," the deist Thomas Paine claimed. One Christian clergyman wrote that "the Deist is one who denies the Divinity, the Incarnation, and the Atonement of Christ ... and believes in the God of nature." Many of the Founding Fathers accepted some elements of deism.[9]

When Jefferson wrote the Declaration of Independence, his references to the Creator and Nature's God was not the God of any particular religion. His fellow authors of that Declaration, including Franklin and Adams, made no attempt to change those words, perhaps because they too had a less than orthodox view of religion. Franklin is often described as a deist, although he was more of a freethinker and a man of science. When he was young, he envisioned there were multiple gods that governed different solar systems, with one overarching and all-powerful God that "expects or requires no worship or praise from us." But the individual God of each solar system was "pleased and delights in the happiness of those he created," a personal God at odds with a pure deist. Later in life, Franklin indicated his support for the Trinity, and just before he died, Franklin had simplified his faith even further. "Here is my creed," he stated. "I believe in one God, Creator of the Universe. That he governs it by his Providence. That he ought to be worshipped."[10] John Adams was also much less orthodox than one who was raised in Puritan New England. He rejected the notion of eternal damnation, stating "I believe in no such thing," and that "the love of God and his creation ... these are my religion." He also questioned the divinity of Jesus and the Trinity, placing him outside traditional Christianity, but within the mainstream of Unitarianism. Adams and many of the other founders also strongly supported the idea that religion was essential in inculcating virtue into mankind, as we shall explore in greater detail later in this chapter.[11]

The other members of the Continental Congress, who went through an extensive editing job on the balance of the Declaration, made no changes to Jefferson's use of "Nature's God." As Jon Meacham has pointed out, they did add two other references to God, but both were along the same lines as those that Jefferson had used, including referring to the "supreme judge of the world" and to a "firm reliance on the protection of divine providence." Perhaps many of them too subscribed to an unorthodox view of religion. The Continental Congress was also made up of men from thirteen separate colonies who subscribed to many different Christian sects. Religion could have added to their already extensive disagreements if they were not careful. "In the public business of the nation ... it was important to the founders to speak of God in a way that was unifying, not divisive. 'Nature's God' was the path they chose, and it has served the nation admirably," Meacham has written.[12]

Classical liberalism was one of the Enlightenment ideas that animated the American Revolution. Those ideas were most forcefully presented by John Locke. As historians Isaac Kramnick and R. Laurence Moore point out, the liberalism of the founders placed not only political and economic liberty at the forefront of their struggles, but also religious liberty. "For these historical liberals, like the American founders, the state was best kept out of people's houses, out of the marketplace, and out of spiritual life," the authors write. Jefferson was an adherent of Locke, who wanted to separate civil and religious power when he wrote: "And upon this ground, I affirm that the magistrate's power extends not to the establishing of any articles of faith, or form of worship, by the force of his laws." For Locke, a church was a "free and voluntary society." Jefferson shared this belief, writing in *Notes on the State of Virginia* that "the rights of conscience, we never submitted, we could not submit," to governmental power. Jefferson went on: "But it does no injury to me for my neighbor to say there are twenty gods, or no God. It neither picks my pocket nor breaks my leg." Kramnick and Moore argue that for Jefferson, there were two sources of tyranny—"kings, such as mad George III, and priests." The real danger occurred when these two sources of power became joined. Both Locke and the founders were well aware that "millions of Europeans had died in the two centuries of religious wars between Protestants and Catholics that followed Martin Luther's break from Rome," the authors write. The founders wanted to avoid a similar fate.[13]

It should come as no surprise that Jefferson would set out to eliminate Anglicanism as the established religion of Virginia when he proposed the Statute for Religious Freedom in 1776. In it, Jefferson argued that no one should be subject to "temporal punishments" for following their own conscience on religious matters, since to do so is "a departure from the plan of the holy Author of our religion." The act would have made it illegal to require anyone "to frequent or support any religious worship, place, or ministry." As Jefferson later wrote, it "brought on the severest contest in which I have ever been engaged." It would take ten years, and the efforts of his good friend James Madison, to finally get the statute passed in Virginia. Madison was no stranger to efforts to promote religious liberty. He had chafed at the way non-Anglicans had been treated in his home state, and one of his first legislative acts was to strengthen George Mason's section on religious freedom in the Virginia Declaration of Rights in 1776, which had essentially ended Anglicanism as the established church in Virginia. In 1785, Madison became engaged in a battle to stop the implementation of a bill sponsored by Patrick Henry to tax Virginians to pay for religious teachers on a nonsectarian basis, which the Declaration of Rights had left as an open question. As part of that fight, Madison was able to defeat Henry's bill and get Jefferson's statute finally passed, while he (Jefferson) was serving as minister to France.[14]

Jefferson was labeled an atheist in the election of 1800, partly due to his actions in separating church from state in Virginia, and partly because of his writings in *Notes on the State of Virginia*. But Jefferson was no atheist. He was a vestryman in his local Anglican Parish, St. Anne's, and gave generously to other churches as well. He was married by an Anglican priest, and a minister was at his bedside when he died. As stated earlier, he rejected combining the power of the state with the power of religion, which he believed had led to the corruption of Christianity. His rational nature and belief in science and reason led him to reject many of the precepts of Christianity: miracles, the virgin birth of Jesus, the Trinity, and Jesus as God. "And the day will come when the mystical generation of Jesus by the supreme being as his father in the womb of a virgin will be classed with the fable of the generations of Minerva in the brain of Jupiter," he wrote to John Adams in 1823. Yet he also believed that Jesus was a great moral teacher, "the most pure, benevolent, and sublime which has ever preached to man." He wrote his own Bible, excising the miracles and highlighting the moral teachings of Jesus. Jefferson thought that religion was a private matter, "a subject of accountability to our God alone," and that no one should be forced to believe in God. Perhaps his most enduring legacy on religion was reflected in a letter he sent to the Baptists in Danbury, Connecticut, shortly after he was elected president, when he wrote that the First Amendment created "a wall of separation between church and state."[15]

The American Constitution is a remarkably secular document. Whereas the Declaration of Independence referred to the Creator, Nature's God, and divine providence, the Framers of the Constitution placed their trust in "We the People." The one explicit reference in the document, in fact, places a limitation on religion. Introduced on August 20, near the end of the convention, it was eventually incorporated in Article VI to state that "no religious test shall ever be required as a Qualification to any office or public Trust under the United States." The proposal elicited little debate among the delegates, with only one state (North Carolina) opposed and Maryland divided in its vote. Hamilton's draft constitution, which he shared with his then friend Madison prior to the convention, included very similar language.[16]

The state ratifying conventions proved to be more contentious over the issue. In a country where nine of the thirteen states still had established religions, and eleven states required a religious test to hold office, the opposition was not surprising. There was fear that "Atheists, Deists, Papists or abettors of any false religion" would take over the new nation, as one critic in the Massachusetts convention framed it. "The absence of religious tests, it was feared, would open up the national government to control by Jews, Catholics, and Quakers," Kramnick and Moore write. One delegate in Connecticut proposed that the preamble be changed to the following: "We the people of the United States in a firm belief of the being and perfection of the one living and true God ... do ordain." His motion was voted down. In response to concerns expressed in North Carolina, future Supreme Court Justice James Iredell defended the Constitution, telling the delegates "that a man may be of different religious sentiments from our own, without being a bad member of society," and that banning such tests would "secure religious liberty, by putting all sects on a level—the only way to prevent persecution." There were also ministers who supported the ban, as did those who were of a more secular nature. One delegate to the Constitutional Convention wrote that religious tests "are useless, tyrannical, and peculiarly unfit for the people of this country" and that "civil government has no business to meddle with the private operations of the people." Ultimately, sentiments like these would prevail, and the Article VI ban on religious tests survived.[17]

As part of the outcome from the Virginia ratifying convention and his later campaign for the House of Representatives, James Madison pledged to fix the major blunder the Constitutional Convention had made; this was to add what we have come to call the Bill of Rights. His original proposal to Congress on religious freedom stated: "The Civil Rights of none shall be abridged on account of religious belief or worship, nor shall any national religion be established, nor shall the full and equal rights of conscience be in any manner, or any pretext, infringed." The House would change this wording to a prohibition that "Congress shall make no law establishing religion or prohibiting the free exercise thereof," and the Senate would ultimately combine that with freedom of speech and of the press as the First Amendment now states. Madison also included a provision that would limit the right of states to interfere in certain private matters, including religion. "No state shall infringe the right of trial by jury in criminal cases, nor the rights of conscience, nor the freedom of speech, or of the press." While Madison would successfully steer the latter amendment through the House, the Senate would strip this out. Congress could not establish a religion, and as the constitutional scholar Akhil Reed Amar has written, the First Amendment also "prohibited the national legislature from interfering with, or trying to disestablish, churches established by state and local governments."[18]

Madison thought that the restriction on the states was the most "valuable amendment on the whole list," but he may have been somewhat assuaged by the fact that the states had begun to liberalize their religious establishment practices since colonial times. While Jefferson and Madison were pursuing the disestablishment of religion in Virginia, John Adams was taking a different tack in Massachusetts, where he was attempting to balance "Publick religion," based on "honesty, diligence, devotion, obedience, virtue, and love of God, neighbor, and self," as the legal scholar John Witte Jr. has written. Adams wanted to "countenance a plurality of forms of religious exercise and association" in the Massachusetts Constitution of 1776. That constitution ultimately placed the responsibility for ensuring religious worship on its "several Towns, Parishes, precincts ... religious societies, to make suitable provision ... for the Public worship of GOD." But the Massachusetts Constitution did not make Congregationalism the sole established religion for the state and included a provision that "no subordination of any one sect or denomination to the other shall ever be established by law." By 1791, there were seven states "with multiple establishments" in which religion was supported by government without restricting this to one particular sect. While Madison would have preferred the anti-establishment clause to have been extended to the states, he could at least take solace that there were multiple sects competing against one another in a nonfavored way by many of the states. He had in fact told the Virginia ratifying convention in 1788 that the protection of religion flows "from the multiplicity of sects, which pervades America, and which is the best and only security for religious liberty in any society. For where there is a variety of sects, there cannot be a majority of any one sect to oppress and persecute the rest." As the historian Leonard W. Levy has written, the establishment clause in the federal Constitution "was meant to depoliticize religion, thereby defusing the potentially explosive condition of a religiously heterogeneous society ... and to protect religion from government, and government from religion."[19]

❦ ❦ ❦

The founders also thought that religion was an important building block in establishing a stable republic. As we have seen, Lockean liberalism was one strain of political thought that informed the founders, the view that governments exist to protect the rights of individuals, particularly their property rights. Another strain of thought was classical republicanism, which "conceived of man as naturally social, with a need to participate in political life and display a capacity for public virtue," Garrett Ward Sheldon wrote. Public virtue was at the core of John Adams's view of republicanism, which was grounded in his view of private virtue. "Public virtue cannot exist in a Nation without private (virtue), and public virtue is the only foundation of Republics," Adams wrote in 1776. "There must be a positive passion for the public good, public interest ... established in the minds of the people, or there can be no Republican government." At the Virginia ratifying convention in June of 1788, Madison said: "Is there no virtue among us? If there be not, then we are in a wretched situation." Washington, in his farewell address in 1796, wrote that "virtue or morality is a necessary spring of popular government."[20]

Religion was one of the main sources for creating private virtue in the public. Alexander Hamilton believed that virtue sprang from morality and "morality *must* fall with religion," because religion can help "confine" man "within the bounds of social duty," quotes constitutional scholar Geoffrey R. Stone. Franklin thought that religion was needed to "restrain [people] from vice," and wondered "if Men are so wicked as we now see them *with* religion what would they be *without* it?" Adams had a ready answer for that, writing to Jefferson in 1817 that "without Religion this World would be Something not fit to be mentioned in polite Company, I mean Hell." For his part, Jefferson once wrote "while I claim a right to believe in one God, I yield as freely to others that of believing in three. Both religions, I find, make honest men, and that is the only point society has any right to look to."[21]

The founders believed that both civil society and religion would thrive best without government interference. They had come to believe that "civil societies dominated by compulsory religious rigidity were unhappy and intolerant, while religious liberty seemed to produce more prosperous, stable, and popular cultures," Meacham has observed. Madison, for example, applauded Pennsylvania as a place where the "public has long felt the good effects of the religious as well as civil liberty," compared to places where "religious bondage shackles and debilitates the mind and unfits it for every noble enterprise." By the 1830s, Tocqueville observed that ministers "all attributed the peaceful domination that religion exercises in their country principally to the complete separation of church and state." Both religion and democracy would grow and expand in the early American republic.[22]

The Second Great Awakening

They came in droves, with estimates as high as twenty thousand people in attendance at Cane Ridge, Kentucky, in the summer of 1801 for a week of religious proselytizing. A Presbyterian minister who preached at the event remembered that "all distinctions of name was laid aside."

All were "welcome to sign, pray, or call sinners to repentance. Neither was there any distinction as to age, sex, color or any thing of a temporary nature ... [and all] had equal privilege to minister the light which they received, in whatever way the sprit directed." Another observer noted how people "fell in droves," were "affected with the jerks" and would scream with ecstasy at the personal religious experience they underwent. Throughout the day, multiple preachers gave sermons all at the same time. Cane Ridge may have been the largest of these camp meetings, but it was far from the only one. One Methodist bishop claimed that camp meetings "brought together three to four million Americans annually—an estimated one-third of the population," according to the religious historian Nathan O. Hatch. One Methodist preacher called it "fishing with a large net."[23]

Indeed, religion flourished in the aftermath of the founders' efforts to split church from state at the national level. The Second Great Awakening, a period that roughly ran from the 1790s through the 1830s, saw the growth of new evangelical churches like the Baptists and the Methodists that competed for adherents with the older mainline churches, including the Congregationalists in New England and the Anglican church in the South. The Baptists went from 100 churches in 1750 to 858 in the 1790s, and then to 2,500 by the 1830s. Methodism barely existed in America prior to the revolution, but by the 1820s it had approximately 250,000 members, with that number doubling by the 1830s.[24]

Some of the new evangelical ministers were strongly supportive of the separation of church and state. The Baptist minister Isaac Backus from Connecticut believed that religion had to be based on "a voluntary obedience to God's revealed will," and not based on government intervention and support, as Gordon Wood has written. The Presbyterian minister Lyman Beecher originally bemoaned Connecticut's 1818 law that disestablished the Congregational Church, saying "it was as dark a day as I ever saw." But he soon changed his mind and came to believe that it was "the best thing that ever happened," since it "cut the churches loose from dependence on the state." Instead of losing influence, ministers had in fact gained it, Beecher went on to say.[25]

Perhaps one of the reasons these new evangelical churches did so well was that they were in sync with certain elements of the Republicanism of Jefferson, including placing the common person in a central role. Many of the new evangelical ministers believed that individuals needed to find their own path to God. By the 1800s, "it took little creativity for some to begin to reexamine the social function of the clergy and to question the right of any order of men to claim authority to interpret God's word," Hatch writes. The evangelical preacher Lorenzo Dow may have gone the furthest in promoting the common person's religious experience in the language of Jefferson. "But if all are 'BORN EQUAL,' and endowed with unalienable RIGHTS by their Creator ... [then] there can be no just reason, as a cause, why he should not think, and judge, and act for himself in matters of religion, opinion, and private judgement." Dow did much to expand Methodism, traveling throughout the country in the early 1800s. He attracted large crowds, and many people thought he "was the most memorable preacher they had ever heard," according to Hatch.[26]

The evangelical movement spread the widest in the newly developing areas of the West and the South where the existing mainline churches were the weakest and where there were few members of the elite or well-educated clergy. As early as 1780, the president of Yale "counted sixty destitute parishes in Vermont, sixty in New Hampshire, and eighty in Massachusetts and Maine, most of them in rural areas and new settlements," Hatch reports. In Virginia, less than 40 percent of the parishes could support ministers by the early

1800s. Where mainline churches and trained pastors failed to go, the evangelical movement spread. As we have seen, people would gather in camp meetings, "in fields, barns, taverns, or homes, to lay hands on one another, to bathe each other's feet ... and to form new bonds of friendship," according to Wood. Many of the preachers, like Dow, were without formal training and developed "large followings by the democratic art of persuasion," Hatch writes. This created a rivalry with elite and educated ministers. It also reflected the larger social forces underway that were breaking down the hierarchy of the colonial era and that were helping to usher in a more populist and democratic age.[27]

The evangelical movement was based on the idea that people should be able to make up their own minds about their relationship to God without the need to be told what to believe by an elite clergy. Hatch frames the issue as a question. "If opinions about politics and society were no longer the monopoly of the few, why could not people begin to think for themselves in matters of religion?" Many of the newly minted preachers looked to the Gospels for inspiration, pointing to the fact that Jesus and his disciples were poor people who lived on the fringes of their society. The Evangelicals "appropriated Christ's teaching that power in the church should emanate from below, that the first should be last, and that the chief should not lord it over others but become a servant to all," according to Hatch. As one of the Evangelicals wrote, Jesus and his followers "were not college learnt."[28]

There was also a large role for women in the evangelical movement. In the Methodist church, women could lead "classes," small groupings of about thirty people each in which worship services were undertaken. Women could also be exhorters, which is the "term for laypeople who delivered what were in effect mini-sermons," according to Howe. One of the most famous female exhorters was Phoebe

Palmer, who had been converted by the founder of Methodism, John Wesley. Traveling throughout the country, she preached in homes and at camp revivals until her death in 1873. Other women also played a large role in the evangelical movement, including Harriet Livermore, who spoke before a joint session of Congress in 1827, with President John Quincy Adams in attendance. These women were at the cutting edge of "the next generation of women's-rights activists," Howe argues, although most women were not in positions of leadership in the church. Women would also go on to be actively involved in many of the moral improvement societies that the Christian churches would soon undertake, as we will explore further.[29]

Evangelical Christianity also spread among both free blacks and slaves. Before the revolution, there were very few black Christians. But the earliest evangelical leaders were able to appeal to African Americans because they were antislavery. Hatch writes that both Baptist and Methodist ministers in the post-revolutionary era were "militant about converting slaves, they forthrightly identified with the slaves' plight, and they gave clear antislavery testimony." Some of these ministers freed their own slaves. Another major appeal was that African American men could be ministers in the Methodist church and could openly preach in the Baptist Church. But by the early 1800s, there was the beginning of a backlash among whites, who were increasingly uncomfortable with worship services attended by blacks. This led to independent black churches, including the African Methodist Episcopal Church (AME), which was the first all-African congregation when it was founded in Philadelphia in 1816. A former slave who converted to Methodism during the American Revolution, and then went on to buy his way out of slavery, became the first bishop of the AME Church.[30]

Evangelical movements that rely so much on itinerant preachers and camp revivals cannot last forever, and so it was that by the 1820s many of these movements began to become more mainline. The Methodists began to open churches that were managed by ministers who settled down and married. They also established colleges and seminaries, and their base of support increasingly moved toward middle-class people. Baptists did not have a formal church organization and were increasingly split into numerous subsects and factions. There was an attempt to bring order to the Baptists in 1814, when the General Missionary Convention met in Philadelphia. In 1817, the president of the convention proposed the creation of a "national seminary of learning" to train a cadre of young professional ministers. While some supported the creation of colleges and seminaries, particularly in New England, in other areas of the country Baptists remained "unashamedly anti-intellectual," Howe writes. There was also blowback against the movement to centrally organize the Baptists, most vociferously from John Leland. Leland was a Republican and a fan of Jefferson who famously gave the president a 1,235-pound "Mammoth Cheese" in 1802. His opposition "flowed out of a passion for religious liberty that exalted the individual conscience over creedal systems, local control over powerful ecclesiastical structures, and popular sensibility over the instincts of the educated and powerful," according to Hatch. While the Methodists began to attract more middle-class adherents, the Baptists' major base of operation continued to be in rural areas with outreach mainly to poor people.[31]

Moral Quests and Breaching Walls

The expansion of religion during the Second Great Awakening was accompanied by efforts to improve the morals of American society. Movements and associations were formed to reduce the consumption of alcohol, to prosecute laws against blasphemy, and to regulate sexual conduct. Inevitably, this led some to attempt to breach the wall that had been erected between church and state.

Lyman Beecher became one of the foremost advocates of moral reform. Beecher believed that "the great aim of the Christian Church in its relation to the present life is not only to renew the individual man, but also to reform human society." He was one of the leaders of the temperance movement, whose goal initially was to reduce the consumption of alcohol. As we saw in the previous chapter, alcohol abuse was widespread in early America. "The annual per capita consumption of spirits by those fifteen or older in 1820 was four times that of today," Appleby reports. What began as a movement to reduce drinking soon evolved into proposals for total abstinence. By 1826, Beecher had come to support "the banishment of ardent spirits from the lawful articles of commerce," and in 1836 the American Temperance Movement was formed to advocate for a total ban on the use of alcohol. While the movement was unsuccessful at the national level until the Eighteenth Amendment to the Constitution was ratified in 1919, which instituted the era of Prohibition, twelve states had banned alcohol by the 1850s. The consumption of alcohol declined dramatically in the aftermath of the temperance movement.[32]

"The fierce intensity of committed Christians introduced an urgency into public discussions of values and behavior that blurred the line between religion and politics," according to Appleby. This could be seen in attempts to enforce blasphemy laws, many of which remained on the books in the post-revolutionary period, even though they were viewed as a "relic of a dead age" during the founding era. One New York jurist and legal scholar argued that blasphemy, specifically against Christianity, was "a gross violation of decency and good order" since "we are a Christian people." In 1824, Pennsylvania prosecuted a man for calling the Bible a "mere fable." Another was prosecuted for writing an article that claimed, "the miracles in the Bible were nothing more than 'trick and imposture,'" according to Stone. Prosecutions of this type were condemned by both Jefferson and Adams. They also marked the beginning of attempts to recast the United States as a Christian nation.[33]

Ideas about the morality of sex also became more constrained than they had been during the revolutionary era. The first ever trial in the United States was held in Philadelphia for a bar owner who was charged with showing a picture of "a man in an obscene, impudent, and indecent posture with a woman." A doctor in Massachusetts was convicted to hard labor for writing a book about the use of contraceptives. "The nation's first statutes prohibiting the distribution of obscene literature were enacted in the 1820s, at the height of the Second Great Awakening, in Vermont, Connecticut, and Massachusetts," Stone writes. The movement to crack down on permissive sexual activity caused a counterattack by those that have variously been described as freethinkers and rationalists, who "countered that sex was a natural and vital part of life."[34]

But perhaps the most important conflict that traversed the boundaries of church/state relations was over Sunday mail delivery. The battle was initially joined in 1809, when religious leaders petitioned Congress to end delivery of mail on Sunday out of respect for the sabbath. The first rumblings that America was a Christian nation could be seen in the language that some of the petitioners used. "Our Government is a Christian Government formed and established by Christians" one petition read. While the proposal to end Sunday mail delivery died in 1817, a second round of lobbying began in 1828. It was led by none other than Lyman Beecher, who had previously seen the good that separating church and state had achieved. He formed the

General Union for the Promotion of the Christian Sabbath (GUPCS). The GUPCS began a much more sophisticated petition campaign that recruited merchants, many of whom supported Sunday mail for economic reasons. Once again, a recurring theme was, as one petition from North Carolina put it, that America was "a Christian Community [which] recognizes the authority of the Christian religion."[35]

There were also many that stood on the other side of the issue, including the state of Indiana, which argued that "any legislative interference in matters of religion [constituted] a violation of both the letter and the spirit of the Constitution." Opposition to the proposal to end mail service on Sunday was led by Richard M. Johnson, the chairman of the Senate committee that handled such matters. Johnson had fought in the War of 1812 and was widely credited with killing the Indian leader Tecumseh at the Battle of the Thames in Canada. Johnson, who was a devout Baptist, was also a firm supporter of the separation of church and state. He issued a report that stated, in part, that "the Framers of the Constitution recognized the eternal principle that man's relation with God is above human legislation and his rights of conscience unalienable." A repeal of the law allowing for Sunday mail delivery "would be to sanction by law religious opinions and observances," Kramnick and Moore argue. The Johnson report ended by stating that "the line cannot be too strongly drawn between church and state." It would not be until 1912 that Sunday mail delivery ended, and by then the economic necessity for it no longer existed.[36]

❦ ❦ ❦

One of the most important roles that religious leaders would play in the early republic was over slavery. The abolitionist movement would be fostered by many religious groups, as we shall see later in this book.

Endnotes

1   David L. Holmes, *The Faiths of the Founding Fathers* (Oxford, 2006), p. 1; Alexis de Tocqueville, *Democracy in America* (London, 2003), p. 513.

2   Caleb Johnson, "Voyage of the Mayflower," retrieved June 14, 2017, from http://mayflowerhistory.com/voyage/; Alan Taylor, *American Colonies: The Settling of North America* (New York, 2001), p. 165.

3   Taylor, p. 164–169 and p. 339–340; Daniel J. Boorstin, *The Americans: The Colonial Experience* (New York, 1958), p. 3–8; Holmes, p. 13; Jon Meacham, *American Gospel: God, the Founding Fathers, and the Making of a Nation* (New York, 2006), p. 54.

4   Taylor, p. 180 and p. 343; also see Wood, *Empire*, p. 579–580.

5   Meacham, *American Gospel*, p. 42–43; Taylor, p. 341.

6   Taylor, p. 341; Holmes, p. 15–16 and p. 23–25.

7   Taylor, p. 346–361; Holmes, p. 25–30.

8   Holmes, p. 9–25.

9   Holmes, p. 39–40.

10 Alf J. Mapp Jr., *The Faiths of Our Fathers: What America's Founders Really Believed* (New York, 2003), p. 22–39.

11 Mapp, p. 54–65; Holmes, p. 73–78.

12 Meacham, *American Gospel*, p. 73 and p. 23.

13 Isaac Kramnick and R. Laurence Moore, *The Godless Constitution: A Moral Defense of the Liberal State* (New York, 2005), p. 69–76. I am indebted to the authors for the insights contained in their book that are expressed in this paragraph.

14 Edward Dumbauld, ed., *The Political Writings of Thomas Jefferson* (Indianapolis, 1976), p. 33–35; Meacham, *Jefferson*, p. 123; Ketcham, p. 162–165; Leonard W. Levy, *Origins of the Bill of Rights* (New Haven, 1999), p. 100, makes the case that the Virginia had essentially disestablished Anglicanism with Mason's Declaration of Rights.

15 Holmes, p. 80–87; Mapp, p. 19 and p. 13; Kramnick and Moore, p. 96.

16 Kramnick and Moore, p. 29; Richard Beeman, *Plain, Honest Men: The Making of the American Constitution* (New York, 2009), p. 179.

17 Kramnick and Moore, p. 32–42; Pauline Maier, *Ratification: The People Debate the Constitution 1787–1788* (New York, 2010), p. 152 and p. 420.

18 Fraser, p. 404; Robert A. Goldwin, *From Parchment to Power: How James Madison Used the Bill of Rights to Save the Constitution* (Washington, DC, 1997), p. 158 contains Madison's original language as approved by the House; Akhil Reed Amar, *The Bill of Rights* (New Haven, 1998), p. 32.

19 Akhil Reed Amar, *America's Constitution: A Biography* (New Haven, 2005), p. 316–317; John Witte Jr., "'A Most Mild and Equitable Establishment of Religion' John Adams and the Massachusetts Experiment," in *Religion and the New Republic:*

Faith in the Founding of America, James H. Hutson, ed., (Plymouth, 2000), p. 3 and p. 13; Ketcham, p. 166; Levy, p. 98 and p. 101–102.

20 John Adams to Mercy Otis Warren, 16 April 1776, retrieved June 26, 2017, from https://founders.archives.gov/documents/Adams/06-04-02-0044; the quotes from Madison and Washington were retrieved June 28, 2017, from http://www. westillholdthesetruths.org/quotes/category/virtue.

21 Geoffrey R. Stone, *Sex and the Constitution: Sex, Religion, and Law from America's Origins to the Twenty-First Century* (New York, 2017), p. 107; Holmes, p. 78; Meacham, p. 75.

22 Meacham, p. 56–57 and p. 79–80.

23 Wood, *Empire,* p. 596–597; Stone, p. 133–134; Nathan O. Hatch, *The Democratization of American Christianity* (New Haven, 1989), p. 49 and p. 55.

24 Wood, p. 581; Hatch, p. 3.

25 Howe, p. 164–165; see also "God in America: People & Ideas: Lyman Beecher," retrieved June 28, 2017, from http://www.pbs.org/godinamerica/people/lyman-beecher.html.

26 Hatch, p. 36–37.

27 Wood, p. 595; Hatch, p. 13–22 and p. 59–60.

28 Hatch, p. 45.

29 Howe, p. 178–190; Robert H. Abzug, *Cosmos Crumbling: American Reform and the Religious Imagination* (New York, 1994), p. 184.

30 Hatch, p. 102–113.

31 Hatch, p. 93–97; Howe, p. 180–181.

32 Howe, p. 167–168; Stone, p. 143; Appleby, *Inheriting,* p. 204–215.

33 Stone, p. 140–142.

34 Stone, p. 145–149.

35 Kramnick and Moore, p. 134–138.

36 Kramnick and Moore, p. 138–142; Hickey, p. 139.

CHAPTER 8

Andrew Jackson, American Nationhood, and the Expansion of Democracy

Our government is founded upon the intelligence of the people.
I for one do not despair of the republic. I have great confidence
in the virtue of the great majority of the people, and cannot fear
the result.[1]

—ANDREW JACKSON

The Era of Good Feelings did not end well, in large part because it masked the underlying tensions that had existed in America since the beginning of the revolution: centralization versus decentralization of governmental powers. The break from Great Britain had been launched with a declaration that created thirteen separate states, loosely held together by the Articles of Confederation, which brought its own problems. The Constitution had been designed to fix this problem by centralizing more power in the federal government.[2] The 1790s revealed that the ideological battle to determine just how much power should reside in the federal government had not ended with the Constitution, as Jefferson and Hamilton led two opposing camps with the establishment of the first party system. In the aftermath of Jefferson's victory in 1800, the Federalists had begun to disappear. But the old disputes resurrected themselves in the Republican Party, as the elections of 1824 and 1828 would reveal. Finally, the essence of what makes America a nation would continue to be in dispute.

Two Views of American Nationhood

As discussed in the introduction, America did not begin as one nation, far from it. There have also been two underlying notions of what makes America a nation: the ethnonationalist view and the creedal view. Andrew Jackson and his followers typify the ethnonationalist point of view.

There were then and are still today people who view America from an ethnic and religious perspective. Walter Russell Mead argues that they are largely Jacksonian in their orientation. "Through most of American history, the Jacksonian community was one from which many Americans were automatically and absolutely excluded: Indians, Mexicans, Asians, African-Americans ... and recent immigrants of non-Protestant heritage ... " The core of this group is, surprisingly, made up of the descendants of the Scotch Irish ... surprising because so much of the discrimination that took place during the Age of Jackson was directed toward the Irish. But the Scotch Irish are a distinct group made up of those people that first immigrated from Scotland to Northern Ireland, and then came to America. They "settled the backcountry regions of the Carolinas and Virginia ... and went on to settle much of the Old West—which would become West Virginia, Kentucky, parts of Indiana—and the south and south central states of Tennessee, Missouri, Alabama, Mississippi, and Texas," Mead writes. It is also ironic that it was within the Democratic Party, Jackson's party, that large numbers of Irish who settled in the United States after he left office in the 1840s would find a home.[3]

There are many elements of the American Creed that Jackson and his followers supported. Jackson expanded American democracy, defending the right of the people to rule themselves without interference or direction from elites, an early form of populism. Jacksonians are fiercely egalitarian, at least for those that are within the "folk community." They believe in hard work, individualism, self-reliance, and they respect the elderly. They also fear the corruption of government, and "when this becomes unbearable, they look to a popular hero to restore government to its proper function," Mead states.[4]

As for Andrew Jackson, his view of ethnic and racial differences was typical for the times that he lived in. "Inequalities that others deemed artificial—especially between blacks and whites, Indians and settlers, men and women—appeared to Jackson, as they did to most American contemporaries, perfectly natural," Wilentz writes. Still, he lacked the subtly of Jefferson, who knew that slavery was wrong and attempted to implement an enlightened, if paternalistic, policy toward the Indians. Particularly on Indian policy, Jackson's "campaign for Indian removal tied the movements for economic development, territorial expansion, racial discrimination, white democracy, and the spread of slavery together," historian Harry Watson argues. Like Jefferson, Jackson stood against the privilege of the elites and feared the return of aristocratic politics. He believed it was his duty to protect "the independent rights of our nation," and the legacy of the revolution, an inherently Jeffersonian perspective. Unlike his main opponent in both 1824 and 1828, John Quincy Adams, Jackson would never see that slavery was wrong.[5]

Two Fateful Elections

The method for selecting the president was gradually evolving, and the elections of 1824 and 1828 saw some major changes. Initially, electoral college candidates were selected by state legislatures. By 1824, eighteen of the twenty-four states assigned presidential electors by popular vote, and fourteen of these used a winner-take-all approach where the top vote getter received all that state's electoral votes. Still, the total number of people that voted in the presidential election of 1824 was quite small, with a total of 350,000 ballots cast. By way of comparison, in 1828 there were almost 1.2 million votes recorded. The method for selecting a presidential candidate was also undergoing change. Since 1796, the Republican Party had selected its presidential candidate by a caucus of its congressional members, referred to as King Caucus. But this system collapsed in 1824 and would eventually be replaced by a somewhat more democratic convention in which party members and officeholders together selected the presidential candidate.[6]

The year 1824 was also a change election. There was a strong hangover from the 1819 economic panic, and concern in both the North and South over the future of the union in the aftermath of the Missouri Compromise. Calhoun told Adams in 1820 that there was "a general mass of disaffection to Government ... ready to seize on any event and looking out anywhere for a leader." The role of the BUS, and banks generally, caused part of this feeling of unease. Banking had always had its detractors, particularly in the South, but the actions of the BUS had caused some people to believe that the federal government was corrupt. Historian Robert V. Remini writes that "it soon appeared that many men in Washington regularly plundered the treasury as well. Those who disbursed funds or otherwise handled public money skimmed off a little something for themselves as a regular matter." Whether this was true or not is beyond the scope of this book, but it provided an opportunity for an outsider to ride to the rescue. There was a perceived need for someone who could clean "[t]he Giant Augean Stable at Washington" of corruption, as one Pennsylvania supporter of Andrew Jackson put it, which might remind readers of the slogan from the 2016 election to "drain the swamp," which candidate Donald Trump used. King Caucus was also viewed as an insider's game, meant to maintain those already in power, especially in a system where there was only one political party. "That fact rendered a congressional caucus totally improper and dangerous," Remini writes. "It negated the idea of free elections."[7]

Jefferson had selected Madison to succeed him, and Madison had selected Monroe, continuing the Virginia dynasty. But in 1824, there was no clear heir apparent to James Monroe, and he showed no sign of who he favored. Five men vied for the presidency: William Crawford, John Calhoun, Henry Clay, John Quincy Adams, and Andrew Jackson.

Crawford was the initial front-runner. A cotton farmer from Georgia, he was a former senator and the secretary of the treasury under both Madison and Monroe. In 1816, he had unsuccessfully challenged Monroe for the presidency, and by 1824 he thought it was his turn. In the aftermath of the Panic of 1819, he had recast himself as a traditional Republican, a Quid. "Crawford turned the Treasury Department into the headquarters for neo-Jeffersonian efforts to slash federal expenditures and curb the alleged financial profligacy of the postwar nationalists," Wilentz has written. This made him unpopular in Monroe's cabinet, appearing as a man out to fulfill his ambition at the price of being disloyal to the cabinet he served in. Crawford was a "worm preying upon the vitals of the Administration within its own body," according to Adams. Both Jefferson and Madison thought him the best choice, although he had limited support outside of the South. But his fate was sealed when he suffered a serious stroke in September of 1823, "which left him a partially paralyzed, semi-blind hulk," according to Wilentz. He was, in part, also done in by his attempt to rely on King Caucus as a route to the presidency, which by 1824 had fallen out of favor. None of the supporters of the other candidates attended the caucus, which he won, making the outcome less than legitimate and leaving his opponents still in the race.[8]

John C. Calhoun was a young man on the rise. Monroe had made him secretary of war when he was thirty-four years old. As his stint in the office was coming to an end, he looked to the presidency as the next logical step. At this point, he was still a fervent nationalist, which differentiated him from Crawford, who he thought unqualified to be president. In 1820, he went on a tour of the Northern states of Pennsylvania and New York, ostensibly in his official capacity as a cabinet member, but also to gauge support for a Southern nationalist. His candidacy was ultimately undone by popular support for Jackson, when North Carolina and Pennsylvania came out for the hero of New Orleans. "Pleased to have him out of the race and hoping to pick up his supporters, both Jackson and Adams agreed to take [Calhoun] as their running mate," according to Howe.[9]

Henry Clay was an extremely ambitious politician who turned his sights to the presidency in 1824. "For many, Clay's lust—no other word suffices—for the presidency had become so palpable, so obvious, so relentless" that it even troubled his supporters, according to his biographer Robert V. Remini. It was an office that would elude his grasp many times, in part because of the role he would play in the outcome of the 1824 election. Clay had briefly left the House of Representatives in 1821 to put his financial affairs in order but returned in 1822 as he prepared to run for the presidency. His best hope was as the western candidate, and then to try to pick up electoral votes in New York or Pennsylvania. While this would not bring him an outright victory, he hoped to be one of the top three vote getters and throw the election to the House. "In this event your [being] a member will be very importan[t]," as one of his supporters framed it. Clay had the most well-defined policy positions of all the candidates as represented by his "American System, [which] was intended to strengthen the bonds that tied the nation together into a single whole," as Remini writes. There were three main planks to the American System: 1) the installation of major internal improvements to knit the nation together; 2) support for tariffs designed to protect domestic industry; and 3) the sale of public lands to promote westward expansion and to generate revenue to pay for internal improvements. Clay wanted to "encourage urban and commercial growth to complement the nation's strong rural and agricultural society," Watson writes. It was a Hamiltonian vision for the future, one that would compete with Andrew Jackson's more Jeffersonian themes.[10]

John Quincy Adams had been bred to be president. He was probably both the most- and least-prepared person to pursue the highest office in the land. From an early age, his parents had instilled in him the need to strive for a position of leadership. As one of his biographers writes, JQA "wished to emulate—or surpass—his revered father's distinguished career," something he would never quite accomplish. At the age of twenty-seven he had first been appointed a foreign ambassador by Washington; he then served in the United States Senate, helped negotiate an end to the War of 1812, and served for eight years as Monroe's secretary of state. Yet, if he was well prepared for the office of the presidency, his own personality did not suit it or politics particularly well. He was generally introverted, and later in life he admitted he was "a man of reserved, cold, austere and forbidding manners." As we have seen, he also struggled with severe bouts of depression brought on in part by the enormous expectations thrust on him by his parents. As he told his wife prior to the election: "There are candidates enough for the Presidency without me—and my delicacy is not suited to the times." Adams knew he was not a "popular man" and that "I have not the pliability to reform it."[11]

Yet by 1822, he had begun to explore his election possibilities. The temper of the times was still such that no man could openly run for the office, but Adams began "to remind his allies that whenever citizens might form a movement in behalf of his election, he would 'leave it to take its course,'" Nagel writes. He also urged Monroe to dispatch Jackson, Clay, and Calhoun overseas as foreign ministers to clear the field, and when that failed, he offered an alliance with Jackson, whom he would make his vice president. On policy matters, Adams was an open nationalist who strongly supported the federal construction of internal improvements. He took a more moderate approach on the tariff than Clay, since the Southern states were opposed to higher tariffs, which increased the price of the goods they purchased. But perhaps his biggest weakness, aside from his own ambivalence about the office, was geographical. Other than the New England states, he had no base of support outside his home region, and Southerners distrusted him because he was not a slave owner.[12]

This leaves the final candidate, Andrew Jackson. In 1821, he was not a healthy man. He had two bullets still in his body from duels he fought, and he had contracted dysentery and malaria during his battles with the Creek Indians. His doctor at the time treated him with a combination that included sugar and lead, which was slowly poisoning him. He claimed he did not want to be president, writing to one of his supporters in 1822, "Let the people do as it seemth good unto them." But he also had a very strong ambition for the office. Jackson was a man who hated the rhythm of life as a legislator, having served in both the House and the Senate in the late 1790s. He did not last long, since he "wasn't cut out for politics, at least not legislative politics," H. W. Brands observes. "His was an executive temperament."[13]

At first, none of his opponents took his candidacy seriously. By the time they did, it was too late. Jackson had numerous advantages that soon became apparent. He was the first outsider to run for president, a man who could clean up the corruption in Washington, a most important quality in a change election. He feared the power of elites and stood against the caucus system for selecting presidents, which he believed was an "unconstitutional proceeding" that could, if allowed to continue, lead to a "system of intrigue and corruption ... that will ultimately destroy the liberty of our country." Like Washington, Jackson was a war hero, and he would be the second general elected president of the United States. He shared much of Jefferson's political philosophy in terms of the need for smaller government, and, like Jefferson, was a staunch supporter of the Union and the Constitution.[14]

Jackson's philosophy on economic development in the mid-1820s appears pragmatic, since he voted to support higher tariffs and internal improvements while a member of the Senate. But the outline of where he was going can be seen. He opposed debt and had a longstanding fear of bankers and banking, which would ultimately lead to the bank wars when he was later elected president. While in the Senate, he voted for a modest increase in the tariff, but he did this mostly to raise revenue for national defense and to pay off the nation's accumulated debt. He saw the tariff as placing our "own Manufacturers ... on a footing of fair competition" with those of Europe, but this was largely to benefit "domestic Labour" and not business owners. He supported internal improvements, so long as they were "deemed National" in scope. While he wanted the country to remain primarily rural, he saw the need for industry. "I find virtue to be found amongst the farmers of the country alone, not about courts where courtiers dwell." The key for Jackson was to ensure that government did not favor the already well-off at the expense of the average people. "Basically, Jackson favored individual enterprise free of government restraint and free of government favoritism," Remini writes. Above all, he believed in individual liberty and the right of the people to participate in their government, and he married this political perspective to an economic view that favored the average white man over the elite. As Richard Hofstadter has written, "the Jacksonian movement grew out of expanding opportunities and a common desire to enlarge these opportunities still further by removing restrictions and privileges that had their origins in acts of government; it was essentially a movement of laissez-faire, an attempt to divorce government and business." Given this, Jackson would eventually oppose most of Clay's American System, in large part because it was government directed and viewed as benefiting the already rich and powerful.[15]

His candidacy was launched in 1822 when Tennessee's Republican Party nominated him for president. A year later, they selected Jackson to serve in the Senate once again, to improve his gravitas on the national stage. Jackson's reputation when he arrived in the Senate was as an uncouth westerner. "I am told that opinion of those whose minds were prepared to see me with a Tomahawk in one hand, and a scalping knife in the other had greatly changed and I am getting on very smoothly," Jackson commented about his return to the Senate. He even made peace with Senator Thomas Hart Benton, whom he had gotten into a gunfight with in 1813 and whose bullet he still carried in his body. As Benton would later recall, "After a deadly feud, I became his confidential advisor." Jackson knew how to use his reputation to his advantage. He was a master chess player, whose moves "could sometimes seem reckless, but more often than not he was playing the games of politics and war with the kind of skill and patience chess requires," Jon Meacham writes. His temper was well known, but "his self-command was always perfect," according to one of his contemporaries.[16]

Jackson's big break came in Pennsylvania, when he won that state's endorsement for president. It proved he had appeal outside of his home base in the West and the South. "Jackson's managers were single minded in promoting their candidate as a national and not merely a sectional candidate," Wilentz writes. Ultimately, Jackson received both the most popular and electoral votes, as shown in the table below, and won ten of twenty-four states. While his strength was centered in the South and West, Jackson won both Pennsylvania and New Jersey. Adams finished second with victory in eight states, most of them in the North and New England. But none of the candidates had enough votes to win the election, which would be settled in the House of Representatives.[17]

1824 Presidential Election		
Candidate	Electoral Votes	Popular Vote
Jackson	99	153,544
Adams	84	108,740
Crawford	41	40,856
Clay	37	47,531
Total	261	350,671

Source: Wikipedia as found on http://www.270towin.com/1824_Election/index.html

The Corrupt Bargain

Washington was shrouded "in rumors of intrigue, plots, deals, arrangements, and plain old vicious gossip," once it became clear that the House would make the presidential selection. And sitting right in the middle of this scene was Henry Clay. The election had not worked out as he had planned. His fourth-place finish meant that, under the Twelfth Amendment to the Constitution, he could not be considered for president, since the House could choose only from the top three finishers. But Clay was still in a central position, given his ability to swing certain states toward one or the other candidate.[18]

Clay had problems with both Jackson and Adams. He and Jackson had disliked each other since Clay's speech in the House of Representatives in which he excoriated Jackson for the invasion of Florida. Beyond this, Clay feared that electing a military leader as president could endanger the republic. It would "be the greatest misfortune that could befall the country [and] give the strongest guaranty that the republic will march in the fatal road which had conducted every republic to ruin." Clay and Adams had also had their differences, both during the negotiations in Ghent to end the War of 1812 and over how to treat the South American republics. But both men shared a nationalist ideology, with Adams supportive of most of the American System, so Clay chose Adams as the lesser of two evils. They met on January 9, 1825, when Clay asked Adams "to satisfy him with regard to some principles of great public importance, but without any personal considerations for myself." The Kentucky legislature, which met a few days later, directed their congressional delegation to vote for Jackson. But Clay, who had won in Kentucky, ignored their decision and convinced the Kentucky representatives to back Adams, who had not won a single vote in that state. Ohio too voted for Adams, which brought him to 114 electoral votes, still short of victory. New York became the deciding vote and pushed Adams over the top when Stephen van Rensselaer broke that state's tie. Van Rensselaer had been lobbied hard by both Martin van Buren, who wanted him to vote for Crawford, and by Clay, on Adams's behalf. Once on the floor of the House to cast his ballot, he bent his head in prayer and when he opened his eyes a ballot with Adams's name stared at him. A deeply religious man, he took it as a sign of divine intervention and cast his ballot for Adams. Adams became the sixth president, with a total of eleven states. The representatives from four states whose voters had selected Jackson instead chose Adams.[19]

On February 10, 1825, one day after the House vote, President Monroe held a party to celebrate the election of Adams as president. Jackson also attended and approached Adams during the affair. No one in the crowded room knew what would happen, whether the ever-tempestuous general would lash out at the newly installed chief executive. Instead, Jackson extended his hand, saying, "How do you do, Mr. Adams?" Adams responded, "Very well, sir. I hope Gen. Jackson is well." Adams later wrote that Jackson "was altogether placid and courteous." Jackson's outward calm masked his true feelings, that the election had been stolen not only from him but from the will of the people. "This you see here, the voice of the people of the west have been disregarded, and demagogues barter them as sheep in the shambles, for their own views and personal agrandisement," Jackson wrote to a friend. His feelings would harden even further when Adams offered Clay the position of secretary of state on February 15. Clay knew the danger of taking the position, since a letter had appeared in a Philadelphia newspaper in late January charging that a "corrupt bargain" had been entered into. While most historians have concluded that no such explicit deal had taken place, and a congressional committee later found no evidence of a "corrupt bargain," much of the public believed it had happened. In politics, appearances can often be as important as reality. Clay equivocated for a week, knowing that taking the job was a major risk to his reputation. But always the gambler, he was willing to risk everything and accepted the position, since he believed it put him in line for the presidency. "It was the worst mistake of his life," Remini writes. And neither he nor John Quincy Adams would ever quite recover from it. Jackson and his supporters were irate. As Jackson said at the time, "So you see, the Judas of the West [Clay] has closed the contract and will receive the thirty pieces of silver ... Was there ever witnessed such a bare faced corruption in any country before?"[20]

✒ ✒ ✒

It is hard to understand how Adams and Clay could make such a major blunder. Both were experienced politicians who knew the danger involved in so clearly overruling the will of the people. Adams was greatly concerned about being a minority president, at one point saying it "would open [me] to a far severer trial than defeat." Yet his ambition to be president overruled his sense of propriety. Clay, for his part, "did not comprehend how much and how quickly the rules were changing in the 1820s along majoritarian lines," Wilentz argues. The same could be said of Adams, as we will see from his first address to Congress. But the actions of both men make more sense when viewed from their underlying political philosophies, as these relate to the core societal dilemmas discussed in chapter 1. Both men were still practicing politics under the rules in play under the Founding Fathers, in which the public will takes a back seat to the judgment of elite leadership. Both men had a top-down view of authority, with power flowing from the leaders to the governed. Jackson's view was more in line with Jefferson's that power should flow from the bottom upward; although he also thought that as president he encompassed the will of the majority.[21]

It is important to recognize that the differences between these men were a matter of degree in terms of how they viewed the flow of power and the role of the people. Both Adams and Clay were less optimistic than Jackson that a majority of the people would always make the right decision. In some ways, these differences were foreshadowed by the differences between Jefferson and Madison. In a 1787 letter, Jefferson had written that the "will of the majority should prevail," a position at odds with Madison's concerns that minority rights be protected in a republic. Adams had similar concerns, which could be seen in the Publicola letters that he wrote when he was just twenty-three years old. Those letters were a response to Thomas Paine's 1791 book *The Rights of Man*, which Paine wrote as a defense of the French Revolution. In the Publicola letters, Adams argued that there were limits on popular sovereignty in cases where the will of the majority endangers the rights of a minority. "If ... [the majority of the people] have no other rule but their sovereign will and pleasure to direct them, what possible security can any citizen of the nation have for the protection of his unalienable rights," Adams wrote. As the political scientist James R. Zink argues, Adams rejected Paine's "view that anything the people will is perforce legitimate by virtue of the fact the people willed it."[22]

Adams also believed in representative government, that the public ultimately delegates a good deal of its power to elected officials. In this, he also shared a Madisonian view of the world. Although Adams had reservations about assuming the presidency without receiving the greatest number of votes from the public, his underlying philosophy was that it was legitimate for elected representatives to substitute their own judgment for that of their constituents. Clay too believed this, and he "behaved as though he knew what was best for the American people, whether they agreed or not," Remini writes. "This condescension, this superior tone, this arrogance seemed to suggest a basic mistrust of the people's capacity for self-government." Both men were following Madison in his view of the superiority of a representative system of government versus a direct democracy. Each of these men were grappling with the age-old problem in democratic governments of whether elected officials should act purely as delegates who simply follow the wishes of their constituents, or whether, as Madison preferred, they should exercise independent judgment, voting based on their conscience and a broader conception of what is in the public interest. Unfortunately for Adams and Clay, they pushed this concept well beyond the original Madisonian approach, and they paid a heavy price. The Adams administration would prove to be a disaster, and Henry Clay would never become president of the United States.[23]

Andrew Jackson, having emerged from the ranks of the common man, identified more closely with them. As he wrote in an 1828 letter, "I have great confidence in the virtue of the great majority of the people, and I cannot fear the result [of their judgment]." Jackson's fear was of elites, of the privileged few, not the great mass of the people. In his first address to Congress in December of 1829, he even went so far as to propose a constitutional amendment that the president should be directly elected by popular vote. "But although no evil of this character should result from such a perversion of the first principle of our system—that the majority is to govern—it must be very certain that a President elected by a minority can not enjoy the confidence necessary to the successful discharge of his duties." This concept of majority rule also began to carry with it a larger meaning during the Age of Jackson. As historian Harry L. Watson writes, "in the early nineteenth century [it] also came to mean a pattern of public customs and attitudes that expressed respect for the tastes, values, and decisions of the mass of ordinary white men, regardless of their incomes, education, or family backgrounds." It was the latest iteration of a process that had been taking place since the start of the

American Revolution to break down the barriers that held back the common man.[24]

Inequality is another core value that these three men disagreed about. Andrew Jackson tied egalitarianism and democracy together. As with Jefferson, he feared that too strong a central government would lead to the rise of "a moneyed aristocracy dangerous to the liberties of the country" that would be inimical to the interests of the general mass of the people. Given this, he supported a more decentralized system of government than either Adams or Clay. As did Jefferson, he also believed that too much government action could end up creating "artificial inequality ... in which some men manufactured privilege for their own benefit," Wilentz writes. Jackson also believed that he was the embodiment of the will of people, and as such, promoted the use of executive power. As Jon Meacham writes, "he made no distinction between himself and a broad idea of the people." But his view of inequality had its limits, as we have seen, and did not include African Americans (whether free or slaves), women, Indians, and other excluded groups. Given this, Wilentz rightly views Jackson as a "transitional democrat," one who does not fit our modern-day sensibilities about democracy and equality, but who nonetheless contributed to an ever-expanding view of the democratic future of the nation. Watson summarizes the Jacksonian view as opposing "inequalities of economic class but" embracing "inequalities of race and gender." Jackson's moral blindness in these areas would lead to some of the greatest failures of his presidency.[25]

Jackson viewed the use of government to promote Clay's American System as feeding into the very types of artificial inequality he most feared. This was long before modern liberals brought forward a view that government could ameliorate the worst conditions of inequality. Neither Clay nor Adams were particularly concerned about inequality. "While [Clay] also claimed to support equality and democracy, he took for granted that some Americans were more capable than others and therefore obligated to guide their countrymen to better things," Watson writes. The policy disputes these men engaged in could ultimately be found in their differing views of how to organize society and contrasting views of the future of the nation, each of which "had deep support among different segments of American society," according to Watson.[26]

The Failures of the Adams Administration

John Quincy Adams was a strange and interesting mixture of the past and the future. As discussed previously, he believed that authority should flow from the top down. It was that view, and his ambition, that had compelled him to pursue the presidency despite the fact he had far less popular support than Andrew Jackson. Both he and Clay had followed the rules as laid out by the Constitution, in which the House of Representatives selects the president. There was no requirement that the top vote getter be the winner, since the Framers of the Constitution had designed a system for the selection of the president that was divorced from the direct will of the people. While both Adams and Clay sensed there was trouble brewing due to the actions they took in resolving the election of 1824, neither man seemed able to stop themselves. As Remini writes, neither man fully recognized "the tremendous changes that had occurred throughout the country since the adoption of the Constitution. The nation was fast evolving from a republic to a democracy." The newly elected president attempted to recognize these changes in his inaugural address, when he was the first to use the term "representative democracy" and also said that the American political creed is "that the will of the people is the ... end of all legitimate government upon earth." Yet Adams had already violated this most sacred principle, and his administration was doomed from the start.[27]

Adams was further hindered by his own political ineptness. He originally attempted to retain Monroe's cabinet, with the exception that Clay would replace him as secretary of state and Jackson would replace vice president Calhoun at the war department. Jackson turned him down, indicating that he would not be a party to this "monstrous union." Crawford also resigned as secretary of the treasury. Adams disdained the use of his power of patronage to reward his friends, preferring instead to "appoint men of character, capacity, and integrity." While at first glance this may seem like the actions of a man of great probity, it wounded him in terms of winning over supporters. Adams even refused to remove the postmaster general, who was an avid supporter of Jackson, because he did a good job. As Traub writes, Adams's "Puritan commitment to a righteous path absolutely precluded him from shoring up his base of support."[28]

His political ineptness and his mixture of the past and future were on full display in his first address to Congress in December of 1825. In it, Adams expressed a very future-oriented and broad vision of what government could accomplish. While Hamilton wanted an energetic government that could stabilize the American financial system and spur industry in order to build what Gordon Wood has called a great fiscal-military state, Adams went even beyond this. The government's role was not just to make physical improvements, but also extended to "moral, political, [and] intellectual" improvements. He wanted the federal government to invest not only in internal improvements, but also in a national university (as Washington originally proposed), and in scientific endeavors, such as an astronomical observatory. In the address, Adams declared that "liberty is power." This was clearly at odds with the standard orthodoxy from the revolutionary period, in which too much centralized power was seen as a danger to liberty. Adams may have been the first president to conceive of the notion of positive liberty, the idea that government could advance the freedom of individuals within society. Negative liberty is typically associated with placing "strong limitations on the activities of the state," as our Bill of Rights generally does. Adams was ahead of his time in terms of his view on positive liberty, and it would not be until the twentieth century that the concept of using government to advance liberty would become both widespread (among liberals) and controversial (among conservatives). Adams's views of the use of government power were at odds with those of Jackson and his supporters, who thought that an active federal government was inimical to liberty. For the Jacksonians "knew that liberty was the exact reverse of power, that the protection of liberty required the restraint of governmental power," Remini writes. Unfortunately for Adams, the notion of an activist federal government, which national Republicans like Clay had championed, was losing favor "and the Democratic belief in limited government was definitely in the ascendancy," according to Eric Foner.[29]

Adams also contributed to the weakening of the address when he slipped back into his outdated view of democracy. He warned Congress that "were we to slumber in indolence or fold up our arms and proclaim to the world that we are palsied by the will of our con-stituents," that the United States would "doom ourselves to perpetual inferiority." Adams's antidemocratic views were on full display with this statement, which helped to fuel his opponents. Traub accurately describes Adams's view as "Federalism in its rankest form: the polit-ical leader does not represent the will of the voter but rather guides it from above and ignores it when need be."[30]

While Henry Clay helped craft the address and generally sup-ported many of the proposals, he had warned Adams to include

"nothing which, from its unpopularity, would be unlikely to succeed."
But Adams decided to plunge ahead, arguing that the "perilous experiment must be made," and that he would "be prepared for the consequences." While "Adams commanded a solid majority in the House,
though not the Senate, [he never] lobbied for his agenda," as Traub
writes. His political opponents, which included the Jacksonians, the
Crawford forces, and even his own vice president, would ensure that
both his domestic and foreign policy agendas would never be enacted.
"All of Adams's scientific and educational proposals were defeated, as
were his efforts to enlarge the road and canal systems," Nagel writes.
Congress bottled up a proposal to participate in the Panama Conference, a meeting of South and Central American countries to discuss
issues of mutual interest. Southerners were particularly concerned
"about sitting at a conference with delegates from Caribbean islands,
some of whom were former slaves," Remini argues. By the time the
Senate confirmed the delegates to Panama, and the House approved
the appropriations for the mission, the conference was over.[31]

The Election of 1828

The election of 1824 almost seemed to never have ended. In October
of 1825, the Tennessee legislature adopted a resolution recommending
that Andrew Jackson be elected president in 1828. The campaign was
formally launched, and Jackson announced his resignation from the
United States Senate.[32]

His campaign would build a coalition that included the supporters
of some of the other candidates from 1824. Vice President John C.
Calhoun, who had been on both Jackson's and Adams's tickets, had
remained neutral during the campaign. But soon after Adams rose
to the presidency, he was one of the first to support Jackson. Calhoun
was undergoing a major shift in his political orientation so as to

survive in South Carolina politics. Support for nationalist policies had once been strong in South Carolina, but this began to change in the aftermath of the slave uprising of Denmark Vesey and the impact of the Panic of 1819 on the state's economy. Any discussion of slavery, even moderate policies of colonization, was no longer acceptable. Tariffs, which Calhoun had supported to protect domestic industry during the War of 1812, were now viewed as being harmful to South Carolina. Most importantly, a nationalist agenda bestowed too much power on the federal government and caused many in the Palmetto State to fear that such power could be turned against the continuation of slavery. As one plantation owner framed it, "acquiescence in these measures [the tariff and internal improvements], on the part of the State sovereignties, sanctions ... the constitutional right to legislate on the local concerns of the States," which would include the potential to abolish slavery.[33]

Calhoun's biographer Irving Bartlett argues that Adams's December address to Congress gave Calhoun the rationale he needed to back Jackson. He was able to depict the new administration's policy approach as "extremist." Calhoun appeared to be specifically concerned with Adams's attempt to equate liberty with power. In a June 1826 letter to Jackson, Calhoun wrote "In my opinion liberty was never in greater danger ... An issue has been made ... between *power* and *liberty*." He went on to write that his concern was over whether the "real governing principle in our political system be the power ... of the Executive, or the voice of the people." Calhoun's backing would be matched by the support of one of Crawford's main lieutenants, Martin van Buren.[34]

Van Buren was a product of the rough-and-tumble politics of New York State. He was born in the small town of Kinderhook, near the state capital of Albany, on December 5, 1782. The Van Buren family had deep roots in New York, with the first of Martin's ancestors arriving in 1631 from Holland. They were also a family of modest means, definitely not part of the Dutch aristocracy that ruled New York. His father Abraham owned a tavern and "was a whig in the Revolution, an anti-federalist in 1788, and an early supporter of Jefferson," one of Van Buren's later campaign biographies declared. Martin followed in his footsteps and became a staunch supporter of Jefferson. With limited schooling, he went to work in a law office when he was fourteen. Seven years later he passed the bar exam and became a successful lawyer. During Jefferson's two terms as president, Van Buren identified with the expansion of democracy. As he wrote in his memoir, "My faith in the capacity of the masses of People of our Country to govern themselves, and in their general integrity in the exercise of that function, was very decided and was more and more strengthened as my intercourse with them extended."[35]

In 1812, Van Buren won a very close election to the New York Senate. The time he spent in Albany taught him the importance of political parties. A very successful organizer, he became the head of the "Bucktails, after a hat worn by Tammany Hall supporters." They were also known as the "Albany Regency," a name bestowed on them by the reporter Thurlow Weed. The party Van Buren led opposed the policies of DeWitt Clinton, the then powerful governor of the state. Van Buren and his followers thought that Clinton was insufficiently loyal to Jefferson and the Republican Party, and they were correct. Clinton had an older vision that harkened back to the founders in which parties were to be avoided if at all possible. Van Buren operated with "ideas about party discipline, communications, and enlarged suffrage, [through which] he had shown other like-minded individuals how to take democracy beyond the periwigs of the eighteenth century," his biographer Ted Widmer writes. In 1821, he won election to the US Senate, where he would take his pro-party views national and be one of the key players in establishing the second American Party system.[36]

Richard Hofstadter, in his seminal study *The Idea of a Party System*, credits Van Buren with two novel approaches. First, he was the first of a new breed of politicians who did not equate political rivalry with personal animosity. "Repeatedly Van Buren would assure an opponent that he held him in high esteem, and he associated on amiable terms with many Federalists," Hofstadter writes. Mutual toleration, "the understanding that competing parties accept one another as legitimate rivals," is one of the basic norms that has allowed our system of checks and balances to operate reasonably well, as the political scientists Steven Levitsky and Daniel Ziblatt write. Second, Van Buren had a coherent vision that political parties could be a force for good in society. In his autobiography, he wrote that "political parties are inseparable from free governments, and that in many and material respects they are highly useful to the country." When he entered the fray in the election of 1828, he "envisaged a party system consisting of Adams and Clay and their friends on one side, advocating Hamiltonian principles, and Jackson, Calhoun, and the Radicals on the other side, committed to Jeffersonian principles," Remini writes. The Little Magician, as Van Buren became known, reached out to Calhoun to combine forces and get Jackson elected in 1828. They became known as the Democratic-Republicans, and soon would be known as the Democrats, while Adams and his supporters became the National Republicans.[37]

Van Buren also hoped that segregating the country along party lines would prevent sectional differences from splitting the nation apart over the issue of slavery. "If the old [party distinctions] are sup-pressed prejudices between free and slave holding states will inevitably take their place," Van Buren wrote. By linking Northern and Southern interests together, Van Buren hoped to revive the old Jeffersonian coalition.[38]

❦ ❦ ❦

While Van Buren may have hoped for a principled campaign, it was instead a very nasty and personal election. While big issues were at stake, including the size and scope of government and the extent to which public power should be used to promote the market revolution, the election devolved into a series of personal attacks. The National Republicans attacked Jackson's relationship with his beloved wife Rachel, charging that he "prevailed upon the wife of Lewis Robards of Mercer County, Kentucky to desert her husband, live with himself, in the character of a wife." The Jacksons had always maintained that they thought Robards had already divorced Rachel before they first married in 1791. Jackson was also attacked for his greatest strength, his military record. It was claimed in a handbill that during the Creek War he had six men shot for desertion, when in fact their enlistment had ended, and they wished to return home. Jackson responded to the "Coffin Handbill" by indicating that the men had "mutinied, broke into a commissary storehouse, stole supplies, burned the bakehouse, and then deserted," Remini writes. Jackson was also charged with threatening the future of the republic as a military man who would become a tyrant in the mold of a Julius Caesar or Napoleon.[39]

Adams did not escape unscathed either. The "corrupt bargain" was used to show that he was an elitist who had flouted the will of the people in order to obtain the presidency. One of the most egregious charges against him was that he had arranged for an American girl to sleep with the Russian czar. "Adams was denounced for his elitist education, his early association with European courts, his former Federalist allegiance, and to crown it all, his purchase of a billiard table and chess set—gambling devices, supposedly—for the White House," as Watson has framed it.[40]

It was also the first election where get-out-the-vote efforts began to appear. By 1828, all states except South Carolina and Delaware selected electors by popular vote. This placed a premium on getting as many supporters as possible to the polls. Given Van Buren's experience as a political organizer, the operations of the Democrats tended to be more sophisticated in this regard. The Jacksonians had a central organizing committee in Nashville, which then relayed campaign advice and messages downward to the state and local level. The men who organized the effort at the state and local levels tended to be elites themselves, "but they sought to persuade the voters rather than command them," according to Watson. The Adams campaign had their own version of organizing their supporters, which was led by Henry Clay and Daniel Webster. Both sides also had newspapers that supported their campaign. But the National Republicans were not nearly as good at the grassroots organizing efforts as the Democrats, who found it their natural venue.[41]

Van Buren also advanced Jackson's cause by pushing through a new round of tariffs in 1828. The tariffs were designed to protect certain industries in Kentucky, Ohio, and Pennsylvania in order to bring those states into the fold. Certain raw materials, like molasses, sail duck, and coarse wool, "were burdened with heavy new duties, a direct attack on pro-Adams Yankees," as Wilentz writes. But the bill almost backfired on Van Buren when the South voted against it, referring to it as the "tariff of abominations." Southerners were forced to swallow their pride along with the bill, since their top priority was ousting Adams first. But the tariff issue would later come back to haunt Jackson, as he and Calhoun would eventually go to war over the issue.[42]

***

For Democrats, the election was a choice between corruption and reform. Adams and Clay represented corruption, not just because of the bargain between the two men that brought them to power, but in a broader sense that harkened back to Jefferson's preference that America remain an agrarian society. As we saw in chapter 1, the Republicans in Jefferson's time questioned whether the movement toward a more urban and industrial society that Hamilton was promoting would equate to progress, or would instead create a great imbalance of wealth and power and ultimately a new aristocracy, along with cities filled with wage workers that were dependent on their employers for their livelihood. Jackson and the Democrats in 1828 saw the election outcome in very much the same way. The word *corruption* had a larger connotation beyond immoral actions, like bribery, but referred to "the changes that could drag a nation from a pure and virtuous stage of cultivation to the state of decay when republicanism became impossible," as Watson writes. To Jackson's followers, the expansion of government power to promote economic development would eventually create such unequal conditions that a republican form of government could not survive. As one of Jackson's supporters framed it, "the parties are Jackson and Adams, democracy and aristocracy." Jackson's program of reform would include preserving "to the people their rightful sovereignty," restoring a system of "proper checks and balances," paying down the public debt, and freeing the government from "the corrupting influence of a monied aristocracy," as Jackson told one of his supporters. It was an election that would pit those in power against those with little power, "the poor man against the rich, the People against the Elite, the rebels against the Establishment," even though the Jacksonian leadership was also made up of society's elite.[43]

Daniel Walker Howe, in his outstanding account of the era entitled *What Hath God Wrought*, puts forward an alternative view of what the National Republicans might have achieved had Adams won a second term. He argues that the American System may have led to a more "diversified economy in place of reliance on the export of slave grown agricultural staples" that could have reduced portions of the South's dependence on the peculiar institution. A more powerful federal government may have also led to a long-term and peaceful solution to the problem of slavery. We will never know if that would have occurred, because the people overwhelmingly elected Andrew Jackson president, as shown in the table below.[44]

1828 Election Results			
Candidate	Party	Electoral Votes	Popular Vote
Jackson	Democrat	178	647,286
Adams	National Republican	83	508,064
Total		261	1,155,350

It was an overwhelming victory for Jackson, who won 56 percent of the popular vote. It also marked the end of an era, when the elites of Washington could select the next presidential candidate who would ultimately occupy the office. With the popular vote ever more important, the people would generally make that decision through the electoral college, except in those instances where the popular and electoral vote differed. The number of white men that participated in the election increased markedly from 1824, with an additional eight hundred thousand people casting their vote.

Jackson swept to victory in the South, and also won throughout most of the new states of the former Northwest Territory. Adams held on to New England and won Maryland and Delaware (where the legislature selected the electors). As Sean Wilentz notes, the election was close in New York, Ohio, and Kentucky. A swing of less than twenty thousand votes in those three states, combined with a change in New York to a winner-take-all system, would have led to an Adams electoral college victory, 133–128. Had this happened, it would have been a stunning outcome, and may have resulted in an amendment to the Constitution to make the popular-vote winner the president. In addition to 1824, the popular-vote winner would lose the election in the electoral college in 1876, 1888, 2000, and most recently 2016, when Hillary Clinton received almost 3 million more votes than the winner, Donald J. Trump.[45]

Endnotes

1 The quote is from Brainy Quote.com, retrieved July 10, 2017, from https://www. brainyquote.com/quotes/quotes/a/andrewjack408994.html.

2 These themes were extensively explored in *The Emergence of One American Nation*. The reader should refer to that work for a complete description of the on-going debate on this issue.

3 Mead, p. 236 and p. 227.

4 Mead, p. 231–239.

5 Sean Wilentz, *Andrew Jackson* (New York, 2005), p. 6–12; Watson, p. 5.

6 For the changes in how electors were selected, see Devin McCarthy, "How the Electoral College Became Winner-Take-All," retrieved October 18, 2013, from www. fairvote.org/how-the-electoral-college-became-winner-take-all.html; for state-by-state breakdown of who voted by popular vote versus state legislature selection, see "President Elect 1824," retrieved June 20, 2017, from http://presidentelect.org/e1824. html; for information on the death of King Caucus, see Richards, p. 29 and Wilentz, *The Rise*, p. 246–247.

7 Bartlett, p. 111; Robert V. Remini, *Andrew Jackson: Volume Two, The Course of American Freedom 1822:1832* (Baltimore, 1981), p. 15–25; Wilentz, *Jackson*, p. 47.

8 Wilentz, *Rise*, p. 241–242; Howe, p. 203–206.

9 Bartlett, p. 108–120; Howe, p. 206.

10 Remini, *Clay*, p. 210–228; Wilentz, *Rise*, p. 243; Watson, p. 113.

11 Nagel, p. 281–285; Robert V. Remini, *John Quincy Adams* (New York, 2002), p. 3 and p. 64.

12 Nagel, p. 282; Remini, p. 65; Traub, p. 291–292.

13 Remini, *Jackson*, p. 1–2; Brands, p. 96–97.

14 Remini, *Jackson*, p. 29–33 has a useful summary of Jackson's main beliefs.

15 Different historians come to differing conclusions about Jackson. My own view of him is generally stated in this paragraph. Hofstadter, in the *American Political Tradition*, p. 56, sees the Jackson movement as primarily one of divorcing government from business, but not as being anti economic development. This view seems generally supported by Jackson's later actions as president. Harry L. Watson, in *Andrew Jackson vs. Henry Clay: Democracy and Development in Antebellum America* (Boston, 1998), puts forward the idea that Jackson feared that economic development would be detrimental to democracy. "Andrew Jackson and his supporters feared that democracy might suffer at the hands of development, while Henry Clay and his supporters worried that the opposite might be true," p. 2. Both views cannot be true, and my own view is closer to Hofstadter's, that Jackson wanted to divorce government from business, since it was the use of governmental power on the side of the rich and powerful that endangered democracy. The quotes in this section on the tariff and internal improvements are from Remini, *Jackson*, p. 68.

16 Remini, *Jackson*, p. 59–60; Meacham, *American Lion*, p. 37–38; Arthur M. Schlesinger Jr., *The Age of Jackson* (New York, 1945), p. 40.

17 Wilentz, *Rise*, p. 248.

18 Remini, *Jackson*, p. 85.

19 Wilentz, *Rise*, p. 248; Nagel, p. 292–293; Remini, *Jackson*, p. 93–94.

20 Remini, *Jackson*, p. 89–90 and p. 96–99; Remini, *Adams*, p. 74; Brands, p. 388.

21 Wilentz, *Rise*, p. 256; Nagel, p. 293.

22 See Fraser, p. 372, for the differing views of Madison and Jefferson on majority rule; my view of Adams's concerns about the abuses of majority rule have been influenced by an article by James R. Zink, *The Publicola Debate and the Role of the French Revolution in American Constitutional Thought*, retrieved July 27, 2017, from http://www.journals.uchicago.edu/doi/pdfplus/10.1086/683203. The Adams quotes are from p. 568.

23 Remini, *Clay*, p. 669; for a more complete discussion of Madison's thoughts on representative government, see Fraser, p. 197–204.

24 Remini, *Jackson*, p. 31; Jackson's proposal for direct election of the president and the quotes shown are from his First Annual Message of December 8, 1829, retrieved July 28, 2017, from http://www.presidency.ucsb.edu/ws/?pid=29471; Watson, p. 15.

25 Remini, *Jackson*, p. 33; Meacham, *American Lion*, p. 250; Wilentz, *Jackson*, p. 11–12; Watson, p. 16.

26 Watson, p. 20–23.

27 Remini, *Clay*, p. 260; Adams's inaugural address was retrieved on August 1, 2017, from http://avalon.law.yale.edu/19th_century/qadams.asp.

28 Remini, *Clay*, p. 260; Traub, p. 318–319.

29 For Hamilton and the fiscal-military state, see Gordon Wood, *Revolutionary Characters: What Made the Founders Different* (New York, 2006), in chapter 4; Adams's First Annual Message was retrieved August 1, 2017, from http://www.presidency.ucsb.edu/ws/?pid=29467; Remini, *Clay*, p. 287; Eric Foner, *The Story of American Freedom* (New York, 1998), p. 54–55.

30 From First Annual Message; Traub, p. 326.

31 Remini, *Clay*, p. 288; Traub, p. 326; Nagel, p. 303; Remini, *Adams*, p. 79 and p. 84.

32 Remini, *Jackson*, p. 105–106.

33 Howe, p. 250; William W. Freehling, *Prelude to Civil War: The Nullification Controversy in South Carolina, 1816-1836* (New York, 1965), p. 127.

34 Bartlett, p. 129; the Calhoun quote is from Watson, *Liberty*, unnumbered page at the beginning of the book.

35 Ted Widmer, *Martin Van Buren* (New York, 2005), p. 19–31.

36 Widmer, p. 39–51; Hofstadter, p. 220–223.

37 Hofstadter, p. 223–225; Levitsky and Ziblatt, p. 8; Remini, *Jackson*, p. 114.

38 Watson, *Liberty*, p. 88.

39 Remini, *Jackson*, p. 118–122; Watson, *Liberty*, p. 91–92.

40 Remini, *Jackson*, p. 133; Watson, *Liberty*, p. 91.

41 Wilentz, *Rise*, p. 302–303; Watson, *Liberty*, p. 90.

42 Wilentz, *Rise*, p. 299–300; Watson, *Liberty*, p. 89.

43 Watson, *Liberty*, p. 46 and p. 62; Remini, *Jackson*, p. 129; Wilentz, *Rise*, p. 302; Burns, p. 320–321.

44 Howe, p. 283.

45 Wilentz, *Rise*, p. 308, points out how close the election was in certain key states, and how a minor change in the popular vote could have led to an Adams electoral college victory. I believe he made a mathematical error that showed that Adams would have won in the electoral college 149–111. Dr. Wilentz appears to have double counted the electoral votes that New York had already cast for Adams, and the actual total is as I have shown. For a general summary of why the Framers of the Constitution chose the electoral college system, see Fraser, p. 287–293.

CHAPTER 9

The First Term: Good Intentions /
Questionable Outcomes

... to the victor belongs the spoils.
—NEW YORK GOVERNOR WILLIAM MARCY

The bank, Mr. Van Buren, is trying to kill me, but I will kill it.
—PRESIDENT ANDREW JACKSON

The people had triumphed, electing their candidate to the highest office in the land. As historian H. W. Brands framed it, Jackson's election was "a hostile takeover of the presidency," the first since Jefferson, at least when viewed from the perspective of the status quo and elite society. But many of the issues he faced were familiar: Indian removal to allow for continued westward expansion; the role of banking; and the continued threat to the nation as the North and South grew apart.

The battles that were to ensue, especially over banking, will look familiar to the reader. They mirror, to a certain extent, the differences between Jefferson and Hamilton over the future direction of the country. Jackson would have preferred that the country remain primarily rural, although he was not opposed to the advancement of industry so long as it occurred in a laissez-faire manner. He wanted the government to be small and frugal, following in the footsteps of

Jefferson. Jackson is often linked to the expansion of democracy in America, but he was also the beneficiary of social changes that had been underway since the revolution, and not the author of those changes. He was a supporter of free markets but wanted to ensure that the government did not contribute to unnatural inequality as part of economic development. The new president feared that "commerce, banking, and industry tended to undermine the independence, virtue and equality that made a republic possible," Harry Watson writes. This harkens back to those Jeffersonian Republicans who did not believe that the development of an industrial society advanced civilization. Jackson's goals were to pay off the national debt and shrink the size of government, which had become a corrupting influence on American life by advancing the interests of only a small group of men. While not absolutely opposed to funding all internal improvements, he opposed those that aided only local interests, or which added to the national debt. His main opponent would be Henry Clay and his American System, which to a large extent built on Hamilton's approach to economic development and on Madison's proposals in the aftermath of the War of 1812. Out of these battles would emerge the second American Party system.[1]

As we saw in the last chapter, Jackson's view was that American policy should be directed toward the advancement of the average white man. His policy toward Indians, specifically his focus on removal, illustrated his view that America was primarily a white man's nation.

Jackson would also implement his own vision for how to administer the government, reflecting American distrust of centralized power, which is where we begin.

Jacksonian-Style Administration

Andrew Jackson did not want to attend his own inauguration, telling friends he was depressed after the election results came in. These feelings became overwhelming when his beloved Rachel died of a heart attack in late December of 1828. Blaming himself in part, Jackson came to "the inescapable suspicion that this wouldn't have happened, that she would still be living, if he had heeded her wishes and kept clear of politics." More than that, he blamed his political enemies, who had cast such vicious attacks on Rachel during the recent campaign.[2]

The president-elect finally tore himself away from the gravesite and arrived in Washington in mid-February. Thousands of people descended upon the Capitol for the inauguration of the people's president. By some estimates, fifteen to twenty thousand people attended the swearing-in ceremonies that took place on March 4, 1829. Still in mourning, Jackson was dressed all in black as he gave his inaugural address, which preceded his taking the oath of office in those days. He delivered a barely audible address in which he recognized his appointment "by the choice of a free people." He promised to keep "in view the limitations as well as the extent of the Executive power" and to respect the sovereignty of states while balancing the "interests of agriculture, commerce, and manufacturing." In a somewhat surprising statement for the feared Indian fighter, he also promised "a just and liberal policy toward the Indians." Most importantly, he planned to reform the government and rid it of corruption. His critics would later say he violated each of these promises, as Sean Wilentz notes. Chief Justice John Marshall then swore Jackson in as the seventh president.[3]

For Jackson, reforming the government was first and foremost about the men who filled the ranks of the various governmental positions. While most previous presidents, except for the Adams men, had filled their cabinet posts with supporters, Jackson would go further and implement what would become known as the "spoils system," where individuals are appointed to government jobs because of their loyalty to a political party and not due to a particular level of expertise. As Howe points out, there was no civil service system in the early republic, but the "prevailing custom was to leave one's predecessor's appointees in office (except for the top tier)," and replace the lower-level employees gradually through attrition. Jefferson, for example, had replaced some Federalist officeholders, an early version of a spoils system. "The politically neutral quality of [public] service generally sustained from 1789 to 1829 was impaired and in some quarters destroyed," historian Leonard D. White has written. The core of Jackson's reform was a system of rotation in office. "Rotation in office will perpetuate our liberty," according to Jackson. The newly elected president believed that long terms in office led to government officials that promoted their "individual interests" rather than serving the public. Historians have long argued whether Jackson's policy of rotation in office promoted or eliminated corruption, although Jackson's intent seemed to be generally reformist, to remove "only those who had been appointed against the manifest will of the people." Rotation in office was part and parcel of the expansion of democracy under Jackson, and "it was demanded from below" and implemented "not merely because it was advocated from above," according to White. Overall, Jackson replaced about one in ten federal employees, which Howe argues "was more than all of his predecessors had done in the previous forty years." Sean Wilentz indicates that those numbers were generally in line with Jefferson's approach, although as stated above, some attributed a limited spoils system to the third president as well. Wilentz, too, recognizes that Jackson's approach "led to sweeping changes" among "customs officials, federal marshals and attorneys ... [and among] local postmasterships," positions that previously had been nonpolitical. While the overall number of people who were replaced was small, part of this can be attributed to the fact that "many officeholders who saw Jackson inaugurated ... were of course his partisans."[4]

Given Jackson's approach to filling his administration with supporters, many of those who attended the inaugural were job seekers. The White House was thrown open for all to visit on inauguration day. Wilentz calls the ensuing scene "one of the set pieces of American political lore," as the White House was soon overrun with Jackson supporters. Margaret Bayard Smith, a friend to Jefferson who attended many prior inaugurals and was at the center of the social swirl of Washington, DC, wrote: "What a scene did we witness! The Majesty of the People had disappeared ... and the whole house had been inundated by the rabble mob ... Cut glass and china to the amount of several thousand dollars had been broken in the struggle to get to the refreshments." Jackson himself, after greeting his admirers, was forced to retreat out a back stairway. One justice of the Supreme Court succinctly said that "the reign of 'King Mob' seemed triumphant."[5]

Based on the scene at the White House that day, and the backwoods image of the new president, one might expect that the government would soon be stocked from the ranks of the humble and lowly. But, in fact, those Jackson appointed to office did not differ substantially from their predecessors, especially the Jefferson administration. "The crowd that followed Jackson contained not only the most vulgar and gross, who ruined White House upholstery," political scientist Matthew Crenson writes, but it also included "the highest and most polished ... and some of them stayed on as Old Hickory's administrators." Most came from families whose fathers had held high-ranking occupations, and they had attended college and been trained in a professional field. "They were not men of humble origins," Crenson found. And Jackson's selection criteria seemed to have less to do with political principles and more to do with personal loyalty.[6]

The other hallmark of Jackson's approach was a sense that it was a simple matter to administer the government. "The duties of all public offices are, or at least admit being so plain and simple that men of intelligence may readily qualify themselves for their performance," he said in his first address to Congress. While this was an admirable goal, intended to ensure that an "official aristocracy" did not come to dominate government affairs, it also fit within an anti-government perspective that some had ascribed to since before independence. Our own revolution was born as a protest against the strong actions of the British central government to tax the colonies for their own defense. Given the nation's birth in protest against centralized power, it has always been difficult to establish a strong governmental presence in the United States. Garry Wills has written that there are a set of values that recur "whenever government is opposed: a belief that government, as a necessary evil, should be kept at a minimum ... and should be provincial, amateur ... popular ... and rotational." On the other side are those who view government as "a positive good, and that it should be cosmopolitan, expert, authoritative ... progressive [and] elite." Jackson was the latest to hold the former view, following in the path of the antifederalists and the Jeffersonians, who stood on one side of that divide. Others took the opposite view, including the Federalists, who supported a new Constitution that strengthened the federal government, and the National Republicans, men like Clay and Adams, who wanted to use government to advance what they viewed as the public interest.[7]

Given Jackson's view that running the government is a simple matter, it's little wonder that the cabinet officials ultimately selected, most of whom were considered subpar, have been widely panned by historians. Remini writes that "the cabinet was uniformly second-rate with the single exception of Martin Van Buren," who was selected to serve as secretary of state. Perhaps Jackson's worst pick was his close friend, John Eaton, to head the department of war. Eaton's relationship with the widower Margaret Timberlake would immediately engulf the administration in scandal. Timberlake was a thirty-year-old beauty with a reputation as "an allegedly loose woman of low origins." It was rumored that she and Eaton had been intimate prior to the death of her husband. The two married in January of 1829, causing a major scandal in the capital. Led by Calhoun's wife, "the imperious Floride," Margaret was snubbed by the women of Washington society. Jackson saw the attacks on Margaret Eaton as like those that had been made on Rachel during the campaign and defended the couple. "At bottom it was a cultural divide, pitting pious, self-important Washington fixtures against new arrivals and local commoners whom they deemed vulgar, loose in morals, and uppity," according to Wilentz. The scandal would contribute to the divide between Jackson and his vice president, which Van Buren would use to his advantage. The weakness of Jackson's cabinet would lead to substantial turnover during the eight years of his presidency, including the wholesale dismissal of the cabinet prior to the 1832 election.[8]

Rotation in office would come in for criticism from Jackson's opponents, the National Republicans, who by 1834 would take the name Whigs. Daniel Webster was one of the most vociferous critics.

Originally a federalist with a conservative bent, he had grave concerns that the Jeffersonian revolution of 1801 would lead to "licentiousness, tyranny, death and destruction," according to one of his biographers. But the New Englander had become a strong nationalist in the aftermath of the War of 1812, and with federalism all but dead, he became a Republican, albeit a National Republican. His ability as an orator may have been unequaled in the early republic. In the aftermath of a speech Webster gave in 1820 marking the two hundredth anniversary of the Pilgrims landing in the New World, John Adams called him "the most consummate orator of modern times." He was not only a successful politician, but a lawyer with a long record of appearances before the Supreme Court. "Altogether from 1814 to 1852 Webster argued 168 cases before the Supreme Court," according to historian Merrill D. Peterson. This included the all-important McCullough case discussed in chapter 5, which established the legal principal of federal supremacy.[9]

Webster was a staunch supporter of an activist federal government in the mold of Hamilton and John Quincy Adams, which put him at odds with Jackson's small-government philosophy. While Jackson's supporters seemed "to think the country is rescued from some dreadful danger," as Webster said, he thought the real danger was from Jackson and his supporters. Webster was especially concerned about Jackson's theory of rotation in office, "which could only be prelude to partisan despoliation of public offices," Peterson writes. In congressional debates in 1835, Webster worried that many of the "institutions of the country," which had been "established for the good of the people" had become nothing but the "spoils of victory."[10]

Despite Webster's pleas, the Whigs would also take advantage of the emerging spoils system. While they condemned the system in theory "because it corrupted public and private morals, and because it lowered the competence and impartiality of the public service, reducing it to a mere party agency," they would also take advantage of the system, as White has written. William Henry Harrison was the first Whig elected president, in 1840. By then, "the Whigs adopted all the characteristic practices of the spoils system," according to White. By 1856, "the theory of rotation had finally been perfected" under the Buchanan administration.[11]

While Jackson's reformist motivations were genuine, hoping to open government service to a range of new people, the spoils system came at a high price. Governmental positions were often filled with people who had little or no experience. In 1842, a House committee found that "it very often happens that individuals are brought from a distance, perfect strangers to the duties and details of their office." When asked about his experience, one clerk in the naval storekeeper's office admitted he did not know much about the work he was asked to perform since he was a bricklayer by trade. Some of those that filled the civil service worked very little, no more than a few hours a week, and one clerk in the post office admitted he worked an hour a day. "In short, the efficiency of the public service fell as men were placed on the payroll because they had influential political connections, or worked for a partisan newspaper, or distinguished themselves in local politics," White found. Faith in governmental service declined, and those employed in the public sector were expected to contribute to the political party that put them in office and to assist in getting party members elected.[12]

There were several developments that helped to preserve the public service from complete annihilation. For one thing, both parties looked for "men of integrity and skill" to fill many positions. Some of those that filled civil service positions were successful politicians at the local level who could "augment the popular support and authority of the federal establishment," according to Crenson. Most importantly, a shadow public service system continued despite the introduction of the spoils system. As White points out, there was a dual system in existence from 1829 to 1861: "one sector partisan, rotating its personnel; the other, based in part on examinations and in part on custom, neutral and permanent." The career civil service, as it would later come to be known, was a product of the need to get things done in the public sector. While some of those appointed through the spoils system would prove to be capable, there was still the need for a cadre of "men who knew the precedents, who were familiar with the flow of work, and who could be counted on to avoid the errors and misjudgments of novices." It was these men who represented the future of public administration, which would gradually emerge as a field separate and distinct from politics.[13]

Indian Removal

As with rotation in office, Andrew Jackson's intent with Indian removal would differ from the practical application of the policy. Rotation in office was designed to make the process of filling government jobs open to more people, to eliminate corruption, and to fight elitism, although that was not the outcome of the policy. Jackson's policy about Indian removal was designed, in the president's opinion, to protect the tribes from the predatory practices of the states. As with rotation, the end result would be far different. The Washington administration under Henry Knox and Thomas Jefferson had also struggled with Indian policy. Yet they had attempted to treat the tribes with the respect that is owed to sovereign nations, and Jefferson envisioned the assimilation of native peoples into white society. While Jackson believed he was acting in the interests of the tribes, there was little subtly to his policy, and it clearly reflected his view that America was a nation for white people and the Indian tribes would need to be removed. "Jackson's memory of wars against Indians allied with the Spanish and British, his hunger for expansion, and his own residence in the Southwest all led him to feel the grievance of stymied state governments and land-hungry frontiersmen more than the plight of threatened tribes," historian Daniel Feller explains.[14]

The conflict erupted between native tribes and white people during the Monroe administration, this time in the Southern states of Georgia, Alabama, and Mississippi. The Five Civilized Tribes, which included the Cherokee, Creek, Choctaw, Chickasaw, and Seminole, who numbered sixty thousand people, occupied a good deal of cotton-growing land in these states. Near the end of Monroe's term, the Georgians had negotiated the fraudulent Indian Springs Treaty, which Adams signed once he became president. But Adams, who had also never been sympathetic to the plight of the Indians, soon had a change of heart when he "realized that the Creek Nation in Georgia had been betrayed by scheming Indian chiefs and their white allies," Remini writes. Adams tried to negotiate better terms for the Creeks under a new treaty, an idea which was opposed by Clay, who believed that the Indians could not be civilized and "that their disappearance from the human family will be no great loss to the world." Adams persisted nonetheless and reached agreement with the Creeks on a new and more generous treaty, which he proposed to the Senate "in the interest of justice and humanity." Neither the Georgians nor the Senate supported the new treaty, and the Creeks were finally forced to accept changes that provided the Georgians with all the land they had demanded, in return for a small amount of cash. Adams was not about to risk a war with the state of Georgia in order to protect the Creeks or any other tribes. And his efforts to achieve a fairer outcome "gained him nothing but the hatred of those southerners who lusted after Indian territory and could hardly wait for the next election to replace him in the White House with Andrew Jackson," according to Remini. Adams soon realized that American policy had done "more harm to the Indians than the British or the French or the Spanish combined," later writing that "these are crying sins for which we are answerable before a higher jurisdiction."[15]

In many ways, the Cherokees fit the ideal that Jefferson had laid out for the integration of Indians into American society. They had long practiced agriculture, and in 1806 Jefferson had encouraged them "to go on learning to cultivate the earth." There was some intermarriage between the Cherokees and whites, as shown in an 1825 census that counted over 200 white men and women, along with 1,200 slaves, living among the Cherokees, who numbered 13,500. The one thing the Cherokees would not do is sell any more land to white settlers in the parts of Georgia, Alabama, Tennessee, and North Carolina they occupied, fearing a further loss of independence if they did so. To this end, in 1827 the tribe declared themselves an independent republic and adopted a written constitution modeled on the American Constitution. In the spring of 1829, gold was discovered on Cherokee land, and whites "surged over Cherokee country, seizing Indian farms, homes and gold mines." In June of 1830, the Georgia legislature passed a bill that invalidated the Cherokees' constitution and made the Indians subject to state laws, effectively removing all protections in an attempt to make "life miserable for the Cherokees, in order that they abandon their lands and follow their cousins west across the Mississippi," as Brands writes. The Cherokees looked to the federal government for protection, but they would not find support from the White House.[16]

Andrew Jackson had a different approach to the Indians. He

announced, in his first address to Congress, that he had "informed the Indians inhabiting parts of Georgia and Alabama that their attempt to establish an independent government would not be countenanced" by the president and they "should emigrate beyond the Mississippi or submit to the laws of those states." It wasn't that Jackson hated individual Indians. As his biographers point out, he sincerely believed that a policy of removal was in the best interest of the Indians. Jackson, who had adopted Indian children, "had good intentions toward Indians as individuals," Brands writes, even if he was paternalistic. There had also been some form of Indian removal floating around since the Monroe administration, and Adams too had accepted that there was little alternative, although neither man had proposed legislation to implement it. Jackson would effectuate the policy out of a belief that the federal government could not force a state to accept an independent government within its boundaries. This was based on his reading of the Constitution, which included a clause that: "no new State shall be formed or erected within the Jurisdiction of any other State" without the permission of that state's legislature. Given this, Jackson argued that the federal government could not force a state to accept "a foreign and independent government to establish itself there." The president proposed that Congress set aside land west of the Mississippi River for the tribes, but that relocation of the tribes would be voluntary. If this represented the carrot, then the stick was "that if they remain within the limits of the States they must be subject their laws."[17]

A modern historian needs to be careful in judging our ancestors based on the moral climate of today. But, in fact, Jackson's proposal, which was converted into the Indian Removal Act of 1830, also generated a storm of protest both within Congress and in the country at the time. "Men and women, all across the country (including Georgia), joined in massive petition campaigns demanding that Congress defeat Jackson's plans and uphold the Indians' property rights," Wilentz writes. The grassroots groups were led by the American Board of Commissioners for Foreign Missions (ABCFM), which typically placed missionaries in other countries, but also saw a role for their members in civilizing the Indian tribes. The ABCFM had earlier supported a plan to colonize "smaller tribes, and remnants of tribes," to the lands west of the Mississippi, but this was to be accompanied by a comprehensive plan of "state-building [and] education" that would ultimately incorporate these Indians as citizens into the United States. And it was restricted to only the smallest tribes. The ABCFM was joined in its opposition by Catharine Beecher, the daughter of Lyman Beecher and the sister of Harriet Beecher Stowe. They opposed the Jackson policy as "dispossession and deportation," which "they condemned as a cruel betrayal" of the Indians and as a means of "undercutting efforts to 'enlighten and Christianize' the Indians," Howe writes.[18]

In the Senate, Theodore Frelinghuysen of New Jersey led the campaign to defeat the bill. He argued that the United States must respect the rights of the Indians and stand against the greed that compelled men to take more and more land. The Indians had listened to "our profession of friendship ... and yet we crave more" land, leaving the tribes to a "few miserable acres of our Southern frontier." He proposed an amendment to the bill that would continue to provide federal protection to the tribes. These arguments were countered by John Forsyth of Georgia, who "responded with savage sectional rage," according to Remini. Forsyth reminded the opponents of the bill that Georgia was simply doing what the eastern and Northern states had done to their Indians, which certainly had a measure of truth to it. He was taking a page from Jackson's first annual message, when he questioned whether "the people of Maine [would] permit the Penobscot tribe to erect an independent government within their State." As with the later controversy over tariffs and nullification, the debate in Congress took a very strong sectional cast between the East and the South.[19]

Jackson placed a great deal of pressure on his fellow party members, telling them that he "staked the success of his administration upon the measure." Given this, the Indian Removal Act passed the Senate on a party-line vote of 28–19. The vote in the House was much closer, motivated by the twin concerns of Northern representatives about the morality of the removal policy and its potential cost. Some feared that, to the extent that Indian removal depleted the treasury of funds, there would be that many fewer dollars available to build internal improvements. Party loyalty did not seem to play as much of a role as sectionalism in the House, with twenty-four Jacksonian Democrats voting against the bill. Overall, "the slave states voted 61 to 15 for Removal, the free states opposed it, 41–82," Howe writes. Jackson signed the bill on May 28, 1830, making it the law of the land. It would have devastating impacts on the Indian tribes of the South.[20]

Perhaps had the president continued the policy of his predecessors in protecting the Indian tribes from state interference, the results and impacts may have been different. But Jackson's priority was the protection of white Americans. While Jackson had declared that Indian removal would be voluntary, the tribes knew that being placed under state control would make them little more than second-class citizens. As Howe writes, "submission to the laws of Georgia for a Creek or Cherokee meant not being able to vote, sue, own property, testify against a white person, or obtain credit." Jackson also placed significant pressure on the tribes to submit to removal. He threatened that if they did not relocate when asked, they would be on their own in the future. "When they find that they cannot live under the laws of Alabama, they must find, at their own expence ... a country and a home," Jackson said.[21]

Still the Cherokee would not submit, and they hired the former attorney general under Monroe and Adams to sue the federal government over its treaty rights. The aging John Marshall was sympathetic to the Cherokees, but ultimately found that all Indian tribes were "domestic dependent nations," similar to "a ward to his guardian" and as such lacked standing to sue. But in a follow-up suit a year later, the Supreme Court got its opportunity to weigh in on the rights of the Indians. Georgia had passed a law making it illegal for whites to live on tribal lands, and then arrested two missionaries who had proceeded to do so. The men clearly had standing. Marshall took the opportunity to strike down the Georgia law as unconstitutional and found that the whole "system of legislation lately adopted by the Legislature of Georgia in relation to the Cherokee Nation [was] repugnant to the Constitution, laws, and treaties of the United States." But alas, Jackson refused to implement the court's decision, reportedly saying, "Well, John Marshall has made his decision: now let him enforce it." While historians doubt that Jackson said this, it certainly reflected his point of view. And some at the time thought that Jackson had encouraged the behavior of Georgia and the other states, like Alabama and Mississippi, which passed similar laws. "Gen Jackson could by a nod of the head or a crook of the finger induce Georgia to submit to the law," one North Carolina congressman observed.[22]

❦❦❦

Jackson wasted little time implementing the Removal Act. By the summer of 1830, the Choctaws were essentially forced to sell some 10 million acres in Mississippi and move to present-day Oklahoma. The tribe was threatened with military force if it chose to remain and not submit to state law. Bribes were offered to tribal leaders in order to get them to comply. "From start to finish the operation was a fraud," Remini writes. "Corruption, theft, mismanagement, inefficiency—all contributed to the destruction of a once great people." Removal of the Creeks and Chickasaws soon followed under similar circumstances. The Creek Treaty, signed in 1832, led some members of the tribe to take up arms once again in what became known as the Second Creek War, which broke out in 1836. The army put down the rebellion in short order. Up to half of the Creeks may have died from the war and in the process of removal.[23]

Still the Cherokees held out. They were led by John Ross, a man of Scottish descent who was only one-eighth Indian. "He was rich, lived in a fine house, was served by black slaves, and virtually controlled the annuities paid by the United States to the tribal government for former land cessions," according to Remini. Ross and most of the Cherokees opposed the policy of removal. A smaller group, known as the Treaty Party, entered negotiations with the government over the terms of removal. It was an unpopular decision with the majority of the Cherokees, and some of the leaders of the Treaty Party were later killed for their role in removal. Jackson and his negotiators were playing a classic divide-and-conquer strategy, exploiting tribal disunity. Negotiations yielded the Treaty of New Echota, which required the Cherokees to give up some 7 million acres of land that covered parts of Georgia, Alabama, North Carolina, and Tennessee, in exchange for $5 million.[24]

The Cherokee National Council formally rejected the treaty in the fall of 1835, but it was approved by the Treaty Party on a vote of 79–7. Only a handful of the Cherokees voted to ratify the treaty, making the entire process a sham. There was also substantial opposition in the

Senate from Henry Clay and Daniel Webster. Clay would later recall that he opposed the treaty because it was "induced by corruption." Despite their opposition, it passed by one vote in the Senate. The treaty required removal to begin within two years of its approval, or May of 1838. Most of the Cherokees refused to comply and were summarily rounded up and forced into prison camps. One observer wrote that "men were seized in their fields, women were taken from their wheels and children from their play," and watched as their homes were burned behind them. Of the eighteen thousand that were forced to relocate, four thousand lost their lives in what became known as the Trail of Tears. "I fought through the Civil War and have seen men shot to pieces and slaughtered by thousands, but the Cherokee removal was the cruelest I ever saw," according to one eyewitness.[25]

While the Trail of Tears occurred after Jackson left the White House, he bears responsibility for what occurred. Despite his intent to save the Indians, the policy of removal led to their eventual destruction. In total, forty-six thousand Indians were removed during the Jackson administration, with a like number slated for future removal. A total of 100 million acres were acquired at a cost of $70 million, "yet little of the money ended up with the American Indians," according to Howe. The treaty-making process was marked by coercion, bribery, and corruption. It was a shameful process, marked by the greed of white settlers for ever more land, and a racist attitude toward the tribes. If done today, we would call it "ethnic cleansing," Howe writes.[26]

Bank Wars and Reelection

The controversy over banking did not begin with Hamilton and Jefferson nor in the aftermath of the Panic of 1819 but extends far back in history. In the days before his death by crucifixion, the Gospels report that Jesus overturned the tables of the moneychangers outside the temple, telling them, "My house shall be a house of prayer, but you are making it a den of thieves." Shakespeare wrote in Hamlet: "neither a borrower nor a lender be," reflecting a fear of debt. In the middle ages, the Catholic Church forbade Christians from charging interest, referring to it as usury. Yet there was still a need for financiers, and so the Jews became the moneylenders and later the bankers of Europe. In the eighteenth century, the Rothschilds built an international banking system, and other Jews held prominent positions in finance. Given the prominent role that Jews played, there developed an anti-Semitic element underlying the criticism of banking that continues in our time. "When Donald J. Trump, campaigning for the presidency in 2016, charged that his rival, former Secretary of State Hillary Clinton, 'meets in secret with international banks to plot the destruction of U.S. sovereignty in order to enrich these global financial powers,' some saw an evocation of anti-Semitic stereotyping," according to the website My Jewish Learning.[27]

Yet banking is essential in a modern economy. Bankers bring together those with money who are looking to invest it and those who need to borrow money for any number of purposes. In the absence of banks, the only recourse for those who lack money is to borrow from another individual or family member, who may lack the knowledge and skill to evaluate the risk inherent in making loans. In colonial America, there were no banks. Benjamin Franklin, after running away to Philadelphia as a teenager, returned to Boston to borrow money from his father so he could open his own print shop. His father refused, telling him he was "too young to be trusted with the management of a business so important." Perhaps his father refused in part because he could not properly evaluate his son as a credit risk, or because he could not separate his emotions from the decision, given that his son had run away from home. Banks can help resolve this problem by evaluating risk and spreading it among large numbers of lenders and borrowers. Banks also provide a convenient payment system between individuals, with most people paying for purchases in the modern world through bank checks, credit/debit cards, and through online banking.[28]

Banks can be controversial because they use other people's money to make loans, which sometimes go into default. To mitigate the risk of loan defaults, banks typically hold on to a certain level of cash reserves from their depositors and from their own capital, a concept referred to as fractional reserves. For example, a bank may decide that it can loan out 50 percent of its capital and deposits, and thus operate on a 50 percent fractional reserve system. In the eighteenth century, these reserves were held in specie, such as gold or silver. A borrower would receive banknotes (essentially paper money) and not specie, which could be used to purchase goods, invest in land, or open or expand a business or farm. Those who received the banknotes could then redeem these for specie at the bank that issued them or use them for other purchases. Banking was grounded in the assumption that not all depositors would seek to withdraw their funds at the same time, and so only a portion of the deposits need be held. "As a result of their ability to make loans, banks had considerable power over the supply of money flowing through the economy," financial historian Sharon Ann Murphy explains. "They could use this power to expand (increase) or contract (decrease) the money supply."[29]

There is one major problem with the fractional reserve system. In the absence of regulation, some banks hold little or no reserves and make highly risky loans prone to default. If it becomes known that a bank is in trouble, depositors will attempt to withdraw their money simultaneously, which creates a classic bank run. Only the very first people to arrive would receive their money, and even the very best banks could not withstand a bank run due to the way fractional banking works. During economic downturns, bank runs can become widespread and hit even solvent banks, causing them to fail. In the Frank Capra classic *It's a Wonderful Life*, George Bailey (played by Jimmy Stewart) confronts a bank run. Facing his friends and neighbors who are demanding their money, he tells them: "You're thinking of this place all wrong. Your money is not here. It's in Joe's house, in the Kennedy house ... and a hundred others." In the aftermath of the Great Depression of 1929, the federal government largely resolved the problem of bank runs by establishing the Federal Deposit Insurance Agency, which today provides insurance up to $250,000 for deposits per bank.

In the early republic, the federal government did not issue paper money because it was believed that the Constitution forbade this. The only paper money were banknotes, which create their own problems, not the least being a rather chaotic currency system. Different banknotes would trade at only a portion of their face value, depending on the strength of the bank and its location. The further a holder of banknotes was from the issuing bank, the less in specie the holder would receive from another bank, a concept known as discounting. This occurred because the reputation of the bank issuing the notes, and the level of reserves it held, may be unknown. "As a result, people valued most highly banknotes issued by institutions close to home, about which they possessed the most knowledge," Murphy writes. There was also a cost of returning banknotes to a distant bank. There arose a whole business of note brokers who "earned a living by buying bank notes at a discount and returning them *en masse* to the issuing bank for payment in coin," according to Richard Sylla. Counterfeiting was an ongoing problem, with banknotes that were often "inscribed with the names of seemingly legitimate but actually fictitious banks."[30]

A common conundrum for most governments was to find a way to create a stable currency. If banks, or the government itself, issued too much paper money, inflation would ensue. Yet if too little money was in circulation, which happened when only specie was used, then deflation would result, dampening economic growth. Over time, governments would establish central banks designed to control the money supply, regulate banks, and act as a lender of last resort to other banks during an economic downturn. But central banks created their own controversies, as we shall see with the experience of the United States.

⚓ ⚓ ⚓

The Continental Congress had financed the Revolutionary War primarily through the issuance of paper money, which led to hyperinflation and a currency that eventually became worthless. The young Alexander Hamilton, who was an aide-de-camp to General Washington during the war, was one of the first people to propose the formation of a national bank to stabilize the country's currency and restore its credit worthiness by marrying "private wealth and governmental authority." At the end of 1781, the Confederation Congress incorporated the Bank of North America, the first bank to be established in the fledgling country. While it helped to stabilize the economy, it could not overcome the manifest weaknesses built into the government under the Articles of Confederation, especially the lack of authority for the central government to levy taxes in order to pay for the war. The bank eventually floundered in 1785 when opposition to it formed in Pennsylvania from farmers who believed it placed too much power in the hands of the few and was inimical to a democratic society. It would not be the last time a central bank came under attack over these issues.[31]

Hamilton once again returned to the need for a national bank while serving as the first treasury secretary to President Washington. As we saw in chapter 1, Hamilton helped to stabilize the finances of the new nation, but also spurred the first party system. Both Jefferson and Madison argued that the Constitution did not authorize the federal government to establish a bank, while Hamilton relied on a broad reading of the necessary-and-proper clause to support creation of the bank. Washington ultimately sided with Hamilton, and the Bank of the United States went into operation in 1791. Hamilton "hoped that it would serve as [a] depository for government funds, provide loans to the government, and create a stable, uniform national currency," Murphy writes. The bank was also useful in filling a void for issuing paper money, which was thought to be impermissible for the government to do under the Constitution. Given this, the federal government only issued gold and silver coins. An 1871 Supreme Court decision would find that Congress in fact had the power to issue paper money under the necessary-and-proper clause. While the bank did not directly implement the monetary policies of the government, as modern central banks do, it did help to regulate the note issues of other banks and thereby stabilize the money supply of the country.[32]

Questions about the constitutionality of the first Bank of the United States never completely faded. By the time its charter came up for renewal in 1811, constitutional concerns once again resurfaced. In addition, an odd coalition formed in opposition to the bank that included certain business interests that wanted access to easier credit and included parts of the original Republican Party that were wedded to agrarianism. The recharter of the bank failed in the Senate when Vice President George Clinton broke the tie and voted against the bill. The lack of a central bank caused the United States major problems in financing the War of 1812, leading James Madison to support the creation of the Second Bank of the United States in 1816.[33]

The Irresistible Force Meets the Immovable Object

The next round of bank wars featured President Andrew Jackson, the irresistible force, against Nicholas Biddle, the president of the Second BUS, in the role of the immovable object. Being immovable can often be a vice rather than a virtue, especially in politics. And attempts to find compromise would falter in the face of election-year politics.

The president had, for many years, harbored a distrust of banks, paper money, and debt. Perhaps this went back to his early business dealings. In 1795, Jackson had sold some land in the West to finance his mercantile business. Because there was little demand for the land, he was forced to accept a personal note from the buyer, David Addison. What Jackson didn't know was that Addison was essentially bankrupt and his note worthless. Jackson was forced to sell his mercantile business to repay those he had purchased goods from. During the Panic of 1819, he had seen how the lack of money had affected the West. "Confidence entirely destroyed, specie payments suspended," he wrote. "Eastern paper is not to be obtained here." There was a substantial discounting of notes issued by western banks after the panic, making "the western states ... a separate country from the east with respect to the money supply," Brands writes. Jackson's firsthand experience of these events contributed to his hard-money sentiments, to a belief that only specie should be used as money.[34]

One of Jackson's main concerns about the Second BUS was that it contributed to the corruption of American democracy and was a threat to liberty. He had become aware that the two Kentucky branches of the BUS, along with the New Orleans branch, had supported Adams in the 1828 election. How could democracy survive if a small group of very rich men could sway elections? Their influence "if not curbed, must destroy the purity of the right to suffrage." To Jackson, the bank placed too much power "in the hands of a few men, a power over the money of the country," and was part of the growth in government that was having a corrupting influence on American society. In 1833, he would write that "every one that knows me, does know that I have always been opposed to the U. States Bank, nay all Banks." His views touch on two of the core societal dilemmas that were discussed in chapter 1. One is whether society is better served by a top-down decision-making process, or a bottom-up process. On this issue, Jackson was a strange hybrid, believing "in the virtue of a great majority of the people" as he wrote in 1828, but also believing that he, as president, encompassed the will of that majority. As Jon Meacham has written, Jackson thought that "the idea of the sovereignty of the many was compatible with a powerful executive" and he wasn't above using autocratic methods "to preserve democracy." Such an approach would bring charges from his political opponents that he was acting like a king, especially in his veto of the extension of the bank's charter.[35]

Jackson placed great importance on fighting inequality, and he believed that the BUS created further inequality. He closely followed the view of Jefferson and other liberals, who placed significant importance on the structural causes of inequality. While Jackson believed that inequality was sown into the nature of man and that "distinctions in society will always exist," he also opposed laws that "add to these natural and just advantages" any type of "artificial distinctions ... [that] make the rich richer and the potent more powerful," as he wrote in his veto message of the Second BUS's charter extension. He was not alone in his concern about the BUS creating further inequality. A committee formed by a group of Philadelphia workingmen, which included economists and other intellectuals, concluded that banks laid "the foundation of artificial inequality of wealth, and thereby artificial inequality of power ..." Senator Thomas Hart Benton, once a

Jackson opponent who had fought a duel against him, but had become an ally, said in an 1831 speech that he looked "upon the bank as an institution too great and powerful to be tolerated in a Government of free and equal laws."[36]

The coalition that opposed the BUS included an interesting mix of working-class people and hard-money men, those like Jackson who were opposed to all forms of paper money. They were joined by many in the West, including local bankers who chafed at the limitations the BUS placed on their ability to expand and who wanted easier credit and a more expansionary paper-money system.[37]

Jackson's comments on the BUS were initially muted. In his first annual message to Congress in 1829, he wrote that "both the constitutionality and the expediency of the law creating the Bank are well questioned by a large portion of our fellow citizens; and it must be admitted by all that it failed in great end of establishing a uniform and sound currency." Both parts of the statement were either misleading or flat wrong. While there were people who still questioned the constitutionality of the bank, even James Madison, its original opponent, had concluded the bank was constitutional based on the long-term existence of the first BUS, which established a clear precedent. The Supreme Court had also weighed in on the question in the affirmative. The second part of Jackson's statement, that the BUS had failed in establishing a stable currency, was absurd. As Remini writes, the BUS "had developed into a powerful central banking institution in full control of the credit of the currency facilities of the nation and adding to their strength and soundness." One need look no further than those critics who demanded easier money, including state-chartered banks, to see that the BUS had been quite successful in its role of managing the money supply.[38]

A year later, in his second annual message, the president expanded his attack on the BUS and laid out his vision for an alternative institution. He proposed to bring the banking functions under the control of the federal government, making it an arm of the treasury. It would continue as the depository for both the federal government and private funds, but "without the power to make loans or purchase property." This new bank would not have the ability to issue its own paper money but would have the authority to continue to restrain state banks from printing too many banknotes. It was largely an unworkable plan for central banking, since it would be subject to direct political interference. But it did show that Jackson was willing to compromise on the changes he requested, if only his opponents also would.

The BUS had powerful supporters, including a majority of Congress and the backing of two of its most important members, Senators Henry Clay and Daniel Webster. Its president, Nicholas Biddle, was a wunderkind. Born in 1786 to a well-established Philadelphia family, he first attended the University of Pennsylvania when he was ten years old, and eventually graduated from Princeton at fifteen. He studied law but did not feel it was his calling. He served as the secretary to the American minister in Paris and attended the coronation of Napoleon in 1804. Returning to the United States in 1807, he began a stint as a writer for a magazine and wrote a history of the Lewis and Clark expedition from their journals. He was elected to the Pennsylvania state legislature in 1810. Monroe nominated Biddle to serve on the board of the BUS in 1819. Four years later, when he was thirty-seven, Biddle became its president. He would bring great stability to the bank in the aftermath of the Panic of 1819 and to the monetary policy of the country, allowing for economic growth without inflation. Biddle was interested "in banks generally; and this interest was less in banking as a means of making money than as a function of the economy," Hammond writes.[39]

Despite his brilliance, Biddle had a major problem in the battle to come with Jackson. He was both arrogant and inflexible. "His chief flaws were his hubris and his excitability," Wilentz writes, "both of which proved disastrous in national politics." Biddle was unable to see that in a democratic society, especially one so grounded in solid mistrust of concentrated power, the bank was an easy target for its opponents. Biddle "insisted flatly that the Bank was not accountable to the government or the people," according to Arthur Schlesinger Jr. Prior to becoming president of the bank in 1824, he had written that the only role for the government was the appointment of five of the twenty-five directors. "The entire responsibility is thenceforward in the directors, and no officer of the Government, from the President downwards, has the least right, the least authority ... for interference in the concerns of the bank ..." His view confirmed that the bank had indeed become too powerful.[40]

Perhaps a compromise could have been engineered, something more along the lines of today's Federal Reserve System, if the issue of the bank had been postponed until after the 1832 election. The modern Federal Reserve System is decentralized, with twelve reserve branches around the country and a central governing board whose members are appointed by the president, with the advice and consent of the Senate. While the Fed has both public and private elements, it is designed to operate broadly in the public interest. It also needs to take into account the policy preferences of the government. As Frank E. Morris, president of the Boston Federal Reserve Bank from 1968 to 1988, once wrote: "the Federal Reserve cannot follow, *for any extended period of time*, a policy that is not acceptable to the Congress." The Fed can act independently in the short term, sometimes following policies that are painful but needed, but this independence is constrained by its need to be responsive to elected representatives. In the late 1970s, President Carter selected Paul Volker as chairman of the Fed during a time of stagnation. Under Volker, the Fed raised interest rates substantially, triggering a significant recession in the short term, and may have been part of the cause of Carter's loss to Ronald Reagan in 1980. But the Fed's actions also broke the inflationary cycle and ultimately led to an environment where the economy could grow over the long term. Morris argues that the Fed was able to do this because both Carter and Reagan accepted the Fed's actions, painful as they were, because controlling inflation had become the most important goal for the American people.[41]

Reelection and the Bank War

There had been speculation that Jackson would serve only one term, largely due to his bad health. This created considerable jockeying in the cabinet to replace him, especially between Calhoun and Van Buren. But both men underestimated Jackson's own ambition, because he did decide to run for reelection. One of his first actions was to start his own party newspaper, the *Washington Globe*. The existing newspaper that the Democrats used, the *Telegraph*, took its editorial direction from Calhoun. Jackson's second step was to purge his cabinet, whose members were Calhoun loyalists. Ever since the Eaton affair, Jackson and Calhoun had been at odds. Jackson had also become aware "that Calhoun had secretly denounced him during the Florida expedition fracas in 1818," Wilentz writes. Jackson also knew that Calhoun had become one of the leaders of the South Carolina nullification movement, which will be discussed in detail in the next chapter.[42]

Van Buren, who was Jackson's most capable cabinet member, and now his closest confidant, provided the president with the excuse he needed to clean house when he offered to resign. Many thought that Van Buren was to blame for the division between Calhoun and Jackson and saw the Little Magician as a master manipulator. In this view, Jackson was little more than an "ignorant weak superannuated man," according to one senator, and "Van Buren is President *de facto*." That these charges were untrue didn't matter, and they placed Van Buren under great pressure to resign, an offer that Jackson originally refused. "Never sir," he exclaimed, but he also knew that he ultimately must accept the resignation in order to "improve the quality of the entire cabinet," according to Remini. The ensuing purge was a shock to the nation. Not only were the three disloyal cabinet members gone, but so were Van Buren and Eaton, who were appointed minister to England and governor of the Florida territories respectively.[43]

The cabinet shakeup provided one last chance at compromise over the bank. Louis McLane, the newly appointed treasury secretary, saw the need for the bank and offered his boss a comprehensive solution. McLane, who had come from a federalist family, had served as the chairman of the House Ways and Means Committee and was therefore familiar with finance and banking. He also knew Biddle, which meant that he could serve as an honest broker between the bank president and the United States president, whom he had supported in 1828. McLane's plan involved paying off the federal debt, a goal near and dear to Jackson, in part by selling off the government's stock in the bank. The bank recharter would be delayed until after the election and then be considered with appropriate modifications. Both Jackson and Biddle appeared satisfied with the proposal. Unfortunately, neither man's supporters accepted the compromise. When McLane's *Treasury Report of 1831* was published, antibank Democrats attacked it. One critic wrote that it was Hamiltonian in nature and "totally unsuited to *this age of democracy and reform*." The new attorney general, Roger

Taney, who had been opposed to McLane's plan from the beginning, provided an antibank voice within the cabinet. Even the *Globe*, Jackson's own newspaper, reprinted articles critical of the plan. McLane had his own ambitions to become president, and he overreached when he attempted to have the *Globe*'s editor, Francis Blair, fired. Blair was a close friend of the president, and McLane undertook this action without the support or even the knowledge of Jackson, which cost him his support and influence within the administration. "Disloyalty to Blair was, in Jackson's eyes, tantamount to disloyalty to Jackson himself, as well as the larger cause of reform," Wilentz writes. Not only was the chance at compromise lost, but McLane's actions led Jackson to begin to rely on his closest friends, what became known as his Kitchen Cabinet, men like Van Buren and Blair. Amos Kendall was another of Jackson's closest friends and a member of the Kitchen Cabinet. He was originally from Massachusetts, a graduate of Dartmouth, who moved to Kentucky and had been a friend of Henry Clay. But he changed his mind about banking after the Panic of 1819, denouncing it as an unconstitutional "monied aristocracy," and became a fervent Jacksonian.[44]

With the McLane compromise dead, the Bank War became entangled in the 1832 election. By their very nature, elections magnify differences since there can only be one winner, which meant both sides were unwilling or unable to reach any form of compromise, despite their continuing efforts. Henry Clay was the leading figure in promoting the extension of the bank's charter in the run-up to the election. His initial instinct had been to defer the issue until after the election, telling Biddle in 1830 to wait, lest it become "the controlling question in American politics." Clay, who had been out of office after Adams's loss in 1828, returned to the Senate in 1831. When the National Republicans nominated Clay as their presidential candidate at the end of 1831, he made an abrupt about-face on the timing for the recharter issue. Clay "wanted his American System made the crux of the struggle between Democrats and National Republicans," and "was certain he could defeat Jackson on the issue if the President dared veto a recharter bill," Remini writes. "It was a blatant act of political self-interest." It would also prove to be a losing strategy, but then Clay was always a gambler.[45]

The bank wasn't the only issue on which Clay and Jackson disagreed. Internal improvements were another key element in Clay's American System. Jackson had hewn a middle course on the issue of internal improvements. As a senator in 1824, he had supported the construction of such improvements so long as they were "deemed National." As president, he vetoed a bill that would have funded the extension of the Maysville Road that ran solely through Kentucky, since it violated this principle. "I am not able to view it in any other light than as [a] measure of purely local character," Jackson wrote. Its supporters in Congress "called it a national measure because it would extend the reach of the National Road, linking the Midwest to the Chesapeake basin," according to Watson. The very concept of national versus local could be interpreted in many different ways. In addition to his principled concern, the president was aware that funding the Maysville Road project would be a major victory for Clay. As part of his veto message, he also expressed constitutional objections to the road and requested an amendment to clarify the power of the federal government to undertake such improvements and under what conditions. Jackson also indicated that even if the project did meet the test of being of national importance, he would still veto it, because there was no money to fund it, thereby adding to the national debt, which he intended to pay off. Finally, both Van Buren and the president were concerned that congressional legislation promoting internal improvements would result in wasteful pork barrel legislation in the future. Jackson was clearly not opposed to all spending for internal improvements, but it was not his highest priority, and like many of his predecessors, he wanted clear constitutional authority to undertake them.[46]

The Veto Message

Biddle felt he needed to maintain the support of both Clay and Daniel Webster, who were pushing him to submit a request for recharter. On January 6, 1832, he submitted the request, which included certain modifications that were intended to assuage the president. "But the reforms were too little, too late," Wilentz writes. Van Buren, whose nomination as minister to England had been rejected by the Senate based on the urging of Clay, returned to the United States and went to see Jackson in early July. By then, the bank recharter bill had cleared Congress. The old warrior, although terribly sick, was still geared for battle. "The bank, Mr. Van Buren, is trying to kill me, but I will kill it," the president told him as his closest advisors prepared a veto message.[47]

Historians of differing perspectives agree that the veto message was more powerful from a political perspective than an economic one. Economically, the veto provided no alternative to the BUS and "removed restraints from regional and local banks, enabling them to behave more irresponsibly than ever," according to Howe. Politically, it played to the fears of many that the bank was simply too powerful and helped to enrich a small number of people. "Many of our rich men have not been content with equal protection and equal benefits but have besought us to make them richer by acts of Congress," Jackson wrote in the veto message. The bank represented the ultimate grant of a corporate charter, but it was far from the only one, as Richard Hofstadter has written. States issued most of these, but "men whose capital or influence was too small to gain charters from lawmakers were barred from such profitable and strategic lines of corporate enterprise as banks," Hofstadter argues. Only the already rich, powerful, and connected could receive these benefits.[48]

Jackson opened the veto message by recognizing that the bank could be "convenient for the Government and useful to the people." But the government simply received too little in return for the value of the corporate charter, which instead flowed to "foreigners" and "a few hundred of our own citizens, chiefly of the richest class." The veto message specifically challenged stockownership by foreigners, even though they were not allowed to vote and provided a source of outside investment capital. The tone of the message was a bit paranoid regarding foreigners, according to Watson, creating the specter that "the Bank would recolonize America, reverse the results of the American Revolution, and deliver the Republic into the hands of British financers."[49]

Jackson had always questioned the constitutionality of the bank. He had never accepted, as Madison did, that precedent had established its legality. Nor did he accept that the Supreme Court was the final arbiter of what was constitutional. "The Congress, the Executive, and the Court must each for itself be guided by its own opinion of the Constitution." As we have seen, this was not an unusual position in the early republic. Jackson concludes his review of the constitutional question by finding that there was "nothing in [the bank's] legitimate functions that make it necessary or proper."

The heart of the veto came at the end, when Jackson attacked the bank for contributing to artificial inequality. If written today, conservatives would charge Jackson with playing the class-warfare card, which he indeed did. The president indicated that "distinctions in society will always exist under every just government." Reading these words, one is reminded of Jefferson's reliance on a natural aristocracy to rule at the state and national level. "There is a natural aristocracy among men. The grounds of this are virtue and talent. There is also an artificial aristocracy, founded on wealth and birth, without either virtue or talents," Jefferson wrote to John Adams in 1813. "The natural aristocracy I consider as the most precious gift of nature, for the instruction, the trusts, and government of society." Both Jefferson and Jackson understood that people have differing skills and abilities, and both wanted to avoid an aristocracy tied to either birth or social connections. The monarchies of Europe controlled both the government and the economy and blocked the average person, regardless of ability, from reaching their full potential. Jackson saw the bank as an institution that granted a privileged position to a select few. "But when the laws undertake to add to these natural and just advantages artificial distinctions ... to make the rich richer and the potent more powerful," then average people "have a right to complain of the injustice to their Government." For both Jefferson and Jackson, a smaller government with less power would ameliorate such situations. Both viewed active government as the worst form of corruption, since it aided the already wealthy and powerful. One must remember that this was a period before liberals believed that government had the ability to aid the common person. Jackson could point to the recent election, when certain powerful bankers had supported his opponent, making one "tremble for the purity of our elections." (Of course, Jackson does not mention that Biddle supported him for president in 1828.) The bank also loaned money to favored politicians and paid a retainer to one of its prime supporters, Daniel Webster. Jackson also looked on aghast as Biddle attempted to influence the legislative process during the passage of the bank recharter bill. "The action proved all of the President's fears and past warnings," Remini writes.[50]

The debate over the size, scope, and role of government is deeply embedded in American history. For many, including Jackson, too much centralized governmental power was viewed as inimical to liberty. Power and liberty were viewed as polar opposites, two distinct ends of a continuum. "The central fact of civic life, by which every political collision and its outcome could be understood, was the irreconcilable antinomy of liberty and power," Elkins and McKitrick have written about eighteenth-century politics. But the same could be said of the nineteenth century, and of American politics in general. The battle between Jackson and the Democrats on one side, and Clay and the National Republicans on the other, was a continuation of an ongoing American debate.[51]

Jackson was, in his own way, expanding centralized power in the authority of a president to have a role in legislation. Prior to Jackson, only nine vetoes had been issued, and all of these were strictly over constitutional questions. Generally, it was assumed that this was the only proper reason for a veto, and that presidents should abstain from interfering in the legislative process. But Jackson "believed that a President could kill a bill for any reason—political, social, economic … when he felt it injured the nation and the people," Remini argues. In the future, the president would need to be consulted on the content of legislation.[52]

❦ ❦ ❦

The veto elicited an immediate response from Clay, Webster, and Biddle. They homed in on Jackson's class-warfare language. Webster claimed that the veto message "attacked whole classes of the people, for the purpose of turning against them the prejudices and resentments of other classes." Biddle said that "it is really a manifesto of anarchy—such as Marat or Robespierre might have issued to the mob ..." And Clay challenged Jackson for attempting a power grab by using the veto for "ordinary cases," in contravention of the founders. "It was designed for instances of precipitate legislation, in unguarded moments," a power that should be used rarely. But none of this mattered, because Clay and Webster lacked the votes needed to override the veto. On July 13, the bank recharter bill passed the Senate on a vote of 22–19, "far short of the two-thirds' majority required to override Jackson's veto," Wilentz writes.[53]

Clay's election-year gamble also failed. Jackson easily defeated him in the electoral college 219–49 and won 52 percent of the popular vote to Clay's 40 percent. It may have also hurt Clay's cause that a new third party had entered the contest, the Anti-Masons, which peeled off seven electoral votes. But the Democrats could not celebrate too much, since their majority in the House had fallen and the Senate was now controlled by the National Republicans (soon to be the Whigs). There was also one other ominous note. All of South Carolina's electoral votes were cast for John Floyd of Virginia, its "extremist state-rights governor." Jackson now faced a major challenge from South Carolina over the issue of tariffs. They were led by none other than John C. Calhoun, who had developed a theory that justified the nullification of federal laws by a state. It is to that story we now turn.[54]

Endnotes

1   Watson, p. 133.

2   Brands, p. 406.

3   Remini, *Jackson*, p. 174; Wilentz, *Jackson*, p. 56; the First Inaugural Address of Andrew Jackson was retrieved on September 20, 2017, from http://avalon.law.yale.edu/19th_century/jackson1.asp.

4   Remini, Jackson, p. 183; for a comparison of different historians' views, see Remini, *Jackson*, p. 183–186, for a defense of the Jackson rotation system. For a more critical view, see Howe, p. 331–333; Leonard D. White, *The Jacksonians: A Study*

in Administrative History 1829-1861 (New York, 1954), p. 346, p. 301, and p. 308; Wilentz, *Jackson,* p. 57.

5   Wilentz, *Jackson,* p. 55; Brands, p. 412.

6   Matthew A. Crenson, *The Federal Machine: Beginnings of Bureaucracy in Jacksonian America* (Baltimore, 1975), p. 11–13 and p. 36.

7   Garry Wills, *A Necessary Evil: A History of American Distrust of Government* (New York, 1999), p. 17–18.

8   Remini, *Jackson,* p. 161–165; Wilentz, *The Rise,* p. 317–318.

9   Peterson, p. 98 and p. 107.

10 Peterson, p. 165–166; White, p. 323.

11 White, p. 309–313.

12 White, p. 327–337.

13 White, p. 315 and p. 349; Crenson, p. 168–171.

14 Daniel Feller, *The Jacksonian Promise: America 1815–1840* (Baltimore, 1995), p.180.

15 Remini, *Adams,* p. 91–100.

16 Watson, p. 105–108; Howe, p. 342–346; Brands, p. 488.

17 Brands, p. 490–491; Wilentz, *Rise,* p. 324–325; the quotes shown are from his First Annual Message of December 8, 1829, retrieved July 28, 2017, from http://www.presidency.ucsb.edu/ws/?pid=29471; Nicholas Guyatt, *Bind Us Apart: How Enlightened Americans Invented Racial Segregation* (New York, 2016), p. 287–294.

18 Guyatt, p. 282–284 and p. 296–303; Howe, p. 349.

19 Wilentz, *Rise,* p.323; Remini, *Jackson,* p. 260.

20 Howe, p. 352; Wilentz, *Rise,* p. 326; Remini, *Jackson,* p. 263.

21 Howe, p. 348 and p. 353; Remini, *Jackson,* p. 272.

22 Howe, p. 354–357; Smith, p. 518; Remini, *Jackson,* p. 277.

23 Remini, *Jackson,* p. 272–273; Howe, p. 416–417.

24 Robert V. Remini, *Andrew Jackson and the Course of American Democracy: 1833-1845, Volume III* (New York, 1984), p. 293–294.

25 Remini, *Jackson Volume III,* p. 299–303; Remini, *Clay,* p. 636.

26 Howe, p. 420–422.

27 The quote is from My Jewish Learning, retrieved November 20, 2017, from https://www.myjewishlearning.com/article/usury-and-moneylending-in-judaism/.

28 For an excellent overview of banking in general, and specifically in the early Republic, see Sharon Ann Murphy, *Other People's Money: How Banking Worked in the Early American Republic* (Baltimore, 2017). The Franklin example was taken from this book at p. 40. Chapter 2 contains a useful overview of banking that has informed this section of the book.

29 Murphy, p. 45.

30 Murphy, p. 58 and p. 72; Richard Sylla, "The US Banking System: Origin, Development, and Regulation," retrieved November 20, 2017, from https://www.gilderlehrman.org/history-by-era/hamiltoneconomics/essays/us-banking-system-origin-development-and-regulation; see also Howe, p. 382, for problems with the banking system.

31 Hammond, p. 41 and p. 53–54.

32 Murphy, p. 64–65 and p. 30, for information about the view that the Constitution initially forbade the issuing of paper money. See also Constitutional FAQ Answer #154, retrieved December 4, 2017, from https://www.usconstitution.net/constfaq_q154.html, which includes a discussion that took place at the Constitutional Convention regarding the unpopularity of allowing Congress to issue paper money, given the experience under the Articles of Confederation, and also includes information on the 1871 Court decision.

33 Hammond, p. 219–220; Murphy, p. 67.

34 Brands, p. 70, p. 346, and p. 364.

35 Wilentz, *Rise*, p. 360–361; Remini, *Jackson II*, p. 200; Schlesinger, p. 76–77; Meacham, p. 48.

36 Wilentz, *Rise*, p. 370; Schlesinger, p. 79–81.

37 Wilentz, *Rise*, p. 362–364; Schlesinger, p. 77–79.

38 Hammond, p. 374; Remini, p. 229.

39 Hammond, p. 287–291; Wilentz, *Rise*, p. 364–365.

40 Wilentz, *Rise*, p. 364–365; Schlesinger, p. 76.

41 For an overview of the Federal Reserve System, see https://www.federalreserve.gov/aboutthefed/files/pf_1.pdf; the views of Frank E. Morris can be found as part of the publication of Donald R. Hodgman, ed., (July 1983), *The Political Economy of Monetary Policy: National and International Aspects*, p.141, retrieved December 15, 2017, from https://pdfs.semanticscholar.org/8a9d/4e9b1aa930c286f4c765db97e719a69b716e.pdf.

42 Harry L. Watson, *Jackson vs. Clay* p. 72; Wilentz, *Rise*, p. 359.

43 Remini, *Jackson II*, p. 311–312.

44 Remini, *Jackson II*, p. 336–343; Wilentz, *Rise*, p. 360 and p. 367. For background on Blair, see Wilentz, *Rise*, p. 289–291.

45 Remini, *Clay*, p. 367 and p. 379.

46 Watson, *Jackson vs. Clay*, p. 77–78; Howe, p. 358–359; Wilentz, *Rise*, p. 328.

47 Wilentz, *Rise*, p. 369; Watson, *Liberty*, p. 143.

48 Both Wilentz in *Rise* and Howe make similar points on the economic message. See p. 371 and p. 379 respectively. Hofstadter, p. 58. The quotation from the veto message can be found in Watson, *Jackson vs. Clay*, p. 187. That book contains several very useful primary source documents.

49 Watson, *Jackson vs. Clay*, p. 183; Watson, *Liberty*, p. 144.

50 The quotes from Jefferson can found in Koch and Peden, p. 632–633. All quotations from the veto message are found in Watson, *Jackson vs. Clay*, p. 187. Remini, *Jackson II*, p. 364.

51 Elkins and McKitrick, p. 6.

52 I find Remini's argument to be persuasive on the issue of the veto. See *Jackson II*, p. 369–370.

53 Wilentz, *Rise*, p. 371; Remini, *Clay*, p. 399.

54 Wilentz, *Rise*, p. 373–374; elections results were retrieved December 26, 2017, from https://www.270towin.com/1832_Election/.

CHAPTER 10

Nullifiers, Bank Wars Redux, and the King

... that the Constitution of the United States is, in fact, a compact, to which each State is a party ...
—JOHN C. CALHOUN, FORT HILL ADDRESS, 1831[1]

The people of the United States formed the Constitution, acting through the State legislatures in making the compact ...but the terms used in its construction show it to be a Government in which the people of all the States, collectively, are represented.
—ANDREW JACKSON, NULLIFICATION PROCLAMATION, 1832[2]

*I*f the nullification crisis shows Jackson at his finest, the continuing Bank War showed the opposite. The president handled nullification deftly, keeping the personal separate from the political, and showed a command of the concept of America as a nation that was in keeping with the best traditions of the Framers of the Constitution. While Jackson was genuinely concerned that the bank was a corrupting influence on the country, his inability to find a realistic alternative would bedevil the American economy for many years.

The Nullification Crisis

The nullification crisis that occurred between the state of South Carolina and the Jackson administration was, in many ways, baked into the American constitutional system. It reflected the two major pieces of unfinished business from the founding era, federalism and slavery, which would once again be entwined during the nullification crisis. Federalism dealt with the nature of a divided system of sovereignty: how much power should be allocated to the national government, and how much should be left to the states. During the revolution, two competing ideological approaches had come to the forefront. One maintained that too much centralized power was a danger to the survival of republican government and liberty. The other, that only through a more powerful centralized government could the United States defeat the British. Under the Articles of Confederation, the balance was tipped too far toward the states, with the document declaring that the states were sovereign. The Framers of the Constitution took a major step in moving the balance toward centralization, but they too did not ultimately establish the precise boundaries for where sovereignty resided between the states and the federal government. They needed to obscure the issue in order to get the Constitution ratified, since the Framers were undertaking an unprecedented attempt to establish a dual-tiered government, something considered impossible before this time. Such a government was sometimes referred to as *imperium in imperio* (a government within a government). James Wilson, speaking before the ratifying convention in Pennsylvania, had come up with the novel approach that sovereignty resided in the people, who doled it out to both the federal and state governments. Madison expressed a similar view in *Federalist* No. 46: "The federal and State governments are in fact but different agents and trustees of the people." Yet references to the people provide no clear answer to the question: who decides interpretive questions about the Constitution? And as Joseph Ellis has pointed out, the demarcation between state and federal sovereignty is but the most obvious of the disagreements that mark the ongoing debate in America. "The source of the disagreement goes much deeper, however, involving conflicting attitudes toward government itself, competing versions of citizenship [and, I would add, who can be an American], differing postures toward the twin goals of freedom and equality."[3]

The other major issue was slavery. Rather than placing restrictions on slavery, the Constitution provided additional protections in several areas and in return the union was strengthened. This included counting slaves as three-fifths of a person for the purpose of allocating representatives to the House, and by extension to the process for electing the president through the electoral college. It also included a twenty-year window for the importation of slaves into the country, and a provision requiring the return of runaway slaves. These protections were added without ever mentioning the word slavery in the document. The Framers also refused to overtly recognize in the Constitution that slaves were property. Madison had indicated at the convention that it would be wrong "to admit in the Constitution the idea that there could be property in men." The three-fifths clause had allowed the South to dominate the presidency in the early republic, and the extension of the slave trade would double the number of slaves in the country during the first twenty years of the Constitution, making its later peaceful eradication all but impossible.[4]

Part of the dispute over federalism hinged on whether the states had preceded the federal government or whether the reverse was true, and whether the constitutional compact was between the people or the states. Abraham Lincoln believed that the federal government preceded the states, arguing that no state had ever existed outside of the union. "The original ones passed into the Union even before they cast off their British colonial dependence; and the new ones each came into the Union directly from a condition of dependence, excepting Texas." Ronald Reagan thought that the states had formed the federal government, a position supported by states'-rights advocates. This is no minor distinction, since those who believed the states were the originators of the federal government would also conclude that the Constitution was a compact between the states. Jefferson took this position in the Kentucky resolution that protested the Alien and Sedition Acts of 1798. "Jefferson said that no one but the partners to the compact can interpret it, and any state can nullify a law," Garry Wills points out. Jefferson's view was particularly dangerous to the continuation of the union, since it could lead to secession.[5]

Madison and Jefferson had met in July and October of 1798 over the best response to the Alien and Sedition Acts. "Both men agreed in their fundamental view of the Constitution as a compact among the states vesting certain limited powers in a national government," Jack Rakove writes. Just about all people at the time thought of the Constitution as some form of a compact, since they were followers of Locke's social contract theory (in which each individual gives up some of their freedom to the state in return for collective safety). The question was whether it was a compact between the states or between the federal government and the people. Madison's position in 1798 was inconsistent with both his earlier and later nationalist views that it was a compact with the people, as formulated through the state ratifying conventions. In the run-up to the Constitutional Convention, he had envisioned a federal government that would act directly upon the people and be responsible to them. He had even gone so far as to recommend that the federal government have a veto power over state legislation. He eventually signed a Constitution that began with the words "We the People," not "We the States." While Madison rejected Jefferson's notion of nullification, he did propose that the states could interpose themselves in "arresting the progress of the evil," as he referred to the Alien and Sedition Act. In the Virginia resolution, he wrote that the state "views the powers of the federal government as resulting from the compact to which the states are parties." Perhaps he was simply reacting to the overheated passions of the time, with the Federalists attempting to muzzle the Republican opposition as war fever swept the country. Or perhaps he was struggling with where the final authority for deciding constitutional questions should reside, as historian Jonathan Gienapp argues. Madison had already rejected the idea that the Supreme Court should have the final say when major constitutional questions were raised, since this would place the court in a superior position to the legislative and executive branches. "If the constitutional boundary of either be brought into question, I do not see that any one of the independent departments had more right than another to declare their sentiments on that point," he wrote in 1789. Gienapp maintains that Madison did not intend to place the states in the role of final arbiter of the constitutionality of laws either, but rather saw them as alerting the people, who were the final arbiters, to unconstitutional laws. "The people, not the government, possess the absolute sovereignty," Madison had written in the report that went along with the Virginia resolution. "The state's role was less to exert their own primacy than to activate this more fundamental source of authority," which was the people, Gienapp writes. Whether this worked in practice, the South Carolina nullifiers were well aware of the Kentucky and Virginia resolutions, and would build on them in their attempt to nullify federal tariff laws. As we shall see, the Madison of the 1830s would oppose these efforts.[6]

☞ ☞ ☞

Southerners had always been sensitive about duties on imports, viewing them as a tax they paid when purchasing consumer goods, but which only benefited and shielded Northern industry from global competition. Their own major cash crops, cotton and rice, had no such protections and were subject to the whims of international trade and retaliatory tariffs from foreign governments. Ironically, tariffs had been chosen as the primary source for funding the federal government "based on a political accommodation to slavery during the Revolution," according to historian Robin L. Einhorn. Prior to the ratification of the Constitution, the Confederation Congress had attempted to implement the impost, a general tax on imports, because "it was the only tax Congress could adopt without talking about slavery," Einhorn writes. All other forms of taxation required decisions about how to tax and count slaves.[7]

At the Constitutional Convention, the North and the South struck a bargain over navigation acts, those laws that regulate shipping and trade, including the impost. The South dropped its demand that navigation acts must receive a two-thirds vote of Congress to become effective in exchange for a twenty-year extension of the slave trade. When the new Congress met in 1789, the impost was transformed into a tariff. "Rather than the flat ad valorem tax on all imported goods ... the first session of the first Congress adopted the protective tariff—a tax that subsidized ("protected") domestic manufacturers by hiking the prices of competing imported products," according to Einhorn. While the first Congress was able to negotiate the first tariff so that both the North and South felt they were winners, this type of accommodation would collapse by 1828 when the Tariff of Abominations was approved.[8]

As we have seen, John C. Calhoun had originally been a nationalist who supported much of the Madisonian Platform that later led to Clay's American System. He supported the tariff of 1816, although he justified it on the basis of national defense. He also supported the construction of internal improvements. The nationalist view predominated in South Carolina at the time, although there was some opposition from the planter class to the protective tariff. Correspondingly, Calhoun and most of the state generally backed a broad construction of the Constitution. This began to change in the mid-1820s as Northern manufacturers requested ever higher tariffs, which raised the price of consumer goods. There was also concern that "tariffs would inevitably destroy demand for rice and cotton," according to historian William W. Freehling. These concerns were set in the context of a weak South Carolina economy that had not completely recovered from the Panic of 1819.[9]

Slavery became entwined in the debates in South Carolina, especially in the aftermath of the Denmark Vesey uprising in 1822. Vesey was a literate freed black man. He may well have been inspired by the debates in Congress over the Missouri Controversy, and he "hated the whites for what they had done to him and his people," Howe writes. Vesey led a potential slave uprising in Charleston in 1822, for which he was later put to death. But the fear of further slave rebellions, when combined with an emerging opposition to the protective tariffs, began to change the political environment in South Carolina. In 1824, a resolution was introduced in the state senate "stating the principle of strict construction and proclaiming protective tariffs and internal improvements unconstitutional," Freehling writes. By 1827, debates in Congress over higher tariffs for woolen products, and potential assistance to the American Colonization Society to free and colonize slaves, pushed the South Carolinians ever further away from their nationalist leanings.[10]

In the run-up to the 1828 election, "President Adams allowed Clay and his Secretary of the Treasury, Richard Rush of Pennsylvania, to take the lead in pressing for tariff protection," Howe writes. Not to be outdone, the supporters of Andrew Jackson in Congress, led by Van Buren, pushed through a new set of tariffs, raising them "by about 30 to 50 percent." The intent was to provide additional protections to industries in New York, Pennsylvania, Kentucky, and Ohio as a way to build support for Jackson outside of his base in the South. The Jacksonians also targeted the bill in such a way that it harmed the New England states, who were sure to vote for Adams. As one Southern representative put it, the tariff had been "changed into a machine for manufacturing Presidents, instead of broadcloths, and bed blankets." Southerners attempted to amend the bill so it would fail, voting "with protection-minded producers of raw materials to keep rates high on nonindustrial products," then voting "with New England manufacturers to defeat the entire bill," according to Freehling. But the strategy failed when Van Buren was able to amend the bill and obtain sufficient votes to get it passed. Southerners were irate over the Tariff of Abominations, as they now referred to it. But they still supported Jackson in the election, fearing they would divide their ranks if they protested before the election, and hopeful that the team of Jackson and Calhoun (as vice president), would overturn the bill. Calhoun returned home to South Carolina during the election campaign, where he began to work on a theory that would threaten the union.[11]

Initially Calhoun tried to keep quiet about his role in developing the theory of nullification as he set about to compose the *South Carolina Exposition*. He hoped to preserve his national status in order to make another run for the presidency, and so he attempted to maintain a middle ground between the radicals in his home state and the remaining unionists. He had been considering some form of nullification since as early as 1824, writing, "The despotism founded on combined geographical interest admits of but one effective remedy, a veto on the part of the local interest, or under our system, on the part of the states." In the *Exposition*, Calhoun first attacked the legality of a protective tariff, arguing that the Constitution only granted Congress "the power of imposing a duty on imports for revenue" and not the power to protect one industry or region over another. He made it clear that states are the parties to the constitutional compact. "The Constitution of the United States was formed by sanction of the States," and "being parties to the constitutional compact ... there can be no tribunal above their authority to decide, in the last resort, whether the compact made by them be violated." The only way to check "the abuse of authority on the part of the absolute majority [is] by leaving to the States an efficient power, by a veto, the minor against the major interests of the community." In the *Exposition*, Calhoun was not only rejecting his own earlier nationalist sentiments, but also majority rule, since under his theory a minority of one state could veto a federal law. A state could call for a convention, similar to the state ratifying conventions for the Constitution, that would be bestowed with the ultimate power to decide on the question of the constitutionality of laws. "This state convention could also issue a call for a national convention to meet and clarify the issue, proposing amendments to the Constitution if necessary," according to Howe. Calhoun was silent on what a state convention could do if the national convention disagreed with its conclusion or the Constitution were amended to give the federal government the power in question, shrinking from the logical conclusion that this would lead to secession. South Carolina only issued a protest in 1828, hoping that the newly elected president would lead an effort to overturn the Tariff of Abominations. They would be sorely disappointed when tariff reduction was not at the top of Jackson's agenda. Calhoun's role in drafting the *Exposition* remained secret until 1831, although many speculated about his role.[12]

Calhoun wasn't the only one contemplating the nature of the federal union, as the Hayne–Webster debate would show.

Hayne versus Webster

It began in the Senate on January 19, 1830, over public-land sales. It would soon expand into a debate between those who believed in states' rights and the compact theory of the Constitution, led by Robert Hayne of South Carolina, against the strong nationalist views put forward by Daniel Webster. Their positions would emerge gradually over the next week.

Initially, the issue was the price that should be paid for western lands. Thomas Hart Benton of Missouri introduced a policy he called "graduation" in which the price would be gradually reduced until a buyer was found, to as low as $0.25 an acre from the then minimum price of $1.25 per acre. The proposal was intended to speed westward expansion, but it would deprive the government of needed revenue to fund one of the major planks of the American System, internal improvements. "Not surprisingly, some argued that Americans would be better off pushing industrialization and developing more infrastructure, instead of trying to expand the agricultural sector with more land," Howe writes. It was, in some ways, a repeat of the debate between Hamilton and Jefferson over the future direction of the country. With the West awash in land sales already, a senator from

Connecticut proposed a moratorium on new land sales until the old land had been sold. This caused Robert Hayne of South Carolina to join the debate, who began by attacking the high price placed on western land, linking the exploitation of the West with the exploitation of the South via the protective tariff. He saw these as "parallel oppressions." Hayne was attempting to align the South and West against the East and proposed that western lands be given to the states for disposition.[13]

"Sir, I rise to defend the East," Daniel Webster replied the next day. He defended the current system for western land sales, but, seeing the danger of Hayne's sectional approach of dividing the South and West from the East, he went beyond this to defend the union. Webster had undergone a transition not too dissimilar from Calhoun's, although in the opposite direction. During the War of 1812, he had been a states'-rights proponent, but now Webster "emerged as a leading defender of nationalism and the protective tariff," in large part because the economy of New England depended on it. He declared "I am a unionist, and, in this sense, a national republican. I would strengthen the ties that hold us together." Webster also defended the activism of the federal government under the American System against charges of corruption. He argued that the role of government was "actively good," that it spreads "benefits and blessings" and opens "channels of intercourse, augments population, enhances the value of property, and diffuses knowledge."[14]

Hayne's response came over a two-day period, with the weekend in between. He took Webster's argument as an attack on the South. "He has crossed the border, he has invaded the State of South Carolina, is making war upon her citizens, and endeavoring to overthrow her principles and institutions." This last reference was clearly pointed toward slavery, which Hayne defended. He also supported the principles outlined in the *South Carolina Exposition*, which people suspected had come from the pen of Calhoun. The vice president, in his role as president of the Senate, was in attendance during these speeches, and was seen passing notes to Hayne as he spoke. In referring to the *South Carolina Exposition*, the debate had been transformed from one about western land sales to one that went to the heart of the American nation.[15]

Daniel Webster saw that the debate was now about "nullification, secession, the very nature of the American Constitution," Burns writes. And so, the "godlike Daniel" began to dismantle the notion that the Constitution was nothing more than a compact among the states. In his "Second Reply to Hayne" Webster laid out an alternative vision of the Constitution. "It is, Sir, the people's Constitution, the people's government, made for the people, made by the people, and answerable to the people." It was not, as Calhoun and Hayne thought, a creature of the states, but rather the people had formed the Constitution and allocated a portion of their sovereignty to it. This was certainly closer to the view put forward by both James Wilson at the Pennsylvania ratifying convention and by Madison in the *Federalist*. Lincoln would later use Webster's words as inspiration in his first inaugural and echo his sentiments at Gettysburg. Webster concluded his reply by stating "Liberty and Union, now and forever, one and inseparable." Even Hayne was impressed and would later remark that Webster was "the most consummate orator of either ancient or modern times."[16]

Southern politicians could dismiss Webster "as a New Englander and an old Federalist," as Burns writes. But what of President Jackson, who had dragged his feet on tariff reform and despised the idea of nullification, as he made clear at a dinner held on April 13, 1830, to celebrate Jefferson's birthday. Jackson was forced to listen to a series of toasts that celebrated the Southern view of states' rights, with Hayne offering a concluding toast to "the *Union* of the States, and the *Sovereignty* of the States." When it came time for Jackson's toast, he made clear his position on nullification and secession. As he stared at Calhoun, Jackson declared: "Our Union, *it must be preserved*." Calhoun, his glass shaky as he lifted it for the toast, responded: "The Union. Next to our liberty the most dear. May we always remember that it can only be preserved by respecting the rights of the states and by distributing equally the benefits and the burdens of the Union."[17]

Calhoun versus Jackson

By the spring of 1831, Calhoun was facing a serious dilemma. The forces for nullification had strengthened, and South Carolina was heading for a confrontation with Jackson and the federal government. James Hamilton, who strongly supported nullification, had been elected governor, and the legislature was under the control of the nullifiers as well. Still, Calhoun harbored hopes of being elected president in 1832, and of finding some middle ground, which was rapidly shrinking. He told a local newspaperman of his "plan of reconciliation" between the various sections of the country. For the West, internal improvements would be constructed through the proceeds of the sale of public lands and given final sanction through an amendment to the Constitution. A compromise would be fashioned with the East over the tariff along the lines of the 1816 tariff. But alas, Calhoun was fooling himself, since there was little support for his position. His real choice was to either join the nullifiers and attempt to moderate their proposals, or to see his political career end.[18]

Not surprisingly, he chose to join the nullifiers and went public with his view on nullification in the *Fort Hill Address*, which he released in July 1831. It was the next iteration in his evolving view on the relations between the states and the federal government and of the right of a state to veto a federal law. Calhoun expounded on his compact theory of the Constitution. "The great and leading principle is, that the General Government emanated from the people of the several States forming distinct political communities, and acting in their separate and sovereign capacity, and not from all of the people forming one aggregate political community; that the Constitution of the United States is, in fact, a compact, to which each State is a party ..." Leaning on the work that Jefferson and Madison had previously done, he declared that the "right of interposition ... be it called what it may,—State-right, veto, nullification, or by any other name,—I conceive to be the fundamental principle of our system." Since the states were the original parties to the Constitution, they have the right to judge whether the compact has been violated, and if it has, to nullify federal law. In the address, he laid out his theory for why majority rule should not always be followed. Calhoun argued that when interests are the same between the sections of the country, "it is just and proper to place them under the control of the majority." But this was not the case when laws impacted the interests of different sections of the country in different ways, as was the case with the tariff. "It would be vain to attempt to conceal, that it has divided the country into two great geographical divisions." Calhoun went so far as to posit that the federal government was not "a party to the constitutional compact," but a creature of the states.[19]

The *Fort Hill Address* ended any hope that Calhoun had of becoming president. "Exchanging one delusion for another, he entered heart and soul into the South Carolina crusade," Peterson writes.[20]

Andrew Jackson was pragmatic about the tariff. In 1824, he had called for a judicious tariff, a rather vague position designed to alienate as few people as possible. He also knew that part of his support in states like Pennsylvania and New York was built on backing some level of protectionism. Like Calhoun, he tried to walk a middle path, knowing that the tariff was extremely unpopular among his Southern constituents. Jackson wanted to ensure "that the great interests of agriculture, commerce, and manufactures should be equally favored," as he indicated in his first inaugural address, something that was easier said than done. Unlike Calhoun, he also believed that a protective tariff was clearly consistent "with the letter and spirit of the Constitution."[21]

At times, the president felt that both sides in the dispute, those in the North that supported protective tariffs, and those in the South that opposed them, overstated the impact of the tariff. "The effects of the tariff are doubtless overrated, both in its evils and its advantages," he wrote in his second address to Congress in 1830. Yet he also knew the tariff was a clear political problem. Jackson saw two purposes for the tariff: one was as a source of revenue to pay down the national debt. The second was "to protect that portion of our manufacturers and labor whose prosperity is essential to our national safety and independence." As the national debt came closer to being paid off, and as the controversy in South Carolina worsened, Jackson threw his support behind a downward revision in the tariff prior to the 1832 election. Secretary of the Treasury McLane prepared a report on tariff reductions in the spring of 1832. His proposal was modified by John Quincy Adams, newly elected to the House and the chairman of the Committee on Manufacturing. Adams had been lobbied by friends to stand for election to the House as the representative from Plymouth, a rather unusual move for a former president. Adams was concerned about the brewing nullification crisis and had given a speech in Quincy on the subject during its celebration of the fiftieth-fifth anniversary of the Declaration of Independence in which he denounced the idea that a state has the right to nullify federal law. "Stripped of the sophisticated argumentation in which this doctrine has been habited, its naked nature is an effort to organize insurrection against the laws of the United States," Adams asserted. It was a clear reference to the theory of nullification his former vice president was putting forth.[22]

Yet Adams shared Jackson's concern that some reductions in the tariff were warranted, and so he worked with McLane on a bill that ultimately passed Congress. Adams inserted a provision that reduced tariffs on woolen products, which slaves primarily wore, as a way to appease the South, while still maintaining a level of protectionism for cotton and iron, to satisfy the North. "In effect it restored the tariff to what it had been in 1824 when the average rate on dutiable articles was about 33 percent," Ellis writes. In July of 1832, Jackson signed the bill, hoping it would quell the controversy. While it helped to remove the issue from the upcoming election, it failed to end the controversy.[23]

❦ ❦ ❦

South Carolina's governor, James Hamilton, was leading the nullification movement in the run-up to the fall election. His goal was to elect enough nullifiers to the legislature to reach the two-thirds vote needed to call for a nullification convention. Though he was once a nationalist who had served in Congress, the 1828 Tariff of Abominations had converted him into one of the leading proponents for nullification. Hamilton "rallied thousands of Carolinians to his banner through state conventions, mass meetings, barbecues, a well-disciplined newspaper network, and a multitude of states'-rights clubs spread throughout the state," according to Calhoun biographer Irving H. Bartlett. But he needed a strong justification for the actions he hoped his state would take, and so in July of 1832 he requested that Calhoun provide him with a paper on the "principles and consequences of nullification."[24]

Calhoun responded at the end of August with his most detailed and far-reaching analysis to date. In a letter titled: "To General Hamilton on the subject of State Interposition," Calhoun denied that the United States was a nation. "So far from the Constitution being the work of the American people collectively, no such political body either now or ever did exist." It was an assertion at complete odds with the opening words of the preamble to the Constitution, "We the people." The antifederalists, those who had opposed the Constitution, took the opening words quite seriously and found them to be a major barrier to support for the document. The antifederalists viewed the Constitution as creating a consolidated national government with too much power, one that would act directly on the people, and strip the states of too much of their sovereignty. But they lost that debate, and now Calhoun was attempting to deny the very existence of a national political community in America, which the Constitution had created.[25]

One of the core elements of Calhoun's nullification theory was that states had the final authority to judge the constitutionality of federal laws. Essentially, unless three-quarters of the states condoned the federal law in question by amending the Constitution, the action of the state in nullifying federal law would stand. This created two problems for Calhoun. The first was, What could a state do that found itself in such a situation? "In the case stated, should the other members undertake to grant the power nullified," then that state would have the power to secede from the union. Whereas Calhoun had previously shied away from that answer, in the letter to Hamilton, he embraced it.[26]

The second problem was that Calhoun needed to develop a justification for why a minority should hold sway over the majority. The answer lay in his concept of the concurring majority. Calhoun argued that there were really two majorities. One was the absolute majority, which held sway over basic "law making." But there was also a concurrent majority that represents "each class or community of which [the absolute majority] is composed,—the assent of each taken separately,—and concurrence of all constituting the majority" is required when constitutional questions arise. Calhoun maintained that the Constitution itself was approved by the concurring majority. The concurring majority was needed in order to "COMPEL THE PARTS OF SOCIETY TO BE JUST TO ONE ANOTHER, BY COMPELLING THEM TO CONSULT THE INTEREST OF EACH OTHER." Calhoun went so far as to spell this out in all capitalized letters in the document he had produced, reflecting the importance he attached to the idea that each state formed its own majority which must be consulted and which must approve any laws, like the tariff, that affected the interests of a particular state. By extension, this would also extend to any law that affected slavery. "The theory was ingenious," Peterson writes, "but it was at war with reason, republicanism, and the Constitution."[27]

Political scientists James H. Read and Neal Allen have succinctly written that nullification, both in Calhoun's conception and in its later iterations, relies on three general axioms:

1. That there is no such thing as the "People of the United States." Calhoun certainly put forth this concept in his

letter to Hamilton and would later follow this up in his *Discourse on the Constitution*, which was published just after his death. "There is, indeed, no such community, politically speaking, as the people of the United States, regarded in the light of, and as constituting one people or nation."

2. That sovereignty cannot be divided. This was a very old concern that the Federalists had grappled with and harkened back to the antifederalist critique that the Constitution established a consolidated government, based on the theory that sovereignty could not be divided; that it was impossible to create a government within a government, what they referred to as *imperium in imperio*. James Wilson had been the first to come up with an answer to this question when he argued that it was the people who were sovereign and who could allocate their sovereignty to both the states and the federal government. "By adopting this system, we become a NATION; at present we are not one," Wilson said in 1787 at the Pennsylvania ratifying convention.

3. That the states are sovereign and are the final judge of the Constitution. As Read and Allen write, "if each individual state is fully sovereign in this sense [having the right of final judgment], then it follows that each state is final judge, for itself, of the Constitution's meaning and entitled to act of that judgement."[28]

Nullification was also at odds with the position of the Father of the Constitution, James Madison. In his various writings, Calhoun had leaned on the Kentucky and Virginia resolutions, and on the authority of Jefferson and Madison, who had prepared them. While Jefferson had died on July 4, 1826, Madison was still very much alive and ready to debunk the theory of nullification. In an 1828 letter to the leader of the antinullification movement in Virginia, Madison made it clear that a tariff imposed to protect domestic industry was constitutional. At the conclusion of the debate between Hayne and Webster, Hayne had looked to Madison to support his position. Madison responded politely, telling Hayne that his speech showed "ability and eloquence" but that he was "constrained to dissent ... from the doctrines espoused in them."[29]

Madison's response to Hayne was later recast in an 1831 letter. While Madison continued to view the Constitution as a compact among the states, he clarified that it was not formed "by the Governments of the component States," but rather "by the people in each of the States, acting in their highest sovereign capacity." Since it was not "formed by a majority of the people of the U.S. as a single community" it could not be considered a consolidated government, as the antifederalists had charged during the ratification debates. This made sense, since the Constitution was ratified by the people of each of the states through special ratifying conventions, and not by one national convention or referendum. Madison also recognized that the United States formed one nation, or as he framed it, "one people for certain purposes," those purposes being the enumerated powers provided to the federal government in the Constitution. As for the issue of sovereignty, the federal government was sovereign within its sphere, since the people had divided "the supreme powers of Govt between the States in their united capacity and the States in their individual capacities."[30]

Madison thought it absurd to leave the final decision on consti-tutional questions to individual states, since it would "speedily put an end to the Union itself." Madison pointed to two solutions for solving problems of constitutional interpretation. One was elections, which harkened back to his position on the Virginia resolutions in which he felt that state governments could awaken the people to the danger of certain federal laws. "When the Alien & Sedition laws were passed in contravention to the opinions and feelings of the community, the first elections that ensued put an end to them," Madison stated in reference to Jefferson's election as president in 1800. The second was to amend the Constitution. Madison was greatly concerned about the ability of one state to overrule "the law of the U.S. unless overruled by ¾ of the States." A process that allows a minority to dictate to the majority "would overturn the first principle of free Govt. and in prac-tice necessarily overturn the Govt. itself." Madison's views would soon have an influence over Jackson's Nullification Proclamation through Secretary of State Edward Livingston, its prime author and an old friend of Madison's.[31]

❦ ❦ ❦

In October of 1832, the nullifiers swept to victory in the legislative elections in South Carolina. They now had the two-thirds vote they needed to call for a convention to consider the issue of nullification. Governor Hamilton called a special legislative session on October 22, which quickly approved the calling of elections for the convention to be held on November 19.

Why was the tariff of such importance that South Carolina was willing to risk the possible dissolution of the union and a civil war? Because the tariff was tied in the minds of many of the nullifiers to slavery. "Nullifiers considered protective tariffs not only an inherently onerous burden but also an integral pattern of sectional exploitation which would lead to slave revolts, colonization schemes, and ultimately the abolition of slavery," according to Freehling. In 1827, a pamphlet entitled *The Crisis* was widely circulated in the state. The author, writing under the pen name Brutus, argued that the tariff was linked with the slavery issue and that the American Colonization Society's real goal was the elimination of slavery. Others feared that the broad construction of the Constitution, which they believed was how the protective tariff had been justified, would eventually be used to attack slavery.[32]

On November 24, 1832, five days after the convention opened, it issued its Ordinance of Nullification. As of February 1, 1833, the tariffs of 1828 and 1832 would be "null, void, no law, nor binding upon" South Carolina. It was illegal for any officer of the state or the federal government "to enforce the payment of duties" required under the various tariff acts. State officials would be required to take an oath that they would enforce the provisions of the ordinance. If the federal government were to threaten to use force against South Carolina, the state would "hold themselves absolved from all further obligation to maintain their political connection with the people of the other States." In other words, South Carolina would secede from the union.[33]

Calhoun and the other leaders of the nullification movement had always maintained that it provided a peaceful way for a state to stand against unconstitutional acts of the federal government. Yet Hamilton now called on the legislature to raise a volunteer army of 12,000 men. The action was justified at the time by pointing out that President Jackson "had repeatedly sworn to enforce the laws, using coercion if necessary, and to hang the leading nullifiers as traitors," according to Ellis. Shortly thereafter, Robert Hayne resigned from the Senate and was elected governor to replace Hamilton. Calhoun then resigned as vice president (he was a lame duck after the election of 1832, since Van Buren had replaced him as Jackson's running mate) and was elected by the legislature to take Hayne's seat in the Senate. Matters were now in the president's court.[34]

‍ ‍ ‍ ‍

Andrew Jackson faced his most difficult challenge yet. The hero of New Orleans, of numerous battles with enemy troops and Indians, knew how to directly confront an enemy. As a candidate for office, he had learned the fine political art of obfuscation. As president, he had faced multiple challenges, from reshuffling his cabinet, to Indian removal, to the bank wars. In facing the nullification crisis, Jackson would need to combine all that he had learned in his life. As the crisis unfolded, he revealed an ability to separate the personal from the political; to state his principles clearly on the importance of the union; and to combine this with a willingness to compromise on issues of interest. Many historians have called his handling of the crisis his finest moment.[35]

On the personal level, he had grown to despise Calhoun. The rift had begun when he became aware of Calhoun's denunciation of his handling of the Florida invasion during the Monroe administration. He also blamed Calhoun and his wife for isolating the Eatons during the early part of his presidency. Both Jackson and his advisors thought that Calhoun's role in the nullification crisis was an outgrowth of his failure to achieve his ambition to be president. "He strove, schemed, dreamed, lived, only for the presidency," was the view from the White House, and he was willing to ruin the country since he was unable to reach his highest goal. Jackson would later lament that he had not hung Calhoun for his role in the crisis. "My country would have sustained me in the act, and his fate would have been a warning to traitors in all time to come."[36]

Yet he refrained from such a precipitate act due to very real political considerations. The president was attempting to find a middle course in order to "preserve the Union without appearing so tyrannical and power-hungry that other Southern states might join with South Carolina, precipitating an even graver crisis that could lead to the secession of several states," as Meacham writes. Georgia was a particular problem, since the Supreme Court had recently issued its decision in the Worcester case, which called into question Georgian law on the Cherokees. But Jackson had no intention of implementing that decision, since he fully supported Indian removal, and so the threat from Georgia was removed. Other Southern states would soon fall in line given Jackson's adept handling of the crisis.[37]

Jackson strongly supported the principle of an enduring union and the idea of majority rule. He thought that nullification was essentially treason. "It leads to civil war and bloodshed and deserves the execration of every friend of the country." In early December, he began to work on a proclamation that "was meant to reach out to all Americans ... and rally them to the defense of the Union and the Constitution," according to Remini. Livingston served as the editor, polishing and finalizing the document, and incorporating input from Madison. He worked from numerous pages Jackson had written that expressed his thoughts on the matter of nullification and the very nature of the union. At one point, Jackson sent back the draft that Livingston had prepared for further revision, since it did not express his true feelings. On December 10, 1832, the Nullification Proclamation was released.[38]

Jackson's proclamation is a ringing endorsement of the idea that the United States is one nation, and a complete repudiation of nullification and secession. The Constitution was formed "for important objects that are announced in the preamble, made in the name and by the authority of the people of the United States, whose delegates framed and whose conventions approved it." The most important of these objects was to "form a more perfect union." If one state has the power to annul a federal law, the more perfect union described in the preamble would be destroyed. Jackson repudiates the right of a state to secede on the basis that the Constitution "forms a *government*, not a league ... Each State, having expressly parted with so many powers as to constitute, jointly with the other States, a single nation, cannot, from that period, possess any right to secede, because such secession does not break a league, but destroys the unity of a nation." If any individual state could secede, then the United States was "not a nation." For Jackson, as for Madison, elections were the proper venue for a state to change federal law. In an 1831 letter to Robert Hayne, Jackson had written that if the federal government oversteps its boundaries, "the remedy is with the people ... [by] submitting the whole matter to them at their elections." The people "will always, in the end, bring about the repeal of any obnoxious laws which violate the constitution." Jackson also reminded Hayne that in "all Republics the voice of a majority must prevail," a not so subtle swipe at the idea that one state can overturn the will of the majority.[39]

Jackson closed the proclamation with an appeal to his "Fellow-Citizens of my native State," speaking as a parent attempting to keep his children from committing a major blunder. "In that paternal language, with that paternal feeling, let me tell you, my countrymen, that you are deluded by men who are either deceived themselves or wish to deceive you ..." Jackson recognized that the tariff had affected South Carolina in an unequal way, but that the state was heading down a disastrous path just at the moment that "a change in public opinion had commenced" in regards to the tariff. This was a reference to the very conciliatory position the president had taken only a few days before in his annual address to Congress. But he also closed with a warning that "disunion by armed force is *treason*."[40]

The proclamation is a remarkable document for many reasons. In it, Jackson implies that the union preceded the states. "Under the royal Government we had no separate character; our opposition to its oppressions began as *united colonies*." In *Federalist* No. 2, John Jay had made a similar argument. "A strong sense of the value and blessings of union induced the people, at a very early period, to institute a federal government to preserve and perpetuate it." Lincoln also believed that the Union came first, and at Gettysburg he dated the birth of the nation to 1776 when he declared: "Four score and seven years ago our fathers brought forth on this continent, a new nation, conceived in Liberty, and dedicated to the proposition that all men are created equal." This was questionable history, as Joseph Ellis has pointed out. "In 1863 Lincoln had compelling reasons for bending the arc of American history in a national direction, since he then [was] waging a civil war on behalf of a union that he claimed predated the existence of the states." The ambiguous nature of America's birth could lead different men to draw very different conclusions about the nature of the union that bound them together, since the truth existed somewhere between extremes. This author's view, developed extensively in *The Emergence of One American Nation*, is that the United States did not begin as one nation. Rather, the multiple acts of declaring independence, fighting a war, and especially the framing and ratification of the Constitution had begun to knit us together into one nation. Ratification was not the end, but the continuation of the process of nation building that was once again being tested during the nullification crisis.[41]

Remini argues that Jackson "was the first American statesman to offer the doctrine of the Union as a perpetual entity." But this was not true. During the New York ratification convention, Alexander Hamilton had asked Madison whether a state could vote for a contingent ratification and then withdraw from the union if the contingency, in this case a call for a second convention, was not met. Madison's reply is revealing. "The Constitution requires an adoption *in toto* and forever." It is certainly true that Jackson's proclamation provided Lincoln with the inspiration he used in his first inaugural address. "I hold, that in contemplation of universal law, and of the Constitution, the Union of the States is perpetual."[42]

☞ ☞ ☞

President Jackson followed a two-prong strategy during the crisis. He stood strongly opposed to nullification and was willing to use force as a last resort to put it down, although if violence erupted, he wanted South Carolina to fire the first shot. A unionist in South Carolina advised Jackson "that possibly 500 to 1,000 unionists could be mustered, provided they could be armed, but predicted that no violence was likely until February 1," according to Remini. Rifles were sent to Castle Pinckney, and General Winfield Scott traveled to South Carolina to oversee the operation. Jackson wanted to ensure that force be used only once all other means for resolving the problem had been exhausted. To avoid conflict, Jackson also sent "revenue cutters to the waters off the South Carolina coast to collect the tariff before merchant ships came to shore," Wilentz writes. The second part of the strategy was a willingness to compromise on the tariff, which he had indicated even before the proclamation was released as part of his December 4 address to Congress. Jackson's two-prong strategy confused some during his day, and later historians as well. Henry Clay indicated this when he wrote that "one short week produced the message and the proclamation, the former ultra, on the side of State rights—and the latter ultra, on the side of Consolidation. How can they be reconciled?"[43]

The clearest answer is that "Jackson saw nullification and tariff reform as completely separate issues," according to Richard Ellis, "and he handled them in different ways." In the address to Congress, Jackson's goal was to isolate South Carolina by showing his support for states' rights and his sympathy for tariff relief, which he hoped would assuage the rest of the South from standing with the nullifiers. Jackson proposed a substantial tariff reduction in the address to Congress, arguing that since the national debt was almost repaid, the revenue generated from high tariffs was no longer justified. Whereas he had previously been for some level of protectionism, he had now changed his mind and argued that the high rates had caused "a large portion of our countrymen a spirit of discontent and jealousy dangerous to the stability of the Union." Despite unhappiness in the South with Jackson's proclamation, and some support for nullification in Virginia and Georgia, "no southern state came to the nullifiers' support," Wilentz states. Jackson also had his treasury secretary, Louis McLane, begin work on a tariff reduction bill, which was submitted on January 8, 1833.[44]

By mid-January, Jackson concluded he needed congressional support to manage the crisis, especially if force were needed. His efforts to organize the unionists in South Carolina into a militia, what he called a "posse comitatus" had largely failed. He therefore submitted what came to be known as the Force Bill to Congress on January 16, 1833, requesting to use force against South Carolina if the state were to use its military to block the collection of federal revenues or otherwise interfere in the implementation of federal law. Much of the message that accompanied the bill was focused on documenting South Carolina's actions to that point and in avoiding force, such as moving collection points for the tariff to federal property or off the coast. As soon as the bill was introduced in the Senate, Calhoun rose to oppose it, opening another round of intense debate. Webster countered his arguments, but many historians have concluded that Calhoun got the better of him in this debate. Still, Webster made a strong nationalist appeal. "The people of the United States are one people," Webster argued. "The very end and purpose of the Constitution was to make them one people ... and it has effectively accomplished its object."[45]

With the tariff bill being debated in Congress, the leadership in South Carolina decided to turn down the heat and put off any attempt to implement the Nullification Ordinance, "pending the completion of Congress' deliberation on the tariff." While Calhoun was publicly confronting the Force Bill, he was also looking for a way out of the crisis, and so he turned to Henry Clay to forge a compromise measure. "Neither Calhoun nor the National Republicans wanted to have anything to do with the administration's latest tariff bill," Wilentz writes, since they did not want Andrew Jackson to be able to claim victory in the crisis. Clay's compromise would gradually lower tariffs over the next decade until they reached 20 percent for all products, which allowed Calhoun to claim victory, since the tariff would eventually no longer protect specific items. In return, Calhoun and South Carolina agreed to rescind the Nullification Ordinance. Clay called it "a nominal triumph" for Calhoun, although he felt that "all the substantial advantages have been secured in the Tariff States," since the bill gave protected industries ten years to adjust, and a future Congress could always change its provisions. In addition, the Clay bill "offered far slower reductions than the original ... bill and much less than the minimum demands of the Nullification Convention," in Freehling's opinion.[46]

While Jackson had to accept the Clay compromise bill, he also was successful in getting the Force Bill through Congress, both of which passed on March 1, 1833. The crisis was over. Freehling argues that it was "his greatest victory as President" since he was the only one of the nation's leaders who insisted on both measures, "and his masterful statesmanship had played a crucial role in gaining the final settlement." Yet the idea of nullification, and certainly secession, was far from dead. In our own time, issues ranging from immigration (sanctuary cities and states), marijuana legalization, and gun laws test whether the concept of nullification is truly dead. And Jackson himself worried that the "tariff was only the pretext, and disunion and southern confederacy the real object. The next pretext will be the negro, or slavery question." Jackson had also generated some enmity from his own party in the South and some goodwill from his opponents on the National Republican side. But that goodwill would not last as the next round of the bank wars would soon heat up.[47]

Killing the Bank Once and For All

With the nullification crisis behind him, Jackson turned his attention back to the Bank of the United States. His next set of actions would further tear at the fabric of the Democratic Party, which was already split over the issue of states' rights versus union, and lead to the creation of the second party system in the United States. As we have seen, Jackson was willing to do this because he believed that the bank was a corrupting influence on the nation. In fact, Jackson thought that the bank endangered the twin American values of liberty and equality, which he equated with each other. The bank strengthened "the predatory portion of [the] community," which threatened equality and "the freedom of the American people," as Remini writes. While much of this seems like hyperbole today in a world of large and varied financial institutions, Jackson clearly believed his own rhetoric and was willing to take great risks to kill the bank.[48]

The president knew that Nicholas Biddle and the bank's directors had supported Clay and the National Republicans in the recently completed 1832 election. "A report from the government's directors on the BUS board affirmed that the bank had spent eighty thousand dollars on printing campaign materials hostile to Jackson ... and that Biddle himself had spent twenty thousand dollars, with no accounting records whatever," Wilentz writes. Jackson's greatest fear was that the BUS would eventually influence Congress to pass a new bank recharter with sufficient votes to override his veto. The president was determined to kill "the hydra of corruption," once and for all, as he told James K. Polk, his ally and the chairman of the House Ways and Means Committee. Polk, who was born in the backcountry of North Carolina of humble origins, had become a successful lawyer before entering politics. His nickname was "Young Hickory," and he would go on to become the Speaker of the House in 1835 and then president in 1844. He assisted Jackson in his attempt to undermine the bank. The plan was to gradually remove the federal government's deposits from the BUS, as a way to weaken it, since "the Bank would have insufficient funds to corrupt Congress," according to Watson. In 1832, federal deposits represented about 40 percent of the bank's overall deposits.[49]

Jackson faced two problems. The first and easier issue was to find an alternative to the BUS for the deposits. Jackson sent his close advisor, Amos Kendall, on a mission to find state banks that would accept new federal revenue as it came in. Existing deposits on hand at the bank would be used to pay the governments bills and debts, which would gradually drain the BUS of federal money as new revenue went to the state banks. Kendall had no trouble finding seven interested "pet banks," located in Baltimore, Philadelphia, New York, and Boston. "Over the next three years some ninety-odd banks were added to system, and in each case those selected were regarded as 'friendly' to the Democratic creed," according to Remini. Banking was moving in the same partisan direction as the federal workforce.[50]

The second problem was far trickier since by law the decision to remove the deposits was not the president's to make, but rather the treasury secretary's. Since the House of Representatives had recently issued a report that federal deposits were indeed safe, any action by the Jackson administration would be seen as violating the wishes of Congress. The president and Treasury Secretary McLane had already had one falling out over the bank, and McLane (along with other cabinet members) opposed removal of the deposits, fearing it would damage the economy. McLane also believed that the treasury secretary was directly responsible to the Congress on this issue. Since Edward Livingston was leaving as secretary of state, Jackson moved McLane to the senior cabinet position. Jackson decided to select William Duane to serve as treasury secretary, a man known to be antibank. But the president made a major mistake, never asking Duane his views on deposit removal.[51]

As it turned out, Duane shared McLane's view on the issue. Jackson then met with Duane and explained to him that his objective was "to save the country, and it will be lost if we permit the bank to exist." Duane was challenging Jackson's authority, which would prove an untenable position to be in. Yet Duane's position was understandable. Since the creation of the Treasury Department in 1789, there had been tension between Congress and the president over the precise boundary of executive versus legislative control. "When [Congress] created the Treasury Department ... it made no mention of the president and instead required the secretary to report directly to the Congress," Gordon Wood writes. This differed from the secretaries of state and war, which clearly reported to the chief executive.[52]

Jackson was willing to push the boundaries of executive power since he believed it went hand in hand with the will of the people. He was the only constitutional officer elected by all of the people, and in his mind the last election gave him a mandate to act as he wished on the issue of removal of the deposits. "The President considers his reelection as a decision of the people against the banks," Jackson said. Jackson believed it was his duty to protect the American people "from combinations of the wealthy and professional classes—from an aristocracy" that prevents the government "from securing the freedom of the citizen." Even though Congress had designated the treasury secretary to make the decision on deposit removal, Jackson now assumed that authority. When the president was told by one of his cabinet members that Duane would be facing a heavy responsibility if he ignored the will of Congress, Jackson responded "I don't want him to assume the responsibility. Have I not said I would take the responsibility?"[53]

Duane continued to resist the president's direction, and he also refused to resign, and so Jackson fired him. Roger Taney, an enthusiastic supporter of deposit removal, was moved from attorney general to treasury secretary, and the deposit removal process was launched. It was the first time a president had fired a cabinet secretary, since they were typically forced to resign. Jackson was settling the issue of who had responsibility for cabinet officers: the president did. As Remini writes, "Jackson established a new dimension of presidential power."[54]

Jackson's actions showed a willingness to grab power and to ignore the law and the system of checks and balances when it suited his purposes. In some ways his conduct represents what the journalist Fareed Zakaria has referred to as an "illiberal democracy," one in which free and fair elections occur but thereafter the rule of law is ignored. Jackson "did not manifest a general respect for the authority of the law when it got in the way of the policies he chose to pursue," Howe writes.[55]

Nicholas Biddle's response was to tighten credit by calling in loans as federal money began to flow out of the BUS in October of 1833. "Biddle consciously pushed the contraction further than necessary," Watson writes. "A short and sharp recession became his deliberate tool for political influence." While Biddle's actions caused harm to the economy, he was soon forced to back down, as business executives turned against him. By 1834, Biddle reversed his policy and began to expand credit, ending the panic. But the political influence of the bank was on the wane, and when its charter finally ended in 1836, so too did the experiment in central banking in the United States, at least during the nineteenth century. Over the next seventy-five years, "the U.S. economy seemed to move from one financial crisis to another," as the Philadelphia Federal Reserve Bank noted in a December 2010 report on the BUS. Central banking would not appear again until the Federal Reserve System was established by Woodrow Wilson in 1913. The inability of Jackson and Biddle to find some middle ground would be a very costly mistake.[56]

There was also a political price to pay for Jackson. His actions on the bank veto, deposit removal, and nullification had split the Democratic Party. Henry Clay, his major rival for power during this period, used the president's actions to pursue a censure of Jackson in the Senate, now controlled by the National Republicans in the aftermath of the 1832 election. It was a novel approach, given that impeachment proceedings were off the table with the Democrats still in majority control of the House.[57]

On December 26, 1832, Clay began his attack on Jackson in the Senate. He proposed two censure resolutions, one against Jackson for executive usurpation of legislative powers and the second against Taney as treasury secretary for "unsatisfactory and insufficient" reason for removing the deposits. Over the next three days, Clay would excoriate Jackson for "the exercise of power over the treasury of United States, not granted to him by the constitution and laws, and dangerous to the liberties of the people." He charged Jackson with leading a revolution that endangered "the pure republican character of the Government." His ultimate fear was "the concentration of all power in the hands of one man," that Jackson was transforming the presidency into an "elective monarchy." Clay also questioned Jackson's assertion that the recent election provided him with a mandate to pursue his policies. "I am surprised and alarmed at the new source of executive power, which is found in the result of a presidential election," arguing that elections are merely a way "to place the Chief Magistrate in the post assigned to him." Clay received support from both Webster and Calhoun.[58]

Jackson viewed the presidency as the center of the American political system, which was a totally different perspective from both the Founding Fathers and his opponents, led by Clay. These men were opposed to expansive executive power and continued to believe that the Congress should be the central institution that dominated the American political system. Clay and the National Republicans now decided to rename themselves the Whig Party, harkening back to those in Great Britain who stood against the power of the monarchy, and the American Revolutionaries who had fought King George III. Fittingly, the Whigs began to refer to Jackson as King Andrew. Henry Clay would soon hold a series of dinners over the next several years, "assembling nullifiers, his own National Republicans, and Anti-Masons ... to discuss strategy for the presidential contest in 1836," Wilentz writes.[59]

The rise of an opposition party showed that the American system of checks on power, as envisioned at least partly by Madison, was working. While Madison had not anticipated the rise of political parties, in *Federalist* No. 51 he put forward a theory of countervailing power between ambitious men. The way to avoid a "gradual concentration" of power is to give each branch of the government "the necessary constitutional means and personal motives to resist the encroachments of the other," Madison wrote. "Ambition must be made to counteract ambition. The interest of the man must be connected with the constitutional rights of the place." His words seemed to be coming to fruition over the issue of the bank. Each of these men (Clay, Webster, Calhoun) were ambitious politicians, who were sometimes referred to as the Great Triumvirate, and each desired to be president. The three were also, each in his own way, attempting to defend the constitutional prerogatives of the legislature in their battle with the executive, even though they were not in agreement over how best to do this. Clay believed that Jackson was usurping Congress's power of the purse, arguing that neither the law "creating the treasury department, nor ... the bank charter, [gives the president] any power over the public treasury." Calhoun also believed that Jackson had committed "a robbery of the treasury." He, too, feared that Jackson had garnered too much power to himself; but whereas Clay wanted to focus solely on Jackson's despotism, Calhoun also criticized the entire American System, including the tariff, that was leading to a consolidated government. Webster, for his part, wished to show that a national bank was necessary. As one senator framed it, Webster "was the real representative of the great manufacturing and capitalist interests of New England and the North generally." Without a national bank and a resulting stable currency, business interests would suffer. These men were indeed strange bedfellows.[60]

As we explored in chapter 1, there are a series of "bedrock social dilemmas" that divide people. The Democrats and Whigs, too, would split over these issues. The Whig approach was much more top-down in terms of decision-making, evoking an earlier era of politics. As Senator Peleg Sprague of Maine framed it, the people "are not infallible," and legislators needed to use their independent judgment when the people fell victim to "the paroxysm of their devotion" to a leader like Jackson, which caused them to "sacrifice their rights, their liberties, their children and themselves." Whigs were elitist when it came to governmental decision-making and feared that the people could not run their own affairs. On the other hand, Democrats were oriented to a more bottom-up approach, in expanding democracy for white men, "including the popular election of senators and judges, the abolition of the electoral college, limitation of presidential tenure, and regular rotation of governmental officers," Remini writes. But in a strange twist, Jackson thought himself to be the true representative of the American people and was willing to use his power to expand the office of the presidency. He was committed to majority rule, if not necessarily the rule of law, at least when it didn't suit his goals.[61]

Correspondingly, the Democrats placed much greater value on equality, and generally preferred a society that retained much of its rural character. Whigs were tied more closely with the market revolution, and the use of government to expand the economy. Democrats would often say that the difference between the two parties was tied to the "rich versus the poor." These divisions between the parties came into focus during the Senate censure vote, which passed on March 28, 1834, on a vote of 26–20. Jackson responded with his own protest, contesting the Senate's authority to censure him, since the Constitution only provided for impeachment proceedings, which needed to be brought first in the House, still under Democratic control, foreclosing such an action. Jackson's protest made overt what had been implicit, stating that he was "the direct representative of the American people." His goal was to undo "the splendid government supported by powerful monopolies and aristocratical establishments," and to return it to "a plain system, void of pomp, protecting all and granting favors to none." Daniel Webster responded in the Senate, denouncing Jackson for claiming to be the "tribune of the people." Given that the president was also indirectly elected, he asked "where, then, is the authority for saying that the President is the direct representative of the people?" Yet Jackson refused to back down, except in one area. In the protest, Jackson implied he had unlimited power that went beyond any constitutional restraints. Ultimately, he issued what he called a "codicil" clarifying that he did not claim any power not granted by the Constitution. Still, Jackson's actions were gradually moving the country toward "the president [as] the central player in the American political order," as Arthur Schlesinger Jr. has written.[62]

☞☞☞

Despite the differences between the Democrats of Jackson and the Whigs of Clay, the one issue both sides wished to avoid was slavery. Politicians of the era attempted to keep slavery "at the margins of political discourse," as Watson writes, because the issue was too divisive. Yet there was a group of people, the abolitionists, who had begun to make their voices heard ever more strongly during the Age of Jackson. It's to their story we now turn.[63]

Endnotes

1   John C. Calhoun, Fort Hill Address, retrieved February 7, 2018, from http://teachingamericanhistory.org/library/document/fort-hill-address/.

2   Watson, *Jackson vs. Clay*, p. 205.

3   *The Emergence of One American Nation* delves into the competing ideologies of the American Revolution on the issue of centralization. See p. 361 for Wilson's view of sovereignty. The Madison quote is from Rossiter, p. 294. Joseph J. Ellis, *Founding Brothers: The Revolutionary Generation* (New York, 2000), p. 16.

4   Fraser, p. 302–309; Sean Wilentz, *No Property in Man: Slavery and Antislavery at the Nation's Founding* (Cambridge, 2018), p. 97, provides the evidence.

5   Wills, p. 59–60 and p. 141–142.

6   Rakove, *Madison*, p. 151. On Madison's view that the federal government should act directly on the people, see Fraser, p. 199, and Rakove, *Madison*, p. 57. Wills also deals with how Madison had changed his mind over the ten-year period from 1788 to 1798 on p. 145–146. On the issue of constitutional maintenance, see Jonathan Gienapp, "How to Maintain a Constitution: The Virginia and Kentucky Resolutions and James Madison's Struggle with the Problem of Constitutional Maintenance," in Sanford Levinson, ed., *Nullification and Secession in Modern Constitutional Thought* (Lawrence, 2016).

7   Robin Einhorn, *American Taxation, American Slavery* (Chicago, 2006), p. 11 and p. 120.

8   On the bargain between North and South on navigation acts, see Richard Beeman, *Plain, Honest Men: The Making of the American Constitution* (New York, 2009), p. 327–328; Einhorn, p. 149 and p. 154.

9   William W. Freehling, *Prelude to Civil War: The Nullification Controversy in South Carolina 1816-1836* (New York, 1966), p. 95–109.

10 Howe, p. 161–163; Freehling, p. 122–131.

11 Wilentz, *Rise*, p. 300–301; Howe, p. 274–275; Freehling, p. 136–137.

12 Freehling, p. 154; the quotes are from John C. Calhoun, *The Works of John C. Calhoun* (New York, 2012), p. 1–59; Howe, p. 396–398.

13 Howe, p. 367–368; Peterson, p. 172.

14 Howe, p. 369; Peterson, p. 173–174.

15 Peterson, p. 174–175.

16 Burns, p. 328; Peterson, p. 177–178; Howe, p. 370–371.

17 Burns, p. 330–331; Howe, p. 372–373.

18 Peterson, p. 191–193.

19 Calhoun, p. 59–94.

20 Peterson, p. 194.

21 The quotes are from Richard Ellis, *The Union at Risk: Jacksonian Democracy, States' Rights and the Nullification Crisis* (Oxford, 1987), p. 42–43.

22 Meacham, *American Lion*, p. 167; Remini, *Jackson II*, p. 359; Traub, p. 389–390 and p. 394–401.

23 Howe, p. 401; Ellis, p. 46.

24 Howe, p. 402; Bartlett, p. 186–187.

25 Fraser, p. 327–328; the Henry quote is from James H. Read and Neal Allen, "Living, Dead, and Undead: Nullification Past and Present," in Levinson, ed., *Nullification and Secession in Modern Constitutional Thought*, p. 104.

26 Calhoun, p. 169.

27 Calhoun, p. 180–190; Peterson, p. 213.

28 Read and Allen, p. 103–105; the quotes from Wilson are in Fraser, p. 361.

29 Ketchum, p. 641.

30 The quotes are in Madison, *Writings*, and come from his letter to Joseph Cabell dated September 18, 1828, p. 813–814, and his letter to Edward Everett dated August 28, 1830, p. 843.

31 Madison, *Writings*, p. 842–849.

32 Ellis, p. 75; on the link between the tariff and slavery, see Howe, p. 402–403, and Freehling, p. 255–259. On the connection between the tariff and broad construction of the Constitution, see Governor Hamilton's quote in Freehling on p. 256.

33 The South Carolina Ordinance of Nullification was retrieved on February 6, 2018, from http://avalon.law.yale.edu/19th_century/ordnull.asp.

34 Ellis, p. 76; Howe, p. 404.

35 The two recent historians who have studied the period seem to agree on this point, even though they view the Jacksonian era very differently. Howe writes that "Jackson's response to the nullification crisis stands as his finest hour," p. 405. Wilentz that "Jackson displayed his style of presidential leadership at its strongest," p. 379.

36 Remini, *Jackson III*, p. 14.

37 Meacham, *American Lion*, p. 223; Remini, *Jackson III*, p. 8–9.

38 Remini, *Jackson III*, p. 13 and p. 17–18.

39 Watson, *Jackson vs. Clay*, contains the text of the Proclamation of Nullification, which is where I have drawn the quotes from, p. 203–206; the quotes from the Hayne letter are in Ellis, p. 47.

40 Proclamation, p. 207–208.

41 Rossiter, p. 39; Joseph J. Ellis, *The Quartet: Orchestrating the Second American Revolution, 1783-1789* (New York, 2015), p. xii.

42 Remini, *Jackson III*, p. 22; Fraser, p, 387; Abraham Lincoln, *Selected Speeches and Writings* (New York, 1992), p. 286.

43 Remini, *Jackson III*, p. 22 and p. 13; Wilentz, *Jackson*, p. 94–95.

44 Ellis, p. 51, p. 81, and p. 93; Wilentz, *Jackson*, p. 98; Remini, *Jackson III*, p. 31.

45 Freehling, p. 286–287; the Webster quote is from Meacham, p. 245.

46 Freehling, p. 288; Wilentz, p. 100; Howe, p. 408.

47 Howe, p. 408–410; Freehling, p. 293–294; on modern-day issues concerning nullification, see Levinson, which contains numerous essays on the subject. Most historians seem to agree that Jackson's handling of the crisis was a victory for him. But Richard Ellis disagrees, finding that Jackson was "increasingly isolated from members of his own party and many of his closest political allies" over the Force Bill and his general stand on the proclamation. He depicts Jackson as having "no choice but to give in" and accept the Clay/Calhoun compromise. See p. 172–177.

48 Remini, *Jackson III*, p. 92–93. Remini uses Jackson's August 20, 1833, letter to Tilghman A. Howard as a source, which is where I became aware of Jackson's sentiments about the danger of the bank and other corporations of this type. The letter can be found at http://memory.loc.gov/service/mss/maj/01084/01084_0354_0357.pdf.

49 Wilentz, *Rise*, p. 394 and p. 571–582; Watson, *Liberty*, p. 154; Watson, *Jackson vs. Clay*, p. 93; the percentage of federal deposits can be found in Appendix F of the 1910

Senate report of the National Monetary Commission retrieved April 4, 2018, from https://fraser.stlouisfed.org/files/docs/historical/nmc/nmc_571_1910.pdf.

50 Remini, *Jackson III*, p. 93–94 and p. 106.

51 Remini, *Jackson III*, p. 55–58.

52 Remini, *Jackson III*, p. 85 and p. 93; Meacham, *Jackson*, p. 264; Wood, *Empire*, p. 91; Elkins and McKitrick, p. 52.

53 Meacham, *Jackson*, p. 264; Remini, *Jackson III*, p.99.

54 Remini, *Jackson III*, p. 101.

55 Howe, p. 411.

56 Wilentz, *Rise*, p. 399–400; Watson, *Liberty*, p. 157–159.

57 Remini, *Clay*, p. 447.

58 Remini, *Clay*, p. 449; Remini, *Jackson III*, p. 124–127.

59 Wilentz, *Rise*, p. 402.

60 Rossiter, p. 322; Remini, *Clay*, p. 449; Peterson, p. 241–243.

61 Remini, *Jackson III*, p. 149–150; Remini, *Clay*, p. 462.

62 Remini, *Jackson III*, p. 153–159; Remini, *Clay*, p. 465; the Schlesinger quote can be found in any of the American Presidents series. See for example, Appleby, *Jefferson*, p. xv.

63 Watson, *Jackson vs. Clay*, p. 5.

CHAPTER 11

The Abolitionists

I am in earnest—I will not equivocate—I will not excuse—I will not retreat a single inch—AND I WILL BE HEARD.
—William Lloyd Garrison

The Constitution found slavery and left it a State institution—the creature and dependent of State law—wholly local in its existence and character. It did not make it a national institution.
—Salmon P. Chase

Abolitionism in the United States occurred in the context of the movement in the Western world to eradicate slavery. In 1750, slavery was common in the colonies established by the Spanish, French, British, and Dutch. Yet over the next 150 years, slavery would end everywhere in the Western world. By the 1830s, the American South was one of the last holdouts and had become ever more dependent on the peculiar institution for its wealth as the growth of cotton expanded into newly added states. Due to slavery, the South was also increasingly isolated from the rest of the nation, developing a distinctive culture. The abolitionists of this period played a key role in the transformation of attitudes toward slavery, viewing it as immoral and demanding the immediate end to the practice and that African Americans be treated as equals. Their radical approach alienated many in the North and South, but they also began to change the terms of the national debate, especially once the movement became politically engaged.[1]

Early Abolitionist Movements

The abolitionist movement that surfaced in the 1830s was not new. In fact, resistance to slavery in America was as old as the practice itself. "The story of the rise of abolition is an interracial one," as well, the historian Manisha Sinha has written, and it also included many women. Some of the earliest actions against slavery during the colonial era were led by Africans attempting to free themselves, including revolts in 1676 in Virginia, in New York City in 1712, and in South Carolina in 1739. The goal of these actions was freedom for the individuals involved, not the abolition of slavery. These rebellions were quickly and harshly ended, but they had a lasting effect in the South, which always feared that the slaves would rise up and kill their white masters.[2]

In the 1730s, some members of the Quaker religion began to call into question the practice of slavery. Benjamin Lay published a book on the evils of slavery and once interrupted a Quaker service by "splattering the Bible with pokeberry juice, representing the blood of slaves," according to Sinha. By 1758, the abolitionists John Woolman and Anthony Benezet had gained control of the Philadelphia chapter of the Quakers. They voted to remove from leadership positions anyone who owned slaves. "By the end of the Revolution, it was practically impossible to locate a Quaker living north of Virginia who dealt in slaves," according to historian James Brewer Stewart.[3]

The Quakers were just the first of many who began to question the continued existence of slavery as the American Revolution unfolded in the 1770s. Suffused as the era was with Enlightenment thought, the leaders of the founding generation, many of whom subscribed to ideals of liberty and equality, knew that slavery was inconsistent with their own concept of right and wrong and violated the individual rights of the enslaved. As we saw in chapter 3, the Northern states had largely taken steps to outlaw or gradually emancipate their slaves by the early 1800s. At least part of the movement toward emancipation in the North was inspired by African Americans. For example, lawsuits brought by two slaves, Mumbet and Quok Walker, eventually led the Massachusetts Supreme Court to rule that slavery was abolished by their own state Constitution, which declared that "all men are born free and equal."[4]

Yet while the North was abolishing slavery, which was an easier matter since there were fewer slaves there, the South had begun the expansion of slavery in the years after the revolution. The Founding Fathers from the upper South, men like Washington, Jefferson, and Madison, knew that slavery was immoral, yet they also felt trapped in the system. Only Washington freed his slaves after he died, and Jefferson kept delaying emancipation ever further into the future. But that attitude did not exist in the Deep South, which had fought for protections of slavery at the Constitutional Convention, including the three-fifths clause for counting slaves for purposes of representation in Congress and the continuation of the slave trade until 1808. The growth of the cotton kingdom and the westward expansion of slavery into new states like Alabama and Mississippi made any movement toward ending slavery in the South all but impossible.

※ ※ ※

In the aftermath of the War of 1812, a new movement arose whose goal was to emancipate black slaves and colonize them in

Africa. The American Colonization Society (ACS) was launched in December of 1816 and included "a large bisectional coalition of religious and political leaders from the North and upper South" Sinha writes. Henry Clay, James Monroe, and Daniel Webster, among others, were members of the ACS. Former President Madison served as its second president and held similar views to Jefferson's: that slavery was immoral but that freed blacks could never fully integrate equally into American society. His view was typical of many men of the time, believing that "existing and probably unalterable prejudices in the United States" would require that freed slaves "be permanently removed" either to the American West or preferably to West Africa. To this end, the Monroe administration acquired land in what became known as Liberia in West Africa, whose capital, Monrovia, was named for the president.[5]

Opposition to the ACS arose from plantation owners in the Deep South, who "feared involving the federal government in any solution to the problem of slavery, even on a voluntary basis, lest it move in more threatening directions later," Howe writes. Not only slaveowners, but also freed blacks opposed colonization. Probably no more than 20 percent of freed blacks ever supported the idea, and many thought it was simply a way for slave owners "to get rid of them [free blacks] so as to make their property more secure," according to James Forten, who had organized a meeting on colonization attended by over three thousand free blacks in 1817. Forten, who was born a free black in Philadelphia in 1766, served in the Revolutionary War and became a successful sailmaker. In 1798, the owner of the sail loft he worked for loaned him the money to purchase the business and he went on to become one of the richest men in the United States, and one of the foremost leaders among black abolitionists. Forten, who originally supported colonization at the time of the 1817 meeting, was forced to backtrack due to large-scale opposition from free blacks, and he later became an opponent of colonization.[6]

Those that wanted to gradually emancipate the slaves had to deal with their own and their society's pervasive racism, which held that blacks could never fully integrate into white American society. Colonizers melded support for the gradual elimination of slavery with the racist belief that one ethnic group is superior to another. Racism may have emerged as a natural tendency to identify the group we are members of in opposition to that of an outside group. Aristotle, for example, believed that the Greeks were superior to all other people. Racism took on particular relevance in the West as light-skinned people came to view themselves as superior to dark-skinned people. Historically, not all slaves in Western society were black, and in fact the Latin origin of the word *slave* means "Slavic person." "By the mid-1400's, Slavic communities had built forts against slave raiders, causing the supply of Slavs in Western Europe's slave market to plunge at around the same time that the supply of Africans was increasing," historian Ibram X. Kendi writes. Thereafter, slavery increasingly came to be identified with black Africans. Even serfs and peasants in medieval Europe "were commonly depicted as subhuman and even 'black,' as a result of their constant exposure to the sun, soil, and manure," historian David Brion Davis writes.[7]

Slavery and racism were not isolated to the United States. The practice of slavery had existed in numerous parts of the world as civilizations emerged. Both the ancient Greeks and Romans had utilized slaves extensively, as did the T'ang Dynasty in China, which enslaved Koreans, Turks, Persians, and Indonesians. Muslims enslaved both sub-Saharan Africans and also Slavic people. Slavery in Western society was sometimes justified on climate theory, which was introduced by Aristotle, who believed "that extreme hot or cold climates produced intellectually, physically and morally inferior people who were ugly and lacked the capacity for freedom and self-government," according to Kendi. In 1377, Ibn Khaldun of Tunisia refined the climate theory by stating that the inferiority of Africans was not permanent and could be reversed if they moved to cooler climates, since their descendants' skin "gradually turns white." Climate theory was used to justify the assimilation of blacks into white society by the abolitionists of the 1830s, since they viewed the inferiority of blacks not as permanent but rather as caused by slavery.[8]

Segregationists, on the other hand, justified their view of the inferiority of blacks based on the biblical story of Ham, who had sinned against his father, Noah. In retaliation, Noah had cursed Canaan, the son of Ham, to life as a slave. Legend has it that Ham was "dusky" or black. Segregationists believed that blacks were "naturally and permanently inferior, and totally incapable of becoming White," according to Kendi. The story of Ham "would become absolutely central in the history of antiblack racism ... the Curse of Ham was repeatedly used as the most authoritative justification for Negro Slavery by nineteenth century Southern Christians," Davis writes. Segregation was part of the colonization movement and encapsulated the idea that free blacks needed to be removed from the United States since they could not be integrated.[9]

Segregationists justified slavery based on the theory that blacks were "inherently inferior and even closer to African apes than to fully human white Christians," Davis writes. Many subscribed to the theory of polygenesis, that black and whites were in fact separate species. They went so far as to say that the children born of biracial parents would be infertile, which gave rise to the word *mulatto*, derived from the word *mule*. To the extent that blacks were viewed as less than human, their harsh treatment as slaves was justified, since they were just another form of property, no different from cows, pigs, or goats. As one ex-slave would later recall: "Speculators uster buy up [slaves] jest lak dey was animals ... I've seen 'em come through in droves lak cattle.'" Another fugitive slave, Henry Highland Garner, wrote that slave owners "endeavor to make you as much like brutes as possible," a theme that Frederick Douglass echoed when writing about his experience with the slave breaker Edward Covey. "I was broken in body soul and spirit ... behold a man transformed into a brute."[10]

The next wave of abolitionism would challenge not only the idea of gradual emancipation accompanied by colonization, but also the very idea that freed slaves could not fully participate in American society.[11] These ideas would be deeply unpopular and cause a major uproar, not only in the South, but also in the North, which harbored its own continuing racism.

The Second Wave: Immediatism

On September 28, 1829, David Walker published his *Appeal*, a scathing criticism of slavery and those who practiced it. Walker was born in Wilmington, North Carolina, to a free black woman and a slave father, which made him a free man. He may have met Denmark Vesey when they attended the same church in Charleston. Vesey had led a slave revolt in Virginia in 1822. By 1825, Walker had moved to Boston and become involved in the black abolitionist movement, joining the Massachusetts General Colored Association and working as a writer for *Freedom's Journal*, the first African American–owned newspaper in the United States.[12]

The *Appeal* was a complete denunciation of the treatment of blacks in America. "We, (coloured people of these United States,) are the most degraded, wretched, and abject set of beings that ever lived since the world began," far worse than the "Israelites in Egypt" or the "Roman Slaves,"Walker wrote. Such conditions were imposed on African Americans by so-called "*Christian Americans*."White Americans told blacks "they were not of the human family" but rather descended from "*Monkeys or Orang-Outangs*."Walker was disparaging toward white society, writing that "whites have always been an unjust, jealous, unmerciful, avaricious and blood-thirsty set of beings, always seeking after power and authority."If Americans do not change, then "you and your *Country are gone*,"Walker warned. He subtly called for the slaves to rise up and break their chains, telling them they should not wait for God to "take us by the hair of our heads and drag us out of abject wretchedness and slavery."It was better to die than to remain as a slave. In addition to blacks taking responsibility for their own liberation, Walker thought that African Americans needed to conquer the ignorance that whites had forced upon them. Eventually, Walker argued, a black leader would arise to lead his people from slavery.[13]

Walker seemed to take great delight in challenging the hypocrisy of Thomas Jefferson, whom he called "one of the great characters as ever lived among the whites." Well aware of *Notes on the State of Virginia*, he questioned Jefferson's view that blacks were inferior to whites. "It is indeed surprising, that a man of such great learning ... should speak so of a set of men in chains."Yet Walker also admired the Declaration of Independence, with its sweeping call that all men are created equal, which he used to close the *Appeal*. David Walker was also a vociferous opponent of colonization, writing that "America is more our country, than it is the whites-we have enriched it with our *blood and tears*."[14]

Manisha Sinha has written that the *Appeal* "was not a lone voice of black radicalism ... but its most effective statement." Perhaps part of its impact came from its widespread distribution in the South, where copies were confiscated in Georgia, Virginia, the Carolinas, and Louisiana and led to laws that outlawed the distribution of antislavery materials and restricted black literacy. Walker's work caused grave concerns in the South that a "godly slave rebellion was coming down directly from the North, written and published with impunity by the ever dangerous free blacks, headquartered safely in New England," Wilentz writes. Rumors swirled that a contract had been taken out by slave owners to kill Walker, leading to speculation that they had succeeded when he died suddenly on August 6, 1830. Walker's work was soon taken up by a young abolitionist whose cause gradually began to change the moral landscape in which slavery existed.[15]

William Lloyd Garrison

He was certainly not the only abolitionist to arise during the late 1820s, but he was perhaps one of the most important. As Abraham Lincoln pointed out in 1865, "the logic and moral power of Garrison, and the anti-slavery people of the country" were responsible, along with the Union Army, for ending slavery in the United States. But it would be a long and hard road from the 1830s to emancipation, which was ultimately delivered through the Civil War.[16]

Garrison was born in December of 1805 in Newburyport, Massachusetts, the youngest of three children. His mother called him Lloyd, which was her maiden name. His father's job as a merchant sailor fell victim to Jefferson's embargo, and he soon abandoned his family, leaving his wife and children almost destitute. Fanny Garrison was a strongly religious woman, and she attempted to hold the family together. Due to financial difficulties, Fanny felt compelled at one point to leave the younger children behind so that she and James, the eldest son, could find jobs in Lynn. "Lloyd wept bitterly when his mother left," his biographer Henry Mayer writes. Within a year he had rejoined his mother, and the family soon thereafter moved to Baltimore, where James fell into alcoholism, and he too abandoned the family. Lloyd was very much the good son, following his mother's religious direction, singing in the choir, and enjoying church services, but he was also unhappy in Baltimore, and so his mother allowed him to move back to Newburyport. In 1818, when he was thirteen, Garrison took a job as an apprentice at the local newspaper. It would prove to be his true calling. Garrison also undertook a process of self-education, primarily in classical literature, which "intensified his faith in words as moral weapons," as Mayer writes.[17]

As we saw in chapter 7, the Second Great Awakening had led to an evangelical Christian quest to reform American society. In late 1826, Garrison moved to Boston, where he became involved in the movement. One of the evangelical leaders was Reverend Lyman Beecher. Garrison regularly attended meetings at his Hanover Street Church, where he got involved in the temperance movement. In 1828, Lloyd became the editor of the *National Philanthropist*, a newspaper dedicated to combatting the use of alcohol. Shortly thereafter, he met the abolitionist Benjamin Lundy, and the arc of his life would change forever. "My soul was on fire then," Garrison wrote, and he threw himself into the antislavery cause. But he was sorely disappointed with the reaction of his fellow Christians, who feared an antislavery society in Boston "would do harm, rather than good, openly to agitate the subject!" and only "enrage the South."[18]

Yet Garrison did not give up, believing as Lundy did that most people in the country were antislavery, including "a majority of the southern people, and even of slaveholders," a position he would come to realize was misplaced. The work he was engaged in required "much patience, immense exertion, and a strong faith in its ultimate accomplishment." He chose July 4, 1829, at Boston's Park Street Church,

in an address to the Colonization Society, to unleash his most comprehensive statement on slavery to that point, calling it "a gangrene
preying upon our vitals." Garrison called for equal treatment for blacks,
who were "born to our soil" and "entitled to all of the privileges of
American citizens." Garrison laid bare the contradiction at the heart
of American society, that a nation dedicated to liberty and equality
could not also own people as property. "Before God, I must say, that
such a glaring contradiction as exists between our creed and practice
[leaves me] ashamed of my country." He called for the free states "to
assist in the overthrow of slavery" through a process of persuasion
and gradual abolition. Garrison knew that the struggle would be
a long one, full of "sharp asperities and bitterness," and even called
into question the continuation of the union, should slavery prevail.
He also envisioned God's wrath falling upon the country if it did not
act to end slavery, alluding to "bloody rebellion, the central fear of
slaveholders," should the North not act. Garrison did not yet call for
the immediate abolition of slavery, instead advocating for its gradual
end over a long time frame and urging the establishment of "auxiliary
colonization societies in every State, county and town."[19]

It would not be long before Garrison began to criticize both
gradual emancipation and colonization. He attended a meeting of
the African Abolition Society ten days after his July 4 address, where
blacks expressed opposition to both gradualism and colonization. By
the time he arrived in Baltimore later that summer to assist Lundy in
editing his newspaper, the *Genius of Emancipation*, his conversion was
complete. "He had realized, moreover, that the question of emancipation could not be addressed without considering the status of black
people in America and the process by which racial prejudice retarded
equal citizenship," Mayer writes. His position on black equality would
put him well outside of the mainstream view that America was a

white man's nation. Perhaps this conversion came about as Garrison directly experienced living among both free and enslaved blacks, who accounted for one in four people in Baltimore. He saw firsthand the racial prejudice that free blacks encountered as they attempted to improve their lives by opening schools and churches, starting businesses, and becoming involved in politics. At one point, Garrison and Lundy met a slave who had just been beaten and "counted thirty-five gashes, from neck to hips, on his bleeding back," according to the historian Robert H. Abzug. Garrison opened up the pages of the *Genius* to black voices and began to work across racial lines in his crusade to abolish slavery.[20]

With the election of Andrew Jackson in 1828, Garrison began to question whether the political system could foster the end of slavery. Garrison greatly admired Henry Clay and thought of him as a "friend to the cause of emancipation." But he soon became disappointed in Clay for his support of colonization and his insistence that blacks and whites be "separated ... in distinct and distant countries." His break with Clay marked the beginning of his movement away from involvement in the political system, to the position of an outside agitator who was determined "to change the climate of opinion in which leaders had to operate," Mayer notes. This would prove to be a long and dangerous journey for Garrison, yet sometimes significant reform is often dependent on changing the hearts and minds of the people, so that political leaders can then follow suit. The American political system, with its checks and balances and multiple layers of national, state, and local governments, is certainly subject to gridlock, especially over moral issues that do not lend themselves to compromise. It would fall to the immediatists to begin to move the moral needle of society, although it would eventually require political action, and ultimately war, to destroy slavery.[21]

In early 1830, Lundy and Garrison were indicted for libel and spent time in a Baltimore jail. Garrison got to know runaway slaves who were serving time in the jail, "and debated masters and slave traders who came to get them," questioning their right to own slaves. He was finally freed from jail by Lewis Tappan, a wealthy New York abolitionist. It was a fateful meeting since Tappan ultimately provided the funds Garrison needed to begin his own newspaper in Boston called the *Liberator*. Returning to Boston was a timely move on Garrison's part since he and Lundy had experienced a falling out over their differing reactions to David Walker's *Appeal*. While Garrison opposed Walker's incendiary language that could foster bloody slave revolts, he still found the work full of "bravery and intelligence." Lundy, on the other hand, condemned it.[22]

The first edition of the *Liberator* was published on January 1, 1831, in Boston. In it, Garrison apologized for his earlier support of gradual abolition and colonization. He made clear that the *Liberator* would be a voice for truth and justice, but not moderation on the issue of slavery. "I am in earnest—I will not equivocate—I will not excuse—I will not retreat a single inch—AND I WILL BE HEARD," he wrote in the first issue. Garrison found financial support for his newspaper from rich philanthropists like Arthur Tappan and James Forten, along with the local black community. Over 90 percent of the subscribers to the *Liberator* in the first year were African Americans, who continued to form a strong core of support even after the subscriber base continued to grow. In return, he published both black and female writers, and he wrote a favorable review of Walker's *Appeal*. "For the next thirty-five years, the weekly publication of the *Liberator* kept Garrison's promise to protest until the ratification of the Thirteenth Amendment purged slavery from the Constitution," Howe writes.[23]

The abolitionist movement entered a period of organizing anti-slavery societies, beginning with the New England Anti-Slavery Society (NEASS) in January of 1832. The founding of the NEASS led to the formation of fifty other organizations, including one in New York in October 1833. By that time, Great Britain had approved legislation abolishing slavery, including compensation to slave owners for the loss of their slaves. Garrison, who was in England at the time, received commitments of both financial and moral support from his brethren in the British Isles. Emboldened by the action of the British, Garrison returned to the United States and helped form the American Anti-Slavery Society (AASS) in December of 1833. It was a multiracial organization, with Arthur Tappan named as president and Garrison the secretary of foreign correspondence. The goals of the organization, which Garrison wrote, were the immediate emancipation of all slaves and the treatment of blacks on an equal basis with whites. Unlike Great Britain, no compensation was to be made to slave owners. Given the abolitionist roots in the evangelical movement, the AASS was devoted to the use of moral suasion to convince slave owners to give up their slaves. As Garrison wrote in the AASS Declaration, the organization would rely solely on "spiritual" means to reach their ends, rejecting the use of violence and instead committing themselves to "the overthrow of prejudice by the power of love—and the abolition of slavery by the spirit of repentance."[24]

The first action of the AASS was to recruit members. "By 1835, the AASS boasted 200 auxiliaries (local chapters), and by 1839, a remarkable 1,350, representing some 250,000 members," Howe writes. While the total number of abolitionists was relatively small, compared to America's 17 million people in 1840, they did find support among the working class, small farmers, and shopkeepers in smaller towns. Black abolitionists were the mainstays of the movement. Still, despite their success in recruiting membership, most whites in the North were hostile to the movement. "By attacking not merely southern slavery but all forms of racial inequality, the abolitionists appeared to the vast majority of white Americans like fanatics, at war with all social order and decency," according to Wilentz.[25]

Antislavery activities in the South were always intertwined with the fear of slave uprisings in the minds of the region's inhabitants. In August of 1831, a slave revolt led by Nat Turner brutally killed fifty-five whites in Virginia. Turner was a thirty-year-old slave, a "mystic religious visionary," who believed he was called by God to lead the revolt. Though quickly put down by the authorities, the Turner rebellion led to a major debate in the Virginia legislature over the future of slavery. Thomas Jefferson Randolph, grandson of the president, led a movement to gradually abolish slavery and relocate all free blacks to Africa. The legislation was ultimately defeated in January 1832 by tidewater plantation owners on a close vote, 67–60, showing that the state was still ambivalent about the peculiar institution. "With the defeat of the Virginia emancipation bill, forthright opposition to slavery in Southern politics ended," Brewer writes, and overt justifications for slavery began to become the norm. Efforts by the Northern abolitionists to convince the South to give up their slaves were just beginning and would result in a predictable outcome.[26]

The Impact of Abolitionism on Politics

The abolitionists now began to force American politicians to confront the issue of slavery. It began in 1835 with a massive Southern mail campaign. Garrison and the AASS hoped to persuade wavering slaveholders, especially those that had been critical of slavery, to join the effort for immediate emancipation. They flooded the Southern mails with 175,000 antislavery tracts. In Charleston, South Carolina, the publications were seized and burned before a crowd of two thousand people. Postmasters asked Amos Kendall, Jackson's postmaster general, what they should do with the material. Kendall, in consultation with Jackson, allowed postmasters to decide whether or not to deliver the tracts. Jackson went one step further, indicating they should only be delivered to people who had subscribed to them, and that their names be made public as supporters of "exciting the negroes to insurrection and massacre." Jackson also proposed legislation to Congress that would ban the distribution of abolition materials, despite the protections of the First Amendment, a proposal that was never adopted. Congress instead passed a law, pushed through by Northern Whigs and Democrats, that required the delivery of all mail. "Yet throughout the South, it went unenforced, and postmasters did as they pleased, with tacit assumption that federal authority over the mails ended at the post office door," Wilentz writes.[27]

American society in the 1830s was particularly susceptible to mob violence. In 1834 and 1835, a total of seventy-three riots were reported, compared to only four in 1830 and 1831. Agitation by abolitionists may have been the single greatest reason for the stark increase during that two-year period, along with the ineffective response of law enforcement. New York experienced three days of riots in 1834 in which Lewis Tappan's home was destroyed. Garrison was nearly killed by a Boston mob in 1835, "Hang him on the Commons" they yelled before he was rescued by two burly men. The mayor eventually had Garrison escorted to the city jail, the only place he could provide protection for him. By 1837, when the abolitionist and publisher Elijah Lovejoy was murdered by a mob in Illinois, "respectable opinion in the North swung away from mob action," according to Howe, and the number of incidents of mob violence began to wane. The murder of Lovejoy was viewed by many in the North as an attack on freedom of speech that "evoked public sympathy" and "helped spike the membership of abolitionist societies in 1837 and 1838," Wilentz writes.[28]

Neither the actions of the abolitionists, nor the death of Lovejoy, elicited any sense of public sympathy in the South. Much of the mob violence in that region was instigated in defense of slavery and out of the fear of slave uprisings. Riots in the South were also targeted against people rather than property, resulting in more deaths than in the North. Mobs were sometimes led by members of society's elite. In Virginia, future President John Tyler spoke before an anti-abolitionists meeting, decrying the attacks on slavery and the social order. In many cases, the crowds that gathered were motivated by the irrational and racist fear that the races would begin to mix, "mulatoizing our posterity." President Jackson denounced the actions of the mob, arguing that it "is becoming much too common and must be checked, or ere long it will become as great an evil as servile war." Yet Jackson himself may well have encouraged a degree of lawlessness, given his actions on banking and his willingness to ignore the law and support the actions of local postmasters who would not deliver the abolitionists' mail. Franklin Delano Roosevelt would later say that the presidency "is preeminently a place of moral leadership." If so, Jackson failed in great measure in reaction to the abolitionist movement, which he considered "an evil force dedicated to the dismemberment of the Union and the discrediting of the democracy," as Remini writes. Jackson, who owned 150 slaves, could be a harsh slave owner, once posting a reward for the return of a fugitive slave that offered an additional "ten dollars for every hundred lashes" laid on him. Jon Meacham writes that Jackson was "blinded by the prejudice of his age, and could not see ... that the promise of the Founding, that all men are created equal, extended to all."[29]

❦ ❦ ❦

Jackson's old rival, John Quincy Adams, stood on the other side of the slavery issue. Although he was no supporter of immediate abolition of slavery and considered men like Garrison to be "fanatics," his sympathies clearly lay with those who wanted to gradually emancipate the slaves. "His parents, and especially his mother, Abigail, had passed along to him their antislavery views," Wilentz writes. During his time serving in the Monroe administration, he had discussed slavery with Calhoun, and concluded that "if the Union must be dissolved, slavery is precisely the question upon which it ought to break." Yet always the strong nationalist and unionist, he attempted to put that day off, supporting the Missouri Compromise. In part, he felt bound to follow the wishes of his constituents, who had little interest in the cause of abolishing slavery.[30]

Adams was dragged into the debate in late 1835 when the abolitionists began to bombard Congress with antislavery petitions in the aftermath of their failure with mass mailings in the South. Southerners proposed that such petitions be accepted but then tabled from further discussion. This was too much for Adams, since it violated "the Constitution of United States, the rules of this House, and the rights of my constituents" to petition Congress. During the debate on the bill, he asked the bill's opponents, "Am I gagged or not?" when they tried to silence him. While the resolution ultimately passed the House in May 1836 on a vote of 117–68, with the support of Southern and Northern Democrats, Adams continued to challenge what became known as the gag rule, so named for his outburst on the House floor. Adams would rise day in and day out to present some new abolitionists' petition. One in particular caused great embarrassment to his opponents, when Adams attempted to have a petition from twenty-two slaves introduced into the House. It turned out that the old politician had sprung a trap for his opponents, who railed against any petition signed by slaves, when it turned out that the petition requested that the slaves be kept in bondage. "Adams had focused the attention of the entire House on the slaveholders' willingness to limit free speech whenever, and wherever, they chose," Wilentz writes. While the gag rule was designed by Southern slaveholders to eliminate discussions about the peculiar institution, it actually fostered them, given Adams's actions. He was also not alone but was joined by other Northern Whigs in the effort to eliminate the gag rule. They were finally successful in having it overturned in 1844. Many in the North began to fear the power of slaveholders, whose actions were seen as a threat to the liberties of white people.[31]

Threats of violence from Southern politicians silenced many Northern congressmen from expressing their displeasure with the gag rule. Due to Adams's age and his status as a former president, he was shielded from such threats emanating from Southern slave owners. Other politicians were not so lucky. One Southern ruffian was Representative Henry Wise of Virginia, a Whig. His father had been a federalist, and Wise was both a college graduate and a lawyer. He was also "a bully of the first order," according to Joanne B. Freeman. Over a four-year period, Wise "fought a duel with a colleague, almost provoked at least two more, and sparked two fistfights on the floor, one time wielding a knife," Freeman writes. One of his main antagonists was the abolitionist Joshua Giddings of Ohio, who was also a Whig. While many Northerners feared speaking out on the slavery issue, Giddings did not. He was a large and imposing figure willing to challenge those he disagreed with. He was also disappointed with his fellow Northerners who he thought were "afraid of these Southern bullies ... This kind of fear I never experienced, nor shall I submit to it now."[32]

❦ ❦ ❦

Adams's antislavery efforts did not end with his fight against the gag rule. In August of 1839, the slave ship *Amistad* was brought into US custody off the coast of New London, Connecticut. The thirty-nine Africans aboard had rebelled against their Spanish capturers, killing all but a few of the sailors. Spain immediately requested that the ship and the men be returned to them under various treaties with the United States, claiming they were slaves and therefore the property of Spain. The case would eventually reach the United States Supreme Court, with Adams serving as part of the legal team defending the right of the men of the *Amistad* to their freedom. Adams made a compelling case before the court that the Africans were illegally seized by the Spanish crew and were not property but people who deserved to have their basic human rights preserved. Adams, pointing to the Declaration of Independence on the wall of the court, argued "that every man has a right to life and liberty, as an inalienable right ... I ask nothing more on behalf of these unfortunate men, than this Declaration" be applied to them. Adams was able to help convince a majority of the court that the men of the *Amistad* had a right to life, liberty, and the pursuit of happiness, and they were granted their freedom.[33]

❦ ❦ ❦

Martin van Buren's actions on abolitionism were distinctly different from those of Adams. In his defense, he was in a very different political position than the former president, since he was running to replace Jackson on the Democratic ticket. Given this, he was attempting to hold together Jackson's coalition of Southern slaveholders and Northern Democrats, or what remained of them in the aftermath of the Nullification Crisis and the bank wars. Van Buren was also the first of a new breed of politicians that saw political parties and the competition for office as natural in a democracy. "Tolerating agitation over slavery would destroy the nation's political fabric," Wilentz writes, and so Van Buren joined with Clay and Jackson in attempting to keep slavery off the political agenda.[34]

Van Buren worked to suppress the distribution of abolitionist material during the mail controversy, and he supported the gag rule in Congress. He wrote to one friend that slave owners were "sincere friends to mankind," while abolitionists were out to undermine the republic. His actions were sufficient to gain him the presidency when the Whigs ran three regional candidates against him. Van Buren was able to hold on to the Southern states of Virginia, North Carolina, Alabama, Mississippi, Louisiana, and Arkansas and gain enough support in the North to win both the popular and electoral college vote. However, his popular-vote total was just over 50 percent, showing the leakage that occurred from Jackson's original Democratic coalition. During his inaugural address, Van Buren promised not to interfere with slavery or to support the movement to eliminate slavery in the District of Columbia, which was a favored cause of the political abolitionists. When the *Amistad* case was decided by the lower courts in favor of the black defendants, Van Buren had the case appealed to the Supreme Court. Yet "despite all he did to shore up his Southern credentials, there was always a lurking fear among Southerners that Van Buren was secretly anti-slavery," his biographer Ted Widmer writes.[35]

Van Buren's outlook on politics was that one's opponents are rivals for power but not enemies, an important norm of American democracy, which has allowed it to thrive. Yet, as the political scientists Steven Levitsky and Daniel Ziblatt note in their book *How Democracies Die*, "America's nascent norms soon unraveled over" the issue of slavery. The type of politics that Van Buren practiced was essential in making a democracy function properly, in producing results based on compromise between differing societal interests. But it works less well, if at all, when the issue is a transcendent moral one, like slavery. "Van Buren approached the intensifying debate over slavery the way most politicians do—he danced around it, trying to placate people and offering various concessions to maintain his support," Widmer writes. Yet, sometimes an issue is of such great moral weight that it requires an extraordinary leader to resolve it, "a new visionary to smash the system ... and build something better in its place."[36]

What ultimately destroyed Van Buren's presidency was the continued instability of the American economy. Almost as soon as he took the oath of office, he faced the Panic of 1837. The economy had been on a major upswing, fueled by the growth of the money supply that was caused by the infusion of silver from Mexico. "With more money in circulation, domestic prices rose, including the price people paid for western land," Howe writes. "On the international market, the prices of cotton and other U.S. export staples soared in the 1830s." When the Bank of England began to reduce credit in the aftermath of a poor harvest, the bubble burst, with banks and businesses going under. While the economy began a tentative rebound in 1838, another panic began in 1839 that would last until 1843. Without a national bank, there was no lender of last resort to shorten the duration of the Panic of 1839. Van Buren's response to the panics was "strict economy and frugality," leading to his defeat in the 1840 election.[37]

☙ ☙ ☙

At the far extreme of pro-slavery politics in the 1830s stood John C. Calhoun, not only in his support of nullification and in his opposition to the abolitionists, but increasingly for espousing slavery as a positive good. Unlike his fellow Southerner, Jefferson, he did not view slavery as "a necessary but temporary evil," as Hofstadter has written. Nor did he share John Quincy Adams's view of the equality of all human beings, since in the South (and much of the North) this only applied to white men. As Calhoun said in the Senate in 1837, slavery "is, instead of an evil, a good, a positive good." Calhoun supported Jackson's efforts to stop the spread of abolitionists' mail, although his fear of a strong central government led him to recommend that this be done pursuant to state laws. He also supported the gag rule.[38]

But perhaps Calhoun's most unique view involved class conflict. "I hold then that there never has yet existed a wealthy and civilized society in which one portion of the community did not in point of fact live on the labor of the other ... There is and always has been in an advanced stage of wealth and civilization a conflict between labor and capital," Calhoun said in a Senate debate in 1837. To Calhoun, the South had solved this problem through slave labor. "The condition in the South exempts us from the disorders resulting from [class] conflicts." Calhoun believed that there should be a "planter-capitalist collaboration against the class enemy," which in his view meant working-class people, a view that caused Richard Hofstadter to refer to Calhoun as the Marx of the Master Class. "Calhoun had an ingenious solution for the section problem: in return for the South's services as a balance wheel against labor agitation, the solid elements in the North should join her in a common front against all agitation of the slavery issue," Hofstadter writes. It was a grand bargain the North ultimately refused to join.[39]

Divisions within the Abolitionist Movement

William Lloyd Garrison had moved in an increasingly radical direction by the mid-1830s. Inspired by his Christian faith, he increasingly turned toward a utopian vision of the moral improvement of society. The heart of Garrison's approach was a belief in the brotherhood of all human beings, black and white, male and female. It was a radical idea for the times (even so in our day), grounded in the notion that all should be treated equally, and it continued to raise a violent uproar from many in society. He rejected the main institutions of society, including the government and the established churches, because he thought they made too many compromises with the Southern Slave Power. Nonresistance, rooted in the Gospels, became the focus for how society would be transformed. The outcome of the positions he took would lead to a schism within abolitionism by the late 1830s over issues related to religion, the role of women, and whether the movement should be involved in politics.

Garrison had married Helen Benson in 1834. She was the youngest daughter of the Benson family of Providence, Rhode Island. He had grown increasingly close to the family, viewing them as a surrogate for his own troubled family life. In Brooklyn in 1836, Lloyd and Helen had their first child, George Thompson. Perhaps it was fatherhood, along with the impact of the mob that nearly killed him in 1835, that caused Garrison to undergo "an intellectual and religious transformation during his interval of seclusion in Brooklyn," while he cared for his wife and new son. He became more estranged from various institutions, including "the church, the law, the political party," as Mayer writes.[40]

Garrison had always viewed religion as an internal journey toward the perfection of the soul. It was a bottom-up rather than a top-down approach in which each person needed to reach their own private judgment about what is right and what God expected. He may well have been influenced by the Englishman John Milton, who in 1644 wrote: "Give me the liberty to know, to utter, and to argue freely according to conscience, above all liberties." Garrison believed that the clergy could not impose their moral code from above, but that each person must pursue their own spiritual journey. He increasingly rejected the moral leadership of the clergy, especially those that opposed the immediate abolition of slavery. Garrison may have been partly motivated by his own rejection by organized religion in the early 1830s, when many ministers would not allow him to speak in their churches. At one point, Lyman Beecher had told him: "Your zeal is commendable, but you are misguided. If you will give up your fanatical notions and be guided by us (the clergy), we will make you the Wilberforce of America." William Wilberforce had led the movement in Great Britain to end slavery.[41]

It's not a surprise then that Garrison's first attack against organized religion focused on Beecher. Beecher was no supporter of slavery and had delivered a speech in Cincinnati in 1834 to the Colonization Society that "it is manifest that slavery must terminate quickly." But Beecher also looked for compromise, as he did during a dispute at Cincinnati's Lane University that occurred in 1834 while he was president of the school. Theodore Dwight Weld had been sent by Tappan to organize abolitionists on the campus, which he was wildly successful at. When many in the local community protested against those students who had formed an abolitionist society, "President Beecher, proclaiming his devotion to free speech and discussion, tried to mediate, but to no avail," Wilentz writes. Weld and the students were expelled from Lane, and many of them moved to Oberlin College. Perhaps influenced by these events, in 1836 Beecher came out against the abolitionists, urging that slavery should not be discussed by religious leaders. He also defended the moral authority of the clergy and praised the "silken ties" between Christians of the North and South.[42]

Garrison responded by charging Beecher with siding "with the South" and that those "silken ties" were "literally the chains of slaves." His attacks on Beecher covered ten columns in the *Liberator*, in which he charged that the aged minister "goes with the South" and those churches that were silent on the issue of slavery were "clotted with innocent blood." The only way for the evangelical movement to regain its gospel purity was to divorce themselves from any relationship with the defenders of slavery. He also assailed the clergy for supporting society's "rich and powerful." Garrison wrote that "all classes know and some feel that there is a growing aristocracy in our land, that privileges are granted to the wealthy few, to the injury and impoverishment of the laborious many." He was attempting to "link the working classes of the North with the slaves of the South," Mayer states.[43]

Increasingly, Garrison was committed to the principle of non-resistance. In September of 1838, he helped launch the New England Non-Resistance Society, which was dedicated to pacifism and nonviolent resistance, including opposition to standing armies, military service, and capital punishment. The organization was inspired by the Sermon on the Mount, specifically the section of Matthew's Gospel where Jesus says: "Offer no resistance to one who is evil.

When someone strikes you on your right cheek, turn the other one to him as well." Garrison and his followers extended nonresistance to the political sphere, shunning voting and campaigns in the belief that until individual hearts were changed, politics was meaningless. As James Brewer Stewart frames it, "appeals to conscience had to be expanded to induce a total reshaping of the nation's ethical values and institutional practices." This was a new approach for Garrison, who had previously been involved with the mailing campaign in the South, had voted, and had participated in opposition to the gag rule.[44]

Among Garrison's strongest supporters were women abolitionists, especially the Grimke sisters. Sarah and Angelina were originally from Charleston, South Carolina. They were thirteen years apart, and Sarah served as a mother figure toward her younger sister. Their father was an affluent lawyer, judge, and plantation owner. Sarah accompanied her father North when he became ill in 1819, and after his death two years later, she remained in Philadelphia, converting to Quakerism. Eight years later, Angelina also left the South to join her sister. Both viewed slavery as evil, with Sarah later remembering that "slavery was a millstone about my neck, and marred my comfort from the time I can remember myself." When Sarah was young, she got into trouble when she taught her "little waiting-maid" to read, a practice that was illegal in South Carolina. Both sisters had firsthand experience with the brutality of slaves being beaten. Angelina once fainted after seeing a small slave boy whose "back and legs were scarred by whipmarks," according to their biographer Gerda Lerner. Given their Southern roots and direct knowledge of the world of the slave, they would soon become an especially potent voice in the abolitionist movement.[45]

Their brother Thomas, who was six years older than Sarah, had become "a prominent peace, temperance, and colonization reformer," and when he died in the mid-1830s, the sisters joined the abolitionist movement partly in tribute to him. In August 1835, Angelina wrote a letter to Garrison in which she said that abolishing slavery "is a cause worth dying for." When he published the letter in the *Liberator*, she became a celebrity. Both sisters attended a training session for seventy agents led by Theodore Dwight Weld in November of 1836. Angelina and Sarah were not actually part of the "seventy," but were allowed to participate in three weeks of training "that addressed slavery as a moral wrong, the shortcomings of colonization and gradualism, conditions in the South, the needs of the free black population, and the relationship between prejudice and abolition," Mayer writes. Angelina and Weld fell in love and married in 1838. In the aftermath of the training session, the sisters began to organize and speak at abolitionist events that included mixed-race audiences of men and women. The sisters also began to advance a feminist agenda as part of their antislavery work. At a meeting of women abolitionists in May 1837, Angelina introduced a resolution stating "the time has come for woman to [assume] the rights and duties common to all moral beings ... and no longer remain satisfied in the circumscribed limits which corrupt custom and a perverted application of Scripture have encircled her ..." Not to be outdone, Sarah published a series of letters on the equality of women in 1837 that was grounded in a reading of the Bible in which she argued that Eve was "in all respects his [Adam's] equal." The Grimkes would be part of a movement to promote the rights of women that would culminate in the Seneca Falls Convention of 1848, which was intended to "discuss the social, civil, and religious condition and rights of women," as advertising for the convention proclaimed.[46]

Garrison elicited strong opposition within the abolitionist movement due to his views on nonresistance, especially nonparticipation in the political system, his attacks on evangelical ministers, and most importantly, his support for the active and equal participation of women. In June 1837, the Congregational General Association issued a pastoral letter stating that the Grimke sisters were violating "the natural role accorded to women," by publicly speaking before mixed groups of men and women. A month later, a group of evangelical ministers attacked Garrison and the *Liberator* for his "abuse of ministers who would not act against slavery to its editor's satisfaction." The executive committee of the AASS was also uncomfortable with "extraneous causes like women's rights and non-resistance," according to Stewart. Men like Lewis Tappan and even Weld wanted the women to tone down their participation. While Weld supported women's rights generally (how could he not, being married to Angelina), he did not think they "were in as dire a need of agitation as abolitionism."[47]

❧ ❧ ❧

Frederick Douglass and his wife, Anna, had escaped from slavery in the fall of 1838 and settled in New Bedford, Massachusetts. It was a congenial place for free blacks and escaped slaves, "the best city in America for an ambitious young black man," according to Douglass's biographer William McFeely. But New Bedford had its own problems with discrimination, as Douglass quickly found out after taking a job as a caulker at a shipyard. "Every white man would leave the ship ... unfinished ... if I struck a blow at my trade upon her," Douglass wrote, and so he was forced to take an unskilled job at half the pay.[48]

At a church meeting the following spring, Douglass spoke out against colonization and of "what slavery was like and why slaves should be set free, right here in America," McFeely writes. Garrison published the comments in the *Liberator*. In August 1841, the Massachusetts Anti-Slavery Society (MAS) held a convention in

Nantucket, which both Garrison and Douglass attended. Near the end of one session, Douglass rose to tell his story. Nervous to the very core of his being, Douglass explained that he was an escaped slave "and telling of the cruelties he had witnessed and suffered," he mesmerized the audience. Garrison reacted by pointing to Douglass and asking, "Have we been listening to [a] thing, a piece of property, or to man?" and "Should such a man be held a slave in a republican and Christian land?" The crowd reacted with cries of "Never! Never!" With this speech, the abolitionist movement had found its most important black voice. Douglass was recruited to be an agent for the MAS, and he and Garrison began an on-again, off-again relationship that would continue for many years.[49]

❦ ❦ ❦

Garrison's decision to avoid politics came under attack in January 1838 at a meeting of the MAS. Interestingly, Garrison never insisted that others follow his lead. This became clear at the meeting, when he was confronted by Henry Stanton, who had concluded that forcing the political system to confront slavery was the only way to end it. Stanton, who had been trained by Weld and been part of the Lane Controversy, caught Garrison off guard with his criticism, since Stanton had "stayed with the Garrison's and given no hint of his shifting allegiance," Mayer writes. At one point during the meeting, Stanton asked, "Mr. Garrison! Do you or do you not believe it a sin to go to the polls?" Garrison responded, "Sin for me," indicating that while he would not participate in the political system, he was not willing to judge others. Stanton wanted to make it mandatory that abolitionists vote, and he was joined by Tappan. But neither man was able to add this as a requirement to the various abolitionist organizations, and so they attacked the unorthodox role that women were playing with Garrison's support. As with most large-scale organizations, there were people with a variety of views. "Some political abolitionists endorsed women's rights, and some Garrisonians supported political action, but the schism forced them to choose sides," Sinha writes. At the annual meeting of the AASS in July 1840, the feminist Abby Kelley was elected to the executive committee, which caused the losing side to walk out. They soon formed the American and Foreign Anti-Slavery Society (AFASS), which was led by the Tappans. Some, like Theodore Weld, rejected both sides. When later asked to join the AFASS, he refused due to their "denial of the equal membership of women." Black abolitionists also "deplored the schism as distracting and unnecessary."[50]

While Garrison may have occupied the moral high ground in many of these issues, it would ultimately take political action to finally move the abolitionist agenda forward. "Progress in America does not usually begin at the top and among the few, but from the bottom and among the many," historian Jon Meacham has written. "It comes when the whispered hopes of those outside the mainstream rise in volume to reach the ears and hearts and minds of the powerful." Garrison had helped to launch a bottom-up movement to end slavery. But it would ultimately take the political abolitionists, those who engaged in the political arena, to gradually transform the terms of the debate. Their first experience with forming a third party would have no impact on presidential politics, but during the ensuing twenty years they would lay "the groundwork for the broader antislavery coalitions that became the Free Soil and then the Republican Party," according to historian Corey M. Brooks.[51]

Antislavery Politics and Third Parties in the 1840s

The twin economic depressions of 1837 and 1839 left Martin van Buren in a precarious position from which to seek reelection, as did his lack of positive action to staunch or reverse the economic slide. He must have known there was trouble when the opposition Whigs hung the nickname "Martin van Ruin" upon him. For the first time, the Whigs were organized to run a credible political campaign for the presidency. The party, which in 1836 had been viewed as made up of the rich and powerful, now put their candidate forward as a populist man of the people. The Whigs united around William Henry Harrison, the general who had claimed a major victory over Tecumseh at the Battle of Tippecanoe in 1811, selecting him over Henry Clay for his party's nomination. Clay had never been pro-slavery, but he also knew that for the Whigs to be successful, they would need to pursue a nationwide campaign. He attempted to burnish his anti-abolitionist credentials with a speech in February 1839 in which he "charged that immediate emancipation would lead either to war between the races, causing extermination of one or the other, or to mongrelization and the ruination of both races," Wilentz writes. Harrison defeated Clay on the third ballot at the Whig convention in late 1839, and when Clay refused the second slot, his fellow Virginian John Tyler was named the vice-presidential candidate. Tyler's selection was "one of the worst mistakes ever made by any political party," Howe writes, as we shall see.[52]

Historians disagree over whether the Democrats were the party of slavery, although there does seem to be a consensus that there were more Whigs that were antislavery, even if they were still a minority in the party. Still, it is not surprising that both the Democratic and Whig tickets were opposed to the abolitionist movement during the

1840 election, since they each needed to compete in both the North and the South if they wanted to succeed. As we saw during Jackson's time in office, both sides generally preferred that the issue not be discussed. The 1840 campaign was largely waged over the elements of Clay's American System, with the Whigs supporting a new national bank to replace the BUS, a more activist government to help end the depression, and investment in internal improvements. The Democrats opposed these Whig policies and supported hard money, a Treasury Department that managed the fiscal affairs of the nation without banks by using specie to pay bills (known as an Independent Treasury), and limited government. Even more interesting, the Whigs inadvertently stole the populist image of the Democrats as the champion of average people. A Democratic newspaperman attacked both Harrison's age (he was sixty-six) and his intellect when he wrote: "Give him a barrel of hard cider, and settle a pension of two thousand a year on him, and my word for it, he will sit the remainder of his days in his log cabin." The criticism backfired when the Whigs used the symbolism of the log cabin and cider to show Harrison as a man of the people compared to the imperious Van Buren. Harrison was in fact born into a family that was part of the Virginia planter aristocracy, and his father had signed the Declaration of Independence. As a young adult he had moved to Ohio, where he made his mark first as a military man and then later in politics. "It became the first true use of political handling, or public image-making, in an American presidential race," historian William Freehling has observed. The Whigs even developed a slogan: "Tippecanoe and Tyler too."[53]

Given the hostility toward the abolitionists from the Democrats and the Whigs, the abolitionists organized the Liberty Party. They ran James G. Birney, a Southerner from Alabama who had freed his slaves and joined the abolitionist cause in the early 1830s. Their goal was "to make the question of slavery the grand question of national politics." The party supported the elimination of slavery in the areas controlled by the federal government, specifically in new territories and the District of Columbia, and wanted to ban slavery in new states. They also proposed termination of the slave trade between states. But abolitionists were split over the wisdom of forming a third party, and Birney garnered only seven thousand votes. Not surprisingly, Harrison swept to victory over Van Buren, winning the electoral college 234–60 and 53 percent of the popular vote. The Whigs also swept to victory in the congressional races and controlled both the House and the Senate.[54]

While the political abolitionists were unsuccessful with their first foray into electoral politics, they would gradually begin to change the terms of the debate by making "the claim that slaveholders wielded disproportionate political power and threatened the liberties of white Northern men," Brooks argues. The reaction of the South to the mailing of abolitionist literature, and the enforcement of the gag rule in Congress, gave credence to the thesis that a malevolent "Slave Power" existed and threatened the North. Since the mid-1830s, the political abolitionists believed they needed to upend the two dominant existing parties, since both the Whigs and Democrats were complicit in continuing slavery.[55]

Salmon P. Chase, one of the emerging leaders of the antislavery movement in the 1840s, claimed that he became aware of the "Slave Power and the need for political organization to combat its influences" from Senator Thomas Morris of Ohio. Chase was born in New Hampshire in 1808, the eighth of eleven children. His father died when he was nine, leaving the family in poverty, and young Chase was forced to live in Ohio with his uncle, an Episcopal bishop. The bishop was "often very harsh and severe" Chase recalled, unlike his father, who was gentle and nurturing. A serious and ambitious young man, Chase eventually graduated from Dartmouth, and then went on to study law under William Wirt, Monroe's attorney general. In 1829, he moved to Cincinnati and established a successful law practice.[56]

Chase became involved in antislavery politics in Ohio. Cincinnati, which was just across the Ohio River from Kentucky, was a city with clear Southern sympathies. When James Birney began to publish an antislavery newspaper in the city, a mob attacked him and destroyed his printing press. Chase, showing great bravery, rescued Birney from the mob. "His passionate awakening to the antislavery cause was not surprising, given his receptiveness to religious arguments in favor of emancipation and equality," Doris Kearns Goodwin writes. In 1841, Chase joined the Liberty Party, motivated both by his sense of the immorality of slavery, but also by personal ambition to make a name for himself.[57]

Chase's contributions to the antislavery cause were twofold. First, he believed that the Constitution was an antislavery document, a view markedly different from Garrison, who called the document "a covenant with death, an agreement with hell" that sanctioned slavery. Chase pointed to both Jefferson's Declaration of Independence and also the Northwest Ordinance to make the case that the founders "regarded freedom and equality as the natural condition of men, and viewed slavery as a temporary abnormal state," Eric Foner writes. Chase argued that the Framers of the Constitution had in mind the Declaration's call for liberty and equality and wanted to keep the federal government out of the business of slavery as much as possible. That was why the document never mentions slavery. Chase's view of the Constitution could be summed up in an address he wrote for the Liberty Party in 1841: "The Constitution found slavery and left it a State institution—the creature and dependent of State law—wholly local in its existence and character. It did not make it a national institution." Chase may have been a better lawyer than historian since, as we have seen, slavery was one of the issues the founders were unable to resolve. The Framers placed numerous protections in the Constitution to create a stronger national union, although they refused to recognize that people were property. Still, Chase's argument would resonate in the North. He also distinguished between abolitionists, who seek "to abolish slavery everywhere," and those like himself who were antislavery. "Antislavery aimed at the separation of the federal government from slavery, and its deliverance from control by the Slave Power," according to Foner.[58]

Chase also helped spread the idea that there was a Slave Power conspiracy, that Southern slaveowners had taken control over the federal government and had spread slavery in opposition to the wishes of the founding generation. He and other Liberty Party members argued that there were only 350,000 slaveholders, less than 1 percent of the nation's population, which held disproportionate political power due to the three-fifths clause and the impact it had on both Congress and presidential elections (due to the electoral college). The Constitution had been transformed from "the safeguard of Liberty ... into a bulwark of slavery." But what made the Slave Power argument so powerful and would begin to change the terms of the political debate in the 1840s and 1850s was that the South began to be seen as a threat to Northern white men. The Liberty Party advanced the idea "that the ultimate intention of the South was to spread slavery into the North, and to destroy the civil liberties in the free states," Foner writes. While this idea may have been fanciful, it did change the politics of the antislavery movement, broadening its appeal.[59]

❧ ❧ ❧

The Whig ascendancy was short-lived. After being sworn in, President Harrison gave an inaugural address that lasted almost two hours. Eschewing a coat in a driving snowstorm, Harrison contracted a severe cold and was dead within thirty days of assuming office. John Tyler, more Democrat than Whig, "insisted on being considered the new, constitutional President, rather than a Vice-President acting as President, thus setting a precedent for all later Presidents elevated by chance," according to James MacGregor Burns. Tyler, who was a Virginia slave owner, was a follower of Jefferson and believed in states' rights. He had become a Whig due to his opposition to Jackson's policy on nullification and his power grab during the controversy over removing federal deposits from the BUS. But he soon proved to be unsympathetic to many of the core policy preferences of the Whigs.[60]

While Tyler may have opposed Jackson on the removal of federal deposits, he was no fan of a national bank and considered it unconstitutional. The top priority for Clay and the Whigs, their main proposal to fix the economy, was the resurrection of the BUS. Tyler vetoed two bills that would have done that. Not only did Tyler veto the bills as a matter of principle, but he also feared that the credit for a bank bill would redound to Clay, who would emerge as the clear leader of the Whigs and the party's presidential nominee in 1844. While the two men considered each other friends, politics came first. In response to the bank vetoes, five members of the Harrison cabinet resigned, and a caucus of congressional Whigs kicked Tyler out of the party. Tyler decided to form his own party and began to push for the annexation of Texas as a way to enable a "run for President in 1844 as the candidate of a new pro-Texas third party, or better yet as the Democratic nominee," Leonard Richards writes.[61]

The annexation of Texas, and the resulting war with Mexico, would change antislavery politics in the United State irreversibly.

Endnotes

1   Stanley Harrold, *American Abolitionists* (Essex, 2001), p. 8; David Brion Davis, *Inhuman Bondage: The Rise and Fall of Slavery in the New World* (New York, 2006), p. 1.

2   Manisha Sinha, *The Slave's Cause: A History of Abolition* (New Haven, 2016), p. 9; Harrold, p. 16.

3   Sinha, p. 18; James Brewer Stewart, *Holy Warriors: The Abolitionists and American Slavery* (New York, 1996), p. 17.

4   Sinha, p. 68–69.

5   Sinha, p. 163; Ketchum, p. 626.

6   Howe, p. 265; information on James Forten was retrieved on May 10, 2018, from http://explorepahistory.com/hmarker.php?markerId=1-A-28C; David Brion Davis, *The Problem of Slavery in the Age of Emancipation* (New York, 2014), p. 173–174.

7   David Brion Davis, *Inhuman Bondage*, p. 48–50; for a brief discussion of in- and out-groups as part of the origin of racism, see Rob Brooks, "The Origins of Racism," retrieved May 10, 2018, from https://www.huffingtonpost.com/rob-brooks/the-origins-of-racism_b_1700504.html. Brooks summarizes the work of Elizabeth Culotta, which shows how racism may have evolved from living and working in groups. Ibram X. Kendi, *Stamped from the Beginning: The Definitive History of Racist Ideas in America* (New York, 2016), p. 23.

8   I am indebted to Kendi for his descriptions of the racist underpinnings of both the assimilationists' and segregationists' views that have been held in the past. This summary description of climate theory can be found on p. 17–20.

9   Davis, *The Problem*, p. 40 and p. 64–67; Kendi, p. 32.

10 Davis, *The Problem*, p. 3–13 and p. 38–40; Kendi, p. 84–85.

11 Kendi also argues that the assimilationists, which includes the abolitionists who favored the immediate end to slavery, advanced racist ideas by encouraging "Black adoption of White cultural traits." He points to William Lloyd Garrison's preface to *The Narrative of the Life of Frederick Douglass, An American Slave*. In it, Garrison wrote that slavery had "degraded" Black people "in the scale of humanity. Nothing has been left undone to cripple their intellects, darken their minds, debase their moral nature, obliterate all traces of their relationship to mankind." See p. 184. Yet, in that same paragraph, Garrison pointed out that slavery can degrade white people as well: "it proves at least that the white slave can sink as low in the scale of humanity as the black one." In the preface, Garrison also writes of Douglass as an "intellect richly endowed—in natural eloquence a prodigy," hardly the words of a racist. Kendi also argues that Garrison and the other abolitionists fought for "gradual equality" and not immediate equality, although he does not provide any direct quotes from Garrison on this point. See p. 168–168. I did not find Kendi's argument that the assimilationists were also racist particularly persuasive, especially given the time that they lived and

how far outside of the mainstream they were on issues of black equality. In 1843, Garrison urged those held in bondage to run away and said that the abolitionists would demand for them "all that we claim for ourselves—liberty, equal rights, equal privileges." See Mayer, p, 320.

12 Wilentz, *Rise*, p. 332–333.

13 The quotes are from David Walker, "Appeal, in Four Articles," retrieved May 11, 2018, from http://docsouth.unc.edu/nc/walker/walker.html p. 1–34.

14 Walker, p. 1–34.

15 Sinha, p. 205; Howe, p. 424–425; Wilentz, *Rise*, p. 334.

16 Robert H. Abzug, *Cosmos Crumbling: American Reform and the Religious Imagination* (Oxford, 1994), p. 130.

17 Henry Mayer, *All on Fire: William Lloyd Garrison and Abolition of Slavery* (New York, 1998), p. 3–43; Abzug, p. 136–137.

18 Mayer, p. 55–56; Abzug, p. 140.

19 Abzug, p. 141–144; Mayer, p. 62–68; the quotes are from William Lloyd Garrison, Address to the Colonization Society, retrieved May 15, 2018, from http://teachingamericanhistory.org/library/document/address-to-the-colonization-society/.

20 Mayer, p. 71–82; Abzug, p. 146.

21 Mayer, p. 78. Mayer frames Garrison's position on politics in the following way in his introduction: "His career is a landmark in the American dissenting tradition and exemplifies that fault line that in democratic politics separates the insiders, who think progress comes from [quiet] lobbying within the halls of power, from the outsiders, who insist that only public manifestations of dissatisfaction can overcome institutional inertia."

22 Mayer, p. 83–94; Abzug, p. 147–151.

23 Sinha, p. 217; Howe, p. 425–426.

24 Sinha, p. 225–226; Wilentz, *Rise*, p. 403; Stewart, p. 55–56.

25 Howe, p. 426; Wilentz, *Rise*, p. 403 and p. 406–407; Stewart, p. 65.

26 Howe, p. 323–327; Wilentz, *Rise*, p. 339–347; Stewart, p. 63.

27 Wilentz, *Rise*, p. 410–411.

28 Howe, p. 430–433; Richards, p. 156–157; Mayer, p. 200–205; Wilentz, *Rise*, p. 468.

29 Howe, p. 433–447; Richards, p. 157; Remini, *Jackson III*, p. 272–273; Meacham, p. 302–303.

30 Wilentz, *Rise*, p. 471; Traub, p. 432.

31 Wilentz, *Rise*, p. 472; Traub, p. 434; Howe, p. 514–515, indicates that the number of petitions submitted to Congress during the winter of 1838–39 grew to 1,496.

32 Freeman, *The Field of Blood*, p. 80, p. 115, p. 130–132.

33 Remini, *Adams*, has a useful summary of the case on p. 146–148. For more details, see

Traub, p. 464–480.

34 Wilentz, *Rise*, p. 447.

35 Widmer, p. 112–113; Howe, p. 486–487; Wilentz, *Rise*, p. 451; election results for 1836 were retrieved May 22, 2018, from https://www.270towin.com/1836_Election/; Martin van Buren, "Inaugural Address," March 4, 1837. Online by Gerhard Peters and John T. Wooley, "The American Presidency Project," retrieved May 22, 2018, from http://www.presidency.ucsb.edu/ws/index.php?pid=25812.

36 Levitsky and Ziblatt, p. 121 and p. 143; Widmer, p. 122.

37 Howe, p. 502–505, has the most useful summary of the two panics and Van Buren's reaction to them.

38 Hofstadter, *American Political Tradition*, p. 79; Bartlett, p. 217–226.

39 Hofstadter, *American Political Tradition*, p. 81–84; Bartlett, p. 226–227.

40 Mayer, p. 179 and p. 214–222.

41 Mayer, p. 222–226; Abzug, p. 152.

42 Mayer, p. 226; Beecher's speech to the colonization society from 1834 was retrieved May 29, 2018, from http://utc.iath.virginia.edu/abolitn/abes38at.html; Wilentz, *Rise*, p. 405.

43 Mayer, p. 226–227.

44 Mayer, p. 249–251; Stewart, p. 90; Sinha, p. 259.

45 Abzug, p. 204–209; Gerda Lerner, *The Grimke Sisters from South Carolina: Pioneers for Women's Rights and Abolition* (Chapel Hill, 2004), p. 3–28.

46 Abzug, p. 209–216; Mayer, p. 230–233.

47 Abzug, p. 217 and p. 233; Mayer, p. 233–236; Stewart, p. 91.

48 McFeely, p. 74–80.

49 Mayer, p. 305–306.

50 Mayer, p. 256–257 and p. 281–284; Sinha, p. 263–265.

51 Jon Meacham, *The Soul of America: The Battle for Our Better Angels* (New York, 2018), Kindle version p. 61; Corey M. Brooks, *Liberty Power: Antislavery Third Parties and the Transformation of American Politics* (Chicago, 2016), p. 2.

52 Wilentz. *Rise*, p. 152, p. 482, and p. 495; Howe, p. 572.

53 On the issue of the Democrats and slavery, Wilentz, *Rise*, p. 512–513, does not see the party as necessarily pro-slavery but rather that "they wanted, as the Whigs did, to keep slavery out of politics to protect constitutional order, national harmony, and party unity." Alternatively, Howe writes: "Virtually every aspect of the Democratic political outlook supported white supremacy and slavery," on p. 510. Between the two views, I tend to see the Democrats of this era as generally more supportive of slavery than the Whigs, although I think Wilentz and Howe agree that both sides wanted to suppress any debate over the issue. For a general description of the 1840 election, see Wilentz,

Rise, p. 496–507 and Howe, p. 573–575. William Freehling, "William Harrison: Campaigns and Elections," retrieved June 7, 2018, from https://millercenter.org/president/harrison/campaigns-and-elections.

54 Howe, p. 575 and p. 652; Brooks, p. 38–41.

55 Brooks, p. 3; Eric Foner, *Free Soil, Free Labor, Free Men: The Ideology of the Republican Party before the Civil War* (Oxford, 1970), p. 90–91.

56 Foner, *Free Soil*, p. 91; Goodwin, p. 34–41.

57 Goodwin, p. 108–109.

58 Foner, *Free Soil*, p. 75–76; Sean Wilentz, *No Property*, p. 97–99.

59 Foner, *Free Soil*, p. 87–101.

60 Wilentz, *Rise*, p. 522; Howe, p. 590; Burns, *Vineyard*, p. 423.

61 Howe, p. 591–595; Richards, p. 168.

CHAPTER 12

Texas and the Mexican-American War

*...the re-occupation of Oregon and the re-annexation of Texas
at the earliest practicable period are great American measures ...*
—From the Democratic Platform of 1844

*...as an express and fundamental condition to acquisition of
any territory from the Republic of Mexico ... neither slavery
nor involuntary servitude shall ever exist in any part of said
territory ...*
—The Wilmot Proviso of 1846

The divisions between North and South had been managed so far, even though there had been some major disputes, including the battles over Missouri and nullification. Westward expansion was another tension point between North and South, with the addition of new territories tightly balanced between slave and free states, since such additions converted into political power. As we saw in chapter 11, the abolitionists had placed the morality of slavery back on the national agenda, with political abolitionists making arguments that were beginning to resonate in the North. Each of these threads will come together over the annexation of Texas, lead to war with Mexico, and to a major expansion of the boundaries of the United States. With ever more territory to argue over, sectional politics would begin to spin out of control between 1844 and 1860.

Texas Independence

Settlers began to stream into Texas from the American South in 1821. Moses Austin had been granted a large tract of land from the Spanish and permission to colonize the lightly populated Texas frontier. When Moses died unexpectedly, his twenty-eight-year-old son Steven took over the venture. A month after the colonization process began, Mexico achieved independence from Spain, but the new government continued to allow immigrants to settle the land. Trouble began when Mexico banned slavery throughout the country, including in Texas. Yet, those Americans that had brought slaves with them found ways around the ban, and their growing population made it difficult for the Mexican government to exercise any control in Texas. By 1830, Anglos outnumbered Hispanics by two to one, which would grow to ten to one by 1836. Mexican authorities also feared that the United States was eyeing Texas, and so in 1830 they passed a law restricting immigration into the territory.[1]

Mexican authorities were right in their suspicions that some in the United States coveted Texas. Andrew Jackson thought it was a part of the United States based on the Louisiana Purchase, and blamed Adams for the 1819 treaty that recognized Texas as a part of Spain. In the early 1830s, Jackson sent an emissary to negotiate the acquisition of Texas from Mexico. The attempt was badly bungled, and the effort failed. When General Antonio López de Santa Anna made himself dictator in Mexico, the settlers in Texas declared their independence. Santa Anna led six thousand Mexican troops into Texas, laying siege to the Alamo in San Antonio, ultimately killing 188 rebel soldiers, including frontiersman/politician Davy Crockett and James Bowie. Ultimately, the rebel army led by Sam Houston defeated Santa Anna at the battle of San Jacinto. To save his own life, Santa Anna signed a treaty that recognized Texas's independence, although the Mexican Congress failed to ratify the treaty and continued to dispute Texas's independence.[2]

While the Jackson administration maintained a formal policy of being neutral, they had in fact aided the rebels by allowing "the Texans to enlist recruits and raise money and supplies in the United States," according to Richards. Once Santa Anna was defeated, Jackson also moved American troops from the border into Texas, causing the Mexican government to protest. Still, Jackson hesitated on the request from the Texas republic to annex them into the United States. His concerns were twofold. On the one hand, he was concerned about international reaction should he act in violation of the "law of nations." The United States had "a treaty with Mexico," and so American neutrality "must be faithfully maintained." Equally important, Jackson was concerned about the impact that annexation would have on Martin van Buren's election prospects in 1836. The abolitionists opposed the annexation of Texas since it could be split into multiple slave states. As Benjamin Lundy wrote, the South and the Texans were in league to "open a vast and profitable SLAVEMARKET therein." Adams was also opposed to the annexation of Texas and argued that the war there was intended to reestablish "slavery where it was abolished." Jackson waited until after Van Buren was elected before recognizing Texas independence.[3]

The Election of 1844

Texas remained an independent republic, with a growing population that by 1845 had reached 125,000, of which 27,000 were slaves. The leaders of Texas, including their president Sam Houston, continued to be interested in becoming a part of the United States. The issue of annexation did not disappear from American politics either, especially when Houston flirted with the British as a potential supporter. "Even now it is by no means clear when Texan statesmen like Sam Houston were courting British aid to achieve long-term independence and when they were doing it to get the attention of policymakers in Washington," Howe writes. The British clearly had an interest in Texas, since many of their people had investments there and in Mexico, and they wished to see the two sides achieve peace and create a stable economic environment. But British interest in Texas was also tied to the elimination of slavery, which caused grave concern among Southern politicians, including President Tyler.[4]

As we have seen, Tyler had decided to use the issue of Texas annexation to win reelection. This caused problems with Secretary of State Daniel Webster, who had been appointed by Harrison. Webster had remained in Tyler's cabinet when the other Whig members resigned, since he was engaged in delicate negotiations with Great Britain over certain boundary issues in Maine and Minnesota. Once those negotiations were completed, Webster, who opposed the annexation of Texas, resigned from the job in May of 1843. Tyler selected Abel Upshur to replace him, "a proslavery radical of the Calhoun school," according to Howe. Tyler hoped to gain support from Calhoun in order to secure the nomination of the Democrats for president. In October of 1843, Upshur entered annexation negotiations with a representative of Texas. But Houston continued to drag his feet, playing the Americans and the British off against each other for the best deal. He did not relent until early 1844, and by then an act of God changed everything.[5]

On February 28, 1844, Upshur was killed on the USS *Princeton* while attending a demonstration of a giant gun, known as the Peacemaker, that exploded. Tyler then turned to Calhoun to step in as secretary of state, and he quickly completed the secret negotiations over the treaty and then sent it to the Senate for confirmation. He also included with the Treaty that went to the Senate a letter he had sent to Great Britain's minister to the United States in which he declared that "the United States acquired Texas in order to protect slavery there from British interference," Howe writes. Calhoun went on to expound his new pet theory, that slavery was a positive good and "that in no other condition or in any other country had the negro race ever attained so high an elevation in morals, intelligence or civilization," as in the American South. When the letter was leaked, the proposed annexation of Texas not only became public knowledge, it also became the major issue of the 1844 election. Both major parties were now faced with a choice: "support Texas annexation and its pro-slavery rationale and alienate the north, or oppose it and forever lose the South," according to Wilentz.[6]

The decision for Henry Clay was not difficult. Clay, who was running once again for president under the Whig banner, prepared a letter from Raleigh, North Carolina, that was published on April 27, 1844. In the letter, Clay expressed his opposition to the annexation of Texas for two reasons. One was that it would lead to war with Mexico, whose government had never conceded the independence of Texas. "Annexation and war with Mexico are identical," Clay wrote. He also feared the impact that annexation would have on the Union, since a "considerable and respectable portion of the Confederacy" were opposed to the incorporation of Texas. Clay's stand did not affect his nomination as the Whig standard-bearer, which occurred by acclimation at their convention on May 1 in Baltimore. The Whigs were generally opposed to further expansion of the boundaries of the nation, which included the annexation of Texas. "Whigs preferred for the United States to concentrate its energies internally, on economic development, education, and social reform," according to Howe. While it did not harm his nomination, Clay's stand on Texas would come back to haunt him in the general election.[7]

On the Democratic side, Martin van Buren was the front-runner for his party's nomination for president once again. Democrats were divided over the issue of Texas. Unlike the Whigs, there was a strong contingent of Northern Democrats, sometimes referred to as Young America, that supported the newly emerging concept of manifest destiny and the annexation of Texas. That term was not actually used by its author, John L. O'Sullivan, until 1845, one year after the 1844 election. But the sentiments it expressed, that the United States "enjoyed the right of our manifest destiny to overspread and to possess the whole of the continent which Providence has given us for the ... great experiment of liberty," was clearly present among a portion of the Democratic Party in the North. The Young America movement was agnostic on slavery, although O'Sullivan believed that Texas annexation would lead to the eventual end of slavery by dispersing the slave population. Southern Democrats, on the other hand, clearly supported the annexation of Texas and the extension of slavery. Still other Northern Democrats "strongly objected to Texas annexation," according to Wilentz.[8]

This placed Van Buren in an awkward position, with the party split over the issue. Van Buren, who had tried to keep slavery off the national agenda, and who had made major efforts to placate Southern slaveholders during his last run and tenure in the White House, now decided to take a principled stand on Texas annexation. In a letter that was released on the same day as Clay's Raleigh letter, Van Buren came out against annexation. It was the "most courageous act of his political career," in the words of Sean Wilentz. Citing similar concerns to Clay, Van Buren argued that annexation would lead to war with Mexico and be an act of aggression that reflected a "lust for power, with fraud and violence in the train." Always the politician, Van Buren could not resist adding that he might support a future annexation of Texas under the right circumstances. Still, his April letter would ultimately cost Van Buren the Democratic nomination.[9]

The Democrats, too, gathered in Baltimore later in May for their convention. While Van Burn held a majority of the delegates, he did not control two-thirds, which had been required for the Democratic nomination since 1832. Van Buren's main challenger was initially Lewis Cass, who had served as Jackson's secretary of war and strongly favored the annexation of Texas. As neither man was able to garner the necessary votes, a dark horse candidate arose, James K. Polk. Polk had originally come to the convention hoping to secure the second spot on a Van Buren ticket, but he now had the support of Andrew Jackson for the top spot. Jackson, who had reservations about Van Buren's ability to win in the South even before his public opposition to the Texas annexation, now abandoned him. The ex-president was also concerned that the British would come to dominate Texas, which would be "highly injurious and probably hostile to this country." Jackson had summoned Polk to the Hermitage prior to the Democratic Convention and urged him to be a "candidate for the first office." Polk initially demurred, thinking "the attempt to place me in the first position would be utterly abortive." But he soon warmed to the idea, and when Van Buren withdrew his name from nomination after the ninth ballet, Polk became the Democratic nominee.[10]

While the Whig platform was dedicated to the promotion of Clay's American System, the Democratic platform highlighted further westward expansion. Not only was the annexation of Texas on the table for the Democrats, but also the Oregon Territory. A key passage of the platform read:

That our title to [the] whole of the Territory of Oregon is clear and unquestionable ... the re-occupation of Oregon and the re-annexation of Texas at the earliest practicable period are great American measures, which this Convention recommends ...

The addition of Oregon was intentional, designed to appeal to Northern Democrats who might oppose Texas annexation. So, too, was the use of the words *re-occupation* and *re-annexation*, which "implied that the United States had once enjoyed clear title to all of Oregon and Texas but had foolishly agreed to the joint occupation of the former in 1818 and surrendered the latter altogether in the Florida treaty of 1819," Howe writes. Both were subtle attacks on the handiwork of John Quincy Adams, who was now a Whig that opposed Texas annexation, and who was increasingly a strong anti-slavery proponent.[11]

In the aftermath of the conventions, the Senate voted against the annexation of Texas on a vote of 35–16. A treaty requires a two-thirds vote, and this one had not even garnered a majority. The vote was largely along sectional lines, with Northern Whigs and Democrats providing 20 votes against, although Southern Whigs also opposed the treaty 14–1. It would not be until after the election that the issue of Texas would be settled.[12]

"Who's Polk?" the Whigs asked, initially delighted to face a virtual unknown. James K. Polk had, in fact, been actively involved in politics both at the state and federal levels for quite some time. Polk was born in 1795 near Charlotte, North Carolina, and his family were followers of Thomas Jefferson. His great uncle was part of a syndicate that controlled over three million acres of land between the Great Smoky Mountains and the Mississippi River. Polk's grandfather was an explorer who surveyed western land and ultimately settled in Tennessee. By the time young James was eleven, he and his family also moved to the Tennessee frontier, where his father became a successful land speculator and businessman. Polk's interest in westward expansion came naturally to him, an inheritance from his family, and perhaps to honor Jefferson's empire of liberty. Howe writes that Polk "identified the acquisition of land with wealth and power, on a national as well as [an] individual scale."[13]

James was a sickly youth who suffered from urinary stones, which were removed in a very painful operation when he was seventeen. The procedure left him sterile, which explains why he and his wife, Sarah, never had children. Given his father's success in business, the family was able to provide James with a classical education, and he ultimately graduated from the University of North Carolina. He then began his legal training under a "giant of the state's bar," according to Polk biographer John Seigenthaler. Building on his success as a lawyer, Polk entered politics and became a disciple of Andrew Jackson.[14]

In 1824, as a member of the Tennessee legislature, Polk backed Jackson's run for the presidency, which culminated in the corrupt bargain. Polk was a true believer in the Democratic Party of Jefferson and Jackson, "that if democracy was to have meaning the great mass of people were as entitled as the wealthy few to vote and to serve in public office," as Seigenthaler writes. Polk rejected the perceived elitism of the old Federalists, including Alexander Hamilton. With his election to the House in 1824 at the age of thirty, he stood in opposition to the minority government of Adams. "The majority should rule and the minority should submit," Polk argued. After Jackson's 1828 electoral triumph, Polk supported him on issues that ranged from opposition to internal improvements, to nullification, to banking. In the powerful position on the House Ways and Means Committee, and ultimately as its chairman, Polk played an integral role in investigating the perceived corruption of Biddle's Second Bank of the United States.[15]

During the Van Buren administration, Polk served as Speaker of the House. He inherited the struggle over the gag rule, which continued in effect and led to numerous caustic debates in the House. He also had to confront the economic panic that had begun in 1837. Realizing that the Speaker's position was a poor platform to gain the presidency, Polk returned to Tennessee and was elected governor in 1839. But his two-year tenure was a flop, with the ongoing financial collapse leaving little money to tackle the problems at the top of his agenda, including improving education and investing in internal improvements. When Polk lost reelection in 1841, and then lost the governor's race again in 1843, his political future looked bleak. Yet a year later he was the Democratic candidate for president in 1844. He would ride the issue of Texas annexation, and westward expansion, to a narrow victory.[16]

❦ ❦ ❦

Why was western expansion so pivotal in the 1844 election? It wasn't just the annexation of Texas, which was popular in the South and controversial in the North. But it was also about annexing the Oregon country, which was quite popular in the Midwest, and had been added to the Democratic Party's platform. Unbeknownst to anyone, Polk also had ambitions toward California.[17]

Expansion into the Oregon country and California by American settlers had begun in earnest in the aftermath of the economic depression in 1839. Most came in covered wagons along the Oregon Trail, which ran from Independence, Missouri, to Fort Hall in present-day Idaho. At that point, the wagon trains had a choice: either head north toward the Willamette Valley of Oregon, or south toward settlements that had been established in Sacramento and San Francisco. By 1844, around five thousand Americans had settled in Oregon.[18]

Since 1818, the United States and Great Britain had both claimed the Oregon Territory, which extended from the forty-second parallel (the present boundary between Oregon and California) all the way to the fifty-fourth parallel in British Columbia. Many Northern and midwestern Democrats in the United States wanted to claim the entire Oregon Territory and adopted the slogan "Fifty-Four Forty or Fight," including a young congressman, Stephen A. Douglas of Illinois. Douglas thought that the United States should evict "Great Britain and the last vestiges of royal authority from the continent of North America" by obtaining a portion of Canada. This was an unrealistic plan, and the real area of negotiation would take place over what was sometimes referred to as the Disputed Triangle, an area that included what would later become Washington state.[19]

Several European powers, including Russia, Great Britain, and France had an interest in California, as did the United States. The state had numerous ports, from San Diego to San Francisco, that would make a great jumping-off point for trade with Asia. As with Texas, the Mexican government had little control over faraway California. In 1835, Andrew Jackson had attempted to acquire San Francisco. By 1841, the American navy was exploring the Bay Area and the Sacramento River. When Commodore Thomas ap Catesby Jones received an erroneous report in October of 1842 that the United States and Mexico were at war, he seized Monterey Bay, the capital of Mexican California. When it became clear that war had not broken out, Jones was forced to withdraw his men and apologize. But Jones's action did reveal Tyler and Webster's interest in California. Webster had made an offer to acquire San Francisco Bay and whatever part of the balance of California that came with it from Mexico and envisioned a grand bargain in which the British would help convince Mexico to complete the sale, and in return the United States would accept the British boundary for Oregon at the Columbia River. That deal never came to fruition.[20]

American settlers were also arriving overland in California. "The trip took months, and it had to be timed for crossing the Sierra Nevada into California before the snows came," Howe writes. Many stopped at the settlement established by John Sutter in Sacramento in 1839. By 1842, the Mexican government prohibited immigrants from buying land, but still the settlers came. While the non-Indian population in California only totaled eight thousand people in 1840, by 1850 the population had swelled to over ninety thousand. Many of these people came in the aftermath of the discovery of gold in 1848 at Sutter's Mill in the foothills of the Sierra Nevada mountains.[21]

❧ ❧ ❧

Immigration also had an impact on the 1844 election. Beginning in the 1840s, immigration surged in the United States, with 1.7 million new arrivals during the decade. This compared to approximately 600,000 immigrants in the 1830s and 150,000 in the 1820s. Nearly half were Irish, even prior to the potato famine that began in 1845. The Irish filled many jobs as laborers, helping to construct canals and other infrastructure, although many experienced discrimination and confronted employment signs that read "No Irish need apply." Most settled in the cities of the Northeast, like Boston and New York, although some also made their way to the Far West. As one

Irish family framed it in 1844 as they made their way to California, they hoped they "would find themselves under more sympathetic conditions than obtained in the United States," given the rise of a nativist backlash.[22]

In 1844, rioting broke out between Protestants and Catholics in Philadelphia. A new nativist party, the American Republicans (not to be confused with the antislavery Republican Party of the 1850s), arose in New York and Pennsylvania. Some Whigs sided with the nativists, putting Clay in an awkward position. He did not want to alienate either side and was especially concerned about losing the Catholic vote in New York. In late October, Clay sent a letter to a New York newspaper editor in an attempt to placate both immigrants and the nativists. "I am utterly opposed to all foreign influence in every form and shape," Clay wrote, playing to the anti-immigrant side. But then he went on to say, "I wish our Country, forever, to remain a sacred asylum for all unfortunate and oppressed men whether from religion or political causes," language meant to yield support from those that had recently immigrated. As with his attempts at clarifying his position on Texas annexation, the letter made neither side happy.[23]

Not all Whigs were anti-immigrant. William Seward, who had been elected governor of New York in 1838, supported improved education for immigrants and for blacks. Seward was born in May of 1801 to an affluent New York family that owned slaves. As a child, he had made friends with the slave children, and it left a lasting impression on him. "Seward later would credit this early unease and personal awareness of the slaves' plight for his resolve to fight against slavery," Doris Kearns Goodwin writes. Seward attended Union College, and then studied law. Yet, like so many leaders of his era, Seward found the law boring and politics his true calling. His affiliation with the newspaperman Thurlow Weed would prove to be advantageous to both men. Weed helped Seward get elected to the New York Senate in 1830 at the age of twenty-nine. Seward was a strong supporter of Henry Clay's American System.[24]

As governor, Seward hoped to "broaden the appeal of the Whig Party" by proposing measures "to attract Irish and German Catholic immigrants who formed the backbone of the state Democratic Party," Goodwin writes. He also displayed his antislavery credentials when Virginia requested that three free black sailors be sent to the state to stand trial for hiding a fugitive slave on their ship. Seward made the case that "since people were not property ... no crime had been committed," according to Goodwin. The Liberty Party considered Seward for their nomination in 1844, but he was not yet ready to leave the Whig Party.[25]

Seward's pro-immigration views ultimately could not swing New York to Clay. In an incredibly close election, Polk won the electoral college 170–105, but the popular vote by only 38,000 votes out of 2.6 million cast. Polk carried New York by 5,106 votes, with Birney of the Liberty Party garnering 15,812 votes. Had Clay prevailed in New York, he would have won the electoral college by one vote. In the ultimate irony, the political abolitionists had helped to elect Polk, whose actions with Texas annexation and the coming Mexican-American War would do so much to expand the debate over the extension of slavery and the divide between North and South. One historian of the era, Daniel Walker Howe, argues that a Clay victory in 1844 may have "avoided the Civil War of the 1860s." As with so many untaken paths in history, this is one we will never know.[26]

Expansionism through Peace and War

President Tyler did not wait for Polk to take office before continuing his efforts to annex Texas. He proposed a "constitutionally dubious strategy," in the words of Wilentz, in which each house of Congress would adopt a resolution supporting the annexation of Texas, rather than making another attempt at a treaty requiring approval by a two-thirds vote of the Senate. While there was sufficient support in the Democratic House for approval, the lame-duck Senate proved more problematic, since it was still in Whig hands. The tide turned when Thomas Hart Benton, one of the Democrats who voted against the treaty, changed his mind, given that his constituents in Missouri had voted for Polk. His amendment to the resolution would have split Texas into two states, one slave and one free, and garnered enough votes when three Whigs joined all Democrats in voting for it. The House concurred in the change and Tyler signed it, although neither he nor Polk intended to follow the two-state solution.[27]

Polk was sworn in to office on March 4, 1845. In his inaugural address, the new president revealed part of his expansionist goals, framing Texas annexation as simply adding territory that was "once a part of our country" and the American claim to Oregon as "clear and unquestionable." Polk may have also inadvertently tipped his hand, claiming that "our system may be safely extended to the utmost bounds of our territorial limits." Perhaps this was a reference to his still-secret plans to obtain California and to settle the Texas question by also obtaining the balance of the New Mexico Territory, which would include the future states of Arizona, Nevada, Utah, and New Mexico. He would follow very different approaches to reach his goals, one peaceful and the other leading to war. "Power politics, diplomacy, and war proved as much a part of America's 'manifest destiny,'" Howe writes, as did any attempt at a "truly, a manifest, inevitable destiny."[28]

Oregon proved the easier of the two goals to attain, although not without some saber rattling on Polk's part. The president was initially willing to accept the boundary for Oregon at the forty-ninth parallel, as Tyler had previously agreed to. But then the British minister to the United States, Richard Packenham, rejected the Polk offer, enraging the American president. Howe maintains that Polk never seriously considered war with the British over British Columbia, "since he made no military preparations," although he did withdraw the earlier proposal and maintained a hard-line stand until the British acceded to the American position. "The British responded more to the presence of the American settlers, the decline of the Oregon fur trade, and their eagerness for American imports of cotton and grain than to the president's eyeballing," Howe argues. Other historians have noted that Polk did not want to risk war on two fronts, since he intended to obtain California and New Mexico even if it meant war. In June of 1846 the Senate approved the establishment of the forty-ninth parallel as the boundary for the Oregon Territory, which caused those Northerners that supported "Fifty-Four Forty or Fight" to question Polk's motives, since he "had settled for half of Oregon while pushing to promote the Texas venture," to the point of war, according to historian David Potter.[29]

❧ ❧ ❧

Polk was an incredibly aggressive president in his pursuit of California and the New Mexico territories. In the aftermath of the approval of Texas annexation by the American Congress, Mexico broke off diplomatic relations between the two countries at the end of March 1845. In response, Polk sent General Zachary Taylor and the American army into Texas near the disputed territory between the Nueces and Rio Grande Rivers. By July 4, 1845, Texas had agreed to be annexed by the United States. Polk then attempted to acquire California and New Mexico, sending his minister plenipotentiary to offer $30 million for both. But Mexico refused to receive the minister since diplomatic relations had ended. If they entered into talks with a minster plenipotentiary, Mexico would have been conceding the resumption of diplomatic relations with the United States. "As soon as Polk learned of the rejection of his minister, he ordered General Taylor to advance from the Nueces River (the southern border of Texas) to the Rio Grande," in Mexican territory, according to Potter. When the Mexican general demanded that American troops withdraw from the disputed area, Taylor instead blockaded the Rio Grande. Not surprisingly, shooting broke out between the two sides in the spring of 1846, with several American troops killed or captured.[30]

Polk now had his casus belli, although he had already decided to go to war even before the outbreak of hostilities, directing Secretary of State James Buchanan to draft a declaration of war to be sent to Congress. In May of 1846, Congress voted overwhelmingly to approve the declaration, although Polk's message framed the action as defensive in nature, that Mexico "had invaded our territory ... and that the two nations are now at war." It was a claim that would come back to haunt him. Most historians who have studied the outbreak of the Mexican-American War see Polk as the clear aggressor, ordering Taylor into the disputed territory, which resulted in the blockade, an act of war. Even an American colonel who was part of Taylor's army commented at the time that troop movements were intended to "bring on a war, so as to have a pretext for taking California and so much of this country [Mexico] as it chooses." While the outbreak of war elicited a "patriotic fervor," as Wilentz frames it, the war soon became controversial. But at the outset, only a handful of Whigs, led by Adams, voted against the declaration of war. They "believed that the war was an extension of the Slave Power's thinly veiled plot to extend its territory and power," according to Wilentz. There were also Northern Democrats who had similar concerns. Surprisingly, Calhoun was also opposed to the war, since he believed that the territory the

United States would gain was not suited to the expansion of slavery. Polk too believed this, and actually hoped that the inclusion of California and the Southwest region would act to promote national unity. In this, he was sorely mistaken.[31]

Military and Political Battles

The war was fought largely by volunteers from the South and the West. Despite the original patriotic fervor, the war soon became a political problem for the president. The actual fighting went much better, especially in the early months. In the Far West, fewer than eight hundred American immigrants led a revolt in California in June of 1846. Fueled by rumors that war would soon break out with Mexico (since they had not yet heard the news of the actual declaration) and led by Captain John Frémont, a small American force captured the town of Sonoma, raised a flag with the image of a bear on it, and declared California an independent republic. Three days later, the American navy sailed into Monterey Bay and claimed California for the United States. By August, an American military force had occupied Santa Fe, New Mexico, claiming it too for the United States.[32]

General Taylor and his troops won a major victory in September in Northern Mexico at Monterey. The following February, Taylor won an even more impressive victory at the battle of Buena Vista, despite being outnumbered four to one. The American military had a substantial technological advantage in the war, especially with artillery. The Mexican government was essentially bankrupt, with a shrinking economy and population. "The republic's financial weakness severely restricted its war-making potential; the Mexican army found it easier to raise troops than to feed, clothe, and pay them," Howe writes, and the army "resorted to preying upon local civilians." Yet these military victories were not enough to convince Mexican officials to enter into negotiations to end the war, which dragged on.[33]

Polk next tried a gamble, supporting the return of Santa Anna to Mexico in August, who was supposed to "seize power again and then conclude a treaty of peace along the lines Polk desired," Howe writes. To provide funding for the negotiations, the president requested a $2 million congressional appropriation. Polk hoped to keep the army of Mexico loyal to the government of Santa Anna by providing the $2 million, which could partially be used to pay the army, and to serve as a down payment for the purchase of California and New Mexico. But the plan backfired.[34]

David Wilmot of Pennsylvania, a Jacksonian Democrat, appended a proviso to the appropriation bill requiring that "neither slavery nor involuntary servitude shall ever exist" in any land acquired from Mexico. The wording had been drawn from Jefferson's Northwest Ordinance of 1787. Wilmot had supported the war with Mexico and other elements of Polk's policies. But Northern Democrats like Wilmot had become increasingly dissatisfied with Polk and Southern Democrats, beginning with the defeat of Van Buren for their party's nomination, followed by the failure to fight as hard for the settlement of the fifty-fourth parallel as the boundary of the Oregon Territory as Polk did for Texas. Wilentz writes that the proviso was not meant to promote the "equality of blacks, as favored by the Liberty Party and some of the hard-core antislavery Whigs." Rather, it was designed to promote the interests of working-class whites, "to preserve to free white labor a fair country," in Wilmot's own words, where "the sons of toil, of my own race and own color," could have the ability to be successful. By 1848, the idea of the importance of free labor would lead to the Free Soil Party, which would ultimately become the Republican Party of the 1850s. The Free Soil roots of these parties would ultimately reflect "an affirmation of the superiority of the social system of the North—a dynamic, expanding capitalist society, whose achievements and destiny were almost wholly the result of the dignity and opportunities which it offered the average laboring man," Eric Foner writes. For Whigs who supported the Free Soil movement, the wage worker was of central importance. Those who worked freely for wages had the opportunity to rise up the ranks and ultimately own their own business someday, which slaves could never do. Democrats tended to be less enamored of the idea of the wage laborer, dating back to Jefferson, believing those who were dependent on their employer "could never be truly free, nor could a dependent class constitute the basis of a republican government," historian James McPherson writes. But the way in which the market economy had expanded by the mid-1840s had caused some Northern Democrats to become supporters of "free labor," even if that labor was now largely made up of wage workers. The Wilmot Proviso also exposed a new line of attack, that the Slave Power was "at war with democracy itself," a force which "throttled free discussion of public matters" through measures like the gag rule, as Wilentz argues. It was a line of attack that would become ever more vociferous in the future, and be matched against Southern attempts, led by Calhoun, to divide politics along sectional lines.[35]

The Wilmot Proviso, as it came to be known, passed the House but then stalled in the Senate, where it was blocked by Southerners. The vote in the House was purely sectional and crossed party lines, with all Southern Whigs and most Northern Democrats supporting the bill. When Polk again asked for a $3 million appropriation at the end of 1846, the Senate debated the proviso but was unable to approve it, once again due to Southern opposition. The appropriation bill was finally passed without the Wilmot Proviso, but the sectional divisions it and the expansionist policies of the Polk administration exposed were just beginning. The appropriation also did Polk little good, because by the time it was authorized, Santa Anna had double-crossed him, "rallying the Mexican public to support the war effort," according to Howe, and thereby prolonging the war.[36]

Polk also had problems with both of his generals, Taylor and Winfield Scott. Zachary Taylor, also known as "Old Rough and Ready," was a career military man who had earned his reputation as an Indian fighter since the War of 1812. Polk believed he was a Whig with political ambitions, which caused the president to distrust him. In November 1846, Polk referred to Taylor as "ungrateful," "narrow minded," "bigoted," and "partisan." Since negotiations had failed, with Santa Anna now leading the war effort, the administration decided it needed to strike a blow at the very heart of the capital, Mexico City. "All U.S. strategists agreed, however, on the impracticality of an advance southward from Monterey to the City of Mexico across deserts and mountains," according to Howe, which precluded Taylor from leading the invasion.[37]

The task of leading the invasion to Mexico City fell to the senior general, Scott. Polk distrusted his political ambitions as well, and called Scott "arbitrary, proscriptive, and tyrannical." Scott, too, had served in the military since the War of 1812, becoming a brigadier general at the age of twenty-seven. He was also a Whig who was devoted to "the central government and the rule of law," Howe writes. Despite Polk's reservations about Scott, there really was no one else that could command such a complex military operation, which Scott helped to design. Gathering the American forces on an island off Veracruz in March 1847, Scott led an amphibious landing and siege that lasted three weeks. He and his army then fought their way to Mexico City, entering the city in September. The Mexican-American War ended with the Treaty of Guadalupe Hidalgo, which ceded "500,000 square miles, including the present states of California, Nevada, and Utah, all of New Mexico and Arizona except a strip of the south acquired five years later by the Gadsden Purchase, and part of Wyoming and Colorado," to the United States, as Potter describes it.[38]

Despite the success of Polk's war on the battlefield, politically the tide had turned against him. The midterm elections saw the Whigs narrowly take back the House of Representatives. As one political scientist framed it, the loss of the House "in the midst of a highly successful war [was] a clear measure of the moral protest which had developed against the war." Perhaps this should have been a lesson to future presidents, that wars of aggression and/or choice (like Iraq), or those where the United States is not directly defending its national interest (like Vietnam), can become quite unpopular. One young Whig congressman who was elected during 1846 called it "a war of conquest fought to catch votes," and would begin to grill the Polk administration on how the war began. His name was Abraham Lincoln.[39]

Source: http://umich.edu/~ac213/student_projects06/magsylje/timeline.html

Abraham Lincoln

Other than Jesus, more books have been written about Lincoln than any person in world history, according to Paul Tetreault, the director of Ford's Theatre, where Lincoln was assassinated in 1865. Writing something new or insightful about the sixteenth president is a humbling task when over fifteen thousand books have already been written about him. But Lincoln's role will prove to be pivotal in the coming of the Civil War, and by examining some of the most important recent biographies, I hope to provide the reader with some context to the role he played in the 1850s and to highlight his views on slavery, the American Constitution, and the importance of the Union.[40]

Abraham Lincoln thought his intellect came from his mother's side of the family. Nancy Hicks Lincoln was the illegitimate child of a man that Lincoln described as a "well-bred Virginia farmer or planter." His future law partner, William Herndon, quotes Lincoln as saying, "God bless my mother; all that I am or ever hope to be I owe to her," as much for the genes she transmitted to him as for her giving him life. Lincoln's relationship with his father, Thomas, was rocky. Some of this may have been due to his father's lack of intelligence. "He was an uneducated man, a plain unpretending plodding man," a neighbor recalled, but also honest, a description that would later be applied to his son. Thomas had a difficult time in life from the beginning. He was left out of any share of the family estate due to the law of primogeniture, which meant that his oldest brother received the family wealth upon the death of their father, leaving Thomas to make his own way in the world. Thomas moved the family from Kentucky, where Abraham was born in February 1809, to Indiana in 1816. Lincoln would later recall that the family moved "partly on account of slavery; but chiefly on account of the difficulty of land titles in Ky." Land surveys in Kentucky were often questionable and could lead to lawsuits. But both Thomas and Nancy were also opposed to slavery. They may well have shared the views of many nonslaveholders that lived in the border states who "viewed slavery less as a moral problem than as an institution that degraded white labor, created an unequal distribution of wealth and power, and made it impossible for nonslaveholding farmers to advance," according to Eric Foner. Lincoln would look back in 1864 and remark that he was "naturally anti-slavery. I cannot remember when I did not so think and feel."[41]

Perhaps Lincoln was antislavery due to the views of his parents. Or perhaps it was Lincoln's strained relationship with his father that caused the situation. Thomas always struggled in life due to his disinheritance, and his health seemed to deteriorate as Abraham grew older. In 1818, his mother died from what was known as milk sickness, and his father quickly remarried. While young Abe had a strong and loving relationship with his new stepmother, Sara Bush, the family now consisted of eight people who needed to be fed and clothed. While Sara had encouraged Abraham to pursue an education in the frontier schools of Indiana, where he loved to read and had an interest in history and biography, he was forced to quit school at fifteen to go to work. He would later say that "the aggregate of all his schooling did not amount to one year." The Lincolns were subsistence farmers, and as legend has it, the family lived in a log cabin that Thomas built. He "cleared only enough land for his family's use. Lack of ambition joined with insufficient access to a market for surplus goods to trap Thomas in relentless poverty," Goodwin writes. When Abraham became a teenager, Thomas "regularly hired his son out to work for other farmers in the vicinity, and by law he was entitled to everything the boy earned until he came of age," according to Donald. At a campaign event in the 1850s, Lincoln would say "I used to be a slave," a statement that one of his biographers attributes to his time working for his father without pay.[42]

It's not surprising that Lincoln would strike out on his own at the age of twenty-one. He had already made one journey on a flatboat to New Orleans a few years earlier, and in 1831, he was asked to make the trip once again. While on those trips, he may have first come in contact with slaves. His traveling companion on the second trip later recalled that in New Orleans "we saw negroes chained, maltreated, whipped and scourged. Lincoln saw it. His heart bled ... I can say knowingly that it was on this trip that he formed his opinion of slavery." His friend's memory may have been faulty, because Lincoln later recalled that he had left the trip in St. Louis and had not made it to New Orleans. Still, on an 1841 boat trip Lincoln would refer to how he was tormented by the sight of "ten or a dozen slaves, shackled together with irons."[43]

After returning from New Orleans, Lincoln settled in a small village called New Salem in Illinois, where he managed a store. He was already exhibiting the personality traits that would attract people to him, leading the local schoolmaster to mention his "kindness and honesty." Lincoln was a great storyteller, which endeared him to people. One of his political associates remarked that "several wrinkles would diverge from the inner corners of his eyes, and extend down and diagonally across his nose, his eyes would Sparkle, all terminating in an unrestrained Laugh in which every one present willing or unwilling were compelled to take part." He once told the local townspeople of the time Ethan Allen visited England. While attending a formal dinner, Allen excused himself to use the outhouse, where a picture of General Washington was prominently displayed. Upon his return to the dinner table, he was asked about the picture. Was it placed in an appropriate place, they inquired? According to Lincoln, Allen responded that indeed the picture was in an appropriate place, since "there is nothing that will make an Englishman Shit so quickly as the sight of Genl Washington."[44]

Lincoln was also popular among the young men of New Salem, especially a group known as the Clary's Grove gang. He won them over when he wrestled their leader to a draw, proving "that he had immense strength and courage," Donald writes. In 1834, he was asked to run for the state legislature, and politics became his calling. While he lost this election, he received 277 of 300 votes in New Salem. Two years later, he ran again and was elected to the state legislature, "having widened his set of acquaintances beyond New Salem," according to Goodwin. To prepare himself for the job, Lincoln began to study the law.[45]

The young Lincoln seemed to know his mind politically more than he knew himself personally at this age. "Always a Whig in politics," Lincoln would recall in 1859. He revered Henry Clay and was a strong supporter of the American System. He believed in an active government that would "do for a community of people, whatever they need to have done, but cannot do for themselves," including "building roads and public schools and providing relief to the poor," Foner writes. Perhaps this was another way for him to separate himself from a father who had always been a poor subsistence farmer. The Whigs promoted a market economy and supported the construction of internal improvements to link the market together. Lincoln would hold jobs as a "storekeeper, lawyer and surveyor—essential to the market economy," according to Foner. Because New Salem and then Springfield, where he moved in 1837, were small towns, isolated from the market, businesses often failed. Lincoln had experienced this firsthand when the store he worked at in New Salem went under and he found himself out of work. While in the Illinois legislature, Lincoln was one of the major supporters of building internal improvements in the state through the sale of bonds, a policy which fell victim to the Panic of 1837. By 1840, Illinois was forced to declare bankruptcy when it could no longer pay interest on its debt; yet Lincoln never viewed his support for internal improvements as an error. Likewise, he sided with the Whigs on the need for a national bank and a protective tariff, all designed to promote a capitalist economy.[46]

The young Lincoln was no abolitionist, despite his antislavery views. In 1837, he and a fellow Whig filed a protest against three resolutions that not only condemned the abolitionists but also "offered strong support for owners of slaves," according to Foner. In the protest, the two Whigs wrote that "slavery is founded on both injustice and bad policy; but that the promulgation of abolition doctrines tends rather to increase than abate the evils." Yet the federal government had no power to end slavery where it existed. Foner argues that Lincoln's protest foreshadowed his policies of the 1850s: "slavery was unjust; [and] northerners had an obligation to respect the constitutional compromise that protected the institution." Lincoln's protest of 1837 was clearly an act of political courage in the Illinois of that time, which was openly hostile to criticism of slavery. Still, Lincoln did not believe that blacks were equal to whites. In 1836, he had supported a resolution that voting "should be kept pure from contamination of colored voters." As with other politicians of the Jacksonian era, including his political hero, Henry Clay, Lincoln preferred to keep slavery off the political stage, since it was too divisive an issue. He would later support the idea of colonizing blacks once they were freed from slavery.[47]

Lincoln was also beginning to draw a similar lesson as Salmon Chase did about the danger of the Slave Power. He thought that the violence of the protests against abolitionism, especially the murder of Elijah Lovejoy, endangered "the liberty of all Americans," as Foner writes. In a speech he gave in 1838 to the Young Men's Lyceum of Springfield, Lincoln expressed his fear that mob violence undermined the rule of law, and he urged the nation to eschew emotions and instead follow "reason, cold, calculating, unimpassioned reason." In the speech, Lincoln subtly placed the blame for the mob violence that afflicted the country on slavery.[48]

While Lincoln may have urged that emotions be removed from politics, in his own personal life he struggled to act on the basis of reason. In 1842, Lincoln attacked the Illinois state auditor, James Shields, who would no longer accept notes from the Bank of Illinois for the payment of taxes. Lincoln portrayed him in the press as "a fool as well as a liar." The two men almost fought a duel over the incident, which caused Lincoln permanent embarrassment. His on-again, off-again courtship of Mary Todd was another example of Lincoln attempting to master his own emotions, which sometimes descended into a deep depression, even though outwardly he seemed in total control. Mary was the daughter of a prosperous Kentucky merchant who had "grown up in luxury, attended by family slaves and educated in the best private schools," Donald writes. They seemed to be "the exact reverse" of each other "physically, temperamentally, and emotionally." Yet they shared a love of books and poetry, and both were ambitious. Lincoln had told a friend that he hoped "to link his name with something that would redound to the interest of his fellow man." Mary thought she was "destined to be the wife of some future President." The two were engaged in late 1840, and then Lincoln abruptly broke off the engagement. The pain he caused Mary led him to fall into a deep depression. The two finally reconciled and were married at the end of November 1841.[49]

For those who believe that professional politicians cannot make great leaders, Lincoln serves as a counterpoint, since politics was his main craft. "His life was one of caucuses and conventions, party circulars and speeches, requests, recommendations, stratagems, schemes and ambitions," Richard Hofstadter writes of Lincoln. He was unafraid to get his hands dirty at his avocation and would sometimes bury his principles to achieve his goals. In his second run for the state legislature, he never mentioned his support for Clay's American System, so he could solicit the votes of subsistence farmers who were Democrats and not supportive of expanding the market economy. Illinois was not a Whig-friendly state, which limited Lincoln's ability to move upward to hold a state-wide office, such as governor.[50]

Marriage for Lincoln seems to have lessened his mood swings and particularly his periods of dark depression. While he and Mary fought as any couple did, with her the more demonstrative of the two, they did genuinely love each other. Still, Lincoln's personality seemed to be grounded in melancholy. His law partner, William Herndon, said of Lincoln: "His melancholy dript from him as he walked." Another said that "it was part of his nature and could no more be shaken off than he could part with his brains." Perhaps Lincoln's saving grace was his sense of humor, which he described as a way "to whistle off sadness." Goodwin maintains that Lincoln's melancholy "derived in large part from an acute sensitivity to the pains and injustices he perceived in the world." It gave Lincoln a wide degree of empathy and compassion for his fellow man, and perhaps lay at the core of his antislavery perspective. His ability to put himself in someone else's shoes contributed to his success in politics as well. The daughter of his private secretary thought that Lincoln's empathy "gave him the power to forecast with uncanny accuracy what his opponents were likely to do."[51]

In 1846, Lincoln finally made it onto the national stage, when he was elected to the House of Representatives. Delegates of the Whig Party chose their nominees through conventions, and Lincoln had previously helped to establish the concept of rotation in office. As he reminded everyone, it was now his turn to hold the seat from the Seventh Congressional District, and he was easily elected as the sole Whig representative in Congress from Illinois. As was typical at the time, he would not actually take his seat until December of 1847. He entered Congress just as the parties were beginning to split apart over the issue of the expansion of slavery to the new territories brought in from the Mexican War.[52]

As Lincoln entered the House, he was looking for issues the Whigs could use in the 1848 election. His first target was Polk's rationale for the Mexican War, which Democrats helped to spur by demanding that Congress support "the original justice of the war on the part of the President." Lincoln and his fellow Whigs brought forward a resolution demanding that the president provide "all the facts which go to establish whether the particular spot of soil on which the blood of our *citizens* was so shed, was, or was not, *our own soil*." He was obviously pointing to the disputed territory on which the war began and which Polk used to have Congress declare war. But Lincoln's attack backfired when neither Polk nor the rest of the House of Representatives responded to the resolution or to his speech defending it. Lincoln was attacked by the Democratic press and in public meetings back home, and only received lukewarm support from members of his own party. It would also cost him any chance to be reelected to Congress, since the war had been popular in Illinois.[53]

Free or Slave Labor

Both political parties had begun to weaken with the rise of sectional politics. The major economic issues that had divided the two parties during the years of the Jackson administration had begun to wane, partly due to the policies pursued by Polk. The president had been successful in reestablishing the Independent Treasury plan first introduced by Van Buren, and there was sufficient specie from grain exports in the wake of the Irish Potato Famine to ensure an adequate money supply. Polk's treasury secretary put forth a major reduction to the tariff, which narrowly passed Congress. It would prove damaging to Pennsylvania manufacturers and cost the Democrats votes in that state, but overall the debate on tariffs seemed to be over. Polk vetoed a measure for the dredging of rivers and harbors, which had the support of "Young America." The major policies that Whigs and Democrats had fought over were being replaced by disputes over the expansion of slavery, as reflected in the debates over the Wilmot Proviso.[54]

The recently completed congressional session that occurred over the winter of 1846–47 revealed the deep fissures over the Wilmot Proviso and the expansion of slavery in the new territories. The proposed solutions included the Wilmot Proviso at one end, and Calhoun and his Southern brethren at the other end who believed that the federal government had no power over slavery in the territories. Thomas Hart Benton likened the two positions to a pair of scissors. "Neither blade, by itself, would cut very effectively; but the two together could sever the bonds of Union." Others were looking for a compromise, attempting to impose the Missouri Compromise line, while still others proposed that those who occupied the new territory should be allowed to choose whether slavery should be allowed. None of these positions could garner a majority in both the House and the Senate. "Congress was beginning to lose its character as meeting place for working out problems and to become a cockpit in which rival groups could match their best fighters against one another," Potter writes. Finally, near the end of the session in August of 1848, the Congress approved a bill that Polk signed designating Oregon as a free territory. The president indicated that he approved the bill because Oregon was above the old Missouri Compromise line.[55]

The debates over the new territories were so intense and vociferous because they were about power, the power to decide which social and economic system, free or slave, would prevail in the United States. From the Northern perspective, expansionism had largely helped the South and the Slave Power. "Territorial acquisitions since the Revolution had added the slave states of Louisiana, Missouri, Arkansas, Florida, and Texas to the republic, while only Iowa, just admitted in 1846, had increased the ranks of the free states," McPherson writes. One Northern congressman argued that "everything has taken a Southern shape and been controlled by Southern caprice for years" and so the North must take a stand "that we are not to extend the institution of slavery as a result of the [Mexican] war."[56]

The Free Soil and free labor movements united a part of both the Northern Democrats and the "Conscience Whigs," those who were antislavery. The Conscience Whigs were opposed by the "Cotton Whigs," those who supported "cooperation with southern moderates" and who shared "close financial and political connections with the cotton growers of the South," according to James MacGregor Burns. The Free Soil and free labor movement were still a minority in 1848, but would gradually gain adherents in the North during the 1850s and lead to the creation of the Republican Party that was regional in nature. "The glorification of labor provided a much needed theme of unity" for the Republican Party, according to Foner.[57]

Free labor was wed to Free Soil for many Northern Democrats through westward expansion, which provided a safety valve for those that seemed stuck in low-wage jobs in the Northeast. It was in the small towns and farm communities of the old Northwest Territories where people could obtain property to farm or to open a new business, thereby opening opportunity for upward mobility. The Democrats had long supported low prices for western land "to afford every American citizen of enterprise the opportunity of securing an independent freehold," as Andrew Jackson framed it. The Whigs, for their part, had historically not been particularly interested in further territorial expansion of the United States. But they too favored upward mobility, "which assured that today's laborer would be tomorrow's capitalist," according to Foner. Support for upward mobility and a greater level of equality wed together disaffected Northern Democrats and Whigs.[58]

Those who formed the Republican Party in the 1850s would soon come to believe that the best method to deal with urban poverty in the eastern cities was through "westward migration of the poor," who would be "aided by a homestead act," which would essentially provide free land to those in need. "Republicans believed that the settlement of the western territories by free farmers would prove an effective barrier against the expansion of slavery," as well, Foner writes. Such a view put the Republicans on a collision course with the South.[59]

❧ ❧ ❧

Southerners were also concerned about the loss of power, and that the creation of new free states would endanger their way of life. The population of the North was increasing more rapidly than in the South, which meant that the number of representatives in the House was increasingly shifting power to the free states. As shown in the table below, in 1790, the non-slave states controlled about 55 percent of the representatives to the House, but this only translated to an additional five seats. By 1840, the non-slave states held 61 percent of the seats, and had fifty-two more representatives.

NUMBER OF SEATS IN THE HOUSE OF REPRESENTATIVES					
State	1790	1820	1830	1840	1850
North (no slavery)					
Connecticut	5	6	6	4	4
Illinois	0	1	3	7	9
Indiana	0	3	7	10	11
Iowa	0	0	0	0	2
Maine	0	7	8	7	6
Massachusetts	8	13	12	10	11
Michigan	0	0	0	3	4
New Hampshire	3	6	5	4	3
New Jersey	4	6	6	5	5
New York	6	34	40	34	33
Ohio	0	14	19	21	21
Pennsylvania	8	26	28	24	25
Rhode Island	1	2	2	2	2
Vermont	0	5	5	4	3
Wisconsin	0	0	0	0	3
Total	35	123	141	135	142
% of Total	54%	58%	59%	61%	61%
South (slavery)					
Alabama	0	3	5	7	7
Arkansas	0	0	0	1	2
Delaware	1	1	1	1	1
Florida	0	0	0	0	1
Georgia	3	7	9	8	8
Kentucky	0	12	13	10	10

Louisiana	0	3	3	4	4
Maryland	6	9	8	6	6
Mississippi	0	1	2	4	5
Missouri	0	1	2	5	7
North Carolina	5	13	13	9	8
South Carolina	5	9	9	7	6
Tennessee	0	9	13	11	10
Texas	0	0	0	0	2
Virginia	10	22	21	15	13
Total	30	90	99	88	90
% of Total	46%	42%	41%	39%	39%
Grand Total	**65**	**213**	**240**	**223**	**232**
Source: Office of the Historian US House of Representatives					

To maintain control over national legislation, or at least to block the most egregious bills like the Wilmot Proviso, the South needed to maintain a balance in the Senate. As of 1847, there were fifteen slave states and fourteen free states. While President Polk may have thought that slavery could never exist in the deserts of the New Mexico Territory, nor in California, other Southerners saw it differently. "Cotton was already grown in river valleys in New Mexico," McPherson writes, and a Southern convention thought that "California is peculiarly adapted for slave labor." One Georgia newspaper wrote that introducing slavery would "secure to the South the balance of power in the Confederacy." Southerners were also irate at what they perceived as Northern attacks upon their way of life. One Virginian saw the Wilmot Proviso as saying "in effect to the Southern man, Avaunt! you are not my equal and hence are to be excluded as carrying a moral taint." As we have seen, Southerners were long past the point of thinking that slavery was an evil that would someday need to be ended, and now believed it was "a great moral, social, and political blessing—a blessing to the slave, and a blessing to the master." The Southern way of life was superior to that of Northerners, who were "vulgar, contemptible," and money mad. Should the Wilmot Proviso, or any similar legislation pass, the addition of so many new free states would allow the North to "ride over us rough shod," and endanger slavery where it already existed.[60]

Southerners were also critical of the free labor system of the North, calling wage laborers "the slave of the *community*." Some argued that slavery actually promoted equality for white people, "liberating them from the low menial jobs like factory labor and domestic service performed by wage laborers in the North," Foner writes. This perspective may also have played on the social superiority that non-slave-owning whites felt toward black slaves. Since colonial times, slave owners had elicited the support of non-slave-owners by creating a "shared identity in the psychology of race that held every white man as superior to every black," according to Alan Taylor. This may have contributed to the support that slaveholders received from the yeomen of the South, who were by far the larger group, composing two-thirds of Southern households in 1860. There was also an element of self-interest involved for those who did not own slaves, since "some hired or borrowed slaves. Some took their cotton to wealthier neighbors, who ginned and sold it for them," according to historian Adam Rothman. Many yeomen also hoped to own slaves one day, a form of Southern upward mobility.[61] None of this is to say that the North's position was moral and the South's immoral over the issue of slavery. While slavery was at the heart of the sectional dispute, the North's opposition to the expansion of slavery was rooted in self-interest, in expanding their own economic system and protecting free labor. It was not grounded in moral opposition to slavery, especially where it already existed, other than among the abolitionists like Garrison, who were clearly in the minority. One needs to look no further than the prejudicial way free blacks were treated in the North to see this.

The Election of 1848

Given how seriously each side reacted to the Wilmot Proviso and the question of slavery in the new territories added from the Mexican War, it is surprising that the 1848 election was not fought on this battle-ground. But the nominees from the two major parties attempted to say as little as possible on the subject, especially the Whig candidate.

Lincoln and other Whigs supported Zachary Taylor for the Whig nomination for president. Taylor emerged as the party nominee on the fourth ballot at the party convention in June of 1848. He had bested Henry Clay, who had sealed his fate in November of 1847, when he announced he would not take any land from Mexico except for the undisputed portion of Texas. By February of 1848, the Treaty of Guadalupe Hidalgo made this position a nonstarter. Taylor was a lifelong military man, a Southerner, and a slave owner. But he held no policy positions, and the Whigs decided to run without a party platform. Lincoln convinced him to adopt the traditional Whig view of a weak executive, with power lodged in Congress. "Were I president, I should desire the legislation of the country to rest with Congress, uninfluenced by the executive," Lincoln argued, a position that Taylor adopted. Taylor, the military hero, was an odd choice for a party that largely opposed the Mexican War, but the Whigs wanted to win and felt that selecting the general inoculated them for their opposition to the war. Taylor's lack of a party platform meant he did not have to take a position on the issue of slavery in the newly acquired territories, and his support for a weak executive allowed him to imply he would defer any decision to the Congress.[62]

Polk was true to his word and decided to not seek reelection, since he had promised to serve only one term. The Democrats instead nominated Lewis Cass over Secretary of State James Buchanan. Buchanan's position on the extension of slavery was that the Missouri Compromise line should continue to be used, which would cut California in two. Cass had been Jackson's secretary of war and had a played an important role in implementing the policy of Indian removal. He was also a strong supporter of further expansion of the boundaries of the United States, to include British Columbia and other parts of Mexico. On the issue of slavery in the new territories, he supported the concept of "popular sovereignty." Settlers would be allowed to decide the fate of slavery for themselves. But this position contained its own ambiguity, for neither Cass nor the other supporters of this policy were willing to clarify whether the question of slavery would be decided when a territory was first settled, or only after applying for statehood. "Clearly this was an important distinction, since a ban on slavery in the territorial phase would obviously doom its prospects at the time of statehood," historian John Ashworth writes. The reverse would also be true.[63]

Many people were unhappy with the candidates of both major parties. The Southern followers of John Calhoun had attempted to amend the Democratic platform to state that neither Congress nor a territorial legislature could bar slavery, but this was handily defeated. Even more importantly, a number of antislavery Whigs (the Conscience Whigs) and Democrats decided to leave their party and join up with the members of the Liberty Party to form the new Free Soil Party. They selected Martin van Buren to run for president, with Charles Francis Adams (John Quincy Adams's son) as the vice-presidential candidate. Van Buren, who had attempted in 1836 and again in 1840 to placate the Southern slaveholders, was undergoing a late-life conversion, and now supported limiting slavery in the new territories.

He would be labeled a traitor and hypocrite by his enemies. Liberty men like Salmon Chase had realized after 1844 that they needed to expand their party by attracting antislavery men from the two major parties. The party slogan they emerged with was "Free Soil, Free Speech, Free Labor, and Free Men!" and Chase was allowed to write a party platform that proposed divorcing the federal government from slavery and a commitment to opposing any further expansion of slavery, essentially implementing the Wilmot Proviso.[64]

While there was dissatisfaction among political elites with the position of the two parties on the slavery issue, the rank-and-file voters largely stayed with their own party in the election. Wilentz estimates that 98 percent of Whigs stuck with their party in 1848, while the Democrats retained a somewhat lower percentage of 85 percent. The Free Soil Party garnered approximately three hundred thousand votes, a substantial increase from the Liberty Party total in 1844. But they did not win any states, which meant they received no votes in the electoral college. It was a disappointing result for the antislavery forces. Adams perhaps summed it up best when he wrote that "the people of the Free States are not yet roused so fully as they should be to the necessity of sustaining their principles." Taylor and Cass split the states evenly, but Taylor won the popular vote and more large states for an electoral college victory, 163–127. The center held, but just barely.[65]

General Taylor, a man who owned slaves, would turn out to have a strong and surprising position on the expansion of slavery, as we shall see in the next chapter.

Endnotes

1   Howe, p. 658–660; Richards, p. 165–166.

2   Remini, *Jackson III*, p. 352–353; Howe, p. 666–668; Richards, p. 166–167.

3   Richards, p. 167; Wilentz, *Rise*, p. 435; Traub, p. 438.

4   Howe, p. 671–672.

5   Howe, p. 675–677; Wilentz, *Rise*, p. 566; Peterson, p. 334.

6   Howe, p. 679–680; Wilentz, *Rise*, p. 566–567.

7   Remini, *Clay*, p. 639–640; Howe, p. 686.

8   Wilentz, *Rise*, p. 562–564.

9   Wilentz, *Rise*, p. 562–564; Widmer, p. 149.

10 Howe, p. 682–683; Remini, *Jackson III*, p. 500–501; Wilentz, *Rise*, p. 570.

11 Howe, p. 683–684; John Bicknell, *America 1844: Religious Fervor, Westward Expansion, and the Presidential Election That Transformed the Nation* (Chicago, 2015), p. 94.

12 Howe, p. 680.

13 John Seigenthaler, *James K. Polk* (New York, 2003), p. 11–18; Howe, p. 706.

14 Seigenthaler, p. 18–25.

15 Seigenthaler, p. 29–38 and p. 45–52.

16 Seigenthaler, p. 56–59 and p. 64–69.

17 Steven Hahn, *A Nation without Border: The United States and Its World in an Age of Civil Wars* (New York, 2016), p. 117–122; Howe, p. 708.

18 Howe, p. 710–714.

19 Howe, p. 714–717; Hahn, p. 122.

20 Howe, p. 710; Peterson, p. 333; Hanh, p. 115–122.

21 Howe, p. 710; population information was retrieved July 7, 2018, from https://en.wikipedia.org/wiki/History_of_California_before_1900.

22 Daniels, p. 124–132; Bicknell, p. 135–136.

23 Remini, *Clay*, p. 653–655.

24 Goodwin, p. 29–34 and p. 69–71.

25 Goodwin, p. 82–85.

26 Howe, p. 688–690.

27 Wilentz, *Rise*, p. 575; Howe, p. 698–699.

28 The quotes from Polk's Inaugural Address were retrieved July 14, 2018, from http://avalon.law.yale.edu/19th_century/polk.asp; Howe, p. 707–708.

29 Howe, p. 718–721; for the internal debates within the cabinet over whether to go to war with Great Britain over the boundary of the Oregon territory and Polk's belligerency, see Seigenthaler, p. 122–128; see also David M. Potter, *Division and the*

Stresses of Reunion: 1845–1876 (Glenview, 1973), p. 30, who argues that Polk "did not want two wars at one time."

30 Burns, p. 460–461; Potter, p. 29–30; Howe, p. 735–739.

31 Wilentz, *Rise*, p. 582–585; Polk's war message was retrieved July 16, 2018, from https://www.mtholyoke.edu/acad/intrel/polkswar.htm; Howe, p. 739.

32 Potter, *Division*, p. 41; Howe, p. 754–759.

33 Potter, *Division*, p. 41; Howe, p. 746–749.

34 Howe, p. 766.

35 Wilentz, *Rise*, p. 594–599; Potter, *Impending Crisis*, p. 24–26; Foner, *Free Soil*, p. 11; James McPherson, *Battle Cry of Freedom: The Civil War Era* (Oxford, 1988), p. 23.

36 Howe, p. 766–768.

37 Seigenthaler, p.133; Howe, p. 774.

38 Howe, p. 778–790; Wilentz, *Rise*, p. 603; Potter, *Division*, p. 43; McPherson, p. 50.

39 Howe, p. 762 and p. 770; Seigenthaler, p. 144.

40 For the number of books written about Lincoln and the reference to Paul Tetreault, see the following article retrieved on August 2, 2018, from https://www.npr.org/2012/02/20/147062501/forget-lincoln-logs-a-tower-of-books-to-honor-abe; the two major works I have relied on in this section were also used in the introduction of this book: Donald, *Lincoln*, and Goodwin, *Team of Rivals*. Also helpful was Eric Foner, *The Fiery Trial: Abraham Lincoln and American Slavery* (New York, 2010).

41 Donald, p. 17–24; Foner, *Fiery Trial*, p. 6.

42 Donald, p. 26–33; Goodwin, p. 47; Sidney Blumenthal, *A Self-Made Man: The Political Life of Abraham Lincoln, 1809-1849* (New York, 2016), Kindle location 171.

43 Donald, p. 34–37; Foner, *The Fiery Trial*, p. 8–11.

44 Donald, p. 39–40; Goodwin, p. 88.

45 Donald, p. 40–53; Goodwin, p. 88.

46 Foner, *The Fiery Trial*, p. 33–41.

47 This section has been largely based on and influenced by Foner, *The Fiery Trial*, especially p. 24–32 and p. 41.

48 Foner, *The Fiery Trial*, p. 26–28; Donald, p. 82.

49 Donald, p. 84–93; Goodwin, p. 94–95.

50 Hofstadter, *American Political Tradition*, p. 96; Donald, p. 52; Foner, p. 33.

51 Donald, p. 94 and p. 107–110, describes the Lincoln's early married life; on the issue of Lincoln's melancholy, Goodwin's discussion on p. 102–104 was particularly helpful and insightful.

52 Donald, p. 115; Goodwin, p. 106–108.

53 Donald, p. 123–125; Goodwin, p. 121.

54 Howe, p. 828–829.

55 Potter, *Impending Crisis*, p. 61 and 67–76.

56 McPherson, p. 51–57, has the most useful summary of the contrasting views of North and South and why the Wilmot Proviso had elicited such a dramatic response from each side. I have summarized those views in this and the following paragraph.

57 The entire Free Soil and free labor argument is covered more extensively in the following: McPherson, p. 23–26; Foner, *Free Soil*, chapter 1 and especially p. 18–19; and Foner, *American Freedom*, p. 58–68. The quote from Burns is on p. 468.

58 Foner, *Free Soil*, p. 20.

59 Foner, *Free Soil*, p, 27–28; Foner, *American Freedom*, p. 63.

60 McPherson, p. 51–57.

61 Foner, *American Freedom*, p. 63; Alan Taylor, *American Colonies: The Settling of North America* (New York, 2001), p. 156–157; Adam Rothman, "The Slave Power in the United States, 1783-1865," in Steve Fraser and Gary Gerstle, eds., *Ruling America: A History of Wealth and Power in a Democracy* (Cambridge, 2005), p. 76.

62 Donald, p. 127–128; Howe, p. 828–829.

63 Howe, p. 831; Ashworth, p. 50–51.

64 Ashworth, p. 52–53; Foner, *Free Soil*, p. 124–125; Widmer, p. 153–155.

65 Wilentz, *Rise*, p. 628–631 and footnote 68 on p. 920.

CHAPTER 13

Politics Unravels in the 1850s

The question of slavery in the territories has been avoided. It has not been settled.

—SALMON P. CHASE, IN RESPONSE TO THE COMPROMISE OF 1850

The opening of a new decade would see an attempt to settle the major issues splitting the North and the South, especially the issue of slavery in the new territories added from the Mexican War. Yet, while the Compromise of 1850 initially appeared to successfully settle that issue, it was only a temporary reprieve, which dissolved when new disputes over slavery's expansion erupted over, of all things, building a transcontinental railroad. The outcome would result in the repeal of the Missouri Compromise, spark violence in both the US Senate and in far off Kansas, and lead to the final destruction of the teetering second political party system.

The Compromise of 1850

In December 1849, the new Congress met in an atmosphere of crisis, with North and South splitting apart over the issue of slavery in California and New Mexico. Even before Congress met in October, the Southern states were being called to a convention in Nashville in the spring of 1850 to discuss their options should the Wilmot Proviso pass. Once the House met, they struggled to elect a Speaker, with ten newly elected Free Soil members holding the balance of power in a tightly divided chamber. During the Speaker debates, one Southern representative announced: "I am for disunion" should "you seek to drive us from the territories of California and New Mexico." Violence pervaded the House, with fistfights breaking out. After three weeks, no one could command majority support to be elected Speaker. Howell Cobb of Georgia, a Democrat, was finally elected by a plurality of the House on the sixty-second ballot.[1]

As rancor consumed the House in January of 1850, President Taylor sent his message to Congress. It turned out the slave-owning Southerner was opposed to the expansion of slavery in the territories. The territorial status and statehood for California had become an acute problem, since gold had been discovered at Sutter's Mill in the Sierra Nevada foothills in 1848, and the population exploded the following year as men headed west to seek their fortunes. California formed a state constitution that year which barred slavery, and then petitioned to enter the Union. In his message, Taylor proposed to allow both California and New Mexico to enter the Union as free states, bypassing the territorial phase, ignoring the talk of disunion emanating from the South. The president intended to follow Andrew Jackson's lead and stand against any attempt at secession by the South. When confronted by two Southern politicians, the general threatened to "personally lead an army to enforce the laws and hang any traitors he caught."[2]

The very real threat of disunion hung in the air. Without some compromise, many feared that the Union was doomed, and that civil war could erupt. Into the breach stepped the Great Compromiser, Henry Clay, who had just returned to the Senate. A few months shy of seventy-three, Clay was not in good health, suffering from tuberculosis. As always, his motives were complicated by his ambition, since he was hoping to wrest back control of the Whig Party. But he also intended "to accomplish something for the good of the country during the little time he had left upon the earth," as Daniel Webster would later say. By January 21, 1850, he had formulated his plan and went to Webster to gain his support. The two had never been close, and at times they were rivals, but Webster offered his "general support" at least until he could study the proposals further.[3]

Clay's Compromise of 1850 had something for everybody in a good faith attempt to settle the issues then under dispute. California would enter the Union as a free state, which the Free Soil representatives wanted. Both New Mexico and the newly settled Mormon Territory of Utah would decide for themselves if they wanted slavery banned, based on popular sovereignty. To assuage the abolitionists, the slave trade, but not slavery, would be banned in Washington, DC. The bill resolved a boundary dispute between Texas and New Mexico largely in a manner favorable to New Mexico, and in return the United States would assume the debts Texas had amassed while an independent republic. Finally, a strengthened Fugitive Slave Law would be implemented in order "to enforce more effectively the constitutional provisions" that dealt with this issue. Many Northern states had adopted laws to protect fugitive slaves, and an 1842 Supreme Court decision found that states were not required to assist in enforcing the Fugitive Slave Law. The 1850 provision was meant to strengthen the ability of slaveholders to reclaim their property, and stripped slaves of any ability to testify in their own defense, "to habeas corpus, and to a jury trial," according to McPherson. Of all the proposals, this one would elicit substantial controversy.[4]

❧ ❧ ❧

Clay's bill prompted a round of Senate speeches among both supporters and opponents. First up was John C. Calhoun, who had been sick with pneumonia and was near death. Calhoun was helped into the Senate chamber on March 4 and had James Mason of Virginia deliver his speech. Calhoun spoke of the powerful cords "which bind these states together in one common Union," and how "continued agitation of the slave question" had begun to snap those bonds, leaving only force left to hold them together. Calhoun had given up any hope that the Union could be preserved and placed the blame squarely on the North. The "equilibrium between the two sections in the Government ... had been destroyed," by the North blocking any further expansion of slavery into the new territories, Calhoun maintained. The only answer was a constitutional amendment to restore the sectional equilibrium. While Calhoun did not specify what that amendment should be, most historians believe he was referring to the creation of a dual presidency, with the North and the South each holding one of the offices and having a veto power over national legislation. Calhoun would be dead by the end of the month.[5]

Three days later, Daniel Webster took to the Senate floor and delivered an impassioned appeal for compromise. "I wish to speak today, not as a Massachusetts man, nor as a Northern man, but as an American ... I speak today for the preservation of the Union." Even though he had supported the Wilmot Proviso, he now urged his fellow Northerners to reject what amounted to "a taunt or reproach" to the South. Webster thought it made no sense to split the Union apart over the issue of slavery, especially in the New Mexico Territory, where it could not naturally exist. "I would not take pains uselessly to reaffirm an ordinance of nature, not to re-enact the will of God." Webster also condemned Northerners for obstructing the fugitive slave laws, saying, "the South is right, and the North is wrong," on this issue, which inflamed those opposed to slavery.[6]

On March 11, William Seward provided a response from those who opposed the compromise. It was Seward's initial Senate speech since his election in 1848. Seward lacked great oratorical skills, and he "spoke in a voice so low that it seemed he was talking to himself," Goodwin writes. Yet the power of what he said mesmerized the Senate chamber. Seward argued that the compromise should be rejected. Although the Constitution protected slavery where it existed, there was "a higher law than the Constitution which regulates our authority over" the new territories. The question was "shall we establish human bondage" in those areas, or follow the higher law dictated by God, that slavery was wrong and should eventually be eliminated. Seward's speech placed him in the forefront of the antislavery movement and tied "the egalitarian Declaration of Independence, with its invocation of the Creator," to the Constitution, according to Wilentz.[7]

Seward's higher law speech inflamed the Southerners, who called it "monstrous and diabolical." With the threat of disunion hanging over the capital, relations between individual legislators turned violent. During the debate over the speakership, two congressmen had engaged in a shoving match. In April, Thomas Hart Benton (who as a young man had fought a duel with Andrew Jackson) lunged at Henry Foote, who proceeded to pull a gun on him. Foote was a typical bully, "who fought legislative battles by insult, belittling, and threatening his foes," Freeman writes. Even though Benton was from Missouri, where slavery was legal, he opposed any further expansion of the peculiar institution, which put him on a collision course with Foote of Mississippi. As Freeman has shown, Southerners had in the past used threats and intimidation to force Northerners to go along with them. But by 1850, Northern men were no longer willing to be bullied. "By standing up to slave-state men, they were defending the interests and honor of the North, just as bullying Southerners championed the South," according to Freeman.[8]

In such an environment, finding common ground on the compromise bills was difficult at best. In April, a Select Committee of Thirteen was formed, with Clay as its chair. The committee decided that the best approach was to combine the individual bills into one overall measure, known as the Omnibus bill. "Clay was counting on the Omnibus as a device to induce congressmen to vote for items they did not favor by linking such items with others they did favor," Potter writes. The Omnibus did help to forestall any action from the Nashville Convention, which was meeting to consider whether secession should be pursued, with most Southern representatives unwilling to support such a position and holding out hope that the compromise would prevail. But the bill faced two other major hurdles. One was President Taylor, who felt slighted that his proposals had not been given a fair hearing, and so the threat of a veto from him was possible. The second was that the number of Southern Whigs and Northern Democrats who still supported compromise made up less than one-third of each chamber.[9]

Fate stepped in on July 9, when Taylor died of gastroenteritis after gorging himself during the July 4 celebration. The president had already increased tensions in June when he supported New Mexico's admission as a free state after they held a convention and adopted a constitution, despite the fact that the boundary dispute had not yet been settled with Texas. The governor of Texas threatened to use force to uphold their boundary claims, and Taylor did the same. His death ended the threat of the United States and Texas fighting a war against one another, since the new president, Millard Fillmore, of New York "tilted almost as far South as the southern President Taylor had tilted North," McPherson writes. Fillmore placed the New Mexican application for statehood on hold and firmly supported the Omnibus. But Fillmore's support was not enough, since there simply was not a majority to push the Omnibus bill through in its present form. By July 31, the bill was dead. Clay, in bad health, was spent and left Washington. It fell to a young Senator Stephen A. Douglas to save the compromise.[10]

❧ ❧ ❧

Douglas was a short man with a large head, which earned him the nickname the Little Giant. He was born in western Vermont in 1813, an area distinct from most of federalist New England in that they supported Thomas Jefferson. Stephen's father died when he was two months old, and he was largely raised by his uncle, who was "rather a hard man." The young Douglas loved history and current affairs and was infatuated with Andrew Jackson. When he was seventeen, his mother remarried, and the family moved to New York State.[11]

It was in the Finger Lakes area that Douglas received a classical education, after which he studied law. But he found the requirements to earn a law license in New York too onerous; so, at the age of twenty he headed west, settling in Jackson, Illinois, so named for Douglas's hero. A man could easily become a lawyer on the frontier, and so despite his lack of training or knowledge, Douglas quickly received a license to practice law. He also became involved in Illinois politics, utilizing his great skills as a debater to defend Jackson's bank policies. "Political ambition stirred within him, and he soon began the hard-driving, relentless pursuit of political power that would dominate the rest of his life," his biographer Robert W. Johannsen writes.[12]

Douglas became active in Democratic Party politics and was instrumental in implementing political conventions at the county- and state-wide levels as a means for selecting candidates for office. In 1836, Douglas was elected to the lower house of the Illinois legislature, where he served with Abraham Lincoln. His was a Jacksonian voice in the legislature, where he supported state funding of internal improvements but was opposed to any state role in banking. He also voted in support of the anti-abolitionist petitions that Lincoln had opposed.[13]

In the shadow of the 1837 depression, Douglas ran for Congress against Lincoln's then law partner, John Stuart. He lost the 1838 race in an extremely close vote, and then threw himself into campaigning for Van Buren in 1840. Douglas was a Democrat to his core, believing in "political equality, freedom of thought, speech," and in limited government at the national level. He saw the states as "the pillars of the Republic." As the 1840 race unfolded, Douglas and Lincoln, among others, engaged in a series of debates. Both men "display[ed] the form that would characterize their more celebrated encounter at a later time," Johannsen writes. Douglas was a particularly skilled debater by this time, with an uncanny ability to recall facts and figures.[14]

With the Whigs sweeping to victory in 1840, Douglas was appointed to the Illinois Supreme Court, largely due to "his importance to the Democratic Party" rather than any "recognition of a superior legal talent." In late 1842, Douglas narrowly lost an election to the US Senate but went on to win a seat in the House in 1843. By this point, he had a clearly defined political philosophy that was consistent with Democratic orthodoxy. He believed in majority rule, but that the rights of the minority should be protected, as Jefferson had espoused in his first inaugural. Douglas believed in a bottom-up approach to power, much as Jefferson did. He was opposed to laws that would increase inequality, which was why he objected to the Second

Bank of the United States. Douglas was an ardent expansionist who supported the annexation of Texas and Oregon. Ultimately, Douglas's support of majority rule would make him the great defender of popular sovereignty as the way to resolve the issue of slavery in the new territories.[15]

❧ ❧ ❧

Douglas worked on his own compromise proposal, similar to Clay's, with one major difference: Texas would be split into two states as a way to balance the addition of California as a free state. His proposal elicited little support, and so he set about trying to pass Clay's Omnibus. He spoke after Seward finished, and attempted to steer a middle course. He had already rejected abolitionism in an 1848 speech and he also thought the Free Soil movement would endanger the Union. But Douglas also rejected the Southern position that had been espoused by Calhoun, arguing that "the territories belong to the United States as one people." He also warned that the North would "consent to no amendment of the Constitution which shall be presented under a threat to dissolve the Union." For Douglas, the only answer lay in popular sovereignty. As part of his 1850 speech, he referred to it as "that great Democratic principle, that it is wiser and better to leave each community to determine and regulate its own local and domestic affairs in its own way." Douglas maintained that a reliance on popular sovereignty would actually lead to "the expansion of the area of freedom," as Johannsen writes, as the public rejected slavery in the new territories.[16]

Once Clay's Omnibus bill failed, Douglas set out to pass the measures one at a time. Whereas Clay thought he could cobble together a majority for the entire package, Douglas knew this was impossible.

Instead, he saw "there were strong sectional blocs, in some cases Northern, in others southern, in favor of each of the measures separately, and there was a bloc in favor of compromise," Potter writes. Douglas was able to pull together the compromise bloc with either a Northern or Southern bloc in order to get each bill passed. While the approach worked to get the bills to Fillmore's desk, where he signed the last one on September 17, the compromise was more like a truce, since neither side agreed to the other's terms. Given this, the Compromise of 1850 would not hold.[17]

The nation celebrated the preservation of the Union in the aftermath of Fillmore signing the bills that made up the Compromise of 1850. In Washington, DC, crowds gathered and proclaimed "The Union is Saved," as alcohol flowed freely. President Fillmore declared that "a final settlement" had been achieved over the fate of slavery in the territories, while Daniel Webster proclaimed that "what ever party may prevail ... the Union stands firm." But the Compromise of 1850 was built on sand, with the sea of controversy ready to wash away the settlement.[18]

Some in the North were unhappy with the new fugitive slave provisions, especially abolitionists and members of the Free Soil Party. Those who harbored a fugitive slave or assisted with escape, as many did through the Underground Railroad, were subject to a fine and six months in prison. The law lacked any due process provisions for blacks who were captured. Slaveholders could bring a claim before a federal commissioner, appointed by the courts, who would hear the case. Blacks had no "legal power to prove their freedom," as McPherson writes, and were not allowed to testify on their own behalf and had no habeas corpus rights. The commissioners had a built-in bias against the accused runaway, since they received ten dollars for each claim they found as valid but only five dollars for invalid claims, a provision of the law that abolitionists viewed as a bribe. The bias that was built into the law resulted in 332 fugitives returned to their masters compared to only 11 being set free during the 1850s. Numerous cases of mistaken identity occurred, since slave catchers cared little if they found the right person. Since the law allowed federal marshals to deputize the public to assist with the capture of runaway slaves, Northerners could now be forced by the federal government to assist in implementing the act. "It could hardly have been designed to arouse greater opposition in the North," Foner writes.[19]

The Fugitive Slave Act had numerous consequences, especially in the early years of its implementation. It led to panic among escaped slaves and even free blacks, who feared they would be kidnapped, and many fled to Canada. Abolitionists attempted to thwart enforcement of the law, especially in the upper North and in Boston, the home of Garrison's *Liberator*. Frederick Douglass and other free blacks began to abandon their commitment to nonviolence to prevent the return of fugitive slaves. "The only way to make the Fugitive Slave Law a dead letter is to make a half a dozen or more dead kidnappers," Douglass said in late 1850. "Liberty is worth fighting for," another free black said.[20]

Yet, while the law was unpopular in the North, it appears the great majority of the public was willing to accept it for the sake of the preservation of the Union. This was especially true among the more conservative elements of society. In New York City, a group of merchants and bankers held a public meeting in 1850 and issued a statement in support of enforcement of the Fugitive Slave Act. While the act was difficult to enforce in some parts of the North, like New

Bedford, Massachusetts, where Douglass had settled, "there is no convincing evidence that a preponderant majority in the North were prepared to violate or nullify the law," Potter writes.[21]

Still, there is a difference between being unwilling to violate a law and accepting the law as a good thing. The success of Harriet Beecher Stowe's novel *Uncle Tom's Cabin* illustrates the growing Northern aversion to slavery. Stowe was the daughter of Lyman Beecher and had been exposed to the cruelty of slavery while living in Cincinnati, just across the river from the slave state of Kentucky. The Fugitive Slave Law motivated her to write *Uncle Tom's Cabin*, which was serialized over a nine-month period in an antislavery newspaper (*National Era*), and then appeared as a book, which sold over three hundred thousand copies during its first year of publication. The book broke through "the racism of white America as no one ... had done," Wilentz writes, making the case that "slavery was a national sin" that needed to be eradicated.[22]

❦ ❦ ❦

Southerners, too, were not completely satisfied with the Compromise of 1850, especially the inclusion of California as a free state. There were pockets of Southern resistance among those who were known as the Fire Eaters. "They believed the South must ultimately choose between the Federal Union and the institution of slavery," according to Potter. But in the aftermath of the Compromise of 1850, Southern Unionists now had the upper hand. At the Nashville Convention in November of 1850, only fifty-nine delegates arrived representing just seven of the fourteen slave states. Unsurprisingly, support for secession was strongest in South Carolina and Georgia, but they could not realistically act alone. Instead, Northern enforcement of the Fugitive

Slave Act became the key test of whether the compromise would hold, even among Southern Unionists. As the Georgia Platform declared in December of 1850, "It is the deliberate opinion of this Convention that upon a faithful execution of the *Fugitive Slave Law* ... depends the preservation of our much beloved Union." The Georgia Platform reflected the position of most Southerners. Ominously, the Georgia Platform also announced future resistance to any federal law that eliminated slavery in Washington, DC, or that refused to "admit as a state any territory ... because of the existence of slavery."[23]

Resistance to the Fugitive Slave Law began to wane in the North by 1851. But it still cost Millard Fillmore the Whig nomination for president in 1852, with antislavery Northern Whigs backing General Winfield Scott, who finally came out on top on the fifty-third ballot when a handful of Southern moderates backed him. This caused many Southern Whigs to abandon Scott during the campaign. The Democrats were split at their convention as well, and it took them forty-nine ballots before Franklin Pierce of New Hampshire emerged with the nomination. Pierce was popular in the South, a Northern politician considered safe on the issue of slavery, and he swept to victory. Scott won only four states and forty-two electoral votes, and the Whigs were also routed in the House. It would be the last election that they would compete in nationally.[24]

Pierce's large victory in the electoral college masked his weakness in the North. He barely won the popular vote with 50.9 percent of the total, and he actually received 26,000 fewer votes in the North than the combined total for Scott and the Free Soil candidate, John P. Hale. Pierce, who was born in 1804 in New Hampshire, was the son of Benjamin Pierce, who had been involved in the American Revolution and been elected governor of the state. By the time he was twenty-four, young Pierce was already in the New Hampshire

legislature, and he went on to serve in both the House of Representatives and the Senate. He was a strong supporter of Andrew Jackson,
and no friend to abolitionists or antislavery politicians. A veteran of
the Mexican-American War, he and the Democrats promised their
full support and backing to the Compromise of 1850.[25]

Pierce was a committed expansionist, just as Polk had been. He
was also "one of the so-called 'doughface' Northern Democrats who
gave political cover to slaveholders and their violent supporters in the
1850s," according to Wilentz. His cabinet included Jefferson Davis
of Mississippi as secretary of war, who would, of course, go on to be
the president of the Confederate States of America.[26]

Jefferson Davis

Jefferson Davis's ancestors had been in America since the early 1700s,
when his great-grandfather Evan emigrated to America from Wales.
Jefferson Davis, named for the third president of the United States,
was born in 1808 in Kentucky, the youngest of ten children. His father
moved the family to Mississippi when Davis was two, where he owned
a farm of about four hundred acres and eleven slaves. The farm, known
as Poplar Grove, produced cotton for cash and other crops for consumption, but the Davises were never rich. His education began at an
early age and included time at a Roman Catholic preparatory school.
He attended Transylvania University in Lexington, Kentucky, where
"he received an excellent classical education in ancient languages,
history, and science," according to one of his biographers, William J.
Cooper Jr. When his father died in 1823, his older brother was able
to get Jefferson an appointment to West Point from then Secretary of
War John C. Calhoun. Davis's time at West Point was not particularly
happy for him, as he struggled with a curriculum heavily weighted to
math and engineering, although he eventually completed his course of

study in 1828. Despite his struggles at the academy, he felt important for attending a nationally respected institution, and that those who attended it "are perhaps more free from purely sectional prejudices, and more national in their feelings," than those who did not attend West Point.[27]

Davis spent the next six years in the army, serving in the Northwest frontier. In 1832, he fell in love with Knox Taylor, the daughter of his commanding officer, then Colonel Zachary Taylor. The two were married in June of 1834, just before Davis left the military. His brother Joseph, who had gotten Jefferson into West Point, now owned a highly successful plantation and a large number of slaves. He gave the young couple land to start their own plantation. Unfortunately, after obtaining the land, both Jefferson and Knox contracted malaria in the unhealthful conditions that existed in the Mississippi lowlands, and Knox died soon thereafter. Davis, in deep mourning, continued to establish his own plantation, with Joseph once again helping by providing the money needed to acquire slaves. The two brothers became extremely close and shared in reading books from the large library that Joseph maintained. Their conversations often turned to politics, with both being Democrats who "saw Jackson's Democratic party as a bastion of the state's rights political philosophy they associated with their political saint, Thomas Jefferson." Now thirty-five, Jefferson Davis launched what he hoped would be a political career. Unfortunately, the district he ran in for a seat in the state legislature was largely Whig country, and he lost his first race in 1843.[28]

Bitten by the political bug, Davis went to work in 1844 to help elect Polk as president. It was an experience that helped him develop his political skills, including his ability to deliver a speech. During this period, he once again fell in love and married his second wife Varina. The following July, his work on behalf of Polk led the Mississippi

Democratic Convention to select Davis to run for the House of Representatives. He ran on the typical Democratic issues, including strict construction of the Constitution, limited government, and opposition to high tariffs and a central bank. By this time Texas, whose annexation he supported, was no longer an issue since Polk had already begun that process. In November of 1845, Davis was elected to the House, where he supported Polk's decision to launch a war with Mexico.[29]

Despite the opposition of his wife, Davis decided to rejoin the army to fight in the Mexican-American War. Elected as the regimental commander for the First Mississippi Regiment, Colonel Davis was soon united with his former father-in-law, General Taylor. Davis and his regiment saw action at both Monterey and Buena Vista, where he and his men acquitted themselves well. At Buena Vista, Davis was shot in the "right foot near the ankle, driving shards of brass from his shattered spur and bits of sock into his flesh," Cooper writes. Still, Davis refused to leave the field of battle until it was won. Davis would walk on crutches for the next two years and have occasional problems from the wound for the rest of his life. His war exploits helped to enhance his political ambitions and gave him the status of a war hero.[30]

After returning home from the war, he was quickly elected to the Senate. Davis would become one of the most able defenders of slavery and the rights of Southerners to extend slavery into the new territories that had been obtained from Mexico, including Oregon. He believed that Congress had no authority over slavery in the territories and that the peculiar institution was "sanctioned in the Bible, authorized, regulated, and recognized from Genesis to Revelation." Davis generally opposed the Compromise of 1850, only voting for the fugitive slave provisions. When Franklin Pierce was elected president in 1852, Davis joined his cabinet.[31]

The Kansas-Nebraska Debacle

Pierce unsuccessfully tried to acquire Cuba from Spain, which Southerners had been interested in to balance the inclusion of new free states. In 1848, Senator Davis had said "Cuba must be ours," as a way to "increase the number of slaveholding constituencies." Pierce did succeed in acquiring roughly thirty thousand square miles of land from Mexico that established the Southern boundary of both Arizona and New Mexico. The Gadsden Purchase, so called because James Gadsden negotiated its terms, "was important because ... it provided a feasible route for a railroad across the southern part of the United States," Potter writes. Whether a railroad across the middle of the country should follow a northern or a southern route would soon lead to another controversy that would feature Stephen Douglas on one side and Abraham Lincoln on the other, and that would once again rend the ties of Union.[32]

Railroads and Deals

Pierce's election marked a transition in national politics. He was young, only forty-seven, to that point the youngest president to be elected. A handsome man, he was not particularly smart nor decisive. Pierce would provide only weak leadership, one of a string of mediocre presidents that followed Andrew Jackson before Lincoln was finally elected in 1860. In a 2018 poll of political scientists, the presidents from Van Buren to James Buchanan rank at or near the bottom, with only Polk in the top twenty. In Congress, the men who had dominated politics since the War of 1812 were also gone. Calhoun had died shortly after the debate over the Compromise of 1850, and both Clay and Webster passed away in 1852. "Unlike the men they displaced, whose national perspective had been born of long service, the new Senators were inclined to follow their own personal and sectional dictates," one historian of the period writes.[33]

Stephen Douglas was one of these new leaders, but he had a broader vision than many of those who served with him. He believed that America's future was tied to further westward expansion, a view that mirrored Jefferson's empire of liberty. "An important element of Douglas's program was his dream of connecting the Mississippi valley with the Pacific by a railroad that could be integrated with the valley's river system, the Great Lakes, and the eastern railroads to form a massive transportation network," his biographer Johannsen writes. Douglas wanted that railroad to follow a Northern route, beginning in Chicago and ending at the Pacific Ocean, most likely in San Francisco. In order to achieve this goal, the vast Nebraska Territory would need to be organized. But to achieve that result, Douglas would need the support of Southerners, who preferred a route that would go through New Orleans.[34]

The price for that support would ultimately be the repeal of the Missouri Compromise. The Nebraska Territory was fully above the 36°30′ line, and if the Missouri Compromise remained in place, no new slave states could be created within the area. Douglas was initially opposed to such a move, knowing it would "raise a hell of a storm in the North," and he attempted to finesse the issue in the first Nebraska bill he offered in January of 1854, which simply mimicked the language in the Compromise of 1850 that a territory could be added as a state "with or without slavery, as their constituents may prescribe." But Southerners knew that "if the Missouri Compromise prevailed during the territorial stage, slavery could never gain a foothold," McPherson writes. David R. Atchison of Missouri, who was president pro tempore of the Senate and an ardent defender of slavery, threatened he would rather see Nebraska "sink in hell" than be a free territory, and he was supported by numerous other Southern senators. Douglas ultimately revised his Nebraska bill, renamed the Kansas-Nebraska Act, that explicitly repealed the Missouri Compromise and created one free state (Nebraska) and one potential slave state (Kansas).[35]

Douglas and the Southerners first needed to get the president's support. Pierce and a majority of his cabinet members preferred to let the Supreme Court decide the fate of slavery in the territories. Only the two Southern members of the president's cabinet thought otherwise. Davis had long believed the Missouri Compromise to be unconstitutional, and he arranged for a meeting between the senators and the president on a Sunday afternoon, unusual since Pierce preferred to avoid doing business on the sabbath. After meeting with the senators, Pierce changed his mind and came out in support of the revised Kansas-Nebraska Act, fearing a loss of the Southern support that had put him in the White House. Pierce went so far as to make support of the act a "a test of party orthodoxy."[36]

The reaction of the antislavery forces was swift and certain. The Free Soil Democrats, now going by the name Independent Democrats, issued an appeal on January 19, 1854, drafted and signed by six prominent leaders, including Salmon Chase of Ohio and Charles Sumner, the former Conscience Whig and antislavery leader from Massachusetts. The appeal, which ran in the *National Era*, a weekly paper published in Washington, DC, denounced the Kansas-Nebraska Act as "a gross violation of a sacred pledge" to keep slavery out of any territory north of the Missouri Compromise line. The authors saw the act as a "criminal betrayal of precious rights," and it set off a firestorm of protests in the North as the debate in Congress unfolded. The elimination of the Missouri Compromise was denounced in numerous public meetings, and nine free-state legislatures denounced the bill. It was the beginning of the end for the National Democratic Party, transforming it "into the party of the slaveholders, backed by a sharply reduced number of northern appeasers," according to Wilentz.[37]

Douglas, who was portrayed as a Judas by the Free Soilers, never thought that slavery could take root in the Nebraska Territory. In 1850, he had said, "I think I am safe in assuming that each of these will be free territories and free states, whether Congress shall prohibit slavery or not." In 1854, he wrote to a newspaper in New Hampshire that repeal of the Missouri Compromise was of "no practical importance [since] the laws of climate" would keep slavery out, and if that failed, then popular sovereignty would surely do the trick. But what Douglas failed to take into account was the moral wrong of slavery and how the politics of the issue had shifted so much given the rise of the abolitionists and the antislavery forces that were opposed to any further extension of slavery. Douglas believed that the will of the majority was always right, a very Jeffersonian view and a bottom-up approach to how authority should flow in a society. Yet he failed to uphold the second element of Jefferson's formula that majority will "must be reasonable" and protect the rights of the minority. While Jefferson was surely not referring to black slaves in that passage, it is also true that 1854 was not 1801, and many people now thought that using popular sovereignty to expand slavery was simply wrong. Douglas was attempting to achieve a political compromise on a matter of economic interest to his state (the building of a railroad) and was willing to accept the extension of slavery to achieve it, even if this was not his goal. He also placed great value on the preservation of the Union. "Douglas cared more about the Union than about the eradication of slavery and would never push the slavery issue to [a] point where it imposed too much strain upon the Union," Potter writes. Those who opposed slavery thought that while the Union was important, the extension of slavery was too high a cost. "The Union was formed to establish justice and secure the blessing of liberty. When it fails to accomplish these ends it will be worthless," the Independent Democrats had written in the appeal.[38]

Douglas was able to use the considerable skills he had honed as a legislator to push the Kansas-Nebraska bill through the Senate in March of 1854 on a vote of 41–17. Chase, who had assumed leadership of the forces opposed to the bill, exposed the folly of popular sovereignty "which allows one portion of the people to enslave another portion." The bill now went to the House, where its passage was far from assured. At one point during debate in the House, a fistfight erupted. The press took sides, with both pro- and anti-Nebraska newspapers egging on the congressmen. New York reporter James Pike was at the forefront of an ever-expanding press coverage that encouraged Northern politicians to take a stand against the Slaver Power. "Just as the nation's slavery problem intensified because of western expansion, dangerous words and violent actions in the halls of Congress gained greater reach and influence, stoking regional passions in the process," Freeman writes. Still, Douglas and his forces, supported by the Pierce administration and some bullying of their own, were able to push the bill through the House on a very close vote of 113–100. Pierce then signed the bill. While Douglas got his victory, his purpose in pursuing the bill, the building of a transcontinental railroad, would not begin until after the Civil War began.[39]

❦ ❦ ❦

It was not only the Democrats who were split apart by the Nebraska legislation, but it also marked the death knell of the Whig Party. "The Whig Party has been killed off effectually by that miserable

Nebraska business," one senator from the North opined and would thereafter want nothing to do with "southern Whigs," who felt much the same way. Out of the ruins of the Whig Party the modern Republican Party would eventually emerge, and would contest elections in the fall campaign of 1854. Pike, who wrote for the *New York Tribune*, would presciently see that the debate over the Nebraska legislation "inaugurates the era of geographical division of political parties. It draws the line between North and South. It pits face to face the two opposing forces of slavery and freedom."[40]

Abraham Lincoln, though still a Whig, began to campaign for candidates who opposed the Nebraska legislation. Lincoln said that the Kansas-Nebraska Act had stirred him "as he had never been before." He had supported the Compromise of 1850, which had been spearheaded by his political hero Henry Clay, as a "peaceful solution" to the problem of slavery. After his one term in Congress, Lincoln had not sought office again, although he remained active in the Whig Party. "The fight to stem the spread of slavery would become the great purpose Lincoln had been seeking," Goodwin writes. On October 4, 1854, Lincoln got his chance to state his views when he spoke at the State Fair in Springfield. Douglas had spoken the previous day in defense of the Nebraska act and the principle upon which it was constructed, popular sovereignty. He then sat in the front row to watch Lincoln's rebuttal, which went on for three hours. The two men bantered back and forth, which "helped establish the equality of the challenger and the challenged," in the words of Lincoln biographer David Herbert Donald. Lincoln gave the same speech in response to Douglas a few weeks later in Peoria.[41]

Richard Hofstadter has argued that Lincoln was attempting to find "a formula to reconcile the two opposing points of view held by the great number of white people in the North," that they were opposed to slavery as a moral wrong but "that Negroes must not be given political and social equality." Hofstadter calls Lincoln "among the world's great political propogandists" due to his ability to straddle these two points of view, which, if true, would mean Lincoln was not sincere in his positions. But a more straightforward motive can also be found: that Lincoln believed slavery was wrong, but blacks were not the equal of whites, which put him in the mainstream in the North of the 1850s. Lincoln grounded his argument in much the same terms as Chase had, that slavery was "a violation of the nation's founding principles as enunciated in the Declaration of Independence," as Eric Foner writes, but also at odds with Jefferson's handiwork in the Northwest Ordinance that excluded slavery from the area.[42]

From the perspective of the early twenty-first century, Lincoln's view of the inferiority of blacks was certainly racist. Yet as we have seen, Lincoln was also a practical politician, one who was looking to revive his political career. As Sean Wilentz has observed, Lincoln "was a shrewd and calculating creature of politics, and he achieved historical greatness in his later years because of, and not despite, his political skills." He also had limited contact with African Americans, although while president he would later host important black leaders as well as Frederick Douglass at the White House. Still, "he never became a full-fledged racial egalitarian," according to Foner.[43]

Lincoln opened both his speech in Springfield and in Peoria denouncing the expansion of slavery into the Nebraska Territory as a "zeal for the spread of slavery," which he hated "because of the monstrous injustice of slavery itself." It was the strongest language he had used so far denouncing slavery. Yet he did not attack the "Southern people. They are just what we would be in their situation," Lincoln argued. As for slavery where it existed, he admitted he did not know what the answer was, although his "first impulse would be to free all of the slaves, and send them to Liberia," a proposal he knew was impossible. If not, then "free them, and make them politically and socially, our equals? My own feelings will not admit of this; and if mine would, we well know that those of the great mass of white people will not." This was Lincoln straddling those two great opposing points of view that Hofstadter had recognized.[44]

The highlight in Lincoln's speeches came when he directly took on Douglas's position on popular sovereignty. "The doctrine of self government is right—absolutely and eternally right—but it has no just application" to the issue of slavery, Lincoln said. The reason is that the "negro is a man" and "there CAN be no MORAL RIGHT in the enslaving of one man by another." Lincoln too believed that authority in a society should flow from the people upward, but he also believed there were limits to how far public opinion should dictate policy, especially on a moral issue such as slavery. Lincoln argued that the founders had "rejected" the morality of slavery and were forced to make an accommodation with it because "they found the institution existing among us." The Framers of the Constitution "forbore to so much as mention the word 'slave' or 'slavery' in the whole instrument," and the "earliest Congress, under the Constitution took the same view of slavery. They hedged and hemmed it in to the narrowest limits of necessity." Lincoln believed that Douglas and the Southern politicians he had made cause with were violating the very principles of the Declaration of Independence "that all men are created equal" and were instead converting it into a statement "that for SOME men to enslave OTHERS is a 'sacred right of self-government.'" Lincoln had now found his cause, and he would emerge "as his state's most eloquent opponent of the expansion of slavery," eventually using this as a springboard to reach the White House. Douglas would admit to a friend he did not want to debate "the most difficult and dangerous opponent that I have ever met." Yet debate they would in the 1858 election in Illinois for the US Senate seat.[45]

The Rise of the Republican Party

As we have seen, John C. Calhoun, in his final Senate speech in 1850 regarding Clay's compromise, had stated "the cords which bind the States together in one common Union" were powerful and that "disunion must be the work of time." Calhoun warned that "agitation of the slavery question has snapped" some of the most important cords, and that eventually "nothing will be left to hold the States together except force." It was a prophetic statement from a man who had done so much in his later life to protect the South's interest in slavery and to drive a wedge between the sections.[46]

Political parties were one of those cords that tied the Union together. Both Democrats and Whigs had actively recruited party members from the North and the South, which they needed to compete nationally for votes and power. In fact, since the 1790s political parties had been an essential component in organizing the nation's political life and had helped spread democracy. Potter writes that in twelve of the sixteen "presidential elections held up to 1852, the person elected had been victorious both in the free states and in the slave states; one section had not imposed its choices upon the other." But now both parties were beginning to lose strength, and their ability to compete across the entire nation was being destroyed. Pierce, who won the 1852 election, had not won the popular vote in the free states, and the split in the political parties would be felt acutely in the 1854 midterm elections.[47]

The dissolution of the political parties did not happen all at once;

they had been weakening for some time. Some Northern Democrats had been unhappy with their Southern brethren since Van Buren was denied the party's nomination in 1844. The Free Soil movement had arisen during the Mexican-American War, further weakening the Northern Democratic ties to the South over whether the new territories obtained from the war should be free or slave. While the Compromise of 1850 had tamped down some of this dissatisfaction, the Nebraska legislation reopened these wounds. Part of the South's demand for repeal of the Missouri Compromise was designed to impose Southern control over the Democratic Party. Free Soil Democrats especially resented the Pierce administration for making support for the Kansas-Nebraska Act a test of party loyalty. In addition to slavery, disputes over "internal improvements, temperance, nativism, and the perennial disputes over patronage—were slowly tearing the party apart," Foner writes. Still, it would take another two years before the split would be fully seen with the election of 1856.[48]

Slavery, temperance, and nativism were also rupturing the foundations of the Whig Party. As discussed in chapter 8, Jacksonians tended to exclude racial minorities from their definition of who could be an American. Many, but not all Whigs excluded newly arriving immigrants, especially the Irish, who tended to settle in Northern cities and were attracted to the Democratic Party. The party of Jefferson, which was more sympathetic to the common (white) man, was a natural home for the newly arrived immigrants. Nativism was spurred by the large number of immigrants that had entered the country, beginning in the 1840s. But the 1850s, by far, saw the largest expansion in immigrants to the United States, with 2.6 million arriving. This compared to 1.7 million in the 1840s, a decade that had triggered a previous nativist revolt. Over one-third of the immigrants in the 1850s were Irish Catholic, largely driven from their homes by the potato famine.[49]

Francis Fukuyama, in his book *Identity*, writes that "a modern market economy required something like nationalism and identity based on nation as well." He quotes social anthropologist Ernest Gellner, who wrote that a new type of society was ushered in "based on a high-powered technology and the expectancy of sustained growth, which requires a mobile division of labour, and sustained, frequent and precise communications between strangers." Part of the success of the market economy in the United States was derived from those new immigrants who could fill the jobs being created. But capitalism and modernization can also bring a sense of alienation as people from small, rural areas or villages, where people know each other and share a common culture, begin to migrate to larger urban areas full of different types of people. This process of alienation was well underway in the United States in the 1840s and 1850s and may have been exacerbated by the massive influx of immigrants who came with different cultures and languages (in the case of the Germans). Some people feared that the surge of new immigrants was creating a society of strangers who did not share American values of liberty and democracy, and they feared this threatened national unity. Nativists pointed to the rise of crime and the increasing use of government services to support their claim that the newly arrived were a threat to the American way of life. Many also doubted that the new immigrants would assimilate into America. The United States was, in fact, experiencing the growing pains that would eventually create a new type of multi-ethnic society, one based on universal ideas rather than purely on race, religion, or culture. The appeal of nativism would repeat itself multiple times in the United States, typically during periods when a substantial number of new immigrants entered the country. Each new group would find much the same reception, whether they were Irish, German, Chinese, Japanese, or Hispanic. Yet the ability of each new group to assimilate has been remarkable, as the work of Stanford's Ran Abramitzky has shown. "Lessons from the Age of Mass Migration [1850–1913] suggest that fears immigrants can't fit into American society are misplaced," he argues. "The evidence is clear that assimilation is real and measurable." Part of this assimilation may well hinge on a "a uniform national language, and a state-sponsored educational system to promote national culture," as Fukuyama argues.[50]

Still, during the 1850s Catholicism contributed to the rise of the anti-immigrant movement. The Catholic Church under Pope Pius IX, who was elected in 1846 at the age of fifty-four, was at war with the modern world. "Here was a nineteenth-century leader denying any validity to freedom of conscience, of speech, or of government," Garry Wills has written, and who had stood opposed to the liberalizing movements in Europe in the late 1840s. The archbishop of New York may also have contributed to the rise of nativism when he proclaimed that the church's mission was "to convert the world,—including the inhabitants of the United States," to Catholicism. There had long been opposition to the Catholic Church among American Protestants, who saw the church as a threat to republicanism. By 1854, a blending of nativism and antislavery helped give rise to a secret organization formally known as the American Party. Their members were required, when asked about the party, to respond, "I know nothing." The name stuck, and the Know-Nothing movement was born. As Sean Wilentz has written, "distrust of foreigners, and especially Catholics, had, of course been a feature of American conservative thought dating back to the Federalists and the alien and sedition laws." As we saw in chapter 1, conservatives tend to distrust outsiders, as a threat to one's own group.[51]

In the election of 1854, the Know-Nothings elected 121 members to the House of Representatives. While nativism was on the rise, so too was the antislavery movement, fed by opposition to the Kansas-Nebraska Act. Numerous antislavery parties began to form, none more important than the Republican Party, which was born in Ripon, Wisconsin, prior to the passage of the Nebraska legislation. It combined both Northern Democrats and former Whigs and was named in honor of Jefferson's original Republican Party. A total of 115 antislavery members were elected to the House in 1854 as either Republicans or Whigs. The antislavery members also had a connection to the Know-Nothings. "Since the Know Nothings were partly a secret order, it was possible for a person to be a Know Nothing and a Republican," Potter writes, and that is exactly what happened in the 1854 election. Into this stew of nativism and antislavery, which grew out of "the same cultural soil of evangelical Protestantism," was added the movement to advance temperance, which had been given new life when Maine passed a prohibition law in 1851. Party politics were in great disarray as the elections of 1854 to 1855 were completed, and it was unclear whether the Know-Nothings or the Republican Party would emerge as the dominant party in the North.[52]

The Know-Nothing movement had some things working against it. For one thing, some of the most important politicians emerging in the 1850s opposed nativism. Lincoln, who was still nominally a Whig but would soon join the Republicans, said: "As a nation, we began by declaring that *'all men are created equal.'* We now read it 'all men are created equal, *except negroes.'*... When the Know-Nothings get control, it will read 'all men are created equal, except negroes, *and foreigners, and catholics.*'" Seward, too, had opposed nativism while governor of New York, pushing to assist in the education of Catholics as a means to foster assimilation. Salmon Chase pushed legislation in 1854 "allowing immigrants to benefit from the homestead act," Foner writes. The Homestead Act was a way to advance the Free

Soil movement by allowing people to obtain land inexpensively or for free, a proposal that later passed into law during the Civil War. Lincoln, Seward, and Chase, who emerged as the most important Republican Party leaders, held more liberal attitudes in their view toward outsiders.[53]

The nativists were also attempting to meld together a national party that included both Northern and Southern members opposed to immigration, but they had trouble agreeing among themselves, especially over the issue of the expansion of slavery. In June of 1855, the Know-Nothing national convention met, and the Southern delegates attempted to push through a plank of the platform essentially supporting the Kansas-Nebraska Act. This caused many of the Northern delegates who were antislavery to abandon the party due to its inability to confront the expansion of slavery. In the words of one observer, the nativist party then "gradually melted away" due to its attempt to ignore the slavery issue.[54]

Two other issues also contributed to the demise of the nativist movement and the rise of the Republican Party. One was the reduction in immigration in the years after 1855, "which fell to less than half of the level it had attained in the first half of the decade," according to McPherson. The other was the increasing violence that was occurring in Kansas.[55]

Bloody Kansas

The threat of violence and bullying that underlay the Southern honor code, which had in most cases been implicit, now became explicit. Northern antislavery politicians began to fight back over who would control Kansas. In May of 1854, William Seward announced: "We will engage in competition for the virgin soil of Kansas, and God give victory to the side which is stronger in numbers as it is in right." The competition for control of Kansas would prove that popular sovereignty was not an answer for the problem of the extension of slavery, as two armed camps emerged. In Massachusetts, the New England Emigrant Society was formed to promote the occupation of Kansas by people committed to oppose slavery. Senator Atchison of Missouri, who had pressured Douglas into overturning the Missouri Compromise, helped to organize the pro-slavery forces, who were committed "to assist in removing any and all emigrants who go there [Kansas]," essentially by any means necessary, including the use of force.[56]

In October of 1854, the territorial governor ordered a census in anticipation of the election of a territorial legislature to be held the following March. The census showed there were 2,905 eligible voters in Kansas at the time. Yet when the election was held, 6,307 votes were cast. In the intervening months, a large number of "border ruffians" from Missouri had crossed over the border to vote, casting over 5,000 votes for pro-slavery candidates. As a result of the fraudulent election, which the pro-slavery side may well have won anyway, thirty-six of the thirty-nine legislators favored slavery in Kansas. The three Free Soil legislators, who were joined by other antislavery men when the governor ordered new elections in about one-third of the Districts, were soon evicted from the legislature. "The lawmakers then passed a set of laws that incorporated Missouri's slave code and inflicted heavy penalties against anyone who spoke or wrote against slavery," according to Wilentz.[57]

The antislavery side had no intention of following the dictates of what they considered a fraudulently elected government. Beginning in the summer of 1855, they began to plan for an alternative government which would eventually be elected and hold its first meeting in Topeka by March of 1856. The Free Soilers also began to arm themselves, accepting shipments of Sharp breechloading rifles from their supporters back in Massachusetts. The stage was now set for the two sides to face off against each other with weapons.[58]

A series of violent incidents then occurred over a four-day period in May that connected events in Kansas with the United States Congress. A pro-slavery force of around eight hundred men laid siege to the town of Lawrence on May 21, the headquarters of the antislavery forces. Since the pro-slavery forces were led by a federal marshal, the Free Soil men did not resist. Homes were burned, shops were plundered, and the printing presses of the town's two newspapers destroyed. The Free State Hotel lay in ruins by the time the siege was over. One day later, on May 22, Senator Charles Sumner of Massachusetts was caned by Representative Preston Brooks of South Carolina while he sat at his desk in the United States Senate. The caning came in retaliation for a speech Sumner had delivered over a two-day period between May 19 and May 20 called "The Crime against Kansas." The speech, which was particularly incendiary, had equated Senator Andrew Butler (Brooks's cousin), with "Don Quixote who had chosen a mistress ... the harlot slavery." It was a continuation of the violence that had been increasingly infecting Congress dating back to the time of Andrew Jackson. Congress had become a "bullpen for sectional combat, with armed clusters of Northerners and Southerners defending their interests with fists and weapons as well as legislation," Joanne Freeman writes. The North reacted with horror to the attack, with one journalist writing in the *New York Evening Post*, "Are we too slaves, slaves for life, a target for their brutal blows, when we do not comport ourselves to please them?" Meanwhile Southerners stood in support of Butler's action, with the *Richmond Enquirer* writing that the "vulgar Abolitionists in the Senate ... must be lashed into submission," a fitting description for how slaves were treated by Southerners.[59]

The third incident occurred on May 24, when a man named John Brown led a ghastly attack in Kansas with broadswords that ended with five men dead, many of them dismembered. Brown, who was from New England, had followed his sons to Kansas in 1855. In the aftermath of the sack of Lawrence, he thought that "something must be done to show these barbarians that we, too, have rights." John Brown's massacre touched off further violence in Kansas.[60]

Such was the state of American politics as the 1856 election season began.

The Election of 1856

As violence pervaded Kansas and the halls of Congress, the Know-Nothing Party was attempting the impossible, to build a national party that included both the North and the South. They had support in both the Border South and in Southern cities where immigrants had settled. Now calling themselves the American Party, they met in June of 1855 to establish a party platform. Many Northern delegates left the convention unhappy when the American Party passed a platform supporting the Kansas-Nebraska Act, but then returned for the party nominating convention in February of 1856. When the American Party nominated Millard Fillmore, the former president, as their candidate, men from New England and the Northwest bolted once again and formed their own North American Party. Fillmore, although a New Yorker, was a Southern sympathizer who had signed the 1850 compromise and vigorously enforced the Fugitive Slave Law, making him unacceptable to many in the North.[61]

The North American Party competed with the Republicans to see which would emerge as the antislavery alternative in the North. But the Republicans were more astute than the nativists, and through a series of maneuvers ended up incorporating the North Americans into their party. The most significant maneuver was the selection of presidential candidates for both parties, with the North American Party acting first. Nathaniel P. Banks from Massachusetts, who had been selected Speaker of the House in the current Congress after two months of wrangling, allowed himself to be nominated as the North American Party candidate. He had no intention of running for president, and in fact he planned to withdraw from consideration once the Republicans met to select their candidate. This would leave "the North Americans little choice but to endorse the Republican nominee," according to McPherson.[62]

On June 18, two days after Banks was nominated by the North Americans, the Republicans met in their convention. The Republican platform attempted to balance the various contending factions, including nativists and immigrants, by focusing on the slavery issue. The opening of the document read as follows: "this Convention of Delegates ... are opposed to the repeal of the Missouri Compromise; to the policy of the present Administration, to the extension of slavery into Free Territory; in favor of admission of Kansas as a Free State." The platform also paid homage to the Declaration of Independence and to "restoring the action of the Federal Government to the principles of Washington and Jefferson," a statement designed to make the Republicans the true heirs of the founders, but also ironic in that both were Southern slave owners.[63]

Even more important to the Republicans was the selection of a presidential candidate. Both Seward and Chase were unacceptable to the nativists, and so the convention turned to John C. Frémont, the western explorer known as the "Pathfinder." Frémont had been an army officer in the 1840s and had spent a substantial amount of time exploring the western United States, including the Oregon Trail, the Rocky Mountains, and the Pacific Northwest. He was also one of the leaders of the Bear Flag Rebellion in California in 1847. Frémont was married to Jessie Benton, the daughter of Thomas Hart Benton, and they had been married in the Catholic Church, which should have made him anathema to the nativists. Yet his marriage into the Benton family made him appealing to former Democrats, due to Benton's Jacksonian credentials. He had also not been recently involved in politics and did not carry the stigma that attached to Chase and Seward. Frémont had supported a free California and ran on a slogan of "Free Speech, Free Press, Free Men, Free Labor, Free Territory, and Frémont." Banks, true to his word, withdrew as the North American Party nominee and threw his support to Frémont, leaving party members little choice but to back the Republican.[64]

President Pierce and Stephen Douglas arrived at the Democratic Convention in Cincinnati in June as the perceived frontrunners, with substantial Southern support. Yet neither man had enough votes to lock up the nomination. Finally, on the seventeenth ballot James Buchanan emerged as the Democratic nominee. The sixty-five-year-old Buchanan was born in 1791 in Pennsylvania to an affluent family. Originally a federalist, Buchanan had become a follower of Andrew Jackson, who appointed him as American ambassador to Russia in 1831. Buchanan served in both the House and the Senate, and had been secretary of state under Polk, with whom he had a rather tempestuous relationship, given Buchanan's own political ambitions. The nominee was selected by the Democrats more as a safe pick, "unobjectionable to the North and South, and therefore a potential winner," as Wilentz frames him.[65]

The Democrats threw charges of disunion at the Republicans and used racism to stoke fear in the North of racial equality for blacks. Republicans responded by claiming it was the South that posed a threat to the Union by their threats of secession, and by pointing out that the Slave Power was a threat to democracy. One former Democrat bemoaned that the Slave Power was "aggressively insolent" and "seeks to extend its sway by fire & sword." Republicans answered the racial charges leveled against them by claiming they did not intend "to elevate the African race to complete equality with the white man," which caused abolitionists like Garrison to then denounce the Republicans.[66]

The election came down to a few key Northern states, as shown in the chart below, with Buchanan emerging the winner.

	POPULAR VOTE			ELECTORAL VOTES		
STATE	Buchanan	Frémont	Fillmore	Buchanan	Frémont	Fillmore
NORTH (no slavery)						
California	53,342	20,704	36,195	4	0	0
Connecticut	34,997	42,717	2,615	0	6	0
Illinois	105,528	96,275	37,531	11	0	0
Indiana	118,670	94,375	22,386	13	0	0
Iowa	37,568	45,073	9,669	0	4	0
Maine	39,140	67,279	3,270	0	8	0
Massachusetts	39,244	108,172	19,626	0	13	0
Michigan	52,139	71,762	1,660	0	6	0
New Hampshire	31,891	37,473	410	0	5	0
New Jersey	46,943	28,338	24,115	7	0	0
New York	195,878	276,004	124,604	0	35	0
Ohio	170,874	187,497	28,126	0	23	0
Pennsylvania	230,686	147,286	82,189	27	0	0
Rhode Island	6,680	11,467	1,675	0	4	0
Vermont	10,577	39,561	545	0	5	0
Wisconsin	52,843	66,090	579		5	0
Total	1,227,000	1,340,073	395,195	62	114	0
% of Total	41%	45%	13%			

South *(slavery)*						
South Carolina				8	0	0
Virginia	90,083	Not on ballot	60,150	15	0	0
Georgia	56,581	Not on ballot	42,439	10	0	0
North Carolina	48,243	Not on ballot	36,720	10	0	0
Arkansas	21,910	Not on ballot	10,732	4	0	0
Delaware	8,004	20	6,275	3	0	0
Florida	6,358	Not on ballot	4,833	3	0	0
Alabama	46,739	Not on ballot	28,552	9	0	0
Kentucky	74,642	Not on ballot	67,416	12	0	0
Louisiana	22,164	Not on ballot	20,709	6	0	0
Maryland	39,123	285	47,452	0	0	8
Mississippi	35,456	Not on ballot	24,191	7	0	0
Missouri	57,964	Not on ballot	48,522	9	0	0
Tennessee	69,704	Not on ballot	63,878	12	0	0
Texas	31,169	Not on ballot	15,639	4	0	0
Total	608,140	305	477,508	112	0	8
% of Total	56%	0%	44%			
Grand Total	1,835,140	1,340,378	872,703	174	114	8
% of Total	45%	33%	22%			

Source: The numbers compiled by the author from data retrieved October 25, 2018, from

https://en.wikipedia.org/wiki/United_States_presidential_election,_1856

Percentages may not add to 100% due to rounding.

Frémont had no chance in the South, where he did not even appear on the ballot except in Delaware and Maryland. Buchanan swept the South, except for Maryland, where Fillmore garnered eight electoral votes. In the North, Frémont won 45 percent of the popular vote, compared to 41 percent for Buchanan, with Fillmore gaining the balance. Still, Buchanan was able to win in certain key Northern states, like his home state of Pennsylvania, and he emerged as the winner in both the electoral college and the popular vote. McPherson chalks up the Republican loss to their inability to "convince thousands of voters in the lower North that the party was not, after all, a 'Black Republican' communion ruled by 'a wild and fanatical sentimentality toward the black race.'" Or, in other words, that they were not equally as racist as the Democrats.[67]

Republicans, though defeated, felt they had achieved a milestone, having won a majority of votes in the North. Had Buchanan not been from Pennsylvania, they may have flipped that state, putting them within striking distance of the White House. Still, "it was the conservative Whigs ... from the lower North" that had defeated Frémont, Foner writes. In the future, "conservatives within the Republican Party [would need] to moderate the party's program," in order to extend their constituency. The Democrats, for their part, felt elated. They now controlled all the levers of government, from the White House, to Congress (which they had swept), to the Supreme Court. Still, Northern Democrats had to feel some remorse, since their party was now completely dominated by Southerners who, if they disliked the outcome of policies toward slavery, would bolt the Union. Buchanan, dependent on the South for his political existence, would select "a heavily pro-southern cabinet. But that final conservative effort would end up wrecking what was left of the Democratic Party, and then it would wreck the nation," Wilentz writes.[68]

Endnotes

1 Potter, *Impending Crisis*, p. 90–94; McPherson, p. 68.

2 Potter, *Impending Crisis*, p. 91 and 95; Wilentz, *Rise*, p. 698; McPherson, p. 69.

3 Remini, *Clay*, p. 730–732.

4 McPherson, p. 70–71 and p. 79–80; Potter, *Impending Crisis*, p. 99–100.

5 Peterson, p. 460–461; Bartlett, p. 371–372; Potter, *Impending Crisis*, p. 100–101; Brooks, p. 163.

6 McPherson, p. 71.

7 Goodwin, p. 145–146; McPherson, p. 72–73; Wilentz, *Rise*, p. 640.

8   Freeman, *The Field of Blood*, p. 142–176.

9   Potter, *Impending Crisis*, p. 103–105; McPherson, p. 74.

10 Potter, *Impending Crisis*, p. 107–108; McPherson, p. 75.

11 Robert W. Johannsen, *Stephen A. Douglas* (New York, 1973), p. 3–15.

12 Johannsen, p. 16–35.

13 Johannsen, p. 45–53.

14 Johannsen, p. 61–87.

15 Johannsen, p. 88–147.

16 Johannsen, p. 236–239 and p. 271–294.

17 Potter, *The Impending Crisis*, p. 108–116.

18 Wilentz, *Rise*, p. 643–644; McPherson, p. 75.

19 McPherson, p. 80; Potter, *Impending Crisis*, p. 130–132; Foner, *Gateway*, p. 125.

20 McPherson, p. 84; Potter, *Impending Crisis*, p. 137–139; Foner, *Gateway*, p. 145.

21 McPherson, p. 84; Potter, *Impending Crisis*, p. 137–139; Foner, *Gateway*, p. 129–130.

22 Wilentz, *Rise*, p. 655–657.

23 Potter, *Impending Crisis*, p. 126–128; Wilentz, *Rise*, p. 650.

24 On the end of resistance to the Fugitive Slave Act, see Wilentz, *Rise*, p. 652, and Ashworth, p. 64; for the election of 1852, Wilentz, *Rise*, p. 665, McPherson, p. 117–118; Potter, *Division*, p. 66.

25 Potter, *Division*, p. 66, raises the issue that Pierce had fewer votes than the combined ticket of Scott/Hale. Using data retrieved from Wikipedia on October 4, 2018, at https://en.wikipedia.org/wiki/United_States_presidential_election,_1852, I was able to confirm Potter's contention and determine the number of votes that Pierce would have lost by had all of Hale's votes gone to Scott. On Pierce's life, see https://www.history.com/topics/us-presidents/franklin-pierce retrieved October 4, 2018.

26 Wilentz, *The Politicians*, p. 170.

27 William J. Cooper, *Jefferson Davis: American* (New York, 2000), p. 9–40.

28 Cooper, p. 47–88.

29 Cooper, p. 89–110.

30 Cooper, p. 122–157.

31 Cooper, p. 175 and p. 202–203.

32 Potter, *Division*, p. 66–67; Wilentz, *The Politicians*, p. 170.

33 Potter, *Division*, p. 66; the 2018 rankings of presidents was retrieved October 5, 2018, from https://www.businessinsider.com/greatest-us-presidents-ranked-by-political-scientists-2018-2#13-bill-clinton-32; Johannsen, p. 402.

34 Johannsen, p. 304; McPherson, p. 123.

35 McPherson, p. 123; Potter, *The Impending Crisis*, p. 160–161; Wilentz, p. 671.

36 Wilentz, *Rise*, p. 672; McPherson, p. 123; Potter, *The Impending Crisis*, p. 161–162; Cooper, p. 267–268.

37 Quotations are taken from "Appeal of the Independent Democrats," retrieved October 5, 2018, from http://teachingamericanhistory.org/library/document/appeal-of-the-independent-democrats/; Wilentz, *Rise*, 672–673; Potter, *The Impending Crisis*, p. 162–163.

38 Potter, *The Impending Crisis*, p. 171–173, has the best summary of Douglas's view on the issue.

39 Goodwin, p. 162–163; for the violence in Congress and the role that the press played, see Freeman, *Field*, p. 177–200; Potter, p.

40 McPherson, p. 125–127; Goodwin, p. 163.

41 Goodwin, p. 164; Donald, p. 174 and p. 178.

42 Hofstadter, *American Political Tradition*, p. 111; Foner, *Fiery Trial*, p. 64.

43 Wilentz, *The Politicians*, p. 173; Foner, *Fiery Trial*, p. 256–257.

44 Abraham Lincoln, *Selected Speeches and Writings* (New York, 1992), p. 93–99. The quotes are from Lincoln's speech on the Kansas-Nebraska Act at Peoria, Illinois, on October 16, 1854.

45 Foner, *Fiery Trial*, p. 66–69; Lincoln, p. 93–99; Donald, p. 178.

46 Goodwin, p. 142; Ashworth, p. 46, succinctly summarizes Calhoun's ambivalence toward the Democratic Party and his attempts at various points to create a Southern party.

47 Potter, *The Impending Crisis*, p. 225–238, discusses the importance of party in binding the nation together and how the bisectional nature of the parties began to collapse in the aftermath of the Kansas-Nebraska Act.

48 Foner, *Free Soil*, p. 150–156.

49 Daniels, p. 124–129.

50 Francis Fukuyama, *Identity: The Demand for Dignity and the Politics of Resentment* (New York, 2018), p. 62–63; statistics from Daniels that are on p. 124 and p. 146 show that over 30 percent of new immigrants during the period from 1841 to 1860 were German; Ran Abramitzky, "What history tells us about assimilation of immigrants," retrieved October 21, 2018, from https://siepr.stanford.edu/research/publications/immigrants-assimilate.

51 Garry Wills, *Papal Sin: Structures of Deceit* (New York, 2000), p. 238–244; Wilentz, *Rise*, p. 680–682; Potter, *The Impending Crisis*, p. 252.

52 Potter, *The Impending Crisis*, p. 251; Wilentz, *Rise*, p. 679; Potter, *Division*, p. 80; McPherson, p. 137.

53 Goodwin, p. 180; Foner, *Free Soil*, p. 233–235.

54 Foner, *Free Soil*, p. 240–241; Potter, *The Impending Crisis*, p. 254.

55 McPherson, p. 144.

56 McPherson, p. 145; Potter, *The Impending Crisis*, p. 200.

57 McPherson, p. 146; Potter, *The Impending Crisis*, p. 201–204; Wilentz, *Rise*, p. 686.

58 McPherson, p. 148; Potter, *The Impending Crisis*, p. 204.

59 Potter, *The Impending Crisis*, p. 210; Wilentz, *Rise*, p. 690–691; Joanne B. Freeman, "The Violence at the Heart of Our Politics," *New York Times*, September 7, 2018. Retrieved September 15, 2018, from https://www.nytimes.com/2018/09/07/opinion/sunday/violence-politics-congress.html.

60 Potter, *The Impending Crisis*, p. 211–212; Wilentz, *Rise*, p. 692.

61 Wilentz, *Rise*, p. 693–695.

62 McPherson, p. 154; Wilentz, *Rise*, p. 695.

63 McPherson, p. 155; Wilentz, *Rise*, p. 696; quotes from the Republican Party platform of 1856 were retrieved on October 25, 2018, from https://www.presidency.ucsb.edu/documents/republican-party-platform-1856.

64 Bicknell, p. 109–111; McPherson, p. 156; Wilentz, *Rise*, p. 696.

65 Wilentz, *Rise*, p. 699; for background on Buchanan, see the following, retrieved October 26, 2018, from https://www.whitehouse.gov/about-the-white-house/presidents/james-buchanan/ and https://www.history.com/topics/us-presidents/james-buchanan; for Buchanan's relationship with Polk, see Seigenthaler, p. 128–129.

66 McPherson, p. 159; Wilentz, *Rise*, p. 700–701.

67 McPherson, p. 159.

68 Foner, *Free Soil*, p. 200; Wilentz, *Rise*, p. 706.

CHAPTER 14

The North and South Reach a Tipping Point

A house divided against itself cannot stand.
—ABRAHAM LINCOLN, JUNE 16, 1858

*Virginia is your country ... [the] people of the United States
[was] an imaginary body politic.*
—NATHANIEL BEVERLY TUCKER

*M*alcolm Gladwell argues that a tipping point is "the moment of critical mass, the threshold, the boiling point." For both the North and the South, that tipping point would occur between two presidential elections, one in 1856 and the other in 1860. Sandwiched in between were a series of events, including the infamous *Dred Scott* decision, continuing problems in Kansas over slavery, the rise of Abraham Lincoln as a national figure, and a failed slave revolt at Harpers Ferry by John Brown.

The Failures of James Buchanan

James Buchanan often ranks at or near the bottom in the rankings of presidents. Yet when he entered office, he was filled with great hope that popular sovereignty and the Supreme Court would provide the remedy for sectional disputes over the expansion of slavery that were tearing the nation apart. His goal as president, Buchanan indicated in his March 4, 1857, inaugural address, "was to restore harmony and ancient friendship among the people of the several States." This would be accomplished through "the principle of popular sovereignty" in which "the people of a Territory shall decide this question [of slavery] for themselves." He also held out the promise of a pending Supreme Court decision that would settle the issue of whether slavery should be decided at the territorial or statehood phase. The newly elected president stated that "to their decision, in common with all good citizens, I shall cheerfully submit." Buchanan could not know that he would soon betray the spirit of popular sovereignty, and that the Supreme Court decision, which he had inappropriately interfered with, would add to the divisions between North and South.[1]

President-elect Buchanan, on his way to the podium to take the oath of office on March 4, 1857, stopped to talk briefly with the chief justice of the Supreme Court, Roger Taney. It seemed like an innocuous gesture. Taney was a close associate of Andrew Jackson, who had appointed him chief justice in 1836. The *Dred Scott* decision, issued two days after the inauguration, would go down as one of the worst in Supreme Court history. While Buchanan's sidebar with Taney was indeed harmless, his actions the prior month regarding the court were not.[2]

The facts of the case were straightforward. Dred Scott, born a slave, had been taken in the 1830s by his owner from the slave state of Missouri into the free state of Illinois and then into the Wisconsin Territory, where slavery was banned by the Missouri Compromise. During this time, Scott had married, and in 1846 he and his wife brought a lawsuit claiming they were free due to their residence in Illinois and the Wisconsin Territory, both of which barred slavery.

The case made its way through the court system, eventually landing at the Supreme Court.[3]

The court initially considered issuing a narrow decision pursuant to its 1851 decision in *Strader v. Graham* that "individual states had complete power to decide for themselves if a slave who had lived in the North had been thereby freed," as Wilentz frames it. The problem was that two Northern members of the court intended to issue a dissent that indicated that Congress had the power to ban slavery in the territories and finding that Scott and his wife were both citizens of the United States who were now free. The Southern justices, not wanting to leave such a dissent unanswered, decided that the chief justice should write an opinion that dealt with all the issues raised by the case. Although they wanted to overturn congressional authority over slavery in the territories, they did not want to rule as a Southern bloc and therefore needed at least one Northern judge to join them. Two of the Northern judges were Democrats, Robert Grier of Pennsylvania (Buchanan's home state), and Samuel Nelson of New York, who had been preparing the now-abandoned narrow decision. Buchanan, who had checked in with his contacts on the court about the status of the decision before he took the oath of office, now "brought highly improper but efficacious influence to bear on Grier, who succumbed," McPherson writes. Nelson would also ultimately join them to form a 7–2 vote for Taney's sweeping decision.[4]

Chief Justice Taney, who had freed his own slaves and supported colonization, also thought that the Southern way of life was inextricably linked to slavery and had spent his long tenure on the court defending the peculiar institution. He issued a sweeping decision that took him two hours to read before the court. He first found that no black person, whether free or slave, could be a citizen of the United States. Taney argued that black people were not a part of the "sovereign people" who had created the Constitution, nor were they covered by the Declaration's statement that "all men are created equal." Blacks "had for more than a century before been regarded as being of an inferior order ... so far inferior, that they had no rights which a white man was bound to respect." These assertions were historically inaccurate, as Justices Curtis and McLean pointed out in their dissent. Free blacks had been accorded numerous rights, including the right to own property and to enter into contracts, and had in fact participated in the ratification process for the Constitution. Black people were also treated as citizens in several states, as Justice Curtis pointed out in his dissent. Taney argued that while blacks could be citizens of a state, that did not make them citizens of the United States, despite the provision of the Constitution that "the citizens of each state shall be entitled to all privileges and immunities of citizens in the several states."[5]

Taney then went on to find that the Missouri Compromise was unconstitutional, and that Congress had no power to limit or prohibit slavery in the territories. He ground his argument in the Fifth Amendment's prohibition against taking property without compensation. He reached this decision despite the constitutional provision that Congress had the power to "make all needful rules and regulations" for the territories, arguing that rules and regulations were not laws. He also ignored that both Presidents Washington and Madison, who had been present at the Constitutional Convention, had overseen the exclusion of slavery from certain territories and had not raised any constitutional questions about those actions. Finally, the *Dred Scott* decision also made clear that a territory could not exclude slavery through popular sovereignty, since this would be a denial of a slave owner's Fifth Amendment rights. Buchanan, who had made popular sovereignty the centerpiece for resolving the slavery issue in the territories, now confronted a court decision inimical to his major solution. Stephen Douglas, for one, saw the implications of the *Dred Scott* decision for the implementation of popular sovereignty. Yet he thought that citizens could still be the ultimate arbiters because the right to slaves was "barren and worthless unless sustained, protected and enforced by appropriate police regulations and local legislation." Southern politicians shared in the concern that the public could exclude slavery through other legislative means and demanded that "Congress must pass a federal slave code for the territories" backed up with the use of the army to enforce it.[6]

The Supreme Court had now placed itself into the middle of a political dispute, which was "decided in favor of the southern position by a majority consisting of five southerners," as Potter writes. Rather than quelling the sectional dispute, the *Dred Scott* decision further inflamed it. Not only could the decision be interpreted to eliminate the ability of a territory to exclude slavery, but what would stop a slaveholder from moving to a free state and claim they had a Fifth Amendment right to do so? As Potter observes, the American people saw the United States as "a republic of free people" and that slavery had "only local sanction" while freedom had "national sanction." But *Dred Scott* turned that idea on its head by making "freedom local [and] slavery national."[7]

The Republicans responded to the *Dred Scott* decision in one of two ways. Some thought that Taney's opinion did not establish a precedent and did need not be followed under the theory of obiter dictum, derived from English Common law, that holds that a decision based on a matter not before the court lacks the force of law. Using much of the logic from the two dissents, Republicans argued that the decision was "not binding in law and conscience," since Taney only needed to rule that Scott had no standing to sue. The balance of the decision dealing with the power of Congress to regulate slavery in the territories was obiter dictum. Others, like Seward and Lincoln, thought the decision was another example of a conspiracy at work by the Slave Power, pointing to Buchanan's whispering to Taney before his inaugural. Lincoln, after being nominated by the Republicans to run for the Senate in 1858, cited how "Stephen, Franklin, Roger and James," a reference to Douglas, Pierce, Taney, and Buchanan, had systematically undermined the Missouri Compromise in order to pave the way to expand slavery in the North. Although "Lincoln and the other Republicans who made this charge were mistaken," John Ashworth argues, the perception of a mighty Slave Power conspiracy, which had been gaining currency since at least the time of the Wilmot Proviso, was compelling to many in the North, including Lincoln.[8]

Most constitutional scholars today view *Dred Scott* as "the worst decision ever rendered by the Supreme Court." It pushed the nation ever closer to the Civil War, as did further events that were unfolding in Kansas.[9]

Kansas Redux

Time had passed Buchanan by. As historian Bruce Chadwick argues, the president "was hopelessly stuck in the past and unaware of the deep divisions the slavery issue had created" in both his own Democratic Party and the nation at large. He was a president without a clear agenda, yet unable to see anything but his own point of view. His attorney general said of him "he is a stubborn old gentleman, very fond of having his own way—and I don't know what his way is." President Buchanan was also oblivious of the continuing problems that bedeviled Kansas, telling supporters in 1857, "We shall hear no more of bleeding Kansas." He could not have been more wrong.[10]

The next round of trouble began in January of 1857. The violence in Kansas had to a large degree subsided by then, primarily due to the efforts of Pierce's choice for governor, John Geary. Geary was a large man, brave, a law-and-order governor who seemed to have tamed the worst of the sectarian fight between the pro-slavery and Free Soil forces. But just because the worst of the violence had been quelled did not mean there was the possibility for a political settlement between the two sides. When the territorial legislature passed a bill to form a convention to pass a constitution, the antislavery forces, who now held a two-to-one majority, refused to participate. They did not trust that the election of delegates would be conducted in a fair manner, since the election would be supervised by pro-slavery county sheriffs and commissioners. To top it off, the constitution would go into effect without a referendum. Governor Geary then vetoed the bill, and the legislature overrode his veto. This was too much for Geary, who resigned in March of 1857, calling the territorial government a "felon legislature."[11]

The president decided to appoint Robert J. Walker, who would have little more luck than Geary. Walker was from Mississippi, the former treasury secretary for Polk, who had overseen the lowering of tariffs in the mid-1840s. He quickly realized that the Free Soil men outnumbered the pro-slavery forces, and being a strong Jacksonian who believed in majority rule, he urged the Free Soil forces to participate in the election of delegates to the convention. By doing this, he hoped to preserve Kansas as a Democratic state, since most of those who opposed slavery were Democrats. Yet Walker's appeal fell on deaf ears, and every delegate to the convention that was held in Lecompton, Kansas, ended up being pro-slavery. They ultimately adopted a constitution that could not be amended for seven years, which contained a clause that "no alteration shall be made to affect the rights of property in the ownership of slaves." The convention then sent the proposed constitution and a request for statehood to Congress without including any provision for a referendum, which both Walker and Buchanan had insisted on.[12]

Northern Democratic opposition finally forced the Lecompton convention to add a referendum, but it was limited solely to the issue of whether new slaves could be brought into Kansas. The choice that was to be placed before the voters was essentially "meaningless since the 'no slavery' version guaranteed the ownership of slaves already in the territory—in effect prohibiting the future importation of slaves while formally preserving slavery," as Wilentz writes. Walker denounced the so-called compromise as a "vile fraud, a bare counterfeit," believing that Buchanan would back him up. After all, Buchanan had placed popular sovereignty at the center of his solution to the problem of slavery in the territories. But the president was under pressure from his main source of support in the South, whose voters had essentially placed him into office. Jefferson Davis, now back in the Senate, spoke for much of the South who saw Kansas as a test case for preserving the rights of slaveholders, which had been affirmed in the *Dred Scott* case. Davis thought that the issue of a referendum on the Kansas constitution was irrelevant and that Congress should approve the addition of the territory as a slave state. Absent this outcome, the South would need to take a stand since "submission to such an invasion would cover us with moral leprosy." While Davis only called for "stern resistance," Buchanan was fearful that the South would secede if Kansas were not admitted as a slave state. There was probably something to his fears, as Southern states considered calling conventions to consider secession should Kansas not be admitted as a slave state.[13]

With the antislavery forces sitting out the referendum, the

pro-slavery constitution was approved on a vote of 6,226 to 569 on December 21. A few weeks later, a separate referendum was held by the Free Soil group, who handily rejected the Lecompton Constitution. Under continued pressure from his Southern supporters, Buchanan ultimately sent the pro-slavery constitution to Congress with a recommendation to approve Kansas as a slave state. This action proved too much for Walker, who resigned immediately.[14]

It also caused Stephen Douglas to revolt against Buchanan's decision. Douglas was buffeted by two prevailing political crosswinds. On the one hand, he needed to protect his political base in Illinois, where his support for the Lecompton Constitution, coming on the heels of his role in the Kansas-Nebraska Act and his defense of the *Dred Scott* decision, could doom his reelection chances. Conversely, he would need Southern support if he hoped to be elected president in 1860. Douglas, the great supporter of popular sovereignty, decided to stand on principle, calling the Lecompton Constitution a "fraudulent submission" and a "mockery," complaining that it was a "flagrant violation of popular rights in Kansas." At a meeting with Buchanan on December 3, Douglas lost his temper when the president ordered him to fall in line or face the same fate as Democratic senators that had crossed Andrew Jackson. "Mr. President, I wish you to remember that General Jackson is dead, sir."[15]

Douglas did all he could to defeat the admission of Kansas under the Lecompton Constitution, not because of any concern over slavery, but because it violated his view of popular sovereignty. As he told the Senate, "It is none of my business which way the slavery clause is decided. I care not whether it is voted down or up." But his efforts in the Senate came to naught, as the Southern-dominated chamber approved the bill admitting Kansas as a slave state in March of 1858 on a vote of 33–25. The debate in the House was much more contentious and led to an out-and-out brawl on the floor of the chambers on February 6. During an all-night session, fueled no doubt by the consumption of alcohol, two congressmen got into the "first sectional fight ever had on the floor," according to Alexander Stephens, who would go on to be the vice president of the Confederacy. At its apex, the fight included "roughly thirty sweaty, disheveled, mostly middle-aged congressmen in a no-holds-barred brawl, North against South," as Joanne Freeman writes. Politics, which at its best is designed to settle differences through negotiation and compromise, had now fallen to the violence that would soon engulf the nation. As Freeman notes, Congress is reflective of what is happening in the larger society. "When the nation is polarized and civic commonality dwindles, Congress reflects the image back to the American people," she cogently argues. Ultimately, the Kansas request for statehood was defeated when a number of Northern Democrats joined with the Republicans on a vote of 120–112. Kansas would eventually be admitted as a free state in January of 1861 on the eve of the outbreak of the Civil War.[16]

As the midterm elections for Congress approached, American society was increasingly divided over the issue of the expansion of slavery. No political campaign reflected the differing perspectives in the North more than the Illinois Senate race.

Lincoln versus Douglas

The two men had known each other for over twenty years, acquaintances but not friends, rivals in the political realm. Lincoln had long thought Douglas lacked a moral compass and in fact had attacked him in a series of anonymous newspaper articles that appeared in late 1837 and early 1838 when Douglas first ran for Congress against

Lincoln's then law partner John T. Stuart. Lincoln "accused Douglas of striking a corrupt political bargain to gain the nomination," Sidney Blumenthal writes. The two had also competed for their rival parties over the years, and even represented opposing sides in several court cases. As discussed in chapter 13, the two men had been sparring over the Kansas-Nebraska Act as well. Part of Lincoln's disdain for Douglas may well have been a product of jealousy. Since they first met, the "Little Giant," as Douglas was known, had totally eclipsed Lincoln in terms of political accomplishments. As Lincoln would write: "With *me*, the race of ambition has been a failure—a flat failure, with *him* it has been one of splendid success." Douglas, for his part, spoke of Lincoln in admiring terms. As the campaign opened, and with Lincoln sitting behind him, Douglas called him a "kind, amiable, and intelligent gentleman, a good citizen, and an honorable opponent." Yet Douglas thought Lincoln's position on the issue of slavery was dangerous and that it would lead to "a war of sections, a war of the North against the South."[17]

Since his speech in Peoria in 1854, Lincoln had been building a case that the Declaration of Independence applied to all people, including blacks, and that the founders wanted to contain and gradually eliminate slavery. In the aftermath of the *Dred Scott* decision, Lincoln delivered a speech in Springfield on June 26, 1857, to refute the view both Douglas and Taney shared "that the Declaration of Independence and Constitution had been written for whites" only, as Foner explains. The *Dred Scott* decision had caused Lincoln to think about who was covered by the phrase "all men are created equal." Douglas had said the signers of the Declaration did not include "the negro or ... savage Indians, or the Feejee, or the Malay or any other inferior or degraded race." The senator went so far as to say the Declaration of Independence only applied to people of British descent.[18]

In Springfield, Lincoln asserted that Taney and Douglas did not think the Declaration included "negroes, by the fact that they [the authors] did not at once, actually place them on an equality with whites." But this is specious, Lincoln contended, because the founders "did not at once, *or even afterwards*, actually place all white people on equality with one another." A more cogent way to read the Declaration was that the authors "intended to include all men, but they did not declare all men equal in all respects." People differed in "color, size, intellect," and other qualities. Just because at the time the Declaration was written the natural rights included in it, especially equality, were not a reality did not mean that this would not change in the future. The founding generation had declared "the right, so that the enforcement of it might follow as fast as circumstances should permit." The right to liberty and equality were "a standard maxim for free society" that though "never perfectly attained" should be "constantly spreading and deepening its influence ... to all people of all colors everywhere." It was a remarkable speech, one which took great political courage on Lincoln's part. As a Radical Republican later remarked, "It required some nerve in Lincoln, in a state where prejudice against the negro was so strong ... to stand up and proclaim the right of the negro to all the rights of the Declaration."[19]

Lincoln was greatly disturbed by those who denied that equality was a birthright of all, black and white, rich and poor, native or immigrant. He especially despised the argument first put forward by John C. Calhoun, who in 1848 had said that there was "not a word of truth" to the idea that "all men are born free and equal." As Lincoln would later explain more fully in the debates with Douglas, he was not referring to political or social equality, but rather to the "equal right to the pursuit of happiness [including] the fruits of one's labor," as Foner explains.[20]

❧ ❧ ❧

As Lincoln eyed a run for the Senate in 1858, Douglas at first appeared to threaten his chances for the Republican nomination. Horace Greeley, the *New York Tribune* editor, was leading an effort to get the Republicans to endorse Douglas due to his stand against the Lecompton Constitution. But Illinois Republicans resented the intrusion of eastern Republicans into their affairs and nominated Lincoln as their Senate standard-bearer at their convention.[21]

In accepting his party's senatorial nomination at Springfield on June 16, 1858, Lincoln opened with a series of memorable statements that the United States could not indefinitely remain half slave and half free.

A house divided against itself cannot stand. I believe this government cannot endure, permanently half slave and half free. I do not expect the Union to be dissolved—I do not expect the house to fall—but I do expect it will cease to be divided. It will become all one thing, or all the other.[22]

Lincoln had long been thinking about the theme of a house divided, something that would resonate in a state like Illinois, where people were familiar with the metaphor from the Gospels of Matthew, Mark, and Luke. More importantly, the speech was a way to place pressure on Douglas to stand with the Slave Power. As James MacGregor Burns argues, Lincoln was attempting to "destroy the middle ground on which Douglas was standing and indict the senator as part of a grand conspiracy to spread slavery throughout the nation." It was during this speech that Lincoln had made his reference to "Stephen and Franklin and Roger and James," as being in league with each other to expand slavery, a charge that most historians have dismissed, but which was an effective tool to discourage wayward Republicans from supporting Douglas. Lincoln also thought that the key to stopping the spread of slavery was to be found in educating the public. "Either the *opponents* of slavery, will arrest the further spread of it, and place it where the public mind shall rest in the belief that it is in course of ultimate distinction," Lincoln argued, "or its *advocates*" will make it legal in the "*North* as well as *South*." Lincoln believed that Douglas was failing the test of public leadership on a basic question of morality, of whether slavery was right or wrong, pointing to the senator's statements "that he cares not whether slavery be voted down or voted up." To Lincoln, this was "an *apt definition* of the *policy* he would impress upon the public mind." Stopping the spread of slavery was his ultimate goal, with elimination to occur at some ill-defined future date. Little could Lincoln know, or could he foresee, that his election as president in 1860 would be the final cause that would result in the collapse of the nation.[23]

☞☞☞

A few weeks later, on July 10 in Chicago, Lincoln further developed his theme of connecting all Americans to the Declaration, regardless of race or bloodlines. The speech was a response to one given by Douglas the previous day, where he reiterated his position that "this government of ours is founded on the white basis" and that Lincoln and the Republicans wanted white people to amalgamate "with inferior races," which would lead to "degeneration, demoralization, and degradation." Douglas supported the view that America was exclusively a white nation.[24]

Lincoln stood on the other side of this debate and was perhaps the first politician to clearly pronounce that America was an idea that was best expressed in the Declaration. Lincoln explained to his audience in Chicago that all men were inheritors of the founders, not just those that were connected by birth. "We have ... among us perhaps half our people who are not descendants at all of these men," who came from Germany, Ireland, France, and Scandinavia, and that have no blood connection to the founding generation. Yet they have a "right to claim" a connection with the "moral principle" that all men are created equal. That moral principle, which was universal, "is the electric cord ... that links the hearts of patriotic and liberty-loving men together." Eric Foner has best summarized the essence of this speech. "In opposition to Douglas's racialized definition of American nationhood, Lincoln counterposed a civic nationalism grounded in the ideals of the Declaration of Independence. Not race or ethnicity but principle bound Americans to one another." This is the essence of America as an idea, that we are all tied together by the "electric cord" of the Declaration of Independence, which proclaims that all people have certain natural rights bestowed by the creator, including liberty and equality, and that governing is grounded in the consent of the governed.[25]

The Debates

Lincoln had begun to follow Douglas to each of his speaking engage-ments, listening to what he said and then providing a response to the audience, either later that day or the next. It was a source of great irritation to both Douglas and the Democrats, and the *Chicago Times* suggested that Lincoln did it because he was unable to draw crowds of his own. Finally, Lincoln proposed that the two men engage in a series of debates. As the better-known candidate, one with a national reputation with his sights set on the White House, Douglas had little to gain from debating, which would elevate Lincoln to his level. Yet Douglas feared being branded a coward and "his political pugnacity soon overcame his doubts," Johannsen writes. The two men agreed to seven debates to be held in the remaining congressional districts where they had not yet appeared.[26]

The debates would each follow the same rules. One man would speak for an hour and a half, and then his opponent would get to rebut for one hour. The opening speaker would then conclude for a final half hour. In today's world, candidate's debate specific questions from a moderator for two minutes, with a response from their opponent of the same length. One wonders how today's politicians would react to a three-hour debate, where they had to speak for up to ninety minutes. The debates were well attended, with the first one in Ottawa attracting a crowd of ten thousand people, greater than the population of the town. As one contemporary observed of a later debate in Quincy, "the country people began to stream into town for the great meeting, some singly, on foot or horseback, or small parties of men and women." The more affluent from Chicago came by train. Douglas typically arrived by private railcar, accompanied by his second wife, the twenty-two-year-old "Adele, a great niece of first lady Dolley Madison," according to Foner. Lincoln traveled alone, on a passenger train surrounded by common people, typically dressed in plain clothes that sometimes fit him poorly due to his height.[27]

The debates focused exclusively on one issue: slavery. Each man reiterated familiar positions and tried to exploit the weaknesses of the other's positions.[28] Each debate had its own pattern and highlights, and there was a good deal of repetition from the candidates. In the first debate on August 21 in Ottawa just south of Chicago, Lincoln quickly found himself on the defensive when Douglas opened with a sharp attack. According to Douglas, both the Whig and the Democratic

Parties had historically shared the same position on slavery, which "was the right of the people of each State and each Territory to decide their local and domestic institutions for themselves, subject only to the federal constitution." He claimed that Lincoln had been the one that engaged in a conspiracy to upset this broad consensus by eliminating the old parties in order to create "an Abolition party, under the name and disguise of a Republican Party." He then posed a series of questions to Lincoln on whether he supported "the platform of the Black Republican party," which called for repeal of the Fugitive Slave Law; stood against admitting any more slave states even if their people voted for it; and if he supported the elimination of slavery in Washington, DC. Douglas reiterated his opposition to bestowing citizenship upon blacks, and that "this government was made on the white basis." Lincoln, who was used to having time to think about what his opponent had charged before responding, refused to "give immediate answers to Douglas's questions, even though his position on all these issues had been firmly established for years," according to Donald.[29]

Six days later, in Freeport, Lincoln had the opportunity to be the first speaker. He had been urged by other Republican leaders to attack Douglas, and before a "vast audience as strongly tending to Abolitionism as any audience in the State of Illinois," Lincoln did just that. But first, he had to answer each of the charges that Douglas had levied against him. Lincoln denied that he ever supported repeal of the Fugitive Slave Law, opposed "the admission of any more slave States," or that he supported the "abolition of slavery in the District of Columbia." Lincoln also qualified those answers in certain key ways, especially the one dealing with the admission of more slave states. "I should be exceedingly glad to know that there would never be another slave State admitted into the Union." He then posed a series of his own questions for Douglas, the most important of which was the second one, dealing with the *Dred Scott* decision. "Can the people of a United State[s'] Territory ... exclude slavery from its limits prior to" their formation as a state? Lincoln already knew what Douglas's answer would be, since the senator had made it one of the mainstays of his response to the *Dred Scott* decision. "The people have the lawful means to introduce it or exclude it as they please" since slavery could not survive "unless it is supported by local police regulation," Douglas stated. Lincoln's goal in asking a question which he already knew the answer to was to further divide Douglas's support from Southerners in the Democratic Party.[30]

The next two debates were in Jonesboro and Charleston in the southern part of the state, areas that were more sympathetic to slavery. Douglas's racist charges against Lincoln began to have an impact. Douglas charged that he had seen a carriage in Freeport that carried "Fred Douglass, the Negro," who was sitting with two white women, and that he was campaigning for Lincoln. He also charged that Lincoln "advocated negro citizenship and negro equality, putting the white man and the negro on the same basis under the law." Even prior to these two debates, Lincoln's supporters were urging him to make it clear that neither he nor the Republicans are "in favor of making the blacks socially and politically equal with whites." Lincoln, under pressure from his own backers and from Douglas's incessant race baiting, denied he supported "social and political equality of the white and black races." Lincoln had in the past said he did not think that blacks were equal to whites, and now he further indicated he did not support "making voters or jurors of negroes, nor of qualifying them to hold office, nor to intermarry with white people." At Charleston, he even failed to say that he thought that blacks were entitled to the basic rights contained in the Declaration of Independence. All in all, it was the low point of the debates for Lincoln, with Douglas correctly charging that Lincoln changed his message to suit his audience.[31]

In the final three debates, Lincoln changed the focus of his arguments to the issue of the morality of slavery. In the sixth debate in Quincy, Lincoln argued that the difference between him and Douglas is "the difference between the men who think slavery wrong and those who do not think it is wrong." Those like him and the Republicans wanted to "prevent its [slavery] growing any larger, and so deal with it that in the run of time there may be some promise of an end to it." Douglas, for his part, refused to become engaged in a debate over the morality of slavery. "I tell you why I will not do it," he told the same audience in Quincy. "I hold that under the Constitution of the United States, each state of this Union has a right to do as it pleases on the subject of slavery." As one of Douglas's biographers writes, to introduce morality into the discussion "would strike down the nation's political system, dangerously increase sectionalism at the expense of the national interest, and ultimately destroy the Union."[32]

Douglas may well have been antislavery in private, as historian David Potter indicates. But Potter also takes Douglas to task for his disdain for black people, "a certain callous scorn for the blacks, as people with whom he did not recognize any affinity." As early as 1854, Lincoln had charged that Douglas "has no very vivid impression that the negro is a human." Douglas was essentially unwilling to take any risks in order to slow or stop the spread of slavery, preferring to allow popular sovereignty to keep slavery out of the new territories where the physical conditions made slavery undesirable. Douglas claimed he did not want blacks to be slaves. "I do not hold that because the negro is our inferior that therefore he ought to be a slave." Yet the rights of blacks were to be determined at the state level, and not by national policy. "I would not endanger the perpetuity of the Union," Douglas said. "I would not blot out the great inalienable rights of the white men for all the negroes that ever existed." If Douglas truly believed that slavery was wrong, then he failed the test of moral leadership.[33]

Lincoln took the more principled stand, not only maintaining that slavery was morally wrong, but also extending to all people, including slaves, the natural rights Jefferson recorded in the Declaration of Independence, especially the equal right to be paid for one's work. "But in the right to eat the bread ... which his own hand earns, *he is my equal and the equal of Judge Douglas, and the equal of every living man*," Lincoln emphatically asserted to great applause at the Ottawa debate. Yet Lincoln had his own shortcomings when it came to race. In the Ottawa speech Lincoln said that he had "no purpose to introduce political and social equality between the white and black races," and that physical differences would "forbid their living together upon the footing of perfect equality," which was why he continued to support colonization of freed blacks. Lincoln continued to look for that sweet spot where he could oppose slavery but remain acceptable to white voters, both because it was his lifelong view up to this time but also because he was a shrewd and ambitious politician who wished to be elected. Lincoln went so far as to implicitly support the discriminatory Black Laws of the state of Illinois, which both Seward and Chase had denounced in their home states. At this point, Lincoln had not come to grips with the great question: If slavery was evil, then why not attempt to eliminate it, even in the states where it already existed, by proposing some form of compensated emancipation?[34]

This left a major opening for Douglas, especially in light of Lincoln's oft-repeated claim of placing slavery on the path to "ultimate extinction." Douglas charged that if Lincoln was opposed to interfering with the institution where it existed, then "how does he expect to bring slavery in a course of ultimate extinction"? Lincoln was never an abolitionist in the mold of Garrison, who favored the immediate elimination of slavery. His response to Douglas is revealing. "I do not mean … it will be in a day, nor in a year, nor in two years. I do not suppose that in the most peaceful way ultimate extinction would occur in less than a hundred years." Yet Lincoln thought that public discussion of slavery would eventually lead to its extinction. "[A]n evil can't stand discussion," Lincoln argued. In two years, Lincoln would be elected president, leading to the Civil War and the elimination of slavery in the United States. But it would take almost another hundred years before president Lyndon Johnson would sign civil- and voting-rights legislation that would mark the end of overt discrimination in the United States.[35]

Lincoln's unwillingness to interfere with slavery in the South was largely due to his support of the Constitution, which he believed protected slavery where it already existed. Any attempt to implement a solution consistent with the Constitution would require a two-thirds vote of Congress and ratification by three-quarters of the states, an impossible hurdle to get over in the late 1850s. Instead, Lincoln and the other leaders of the Republican Party pursued a gradual plan for ending slavery by "halting its expansion," which "amounted to a sentence of gradual death" in the words of Sean Wilentz. Slave owners saw the issue very much the same way, which is why the battle over slavery in Kansas and the other new territories that were added by the Mexican-American War was so vociferous. It would also be the primary reason that the South would secede in the aftermath of Lincoln's election in 1860.[36]

Despite Lincoln's shortcomings, he fits the model of a moral leader far better than Douglas, or many of his competitors of the time. James MacGregor Burns, in his book *Leadership*, writes that "at the highest stage of moral development persons are guided by near universal ethical principles of justice such as equality of human rights and respect for individual dignity." Moral leadership "operates at need and value levels higher than those of the potential follower (but not so much higher [as] to lose contact)." This is critical in democratic societies, where the power of a leader is grounded in the consent of the governed. As Burns notes in his introduction, "moral leadership emerges from, and always returns to, the fundamental wants and needs, aspirations, and values of the followers." Neither Lincoln nor his followers were ready to treat black people as their equals. Lincoln seemed to instinctively understand that a leader cannot get too far out in front of his followers. As Wilentz writes, the majority of Northerners were antislavery but "believed, to one degree or another, that blacks were inferior." Both the abolitionists, who were urging the immediate end to slavery, and the "vicious racists who wanted to halt slavery's expansion in order to keep the territories lily white" were much smaller in number.[37]

Finally, when evaluating Lincoln as a moral leader, a historian cannot ignore one of Lincoln's greatest attributes. "At the time of his death, he occupied a very different position with regard to slavery and the place of blacks in American society," than he did at this point in the late 1850s, as Foner writes. Lincoln would continue to change and grow. It is an error to view him either as always ready to free the slaves and then welcome them as full partners into American society, or as "a man with no deep convictions of his own," as Foner writes.[38]

❦ ❦ ❦

Lincoln had established a national reputation, even if he did not ultimately end up winning the Illinois Senate seat. Elections to the Senate were carried out by the state legislatures prior to the

Twenty-Seventh Amendment, ratified in 1913, which called for the direct election of senators. The Democrats retained control of the Illinois legislature in 1858, even though the Republican Party won the popular vote. The apportionment of seats had not kept pace with the growth of population in the Northern part of the state where Republicans were strongest, although the Republicans still would not have taken control since eight of the thirteen holdovers in the Senate were Democrats. Given Democratic control in the Illinois Senate, Stephen Douglas was reelected. Lincoln may have thought his political career was ended, but others in the Republican Party had a different idea. "Now I am for Lincoln for the nomination for president in 1860," one party stalwart remarked.[39]

While Lincoln may have lost, the fortunes of the Republican Party in the rest of the North improved considerably. Playing on voter discontent with the *Dred Scott* decision and events in Kansas, the Republicans gained twenty-five seats in the House of Representatives. The party now held 116 seats, close to 49 percent of the total, compared to 98 for the Democrats. The balance was held by the Know-Nothings and those called the Opposition Party. The Opposition Party was made up of those former Whigs who did not feel at home in either the Republican Party or among Democrats. It was particularly strong in North Carolina, Tennessee, and Kentucky, among those Southerners who continued to cling to the Union. In the Senate, the Republicans gained five seats, and they also controlled a number of state legislatures "for the first time, including New York, Pennsylvania, New Jersey, Indiana and Minnesota" to go along with "their existing majorities in Ohio, Michigan, Iowa and Wisconsin," historian Bruce Chadwick writes.[40]

A tipping point had been reached in 1858 in the North over the issue of slavery. Opposition to slavery, which had once been a minor fringe movement made up of those abolitionists that demanded an immediate end to slavery, now had majority support in the North. The Republican victory in Pennsylvania was particularly impressive, given that it was the home of President Buchanan. Pennsylvania also shared a border with Maryland and Virginia, two slave states, which meant it was less hostile to the peculiar institution than the states farther north. The Republicans were able to combine their antislavery message with some traditional Whig policies, especially a protective tariff and the building of internal improvements, including a transcontinental railroad, which appealed to voters in an industrial state like Pennsylvania. "The Republicans conducted a moral crusade [against slavery] but carefully framed it also as an economic one," Chadwick writes. Buchanan came in for his share of blame, with one critic charging that Democratic losses were due to "the mistakes of the federal administration."[41]

But it wasn't just the North that was experiencing a tipping point, but also the South.

The Tipping Point in the South

On the eve of the 1860 presidential election, the threat of disunion was increasingly becoming a reality in the South. Since the time of the American Revolution, there had always been those who feared centralized power. While they supported independence, they opposed replacing the British system with a strong American federal government. During the ratification debates over the Constitution, the antifederalists had taken this position, charging that the Federalists wanted to institute a consolidated government that would eviscerate the states. The debate over the extent of federal versus state power had not ended with the ratification of the Constitution but had continued throughout the early nineteenth century between the Federalists and the Republicans, the Whigs and the Democrats. The fear of a consolidated government was particularly strong in the South, and opposition to a strong federal government was, at its core, a means to protect slavery. Yet there was also strong support for the Union in the South, and those who wanted to break away and form a separate confederacy were a fringe movement, much as the abolitionists were in the North.

By the early 1850s, those who supported secession were sometimes called the Fire Eaters. While the term was new, the concept was not. One of its earliest proponents, the intellectual grandfather of the movement, was a law professor at the College of William and Mary, Nathaniel Beverly Tucker. His father had been an antifederalist but also an opponent of slavery who thought it "was incompatible with the revolutionary ideal that all men are created equal," historian Eric H. Walther writes. Born in 1784, Nathaniel Tucker, unlike his father, opposed every measure designed to limit the expansion of slavery, and since the time of the Missouri Compromise in 1820 had been working to shatter the Union into "pieces." Like his father, he would have preferred the United States to remain a weak confederacy under the Articles of Confederation. Tucker interpreted the Constitution as a league of friendship under which the states remained sovereign, a position clearly at odds with the intent of the Framers of the document. He taught his law students that "Virginia is your country" and that the "people of the United States [was] an imaginary body politic." Since 1833 and the nullification crisis, "Tucker longed for the creation of a Southern nation," Walther finds, and he had been an early proponent of secession. Although Tucker died in 1851, seven of his former students would vote for secession in 1861.[42]

Robert Barnwell Rhett, born in South Carolina in 1800, was another Fire Eater, a man who advocated secession early on. Originally born Robert Smith, he changed his name to Rhett after an ancestor who had been the governor of the Bahamas. He hoped that "a name of distinction would fetch attention" in the politics of South Carolina. He entered the political arena in 1830, just as the nullification crisis was heating up, warning his fellow Carolinians that "disunion" was preferable "to a union of unlimited powers." Like so many Southern radicals, he viewed life under a Northern-dominated government as nothing less than living as a "fearful slave." While Calhoun worked to preserve Southern rights within the Union, Rhett favored breaking the Union apart. The two men had an on-again, off-again relationship, with Rhett actually running Calhoun's presidential campaign in 1844. But by 1848, the two men had split again over the annexation of Texas, with Rhett once again pushing for secession should Texas not be added to the United States. While Calhoun was the more popular of the two, Rhett clearly had his own following in South Carolina, where he influenced a group of young men "with a baptism of resistance and a benediction of secession," as Walther writes.[43]

When Calhoun died in 1850, Rhett was selected to fill his Senate seat. He did not last long, pushing his idea of secession in the wake of the Compromise of 1850. His ideas were repudiated by the election of an anti-secession convention back home, and Rhett soon resigned his Senate seat. Four years later, he was back at it again after the electoral success of the Republicans in the election of 1856, writing to the governor of South Carolina that the federal government was a "sheer despotism" and that the South should pursue its "glorious destiny" and establish itself as "a great free and independent people!" Rhett was not alone in these views and was joined by men like Laurence Keitt (of fighting fame in the House), Edmund Ruffin, and William Lowndes Yancey.[44]

Yancey was known for his "brilliant oratory and violent temper," according to Walther. Born in Georgia in 1814, he was raised by his stepfather, who had sold his slaves and moved the family north, where he joined the abolitionist movement. Yancey despised him as a traitor to the South. Originally a strong supporter of the Union, Yancey changed his mind once he married into a wealthy slave-owning family. By 1840, he had become a follower of Calhoun's states'-rights philosophy. Elected first to the Alabama General Assembly, and then to the House of Representatives in 1844, Yancey was a major supporter of Texas annexation. When the dispute over the Wilmot Proviso arose, Yancey co-authored the Alabama Platform, which prohibited Congress from banning slavery in the new territories won in the Mexican-American War. He joined Rhett in his opposition to the Compromise of 1850 and worked toward secession in Alabama after it passed.[45]

By the late 1850s, Yancey was working toward building a coalition of Southern states to support secession. Known as the League of United Southerners, it was the brainchild of Edmund Ruffin. Born in 1794, Ruffin was a seventh-generation Virginian. Though not a scientist, Ruffin had developed a method to rejuvenate the exhausted soil of his home state from the destruction caused by tobacco. He first became engaged in politics over opposition to the Tariff Act of 1816 and had become convinced that the federal government was too powerful, a view he shared with his distant cousin, Nathaniel Beverly Tucker. An elitist, he rejected "the concepts of equality and democracy," as did many of the Fire Eaters. While a young man, Ruffin had thought that slavery was "a great and increasing evil." But over time, he had concluded that "slavery made Southern society superior to that of the North," as Walther writes. By the late 1850s, Ruffin, too, had reached the conclusion that secession was the only answer should a Republican be elected president. A realist, he warned Rhett that Virginia would never be the first to secede, but if other states led the way, they "would be forced to join their southern brethren." In May of 1858, Ruffin and Yancey began their campaign for secession.[46]

⚜ ⚜ ⚜

At the other extreme were those who criticized the very basis of Southern society, slavery. Henry Clay's cousin, Cassius Marcellus Clay, opposed slavery and attempted to enlist non-slave-owners in the cause of its elimination during the 1840s and 1850s. As a young man, he had traveled to New England and been impressed by the greater prosperity of the area compared to Kentucky. "I cannot as a stateman shut my eyes to the industry, ingenuity, numbers and wealth which are displayed in adjoining states," he once said, viewing the free labor system of the North as superior. Hinton Rowan Helper, a non-slave-owner from North Carolina, thought that "slavery lies at the root of all the shame, poverty, ignorance, tyranny and imbecility of the South." In 1857, Helper published his book, *The Impending Crisis*, in which he documented, using selected statistics from the 1850 census, that slavery was leading to the economic decline of the South. The prime losers in the system were the non-slave-owning masses, who were denied a decent education and the ability to advance. Helper had challenged one of the dogmas "of the southern creed," which was that "race transcended class," Potter writes. In fact, slave owners were dependent on the willingness of middle- and lower-class whites to maintain their system of plantation slavery. If they turned against the system and rule by the elite, the entire Southern slave aristocracy could come crashing down. Since colonial times, slave owners had elicited the support of the yeomen by appealing to their sense of racial superiority. Still, many feared that Helper's polemic would cause a loss of support for slavery and "several southern states therefore made it a crime to circulate *The Impending Crisis*," McPherson writes. Still, the critics of slavery were a small minority in the 1850s South.[47]

❦ ❦ ❦

The Fire Eaters, too, were outside the mainstream of Southern society until the late 1850s, when their ideas for secession began to hold sway. The question is, Why did the yeoman farmers in the South, who gained so little from slavery, support the move toward secession, and ultimately to a war they would fight and die in?

Southern society was hierarchical, with wealth highly concentrated among the planter elite. By 1860, the top 10 percent held almost 50 percent of the total income in the South, compared to 32 percent in New England and 36 percent in the middle-Atlantic states. "The 1860 census data shows that the median wealth of the richest 1% of Southerners was more than three times higher than for the richest 1% of Northerners," economists Brandon Dupont and Joshua Rosenbloom have found. Much of the wealth held by Southerners was found in the value of their slaves, yet only 25 percent of people owned slaves, and only a small slice had more than 100 slaves (0.1 percent). There was also beginning to emerge a middle class that lived in towns and cities, urban professionals like "merchants, doctors, lawyers, small manufacturers, teachers" and "a growing class of laborers," which had begun to appear as the South made strides to diversify its economy. Yet this group was still small in number, and while they wanted to emulate the North's success with industrialization, they were supporters of slavery. They opposed secession but "were unable to halt or even significantly slow down the region's march to war," according to historian Jonathan Daniel Wells.[48]

In such a hierarchical society, Southern slave owners were dependent on the support of the yeoman farmers to maintain the existing social system grounded in slavery. The yeomen owned few if any slaves but made up most of the population of the South in 1860. As shown in the table below, which is based on the listing of occupations from the census in 1860, farmers and other laborers made up 63 percent of the reported occupations, with planters representing 1 percent. This is based on those states that would secede and form the Confederacy. When combined with two of the other large occupations, overseers and servants, almost 70 percent of the labor force was engaged in some form of work that paid at the lower end of the income scale. Professional and commercial occupations, those typically associated with the middle class, made up around 10 percent of the total reported occupations, although this was higher in urban areas.[49]

STATE	Total Occupations	Planters	Farmers	Farm /Other Laborers	Overseers	Servants
Confederacy						
Alabama	137,419		67,743	14,282	4,141	4,870
Arkansas	85,001	438	48,475	15,394	1,071	567
Florida	21,962	1,175	7,534	3,781	468	178
Georgia	156,514	2,858	67,718	30,842	4,909	5,337
Louisiana	107,498	6,473	14,996	21,976	2,989	5,336
Mississippi	93,208	3,098	46,308	15,088	3,941	416
North Carolina	192,674	191	85,118	37,149	1,782	21,092
South Carolina	81,631	2,521	35,137	12,108	2,737	1,103
Tennessee	215,387	78	103,835	50,347	1,687	5,106
Texas	105,491	265	51,569	16,498	1,254	3,541
Virginia	297,354	80	108,958	74,559	5,459	11,053
TOTAL	1,494,139	17,177	637,391	292,024	30,438	58,599
Percent		1%	43%	20%	2%	4%

The yeomen benefited very little from slavery, yet they supported the system. Some hoped to one day own slaves, although "skyrocketing slave prices seemed to shut the door on their aspirations to climb into the planter class," according to historian James C. Cobb. Those who owned plantations understood the importance of maintaining the support of the yeomen, who formed the slave patrols that captured and returned fugitive slaves. It was also important to maintain the support of the yeomen so they did not vote against slavery. Most slave owners differed in their view from the Fire Eaters, who "rejected the concepts of equality and democracy," Wilentz writes. Fire Eater George Fitzhugh of Virginia, who viewed slavery as "the natural and normal condition of society" also thought that "men are not born entitled to equal rights," even white men. Fitzhugh disparaged the free labor system in the North, writing that "free laborers must work or starve, and slaves are supported whether they work or not." Most planters may have accepted Fitzhugh's view of slavery, believing that Southern society was superior to the North and that slavery improved the lives of blacks; yet they drew the line on white inequality. "Nowhere in this broad Union but in the slaveholding states is there a living breathing, exemplification of the beautiful sentiment, that all men are equal," according to Albert Gallatin Brown of Mississippi, who made it clear he was speaking of all white men. This sentiment was certainly consistent with the views of Jefferson and Jackson.[50]

Most slave owners understood that maintaining their position required them to at least pay lip service to the equality of all white people, and to maintain a social system that allowed poor whites to feel superior to blacks. According to the political scientist Francis Fukuyama, all human beings have a need to be recognized "as equal in dignity to others." For some, this need is expressed as a desire to feel superior to others. Slave owners, who controlled both wealth and power in the antebellum South, seemed to implicitly understand that preserving their status required them to recognize the dignity of poor whites, even if they may not have fully believed it. Unlike black slaves, poor whites were accorded recognition as "fellow human beings," deserving of equal dignity. Perhaps attacks upon slavery by the North elicited a fear among the yeomen that they would lose their superior status should slaves be freed. As Cobb frames it, "the institution of slavery was all that stood between them and a swift and irreversible descent into the unthinkable humiliation of economic, political and social equality with blacks."[51]

☞ ☞ ☞

As the threat of disunion became more real, the South began to develop a series of myths to prove that their society was in fact superior to the North. One was the superiority of the Southern economic system. The Panic of 1857, which had both foreign and domestic roots, was short-lived but hit the North harder than the South. Urban areas and wage laborers were especially impacted. In the South, "cotton and tobacco prices dipped only briefly before returning to their high pre-Panic levels," McPherson writes. In 1858, former Calhoun protégé James Hammond gave a speech proclaiming: "Cotton is king." He argued that cotton had saved the economy, proving the superiority of the South's slave system.[52]

In fact, cotton was becoming less important in the Northeast than it had been in the 1830s, when "the industrial sector was built on the back of enslaved people," Edward Baptist writes. The North had begun to diversify its economy, which was originally dependent on the manufacture of cotton products. By the 1850s, the North had begun to shift to other types of industries. To appeal to Northerners,

Hammond made a similar argument that Calhoun had when he proposed to the businessmen of the North that they should be in league together to keep the working class from taking over. Hammond made the case that "either the rulers in the North could emulate the South by giving all 'mean duties' to enslaved and politically powerless blacks, or they would run the risk" that lower-class whites, armed with the power to vote, would take over.[53]

Southerners began to maintain that they were descended from a superior race of Englishmen. Whereas the Puritans were from "medieval Anglo-Saxons," Southerners were descended from their Norman conquerors, whom they referred to as the Cavaliers. In June of 1860, the *Southern Literary Messenger* wrote that Southerners were "a race distinguished in its earliest history for its warlike and fearless character, a race in all times renowned for its gallantry, chivalry, honor, gentleness, and intellect." Talk of this kind would contribute to the belief that the South could easily defeat the North on the field of battle.[54]

There was one additional myth that pervaded Southern society, and this was that the slaves were happy. Fitzhugh wrote that "the Negro slaves of the South are the happiest and, in some respects, the freest people in the world." Yet even Fitzhugh knew this was largely mythical, confessing to a friend that he saw "great evils in slavery." Southerners also feared that their happy and contented slaves could be riled up by abolitionists from the North, who "would turn inherently loyal slaves into rebellious ones," Ashworth writes. The fear of a slave revolt was about to be put to the test by none other than John Brown.[55]

Harpers Ferry

Some in the abolitionist movement had abandoned nonviolence by the 1850s. One of them, Frederick Douglass, renounced pacifism in the aftermath of the Fugitive Slave Law. Prior to 1850, Douglass had said "the only well grounded hope of the slave for emancipation is the operation of moral force." But he had begun to believe that only "forcible resistance" could end the Fugitive Slave Law. Another was the wealthy New Yorker, Gerrit Smith, who became a member of the "Secret Six" who backed John Brown's intended raid on the federal arsenal at Harpers Ferry, Virginia. Brown's plan was to seize the arsenal and then head south to arm slaves in open rebellion. Yet when Brown formed his "army" to attack Harpers Ferry, it consisted of only twenty-one men, of which only five were black. When Brown approached Douglass to join him, he refused. Douglass could see that Harpers Ferry was a death trap, geographically surrounded by steep hills, telling Brown he would "never get out alive." It was advice that John Brown should have heeded.[56]

The raid, which was a failure, was less important than its aftermath. Even Brown seemed resigned to failure. Despite a quick capture of the arsenal on October 16, 1859, Brown and his small army were soon attacked by townspeople, who were joined by militias from Maryland and Virginia. Brown's troops took refuge in a fire engine house, barricading themselves in. A group of US Marines, led by Colonel Robert E. Lee, stormed the barricade and arrested Brown and his men. In total, fifteen people were killed, including ten of Brown's men. Brown was quickly placed on trial and sentenced to hang on December 2.[57]

While Brown was initially denounced in the North for his actions, his impassioned testimony during and after the trial soon evoked sympathy. "Now if it is deemed necessary that I should forfeit my life for the furtherance of the ends of justice ... I say let it be done," he said. Brown was seen "as a martyr for a noble cause," as McPherson frames it. In some Northern communities, church bells rang and ministers preached that Brown was a man to be admired for trying to free the slaves. Henry David Thoreau called him "a man of ideas and principles," while William Cullen Bryant said history would remember Brown as "among those of its martyrs and heroes." "John Brown had drawn his sword in an attempt to cut out this cancer of shame that tainted the promise of America," McPherson succinctly writes, even if most people denounced his methods.[58]

Some in the South initially felt vindicated over Brown's failure, since slaves had not risen up to throw off their chains, supporting the myth that they were indeed happy and content. Yet the reaction in the North, specifically the extent to which Brown was viewed as a hero, soon led to outrage in the South. Especially galling were abolitionists who seemed to encourage slave insurrections. Garrison, for example, announced, "I am prepared to say 'success to every slave insurrection at the South.'" For most in the North, this was simply too much. They denounced Brown's means (violent slave uprisings) yet shared his ends (eliminating slavery). Leading Republicans like Seward and Lincoln attempted to assuage the South. Seward said that Brown's execution was "necessary and just." For his part, Lincoln applauded Brown for "thinking slavery was wrong" but concluded "that cannot excuse violence, bloodshed and treason."[59]

In the South, such attempts at reassurance did little to staunch the outrage. Southerners lived in overwhelming fear of slave insurrections, and their fellow countrymen appeared to be encouraging such actions. A newspaper in Richmond wrote that "the Harper's Ferry invasion has advanced the cause of disunion more than any other event that has occurred since the formation of the government." They went on to write that "thousands of men ... who a month ago, scoffed at the idea of dissolution of the Union ... now hold the opinion that its days are numbered." For some in the South, the only way to save the Union was for the North to accept that slavery is "a social, moral, and political blessing," as an Atlanta newspaper framed it.[60]

Such was the state of opinion in the North and the South on the eve of the 1860 election. The tipping point had indeed been reached, only a precipitating event was needed to light the flame of disunion.

Endnotes

1   The quotes are from Buchanan's Inaugural Address of March 4, 1857, retrieved November 7, 2018, from https://millercenter.org/the-presidency/presidential-speeches/march-4-1857-inaugural-address.

2   Wilentz, *Rise*, p. 707.

3   Potter, *Impending Crisis*, p. 267–268.

4   Wilentz, *Rise*, p. 711; McPherson, p. 172–173.

5   The quotes are from McPherson, p. 174–175.

6   Wilentz, *Rise*, p. 712–713; McPherson, p. 175–176 and p. 177–178.

7   Wilentz, *Rise*, p. 712, makes the point about slave owners claiming Fifth Amendment rights in the North; Potter, *Impending Crisis*, p. 293. Both historians raise the important point that the court decision, if left intact, placed the United States squarely on the side of slavery, which may have been what the South wanted, but was unacceptable in the North.

8   McPherson, p. 176–179; Ashworth, p. 150.

9   Melvin I. Urofsky, "*Dred Scott* Decision," retrieved November 14, 2018, from https://www.britannica.com/event/Dred-Scott-decision.

10 Bruce Chadwick, *1858: Abraham Lincoln, Jefferson Davis, Robert E. Lee, Ulysses S. Grant and the War They Failed to See* (Naperville, 2011), p. 4–10.

11 McPherson, p. 161–163; Wilentz, *Rise*, p. 715.

12 McPherson, p. 163–165; Wilentz, *Rise*, p. 716.

13 McPherson, p. 166–167; Wilentz, *Rise*, p. 716; Cooper, p. 284–285.

14 McPherson, p. 166–167; Wilentz, *Rise*, p. 716.

15 Johannsen, p. 581–586; McPherson, p. 166; Donald, p. 203–204.

16 Wilentz, *Rise*, p. 718; Freeman, p. 235–240 and p. 283; McPherson, p. 168.

17 Blumenthal, location 3361; Chadwick, p. 109; Donald, p. 208 and p. 210.

18 Foner, *Fiery Trial*, p. 95; Pauline Maier, *American Scripture: Making the Declaration of Independence* (New York, 1997), p. 204.

19 Lincoln, p. 120–121; Foner, *Fiery Trial*, p. 99.

20 Foner, *Fiery Trial*, p. 97; Maier, p. 199.

21 Donald, p. 204–205.

22 Lincoln, p. 131.

23 Donald, p. 206–207; Burns, p. 582; Lincoln, p. 133; for the historian's criticism of Lincoln's conspiracy view, see Foner, *Fiery Trial*, p. 101; Wilentz, *Rise*, p. 738; and Donald, p. 208.

24 Donald, p. 210; Maier, p. 214.

25 Lincoln, p. 145; Foner, *Fiery Trial*, p. 103.

26 Donald, p. 210–211; Johannsen, p. 663–664.

27 Goodwin, p. 200–201; Donald, p. 215; Foner, *Fiery Trial*, p. 104–105.

28 Foner, *Fiery Trial*, p. 107–109, has a very useful summary of the main arguments of the two protagonists.

29 Donald, p. 216–217; the quotes from Douglas are from "First Debate: Ottawa, Illinois," retrieved December 7, 2018, from https://www.nps.gov/liho/learn/historyculture/debate1.htm.

30 Lincoln, p. 154–157; Johannsen, p. 670; Donald, p. 218–219; Wilentz, *Rise*, p. 740.

31 Foner, *Fiery Trial*, p. 107–108; Donald, p. 220.

32 Lincoln, p. 184; Johannsen, p. 672.

33 Potter, *Impending Crisis*, p. 329; Johannsen, p. 673.

34 Lincoln, p. 149; Burns, p. 586–587; Goodwin, p. 205.

35 McPherson, p. 187; Oakes, p. 83.

36 Wilentz, *The Politicians*, p. 191.

37 James MacGregor Burns, *Leadership* (New York, 1978), p. 42 and p. 4; Wilentz, *The Politicians*, p. 188.

38 Foner, *Fiery Trial*, p. xiv.

39 Donald, p. 228; Foner, *Fiery Trial*, p. 111.

40 The results of the 1858 Congressional election were retrieved on December 18, 2018, from https://en.wikipedia.org/wiki/1858_and_1859_United_States_House_of_Representatives_elections; see also Chadwick, p. 209–210; Ashworth, p. 161, for a description of the Opposition party.

41 Chadwick, p. 216.

42 Eric H. Walther, *The Fire-Eaters* (Baton Rouge, 1992), p. 8–47.

43 Walther, p. 121–148.

44 Wilentz, *Rise*, p. 728–729.

45 Walther, p. 48–70.

46 Walther, p. 228–253.

47 Foner, *Free Soil*, p. 42; Potter, *Impending Crisis*, p. 387; McPherson, p. 200.

48 Income statistics are from Lindert and Williamson, p. 116; Brandon Dupont and Joshua Rosenbloom, (2016, June 16), "Impact of the US Civil War on Southern Wealth Holders," retrieved December 23, 2018, from https://voxeu.org/article/impact-us-civil-war-southern-wealth-holders; data on the ownership of slavery is from "Wealth and Culture in the South," retrieved December 27, 2018, from https://courses.lumenlearning.com/ushistory1os2xmaster/chapter/wealth-and-culture-in-the-south/; for information about the emerging Southern middle class, see Jonathan

Daniel Wells, (2009, August), "The Southern Middle Class," *The Journal of Southern History*, retrieved from JStor on December 24, 2018, and Jonathan Daniel Wells, *The Origins of the Southern Middle Class: 1800-1861* (Chapel Hill, 2004), p.151–152.

49 Wells, p. 8, provides the estimate for the middle class. The occupations that make that up are listed in the appendix at p. 239.

50 Wilentz, *Rise*, p. 729–730; Cobb, p. 52; McPherson, p. 196; Ashworth, p. 158.

51 Fukuyama, p. 81–84; Cobb, p. 56.

52 McPherson, p. 196.

53 Wilentz, *Rise*, p. 724–725; Baptist, p. 322; North, p. 205–206.

54 McPherson, p. 197; Cobb, p. 42–43.

55 Cobb, p. 46; Ashworth, p. 158.

56 McPherson, p. 203–205; Wilentz, *Rise*, p. 747–748.

57 McPherson, p. 206.

58 McPherson, p. 209–210; Wilentz, *Rise*, p. 750–751.

59 Potter, *Impending Crisis*, p. 379; McPherson, p. 211–212.

60 McPherson, p. 211–212.

CHAPTER 15

The Union Collapses

The institutions and the happiness of this country are now in greater danger—in more absolute peril—than they have been at any other period in our history.
—STEPHEN DOUGLAS

The South "has come to the conclusion that in case Lincoln should be elected ... she [will] secede from the Union."
—JOHN CRITTENDEN

Carl Von Clausewitz, the Prussian military theorist, wrote that "war is merely the continuation of policy by other means." If true, then civil war seems more like the failure of policy and the political process to resolve problems and disputes. Less than two years after the midterm elections of 1858, the American Civil War began.

A Dysfunctional Congress

The Thirty-Sixth Congress opened on December 5, 1859, three days after John Brown was hanged. Both Northerners and Southerners attended legislative sessions armed with knives and guns. "During the first eight weeks of the first session alone there were nine fights,"

Freeman writes, with "violent outbreaks [occurring] every few weeks." One senator said, "The only persons who do not have a revolver and a knife are those who have two revolvers." Whereas Southern representatives had in the past been allowed to act with impunity, intimidating their Northern brethren, now the Republicans, too, were willing to defend themselves and, in some cases, act as the aggressors.[1]

The first crisis the House faced was the election of a Speaker. While the Republicans held a plurality of seats, they lacked a majority in order to elect their first choice, John Sherman of Ohio. Sherman was no radical and opposed "any interference whatever by the people of the free states with relations of master and slave in the slave states." But he had one major problem: he was among sixty Republicans who had endorsed Helper's book, *The Impending Crisis*. One Democrat from Missouri proposed a resolution that "no member of this House who has endorsed" the book "is fit to be Speaker." While the resolution never passed, neither did Sherman's campaign to be Speaker. While Southerners recoiled generally at the idea of a Republican as Speaker, to put a man in charge who had endorsed Helper's diatribe was considered dangerous. While the Republicans stuck with Sherman for two months, violence and the threat of violence pervaded the people's house. Some expected a shootout on the House floor, and Southerners began to wish "the Union were dissolved and we had a Southern confederacy." Finally, Sherman withdrew and William Pennington of New Jersey, who supported the Fugitive Slave Law, was elected as Speaker of the House with the support of representatives from the border states.[2]

On the policy front, Republicans and some Northern Democrats were interested in promoting a series of bills to encourage economic development and the expansion of free labor into the new territories. One was a Homestead Act, in which each person could gain ownership of 160 acres of land simply by settling on it. The bill passed both houses of Congress, but Buchanan vetoed it due to Southern opposition. It was another example of the split within the Democratic Party. Republicans also pursued an old Whig favorite, a protective tariff, which was passed by the House and defeated in the Senate. Similarly, a bill to build a transcontinental railroad also failed. Policy differences, and the continuing struggle over slavery, portended the future split of the Democratic Party, which was no longer "a single national party" in the 1860 election, as Potter writes.[3]

Southerners had their own policy disagreements. One was over a proposal to reopen the African slave trade, a cause that Rhett had taken up in 1854. Viewed by some as a way to reduce the price of slaves so more yeomen could afford them, it was conversely seen as adding more competition to labor markets that would lead to further impoverishment for those who worked for wages. Slave owners in the upper South, "who found a market for its surplus slaves in the cotton states," were also opposed, as Potter points out. The issue proved to be too divisive, and essentially went nowhere.[4]

There were also disagreements about what the South should do if a Republican was elected president. While some Fire Eaters preferred this as a way to spur secession, more moderate voices were still attempting to tamp down such incendiary talk. Jefferson Davis, who feared that some Republicans were out to destroy "the southern social system" wanted to maintain a middle ground, given his longstanding support of the Union. He was in a difficult position since Mississippi's Democratic Convention had already proclaimed that the election of a Republican president would be "a declaration of hostility" against the state. So, Davis walked a tightrope, telling people that a Republican victory could represent the "despotism of the majority" but also denying that such a victory would automatically cause the state to secede.

Much would depend on who the Republicans elected as president, although he clearly thought Seward, the front-runner, would be the worst of all candidates given his statements about a law higher than the Constitution.[5]

One thing most Southerners agreed on was that Congress should pass a federal slave code that would protect a slaveholder's right to take their property into federal territory. They wanted a law that would codify the *Dred Scott* decision and protect slaveholders from hostile legislation by a territorial government. In essence, they wanted protection from Douglas's Freeport Doctrine (so called because Douglas announced it in his debate with Lincoln in Freeport), in which a territory could vote to exclude slavery based on popular sovereignty, despite the *Dred Scott* decision. On February 2, 1860, Davis introduced a series of resolutions designed to do this. One of the resolutions declared "that neither Congress nor a territorial legislature could prohibit slavery in any territory," according to Davis biographer Cooper. Another made it the "duty of the Federal Government there to afford [slavery], as for other species of property, the needful protection." Interestingly, Davis also allowed a territory to decide for itself whether its constitution should allow for slavery once it applied for statehood. This was a way to continue to support President Buchanan's stand on popular sovereignty. During the territorial phase, the federal government would be required to protect owners who transported slaves into such territory. While the resolutions were adopted by the Senate Democratic caucus, Davis did not attempt to move them through the full Senate. "What he really wanted was a doctrinal test to impose upon Douglas Democrats in the national convention which was less than three months away," Potter writes. Douglas rightly saw it as an attempt to undermine his presidential aspirations, that the proposal to implement a federal slave code for the territories would split the Democratic Party apart. He would soon be proven right.[6]

The Election of 1860

The front-runner for the Republican nomination for president, William Seward had a glaring weakness: he was considered too radical in the eyes of more moderate Republicans. Seward's longtime friend, campaign manager, and power broker, Thurlow Weed, had recommended that "his protégé remove himself from the increasingly contentious debate at home by travelling overseas for eight months," Goodwin writes. Weed hoped that by having Seward travel in Europe for most of 1859 he could avoid any missteps that might cost him the nomination. It was a rare mistake for Weed, since it gave Lincoln time to burnish his appeal to the Republican Party.[7]

Lincoln took advantage of the months Seward was gone, traveling around the country and giving a series of speeches in Ohio, Wisconsin, Iowa, Indiana, and Kansas. A major break came when Lincoln was asked to give a speech in New York by Republican opponents of Seward, including the *Tribune*'s Horace Greeley and William Cullen Bryant, the editor of the *Evening Post*. It was originally to be held at Plymouth Church in Brooklyn in February of 1860. Plymouth's pastor was the abolitionist Henry Ward Beecher, son of Lyman Beecher, and the brother of Harriet Beecher Stowe, the author of *Uncle Tom's Cabin*. But the venue was soon changed to the Cooper Institute (now called Cooper Union), a college for the children of the working class. Lincoln had purchased an expensive black suit for the occasion, yet a member of the audience later commented that the clothes appeared to be "the work of an unskilled tailor" and that the speaker "did not fit in with New York's conception of a finished statesman," given his ill-fitting clothes and his high-pitched voice. Lincoln's oratory, delivered before a full house of sixteen hundred people, soon swayed the audience.[8]

Lincoln had been preparing a response to an article Douglas had published in *Harper's Magazine*. In the article, Douglas attempted to prove that the use of popular sovereignty to decide the question of slavery was consistent with both the views of the founders and with the Constitution. Both men had spent a substantial amount of time studying the founding era, with Douglas checking out reference volumes from the Library of Congress and consulting historian George Bancroft, while Lincoln "went through the records of the Constitutional Convention and the debates in the earliest Congress," Donald writes. Not surprisingly, each man found support for his position, given that the founders had been unable to solve the issue of slavery during their era and had left a mixed record. Douglas found that the "fathers of the Revolution" had determined "that the slavery question was considered by them" to best be decided by the people themselves at the local level.[9]

Lincoln's response, given at the Cooper Institute, was intended to refute "that Congress was powerless to legislate on slavery in the territories" and "that the Constitution affirmed an absolute right to property in man," as Wilentz frames it. Lincoln found in his research that twenty-one of the thirty-nine signers of the Constitution had shown "by their votes that the federal government had the power to control slavery in the national territories," during the convention, according to Donald. This did not include such Framers as Franklin, Hamilton, and Gouverneur Morris, all of whom were antislavery, but who had not voted on this specific issue. The Framers were so embarrassed by the provisions on slavery that were included in the Constitution that they refused to use the word. "Neither the word 'slave' nor 'slavery' is to be found in the Constitution," Lincoln correctly pointed out. Perhaps

Lincoln was aware of the words of John Dickinson at the convention, who wrote in his notebook during one of the debates on slavery that "the omitting [of] the WORD will be regarded as an Endeavour to conceal a principle of which we are ashamed." Lincoln also pointed out that Washington had "signed an act of Congress, enforcing the prohibition of slavery in the Northwestern Territory," and then had sent a letter to Lafayette in which he stated, "that he considered that prohibition a wise measure."[10]

Any attempt to show that the "right of property in a slave is distinctly and expressly affirmed in the Constitution" (which was the wording used by Taney in the *Dred Scott* decision) was false, according to Lincoln. The Framers excluded "from the Constitution the idea that there could be property in man." Lincoln must have been aware of the debate that took place at the Constitutional Convention over taxing the importation of slaves. Roger Sherman had protested that the current wording acknowledged "men to be property, by taxing them as such under the character of slaves." Madison had agreed, saying it would be wrong "to admit in the Constitution the idea that there could be property in men." The convention had therefore amended the subsection to read that "a Tax or duty may be imposed on such Importation, not exceeding ten dollars per *person*." By adding the word *person*, the convention had established that slaves were people, not property.[11]

Lincoln used this finding to great effect. Taney's majority opinion in *Dred Scott* was based on an absolute finding that the Constitution protected slaves as property. This reflected Southern opinion and was at the heart of their claim that their constitutional rights were being violated whenever Congress or a territorial legislature banned slavery. If this position stood, "freedom would be local and slavery national," as Wilentz writes. It was the exact opposite of what had occurred at the

Constitutional Convention. Lincoln maintained that "all Republicans ask[ed] ... in relation to slavery" was that it again be marked "as an evil not to be extended." Since the Republicans were following in the footsteps of the founders, they were the true conservatives, adhering to "the old tried and true." Lincoln was attempting to inoculate the Republicans from the charge that they were radicals in the mold of John Brown.[12]

☞ ☞ ☞

Stephen A. Douglas was in trouble. His ambition to be president, a goal that had seemed within reach just a few short years before, was endangered by the issue he had long sought to finesse—slavery. His break with Buchanan over the Lecompton Constitution, and his unwillingness to fully embrace the implications of the *Dred Scott* decision, had caused a majority in the South to abandon him. To make matters worse, the Democratic Party Convention was held in Charleston, South Carolina, a hotbed of secessionists and Fire Eaters.[13]

The convention opened on April 27, 1860, in an overcrowded city where temperatures had risen into the mid-nineties. The rhetoric of some from the South matched the temperature. Robert Rhett argued that "the Democratic party, as a party, based on principles is dead ... It has not one single principle common to its members North and South." An Illinois delegate complained of "the bitterness of some of our Southern opponents. They go as far as to call us all abolitionists." The delegates from seven states of the Deep South had come to the convention committed to including in the party platform a federal slave code, which Douglas opposed. They planned to walk out if they did not get their way, to be joined by some of the delegates from four other slave states.[14]

The demand for a slave code by the Southern delegates was successful with the platform committee, which passed it on a 17–16 vote. As the full convention began to debate the platform, the Fire Eater William Yancey gave an incendiary speech, telling the Northern Democrats they should have defended slavery as a positive good. Lincoln's warning from the Cooper Institute speech, where he had said that what the South really wanted was for the North to "cease to call slavery *wrong*, and join them in calling it *right*," seemed to be coming true. Northern delegates, who held a solid majority in the convention, rejected the federal slave code and instead "adopted the minority plank, which reaffirmed the 1856 convention's endorsement of popular sovereignty," Sean Wilentz writes. Fifty delegates from the Deep South, true to their word, then walked out of the convention. Douglas still lacked the two-thirds vote needed to secure the nomination, and after fifty-seven ballots, the convention adjourned to meet again six weeks later in Baltimore. Douglas finally secured the nomination there, but without Southern support. The Southern delegates, meeting in Richmond, selected Vice President John C. Breckinridge as their presidential candidate. Breckinridge, who was from Kentucky, had served in the House from 1851 until 1855, and was the youngest vice president in the history of the country when Buchanan selected him at the age of thirty-five. The Democratic Party was now irretrievably split along sectional lines.[15]

❦ ❦ ❦

Lincoln had spent his time wisely in the East and was now considered a possible Republican nominee for president. His strategy was to offer himself as a viable alternative should William Seward, the front-runner, falter on the first ballot. "Our policy, then, is to give no offence to others—leave them in a mood to come over to us, if they shall be compelled to give up their first love," Lincoln told one of his supporters. Since it was still considered unseemly for a man to campaign for himself, Lincoln operated through a group of his loyal friends, who were able to secure the support of the Illinois delegation "to vote as a unit for him." A former Democrat who was helping Lincoln cast the deciding vote that put the Republican Convention in Chicago.[16]

The Windy City was an auspicious choice for Lincoln, allowing his name to emerge as a possible contender in an overwhelmingly friendly environment. Chicago, which had been little more than a backwater fort town in 1830, had a population of over one hundred thousand people when the convention opened in May of 1860. The key to victory for any Republican was to carry three states that bordered the South: Pennsylvania, Indiana, and Illinois, plus New Jersey. In February, Seward had given a major speech in the Senate designed to assuage both Southerners and these important states, who considered him too radical. He talked about his support of the Union and how "the people of the North are not enemies but friends and brethren of the South" and said that the Republican Party did not "seek to force or intrude, our system upon the South." As far as he was concerned, Southerners were "sovereign on the subject of slavery within your own borders." Gone was the talk of the irrepressible conflict or a higher law than the Constitution.[17]

Yet Seward and Weed "failed to anticipate the damage [he] would suffer as a consequence of a rift with Horace Greeley," Goodwin writes. Greeley felt he had been jilted, that his past support of Seward had not been repaid through an appointment to an important government job or assistance in running for office. At the convention, Greeley exacted his revenge, telling the delegates "you couldn't elect Seward if you nominate him." He brought in leading politicians from key Northern states like Iowa, Pennsylvania, and Indiana, who confirmed what Greeley had said.[18]

Meanwhile, Lincoln's men went to work securing the support of delegates from important swing states on the second ballot. Lincoln warned them to "make no contracts that will bind me."[19]

On the day voting began, Lincoln's supporters played a political trick on Seward's people, creating counterfeit tickets to the convention so they could stack the Wigwams gallery, as the venue was known. While Seward's nomination was met with great applause, it paled in comparison to Lincoln's. "The audience like a wild colt with [a] bit between his teeth, rose above all cry of order, and again and again the irrepressible applause broke forth and resounded far and wide" for Lincoln, one reporter noted. Seward fell short of the 233 votes needed on the first ballot, receiving 173½ to 102 for Lincoln. The Pennsylvania delegates then threw their support to Lincoln on the second ballot, putting him within 3½ votes of Seward. On the third ballot, Lincoln secured the nomination when Ohio switched 4 additional votes to put him over the top. Seward was devastated by the loss, but within a week he pledged his support to Lincoln and Hannibal Hamlin, the Republican's vice-presidential pick. Lincoln was informed of his victory while he waited in Springfield. "Well Gentlemen there is a little woman at our house who is probably more interested in this dispatch than I am," he remarked, no doubt suppressing some of the joy he must have felt.[20]

❦ ❦ ❦

As if three parties vying for power were not enough in 1860, a fourth joined the fray. The Constitutional Union Party, formed by Senator John Crittenden of Kentucky, organized those who still hoped to save the Union. Twenty-three of the thirty states, including all the large ones, sent delegates to a convention held in Baltimore in May of 1860. They nominated John Bell of Tennessee, a lifelong slave owner who was nonetheless "not a vigorous exponent of the political rights of slavery," according to Potter. To balance the ticket, Edward Everett of Massachusetts was selected as vice president. The party did not adopt a platform but instead pledged support to "the Constitution as it is, and the Union under it, now and forever ..." While the Constitutional Union Party appealed to those in the border states and the upper South, it lacked what one observer at the time referred to as "any definite principles or opinions" on the major subject for which the election was being contested, slavery.[21]

The Campaign

During an era where it was considered unseemly for a candidate to actively campaign for himself, Lincoln ran a traditional campaign. But this did not stop him from working behind the scenes, "conferring with party chiefs, talking with newspapermen, directing campaign operations by letter, and smoothing frictions within the party organization," Potter writes. The Republican Party consisted of divergent strands, including former Whigs, disgruntled Northern Democrats, and even Know-Nothings. Lincoln needed to hold them together, since a united North would be needed to prevail in the election. Lincoln was depicted in the campaign as a champion of the common man, "Honest Old Abe," "son of the frontier," and "the rail splitter," a reference to his work as a manual laborer when he was young. While the extension of slavery was by far the key issue in the election, Lincoln could not afford to ignore other high-profile issues. In industrial states like Pennsylvania and New Jersey, "a protective tariff was stronger than hostility to slavery," according to Goodwin, and the Republican platform supported such a measure. In the West, passage of homestead legislation was a high priority, especially after Buchanan vetoed the Homestead Act, which the Republican Congress had passed.[22]

Lincoln made it a point to not "write or speak anything about doctrinal points now" that the campaign was underway. He and Seward mended fences, and Lincoln indicated that he intended to name him to the preeminent cabinet post of secretary of state. Seward went on a barnstorming tour of the Midwest on Lincoln's behalf, giving speeches in Michigan, Wisconsin, Minnesota, Iowa, Kansas, Illinois, and Ohio. "Reporters marveled at Seward's ability to make every speech seem spontaneous and vital," Goodwin writes. One observer told Seward that "you are doing more for Lincoln's election than any hundred men in the United States." During a speech in Chicago, Lincoln urged Seward to assure the audience that the Republicans "would not interfere with slavery where it existed." This was targeted toward conservative Republicans, and not to Southerners. Lincoln and the Republicans refused to acknowledge the pending danger the nation was in should Lincoln be elected president. Lincoln thought it was "a sort of political game of bluff gotten by politicians, and meant solely to frighten the North." He thought that the "people of the South have too much good sense, and good temper, to attempt the ruin of the government." Seward joined him in this, telling one audience "they cry out that they will tear the Union to pieces ... Who's afraid? Nobody's afraid." In response to requests from more conservative Northerners, Lincoln rejected any statements that would assuage the South. "What is it I could say which would quiet alarm?" Lincoln had already repeated many times that he would not disturb slavery where it already existed, such that "a repetition of it is but a mockery, bearing an appearance of weakness." Still, the unwillingness of the Republicans to take the threats from the South seriously was a major error in judgment. As historian Alan Nevins has written, the "cardinal error" of the Republicans was the failure to recognize "the now imminent danger of secession."[23]

Perhaps had Lincoln and the Republicans undertaken a national campaign, they would have seen the danger more clearly. Traveling in the South, they may have perceived that this time was different, that the election of Lincoln was indeed the final event that would cause secession. Crittenden warned in August that even the border states, along with the rest of the South, had "come to the conclusion that in case Lincoln should be elected ... she [will] secede from the Union." Potter argues that had the Republicans run a campaign in the South, they may have "stressed Lincoln's recognition of the right of the southern states to determine the question of slavery for themselves," and framed Lincoln more in the mold of his old political hero Henry Clay. This may have given the South an alternative view of Lincoln, one that saw him as "an inveterate enemy of the South." But the Republicans were not welcome in the South and had no chance of winning any of the slave states. There was no reason for them to venture into hostile territory. With a focus on the North, what choice did the Republicans have except to ignore the threat? Nothing Lincoln could have said or done would have assuaged the South, and dwelling on the pending crisis of the Union may well have cost the Republicans the election. As historian James McPherson has argued, it is hard to see what Republicans could have done short of "dissolving their party and proclaiming slavery a positive good."[24]

If Lincoln ran a traditional campaign, Douglas threw the rule book out and directly campaigned all over the country except the Far West. With his party split between North and South, Douglas decided "to carry the issues of the election directly to the people," his biographer writes. While Lincoln was sanguine that the Union would not dissolve, Douglas was fearful. "The institutions and the happiness of this country are now in greater danger—in more absolute peril—than they have been at any other period in our history." His prodigious efforts, along with his heavy drinking and cigar smoking, may have contributed to Douglas's early death in June of 1861 at age forty-eight. He focused his efforts on defeating not only Lincoln but also the Southern wing of his own party and its candidate, Vice President Breckinridge. While traveling in New England, he began to realize the strength that Lincoln had in the North, and he refused to speak badly of him. "I have not the heart to say anything against Abe Lincoln; I have fought him so long that I have respect for him," Douglas told one audience.[25]

In the aftermath of the October elections in Pennsylvania, Ohio, and Indiana, when the Republicans swept to victory, Douglas reached the conclusion that Lincoln would be elected. He was not alone, and some powerful politicians began an effort to create a fusion ticket that combined the forces of Douglas, Breckinridge, and Bell. Jefferson Davis made one attempt to get the three candidates to step aside "in favor of [a] pro-southern Unionist, but Douglas spurned the offer as impractical [and] would rather see Lincoln elected than collaborate with the southerners who had tried to destroy him," according to Wilentz. Instead, Douglas decided to return to the South, where he had already held campaign rallies, to "try to save the Union." He faced a clearly hostile reception in much of the South. One editor in Atlanta indicated that if Lincoln were elected, "the eight cotton states [will] secede immediately on his election." Still, some support remained for the Union, especially in the border states, but even in parts of the Deep South, where Douglas was met by large crowds. In Georgia, he was introduced by his friend of sixteen years, the former representative Alexander Stephens, who opposed secession. He urged the audience to give Douglas "a careful, calm and patient hearing. He comes to address not your passions, but your intellects." Stephens would soon assume the office of vice president for the Confederate States of America once his native Georgia seceded. In Alabama, Douglas directly confronted disunion, warning Southerners that if Lincoln were elected, he must be allowed to assume the office. "I hold that the election of any man on earth by the American people, according to the Constitution, is no justification for breaking up this government." In his campaign appearance in the South, he warned that he would hang all disunionists "higher than Haman" should he be elected.[26]

Douglas's efforts did him little good, either in the North or the South. The one note of hope for those who wanted to preserve the nation was another attempt to fuse the anti-Lincoln forces together. Businessmen and bankers in the Northeast, particularly in New York, New Jersey, Pennsylvania, and Rhode Island, were able to create fusion tickets. "Douglas repudiated any links with Breckinridge but he encouraged merging with the Bell forces, and for a time, it looked as if the alliances might prove just strong enough to affect the outcome," Wilentz writes. Had the fusion party garnered enough votes, they might have caused Lincoln to fall short of the electoral votes needed to win the election, throwing the decision into the House of Representatives. Yet they failed.[27]

It was an outcome that was determined by two very different electorates. In the North, Lincoln swept to victory over Douglas, winning all eighteen free states except New Jersey, which the two men split. Lincoln garnered almost 1.9 million votes, and 180 electors, enough to easily win the election. Yet he won less than 40 percent of the total popular vote, but 54 percent of the total vote in the North. In the South, Breckinridge won 45 percent of the vote and carried eleven states, while Bell won 39 percent of the vote and three states. Douglas, while winning close to 1 million votes (most of the fusion numbers would likely have been his, since they came from the North), only received the full electoral votes of one state. The chart below summarizes the split in the vote.[28]

Candidate	Free States	%	Slave States	%	Total	%
Lincoln	1,838,347	54%	26,388	2%	1,864,736	40%
Douglas	815,857	24%	163,568	13%	979,425	21%
Breckinridge	99,381	3%	570,091	45%	669,472	14%
Bell	76,973	2%	499,441	39%	576,414	12%
Fusion	580,426	17%	15,420	1%	595,846	13%
Total	3,410,984	100%	1,274,908	100%	4,685,893	100%
Source: Potter, Impending Crisis, p. 443						

Lincoln was the president-elect, even though his name did not appear on the ballot in ten states in the South. It was truly a major turnaround for the forces that opposed slavery. From a radical fringe movement in the 1830s, abolitionism was triumphant in the North, electing a president committed to halting the spread of slavery. The Northern electorate was "thoroughly united about the necessity to halt slavery's unchecked spread," Wilentz writes. As for the South, there were still disagreements over whether secession was the immediate answer, but "they were nearly unanimous in their repudiation of the northern candidates and of slavery's restriction." It would not take long for the most vociferous Southern states to make their intentions known.[29]

❦ ❦ ❦

Unsurprisingly, South Carolina went first, calling for a convention to consider secession in mid-January. Under pressure from the radicals, it moved the date up to December 17. Three days later the convention unanimously adopted an ordinance declaring that "the Union now subsisting between South Carolina and other States, under the name of the 'United States of America', is hereby dissolved." By February 1, six other states of the Deep South would join them: Mississippi, Florida, Alabama, Georgia, Louisiana, and Texas. "There can be little doubt that the speed of South Carolina's action gave crucial encouragement to secessionists throughout the South and accelerated the tempo of the disunion movement in [a] decisive way," Potter writes, at least in the Deep South.[30]

It wasn't as if there was no opposition to the movement for immediate secession in these states. Sean Wilentz writes that in states other than South Carolina and Texas, "at least 40 percent" of voters supported candidates that were opposed to immediate secession or who wanted to work in tandem with other states. In those counties where few slaveholders resided, support for secession was weakest. Delegates to the conventions tended to be split into two groupings: the conditional secessionist (also called the "cooperationists") and those who supported immediate secession. The conditional secessionists were further split among themselves. "Some thought it wiser to organize a united southern confederacy first; others wanted to deliver a list of impossible demands to Lincoln and then secede; and still others truly wished to test Lincoln's claims to moderation and await an overt act against the South before dissolving the Union," according to Wilentz. Yet while the voters may have been split between the two sides, the number of delegates that supported immediate secession substantially outnumbered the conditional secessionists, and so they controlled the outcome. Those who supported immediate secession also had the more outspoken supporters on their side, people who were "wild with passion and frenzy," Alexander Stephens observed at the time, who were ready to uphold the "honor or the rights of her [the South's] citizens." The immediate secessionists further appealed to the racism of those who did not own slaves.[31]

Meanwhile, attempts to find a compromise floundered in Washington, DC. In early December, the Senate formed the Committee of Thirteen, which included Douglas, Seward, and Jefferson Davis, among other prominent politicians. The committee's compromise was framed largely by Crittenden, who proposed to revive the Missouri Compromise line and extend it to the Pacific. Since this would mean the possible expansion of slavery, Lincoln lobbied the Republican members of the committee to oppose it. Lincoln wrote to Thurlow Weed on December 17 that he was "inflexible on the territorial question" and that the plan "would lose us everything we gained by the election." All five Republicans on the committee voted against the plan, as did Davis and Toombs. Davis had originally supported the Crittenden Plan, but when the Republicans stood firm, he later wrote "my hope of an honorable peaceable settlement was ... abandoned." Lincoln was willing to support minor concessions, including affirming the constitutionality of the Fugitive Slave Law and an amendment to the Constitution to bar the federal government from interfering with slavery where it already existed, but none of these ended the crisis.[32]

Did the Southern states that seceded see themselves as a new nation? Some people at the time perhaps did, but there were several reasons to believe the answer for most people was no. For one thing, some in the South continued to cling to the notion that the United States was never truly a nation, and they certainly did not want to establish another strong central government or a consolidated nation through the Confederacy. John C. Calhoun had been one of the foremost disciples of such a view, believing that the Constitution was a compact between sovereign states, and that the federal government was a creature of the states. He even denied that the United States was a nation, saying "so far from the Constitution being the work of the American people collectively, no such political body ever did exist." Many of the Fire Eaters shared this view, especially Nathaniel Beverly Tucker. Southerners who espoused this view harkened back to the antifederalists who protested that the Constitution would establish a consolidated national government rather than a federal union of sovereign states.[33]

It's also hard to make a claim for a new Southern nation when the upper and middle South did not yet support secession. Unionism remained strong in the eight slave states of Virginia, Maryland, Delaware, Kentucky, Tennessee, Missouri, Arkansas, and North Carolina. In February of 1861, each of these states either held conventions where the opponents of secession held a majority or refused to even form a state convention. These states "contained most [of] the South's resources for waging war," McPherson writes, including most of the white population and the industrial capacity of the South. It was hard to imagine that the Deep South could succeed independently without these states. The Virginians had deep ties to the formation of the American nation, from Washington to Jefferson to Madison to Monroe, who were esteemed members of the Founding Fathers and represented four of the first five presidents. Virginians supported a Peace Conference in which former President Tyler served as president. Twenty-three states attended the conference that was held at the Willard Hotel in Washington, DC, in February 1861, but they were unable to come up with any original proposals that all could agree on. "After some three weeks of labor, the Peace Conference recommended a seven-part amendment to the Constitution which differed but little from the Crittenden Compromise," according to Potter. Lincoln and the Republicans were not going to sign off on any proposals that allowed for the expansion of slavery, while the border South wanted assurances for the protection of slavery in the new territories and a commitment that the new Lincoln administration would not use force to end the secession crisis.[34]

Rather than a new nation, some in the South saw themselves as "the true Americans," in the words of Ashworth. While the Peace Conference was underway, the states of the Deep South met in Montgomery, Alabama, to form a new confederacy. They elected Jefferson Davis as president and Alexander Stephens as vice president and adopted an interim constitution. Both men were viewed as moderates, selected at least in part "to appeal to the upper South states," according to Wilentz. They then set about to write a permanent constitution that was largely a duplicate of the Constitution the Framers had prepared, with one major exception. Whereas the Framers refused to use the word *slavery* in the document, the Confederate Constitution was explicit in its protections for slavery, stating that no "law denying or impairing the right of property in negro slaves shall be passed." The Confederate Constitution also made it clear, in its preamble, that "each State was acting in its sovereign and independent character," thereby incorporating the theory that the Confederacy was a compact among sovereign states. Surprisingly, the document failed to mention the right of a state to secede. Perhaps this was because the delegates themselves disagreed over the legal basis for secession. "Fire-eater secessionists held the militant view that secession was perfectly legal and represented nothing radical," as Wilentz writes. Others, like Davis, grounded their arguments for secession in Jefferson's right to revolution. In his acceptance speech, Davis argued that Southern secession was based on "the American idea that governments rest upon the consent of the governed, and it is the right of the people to alter or abolish them at will whenever they become destructive of the ends for which they were established," wording similar to that contained in the Declaration of Independence.[35]

If the South did not see itself as forming a new nation, then what was the purpose of secession? In a nation where the North and the South had developed two very different economic systems, and the abolitionists' movement had become so successful, the South no longer believed its system of plantation slavery was safe in the Union. This went hand in hand with the fear of slave uprisings, which was what made the North's reaction to John Brown's death so incendiary. Secession was justified by the South's unique theory of federalism, in which the Union was a compact of sovereign states, and individual states could choose to leave the Union if they felt it was no longer advantageous for them. For those who didn't subscribe fully to the compact theory as a justification for secession, like Jefferson Davis, they fell back on the right of revolution embedded in the Declaration of Independence.

The North and South had always been different economically and culturally, and those differences had increased over time. As a Georgian newspaper wrote: "The differences between North and South have been growing more marked for years, and the mutual repulsion more radical, until not a single sympathy is left," between the sections. The North was increasingly becoming a more diversified economy, with a large farming sector but also an expanding industrial base that had grown between 1815 and 1860. In 1820, only 75,000 workers had been engaged in manufacturing, but that had grown to 1.2 million people by the 1850s, or 15 percent of the workforce. Originally, the industrial sector was centered on cotton mills in New England, which provided an overlap of interests between the North and the South. To a large extent, the American economy had been built on slavery. But as Northern industry diversified, it was no longer as dependent on cotton to fuel its economy. This had an impact politically, as "northern manufacturers no longer needed the South," Baptist writes. "So there was no justification for acceding to continued southern dominance over the political process."[36]

With westward expansion and the growing demand for cotton in the years after 1800, the South had become ever more dependent on slavery. Plantation society had gradually expanded into the new states of Alabama, Mississippi, Louisiana, and ultimately Texas. While the North celebrated its free market labor system, Southerners continued to disparage it. Thomas Jefferson had thought that a republic could only survive where most people owned their own land, which made them independent and free. "A man dependent on others for a living could never be truly free, nor could a dependent class constitute the basis of republican government," McPherson writes. Many Republicans agreed with this but believed that upward mobility would lift wage earners into the middle class, where they could eventually own a business or farm. Southerners looked at the spreading poverty of wage earners in Northern cities and concluded that the basic needs of their slaves were taken care of. This led to the "glorification of plantation life, in which even slavery was idealized" compared to the "impersonal, dehumanized irresponsibility of 'wage slavery,'" found in the North, as Potter writes. Such sentiments led to the view that slavery was not a necessary evil, as the founding generation had believed, but a positive good. John C. Calhoun once said: "Never before has the black race attained a condition so civilized and so improved, not only physically, but morally and intellectually."[37]

Southerners had always had an abiding fear of slave uprisings, dating back to colonial times, and increasingly after the revolution in Santo Domingo. Abolitionists seemed to encourage slaves to revolt, and the reaction of Northerners to John Brown's attempted slave revolt at Harpers Ferry had contributed to Southerners' unease. "From their standpoint, the election to the presidency of a man who stated flatly that slavery was morally wrong might have a more inciting effect upon the slaves than denunciatory rhetoric from the editor of an abolitionist weekly in Boston," Potter writes. Yet, the Southern fear of slave revolts also made clear that the myth they had created, that slaves were happy, was a lie. In 1832, one man had written that "a merrier being does not exist on the face of the globe than the negro slave" in America. The only reason slaves revolted at all was because they were put up to it by abolitionists who "whisper into the ears of such a slave that his situation is degrading and his lot a miserable one." Or so the myth went. As one former slave later said: "A man who has been in slavery knows ... the yearnings to be free, and the fear of making the attempts."[38]

Southerners ultimately seceded from the Union because they had concluded it was the best way to protect and secure their social and economic system, which was grounded in slavery. Once disputes began to arise over slavery, first in the 1830s with the rise of the abolitionist movement, followed by disagreements over whether the addition of new territory should be slave or free in the 1840s and 1850s, the South had begun to feel the peculiar institution might no longer be safe in the Union. Southern politicians attempted to bully their Northern counterparts during this period as a way to quell the disputes over slavery, but they met their match with a new breed of Republican politicians that arose in the 1850s, men unafraid to fight for their beliefs. By 1860, there were still moderates like Alexander Stephens who thought "slavery was more secure in the Union than out of it." But that attitude was increasingly becoming the minority view, and even those Southerner Unionists wanted additional security for slavery. Ultimately, no compromise on the issue could be found that was acceptable to all sides.[39]

The South Carolina convention's declaration on secession was grounded in the theory that the Constitution was merely a compact among sovereign states that the North had violated. "Thus was established, by compact between the States, a Government ... limited to the express words of the grant." The North had violated the compact due to its "increasing hostility ... to the institution of slavery." Secession was therefore warranted. Alexander Stephens had, by the time his state of Georgia seceded, made it explicit that secession was designed to protect slavery. The founders had thought that slavery "was wrong in principle" and an "evil they knew not well how to deal with," Stephens admitted. But the Confederacy held no such qualms, nor did it share in the view that slavery would eventually "pass away ... Our new government is founded upon exactly the opposite idea ... upon the great truth, that the negro is not equal to the white man; that slavery ... is his natural and normal condition."[40]

Slavery was at the heart of secession, justified by the South's interpretation of the Union as a compact among sovereign states. The twin problems left over from the founding era, slavery and federalism, had festered and finally exploded in 1861. After the Civil War, both Davis and Stephens would attempt to obscure the role that slavery played in secession. Davis wrote that "the existence of African servitude was in no way the cause of the conflict." Stephens was even more explicit, stating that the war was not about "African Subordination" but "between the supporters of a strictly Federal Government on the one side, and a thoroughly National one, on the other." While the locus of federal power was certainly in dispute in 1861, it was only relevant because the South wanted to protect and expand slavery. The use of federalism as the cover, the excuse for secession, is what Sean Wilentz calls "one of the most consequential acts of falsification in American history."[41]

Lincoln Takes Office

The president-elect had spent his time in Springfield largely out of the spotlight and remained quiet about the state of affairs, with two major exceptions. Lincoln contemplated his cabinet selections and largely settled on having William Seward serve as his secretary of state. He also ensured that the Republicans did not compromise on any matter of major principle with the South, while maintaining the support of his party, which was internally split over how to proceed on the issue of secession. Lincoln indicated there "was nothing which I have not already said" on the issues, and he refused to take "a position towards the South which might be considered a sort of an apology for [my] election." To do so would allow the secessionists to believe "they had alarmed" him and they would then "clamor all the louder." He unalterably opposed secession, believing that "no state can, in any way lawfully, get out of the Union, without the consent of the" other states. This was the view of Madison, who had written in 1833 during the nullification crisis, when the issue of secession had come up, that individual states "owe fidelity" to the Constitution "till released by consent, or absolved by an intolerable abuse of the power created," in other words, by the right of revolution. Some in Congress, "who were better informed about affairs in the South," according to Donald, urged Lincoln to compromise, which he agreed to do, although not on the issue of the expansion of slavery.[42]

On February 11, Lincoln left for Washington by train on a nine-teen-hundred-mile trip that would take him twelve days to complete. It was intended to cement support for the Union in the North. Lincoln, always subject to bouts of melancholy, "sat alone and depressed" on the first leg of the trip. But his mood seemed to lighten "as he witnessed the friendly crowds lined up along the way," Goodwin writes. Rumors began to spread as the train neared Baltimore, a city seething with sympathy for secession, that Lincoln would be assassinated. He was advised by the private detective, Alan Pinkerton, to secretly take a night train through Baltimore to Washington, DC. Lincoln would later regret the decision, especially when one reporter invented the story that Lincoln "had disguised himself by wearing a Scottish plaid cap and a long military coat," according to Donald. The incident made Lincoln look weak, even cowardly, at a time when he was trying to project strength.[43]

Lincoln arrived in Washington, DC, ten days before the inauguration. Lincoln's presidential rivals, Douglas, Bell, and Breckinridge, each paid him a courtesy visit. Douglas told him he still supported conciliation with the South. "Our Union must be preserved," he told Lincoln, but he would not undermine the president-elect. "I am with you, Mr. President." When he left, Lincoln commented "what a noble man Douglas is." The senator would soon be dead, his heavy drinking, cigar smoking, and all-consuming work habits costing him his life at the age of forty-nine.[44]

Lincoln also finalized his cabinet during this period. He wanted both Salmon Chase and Seward to be part of his government, two men who did not much like each other. When Seward learned that Chase would be treasury secretary, he threatened to resign. Seward had been scheming to control Lincoln and viewed "himself as the premier of the incoming Lincoln administration," according to Donald. In January, Seward had given a major speech in the Senate in an attempt to conciliate the upper South. He came in for substantial criticism from the more radical members of the Republican Party, but believed he was doing Lincoln's bidding, which he was. But Lincoln was "engaged in a more intricate game of political engineering than Seward realized," Goodwin writes, allowing Seward to tamp down secession in the upper South while Lincoln remained at arm's length from the endeavor in order to maintain his support across the party. Lincoln also knew that Seward was attempting to gain control over the new administration, and that his threat to resign over the Chase selection would give Seward too much power. "I can't afford to let Seward to take the first trick," Lincoln told his secretary, John Nicolay. Acting in private, Lincoln tactfully convinced Seward to stay, since he knew he needed him. It would not be the last time Seward would attempt to manipulate Lincoln, but he had in fact met his match.[45]

Seward, along with Lincoln's friend Oroville Browning, proved invaluable in striking the right balance in the inaugural address between defending the nation and mollifying the border states. Lincoln, who relied on the Constitution, Jackson's proclamation on nullification, and Webster's reply to Hayne, had come down too harshly in his first draft of the inaugural address. Specifically, he had pledged to retake federal property that had already fallen into Confederate hands. Browning convinced Lincoln to soften the language and focus on "the properties still belonging to the federal government, including Fort Sumter," Goodwin writes. In the inaugural address, Lincoln said that "the power confided to me, will be used to hold, occupy, and possess the property, and places belonging to the government," and that "there will be no invasion, no using of force." Seward too thought the draft was too belligerent and that Virginia and Maryland would quickly secede if he gave it as written. His influence was present throughout the speech, including a provision in which Lincoln supported a constitutional amendment protecting slavery where it already existed, which had just passed the Congress. Lincoln made it clear that "the Union of these States is perpetual" and that "the idea of secession is the essence of anarchy," which allows a minority of the people to dictate to a majority. Lincoln also made it clear that the federal government would not trigger a conflict, and that the Confederacy would have to be "the aggressors." Perhaps Seward's most important contribution was the closing. Lincoln had originally written a far too bellicose ending. "With *you*, and not with *me*, is the solemn question of 'Shall it be peace or a sword?'" Seward suggested an ending that Lincoln ultimately included, albeit it in his own words.[46]

> *I am loth to close. We are not enemies, but friends. We must not be enemies. Though passion may have strained, it must not break our bonds of affection. The mystic chords of memory, stretching from every battle-field, and patriot grave, to every living heart and hearthstone, all over this broad land, will yet swell the chorus of the Union, when again touched, as surely as they will be, by the better angels of our nature.*

Chief Justice Taney, author of the infamous *Dred Scott* decision, then administered the oath of office to Lincoln. Reaction to the speech was largely predictable, with praise in the North and threats of war in the South. Lincoln would very quickly have to confront that threat.

And the War Came

Lincoln's first morning in office brought immediate bad news. Major Robert Anderson, whose federal troops occupied Fort Sumter in Charleston Harbor, could not hold out much longer. Anderson, who was born in Kentucky, came from a family that had deep roots in America. His father had served under Washington in the Revolutionary War, and he was related to John Marshall. He was a slave owner who sympathized with the South but also a dedicated unionist. He had moved his garrison from the more vulnerable Fort Moultrie to the recently completed Sumter, which was further out in the harbor, just as secession fever swept through South Carolina in December 1860. Buchanan, who had wavered in his response to the demand by South Carolina to surrender all federal forts, finally decided in January to defend Fort Sumter. A relief expedition with supplies for Anderson and his men, who were running out of food, had left New York and was fired upon by the South Carolinians and forced to retreat. Now Lincoln was told that Anderson could hold out for no more than a few weeks.[47]

"Lincoln was not prepared for the emergency," Donald writes. At this point he knew little about how to manage the job of president, and he was trying to do everything himself. He also faced two seemingly contradictory goals. On the one hand, he had promised to "hold, occupy, and possess the property" that was owned by the federal government. On the other hand, he was attempting to avoid bloodshed, fearful that the upper South would secede if he triggered a war. To make matters worse, both Anderson and General Scott maintained it would take a force of twenty thousand to twenty-five thousand men to hold the fort.[48]

When Lincoln assembled his cabinet on March 9, only one member supported an effort to maintain federal control of Fort Sumter. Seward thought that anything short of surrender of the fort would lead to the other Southern states seceding and the onset of a civil war. There were several important opinion makers in the North that agreed with Seward, including Horace Greeley, whose influential New York *Tribune* thought the South should be allowed to leave the Union. But Montgomery Blair from Maryland, who Lincoln had appointed as postmaster general, supported the relief effort. His father, Francis, had told Lincoln that evacuating the fort was "virtually a surrender of the union." Now his son echoed that thought, telling Lincoln the South would view an evacuation of the fort as proof "that the Northern men are deficient in the courage necessary to maintain the government." Lincoln actually shared the concerns of both of the Blairs, and he would later tell Congress that surrendering the fort would "embolden [our] adversaries, and go far to insure to the latter, a recognition abroad ... in fact. It would be our national destruction consummated." Yet Lincoln vacillated, at one point indicating he would gladly surrender Fort Sumter if such a move would keep Virginia in the Union.[49]

Lincoln decided to pursue more fact-finding, sending two men to South Carolina to further explore the situation on the ground. Gustavus Fox, a former naval officer and brother-in-law of Montgomery Blair, visited Anderson at Fort Sumter to see how long the garrison could hold out. Fox had developed a plan to resupply the fort directly from the sea and returned to Washington to inform Lincoln that the troops could hold out until April 15, and that his plan to resupply the fort from the sea at night was doable. Lincoln also sent Stephen Hurlbut, an old friend from Springfield, to check on public opinion in South Carolina. Hurlbut was originally from Charleston, and he "could test Seward's assumption that Unionist sentiment throughout the South would continue to strengthen as long as the government refrained from any provocative action," Goodwin writes. Upon his return, he informed Lincoln that "separate Nationality is a fixed fact, there is no attachment to the Union."[50]

Meanwhile, General Scott told Lincoln that both Sumter and Fort Pickens in Florida should be surrendered as the only means to keep the rest of the South out of the Confederacy. Shocked, Lincoln called his cabinet into emergency session following a state dinner on March 28. "Scott's politically motivated recommendation rendered suspect his initial opinion that reinforcement of Sumter was impossible," McPherson argues. Scott's position was essentially "unconditional surrender" and caused the cabinet members to reverse their position, with six of the eight supporting the resupply effort. Lincoln dismissed the cabinet, and then spent a sleepless night mulling over his decision. When the cabinet met at noon on March 29, the support of a "majority of the cabinet reinforced Lincoln's own view," Donald writes. He ordered that Fort Sumter be resupplied.[51]

This left Seward in an awkward position. Since at least in his Senate speech, he had assumed "he was the power behind a weak president," as Goodwin frames it, and that his actions in appeasing the South would forestall a civil war. Correspondence with people in the South had led to Seward's delusion, as did his conversations with Charles Francis Adams, John Quincy's son, who thought Lincoln was "not equal to the hour" and that the fate of the country lay in Seward's hands. Despite Lincoln's admonition to not deal with the commissioners that had been sent by the Confederacy to negotiate the issue of the forts, Seward had told them that Sumter "would be evacuated in the next five days." Now Lincoln had decided to resupply the fort. On April 1, Seward handed Lincoln his thoughts on what should be done, charging that the president had no clear policy, and recommending that Sumter be evacuated but Pickens reinforced. Seward essentially asked that he take over responsibility for the situation. "Either the President must do it himself ... or Devolve it on some member of his cabinet," no doubt believing he was the right selection. It was an amazing display of hubris.[52]

Lincoln made it clear that he did have a policy that he had announced in his inaugural address "to hold, occupy, and possess" federal property. He then made sure that Seward knew that he was the responsible party. "I remark that if this must be done, *I* must do it." His biographers indicate that Lincoln never actually sent his written response to Seward and instead used it to blow off steam. Lincoln instead discussed the matter in private with Seward.[53]

Meanwhile, the plan to resupply Fort Sumter got underway. Under Lincoln's leadership, the plan had evolved, and now, "instead of trying to shoot its way into the harbor, the task force would first attempt only to carry supplies to Anderson" and only use force if they were fired upon first. As one historian notes, "it was a masterful maneuver, providing the first clear sign of the political genius that would make Lincoln such a formidable president and war leader." Lincoln had found a way to hold federal property without being responsible for firing the first shot. On April 6, Lincoln informed the governor of South Carolina that "an attempt will be made to supply Fort-Sumter with provisions only; and that if such attempt be not resisted, no effort to throw in men, arms or ammunition will be made, without further notice, [except] in case of an attack on the Fort."[54]

If Lincoln was under tremendous pressure from all sides, so too was Jefferson Davis. When his home state of Mississippi seceded on January 9, 1861, Davis concluded that "he was no longer a citizen of the United States," his biographer writes. Even though he revered both the Declaration of Independence and the Constitution, he had always believed in "State sovereignty [and] the right of a State to secede," as he told his Senate colleagues in his final speech. As with many in the South, he believed that Northerners had attacked Southern "social institutions," most importantly slavery, and that the South was simply following the founders by pursuing their right to revolution, "to withdraw from a Government which thus perverted threatens to be destructive of our rights." Davis had also been a strong supporter of the Union and believed that the day he left the Senate for the last time was "the saddest day of my life."[55]

Davis was a natural selection as president, a conservative man who would portray a sense of calm and steadiness upon the rebel cause. At home, when he learned of his selection, his wife Varina reported he acted "as a man might speak of a sentence of death." Now as the president of the Confederacy, he had to decide how to deal with the issue of federal property, and he was prepared to offer compensation both for the property already taken and the remaining forts, like Sumter and Pickens. Meanwhile, "the situation in Charleston was extremely volatile, for South Carolina officials talked about attacking Fort Sumter," Cooper reports. Davis decided to take over the situation, and sent General Beauregard to assume command, directing that force be used only in self-defense.[56]

Yet Davis also believed that the United States no longer had any right to federal property in the Confederate states. He was being pressured by Southern newspapers, the Fire Eaters, and the people of South Carolina to act. Secessionists in Virginia let it be known that the best way to get their state to join the Confederacy was by "the shedding of blood," which "will serve to change many voters in the hesitating states" and lead them to support secession, the Fire Eater Edmund Ruffin wrote. Davis had also been led to believe that Lincoln intended to surrender Fort Sumter based on information he was receiving from those in contact with Seward. When Davis was informed of Lincoln's intent to resupply Fort Sumter, he ordered Beauregard to demand Anderson's surrender or face the consequences. The mortar shell that was fired over Fort Sumter in the early morning hours of April 12, 1861, was lit by none other than Ruffin. "The news galvanized the North" McPherson writes, and Lincoln called for the states to send seventy-five thousand men to fight for the Union on April 15. Two days later Virginia seceded, soon to be followed by Arkansas, North Carolina, and Tennessee. The Civil War had begun.[57]

Endnotes

1 Freeman, p. 249–254; Potter, *Impending Crisis*, p. 383.

2 Potter, *Impending Crisis*, p. 386–390; McPherson, p. 201.

3 Potter, *Impending Crisis*, p. 390–393.

4 Potter, *Impending Crisis*, p. 395–400.

5 Cooper, p. 300–302.

6 Cooper, p. 304–305; Potter, *Impending Crisis*, p. 403.

7 Goodwin, p. 212.

8 Foner, *Fiery Trial*, p. 136; Donald, p. 237–238.

9 Donald, p. 238; Johannsen, p. 707–708.

10 Donald, p. 238; Lincoln, p. 240–248; Fraser, p. 272-273

11 Sean Wilentz, *No Property in Man: Slavery and Antislavery at the Nation's Founding* (Cambridge, 2018), p. 95–97 and p. 252–254.

12 Wilentz, *No Property*, p. 246; Lincoln, p. 241–243.

13 Ashworth, p. 164.

14 Johannsen, p. 748–752.

15 Potter, *Impending Crisis*, p. 409–411; Lincoln, p. 250; Wilentz, *Rise*, p. 757; information on Breckinridge was retrieved January 23, 2019, from https://www.history.com/topics/us-politics/john-L-breckinridge.

16 Goodwin, p. 234–236; Donald, p. 243–244.

17 Goodwin, p. 237–239 and p. 214, where the quotes are from.

18 Goodwin, p. 215 and p. 241–242.

19 Goodwin, p. 246; Donald, p. 242.

20 Goodwin, p. 247–248; Donald, p. 251.

21 Potter, *Division*, p, 91; Foner, *Fiery Trial*, p. 142.

22 Goodwin, p. 267; Potter, *Impending Crisis*, p. 434.

23 Goodwin, p. 270, p. 274–275; Potter, *Impending Crisis*, p. 432; McPherson, p. 230–231.

24 Potter, *Impending Crisis*, p. 439; McPherson, p. 230–231.

25 Johannsen, p. 778–783.

26 Wilentz, *Rise*, p. 765; Johannsen, p. 797–801; McPherson, p. 232.

27 Wilentz, *Rise*, p. 764.

28 Potter, *Impending Crisis*, p. 442–443.

29 Wilentz, *Rise*, p. 765.

30 Wilentz, *Rise*, p. 769; Potter, *Impending Crisis*, p. 491.

31 Wilentz, *Rise*, p. 772 and p. 776; Potter, *Impending Crisis*, p. 495–498.

32 Wilentz, *Rise*, p. 780–781; Lincoln to Weed, in Lincoln, p. 275; Cooper, p. 320; Donald, p. 269.

33 See chapters 10 and 14 for Calhoun's and the Fire Eaters' views. For more information on the Antifederalists, see Fraser, p. 326–329.

34 Potter, *Division*, p. 98; McPherson, p. 276; Potter, *Impending Crisis*, p. 546–547.

35 Ashworth, p. 186; Wilentz, *Rise*, p. 772–777; the Constitution of the Confederate States was retrieved March 26, 2019, from http://avalon.law.yale.edu/19th_century/csa_csa.asp.

36 Potter, *Impending Crisis*, p. 448; see North, especially chapter XII, where he discusses the expanding industrial base in the North. Baptist, p. 318–327.

37 McPherson, p. 23; Foner, *Free Soil*, p. 17; Potter, *Impending Crisis*, p. 457; the Calhoun quote was retrieved March 13, 2019, from http://www.ushistory.org/us/27f.asp.

38 Potter, *Impending Crisis*, p. 454–455; Stanley M. Elkins, *Slavery: A problem in American Institutional and Intellectual Life* (Chicago, 1969), p. 218; Stampp, p, 90.

39 Potter, *Impending Crisis*, p. 475.

40 The South Carolina Declaration of Secession was retrieved March 28, 2019, from http://avalon.law.yale.edu/19th_century/csa_scarsec.asp; Wilentz, *Rise*, p. 774–775.

41 Wilentz, *Rise*, p. 774–775, has influenced my thinking on this subject, although I give greater credence to the idea that secession was about both slavery and federalism.

42 Goodwin, p. 294; Donald, p. 268–269; Madison, letter to Nicholas P. Trist from December 23, 1832, p. 861–862.

43 Goodwin, p. 311–312; Donald, p. 279.

44 Donald, p. 279–280; Johannsen, p. 872–873.

45 Donald, p. 281–282; Goodwin, p. 300–304.

46 Donald, p. 283–284; Goodwin, p. 324–326; Lincoln, p. 284–293.

47 Bechloss, p. 156–164; Potter, *Impending Crisis*, p. 538–543.

48 Donald, p. 285–286.

49 Donald, p. 286–287; Goodwin, p. 336–340.

50 Donald, p. 286–288; Goodwin, p. 337–338; McPherson, p. 268.

51 McPherson, p. 270; Donald, p. 289.

52 Goodwin, p. 341–342; Donald, p. 289–290.

53 Donald, p. 290; Goodwin, p. 342–343.

54 Cooper, p. 339; McPherson, p. 272.

55 Cooper, p. 6–8.

56 Cooper, p. 328 and p. 336–337.

57 Cooper, p. 340; Wilentz, *Rise*, p. 786–788; McPherson, p. 273–274.

Who Can Be an American?

There is nothing more difficult to carry out
nor more doubtful of success,
nor more dangerous to handle,
than to initiate a new order of things.
—MACHIAVELLI[1]

They met on April 9, 1865, at Appomattox Court House in the home of Wilmer McLean, who had witnessed both the first and last major battles of the Civil War. It was Palm Sunday, the start of holy week for Christians throughout the world. General Robert E. Lee arrived first, left with little choice but to surrender, since the last means of subsistence for the Army of Northern Virginia was contained in four rail cars that had been captured by the Union Army. The day after Virginia seceded from the Union in April 1861, Lee had been offered command of the American army. Instead he resigned his commission, saying, "I cannot raise my hand against my birthplace, my home, my children." He instead fought for the Confederacy and the preservation of slavery. Lee was himself a slave owner who had once called slavery "a moral & political evil" but who also thought it was "a greater evil to the white man than to the black race" and that blacks were "better off here than in Africa."[2]

General Ulysses S. Grant reached the McLean home around 1:30 p.m. dressed in "an old suit, without my sword, and without any distinguishing mark of rank," a bit embarrassed about his "dirty boots" he would later record. Lee was dressed "in a spotless gray uniform," the clothing of the two men symbolic of their relative rank prior to the war. While Lee had graduated second in his class at West Point, had been an officer by the time of the Mexican-American War, and was a full colonel in 1861, Grant's record before the war was decidedly mixed. Rising up the ranks to a full captain in 1854, Grant was forced to resign due to rumors about his drinking. Entering the army once again after the Civil War began, Grant's skill as a commander in the West had led to his ultimate selection as the commander of the Union Army. While Lee's brilliance was widely recognized, "Grant surpassed him in grand strategy, crafting the plan that defeated the Confederacy," according to his biographer Ron Chernow.[3]

In the days leading up to the surrender, Lee had made a momentous decision. One of his officers had suggested that they should take to the hills and fight on as guerrillas. Lee rejected such a move out of hand, concerned about the devastation this would bring to Virginia and the country. "We would bring on a state of affairs it would take the country years to recover from." It was a noble decision, although it would only delay the formation of organizations like the Ku Klux Klan (KKK) that would terrorize and murder the newly freed in the South. Instead, Lee accepted Grant's magnanimous terms of surrender that Palm Sunday, remarking, "It is more than I expected." Lee was especially pleased "that officers would be allowed to save face by retaining their sidearms and horses," Chernow writes, "and could return home to resume their lives unmolested."[4]

The shooting war was over, and so too was slavery. In the aftermath of the Union victory at the battle of Antietam in September of 1862,

Lincoln had issued the preliminary language of the Emancipation Proclamation that would go into effect on January 1, 1863. Originally, Lincoln had placed preservation of the Union as the primary goal of the Civil War and slavery on the back burner, fearful of alienating the border states. He even held out "the possibility that [Southerners] could return to the Union with their property, including slaves, intact," Eric Foner writes. But the facts on the ground had changed with the coming of the Union Army in the South, as thousands of slaves streamed toward the troops in search of freedom, forcing first the generals and then Lincoln to deal with the issue. "As the danger of secession by the border states receded, the collapse of slavery accelerated, and the needs of the Union armies increased, pressure mounted for emancipation," according to Foner.[5]

By July of 1862, Lincoln began to see the many advantages of issuing a proclamation freeing the slaves in those states that were part of the Confederacy. Black slaves were used by the South to do work that otherwise would have been done by soldiers, and by freeing the slaves as the Union Army occupied territory, former slaves could instead do that work (and eventually fight) for the North. On July 13, Lincoln told Seward and Gideon Welles, his navy secretary, that he had "come to the conclusion that it was a military necessity absolutely essential for the salvation of the Union, that we must free the slaves or be ourselves subdued." Framing the issue as a military necessity provided Lincoln with the constitutional basis he needed to act. "As commander in chief he could order seizure of enemy slaves just as surely as he could order destruction of enemy railroads," McPherson writes. "Having made war on the Government, they were subject to the incidents and calamities of war," Lincoln responded when asked about the constitutionality of his actions. Seward, who supported the proclamation, advised Lincoln to wait "until you can give it to the country supported by a military success," since the Union was struggling on the field of battle. It was the one issue Lincoln had not "fully anticipated and settled in [his] own mind" and so he waited until after the victory at Antietam. On September 22, 1862, Lincoln announced that the Emancipation Proclamation would free "all persons held as slaves" in any state that was in rebellion against the Union, thereby freeing 3.1 million people from bondage effective January 1, 1863.[6]

Lincoln was gradually redefining the purpose of the Civil War, from a war that was being fought solely to preserve the Union to one to end slavery, advance freedom and equality, and preserve self-government. He took his most famous step in this direction in Gettysburg at the dedication of its cemetery on November 19, 1863. "Four score and seven years ago our fathers brought forth on this continent, a new nation, conceived in Liberty, and dedicated to the proposition that all men are created equal." A beautiful sentiment, if a bit suspect from a historical point of view, since Lincoln dated the formation of the American nation to the signing of the Declaration of Independence, rather than the Constitution. Yet his grounding of American nationhood to the natural-rights section of the Declaration served a larger purpose, to show that the Founding Fathers, too, thought slavery inconsistent with their highest ideals. As Joseph Ellis has framed it, "we may wish to forgive Lincoln, since it was the only way for him to claim the political authority to end slavery." In closing, Lincoln made clear that the cause for which soldiers were dying was a "new birth of freedom" and the preservation of "government of the people, by the people, for the people." It was the clearest statement he ever made that authority flows up from the people in a democracy.[7]

Lincoln's transformation, and that of the North, were far from complete. He was unable to fully embrace the idea that America could be a multiracial society where blacks could be treated equally.

At a meeting with a delegation of black leaders in August of 1862, Lincoln told them "even when you cease to be slaves, you are yet far removed from being on an equality with the white race ... I cannot alter it if I could." David Blight writes that it was "Lincoln's worst racial moment," one in which the "president gave a one-way lecture looking for" blacks to leave the country "to assuage the fears of white people who now had to imagine the end of slavery." Lincoln's ambivalence on black equality, which had clearly been on display during his campaign for the Senate in 1858, remained. Throughout 1862, he continued to support plans for colonization of freed slaves, although after signing the final Emancipation Proclamation in 1863, he made no further public statements on the matter.[8]

Even before the war ended, thoughts had begun to turn toward how to put the nation back together and find the correct balance between justice for freed blacks and sectional reconciliation. At the end of 1863, Lincoln announced his initial plan for Reconstruction of the South in his annual message to Congress. Radical Republicans had insisted that freed blacks be provided equal protection under the law, and some, like Charles Sumner, went so far as to maintain that Congress had "exclusive jurisdiction" over the South. More conservative Republicans eschewed the position of the Radicals, and feared they were promoting the "amalgamation" of the races, as Postmaster General Montgomery Blair asserted in a speech in October. Lincoln attempted to thread the needle with his initial plan, indicating "full pardon ... with restoration of all rights of property, except as to slaves" to all rebels except for high-level Confederate officials. Once the number of rebels taking the loyalty oath to the Union in each state equaled 10 percent of those who had voted in 1860, they could form a new state government. "Voting qualifications from before the war would apply, excluding blacks from the franchise," Foner writes, displaying Lincoln's continued equivocation on full rights for African Americans. Gradual emancipation and compensation would continue to apply to the border states. The Radicals supported Lincoln's approach since it required the South to accept the emancipation of the slaves as a condition of reentering the Union. Conservatives were happy because "he refused to tolerate the radicals' desire to punish the South," Goodwin writes. Reaction in the North was also generally favorable. At this point, Lincoln "did not envision Reconstruction as embodying a social and political revolution beyond the abolition of slavery," according to Foner. The movement for black rights would have to wait until another day.[9]

Lincoln shared the ambivalence of white Americans toward African Americans, and he understood the limitations of moral leadership, especially that a leader cannot get too far out in front of his followers' opinions. While Republicans in the Senate began to push for an amendment to the Constitution to abolish slavery everywhere, "Lincoln remained noncommittal," Foner writes, preferring for individual states to abolish slavery. In April of 1864, the Senate approved the Thirteenth Amendment by more than the required two-thirds vote, but the amendment failed in the House. Lincoln finally changed his mind on the issue, in part to consolidate the Republican Party around his reelection in 1864, calling the Thirteenth Amendment "a fitting, and necessary conclusion" to the war. During the summer of 1864, Lincoln's prospects for reelection seemed dim, as the war dragged on. William Sherman's occupation of Atlanta in early September gave Lincoln the boost he needed, just as Lincoln's campaign against General George B. McClellan heated up. The campaign gave proof to the continued problems of racism in American life, with the Democrats conducting one of the most "explicitly and virulent racist campaign[s] by a major party in American history," according to one historian. Frederick Douglass believed the Republicans too were "ashamed of the Negro," even though he supported Lincoln, who swept to victory, winning 55 percent of the popular vote and 91 percent of the electoral vote.[10]

In the aftermath of his election victory, Lincoln pushed for the adoption of the Thirteenth Amendment. When asked by two of his allies who were assigned to secure the needed votes in the House how they were to proceed, he said, "I leave it to you to determine how it shall be done; but remember that I am President of the United States, clothed with immense power, and I expect you to procure those votes." Ever the practical politician, Lincoln was willing to use whatever means were needed to secure the outcome, including "plum assignments, pardons, campaign contributions, and government jobs," Goodwin writes. By the end of 1865, the Thirteenth Amendment had been ratified, long after Lincoln was assassinated at Ford's Theatre on April 14, 1865.[11]

Antebellum America was an incomplete nation. Much had been achieved to make the United States into one people, including: the peaceful transfer of power; the growth of democracy and political parties; the expansion of equality for white men; the acquisition of territory and the migration over the continent; and the celebration of a shared history, especially the prominent role the founders played in the drive for independence and in establishing the Constitution. Yet the unresolved issues of the founding, slavery, and the nature of federalism, had finally led to the Civil War.

Nation and nationalism are sometimes denigrated today, with good reason. Nationalism can be fused with a hatred of outsiders and used as an excuse to discriminate against certain people. Even worse, it can degenerate into genocide. This is what Francis Fukuyama refers to as ethnonationalism. "This type of identity persecuted people who were not part of the group and committed aggressions against foreigners," he writes. We can see this in the American experience. African Americans were held as slaves and even after the Civil War and Reconstruction were denied their full rights due to the color of their skin. Women, too, were denied certain basic rights, considered the property of their husbands, and could not vote. Native Americans were forcibly removed from their ancestral homes and at times genocide was committed against them.[12]

Yet a sense of nationhood is also crucial to making the modern state work. We have not yet reached a stage in our evolution where identity is tied to the entire human race. Being a part of a nation is the highest level of identity we have achieved, from self, family, tribe, region, state, to nation. Fukuyama lists six reasons why national identity is important, including security, promoting good government, facilitating economic development, promoting trust among citizens, maintaining a strong social safety net, and making liberal democracy possible. Perhaps this final one is the most important in a multi-ethnic country like the United States. Since the time of John Locke, liberal democracies have been built around the concept of a social contract. "If citizens do not believe they are part of the same polity, the system will not function," Fukuyama writes. "Citizens often have to accept outcomes they do not like or prefer, in the interest of the common good." This is difficult to achieve if the other side of the debate is seen as being evil, the enemy, rather than a loyal American citizen who holds a different point of view.[13]

One can see the danger of the collapse of the nation in the run-up to our Civil War. The democratic process ceased working within the citadel of our political system in Washington, DC, with members of Congress confronting each other with weapons. The question this book posed in the introduction was, Why? Why did the ties that bound the young nation together finally crumble?

During the course of this book, we have seen the things that worked to bind the nation together. The introduction to this section highlighted many of those. Yet the unfinished business of the founding generation, the twin problems of slavery and the boundary of federal authority over it, would not go away. Ultimately, all these issues would come to a head over the annexation of Texas and the incorporation of the new territories gained from the Mexican-American War. The underlying theme of much of the period from the 1830s to 1860 was whether slavery was local and freedom national, or slavery national and freedom local.

The Civil War ended slavery, but it did not end the discussion of race and who can be an American. Neither did Reconstruction, that period between the end of the Civil War and 1877, when the North attempted to fulfill the promise of the American Creed for American men, black as well as white. There was an underlying tension during the period of Reconstruction in reaching this goal. On the one hand, many wanted to follow the advice of Lincoln and pursue healing and reconciliation, to "bind up the nation's wounds" and reunite the North and the South. Yet even Lincoln, just before he died, recognized that justice must be given to the newly freed, and he proposed limited voting rights for blacks. "The tragedy of Reconstruction is rooted in this American paradox: the imperative of healing and the imperative of justice could not, ultimately, cohabit the same house," historian David Blight writes.[14]

Reconstruction

Reconstruction was a noble effort to remake the United States along a more creedal path, but it also reflected the limitations of change that can be centrally imposed. In 2019, Harvard professor Henry Louis Gates coproduced and was featured in the PBS documentary entitled *Reconstruction: America After the Civil War*. Reconstruction, he wrote in an article for *Time Magazine,* "was an era filled with great hope and expectations, but it proved far too short to ensure a successful transition from bondage to free labor" for those born as slaves. Eric Foner, who was interviewed extensively for the documentary, at one point said: "After two hundred and fifty years of slavery white Southerners could not accept the four million former slaves as members of their society." The North too was resistant to incorporating the newly freed as full and equal members of American society.[15]

Presidential Reconstruction

As we have seen, Lincoln was conflicted over the role that newly freed African Americans should play in American society. He was initially opposed to any legislation that would require the states to protect the voting rights of freedmen. In his final speech on April 11, 1865, Lincoln supported readmitting Louisiana's newly reconstructed government into the Union, even though it was "unsatisfactory to some that the elective franchise is not given to the colored man. I would myself prefer that it were now conferred on the very intelligent, and on those who served our cause as soldiers." For the first time, an American president had come out in support of voting rights for blacks, even though it was a limited grant of suffrage. This idea proved too much for one man who attended the speech, John Wilkes Booth, who feared that blacks would now be citizens. Booth shot and killed Lincoln three days later.[16]

Andrew Johnson now assumed the office of the presidency. Johnson was originally born in North Carolina in 1808, and his family was part of the lowest rung of white society, people whose status was tied to "white supremacy [which] gave people in the Johnsons' social position a sense of identity that softened the reality of their downtrodden existence," according to Annette Gordon-Reed. Poor whites in the South felt their social position was threatened by the advancement of blacks, a view that shaped Johnson's policies on Reconstruction. After moving to Tennessee, Johnson had climbed the political ladder, serving in local, state, and national offices. By the time Lincoln was running for reelection, Johnson was the Union's military governor in Tennessee. Although he had owned slaves, he was a unionist who had opposed secession. The Republicans were looking to project a "bipartisan dedication to re-union," historian Allen C. Guelzo writes, and so Johnson, a Democrat, was placed on the ticket with Lincoln. Things got off to a rocky start when Johnson showed up at the inauguration drunk. It would only go downhill from there, and Johnson would eventually be impeached by the House of Representatives, although acquitted in the Senate.[17]

Originally, the Radical Republicans, so called because they supported full civil and political rights for African Americans, thought they could work with Johnson. Many of them viewed Lincoln, with his talk of "malice toward none; with charity for all" as too soft on the South. Johnson's hatred of rich Southerners was clear, and he seemed to reassure the congressional leadership that he intended to be tough on the former rebels, since "treason is a crime, and crime must be punished," he told them. Yet it would soon become clear that his hatred of blacks and his commitment to white supremacy would put him at odds with the Radicals.[18]

Between the adjournment of the Thirty-Eighth Congress on March 15, 1865, and the start of the Thirty-Ninth Congress in December of that year, Johnson unfolded his plans for Reconstruction, or what might better be called restoration of the South. Johnson wanted to "bring the Confederate states back into the Union as fast as possible, and to leave matters of citizenship and civil rights to the states to decide," according to historian Jill Lepore. On May 29, barely six weeks after Lincoln was assassinated, Johnson announced his plan for amnesty. It essentially included all former Confederates who were willing to pledge loyalty to the Union and support for the emancipation of slaves, with some notable exceptions. Consistent with the president's hatred of rich Southerners, those with substantial property were excluded and would have to apply to Johnson to be pardoned. Within a year, numerous pardons were granted by the president to the wealthy and others who had originally been excluded. "Most likely, Johnson came to view cooperation with the planters as indispensable to two goals—white supremacy in the South and his own reelection," according to Foner. The president also appointed governors to administer the states in the South who "promised to do little more than return the South, and the freed slaves, to a status only marginally different from what had prevailed in the war," Guelzo writes. Soon thereafter, elections were held to fill state and local offices, with former Confederates dominating the elections. In Georgia, Vice President Alexander Stephens was appointed to serve as a United States senator, and his selection was just the tip of the iceberg. As Guelzo writes, "six Confederate cabinet officers, four Confederate generals, and fifty-eight members of the Confederate Congress" were chosen to return to Congress.[19]

Johnson also stopped the process of land distribution to the newly freed slaves that had begun near the end of the war. In January of 1865, General Sherman had issued Special Field Order No. 15, which set aside forty acres of land for each freedman, along with the loan of mules, in the Sea Islands and parts of the South Carolina low country (thus the phrase "forty acres and a mule"). In March, Congress built on this by establishing the Freedmen's Bureau, which was authorized to confiscate land and distribute it to the freedmen. O. O. Howard, the Bureau commissioner, issued Circular 13 in July, which implemented the congressional mandate to distribute forty-acre tracts of land to African Americans. Johnson rescinded the order and then "ordered the restoration to pardoned owners of all land" that had been seized. Along with providing education, land ownership was the most important element in ensuring the success of former slaves, but Johnson pulled the rug out from under them.[20]

Presidential Reconstruction played into the hands of the South, which had never accepted its loss in the war. Many continued to maintain that the Confederate cause was noble. The South had lost over 250,000 men (the North 325,000), and its economy lay in ruins. The emancipation of the slaves alone had eliminated over $2 billion in value, and the total cost of the war to the South may have exceeded $13 billion. Yet if the South physically lay in ruins, the ideology that had led to the war did not. The commitment to a new and mythical rationale for the war began to emerge in 1866, when Edward A. Pollard released his book entitled *The Lost Cause: A New Southern History of the War of the Confederates*. While the shooting war was over, the war of ideas about its meaning continued unabated. Pollard argued that the war "did not decide negro equality, it did not decide negro suffrage, it did not decide States Rights ... And these things which the war did not decide, the Southern people will still cling to, still claim, and still assert them in their rights and views." Others soon joined the call, including both President Davis and Vice President Stephens, who each now denied that slavery had been the central reason for secession. Pollard made the case that the true issue of the war was "the supremacy of the white race."[21]

To ensure white supremacy and to put the freed people in their place, a series of Black Codes was adopted in the South. The intent of the Black Codes, in the words of W. J. Cash, was to "restore slavery in all but name." The codes provided blacks with some limited rights, including the right to marry and own property, but their main objective was to force freedmen to sign labor contracts under which they worked for white plantation owners. Those not under contract were subject to arrest and imprisonment under vagrancy laws that were implemented as part of the Black Codes. Some young blacks were required to work without pay for plantation owners if they were orphans or if their parents were considered incompetent. The Black Codes were enforced by an all-white police force made up in many cases of former Confederate soldiers who "frequently terrorized the black population," Eric Foner writes.[22]

It was just a short step from implementation of the Black Codes to the Ku Klux Klan, formed in Tennessee in 1866 by former Confederate officers. Disguised in flowing white robes, the Klan served up vigilante justice to keep "impudent negroes" in their place. The Klan often targeted the economically successful, and those who later ran for political office or attempted to vote during Congressional Reconstruction. In 1867, Nathan Bedford Forrest became the grand wizard of the Klan. Forrest was a former Confederate cavalry officer known for his fierce fighting ability. Membership in the Klan knew no class distinctions, with poor white farmers and laborers mixing in with rich planters, merchants, and lawyers, all committed to white supremacy.

Support for the Klan extended beyond its actual membership, with many whites viewing "violence against blacks as something less than a crime," according to Foner.[23]

Violence finally exploded in multiple race riots. The first occurred in Memphis on May 2, 1866, when whites were urged by a city official to "kill every Negro and drive the last one from the city." *Harper's Weekly* reported that blacks were "shot, assaulted, robbed, and in many instances their houses [were] plundered, and then set on fire." Rioting soon followed in Norfolk, Charleston, and New Orleans. Presidential Reconstruction had now reached its logical conclusion, and President Johnson went out of his way to blame the riots on "the Radical members of Congress." A new version of Reconstruction would soon emerge, led by the Republicans in Congress.[24]

Congressional Reconstruction

As we have seen, racism existed in the North as well as the South. Opposition to the war in New York City had led to rioting in July 1863, but quickly "degenerated into a virtual racial pogrom," according to Foner, in which "uncounted numbers of blacks" were murdered. Only five Northern states, all in New England, allowed blacks to vote. Referendums on black suffrage were defeated in Minnesota, Wisconsin, and Connecticut in 1865, albeit on an extremely close vote. Despite Northern racism, there was also unease with President Johnson's Reconstruction policies, especially over whether the South accepted the North's victory in the war, the emancipation of the slaves, and the superiority of free labor. The implementation of the Black Codes, followed by violence against the freedmen, "aroused an indignation that spread far beyond Radical circles," according to Foner. The shifting sands of Northern public opinion helped strengthen the hand of congressional Republicans in implementing policies designed to ensure the legal rights of blacks.[25]

The Republicans began by defining who could be an American, which had never been done before. "The word citizen or citizens is found ten times at least in the Constitution of the United States and no definition of it is given anywhere," wrote a scholar who had been asked to research the definition by Congress in 1866. A Civil Rights Bill was introduced in January of 1866, which established birthright citizenship. All persons born in the United States, except Indians, were considered citizens, regardless of race. The bill reversed the *Dred Scott* decision, and provided for equal protection for all people under the law. The president vetoed the bill, claiming it violated the rights of white people and of the states, since it represented a "stride towards centralization, and the concentration of all legislative powers in the national Government." Johnson also vetoed an extension of the Freedman's Bureau Bill. For the first time in history, Congress overrode both vetoes, thereby ending hope of cooperation between the president and Congress on Reconstruction. The Radical Republicans also began to work on two constitutional amendments, the fourteenth and the fifteenth, that incorporated the Civil Rights Bill and black voting rights into the document. Without political power, black civil rights would be virtually meaningless. There was also self-interest at work, since most blacks would vote for Republicans. Women, who had been such an important part of the abolitionist movement, were excluded from being given voting rights, and were told that "this is the negroes hour."[26]

The Radical Republicans also attempted to resolve the second great question left over from the founding era, federalism, or the precise boundaries between the power of the federal government and the states. They unequivocally believed that the federal government was supreme and set about to completely change not only the governments that had been established in the South, but also Southern society. Having won a substantial victory in the midterm elections in 1866, the Radical Republicans in Congress now had the voting strength to pursue their agenda. Congressmen George W. Julian proposed that what was needed in the South was *"government,* the strong arm of power, outstretched from the central authority here in Washington" to rule in the former Confederate states. The Reconstruction Act of 1867, passed over Johnson's veto, established five military districts governed by a military general. In order to be readmitted to the Union, each state would have to ratify the Fourteenth Amendment, bar for-mer Confederates from voting, and approve new constitutions that included voting rights for blacks. "It was a radical's dream, a centralist's heaven—and a states'-righter's nightmare," Burns writes. "Congress held all the government strings in its hands."[27]

Johnson attempted to undermine the Reconstruction Act by appointing generals who were unsympathetic to the rights of the freed people. In response, Congress began to consider impeachment proceedings against the president. While Johnson wanted "a soft, conciliatory posture toward the South ... the Republicans, both mod-erate and radical, wanted a hard policy," Burns writes. Yet the Radicals were unable to amass enough support to move forward on impeach-ment until Johnson violated the Tenure of Office Act, which stripped the president of the power to fire executive branch officials until a Senate-confirmed appointment had been made. While Johnson was impeached in the House, he was acquitted in the Senate by one vote. A group of influential senators were concerned about "the damage to the separation of powers that would result from conviction," according to Foner, and voted no. The inability to remove Johnson weakened the Radicals and helped contribute to the election of the moderate Ulysses S. Grant as president in 1868, who ran on the slogan "Let Us Have Peace." His opponent, Horatio Seymour of New York, was the Democratic nominee, whose sole campaign issue was opposition to Reconstruction.[28]

It was a time of both hope and fear for the freed people. Many participated in the conventions that were held in the South to write new constitutions under Congressional Reconstruction. They were joined in their efforts by Northerners who had moved south and were disparagingly referred to as *carpetbaggers*, and by Southern Unionists, known as *scalawags*. Many of the constitutions were strongly liberal and democratic, providing for free public education in the South for the first time and protecting the civil and political rights of the freed people. Approximately five hundred thousand blacks in the South turned out to help elect Grant in 1868, who won the popular vote by a margin of only three hundred thousand. This despite attempts by the Klan to discourage voting through their continuing "reign of terror."[29]

In July of 1868, the Fourteenth Amendment was ratified, and two years later, the Fifteenth Amendment went into effect. These led to the election of numerous African American men to political office. Sixteen blacks served in Congress, and Hiram Revels of North Carolina was elected to the Senate in 1870. Black political power at the state level was more hit-and-miss. "In Texas, North Carolina, Alabama, Georgia, and Virginia, none held major political office during Reconstruction," Foner writes, although blacks were more successful in obtaining political office in Mississippi and South Carolina, where a black majority ruled in the House of Representatives. All told, over six hundred blacks were elected as legislators, most of them former slaves. Robert Smalls went from being a slave to a member of the US House of Representatives in just under six years.[30]

But the issue of federalism, which had such deep roots in American history, was far from settled despite the efforts of the Radical Republicans. Support for states' rights, grounded in white supremacy, was far from dead in the South. Many Southerners were outraged by the new governments that had been formed under Congressional Reconstruction. Cracks were also beginning to appear in Northern support for Reconstruction. While seven Southern states were admitted into the Union in July 1868, Virginia, Mississippi, Texas, and Georgia remained under military rule when Grant took the oath of office in March 1869. Grant wanted to move quickly to bring these states back in as well, despite the continuing attempts by Southerners to reinstitute white rule. Democrats in Mississippi renamed themselves the White Man's Party and complained that the Republicans were attempting to place them "under governmental control of ... the African negro." Voters responded by rejecting the new state constitution in that state. Despite resistance of this type, and continuing Klan activity to disenfranchise black voters through violence and intimidation, each of these states were readmitted to the Union by July 1870.[31]

Part of the weakening of Northern support for Reconstruction occurred because some of the most radical members of Congress were passing from the scene. None was more important than Congressman Thaddeus Stevens, who died in August of 1868. Stevens, from Pennsylvania, was one of the leaders in efforts to emancipate the slaves and bring about political and economic equality for black people. He had been a central figure in drafting the Fourteenth Amendment, had proposed a radical plan for land distribution in the South in 1865, and supported black suffrage. He was buried in an integrated cemetery, and he composed his own epitaph, which included his support for "Equality of Man before the Creator."[32]

Even though Grant wanted to restore all of the Southern states to the Union, he had always been opposed to slavery and as the leader of the Union Army had "helped to liberate, feed, house, employ, and arm" blacks during the war, as Chernow writes. He was also a strong supporter of Reconstruction in the South and black voting rights. As Republicans increasingly came to power in the South in the years between 1868 and 1870, they faced a daunting challenge, since they were viewed as, in the words of Foner, "alien impositions," a force outside Southern society. The Klan and other related terrorist organizations increasingly turned to violence, providing a major test for Grant and the Republicans in Washington, DC. "Republicans in 1869 and 1870 stood poised between retreating from Reconstruction and pressing further with its Southern policy," Foner writes, yet the Klan's "campaign of terror overcame Republicans' growing reluctance to intervene in Southern affairs."[33]

Grant was increasingly under pressure from Republican governors in the South to provide assistance in response to the Klan. In North Carolina, the governor indicated that people were too intimidated to testify against KKK activity, making it next to impossible to enforce the law. Governor Robert K. Scott of South Carolina described conditions during the election of 1870. "Colored men and women have been dragged from their homes at the dead hour of night and most cruelly and brutally scourged for the sole reason that they dared to exercise their own opinions upon political subjects." The Klan attacked both blacks who attempted to vote or run for office and also white Republicans. Many in the South did not consider violence against blacks a crime. "If a white man kills a colored man in any of the counties" in Florida, one sheriff indicated, "you cannot convict him."[34]

Congress responded with a series of Enforcement Acts in 1870 and 1871, including the Ku Klux Klan Act of April 1871, which "for the first time designated certain crimes committed by individuals as offenses punishable under federal law," Foner writes. Attorney General Amos T. Akerman began a series of prosecutions of Klan members under the law. Akerman, originally from New Hampshire, had moved to Georgia and served in the Confederate Army. After the war, he had joined the Republican Party, supporting civil and voting rights for blacks. While Akerman's overall success rate in prosecuting cases against the Klan was small, the lawsuits had the impact of defeating the Klan, "restoring order, reinvigorating the morale of Southern Republicans, and enabling blacks to exercise their rights," in the words of Foner.[35]

The Enforcement Acts also obliterated the demarcation lines in the relationship between the federal government and the states, and elicited opposition not just from Democrats but also from a newly emerging group of liberal Republicans. Democrats argued that the laws were "unconstitutional ... so far as they deal with *individuals* and not with *states.*" Liberal Republicans, who arose out of the capitalist expansion of the postwar years and the corruption that went along with it, thought the Radicals had eliminated the need for the states, given the federal government's use of the armed forces to eliminate violence against blacks. Liberal Republicans believed in limited government and a laissez-faire, hands-off attitude toward the economy. In some ways they were Jeffersonian in their views, without Jefferson's commitment to egalitarian policies. They opposed laws that would help the average working person, including an eight-hour day and the ability to strike. Although many liberal Republicans had originally supported Reconstruction, they were beginning to turn against it. "Reconstruction underscored the dangers of unbridled democracy and the political incapacity of the lower orders," according to Foner. They believed that the best men, those with "intelligence and culture" should rule, which included upper-class former Confederates.[36]

The liberal Republicans ultimately nominated the editor of the New York *Tribune*, Horace Greeley, to run against Grant in 1872. Surprisingly, the Democrats also endorsed Greeley. Greeley had always stood on the healing side of the Reconstruction debate. He opposed land confiscation policies and the trial of former Confederates for treason. Yet he also supported black suffrage and the Fourteenth Amendment. Greeley was looking for that sweet spot between justice and healing, but it didn't exist. As David Blight writes, "If only Horace Greeley could have spoken a world into being!" While Grant sailed to victory in his reelection bid, winning 55 percent of the popular vote, Reconstruction would soon "be on the defensive in the North as well as the South," according to Foner.[37]

The End of Reconstruction

Fate, or more precisely the Panic of 1873, now pushed the country toward ending Reconstruction. The postwar years had seen an economic boom, fed by the rapid expansion of the railroad system. In May of 1869, the transcontinental railroad was completed with the symbolic driving of the golden spike in Promontory, Utah. But, as with other technological innovations in the United States, construction of new railroads had created a bubble in the economy. In 1873 the bubble burst, causing a collapse in the nation's financial system and widespread unemployment. Congress responded by passing legislation to expand the money supply, but Grant vetoed the bill. The Republican Party was increasingly moving in the direction of a conservative, pro-business party that believed in limited government, replacing the old ideology of "equality of rights for black citizens as the essence of the party's self-image," according to Foner. As the party in power, the Republicans paid the price in the midterm elections of 1874. Their 110-seat majority in the House became a sixty-vote Democratic majority.[38]

The economic expansion had also led to a significant increase in governmental corruption during the Grant administration, "when

the new financiers were caught distributing bribes and kickbacks,"
Guelzo writes. Reconstruction governments in the South were soon
accused of similar acts of corruption as well, only these charges were
accompanied with blatant overtones of racism against the freed people.
In 1874, James S. Pike published *The Prostrate State*, which depicted
the Reconstruction government of South Carolina as being controlled
by "a mass of black barbarism ... the most ignorant democracy mankind ever saw." Respectable magazines like *Harper's* and *The Atlantic
Monthly* published drawings and cartoons depicting blacks as "vicious
caricatures," little more than uncivilized brutes, as shown in this *Harper's* cover from March 14, 1874.[39]

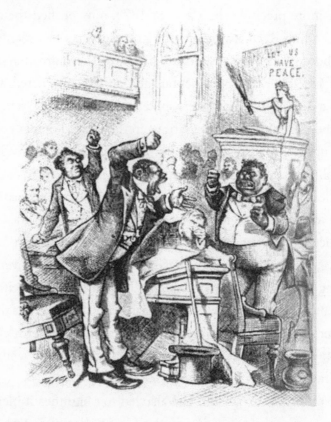

As the North continued its retreat from Reconstruction, Southerners continued their counterrevolution to retake state governments. "The issues of white supremacy, low taxes, and control of the black labor force dominated the Democratic campaigns of the mid-1870s," Foner writes. In Louisiana, the White League was formed, dedicated to re-imposing white supremacy and putting black people in their place. When federal troops stopped members of the White League from assuming five disputed seats in the state legislature, Northern opinion turned against the further use of federal troops in the South. In the aftermath, Grant refused the request of the governor of Mississippi to use the army to protect blacks who were attempting to vote in that state, and the Democrats took back power. The governor was forced to resign, and he later wrote that "a revolution has taken place—by force of arms—and a race are disfranchised—they are to be returned to a condition of serfdom—an era of second slavery."[40]

The Republicans who still supported equality for blacks had one last gasp of effort with their Civil Rights Bill. Senator Charles Sumner, who had been caned on the Senate floor in 1856 because of a speech denouncing slavery, urged his colleagues to not "let my bill fail" as he lay dying in March of 1874. In response, the Senate passed the bill, which "made it illegal for places of public accommodation and entertainment to make any distinction between black and white patrons and outlawed racial discrimination" in a variety of public institutions, as Foner writes. Before the Democrats could take over the chamber, the bill was passed by the lame-duck session of the House in February of 1875, without the requirement prohibiting discrimination in public schools. The bill was never effective in achieving its goals, and in 1883 the Supreme Court struck it down as unconstitutional.[41]

The year 1876 was the one-hundred-year anniversary of American independence. A Centennial Exposition was held in Philadelphia that year, which celebrated American ingenuity and technology, as the United States was entering a period of intense industrialization. Almost without thought, the Exposition largely ignored women, blacks, and Native Americans, highly reflective of a society that still had difficulty coming to grips with the issue of who could be an American. Elizabeth Cady Stanton and Susan B. Anthony reminded the men of their exclusion on July 4, when they read the Women's Declaration of Independence.[42]

It was also a presidential election year. The Republicans selected the two-term governor of Ohio, Rutherford B. Hayes, who originally supported Reconstruction policies. But he had gradually moved away from that position when he realized it would cost him votes. The Democrats selected Samuel J. Tilden of New York, who won the popular vote and appeared to have a lock on the electoral college when he won in New York and certain other East Coast states, along with the solid support of the South. But the Republicans still controlled the election machinery in Louisiana, South Carolina, and Florida, and "voided enough Democratic ballots to claim the electoral votes of those states for Hayes" Guelzo writes, which gave Hayes a one-vote margin in the electoral college. Democrats were ready to take to the streets in protest, believing they had been cheated out of the presidency. In response to the disputed election, Congress created an Electoral Commission in January of 1877, which also confirmed Hayes the winner. To avoid violence in the South, Hayes entered into what has become known as the Compromise of 1877, in which he recognized the new Democratic governors in Louisiana and South Carolina, thus returning those states to home rule. He also agreed to end the military occupation of the South. Southern Democrats were willing to accept the loss of the presidency in return for control of their states, driving the last nail into Reconstruction.[43]

Reconstruction was a lesson in the limits of change that can be imposed from outside of a society. Many historians and writers have commented that the Confederacy was actually born in the aftermath of the war. Robert Penn Warren wrote "only at the moment when Lee handed Grant his sword" did the "conception of Southern identity truly blossom." The cause that bound the South together in the aftermath of the war was white supremacy. Only the use of force by the North could sustain civil and political rights for blacks. The amount of time it would have taken to truly restructure Southern society was daunting. Abolitionist Wendell Phillips seemed to understand this, writing that blacks would only be safe when "more than one-half of the white men of the Southern States are in their graves." But Americans are not very good at long-term military occupations, as later experiences in Vietnam and Iraq would prove, even on our own soil. When the commitment to preserving black civil and political rights began to evaporate, so, too, did Reconstruction. As one Democratic newspaper framed it, Republican rule in the South "will last just as long as the bayonets which ushered them into being, shall keep them in existence, and not one day longer." W. E. B. Du Bois would later write, "the slave went free; stood a brief moment in the sun; then moved back again toward slavery." As the Jim Crow era gradually descended on the South, it would be almost one hundred years before civil rights for African Americans would once again come to the fore. The constitutional amendments that the Radicals had added "made relatively little difference when they were adopted; the changes they prescribed came about only when society itself changed," constitutional scholar David A. Strauss has written.[44]

☞ ☞ ☞

What are the lessons we should take from the history of the early republic? We learned that the sense of being one nation was fragile then, and it continues to be so in the early twenty-first century. It is not that we are near the point of another Civil War, God forbid. That conflict may well have been inevitable, especially as "the revolutionary fires" of 1776 began to wane and slavery expanded westward. Still, the South was an outlier in its reliance on slavery, both in the United States and internationally, as countries like England and France began to give up the practice. Lincoln was right to call slavery evil, but so too is racial prejudice, which continues to afflict our society.

Today we continue to be divided over the question of who can be an American. Donald Trump's election as president in 2016 proved this. He is an adherent of the view that America is made up of a group of people that share certain ethnic, racial, and religious characteristics. Under this view, only certain people can be an American. The other view, discussed throughout this book, is that America is fundamentally an idea, as found in the Declaration of Independence and actualized through the Constitution. The creedal core of America revolves around liberty, equality, self-government, and justice, ideas that have universal appeal. As Americans, our challenge, in the words of Francis Fukuyama, is to avoid "the narrow, ethnically based, intolerant, aggressive, and deeply illiberal form that national identity took" in our past, and which Trump is trying to reignite. Instead, we need "to define an inclusive national identity that fits [our] society's diverse reality."[45]

Race still stands as a barrier to achieving this vision. The end of Reconstruction provides an object lesson in the problems that we must confront. Harvard political scientists Steven Levitsky and Daniel Ziblatt, in their 2017 book *How Democracies Die*, discuss how democracies are dependent for their survival on certain norms. Two of the most important are mutual toleration and institutional forbearance. "Mutual toleration refers to the idea that as long as our rivals play by constitutional rules, we accept that they have an equal right to exist, compete for power, and govern," the authors write. Forbearance means "politicians do not use their institutional prerogatives to the hilt ... since such action could imperil" our democratic system. Both of these guardrails had begun to fray before Donald Trump was elected president, and adherence to them has only worsened, since he neither values nor follows such norms. Levitsky and Ziblatt also raise a very troubling issue. "Mutual toleration was established only after the issue of racial equality was removed from the political agenda," in the aftermath of the Compromise of 1877, which ended Reconstruction, they argue. Could it be that our democracy can only function when race is removed from the discussion?[46]

We cannot accept this. As Martin Luther King Jr. said in his famous "I Have a Dream" speech in 1963, "we refuse to believe that the bank of justice is bankrupt." We have made much progress in race relations since King delivered this speech, even electing an African American, Barack Obama, as president in 2008 and again in 2012. The Grinnell College National Poll, mentioned in the introduction, gives a reason for hope as well. "Most of those polled think that basic agreement with certain ideals, such as treating people equally, valuing difference, and taking responsibility for your own actions, are important to being American," according to Caleb Elfenbein, associate professor of History and Religious Studies at Grinnell College. "I was especially happy to see that support for accepting people of different racial, ethnic, and religious backgrounds far outweighs ideas of being American that focus on a particular background or identity."[47]

The challenge of our times is to continue our commitment to a creedal vision of America. We need to make a reality of the opening words of our Constitution, that "We the People" means all people who share the American Creed, regardless of race, ethnicity, or religion, and to constantly strive to unleash, in Lincoln's words, "the better angels of our nature."

Endnotes

1 Niccolo Machiavelli, *The Prince and the Discourses* (New York, 1950), p. 21.

2 The scenes from Appomattox courthouse are taken from Ron Chernow, *Grant* (New York, 2017), p. 595; Meacham, *The Soul of America*, p. 50; see also McPherson, p. 281, for Lee's decision to side with the South. Adam Serwer, "The Myth of the Kindly General," retrieved April 29, 2019, from https://www.theatlantic.com/politics/archive/2017/06/the-myth-of-the-kindly-general-lee/529038/.

3 Chernow, *Grant*, p. 506, p. 86, p. xxi.

4 Chernow, *Grant*, p. 509.

5 Eric Foner, *Reconstruction: America's Unfinished Revolution, 1863-1877* (New York, 2014), p. 3–5.

6 McPherson, p. 504–505; Goodwin, p. 464–468.

7 Lincoln, p. 405; Joseph J. Ellis, *The Quartet: Orchestrating the Second American Revolution, 1783-1789* (New York, 2015), p. xii.

8 Meacham, *Soul*, p. 56; David W. Blight, *Frederick Douglass: Prophet of Freedom* (New York, 2019), p. 371; Foner, *Fiery Trial*, p. 258.

9 David W. Blight, *Race and Reunion: The Civil War in American History* (Cambridge, 2001), broadly frames the issue of reconstruction as an attempt to balance justice with reconciliation, which I find a compelling framework. Foner, *Fiery Trial*, p. 271–272; Donald, p. 472–473; Lincoln, p. 412–413; Goodwin, p. 589.

10 Foner, *Fiery Trial*, p. 290–311.

11 Goodwin, p. 687–690.

12 Fukuyama, p. 128.

13 Fukuyama, p. 128–131. I am indebted to Dr. Fukuyama for the insights that his book on identity provided to me, especially chapter 12. It has helped to clarify my own thinking on the importance of the nation.

14 Blight, p. 57.

15 Henry Louis Gates, "Reconstruction: America After the Civil War," PBS video at https://www.pbs.org/weta/reconstruction/; Henry Louis Gates, "America's Second Sin," *Time Magazine*, April 15, 2019, p. 43–44.

16 Foner, *Fiery Trial*, p. 330–332, Lincoln, p. 454–458.

17 The Gordon-Reed quote and background on Johnson is from Jon Meacham, Peter Baker, Timothy Naftali, and Jeffrey A. Engel, *Impeachment: An American History* (New York, 2018), p. 52; Allen C. Guelzo, *Reconstruction: A Concise History* (Oxford, 2018), p. 15.

18 James MacGregor Burns, *The Workshop of Democracy: From the Emancipation Proclamation to the Era of the New Deal* (New York, 1985), p. 43–44.

19 Jill Lepore, *These Truths: A History of the United States* (New York, 2018), p. 318; Eric Foner, *A Short History of Reconstruction* (New York, 2014), p. 85–92; Guelzo, p. 22–25.

20 Foner, *Short*, p. 31 and p. 72; Foner, *Reconstruction*, p. 70.

21 McPherson, p. 854; Guelzo, p. 41; Meacham, *Soul*, p. 58–59.

22 W. J. Cash, *The Mind of the South* (New York, 1941), p. 105; Foner, *Short*, p. 93–95.

23 Foner, *Reconstruction*, p. 425–438; Meacham, *Soul*, p. 60–62.

24 Guelzo, p. 35–37.

25 Foner, *Reconstruction*, p. 224–225.

26 Lepore, p. 311–321; Burns, *Workshop*, p. 49; Foner, *Short History*, p. 113.

27 Foner, *Short History*, p. 120–124; Burns, *Workshop*, p. 53.

28 Burns, *Workshop*, p. 55; Guelzo, p. 51–54; Lepore, p. 324; Foner, *Short History*, p. 144–145.

29 Foner, *Short History*, p. 136–142 and p. 145–146; Guelzo, p. 59–65; Gates, "Reconstruction," PBS.

30 Foner, *Short History*, p. 150–151.

31 Guelzo, p. 71–72.

32 Foner, *Reconstruction*, p. 230; Foner, *Short History*, p. 147; Guelzo, p. 72.

33 Chernow, *Grant*, p. xxii and p. 632; Foner, *Short History*, p. 148; Foner, *Reconstruction*, p. 454.

34 Chernow, *Grant*, p. 701–702; Foner, *Reconstruction*, p. 425–435.

35 Chernow, *Grant*, p. 700–709; Foner, *Reconstruction*, p. 454–458.

36 Foner, *Reconstruction*, p. 455–456; Foner, *Short History*, p. 209–213.

37 Foner, *Short History*, p. 213–216; Blight, p. 59–61.

38 Foner, *Short History*, p. 217–221.

39 Foner, *Short History*, p. 222–223; the *Harper's Weekly* cartoon was retrieved May 13, 2019, from https://www.google.com/search?biw=1920&bih=962&tbm=isch&sa=1&ei=XK_

40 Foner, *Short History*, p. 232–237.

41 Foner, *Short History*, p. 228 and p. 234–235; Guelzo, p. 110.

42 Foner, *Short History*, p. 238–239.

43 Guelzo, p. 113–114; Foner, *Short History*, p. 240–245.

44 Potter, *Impending Crisis*, p. 469, writes "The Civil War did far more to produce a southern nationalism which flourished in the cult of the Lost Cause than southern nationalism did to produce the war." Cobb, p. 60; Foner, *Short History*, p. 142 and p. 255; Burns, *The Workshop*, p. 68–69; David A. Strauss, *The Living Constitution*, (Oxford, 2010), p. 127.

45 Fukuyama, p. 128 and p. 143

46 Levitsky and Ziblatt, p. 102, p. 106, p. 124.

47 Caleb Elfenbein, "Who Is a Real American? Overwhelming Agreement on the Answer," retrieved April 16, 2019, from https://www.grinnell.edu/news/who-real-american-overwhelming-agreement-answer.

www.perspectiveshistory.com

CPSIA information can be obtained
at www.ICGtesting.com
Printed in the USA
LVHW110433160720
660703LV00001B/1